JavaServer Pages™

Your visual blueprint for designing dynamic content with JSP™

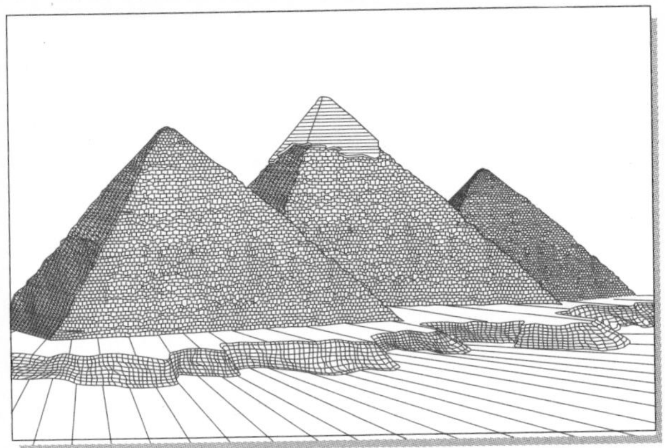

From
maranGraphics®

&

HUNGRY MINDS, INC.
New York, NY • Cleveland, OH • Indianapolis, IN
Chicago, IL • Foster City, CA • San Francisco, CA

JavaServer Pages™: Your visual blueprint for designing dynamic content with JSP™

Published by
Hungry Minds, Inc.
909 Third Avenue
New York, NY 10022
www.hungryminds.com

Library of Congress Control Number: 00-193100
ISBN: 0-7645-3542-0
Printed in the United States of America
10 9 8 7 6 5 4 3 2 1

1V/SR/QT/QR/MG

Distributed in the United States by Hungry Minds, Inc.
Distributed by CDG Books Canada Inc. for Canada; by Transworld Publishers Limited in the United Kingdom; by IDG Norge Books for Norway; by IDG Sweden Books for Sweden; by IDG Books Australia Publishing Corporation Pty. Ltd. for Australia and New Zealand; by TransQuest Publishers Pte Ltd. for Singapore, Malaysia, Thailand, Indonesia, and Hong Kong; by Gotop Information Inc. for Taiwan; by ICG Muse, Inc. for Japan; by Intersoft for South Africa; by Eyrolles for France; by International Thomson Publishing for Germany, Austria and Switzerland; by Distribuidora Cuspide for Argentina; by LR International for Brazil; by Galileo Libros for Chile; by Ediciones ZETA S.C.R. Ltda. for Peru; by WS Computer Publishing Corporation, Inc. for the Philippines; by Contemporanea de Ediciones for Venezuela; by Express Computer Distributors for the Caribbean and West Indies; by Micronesia Media Distributor, Inc. for Micronesia; by Chips Computadoras S.A. de C.V. for Mexico; by Editorial Norma de Panama S.A. for Panama; by American Bookshops for Finland.
For U.S. corporate orders, please call maranGraphics at 800-469-6616 or fax 905-890-9434.
For general information on Hungry Minds' products and services, please contact our Customer Care Department within the U.S. at 800-762-2974, outside the U.S. at 317-572-3993 or fax 317-572-4002.
For sales inquiries and reseller information, including discounts, premium and bulk quantity sales, and foreign-language translations, please contact our Customer Care Department at 800-434-3422, fax 317-572-4002, or write to Hungry Minds, Inc., Attn: Customer Care Department, 10475 Crosspoint Boulevard, Indianapolis, IN 46256.
For information on licensing foreign or domestic rights, please contact our Sub-Rights Customer Care Department at 650-653-7098.
For information on using Hungry Minds' products and services in the classroom or for ordering examination copies, please contact our Educational Sales Department at 800-434-2086 or fax 317-572-4005.
Please contact our Public Relations Department at 212-884-5163 for press review copies or 212-884-5000 for author interviews and other publicity information or fax 212-884-5400.
For authorization to photocopy items for corporate, personal, or educational use, please contact Copyright Clearance Center, 222 Rosewood Drive, Danvers, MA 01923, or fax 978-750-4470.

Trademark Acknowledgments

Permissions

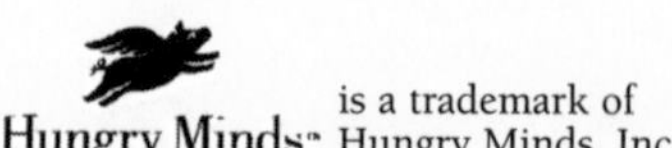

is a trademark of Hungry Minds, Inc.

U.S. Corporate Sales
Contact maranGraphics at (800) 469-6616 or fax (905) 890-9434.

U.S. Trade Sales
Contact Hungry Minds at (800) 434-3422 or fax (317) 572-4002.

JavaServer Pages™

Your visual blueprint for designing dynamic content with JSP™

maranGraphics is a family-run business located near Toronto, Canada.

At maranGraphics, we believe in producing great computer books–one book at a time.

Each maranGraphics book uses the award-winning communication process that we have been developing over the last 25 years. Using this process, we organize screen shots and text in a way that makes it easy for you to learn new concepts and tasks.

We spend hours deciding the best way to perform each task, so you don't have to!

Our clear, easy-to-follow screen shots and instructions walk you through each task from beginning to end.

We want to thank you for purchasing what we feel are the best computer books money can buy. We hope you enjoy using this book as much as we enjoyed creating it!

Sincerely,

The Maran Family

Please visit us on the Web at:

www.maran.com

CREDITS

Author:
Paul Whitehead

Directors of Copy Development:
Kelleigh Johnson
Wanda Lawrie

Copy Developers:
Raquel Scott
Cathy Benn
Luis Lee
Roderick Anatalio

Project Manager:
Judy Maran

Editors:
Teri Lynn Pinsent
Norm Schumacher
Faiza Jagot

Screen Captures & Editing:
Stacey Morrison

Layout Designer:
Treena Lees

Screen Artist:
Dave Thornhill

Cover Illustration:
Russ Marini

Indexer:
Kelleigh Johnson

Permissions Coordinator:
Jennifer Amaral

Senior Vice President and Publisher, Hungry Minds Technology Publishing Group:
Richard Swadley

Publishing Director, Hungry Minds Technology Publishing Group:
Barry Pruett

Editorial Support, Hungry Minds Technology Publishing Group:
Martine Edwards
Lindsay Sandman
Sandy Rodrigues

Post Production:
Robert Maran

ACKNOWLEDGMENTS

Thanks to the dedicated staff of maranGraphics, including Jennifer Amaral, Roderick Anatalio, Paul Baker, Cathy Benn, Joel Desamero, Faiza Jagot, Sean Johannesen, Kelleigh Johnson, Wanda Lawrie, Luis Lee, Treena Lees, Jill Maran, Judy Maran, Robert Maran, Ruth Maran, Russ Marini, Suzana G. Miokovic, Stacey Morrison, Teri Lynn Pinsent, Steven Schaerer, Norm Schumacher, Raquel Scott, Dave Thornhill, Natalie Tweedie, Roxanne Van Damme and Paul Whitehead.

Finally, to Richard Maran who originated the easy-to-use graphic format of this guide. Thank you for your inspiration and guidance.

TABLE OF CONTENTS

3) GETTING STARTED WITH JAVASERVER PAGES

4) WORK WITH JSP IMPLICIT OBJECTS

5) WORK WITH COOKIES

6) HARNESSING JAVABEANS

7) WORK WITH DATABASES

8) HANDLING ERRORS

9) WORK WITH FILES

10) CREATE CUSTOM TAGS

11) DEMYSTIFYING SERVLETS

12) REFERENCE

HOW TO USE THIS BOOK

JavaServer Pages™: Your visual blueprint for designing dynamic content with JSP™ uses simple, straightforward examples to teach you how to create powerful and dynamic Web sites. The coding style and examples used in this book are created for instructional purposes. Once you are more comfortable working with JSP, you can use a method and coding style that suits your needs.

To get the most out of this book, you should read each chapter in order, from beginning to end. Each chapter introduces new ideas and builds on the knowledge learned in previous chapters. Once you become familiar with JavaServer Pages (JSP), this book can be used as an informative desktop reference.

Who This Book Is For

If you are looking for a resource that will help you quickly get started creating JSP pages, *JavaServer Pages™: Your visual blueprint for designing dynamic content with JSP™* is the book for you. This book will walk you through the basics you need to get started and familiarize you with the essentials of coding with JavaServer Pages. This book also demonstrates advanced JavaServer Pages features, such as JavaBeans, custom tags and servlets.

Because you are interested in authoring dynamic Web pages, we assume you have experience using HyperText Markup Language (HTML) to create Web pages.

No prior experience with Web server software is required, but familiarity with the operating system installed on your computer is an asset.

Experience with Java programming is also an asset, but even if you have no programming experience, you can use this book to learn the Java essentials you need to work with the JavaServer Pages examples in this book.

What You Need To Use This Book

To perform the tasks in this book, you need a computer with a Java-capable operating system on which you can install a Java Runtime Environment. The computer will also need to run a JSP-enabled Web server, such as Tomcat version 3.1.

You do not require any special development tools to create JSP pages. All you need is a text editor—we use Notepad in the examples throughout this book—and a Web browser, such as Microsoft Internet Explorer.

The Conventions In This Book

A number of typographic and layout styles have been used throughout *JavaServer Pages™: Your visual blueprint for designing dynamic content with JSP™* to distinguish different types of information.

`Courier Font`

Indicates the use of HTML code such as tags or attributes, programming language code such as statements or operators and JSP code such as objects, methods or properties.

Bold

Indicates information that must be typed by you.

Italics

Indicates a new term being introduced.

Apply It

An Apply It section usually contains a segment of code that takes the lesson you just learned one step further. Apply It sections offer inside information and pointers that can be used to enhance the functionality of your code.

Extra

An Extra section provides additional information about the task you just accomplished. Extra sections often contain interesting tips and useful tricks to make working with JavaServer Pages easier and more efficient.

The Organization Of This Book

JavaServer Pages™: Your visual blueprint for designing dynamic content with JSP™ contains 12 chapters and an appendix.

The first two chapters, Java Basics and Programming With Java, introduce you to the essentials of Java, the programming language used with JavaServer Pages. These chapters also cover the fundamentals of object-oriented programming, which will enable you to use the material in the chapters that follow to create your own JSP pages. If you are already familiar with Java and object-oriented programming, you may want to read over these two chapters quickly before continuing through the book.

Chapter 3, Getting Started With JavaServer Pages, shows you how to install and configure Web server software. Once you have installed the Web server software of your choice, you can immediately begin creating JavaServer Pages code. This chapter also introduces you to some basic JavaServer Pages programming concepts, including topics such as expressions, declarations, scriptlets and directives.

The fourth chapter, Work With JSP Implicit Objects, examines JSP objects, including the `request` object, the `response` object and the `application` object. You will learn how to access and utilize the most commonly used methods of these objects.

Chapter 5, Work With Cookies, provides detailed information about using cookies in your JSP pages to store information about the clients who visit your Web site.

Chapter 6, Harnessing JavaBeans, shows you how to create and use JavaBeans, which allow you to store Java code separately from your JSP pages.

The seventh chapter, Work With Databases, describes how you can use JSP pages to work with information in a database. You will learn the basic principles of connecting to a database and manipulating the data stored in the database.

Chapter 8, Handling Errors, illustrates how to use JavaServer Pages features to deal with errors that may occur in your JSP pages. You will also learn how to create custom error messages for your JSP pages.

Chapter 9, Work With Files, demonstrates how to perform tasks such as writing to a file, creating a directory and reading a file from within a JSP page.

Chapter 10, Create Custom Tags, and Chapter 11, Demystifying Servlets, provide easy-to-understand explanations of high-level JavaServer Pages programming concepts. Creating custom tags allows you to develop your own library of special tags for use in your JSP pages. Servlets enable you to build complete Web sites using only the Java programming language.

The final chapter contains a reference section. Once you are familiar with the contents of this book, you can use the Java and JavaServer Pages references to obtain at-a-glance information for some of the most commonly used Java and JSP statements.

What Is On The CD-ROM

The CD-ROM disc included in this book contains the sample code from each of the two-page lessons. This saves you from having to type the code and helps you quickly get started creating JavaServer Pages code. The CD-ROM disc also contains several shareware and evaluation versions of programs that can be used to work with JavaServer Pages. An e-version of the book and all the URLs mentioned in the book are also available on the disc.

INTRODUCTION TO JAVASERVER PAGES

JavaServer Pages (JSP) is technology developed by Sun Microsystems that is used to create powerful and dynamic Web sites.

Web Servers

You do not require a dedicated Web server to publish the JSP pages you create. You can simply install Web server software on your own computer. A popular example of Web server software that includes support for JavaServer Pages is Tomcat. The Tomcat Web server is commonly used by Web developers who create JSP pages.

You do not require any special development tools to create and view JSP pages. All you need is a text editor and a Web browser.

Versions

JavaServer Pages 1.1 is the current version of JavaServer Pages, although the specification for a newer version 1.2 has been proposed. On average, a new version of JavaServer Pages is produced each year. Each new version offers more features than previous versions of the technology. The Web server you are running will determine the version of JavaServer Pages you can use and the tasks you can perform.

Programming Languages

The Java programming language forms the basis of JavaServer Pages technology. The version of Java you use depends on the Web server you are running and the version of JavaServer Pages technology you are using.

Servlet Technology

JavaServer Pages is based on servlet technology, which allows Web developers to use Java code to create dynamic Web pages. JavaServer Pages simplifies the process of creating dynamic pages using Java.

Server-side Processing

JavaServer Pages uses a JSP engine that is part of the Web server, so the processing of JSP code takes place on the server. When a user requests a JSP page, the JSP engine processes the page and then sends the result as HTML code to the user's Web browser. This allows JSP pages to be viewed by every Web browser.

JSP Implicit Objects

JSP includes implicit objects that can be used to perform specific tasks. For example, the `session` object can be used to store session information about a client computer as the client navigates a Web site. Other commonly used implicit objects include the `response` object, which sends information to a client, and the `request` object, which retrieves and controls information sent from a client to the Web server.

FEATURES OF JAVASERVER PAGES

Create Dynamic Web Sites

Dynamic Web sites contain Web pages that display constantly changing content. Using JavaServer Pages, you can determine the content a Web page displays, depending on many different factors. For example, you can have a page automatically present different content to users depending on the current date or the user's location. Dynamic Web pages are more useful to each individual user than static Web pages.

Create Interactive Web Sites

Interactive Web sites contain Web pages that exchange information between the Web site and the user. JavaServer Pages allows Web developers to easily create Web pages that process information from a user and then generate content depending on the information submitted by the user. Interactive Web sites allow Web developers to tailor the content of Web pages to better appeal to the user.

Increased Security

Because JavaServer Pages code is processed on the Web server, the user cannot access the code used to create a JSP page. This makes it safer to work with sensitive data, such as login names and passwords. If a user views the source code of a JSP page within a Web browser, all the user will see is the HTML code that was generated by the Web server to create the page, not the JavaServer Pages code itself.

Work With Databases

An important feature of JavaServer Pages is the ability to connect to a database. JSP pages can be used to make information stored in a database available to the users who visit a Web site. Using databases to store information and JSP pages to access the information is an efficient method of displaying up-to-date information in a Web site.

JavaServer Pages can also allow users to manipulate the data in a database. For example, a JSP page can be used to add, delete or edit records in a database.

Using JavaBeans

JavaBeans are re-usable components that allow Web developers to keep the Java code for a JSP page separate from the HTML code for the page. This helps prevent the code on a JSP page from becoming long and difficult to work with and allows Web developers to share and re-use Java code. JavaBeans also enable specialization when developing a Web site by allowing experts in Web page design to work with the HTML content for a page while programmers develop the Java code for the page.

Using Custom Tags

JavaServer Pages technology allows Web developers to create their own custom tags that perform specific tasks. Like JavaBeans, tag libraries are re-usable components that help keep the Java code for a JSP page separate from the HTML code for the page. Once a tag library containing the code for a custom tag has been created, the custom tag can be used in JSP pages.

INTRODUCTION TO JAVA

Java is a programming language used to create applications for the World Wide Web. Java was originally developed by Sun Microsystems in 1991 for use in consumer electronics such as handheld computers and television sets, but the language was later modified for use on the Web. Java is now a full-featured programming language that is easy to use and understand.

Java is the main programming language used in JavaServer Pages. While in-depth knowledge of Java is not required, in order to effectively use JavaServer Pages you need to understand the basics of the language. A thorough understanding of Java will enable you to create more sophisticated, versatile and efficient JSP pages.

You can also utilize your knowledge of Java to work with other Java-based technologies, such as JavaBeans.

The popularity of JavaServer Pages is partly due to the fact that people who are already familiar with the Java programming language do not need to learn a new programming language in order to use JavaServer Pages. Since JavaServer Pages uses Java code to create Web pages, programmers can use their existing knowledge of Java to create JSP pages. JavaServer Pages also uses programming code that is unique to JavaServer Pages and is not strictly Java code.

Features

Java includes a number of features that make the language ideal for use on the Web. Java programs transfer quickly over the Web since the language was created to be portable and file sizes are small. In addition, Java is platform independent. This means that a Java program can be run on any computer that has a Java virtual machine, regardless of the operating system the computer uses. This feature is invaluable for use on the Web, where computers using various languages and environments must interact.

Bytecode

When a Java program is compiled, the program is not immediately translated into machine code, which are instructions specific to a particular operating system. Instead, it is compiled into an intermediate language, called bytecode, that can be interpreted by a Java virtual machine. When the Java program is run on a computer that has the Java virtual machine, the Java interpreter translates the bytecode into code that the computer running the program can understand.

Object-Oriented

Java is an object-oriented programming language, so if you understand the fundamentals of how Java works, you will understand the fundamental concepts of object-oriented programming. Object-oriented programming is a type of programming that treats separate pieces of code as distinct modules, or objects. It is often easier to learn object-oriented programming if you do not have vast experience with programming languages that are non-object-oriented. Despite its apparent initial complexity, object-oriented programming is easy to learn.

Security

Java provides a number of advanced security features, such as access controls, which are not offered by many other programming languages. Java programs may contain viruses or code that can cause computer problems. Java's access controls allow programmers to use untrusted Java code in their programs without putting their systems at risk.

PROGRAMS FOR CREATING JAVA CODE

The first step in creating Java programs is to select the method you want to use to create the Java programming code, or *source code*.

Text Editors

Since all Java source code is plain text, you can use a simple text editor to create the source code.

For Non-Windows Operating Systems

There are many text editors that can be used to create Java source code on UNIX computers. Most UNIX computers have multiple text editors installed by default. Text-based editors such as vi and Emacs are very popular and can be configured to suit your needs. If your UNIX system has a graphical interface, like GNOME, then you should already have access to graphical text editors, such as gnotepad+.

On the Macintosh operating system, you can use the SimpleText text editor included with the system.

Notepad

Microsoft Notepad is a simple text editor available on all computers running the Windows operating system. Most operating systems contain a text editor similar to Notepad. While very basic, Notepad is more than adequate for creating source code and is widely used by programmers.

UltraEdit

UltraEdit is a sophisticated text editor popular with many programmers. UltraEdit's advanced features include syntax highlighting, which highlights the Java code to make the code easier to read, and the ability to save Web pages directly to a Web server. UltraEdit is a shareware program available at www.ultraedit.com.

HTML Editors

HTML editors are programs specifically designed to help you create Web pages. Compared to text editors, HTML editors usually offer more advanced features to help you work with HTML and Java code.

BBEdit

BBEdit is a sophisticated HTML editor for the Macintosh operating system. BBEdit makes it easy to create JavaServer pages and is available at www.barebones.com.

HomeSite

Allaire's HomeSite is a comprehensive HTML editor designed for creating Web pages on the Windows operating system. HomeSite is suitable for beginners creating a small number of Web pages and for experienced Web masters producing complicated Web pages and Web sites. HomeSite includes syntax coloring for JavaServer Pages code and allows you to view the results generated by the code within HomeSite. HomeSite is available at www.allaire.com.

Integrated Development Environments

Instead of a text editor, you can use a Java Integrated Development Environment (IDE). An IDE is a program that allows you to create, execute, test and organize your source code. IDEs often contain additional features such as sample code, reusable components and troubleshooting capabilities. IDEs are commonly used to create larger applications and to enable multiple programmers to work on a single project at the same time.

JBuilder

Borland's JBuilder is one of the more popular Java IDEs. JBuilder is a sophisticated, full-featured IDE that can be used to create JSP pages and complex Java applications. JBuilder is also available for various UNIX operating systems. JBuilder is available at www.borland.com/jbuilder.

OBJECT-ORIENTED PROGRAMMING CONCEPTS

Java shares many concepts with other object-oriented programming languages, such as C++ and Perl. While object-oriented programming languages use the same concepts, the terminology and coding systems sometimes differ. For example, in Perl, a single value in an object is referred to as a property. In Java, this is referred to as a field.

The amount of object-oriented programming a Web site requires depends on the size and scope of the Web site. It also depends on where you store the Java code. Storing the Java code in the JSP pages themselves requires much less object-oriented programming than storing the Java code in external modules, referred to as *JavaBeans*.

JAVA CONCEPTS

Classes

A class is the Java code that serves as a template or plan for creating objects, which are the core features of object-oriented programming. A single class can be used to create many objects. For example, a class containing code for generating messages can be used to create an object that displays a welcome message at the top of each Web page. The same class can be used to create another object that displays copyright information at the bottom of a page. Classes can be used and shared by more than one Java program and therefore help programmers avoid having to constantly rewrite the same type of code.

Objects

An object is a package of code that is composed of data and procedures that make use of the data. Objects have two primary functions–to store information and to perform tasks. Objects contain fields, which are used to store information, and methods, which are used to perform tasks. Objects can be created to perform a single task or a range of related tasks. Multiple objects can be created using the same class. When an object is created, it is said to be an instance of the class used to create the object.

Fields

Fields, also known as data fields, are the properties or attributes associated with an object. In comparison to other programming languages, fields can be thought of as variables of the class. Fields can store different types of data, such as strings of text, integers and references to other objects.

Changing the value of an object's fields usually affects the behavior of the object. For example, in an object used to display a changing message on a Web page, a field may be used to specify how often the message changes. With a field value of 1, the message will be updated once every minute. When the field value is changed to 60, the message will be updated once an hour.

When multiple objects are created using the same class, it is typical for the objects to be the same except for the values held in the objects' fields.

Methods

Methods are code that objects use to perform a specific task. A class used to create objects can contain multiple methods. The methods in a class usually perform related tasks. For example, in a class used to format text information on Web pages, one method may be used to generate the code needed to format the headers of paragraphs. Another method may be used to format information in a table. The behavior of methods may be influenced by the values stored in the fields of the object.

Arguments

One or more values, called arguments, may be passed to a method to provide the method with input data or additional information about how to perform a task. For example, when using a method that creates tables on a Web page, you may need to pass the number of rows and columns for a table to the method. Some methods do not require any arguments.

Return Values

A method may return a value after performing a specific task. The return value may indicate the result of a calculation or it could indicate whether or not the task was performed successfully. For example, a method that writes information may return a true or false value, which the program can use to determine the next code that should be executed.

Object Relationships

The following diagram shows how a single class can be used to create multiple objects, each with its own distinct fields and methods.

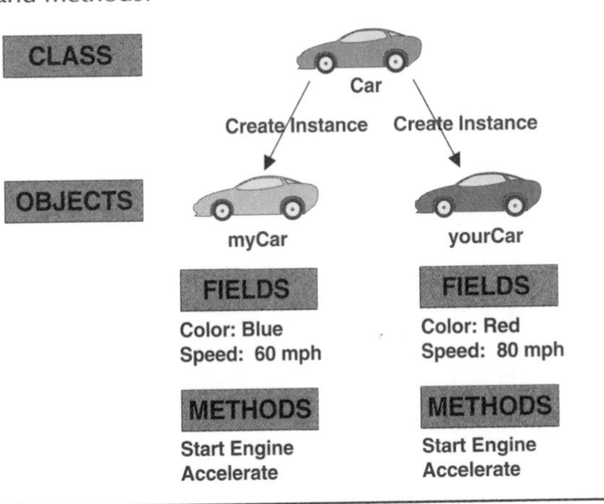

Data Hiding

Data hiding makes classes easier to use by hiding the fields and methods of the classes from other parts of the program. The program then has to know only how to access the class, not the internal workings of the class. Data hiding is often used in programs to protect classes from tampering and to ensure that the methods of the classes are used as originally intended. A programmer can modify and maintain the code within the class without affecting the programs that use the class. This also helps ensure that objects developed by multiple people are compatible.

THE JAVA CLASS LIBRARY

The Java class library is a collection of predefined classes that you can use in your programs. The Java class library is also known as the standard class library or the Java Applications Programming Interface (Java API).

Classes

Some predefined classes are used often in Java programs, such as those used to display output, while other classes are used infrequently, such as the classes used to create Graphical User Interfaces (GUIs). The classes included in the Java class library are available to every Java program you create. Using the predefined classes in the Java class library saves you time and effort when creating programs.

Java Class Library Installation

The Java class library is installed automatically when the Java Software Development Kit is installed on a computer. The Java class library is stored in a Java archive file named rt.jar in the lib subdirectory of the jre directory. The jre directory is located in the main Java SDK directory. You do not need to adjust any settings on your computer to specify the location of the Java class library before using a class from the library in your code.

Packages

The classes that make up the Java class library are organized into packages. A package is a set of related classes stored in a separate directory. For example, classes that are used to generate output are stored in a different package than classes used to process data from a database. Generally, classes stored in the same package can easily access each other.

Package names are based on the directory structure that stores the classes in the package. For example, the classes in the `java.util` package are stored in the util subdirectory of the java directory.

Import Packages

You can import a package from the Java class library into a Java program. This allows you to efficiently use all the classes in the package. The `java.lang` package is automatically imported into every Java program you create. For more information about importing a package, see page 52.

Create Packages

In addition to using predefined classes from Java class library packages, you can author your own classes and store them in packages you create. For example, if you create three classes to work with a Web site, you could store these classes in a package named website. You could then use the classes from the package when creating other Java applications. For more information about creating packages, see page 50.

Commonly Used Java Class Library Packages

The Java class library contains more than 70 packages. The following is a list of some of the most commonly used packages in the library.

`java.io`

Contains classes that allow Java programs to perform data input and output tasks.

`java.lang`

Contains the fundamental classes of the Java programming language and is automatically loaded by the Java compiler.

`java.math`

Contains classes that allow Java programs to perform arbitrary-precision arithmetic.

`java.lang.ref`

Contains classes that allow Java programs to interact with the garbage collector, which performs memory management tasks.

`java.lang.reflect`

Contains classes that allow Java programs to obtain information about the variables and methods of loaded classes.

`java.security`

Contains classes that allow Java programs to carry out security procedures, such as controlling access and encrypting data.

`java.sql`

Contains classes that allow Java programs to access and process data from a database.

`java.text`

Contains classes that allow a Java program to manipulate strings, dates, numbers and characters.

`java.util`

Contains utility classes that allow Java programs to perform various tasks such as date and time operations and random number generation.

`java.util.jar`

Contains utility classes that allow Java programs to read and write Java ARchive (JAR) files.

`java.util.zip`

Contains utility classes that allow Java programs to read and write ZIP files.

`javax.swing`

Contains classes for creating Swing Graphical User Interface (GUI) components. Swing GUI components can be used on all platforms.

JAVA CONVENTIONS

To use the Java programming language effectively, there are several conventions you should know. For more information about the conventions used in Java, you can consult the Java SDK documentation.

Semicolons

Most Java statements end with a semicolon (;). Java statements that include a block of code, known as the body of the statement, are the exception. Examples of these types of statements include methods, conditional statements and statements that create a loop. The Java compiler will stop compiling code and report an error if a required semicolon is missing or a semicolon is used where one is not needed. When an error occurs due to the omission or misplacement of a semicolon, the Java compiler may indicate that the error is in the statement following the actual location of the error. To avoid these types or errors, you should always review your Java code carefully before compiling the code.

Braces

Java statements that include a body use braces {} to indicate the beginning and the end of the body. A body often contains several statements. If a statement block contains only one statement, braces are typically not required. There are two accepted formats that you can use when including braces in your Java code. You should choose one format and then use that format consistently throughout your code.

The most widely used format places the opening brace on the same line as the Java statement. The closing brace is placed on its own line and in the same column as the first character of the Java statement that uses the braces.

Example:

```
public static void main(String[] args) {
      System.out.println("Hello.");
      System.out.println("My name is Bob.");
}
```

The second format places each brace on its own line. The braces are in the same column as the first character of the Java statement that uses the braces. This format is easier to read, but adds more lines to your Java code.

Example:

```
public static void main(String[] args)
{
      System.out.println("Hello.");
      System.out.println("My name is Mary.");
}
```

Indenting

When working with a Java statement that includes a body, you should always indent the code in the body. Indenting makes your code easier to read. Tabs or spaces can be used to indent code. To keep your Java programs consistent, you should use the same indenting style in all your code.

Code without indents:

```
public static void main(String[] args)
{
int counter = 1;
while (counter <= 5)
{
System.out.println(counter);
counter++;
}
}
```

Code with indents:

```
public static void main(String[] args)
{
      int counter = 1;
      while (counter <= 5)
      {
            System.out.println(counter);
            counter++;
      }
}
```

White Space

White space is the term used to describe characters that are not displayed or printed, such as spaces, tabs and newlines. Using white space in your Java code can greatly improve the readability of your code. For example, x + 1 / age is easier to read than x+1/age. The Java compiler ignores white space. This means that using white space will not affect the speed at which your Java code is compiled.

Comments

You can include comments in your Java code to explain important or difficult sections of code. Adding comments to your code is a good programming practice and can help make the code easier to understand. Comments are particularly useful if you or someone else will need to modify or troubleshoot the code in the future. For more information about adding comments to your Java code, see page 15. Using descriptive names for items such as classes, methods and variables can also make your code easier to understand.

Keywords

The Java programming language includes many keywords. A keyword is a word reserved for use only by Java. You cannot use keywords as variable names or values in your code. If you use a Java keyword inappropriately, the Java compiler will usually detect the error and stop compiling the code. The following table displays a listing of Java keywords:

abstract	else	interface	super
boolean	extends	long	switch
break	false	native	synchronized
byte	final	new	this
case	finally	null	throw
catch	float	package	throws
char	for	private	transient
class	goto	protected	true
const	if	public	try
continue	implements	return	void
default	import	short	volatile
do	instanceof	static	while
double	int	strictfp	

INSTALL THE JAVA SOFTWARE DEVELOPMENT KIT

The Java Software Development Kit (SDK) is a collection of programs used to compile and execute Java programs. You need to install the Java SDK in order to install the Tomcat Web server, which allows you to create and test JavaServer Pages.

The Java Software Development Kit is constantly being updated. A recent release of the Java SDK for Windows is included on the CD-ROM disc that accompanies this book, but you should make sure you use the latest release of the kit. More information about the latest release of the Java SDK is available on the Java Web site at java.sun.com. The Java SDK is also currently available for the Sun Solaris and Red Hat Linux platforms. Downloading and installation instructions are available at the Java Web site.

On the Windows platform, the Java SDK is installed using a standard Windows installation program. The Java SDK installation program selects a folder where the kit will be installed for you. It is recommended that you accept this folder. During the installation, you can select which components of the Java SDK you want to install, such as demos. It is recommended that you install all the available components.

The installation program allows you to choose to view a README file that contains information about the release of the Java Software Development Kit you installed and any last minute changes to the documentation. If you choose to display the file, it will open when the installation is complete. You should carefully review the README file for any new release of the Java SDK you install.

Once the Java SDK has been installed, you should restart your computer, particularly if you are upgrading from an older release of the Java SDK.

INSTALL THE JAVA SOFTWARE DEVELOPMENT KIT

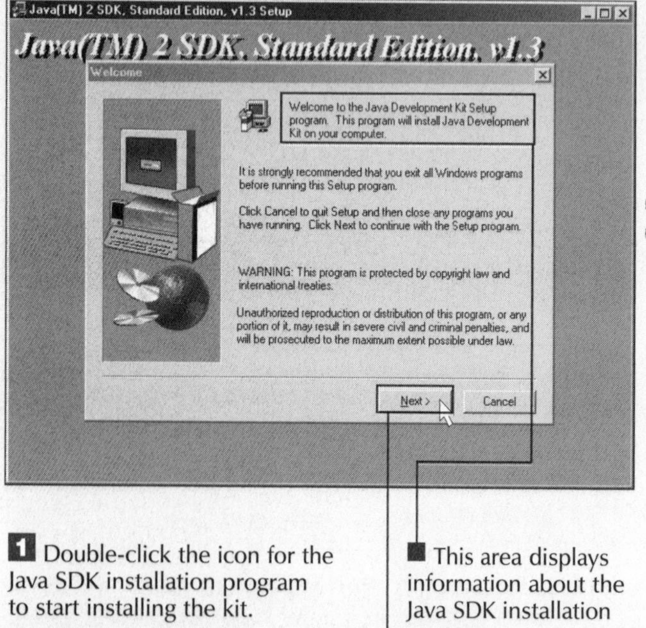

1 Double-click the icon for the Java SDK installation program to start installing the kit.

■ A setup window appears on the screen and a welcome dialog box is displayed.

■ This area displays information about the Java SDK installation program.

2 Click Next to continue.

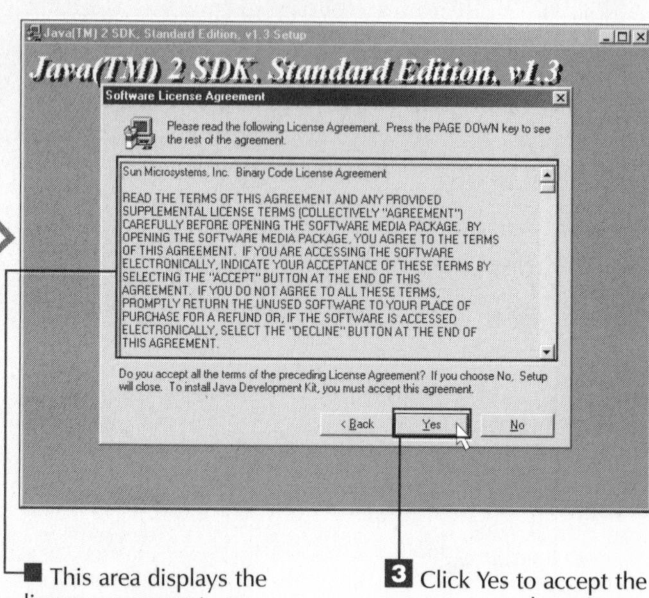

■ This area displays the license agreement you must read and accept before continuing.

3 Click Yes to accept the agreement and continue.

Extra

The Java SDK installation program is over 20 megabytes (MB) in size. If you are using a modem to connect to the Internet, the program can take a few hours to download. For convenience, you may want to start the download and let it continue through the night.

If you already have a previous release of the Java SDK installed on your computer, it is recommended that you uninstall the previous release before upgrading to the latest release of the Java SDK.

The Java SDK documentation can be downloaded separately from the Java Web site. It is recommended that you install and review the Java SDK documentation, particularly if you will be creating your own Java applications.

After installing the Java Software Development Kit, you may want to add the location of the Java SDK programs to the path variable of your computer's operating system. Setting the path variable will allow you to run your Java programs from any folder on the computer without having to type the full path to the Java compiler and interpreter. Refer to the documentation that came with the Java SDK and your operating system documentation for information about changing the path variable.

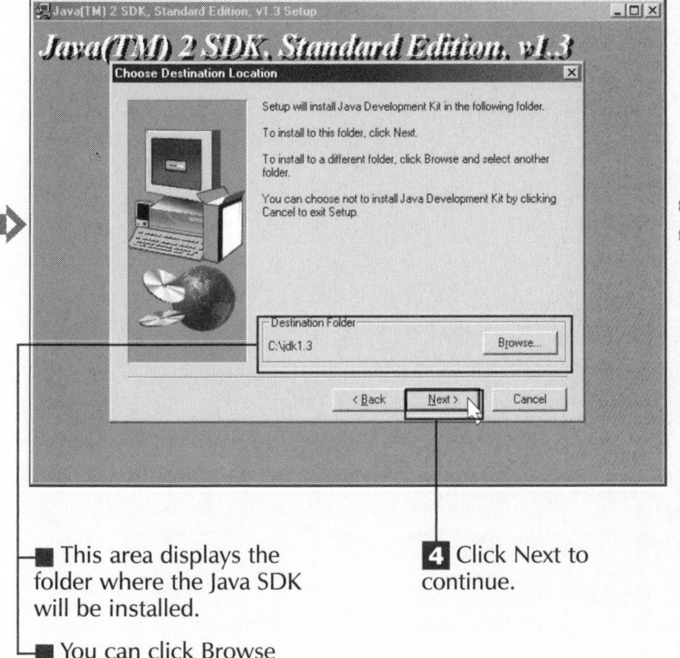

■ This area displays the folder where the Java SDK will be installed.

■ You can click Browse to install the Java SDK in a different folder.

4 Click Next to continue.

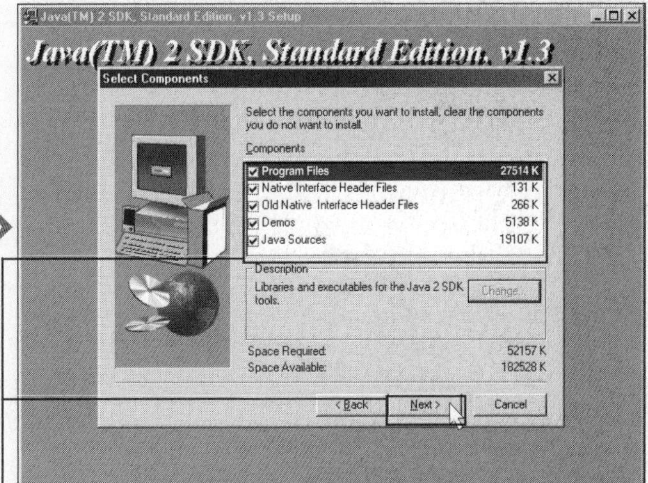

■ Each component in this area that displays a check mark (☑) will be installed. You can click the box beside a component you do not want to install (☑ changes to ☐).

5 Click Next to install the Java SDK components on your computer.

■ A dialog box appears when the installation is complete. Click Finish to close the dialog box and then restart your computer.

DECLARE A CLASS

After installing the Java Software Development Kit, you can begin creating Java programs. When creating Java programs, the first step is to declare a class. A class is the smallest unit of Java code that can be run and is the fundamental structure that Java applications use to group together related code. For example, a class called CheckText may contain all the code required to analyze and validate a string of text. The CheckText class can be used on its own in a program or used in conjunction with other classes. All Java applications must include at least one class.

Java classes are declared using the keyword `class` followed by the class name. The class name should be easy to understand and should indicate the purpose of the class. The class name is followed by a pair of braces `{}`. All methods and Java code in the class must be placed between the braces. The code between the braces is referred to as the body of the class and is made up of methods, which are structures that contain the Java code for specific actions. For more information about declaring a method, see page 16.

The class name you choose must be the same as the filename with which the program is saved. For example, if the class in your Java program is called DisplayText, the program must be saved with the filename DisplayText.java. It is also important to note that Java is a case-sensitive language. If the program is saved with the filename displaytext.java, an error may occur when you attempt to compile the program.

DECLARE A CLASS

1 Start the text editor you will use to create a Java program.

2 Type **class**.

3 Type the name of the class you want to create.

Extra

Class names can begin with any letter, an underscore (_) or the symbol $, £ or ¥. Class names cannot begin with a number or contain any punctuation, such as a period or a comma. Class names also cannot be the same as any of the Java reserved words, such as `do`, `while` or `public`. These naming rules also apply to the naming of methods, fields and parameters in Java code.

You may want to add comments that span multiple lines to your Java code. To do so, type /* before the first line of the comment and */ after the last line of the comment.

Example:

```
/*
This Java application
displays a welcome message when
the program is executed
*/
```

You should always include comments to make your Java code easier to understand. Comments are helpful if you or other people need to modify or troubleshoot the code. Any code you write should include comments that indicate the author's name and the main purpose of the program. Comments are preceded by // and can be included at the end of a line of code or on a separate line.

Example:

```
// Author: Martine Edwards
class DisplayWelcome  // A welcome message
{
     // The body of the class
}
```

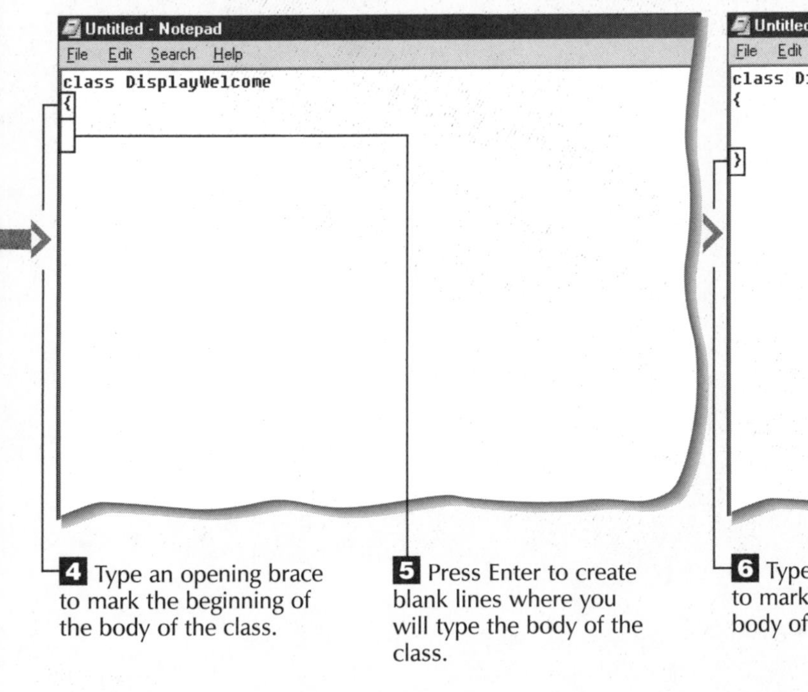

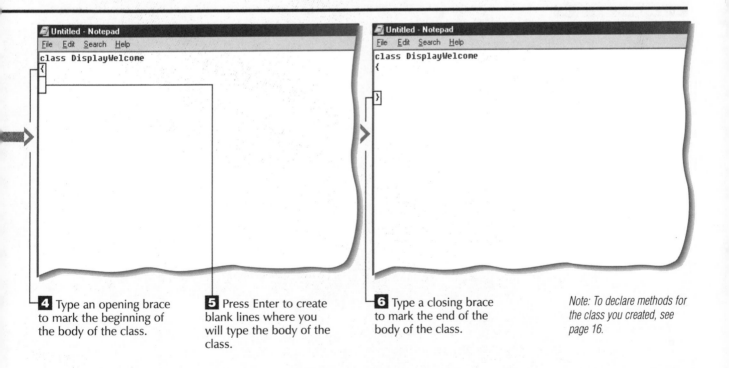

4 Type an opening brace to mark the beginning of the body of the class.

5 Press Enter to create blank lines where you will type the body of the class.

6 Type a closing brace to mark the end of the body of the class.

Note: To declare methods for the class you created, see page 16.

DECLARE A METHOD

Once a class has been declared, methods can be declared for the class. Methods are similar to subroutines and functions that are found in other, non-object-oriented programming languages. Methods contain lines of code that perform a specific task, such as displaying an invoice or calculating the final total of an invoice.

Using methods makes it easy to re-use sections of code and allows you to group lines of code into smaller, more manageable sections. This makes it easier for people to understand and troubleshoot the code.

You can use method modifiers, such as `public` and `static`, to tell Java how a method is to be used. The `public` method modifier is an access modifier that indicates that this method can be used by other classes that you create. A `static` method modifier indicates that the method can be used by any program without having to create an object of the class that declares the method.

A method declaration should also include a return type. A return type specifies the type of value the method returns. If a method does not return a value to the code, the return type should be `void`. For more information about return values in methods, see page 38.

The name of a method is followed by parentheses, such as DisplayInvoice().

Every Java application must have a method called `main`, in which all the other methods required to run the program are called. The argument `String[] args` must be placed within the parentheses at the end of the method name for a `main` method. This argument indicates that the method can accept strings passed from the command line when the Java program is executed.

The method declaration ends with a pair of braces. The code that makes up the body of the method is placed inside the braces.

DECLARE A METHOD

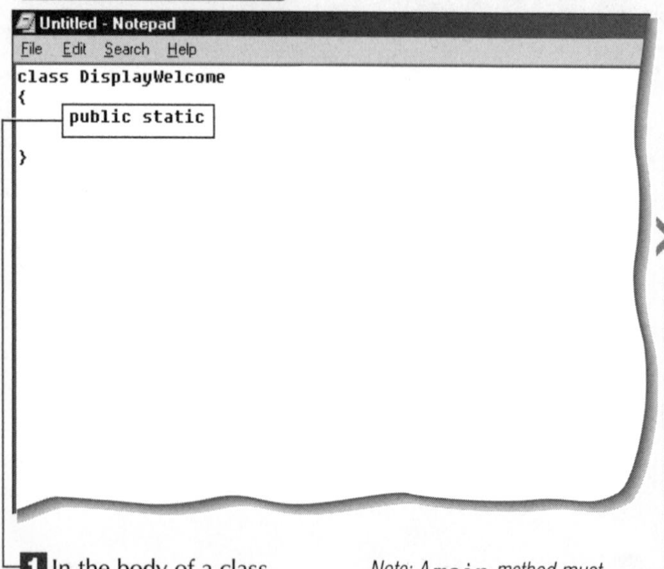

1 In the body of a class, type the method modifiers for the method you want to declare.

Note: A `main` method must include the `public` and `static` method modifiers.

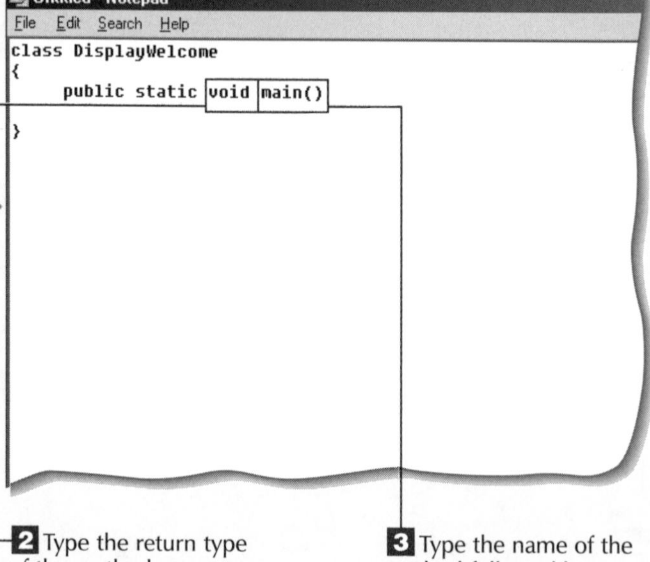

2 Type the return type of the method.

Note: A method that does not return a value must include the `void` return type.

3 Type the name of the method followed by ().

Extra

The name of the method should indicate the purpose of the method. A method name can consist of multiple words. To make the name easier to read, you can capitalize the first letter of each word, such as DisplayMyName.

You can use different access modifiers when declaring a method, depending on how the method will be accessed. The `public` access modifier indicates that the method can be accessed by any class and subclass within any *package*. The `protected` access modifier indicates the method can be accessed by any class within the same package and any subclass of the class that contains the method within a different package. The `private` access modifier indicates the method can be accessed only by the class that contains the method.

A method can generate a result which is returned to the code. The return type for a method that returns a value can be any valid data type in Java, such as `String`, `byte` or `boolean`. The body of a method that returns a value must also include a `return` statement. An error may occur if the data type of the value that is returned does not match the return type specified in the method declaration.

Every `main` method must include the `public`, `static` and `void` method modifiers. If one or more of the method modifiers are entered in a different order, the code may generate an error message.

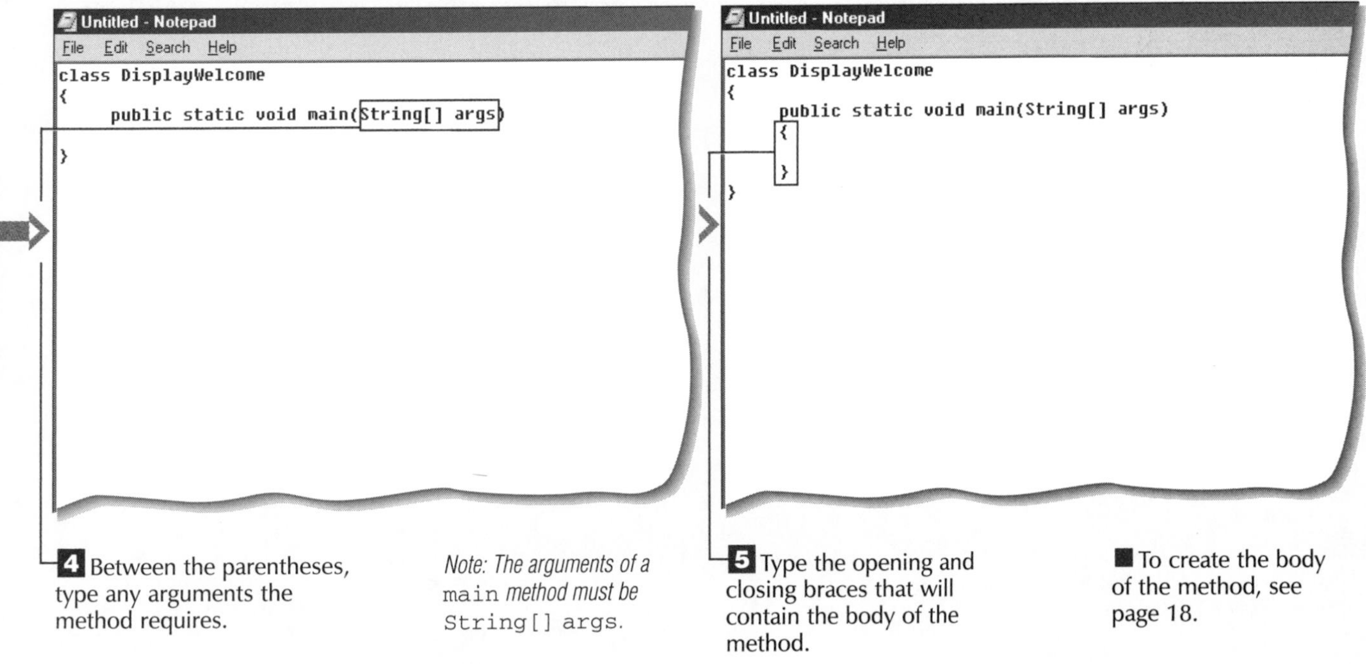

4 Between the parentheses, type any arguments the method requires.

Note: The arguments of a `main` *method must be* `String[] args`.

5 Type the opening and closing braces that will contain the body of the method.

■ To create the body of the method, see page 18.

CREATE THE METHOD BODY

The body of a method contains the Java code that is used to perform a task and must be created within the method's braces `{}`.

The code in the body of a method is often used to *call*, or access, another method. The called method can be declared in the same class or in a different class. Re-using methods saves you time and effort when writing Java programs. For example, if you create a method that displays your name and e-mail address, the same method can be used in any Java application you create.

The Java Software Development Kit includes many classes and methods that can be used to perform a wide variety of common tasks. For example, the Java SDK includes a class called `math`. The `math` class contains several methods that perform mathematical calculations. For example, to determine the square root of a number, you can simply call the `sqrt` method from the `math` class.

Methods can be used to display information on a user's screen. To display information, `System.out.print` can be used. The `System` object is included in the Java SDK and is created automatically when a Java program is executed. The `out` field is used to send information to the standard output device, typically the screen. The `print` member takes an argument that must be enclosed in parentheses. `System.out.print` can be used to display any type of data used in Java. When using `System.out.print` to display a string of text, the string must be enclosed in quotation marks.

Once you have finished creating the code for your Java program, save the code as a text file with the .java extension. The name of the file must be exactly the same as the name of the first class defined in the code.

CREATE THE METHOD BODY

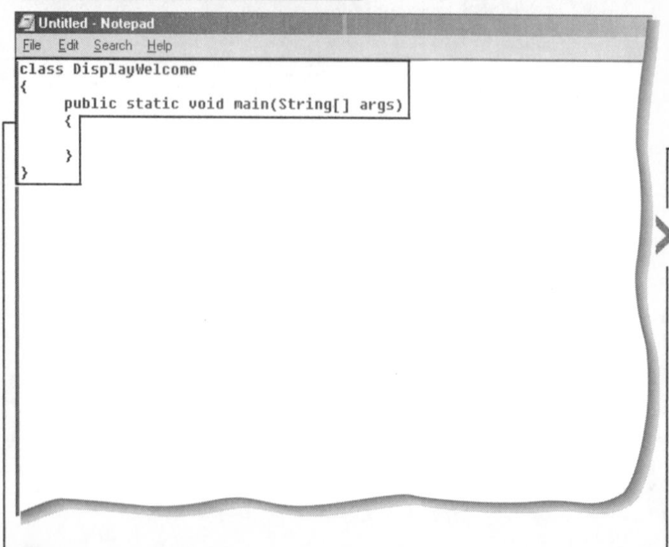

1 Enter the code that declares the class and the method you want to use.

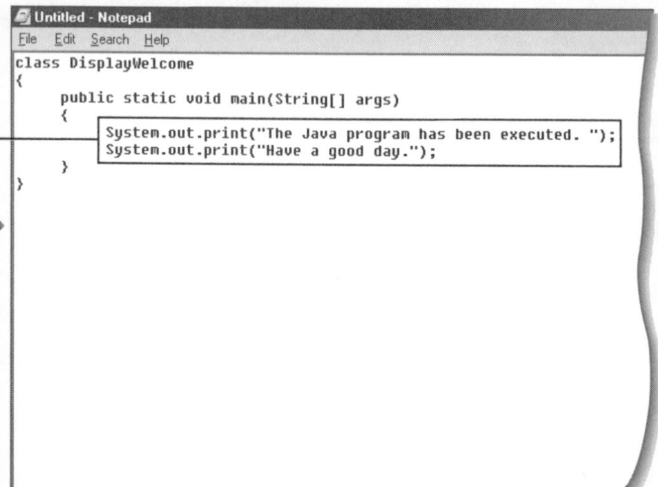

2 In the body of the method, type the code for the task you want to perform.

■ In this example, `System.out.print` is used to display output.

Extra

To start a new line at the end of a line of text, you can use the escape sequence `\n`. Using the escape sequence `\n` allows you to display text over multiple lines.

TYPE THIS:

```
class MyIntroduction
{
     public static void main(String[] args)
     {
          System.out.print("My name is Martine Edwards." + "\n");
          System.out.print("This is my first Java Program." + "\n");
     }
}
```

RESULT:

```
My name is Martine Edwards.
This is my first Java Program.
```

The classes and methods included with the Java Software Development Kit are collectively known as the *Java class library*, also called the Java Application Programming Interface or Java API. The Java SDK documentation describes all the classes and methods available in the Java class library. If you have not already installed the Java SDK documentation, you can obtain the documentation on the Web at java.sun.com.

`System.out.println` can also be used to start a new line.

Example:

```
System.out.println("The Java program has been executed.");
System.out.println("Have a good day.");
```

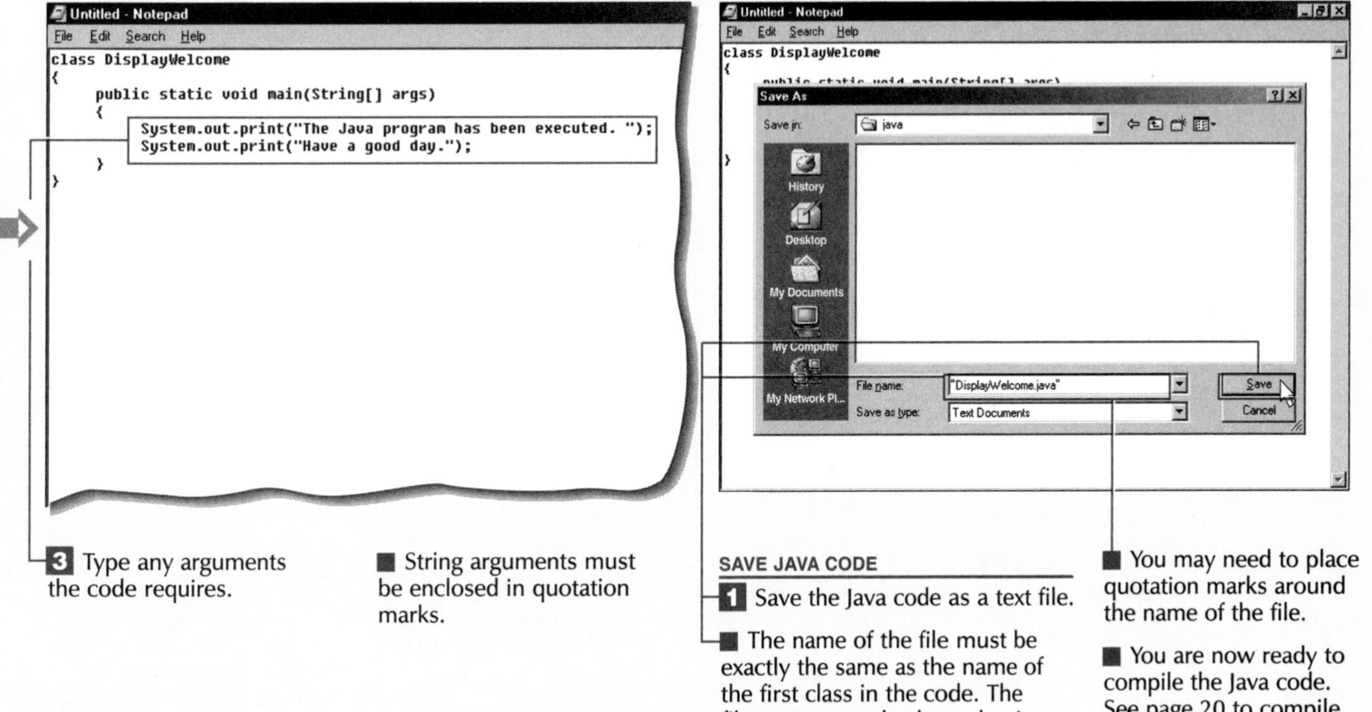

3 Type any arguments the code requires.

■ String arguments must be enclosed in quotation marks.

SAVE JAVA CODE

1 Save the Java code as a text file.

■ The name of the file must be exactly the same as the name of the first class in the code. The filename must also have the .java extension.

■ You may need to place quotation marks around the name of the file.

■ You are now ready to compile the Java code. See page 20 to compile Java code.

COMPILE JAVA CODE

Compiling Java code converts the source code into bytecode. Bytecode contains instructions that the *Java interpreter* executes.

A Java compiler is required to compile Java code. The Java Software Development Kit includes a Java compiler called javac. The javac compiler can only be executed from the command prompt. If you are using a Windows operating system, you will need to open an MS-DOS Prompt or Command Prompt window to use javac.

To compile Java source code, you enter the name of the Java compiler, such as javac, at the command prompt, followed by the name of the file that stores the code you want to compile. The filename must have the .java extension. Depending on whether you have added the location of the Java SDK programs to your operating system's path variable, you may need to specify the full path to the Java compiler, which is typically c:\jdk1.3\bin\javac. For information about setting the path variable, refer to the Java SDK installation instructions or your operating system's documentation.

Before compiling Java code, the Java compiler checks the code for errors. If an error is found, the code will not be compiled and an error message will be displayed.

If the Java code is successfully compiled, the resulting bytecode will be saved in a new file with the .class extension. The name of the new file is taken from the name of the file that stores the Java source code. For example, when the code in a file named Program.java is compiled, the bytecode is saved in a file called Program.class. The filenames of Java programs are case sensitive on most platforms.

Once Java source code has been compiled, the Java program is ready to be executed.

COMPILE JAVA CODE

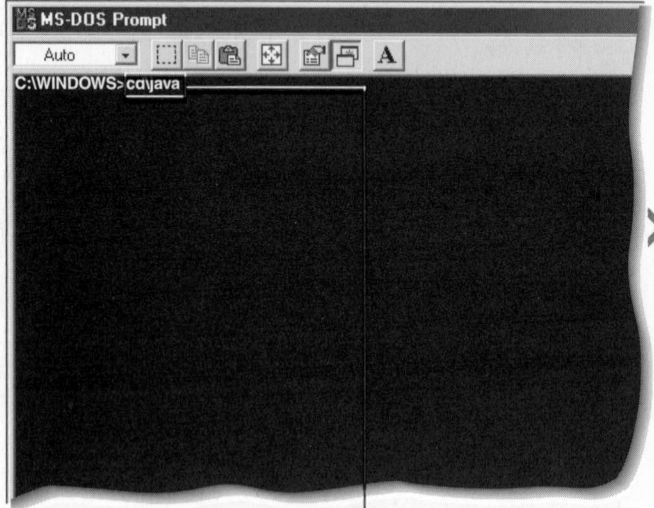

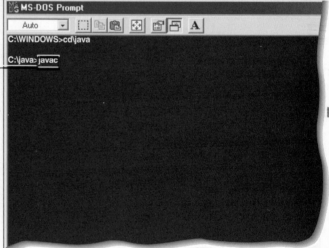

1 Open the window that allows you to work at the command prompt.

2 Move to the directory that stores the Java code you want to compile.

3 To compile the Java code using the javac compiler, type **javac**.

■ If you have not added the location of the javac compiler to your operating system's path variable, you will need to type the full path to the javac program.

Extra

When compiling Java source code, there are two main types of errors that can occur.

Java SDK Errors

If your operating system cannot locate the Java compiler, a problem may have occurred when the Java SDK was installed. Java SDK errors usually result in an error message such as "bad command or file name." To correct this type of error, first determine the correct path to the compiler. If you cannot locate the Java compiler, try re-installing the Java SDK. If you were able to confirm the path to the compiler, ensure that you have not made any typing mistakes in the path.

Source Code Errors

A wide variety of errors can occur in Java source code. When the Java compiler finds an error in source code, the compiler displays an error message that usually specifies the error type and where the error was detected. For example, the error "Program.java:5: invalid method declaration" indicates that an error involving a method declaration was generated at line 5 in the Program.java file. It is important to note that the line number indicates the line that the compiler was processing when the error was detected, which is not necessarily the line that contains the error.

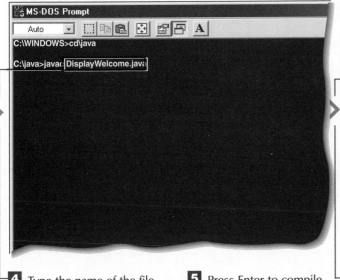

4 Type the name of the file that stores the Java code you want to compile, including the .java extension.

5 Press Enter to compile the Java code.

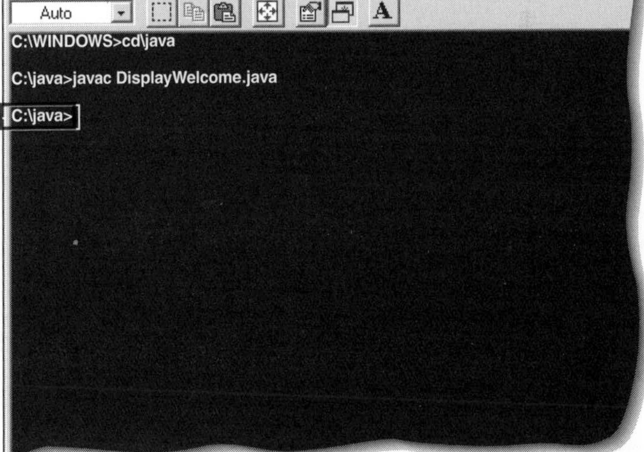

■ If the Java code was successfully compiled, the command prompt re-appears.

■ The Java program is now ready to be executed. See page 22 to execute a Java program.

Note: If an error message appears, the Java code was not successfully compiled.

EXECUTE A JAVA PROGRAM

Once the Java compiler has converted the source code for a Java program into bytecode, the program can be executed.

Bytecode must be processed by the Java interpreter before the code can be executed. When you execute a Java program, the Java interpreter first checks the bytecode to ensure the code is safe to execute and then it interprets and executes the instructions contained within the bytecode.

The instructions in the bytecode are executed by the Java interpreter in what is called the Java Virtual Machine, or JVM. The Java virtual machine enables Java programs to be executed in a controlled environment. This environment may also protect your computer from harmful code that may be included in Java programs.

The Java interpreter that comes with the Java SDK is called java and is typically stored in the c:\jdk1.3\bin directory.

Like the Java compiler, the Java interpreter must be run at the command prompt. The Java interpreter is a stand-alone program, but the interpreter can also be integrated into other programs, such as Web browsers. This allows you to execute your Java programs on different platforms.

To evoke the Java interpreter, type the name of the interpreter followed by the name of the bytecode file. You should not type the .class extension. For example, to execute the instructions in the Program.class file, type **java Program.**

If the Java program executes successfully, the results of the program will be displayed. If the Java interpreter encounters any errors, it will stop executing the program. Most errors encountered at this stage are usually related to the use of incorrect filenames or paths.

EXECUTE A JAVA PROGRAM

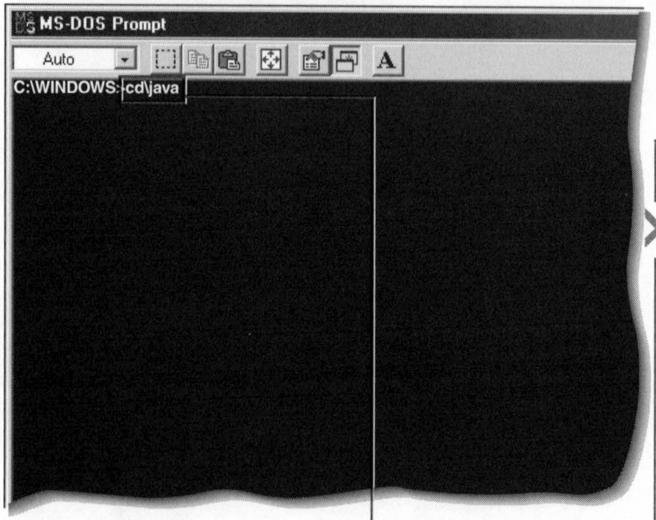

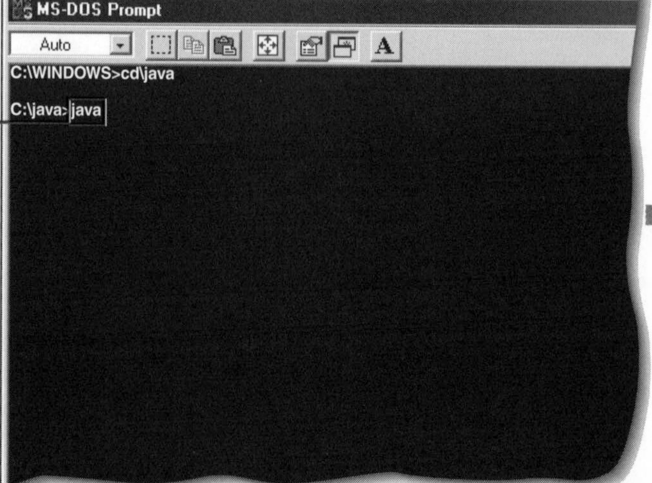

1 Open the window that allows you to work at the command prompt.

2 Move to the directory that stores the bytecode for the Java program you want to execute.

3 To execute the instructions in the bytecode using the Java interpreter, type **java.**

■ If you have not added the location of the Java interpreter to your operating system's path variable, you will need to type the full path to the Java interpreter.

Extra

How Java Code Is Processed

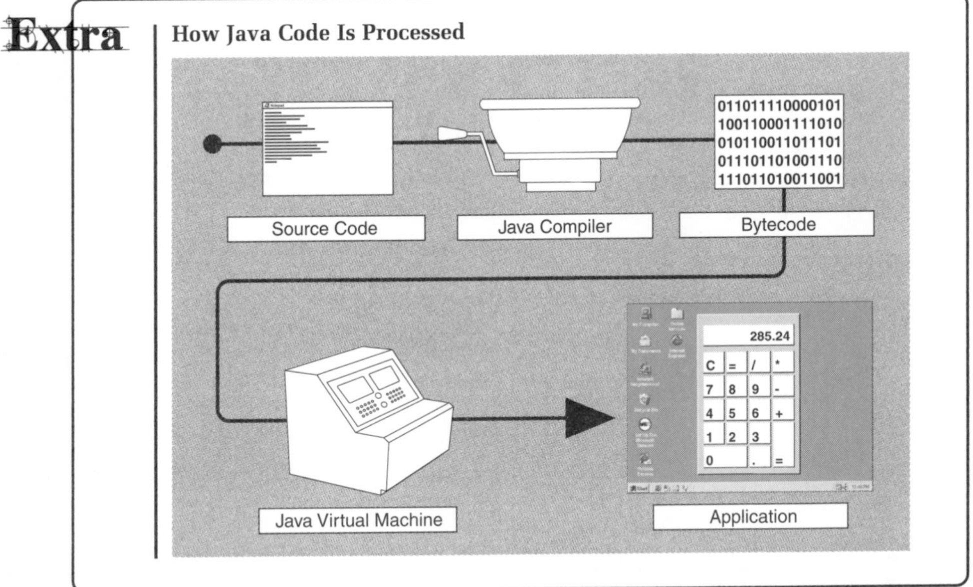

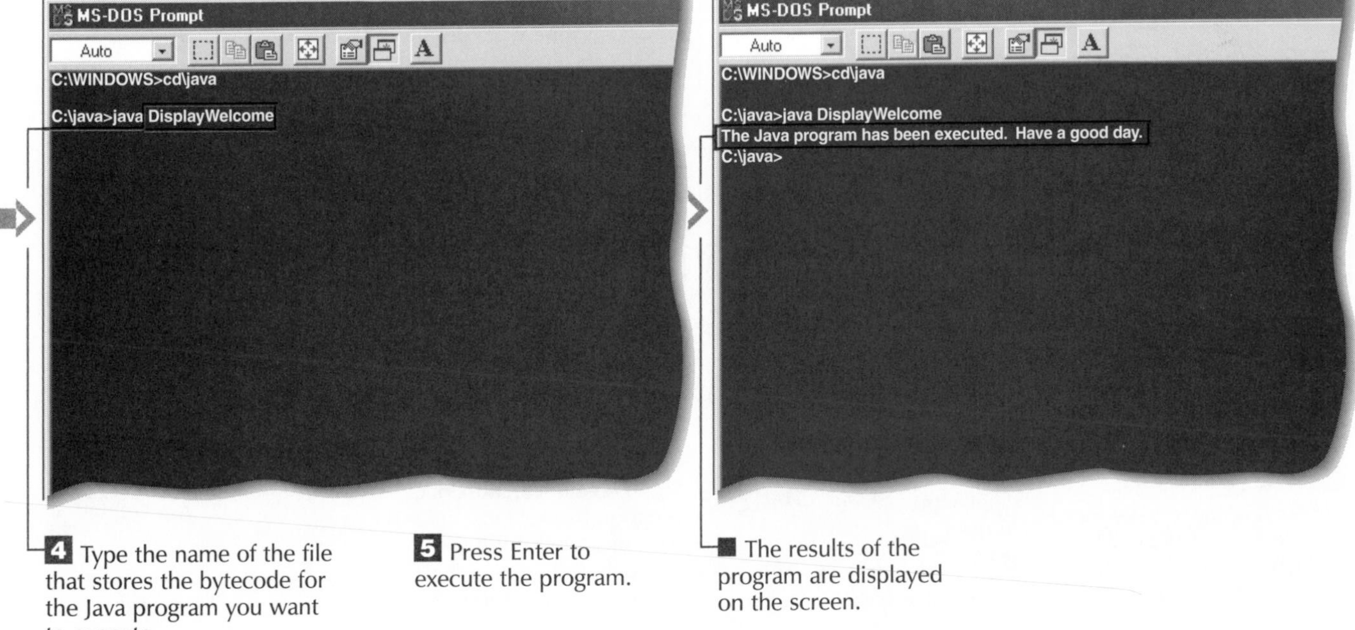

4 Type the name of the file that stores the bytecode for the Java program you want to execute.

5 Press Enter to execute the program.

■ The results of the program are displayed on the screen.

CREATE AN OBJECT

Objects are created using classes. An object usually contains at least one method that specifies the behavior of the object. Objects may also contain fields. For information about fields, see page 26.

The first step in creating an object is to create a class that will serve as a template for the object. In its simplest form, this type of class contains a class declaration, a method declaration and a method body. The method body contains code defining specifications for the object, such as the tasks the object will perform. This type of class is not executed as a stand-alone program and therefore does not need to use the `main` method. Before the class can be used to create an object, you must compile the code for the class.

Once you have created and compiled the class that serves as a template for an object, you can use a stand-alone program to create, or instantiate, the object. To instantiate an object, you must assign the object a name, which is used to access the object. You then use the `new` operator and the name of the class that defines the object to create the object. You can create multiple instances of an object within a program.

After creating an object, you can access a method of the object. This allows the object to take on the characteristics defined in the class. To access a method, you enter the name of the object and the name of the method, separated by a dot. For example, if you create an object named 'employee' that contains a method called DisplayName, you would access the method by entering employee.DisplayName.

CREATE AN OBJECT

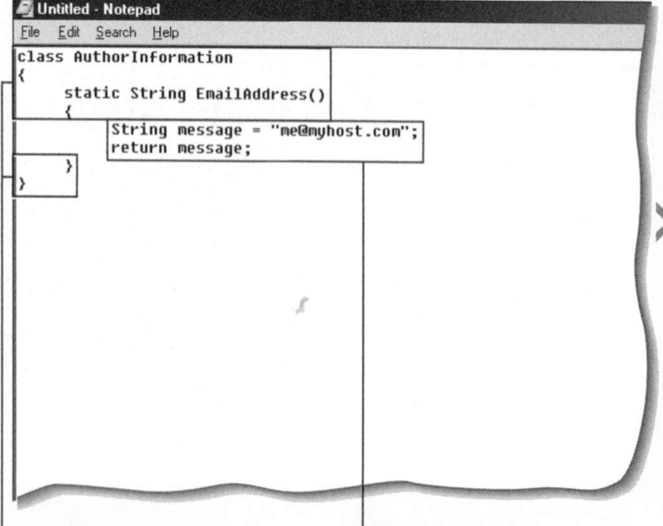

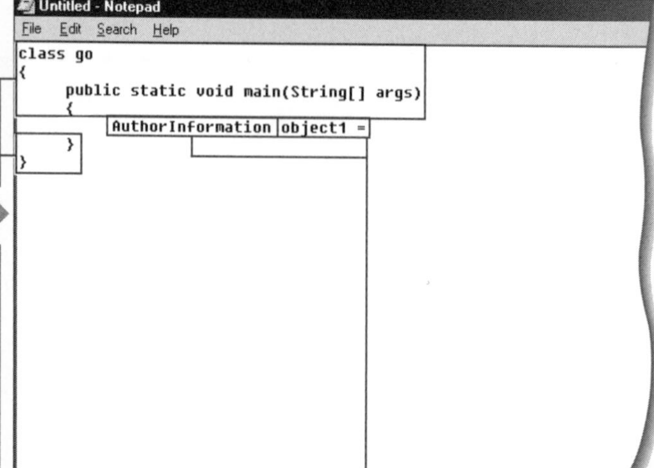

DEFINE THE OBJECT

1 To create a class that will serve as a template for an object, enter the code that defines the class and method you want to use.

Note: This class does not need to use the `main` method.

2 In the body of the method, type the code that defines the object you want to use.

3 Save the class as a text file with the .java extension.

4 Compile the Java code.

INSTANTIATE THE OBJECT

5 To create a stand-alone program that will instantiate the object, enter the code that defines the class and method you want to use.

6 In the body of the method, type the name of the class you created in step 1.

7 Type a name for the object, followed by =.

Extra

The directory you should use to store files you create for Java programs depends on the setup of your computer. In most cases, you should have a specific folder dedicated to Java program development. Regardless of the location you choose, you should always store the class file that defines an object and the file that instantiates the object in the same directory.

It is very rare that an object will be made up of only a single method. In most cases, objects are more complex, containing a wide range of related methods and fields that dictate the behavior of the object.

The fields and methods of an object are also referred to as members. Fields and methods that are available when an object is instantiated and are unique to that object are called instance members.

The ability to create objects is an important feature of JavaServer Pages. JavaServer Pages technology makes use of JavaBeans, which are a form of class file used to create objects. While it is possible to create JSP pages without knowing how to create objects, the flexibility and efficiency of your pages will be limited.

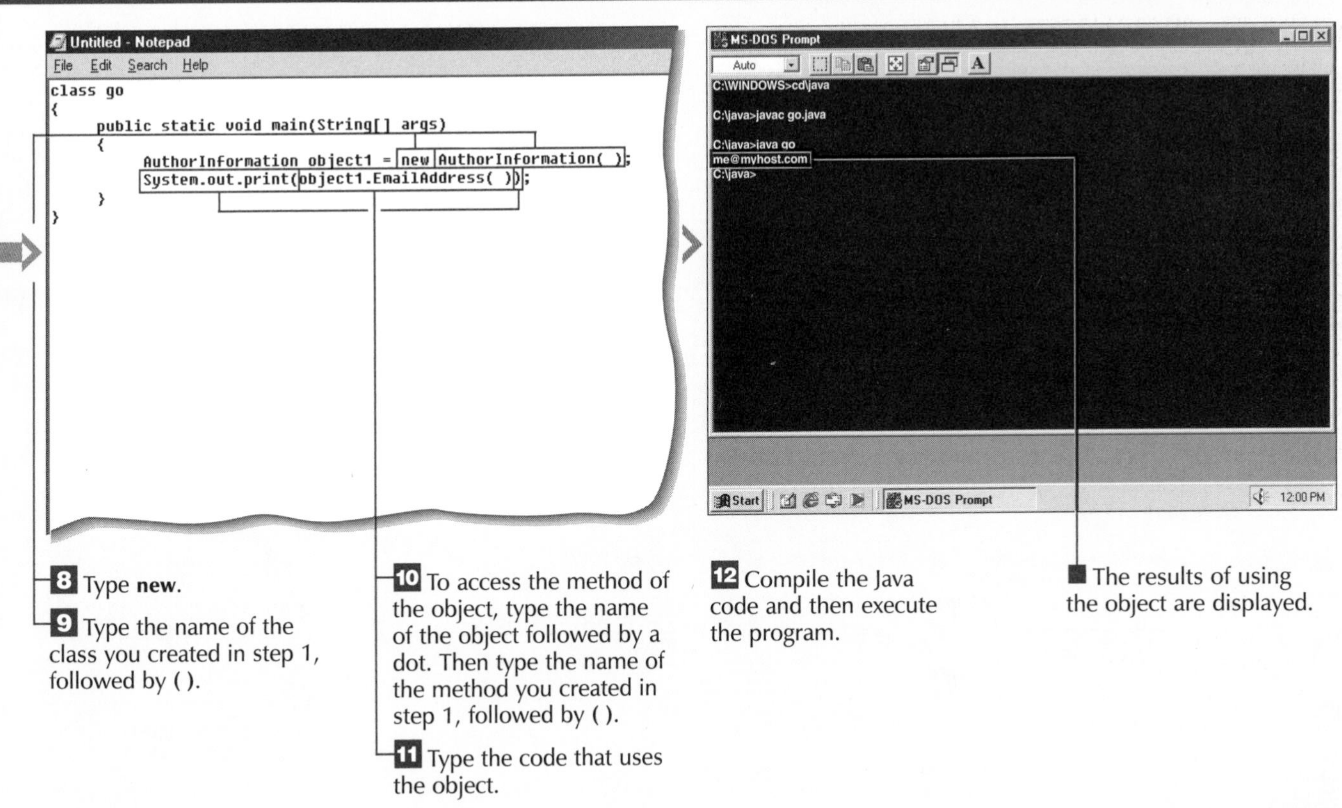

8 Type **new**.

9 Type the name of the class you created in step 1, followed by ( ).

10 To access the method of the object, type the name of the object followed by a dot. Then type the name of the method you created in step 1, followed by ( ).

11 Type the code that uses the object.

12 Compile the Java code and then execute the program.

■ The results of using the object are displayed.

WORK WITH OBJECT FIELDS

You can create an object field, also referred to as data field, to hold information about an object. The information contained in an object's fields determines the properties and attributes of the object.

When objects of the same class are created, the objects have the same methods, but some or all of the object fields may hold different information. For example, each object created from the Employee class may have an object field called empNumber that stores the unique employee number for each object.

Object fields must be declared in the class body, outside of any methods. This allows the field to be used as soon as the object is created. You must specify an access modifier for an object field you create, as well as the data type that the field will store. For information about access modifiers, see page 16. For information about data types, see page 30.

Most object fields are created with an initial value. You can later change the value of an object field as you would change the value of a variable. Changing the value of an object field may change the way some of the methods of the object behave. Object fields may also hold constant data which cannot be changed.

You can use the dot operator (`.`) to access an object field in a program. When specifying the object field, the field name is separated from the object name by a dot, such as object.field. The object name is the name that was given to the object when it was created.

Unlike methods, object field names are not followed by parentheses. It is possible to have object fields and methods that share the same name in a program.

WORK WITH OBJECT FIELDS

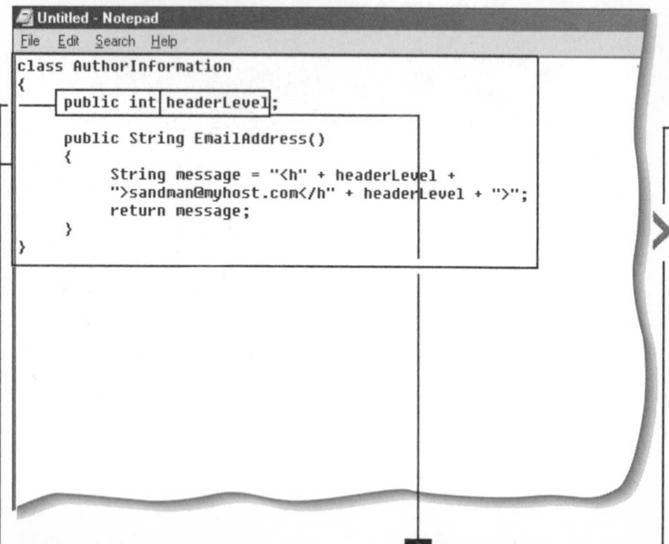

CREATE A FIELD

1 Create a class that will serve as a template for an object.

2 In the body of the class, type the access modifier and data type for the object field you want to create.

3 Type the name of the object field.

4 Save the class as a text file with the .java extension and then compile the Java code.

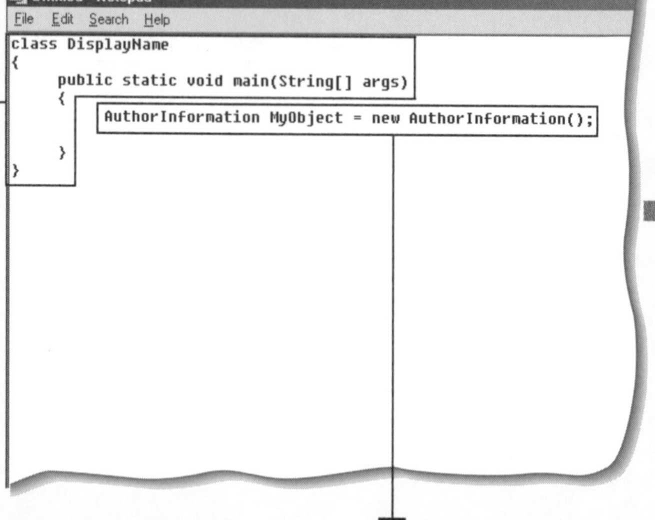

USE AN OBJECT FIELD

5 To create a stand-alone Java program, enter the code that declares the class and `main` method.

6 In the body of the `main` method, type the code to create an object using the class you created in step 1.

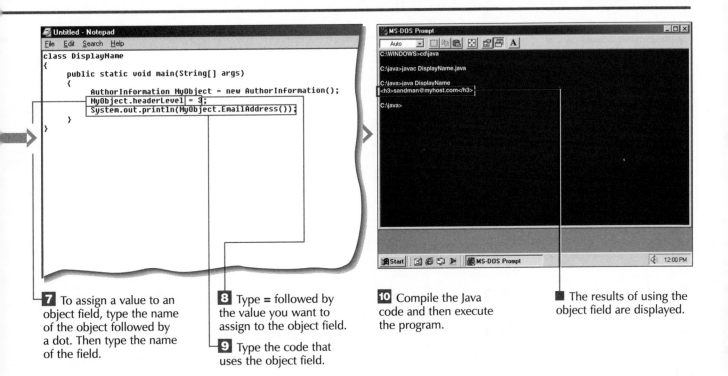

You can set a default value for an object field by using a constructor. A constructor is a special type of method that is always executed each time the class is accessed and an object is created. This makes constructors useful for performing initialization tasks for new objects, such as setting up a connection to a database. A constructor method must have the same name as the class for which it is the constructor.

Example:

```
class AuthorInformation
{
      public int headerLevel;

      public AuthorInformation()
      {
            headerLevel = 3;
      }

      public String EmailAddress()
      {
            String message = "<h" + headerLevel +
            ">sandman@myhost.com</h" + headerLevel + ">";
            return message;
      }
}
```

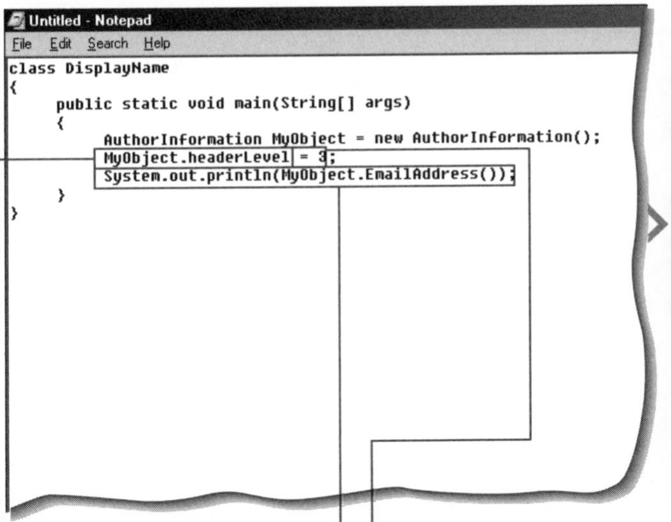

```
class DisplayName
{
      public static void main(String[] args)
      {
            AuthorInformation MyObject = new AuthorInformation();
            MyObject.headerLevel = 3;
            System.out.println(MyObject.EmailAddress());
      }
}
```

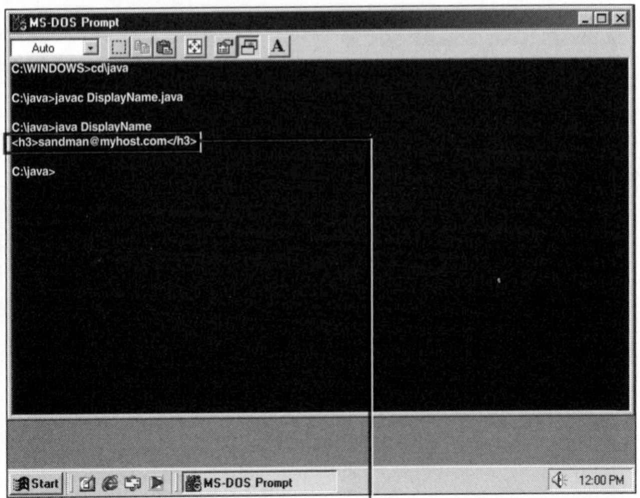

```
C:\WINDOWS>cd\java

C:\java>javac DisplayName.java

C:\java>java DisplayName
<h3>sandman@myhost.com</h3>

C:\java>
```

7 To assign a value to an object field, type the name of the object followed by a dot. Then type the name of the field.

8 Type **=** followed by the value you want to assign to the object field.

9 Type the code that uses the object field.

10 Compile the Java code and then execute the program.

■ The results of using the object field are displayed.

DECLARE A VARIABLE

A variable is a name that represents a value. For example, you could have the variable myAge represent the value 29. Variables can be used to perform many types of calculations. Before a variable can be used in a Java program, you must declare the variable. Declaring a variable tells the computer to set aside an area of memory to store information.

A variable can hold only a specific type of data, such as a text character or a number. When you declare a variable, you specify the type of data the variable can store. For example, to specify that a variable will hold only a whole number that is not a fraction, you would use an integer data type. To declare a variable that will hold an integer, place the keyword `int` before the variable name. For more information about variable data types, see page 30.

A variable name can consist of multiple words. You can use a lowercase first letter and then capitalize the first letter of each of the following words to make the name easy to read. The underscore character (_) can also be used to separate the words in the name, such as `my_age`.

When you declare a variable, you can assign an initial value to the variable. To assign a value to a variable, you use the *assignment operator* (=). For information about operators, see page 34.

If you have multiple variables of the same type, you can declare all the variables on the same line by separating each variable name with a comma.

Once a variable has been declared, it can be used within the method in which it was created. If the variable was created outside of a method, it can be used by any code within the class. Variables declared outside of a method should be declared at the top of the class body. For information about declaring variables in the class body, see page 56.

DECLARE A VARIABLE

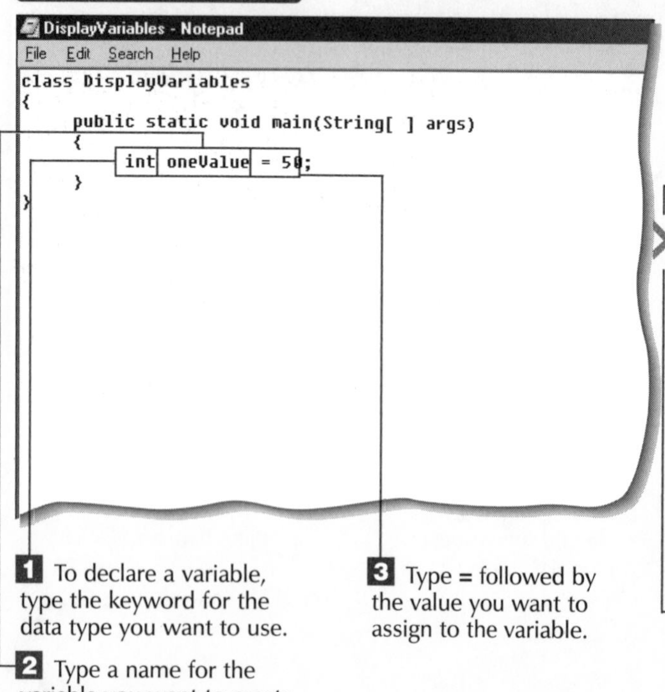

1 To declare a variable, type the keyword for the data type you want to use.

2 Type a name for the variable you want to create.

3 Type = followed by the value you want to assign to the variable.

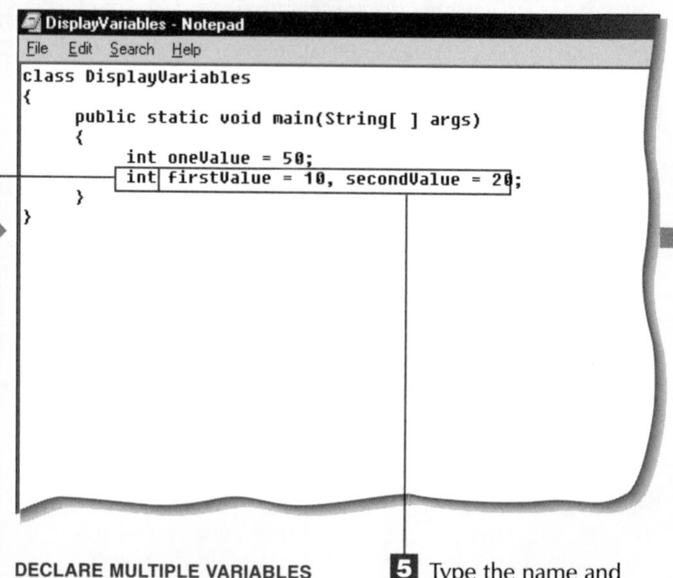

DECLARE MULTIPLE VARIABLES

4 To declare multiple variables, type the keyword for the data type of the variables.

5 Type the name and value of each variable you want to create, separated by a comma.

Extra

If you have not yet determined the value for a variable, you can create a variable without assigning a value. Java will assign a default value to the variable, but you can later assign a value in a separate statement.

Example:

```
int firstValue;
System.out.println("Welcome to my program.");
firstValue = 10;
```

When selecting a variable name, choose a name that describes the value of the variable. For example, `employeeNumber` is more descriptive than `variable1`. Also keep in mind that variable names are case sensitive. This means the variable `AGE` will be different than the variable `age` or `Age`.

Any method you use to determine variable names is acceptable if it makes sense to you and is easy for other people to interpret. You should consistently use the style you choose to make your script easier to understand.

Typing mistakes are a common source of errors in Java code. If the Java compiler displays error messages that refer to undeclared or missing variables, you should first check to make sure you typed each variable name the same way throughout your code.

If the name of a variable is not self-explanatory, you may want to add a comment to the variable declaration to explain the purpose of the variable.

Example:

```
int minutes;    //Minutes to display welcome message
```

DisplayVariables - Notepad

File Edit Search Help

```
class DisplayVariables
{
    public static void main(String[ ] args)
    {
        int oneValue = 50;
        int firstValue = 10, secondValue = 20;

        System.out.println(oneValue);
        System.out.println(firstValue);
        System.out.println(secondValue);
    }
}
```

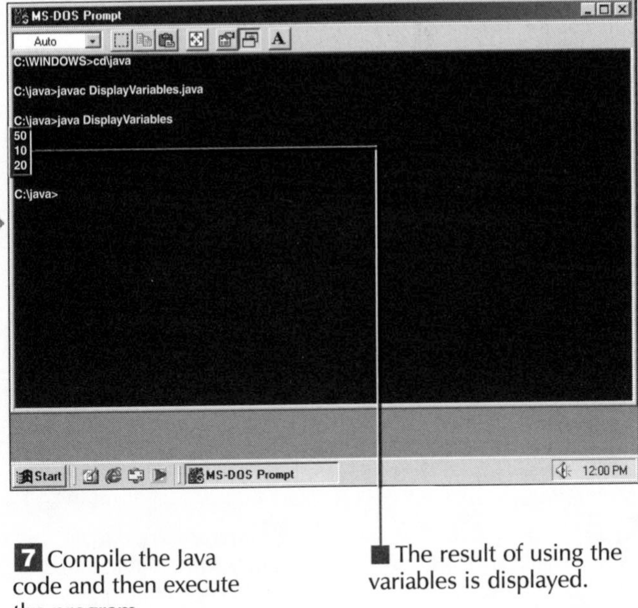

6 Type the code that uses the variables.

7 Compile the Java code and then execute the program.

■ The result of using the variables is displayed.

SPECIFY THE DATA TYPE FOR A VARIABLE

Java is a 'strongly typed language', which means that you must specify a data type for each variable you use in a Java program. This distinguishes Java from many other programming languages such as Perl, which do not require variables to have assigned data types.

There are eight basic data types, called primitive types, that variables can use. The data type you specify for a variable determines the range of values that the variable can store and the amount of memory, measured in bits, that the variable requires. For example, a variable with the `byte` data type can store a number between -128 and 127 and requires 8 bits of memory.

Each primitive data type has a default value. If you declare a variable without assigning a value, the default value for the variable's data type will be assigned to the variable.

The specifications for data types in Java, such as memory requirements and default values, are not affected by the operating system or compiler that is used. This ensures that a data type will have the same meaning when a program is executed on different computers.

Specifying the data type for a variable requires that you know in advance the types of values that will be stored in the variable throughout your program. Once you declare a variable, you cannot change the data type for the variable. If you want to convert the value stored in a variable to a different data type, you must assign the value to a new variable that uses the desired data type. This process is called casting. When converting a value to a new data type, make sure that the conversion will not result in an unintended loss of data. For example, converting the number 13.56 to an integer value will result in a new value of 13.

SPECIFY THE DATA TYPE FOR A VARIABLE

DisplayVariables - Notepad

File Edit Search Help

```
class DisplayVariables
{
     public static void main(String[] args)
          {
          double firstValue = 1.1;
          }
}
```

1 To specify a data type for a variable you want to create, type the name of the data type in the body of the method.

2 Type the code that names the variable and assigns it a value.

Note: If you do not assign a value, the variable will use the default value for its data type.

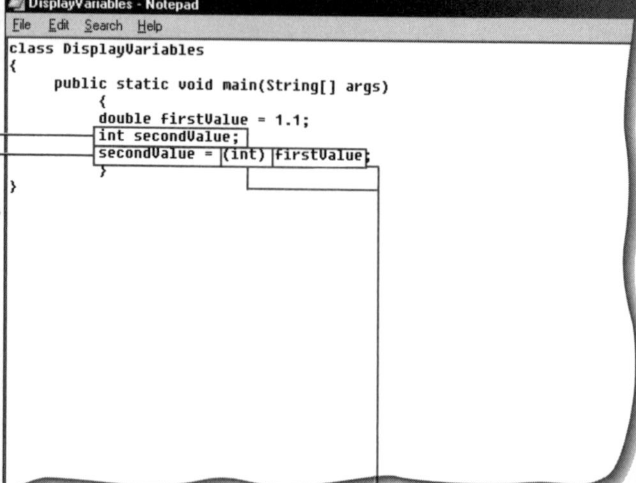

CONVERT A VALUE TO A DIFFERENT DATA TYPE

3 Type the code that declares a variable that will store the converted value.

4 Type the name of the variable you created in step 3, followed by =.

5 Type the data type you want to convert the value to, enclosed in parentheses.

6 Type the name of the variable that stores the value you want to convert.

Extra

Primitive Data Types

TYPE:	SIZE IN BITS:	DEFAULT VALUE:	POSSIBLE VALUES:
boolean	8	false	'true' or 'false'
char	16	\u0000	Unicode character, '\u0000' to 'uFFFF'
byte	8	0	-128 to 127
short	16	0	-32,768 to 32,767
int	32	0	-2,147,483,648 to 2,147,483,647
long	64	0	-9,223,372,036,854,775,808 to 9,223,372,036,854,775,807
float	32	0.0	±1.4E-45 to ±3.4028235E+38
double	64	0.0	±4.9E-324 to ±1.7976931348623157E+308

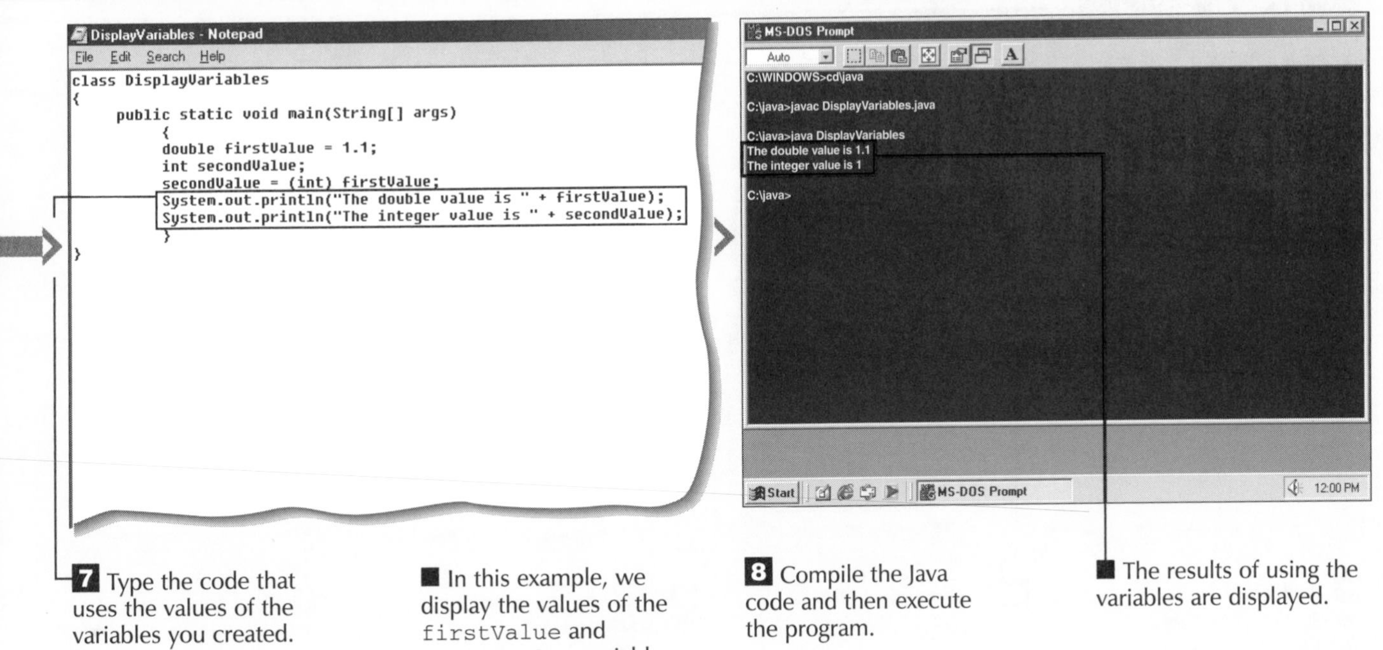

7 Type the code that uses the values of the variables you created.

■ In this example, we display the values of the `firstValue` and `secondValue` variables.

8 Compile the Java code and then execute the program.

■ The results of using the variables are displayed.

WORK WITH STRINGS

A string is a collection of characters, which can contain any combination of letters, numbers and special characters, such as $, & or #.

Before a string variable can be used in a Java program, you must declare the string variable. The process of declaring a string variable is similar to that of declaring other types of variables. To declare a string variable, use the keyword `String` followed by the variable name. The capital S at the beginning of the keyword `String` indicates that a string variable is an object of the `String` class. The `String` class is part of the `java.lang` package that is available to all Java programs as part of the standard class library. For information about the Java standard class library, see page 8.

After a string variable has been declared, a value can be assigned to the variable. To assign a value to a string variable, you use the assignment operator (=). A string value must be enclosed in double quotation marks (""), which identify the beginning and end of the string and allow Java to work with the string as one piece of information.

You can use the concatenation operator (+) to join multiple strings together. The concatenation operator can also be used to join other types of variables and values together.

If you installed the documentation package available for the Java Software Development Kit, you can find more information about the `String` class under the main JDK directory at \docs\api\java\lang\String.html. You can also find documentation for the Java SDK at the java.sun.com Web site.

WORK WITH STRINGS

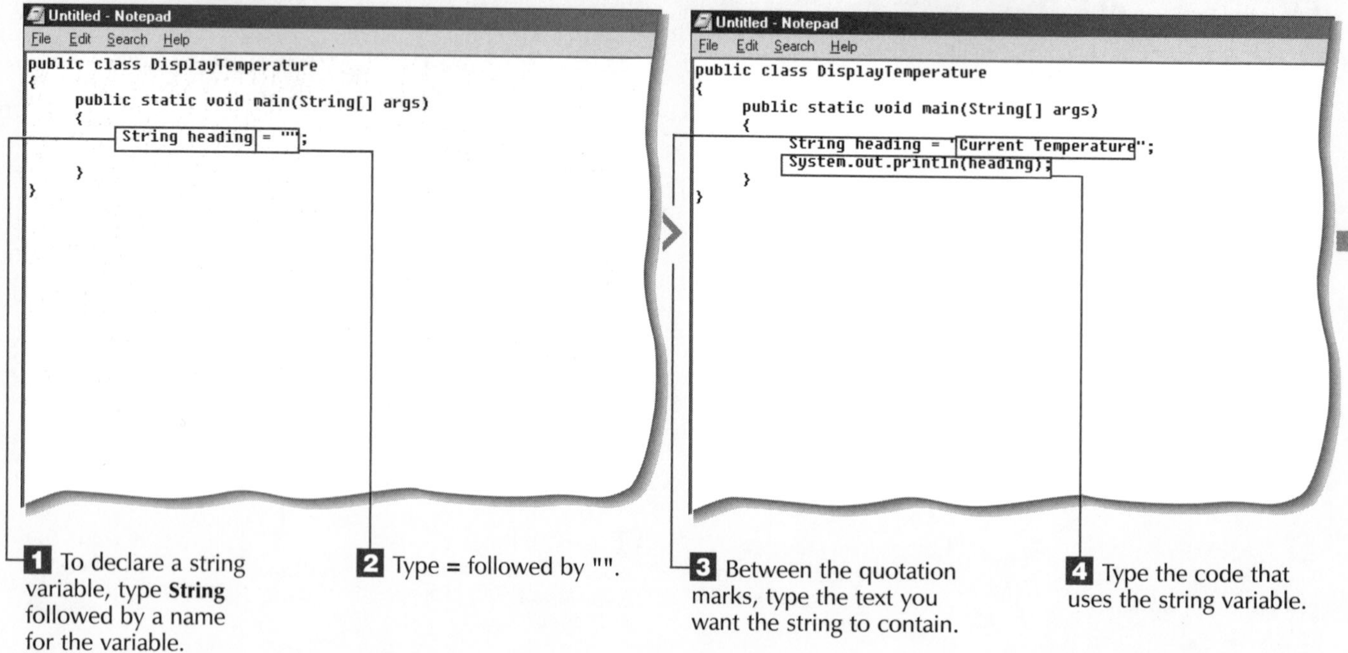

1 To declare a string variable, type **String** followed by a name for the variable.

2 Type = followed by "".

3 Between the quotation marks, type the text you want the string to contain.

4 Type the code that uses the string variable.

Extra

You can determine the number of characters a string contains by using the `length` method of the `String` class.

TYPE THIS:

```
String message = "The temperature is ";
System.out.print("The length of the string is ");
System.out.print(message.length());
```

RESULT:

```
The length of the string is 19
```

You can use the `equals` method of the `String` class to compare two strings and determine if the strings are the same.

TYPE THIS:

```
String message = "weather";
System.out.print(message.equals("temperature"));
```

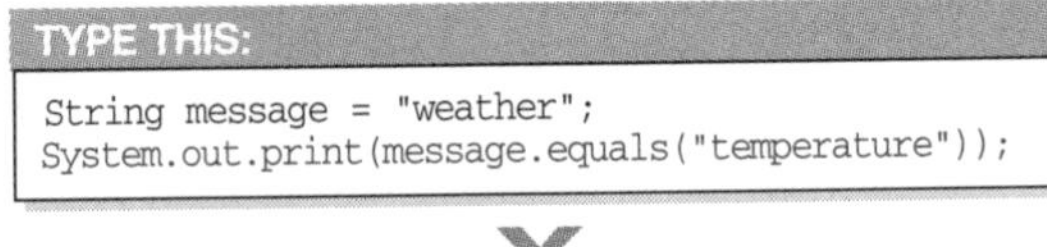

RESULT:

```
false
```

You can insert instructions you want Java to interpret into a string. These instructions begin with the backslash symbol (\) and are called escape sequences. Escape sequences allow you to include special characters, such as tabs, newlines and backspaces in a string. Escape sequences are often used to format text that will be displayed on a screen or stored in a file.

\b	Insert a backspace
\t	Insert a tab
\n	Start a new line
\f	Insert a form feed
\r	Insert a carriage return
\"	Insert a double quotation mark
\'	Insert a single quotation mark
\\	Insert a backslash

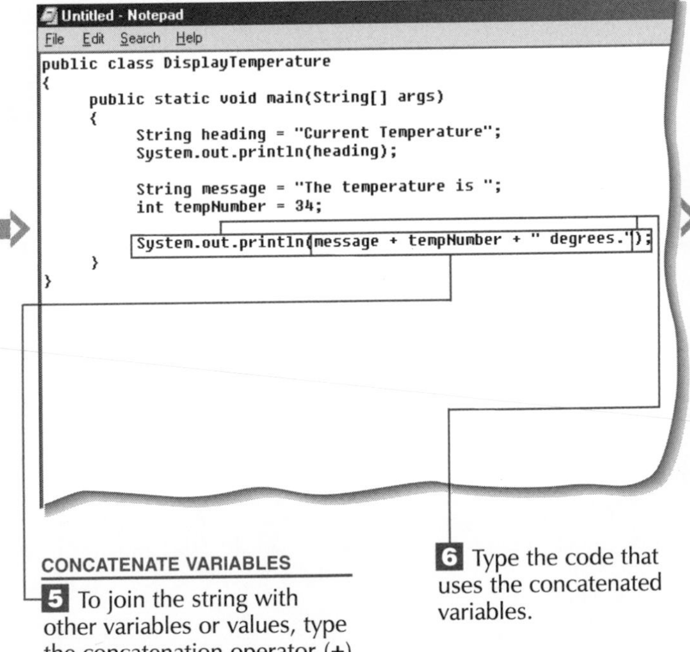

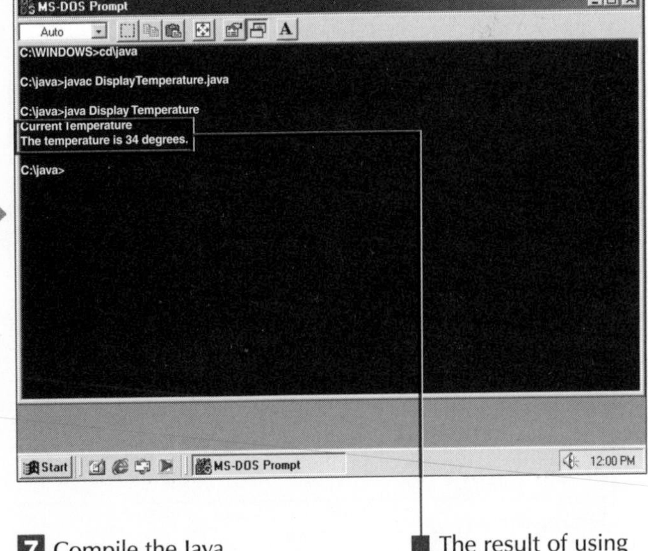

CONCATENATE VARIABLES

5 To join the string with other variables or values, type the concatenation operator (+) between each variable or value you want to join.

6 Type the code that uses the concatenated variables.

7 Compile the Java code and then execute the program.

■ The result of using strings is displayed.

WORKING WITH OPERATORS

Java provides numerous operators that can be used to assign values to variables, perform calculations and create complex expressions. There are several general categories of operators, including assignment, relational, arithmetic, logical, conditional and shift.

TYPES OF OPERATORS

A Java operator can be classified by the number of operands it accepts. An operand is an argument used by an operator. An expression is a sequence of operands separated by one or more operators that produces a result.

Unary

A unary operator accepts a single operand. All unary operators support prefix notation, which means the operator appears before the operand. A commonly used unary operator is `!`, which indicates 'not.' For example, !0 would be used to indicate a value that is not zero.

The increment (++) and decrement (--) operators also support the postfix notation, which means the operator can be placed after the operand. For example, both ++hitCounter and hitCounter++ increment the operand by one.

Binary

The most common type of operator is the binary operator. A binary operator performs calculations based on two operands, with the operator placed between the operands. For example, the expression 2 + 3 contains the operands 2 and 3, separated by the operator, +.

Ternary

The ternary operator `?:` accepts three operands. The `?:` operator tests the first operand and then returns the value of the second or third operand, depending on the result. If the result of the first operand is true, the expression returns the value of the second operand. If the result of the first operand is false, the expression returns the value of the third operand.

PRECEDENCE AND ASSOCIATIVITY

Order of Precedence

When an expression contains several operators, such as 4 - 5 + 2 * 2, Java processes the operators in a specific order, known as the order of precedence. The order of precedence ranks operators from highest to lowest precedence. Operators with higher precedence are evaluated before operators with lower precedence.

Parentheses

Regardless of the precedence and associativity of operators, you can use parentheses to dictate the order in which Java should process operators. In an expression, Java processes operators and operands enclosed in parentheses first.

Associativity

When an expression contains multiple operators that have the same precedence, the associativity of the operators determines which part of the expression will be evaluated first. Operators can have left associativity or right associativity.

If operators have left associativity, then the leftmost operator is processed first. For example, the result of the expression 5 - 3 + 2 is 4 rather than 0. The opposite holds true for operators that have right associativity.

The following table shows the order of precedence from the highest to the lowest, type, category and associativity of operators.

Operator	Type	Category	Associativity
()	parentheses	miscellaneous	left
[]	array subscript	miscellaneous	left
.	member selection	miscellaneous	left
++	unary postfix	arithmetic	right
--	unary postfix	arithmetic	right
++	unary prefix	arithmetic	right
--	unary prefix	arithmetic	right
+	unary plus	arithmetic	right
-	unary minus	arithmetic	right
!	unary negation	conditional	right
~	bitwise complement	logical	right
new	creation	miscellaneous	right
(*type*)	unary cast	miscellaneous	right
*	multiplication	arithmetic	left
/	division	arithmetic	left
%	modulus	arithmetic	left
+	addition	arithmetic	left
-	subtraction	arithmetic	left
<<	bitwise left	shift	left
>>	bitwise right with sign extension	shift	left
>>>	bitwise right with zero extension	shift	left
<	less than	relational	left
<=	less than or equal to	relational	left
>	greater than	relational	left
>=	greater than or equal to	relational	left
instanceof	type comparison	miscellaneous	left
==	is equal to	relational	left
!=	is not equal to	relational	left
&	bitwise AND	logical	left
^	bitwise XOR	logical	left
|	bitwise OR	logical	left
&&	logical AND	conditional	left
||	logical OR	conditional	left
?:	ternary conditional	miscellaneous	right
=	assignment	assignment	right
+=	addition	assignment	right
-=	subtraction	assignment	right
*=	multiplication	assignment	right
/=	division	assignment	right
%=	modulus	assignment	right
&=	bitwise AND	assignment	right
^=	bitwise XOR	assignment	right
|=	bitwise OR	assignment	right
<<=	bitwise left shift	assignment	right
>>=	bitwise right shift with sign extension	assignment	right
>>>=	bitwise right shift with zero extension	assignment	right

CALL A METHOD

Once you have created a method, you need to call the method to tell Java to access and execute the code in the method. The code included in a method will not be executed until the method is called.

To call a method in the same class it was declared in, you type the name of the method followed by a set of parentheses where you want to execute the code specified in the method. You must be sure to type the method name exactly as it was typed in the code that declares the method. Some methods require you to include *arguments* within the parentheses that follow the method name. For information about passing arguments to methods, see page 38.

When a method is called, the code included in the method is executed as if the code was typed in the location where you called the method. Once Java has finished processing the code in the method, Java continues execution from the line following the method call.

In some programs, you may need to call a method that is declared in a different class. The access modifiers used in method declaration determine the locations from which you can call the method. For more information about access modifiers, see page 16.

Classes that contain methods can also be grouped into a *package*. You may need to specify the package that contains the method you want to call. For more information about packages, see page 50.

In addition to calling methods you have created, you can also call methods provided in the Java class library. For example, `System.out.println()` calls a Java class library method which is used to display data. For more information about the Java class library, see page 8.

CALL A METHOD

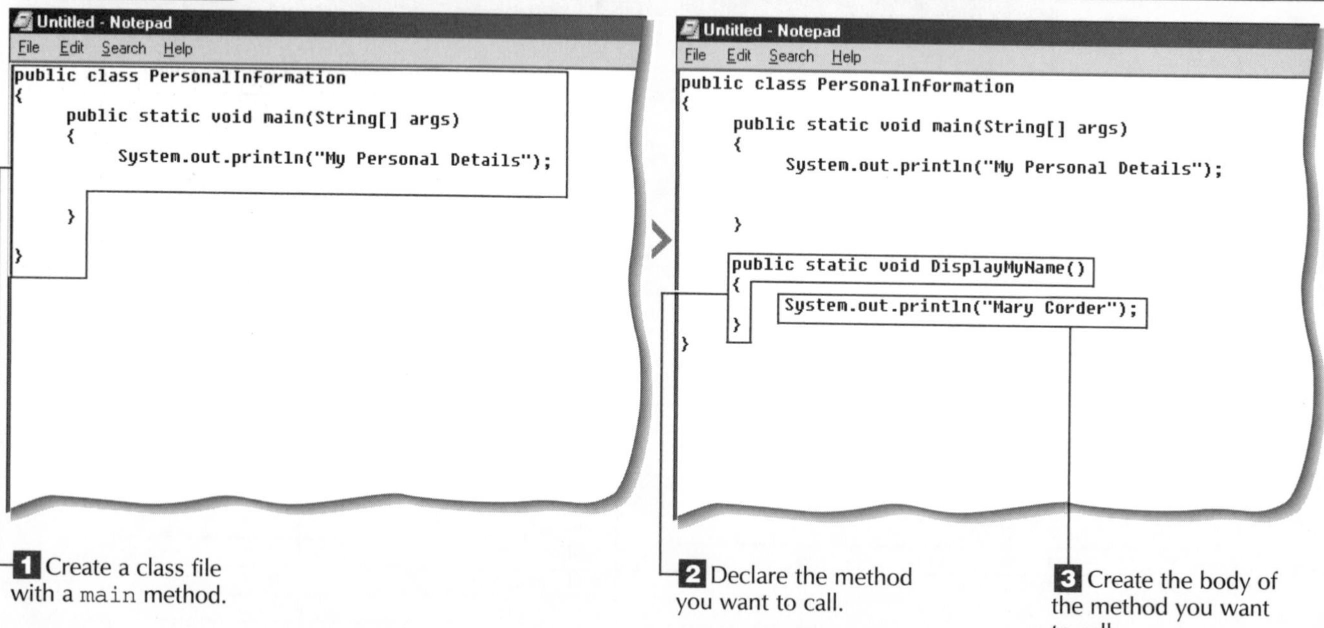
Untitled - Notepad
File Edit Search Help
public class PersonalInformation
{
public static void main(String[] args)
{
System.out.println("My Personal Details");
}
}
Untitled - Notepad
File Edit Search Help
public class PersonalInformation
{
public static void main(String[] args)
{
System.out.println("My Personal Details");
}
public static void DisplayMyName()
{
System.out.println("Mary Corder");
}
}

1 Create a class file with a `main` method.

2 Declare the method you want to call.

3 Create the body of the method you want to call.

Extra

If a method you want to call is declared in a different class, you must specify the class that contains the method you want to call. You use the dot operator (.) to link the class name and the method name. Any methods called from another class should be created with the `public` access modifier.

Example:

```
public class PersonalInformation
{
      public static void DisplayMyName()
      {
            System.out.println("David Gregory");
      }
}

public class CallingClassMethods
{
      public static void main(String[] args)
      {
            System.out.println("My Personal Details");

            PersonalInformation.DisplayMyName();
      }
}
```

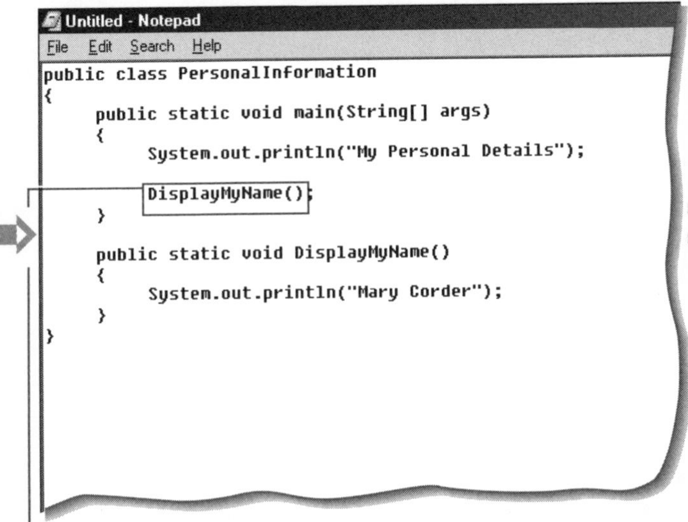

4 In the body of the `main` method, type the name of the method you want to call, followed by a set of parentheses.

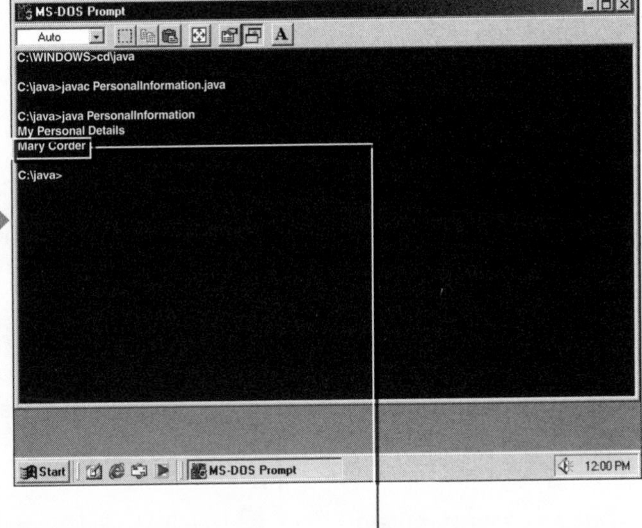

5 Compile the Java code and then execute the program.

■ The result of executing the code in the method is displayed.

USING RETURN VALUES AND ARGUMENTS IN METHODS

You can have a method return a value to the code. A return value may be the result of a calculation or procedure or may indicate whether a process was successfully completed.

The data type of a return value for a method must be specified when the method is declared. Return values can be any valid data type in Java, such as `String`, `byte` or `boolean`. An error may occur if the data type of the value that is returned does not match the return type specified in the method declaration.

Information is returned from a method using the keyword `return`. Once the `return` statement is executed in a method, the processing of the method ends and the value specified in the `return` statement is passed back to the calling statement.

A method with a return value can be used as if it were a variable. For example, you could display the value returned by a method using the `System.out.print` command. You could also assign the value returned by a method to a variable.

You can also pass one or more values, called arguments, to a method you have created. Passing arguments to a method allows you to use one method throughout a program to process different data.

To pass an argument to a method, you include a data type and variable name in the parentheses at the end of the method name in a method declaration. When you call the method, you include the data you want to pass in the parentheses following the method name.

You can pass any type of data to a method, but the type of data must match the data type specified in the method declaration. For example, if a method expects an integer value to be passed for calculation, passing a string value to the method would cause an error to occur.

USING RETURN VALUES AND ARGUMENTS IN METHODS

PersonalInformation.java - Notepad

```
class PersonalInformation
{
	public static void main(String[] args)
	{
		System.out.println("My Personal Information");
		System.out.println();
	}

	public static String DisplayMyName()
	{
		String myInfo;
		myInfo = "My name is: " + name;
		return myInfo;
	}
}
```

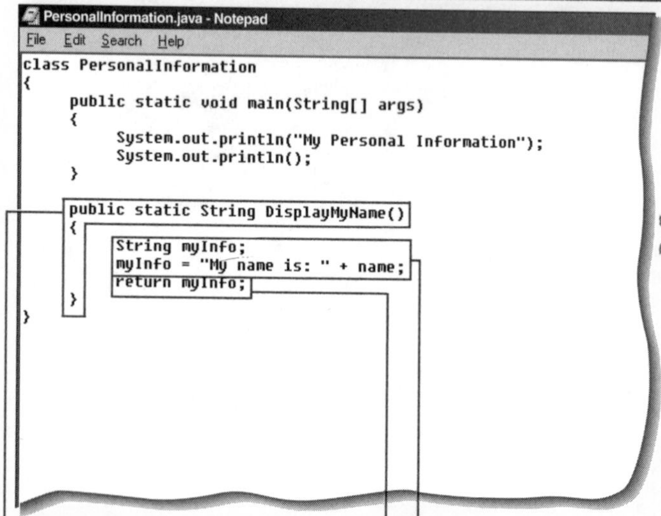

CREATE A RETURN STATEMENT

1 Type the code that declares the method you want to use.

■ The data type of the value the method will return must be specified in this code.

2 Type the code for the body of the method.

3 In the body of the method, type **return** followed by the information you want the method to return.

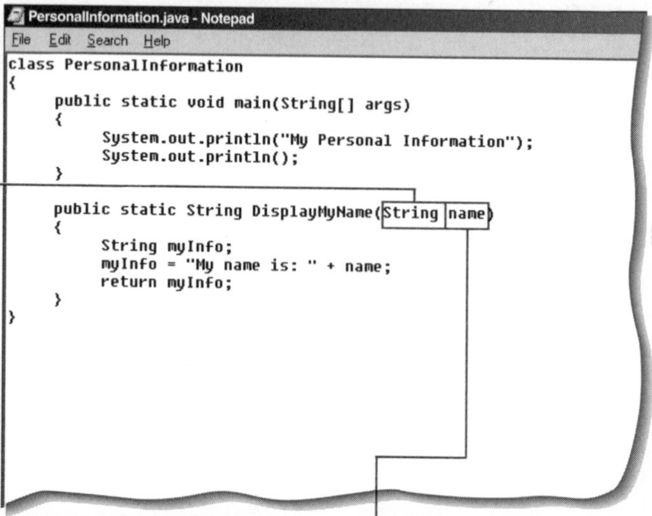

PersonalInformation.java - Notepad

```
class PersonalInformation
{
	public static void main(String[] args)
	{
		System.out.println("My Personal Information");
		System.out.println();
	}

	public static String DisplayMyName(String name)
	{
		String myInfo;
		myInfo = "My name is: " + name;
		return myInfo;
	}
}
```

PREPARE A METHOD TO ACCEPT ARGUMENTS

4 Between the parentheses following the method name in the method declaration, specify the data type of the argument that the method will accept.

5 Type the name of the variable that will store the value of the argument.

Note: When preparing a method to accept multiple arguments, each data type and variable pair must be separated by a comma.

Apply It

A method can have more than one `return` statement. This is commonly found in methods that use conditional statements. Although a method can have more than one `return` statement, only one `return` statement will be executed. When a `return` statement is encountered, the execution of the method is terminated.

TYPE THIS:

```
class MakeList
{
	public static void main(String[] args)
	{
		System.out.println(CheckAge(29));
	}
	static String CheckAge(int age)
	{
		if (age > 21)
		{
			return "You may take the survey";
		}
		else
		{
			return "You are too young to take the survey";
		}
	}
}
```

RESULT:

```
You may take the survey
```

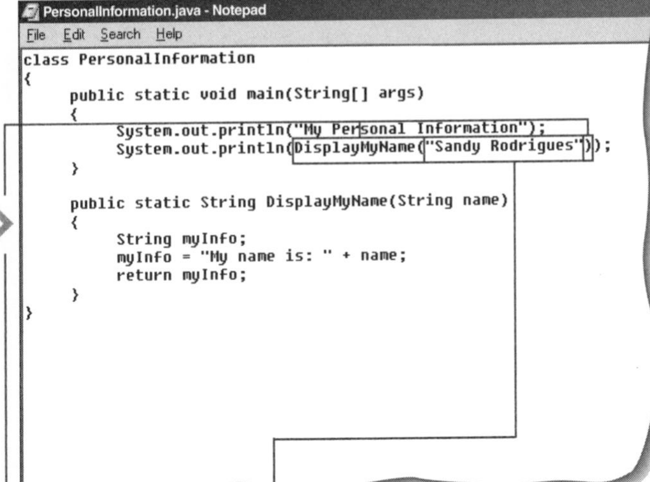

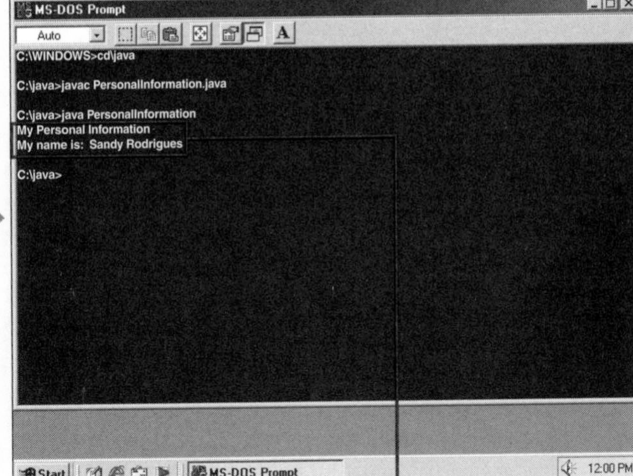

CALL A METHOD USING ARGUMENTS

6 In the body of the `main` method, type the code that calls the method you want to use.

7 Between the parentheses following the method name, type the arguments you want to pass to the method.

■ String arguments must be enclosed in quotation marks.

Note: When passing multiple arguments, the arguments must be separated by a comma.

8 Compile the Java code and then execute the program.

■ The result of passing arguments to a method and using a return value is displayed.

USING THE IF STATEMENT

Using an `if` statement allows you to test a condition to determine whether the condition is true or false. The condition can be as complex as necessary, but it must always produce a value that evaluates to either true or false. When the condition is true, the section of code directly following the `if` statement is executed. For example, you can create a program that displays a Good Morning message when a user runs the program between 5:00 AM and 11:59 AM. If the condition is false, no code from the `if` statement will be executed.

A section of code you want to be executed must be enclosed in braces `{}` and is referred to as a statement block. The condition for an `if` statement must be enclosed in parentheses `()`.

If you want an `if` statement to execute a block when a condition is false, you must include an `else` statement. Using an `if` statement with an `else` statement allows you to execute one of two sections of code, depending on the outcome of testing the condition. If the condition is true, the statement block directly following the `if` statement is executed. If the condition is false, the statement block directly following the `else` statement is executed. Using an `else` statement ensures that a section of code is executed regardless of the outcome of testing the condition. For example, you can have a program display a Good Morning message or a Good Evening message, depending on the time set on the computer that executes the program.

To make your code easier to read and understand, you should always indent the statement block that contains the code to be executed. Many programmers also use spaces within statements to make the statements easier to read. White-space characters, such as tabs and blank lines, are ignored by the Java compiler, so using these characters will not affect the function or performance of your Java program.

USING THE IF STATEMENT

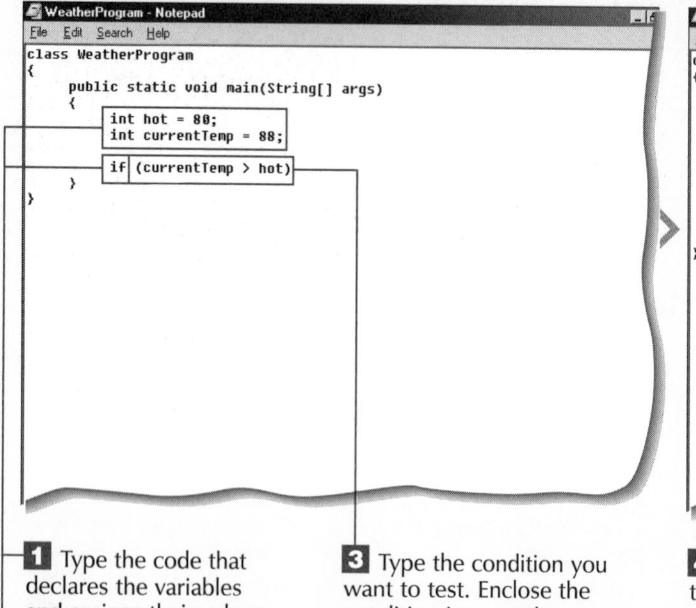


```
class WeatherProgram
{
      public static void main(String[] args)
      {
            int hot = 80;
            int currentTemp = 88;

            if (currentTemp > hot)
            {
                  System.out.println(currentTemp + " degrees. It's hot.");
            }
      }
}
```

1 Type the code that declares the variables and assigns their values.

2 Type **if**.

3 Type the condition you want to test. Enclose the condition in parentheses.

4 Type the code you want to execute if the condition you specified is true. Enclose the code in braces.

If you are going to execute only one line of code based on a condition being true, you can place the code to be executed on the same line as the `if` statement.

FOR EXAMPLE:

```
if (currentTemp > hot)
{
      System.out.println("It's hot.");
}
```

CAN BE TYPED AS:

```
if (currentTemp > hot) System.out.println("It's hot.");
```

Nested `if` statements allow you to specify multiple conditions for an `if` statement at the same time. Each `if` statement will be evaluated only if the previous `if` statement is true. If all the `if` statements are true, a section of code is executed. If any of the `if` statements are false, no code from the `if` statements will be executed.

TYPE THIS:

```
int hot = 80, veryHot = 85, currentTemp = 88;
      if (currentTemp > hot)
      {
            System.out.print(currentTemp + " degrees. It's ");
            if (currentTemp > veryHot)
            {
                  System.out.print("very, very ");
            }
            System.out.println("hot.");
      }
```

RESULT:

88 degrees. It's very, very hot.

WeatherProgram - Notepad

File Edit Search Help

```
class WeatherProgram
{
      public static void main(String[] args)
      {
            int hot = 80;
            int currentTemp = 88;

            if (currentTemp > hot)
            {
                  System.out.println(currentTemp + " degrees. It's hot.");
            }
            else
            {
                  System.out.println(currentTemp + " degrees. It's not that
                  hot.");
            }
      }
}
```

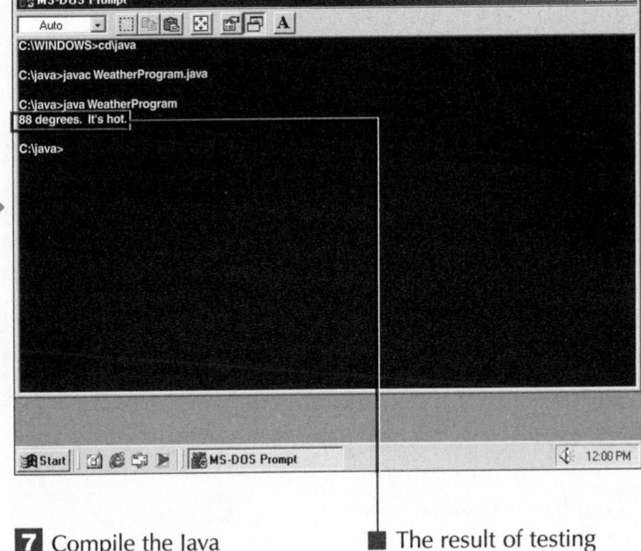

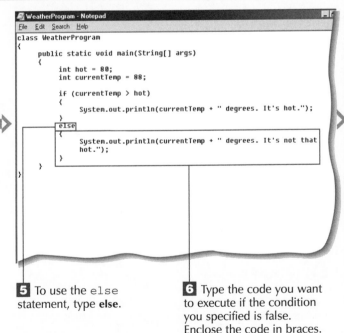

5 To use the `else` statement, type **else**.

6 Type the code you want to execute if the condition you specified is false. Enclose the code in braces.

7 Compile the Java code and then execute the program.

■ The result of testing the condition is displayed on the screen.

USING THE FOR STATEMENT

Programmers often need to execute the same statement or block of statements several times. The `for` statement allows you to create a loop that repeats the execution of code a specific number of times. For example, you may want to create five line breaks on a Web page. Instead of typing the code that creates a line break five times, you can create a loop that executes the code to create a line break and then repeats the loop until the value of a counter reaches 5.

When creating a `for` statement, you usually use a variable, called an iterator, that acts as a counter for the loop. You use an initialization expression to specify a starting value for the iterator.

You must also specify a condition that evaluates the value of the iterator. If the condition is true, the loop is executed and a block of code you specify is processed. If the condition is false, the block of code is not executed and the loop is ended.

The re-initialization expression is used to modify the value of the iterator. For example, if you use the *increment operator* (++) in the re-initialization expression, the value of the iterator will be incremented by one each time the loop is executed. The expression i++ functions the same as i = i + 1.

The block of code you want to execute is placed between braces `{}` and is known as the body of the loop. You should indent the code in the body of a loop to make the code easier to read and understand. The code in the body of a `for` loop can include any valid Java statements, such as calls to other methods. You may also place another loop within the body of a `for` loop. This is referred to as nesting. You should avoid having too many nested loops because it makes the program difficult to read and troubleshoot.

USING THE FOR STATEMENT

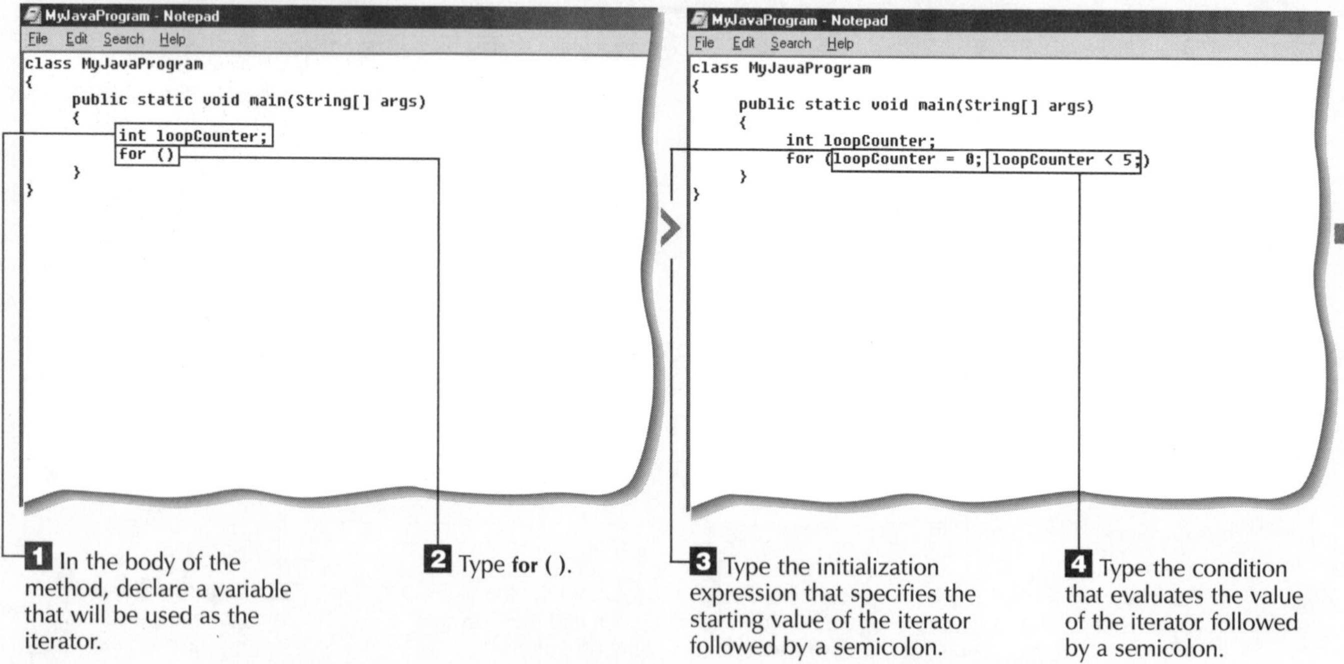

1 In the body of the method, declare a variable that will be used as the iterator.

2 Type **for ( )**.

3 Type the initialization expression that specifies the starting value of the iterator followed by a semicolon.

4 Type the condition that evaluates the value of the iterator followed by a semicolon.

Extra

A loop can still be executed even if one or more expressions are omitted from the `for` statement. However, any expressions you omit from the `for` statement must be specified elsewhere in the code. For example, if you specify the starting value of the iterator in another part of your code, you do not need to include an initialization expression in the `for` statement. Keep in mind that you must still include all the necessary semicolons in the `for` statement.

Example:
```
int loopCounter = 3;
for (; loopCounter < 5; loopCounter++)
{
    System.out.println(loopCounter);
}
```

If a `for` statement does not include a condition and no condition is specified in the body of the loop, Java assumes that the condition is always true and an *infinite loop* is created. You should be careful not to accidentally create an infinite loop.

Example:
```
int loopCounter;
for (loopCounter = 1; ; loopCounter++)
{
    System.out.println(loopCounter);
}
```

If the body of a `for` loop is composed of a single line of code, you do not have to enclose the line in braces. Although the braces are optional in this situation, most programmers use the braces to keep their code consistent.

Example:
```
for (loopCounter = 0; loopCounter < 10; loopCounter++)
    System.out.println(loopCounter);
```

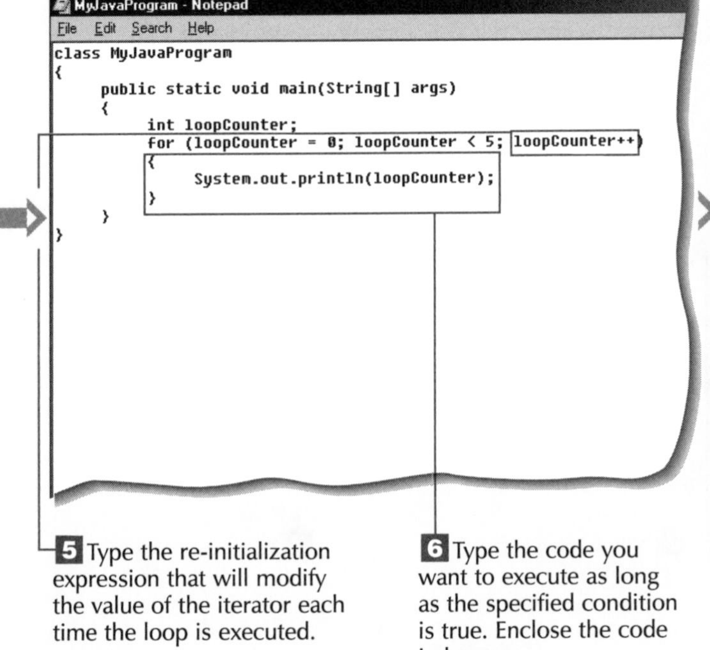

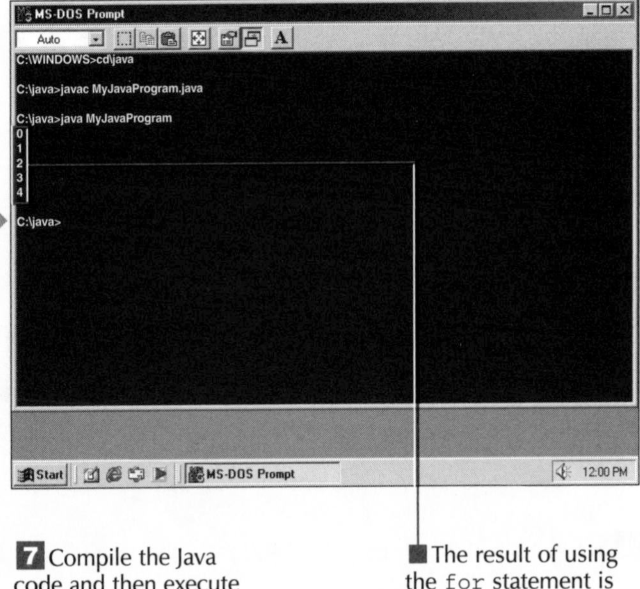

5 Type the re-initialization expression that will modify the value of the iterator each time the loop is executed.

6 Type the code you want to execute as long as the specified condition is true. Enclose the code in braces.

7 Compile the Java code and then execute the program.

■ The result of using the `for` statement is displayed.

USING THE WHILE STATEMENT

The `while` statement allows you to create a conditional loop that will execute a section of code as long as a specified condition is true. Conditions often test the value of an *iterator*. For example, you may want to process a pay statement for each of the 100 employees in a company. Instead of typing the code that processes a pay statement 100 times, you could create a loop to process the pay statement for each employee. The condition would check how many pay statements have been processed. After the 100th pay statement has been processed, the condition would be evaluated as false and the loop would end.

The body of a `while` loop is enclosed in braces `{}` and contains the section of code to be executed. If the condition tests the value of an iterator, the loop body will also contain code to alter the value of the iterator. The value of an iterator can be increased or decreased.

When the condition is true, the section of code in the body of the loop is executed. When Java reaches the end of the loop body, the condition is re-evaluated. If the condition is still true, the section of code is executed again. If the condition is false, the section of code in the loop body is not executed and the loop ends.

When creating a loop using the `while` statement, you must ensure that the condition being tested will be evaluated as false at some time. If the condition is always true, the code in the loop body will be executed indefinitely. This kind of never-ending loop is known as an infinite loop. If an infinite loop is created, you will have to forcibly stop the execution of the Java program.

USING THE WHILE STATEMENT

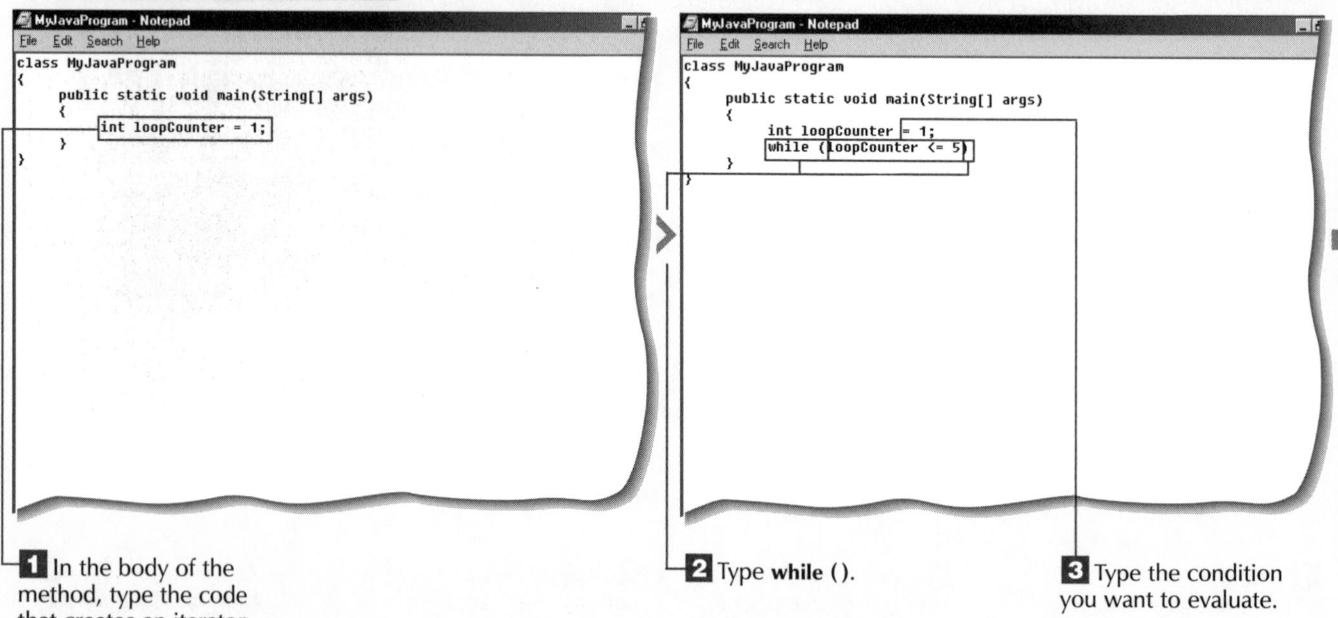

1 In the body of the method, type the code that creates an iterator and assigns it a value.

2 Type **while ()**.

3 Type the condition you want to evaluate.

A `do-while` statement can be used to test a condition after the code in the loop body has been executed. This is useful if you have a section of code that you want to execute at least once, regardless of how the condition is evaluated.

TYPE THIS:

```
int loopCounter = 0;
do
{
      System.out.println("This is line number "
            + loopCounter);
      loopCounter++;
} while (loopCounter < 0);
```

RESULT:

```
This is line number 0
```

You can place another loop within the body of a `do-while` loop to create a nested loop.

TYPE THIS:

```
int loopCounter = 0, dotCounter;
do
{
      System.out.print("This is line number");
      for (dotCounter = 0; dotCounter < 8; dotCounter++)
      {
            System.out.print(".");
      }
      System.out.println(loopCounter);
      loopCounter++;
} while (loopCounter < 3);
```

RESULT:

```
This is line number........0
This is line number........1
This is line number........2
```

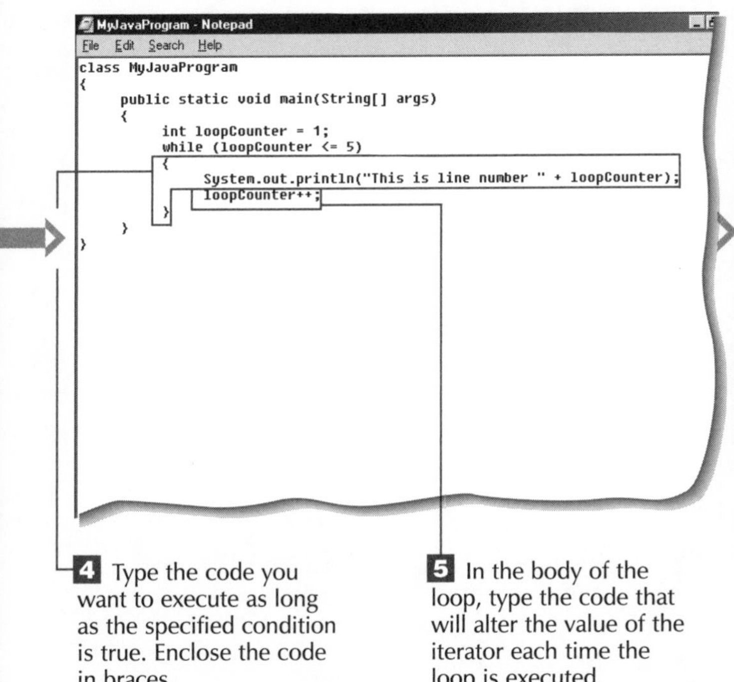

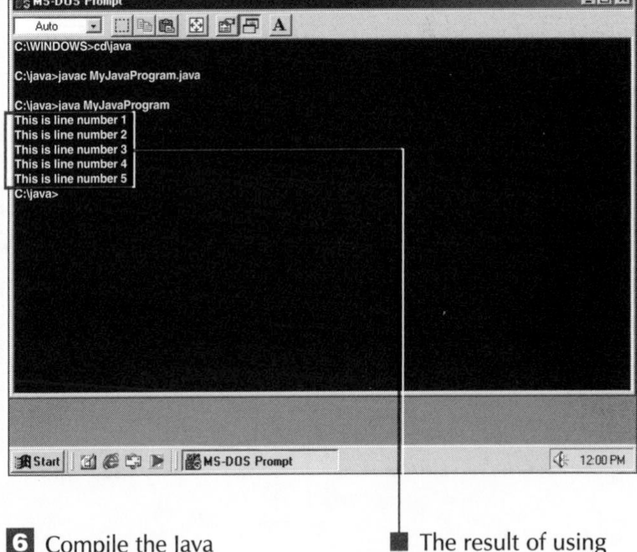

4 Type the code you want to execute as long as the specified condition is true. Enclose the code in braces.

5 In the body of the loop, type the code that will alter the value of the iterator each time the loop is executed.

6 Compile the Java code and then execute the program.

■ The result of using the `while` statement is displayed.

USING THE SWITCH STATEMENT

The `switch` statement allows you to execute a section of code, depending on the value of an expression you specify. When a `switch` statement is executed, the value of the expression is compared to a number of possible choices, called `case` values. If the value of the expression matches a `case` value, the section of code following the `case` value is executed. For example, you can create a `switch` statement that displays a specific message, depending on information entered by a user.

To use the `switch` statement, you must first specify the expression you want to use. The value of the expression must have a `char`, `byte`, `short` or `int` data type. After specifying the expression, you must create the `case` values that the expression will be compared to. The expression must match the `case` value exactly. You cannot use an indefinite expression, such as x > 10, for a `case` value.

The `switch` statement compares the value of the expression to each `case` value in order, from top to bottom. The `case` statements can be in any order, but to make your program more efficient, you should place the most commonly used `case` values first.

To prevent the `switch` statement from testing the remaining `case` values after a match has been made, you should use the `break` statement to skip the remaining `case` statements and continue processing the code after the closing brace of the `switch` statement. The `break` statement should be used as the last statement for each `case` statement. Although the last `case` statement does not require a `break` statement, some programmers include it to be consistent. This can help prevent you from forgetting to include the `break` statement if you later add another `case` statement to the `switch` statement.

USING THE SWITCH STATEMENT

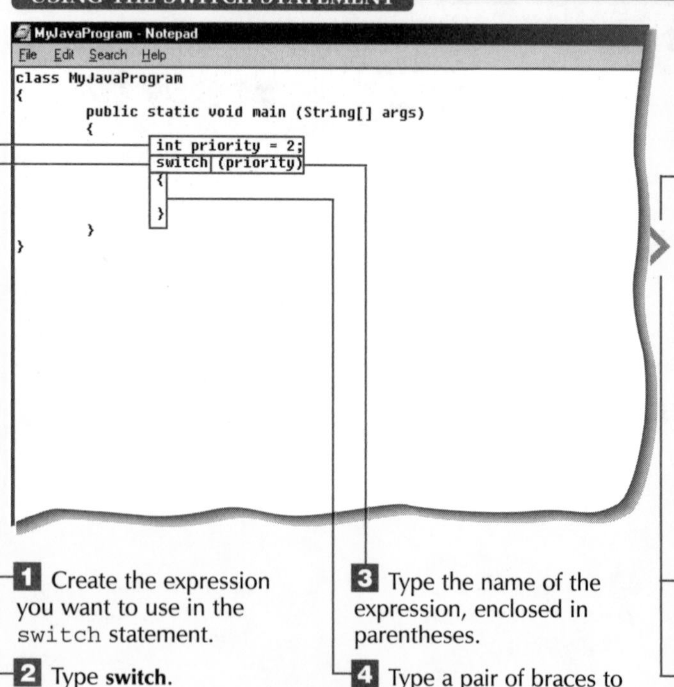

1 Create the expression you want to use in the `switch` statement.

2 Type **switch**.

3 Type the name of the expression, enclosed in parentheses.

4 Type a pair of braces to hold the `case` statements.

```
MyJavaProgram - Notepad
File Edit Search Help
class MyJavaProgram
{
        public static void main (String[] args)
        {
                int priority = 2;
                switch (priority)
                {
                        case 1:
                                System.out.println("Urgent");
                }
        }
}
```

5 Type **case** followed by a value the expression may contain.

6 Type **:** to complete the `case` statement.

7 Type the statements you want to execute if the `case` value matches the expression you specified in step 1.

Extra

You can execute one section of code for multiple `case` statements. Each `case` statement you want to match must be followed by a colon.

Example:

```
switch (gender)
{
      case M: case m:
            System.out.println("Male");
            break;
      case F: case f:
            System.out.println("Female");
            break;
}
```

You can include a `default` statement in a `switch` statement if you want to execute specific code when none of the other `case` values match the specified expression. The `default` statement is usually placed last in the `switch` statement structure.

Example:

```
switch (priority)
{
      case 1:
            System.out.println("Urgent");
            break;
      case 2:
            System.out.println("Not Important");
            break;
      default:
            System.out.println("Ignore");
}
```

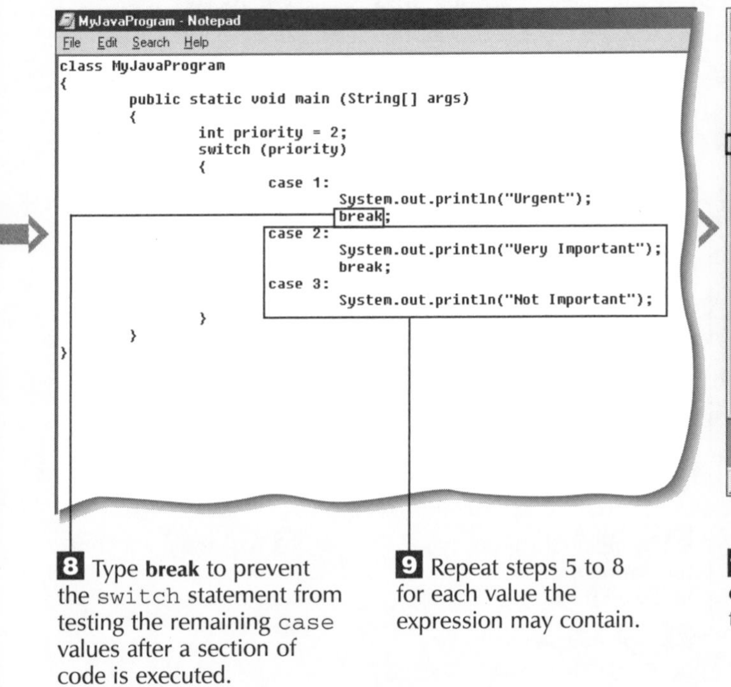

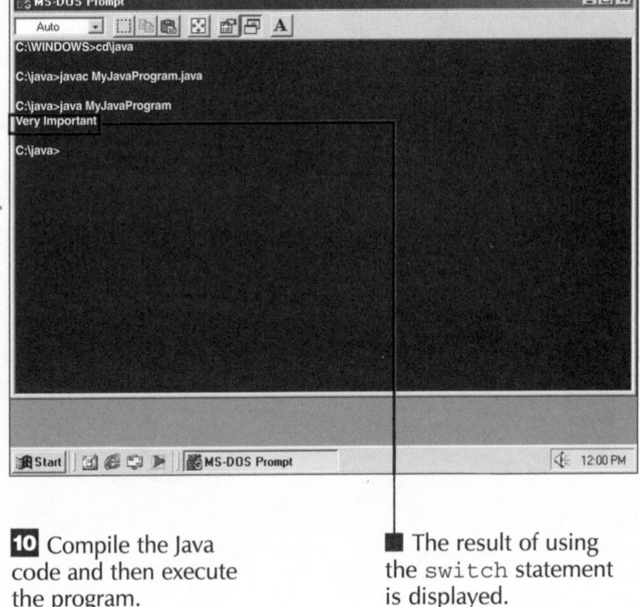

8 Type **break** to prevent the `switch` statement from testing the remaining `case` values after a section of code is executed.

9 Repeat steps 5 to 8 for each value the expression may contain.

10 Compile the Java code and then execute the program.

■ The result of using the `switch` statement is displayed.

CREATE AN ARRAY

An array stores a set of related values, called elements, that are of the same data type. For example, an array could store the name of each day of the week. Using an array allows you to work with multiple values at the same time.

The first step in creating an array is to declare an array variable. To declare an array variable, you specify the data type of the values that the array will store, followed by brackets `[]`. For more information about data types, see page 30. You must also give the array a name. Array names use the same naming conventions as other variables.

Once you have declared the array variable, you can define the array. The `new` operator is used to define an array and indicates that you want to set aside space in memory for the new array. When defining an array, you must also specify the number of elements the array will store.

Each element in an array is uniquely identified by an index number. Index numbers in an array start at 0, not 1. For example, an array defined as items = new int[6] would contain six elements indexed from 0 to 5.

You can specify the values you want each element to store. String values must be enclosed in quotation marks.

To access an individual element in an array, you use the name of the array followed by the index number for the element enclosed in brackets. When brackets are used in this context, they are referred to as the *array access operator*. You can use an array element in a Java program as you would use a variable. Changing the value of an element will not affect the other elements in the array.

CREATE AN ARRAY

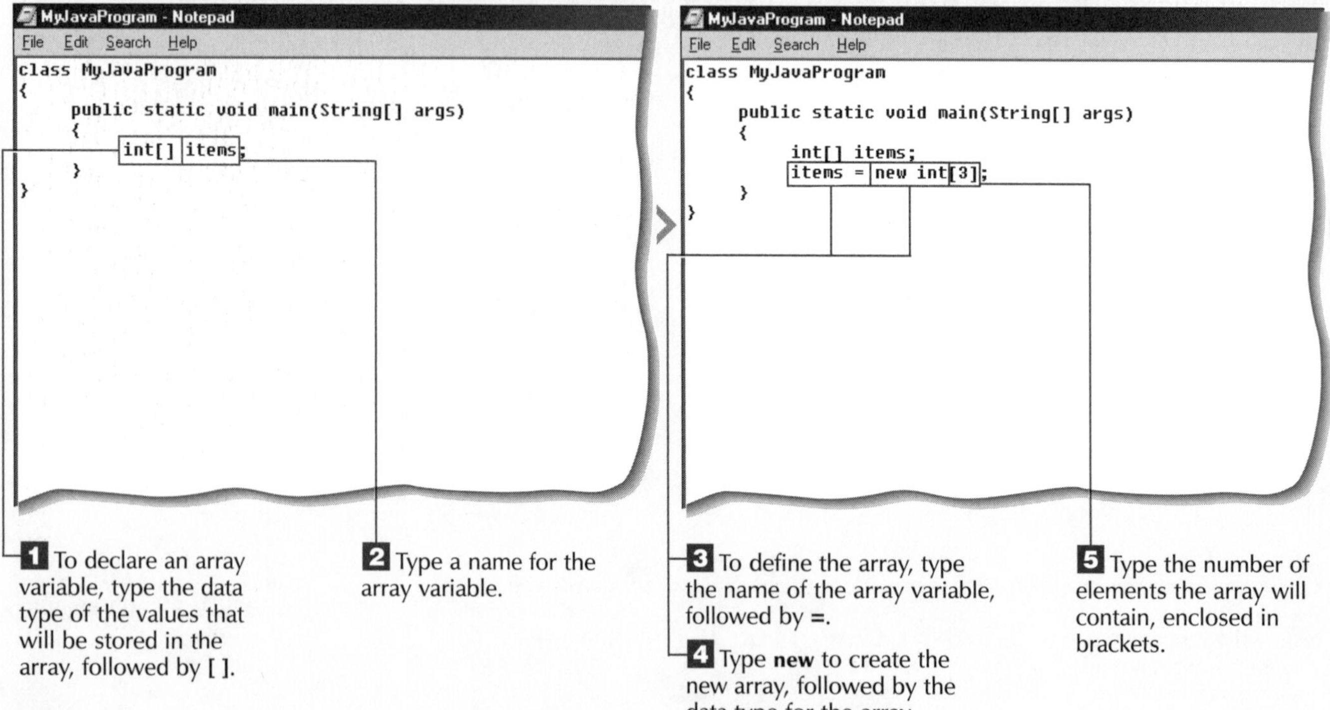

1 To declare an array variable, type the data type of the values that will be stored in the array, followed by [ ].

2 Type a name for the array variable.

3 To define the array, type the name of the array variable, followed by =.

4 Type **new** to create the new array, followed by the data type for the array.

5 Type the number of elements the array will contain, enclosed in brackets.

Apply It

Unlike most other programming languages, Java treats arrays as objects. The `length` member of the `array` object allows you to determine the number of elements in an array.

TYPE THIS:

```
class ArrayLength
{
  public static void main(String[] args)
  {
    int[] items;
    items = new int[3];

    items[0] = 331;
    items[1] = 324;
    items[2] = 298;

    int total = items.length;
    System.out.print("Number of items = " + total);
  }
}
```

RESULT:

```
Number of items = 3
```

You can use code that creates a loop, such as a `for` statement, to work with all the elements in an array at once.

TYPE THIS:

```
class MyArray
{
  public static void main(String[] args)
  {
    int[] items;
    items = new int[3];

    items[0] = 331;
    items[1] = 324;
    items[2] = 298;
    int total = items.length;

    for (int i = 0; i < total; i++)
    System.out.println(items[i]);
  }
}
```

RESULT:

```
331
324
298
```

MyJavaProgram - Notepad

File Edit Search Help

```
class MyJavaProgram
{
     public static void main(String[] args)
     {
          int[] items;
          items = new int[3];

          items[0] = 331;
          items[1] = 324;
          items[2] = 298;

          int total = items[0] + items[1] + items[2];
          System.out.println("Items on hand = " + total);
     }
}
```

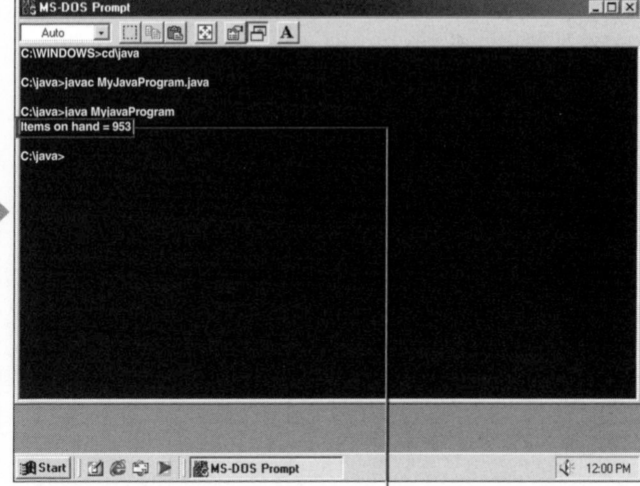

6 To create an element in the array, type the name of the array, followed by the index number of the element enclosed in brackets.

7 Type = followed by the value for the element.

■ If the value for the element is a string, you must enclose the string in quotation marks.

8 Repeat steps 6 and 7 for each element in the array.

9 Type the code that accesses elements in the array.

10 Compile the Java code and then execute the program.

■ The results of creating an array and accessing elements are displayed.

CREATE A PACKAGE

If your Java program contains a large number of class files, you can organize the files by grouping them into packages. A package stores a collection of related classes. For example, all the shipping-related classes in a program could be grouped into a package called shipping.

Packages allow you to use classes with identical names in the same Java program. Using classes with the same name in one program is normally not permitted in Java. However, when you place classes with the same name in different packages, the classes can be used in a single application without conflict.

When creating a package, you must create a directory to store all the classes for the package. Package directories must always be created in the default class directory that was specified when the Java Software Development Kit was installed on your computer. The lib directory, which is located in the main Java SDK directory, is usually the default class directory.

The name of the directory you create should describe the classes the package will store. All the classes belonging to a package must be saved in the same directory.

You add a `package` statement to a class file to specify the name of the package you want the class to belong to. The `package` statement must be the first line of code in the class file. If the package name consists of multiple words, the words are separated by dots. Each word in the name must represent an actual directory on your computer. For example, classes that are placed in a package called myapps.internet would be stored in a directory called internet, located within the myapps directory.

To use a class stored in a package in an application, you specify the package name and the class name.

CREATE A PACKAGE

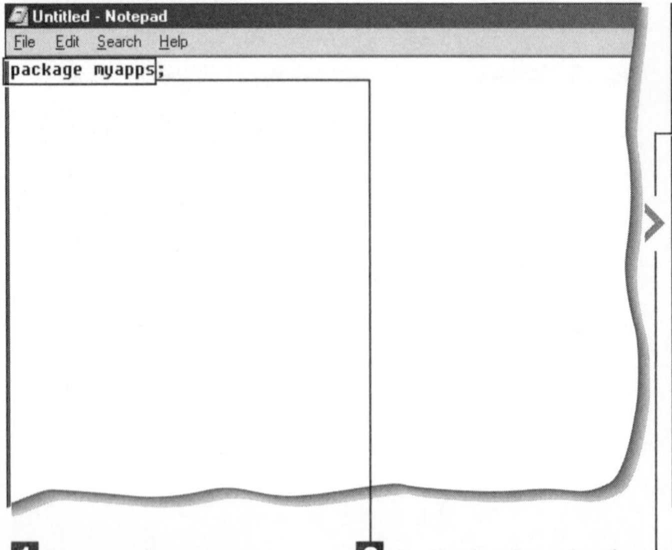

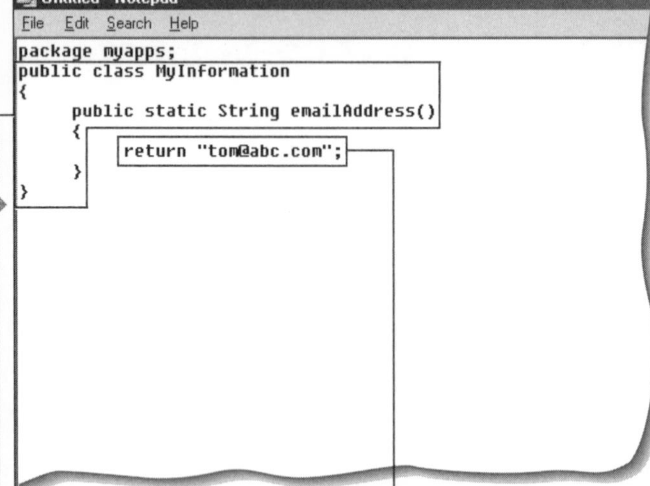

1 Create a directory on your computer that will store classes for the package.

■ In this example, a directory named myapps is created in the lib directory. The lib directory is located in the main Java SDK directory.

2 On the first line of code in a class file, type **package** followed by the name of the package you want to create.

Note: The package name must be the same as the name of the directory you created in step 1.

3 Enter the code that declares a class and a method that you want to use in other Java programs.

4 In the body of the method, type the code for the task you want to perform.

5 Save the code with the .java extension in the directory you created in step 1.

Extra

A class always belongs to a package, even when no package is specified. If a package is not specified for a class, the class will belong to the default package, which is the empty string "".

If you are using a Java development tool, such as an Integrated Development Environment (IDE), package directories may already be set up for you within a main class directory. You can usually change the configuration of the program to specify another directory as the main class directory.

The method you use to create directories will depend on the type of operating system installed on your computer. If you are using a UNIX-based operating system, such as Linux, you might use the `mkdir` command to create directories in a terminal window. If you are using an operating system with a Graphical User Interface (GUI), such as Macintosh or Windows, you would use the graphical tools provided to create directories.

When you use a class stored in a package, you must specify the name of the package in addition to the class name. To avoid having to specify the package name each time you want to use the class, you can *import* the package into your program.

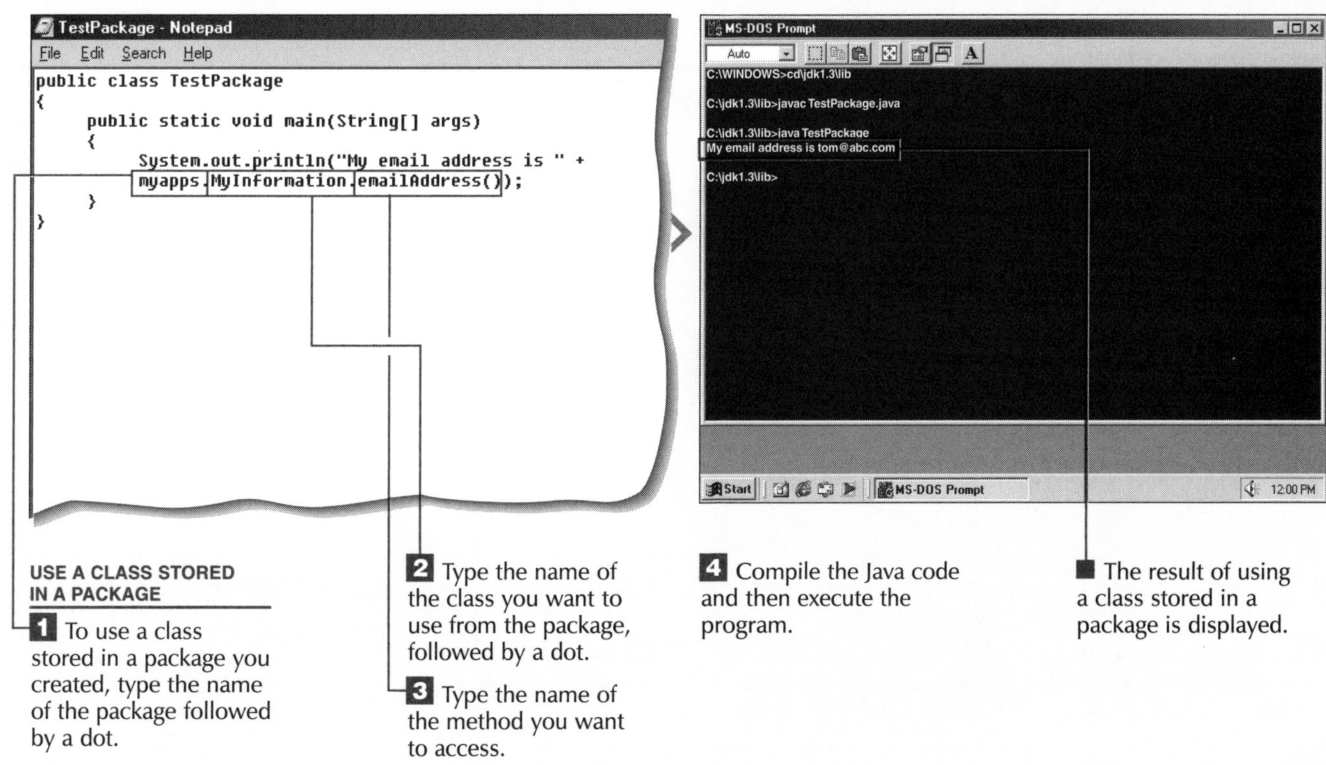

USE A CLASS STORED IN A PACKAGE

1 To use a class stored in a package you created, type the name of the package followed by a dot.

2 Type the name of the class you want to use from the package, followed by a dot.

3 Type the name of the method you want to access.

4 Compile the Java code and then execute the program.

■ The result of using a class stored in a package is displayed.

IMPORT A PACKAGE

You can import a class from a package you have created into a Java program. This is useful if you plan to use the class several times in the program. Once a package and a class have been imported, you do not need to specify the name of the package each time you want to access the class.

The `import` statement is used to import a package and is usually placed at the beginning of your Java program. If your program contains a `package` statement, the `import` statement must be placed after the `package` statement. You can import several packages and classes into one Java program. Each package you want to import must have its own `import` statement. You should not import two classes with the same name into one program.

You must first create the package you want to import. For more information about creating a package, see page 50.

To help ensure an error is not generated when you compile the code for your program, you must ensure that the package directory and the class you want to import are available. In most situations this is not a concern, but it becomes important if you are developing programs on different computers or different platforms.

When importing a class from a package, you must specify the name of the class you want to import. You should only import class files you intend to use. Imported class files increase the size of the bytecode created when you compile Java code.

In addition to packages and classes that you create, you can import packages and classes that are part of the Java class library. You can refer to page 8 for more information about the packages included in the Java class library.

IMPORT A PACKAGE

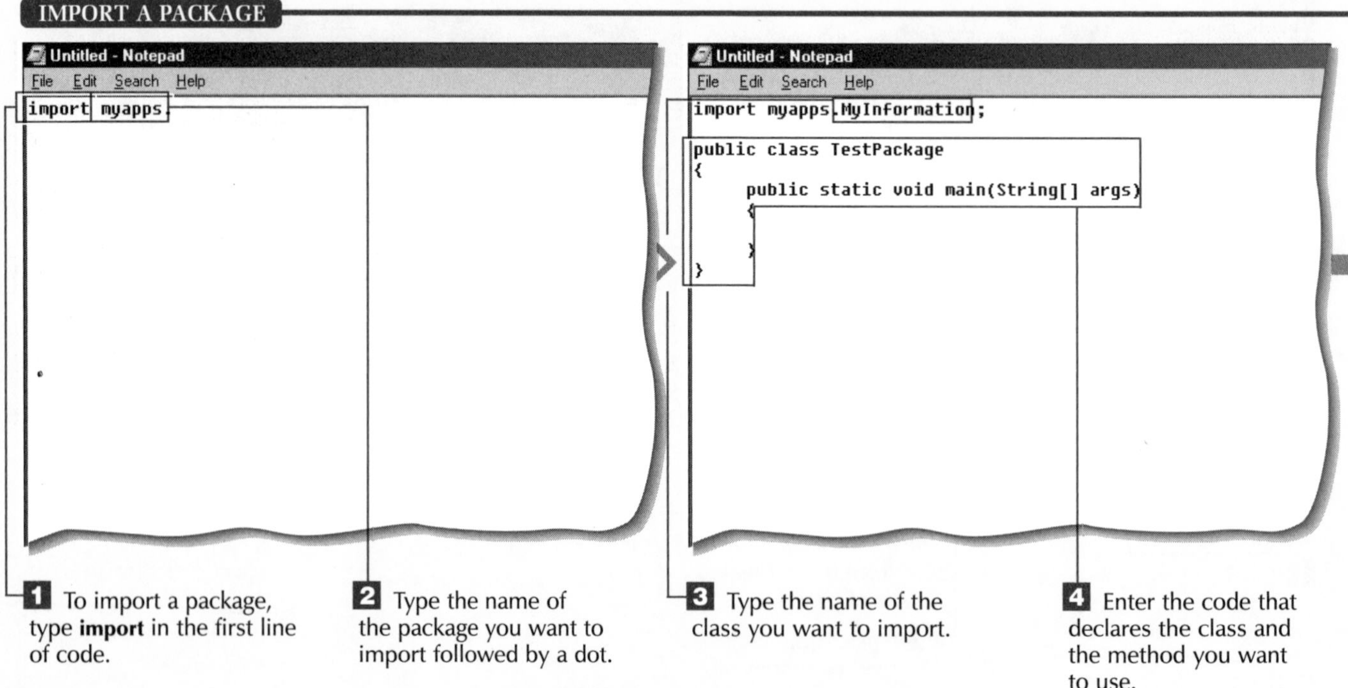
Untitled - Notepad
File Edit Search Help
import myapps
Untitled - Notepad
File Edit Search Help
import myapps.MyInformation;
public class TestPackage
{
public static void main(String[] args)
{
}
}

1 To import a package, type **import** in the first line of code.

2 Type the name of the package you want to import followed by a dot.

3 Type the name of the class you want to import.

4 Enter the code that declares the class and the method you want to use.

Extra

You can use the wildcard character * to have Java import all the classes a package contains. This is useful if you want to access several classes in a package. In the following example, the package is named myapps.webutils.

Example:

```
import myapps.webutils.*
```

When using the wildcard character *, it is important to note that only the classes in the named package will be imported. For example, the import myapps.webutils.* statement will only import the classes found in the myapps.webutils package and will not import any classes found in the myapps.webutils.text package. To import classes from the myapps.webutils.text package, you must use the import myapps.webutils.text.* statement.

Java may not import every class a package contains when you use the wildcard character *. When you compile your code, Java searches the code and imports only the classes that are used. This prevents your bytecode from becoming too large.

Java can automatically import certain packages when you compile code. The `java.lang` package, which is part of the Java class library, is automatically imported whenever you compile code. If your code contains classes that do not belong to a package, Java imports the default package "" and assigns the classes to that package. If your Java code contains a `package` statement, the named package is also automatically imported.

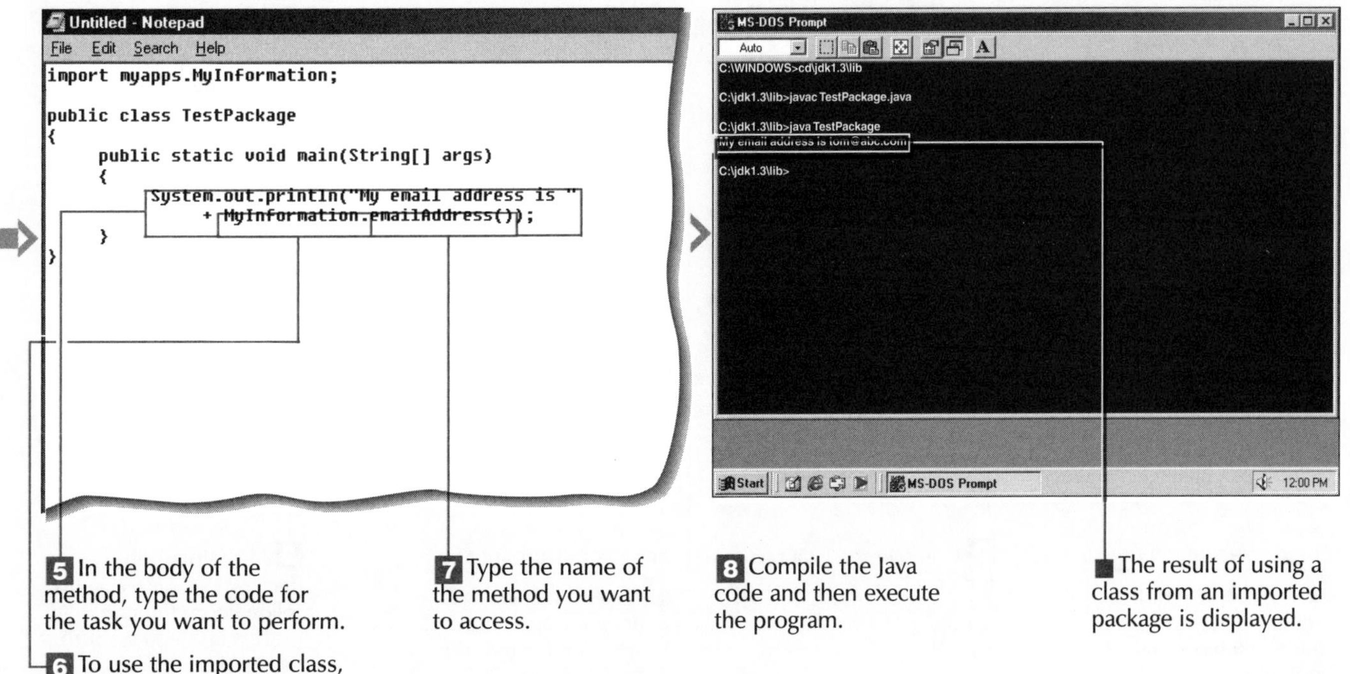

5 In the body of the method, type the code for the task you want to perform.

6 To use the imported class, type the name of the class followed by a dot.

7 Type the name of the method you want to access.

8 Compile the Java code and then execute the program.

■ The result of using a class from an imported package is displayed.

EXTEND A CLASS

If a class you are creating is related to a class you have previously created, you can make the new class an extension of the original class. For example, you can make a new class that performs tasks using a database an extension of the class that connects to the database. This allows you to re-use Java code in the original class without having to retype the code in the new class.

When you extend a class, the original class is usually referred to as the super-class, while the new class is called the sub-class.

When declaring a class you want to use as a sub-class, you must use the `extends` keyword to specify the name of the class that will act as the super-class. The class you specify using the `extends` keyword must be a valid class that will be accessible to the sub-class when the sub-class is compiled.

Whether or not a method within a super-class will be accessible to a sub-class depends on the access modifier the method uses. A method that uses the `public` access modifier will be accessible to any sub-class, while a method that uses the `private` access modifier will not be accessible to sub-classes. A method that does not have an access modifier specified will be accessible only to sub-classes that are stored in the same package as the super-class.

Once you have created a sub-class as an extension of a super-class, you can create a new class that accesses the sub-class. For example, a new class can create an object using the sub-class. The class information from both the sub-class and the super-class will be combined to form a single object, with methods from both the sub-class and the super-class available to the object.

Many of the classes included with the Java SDK extend to other classes. For information about the Java SDK classes, refer to the Java SDK documentation.

EXTEND A CLASS

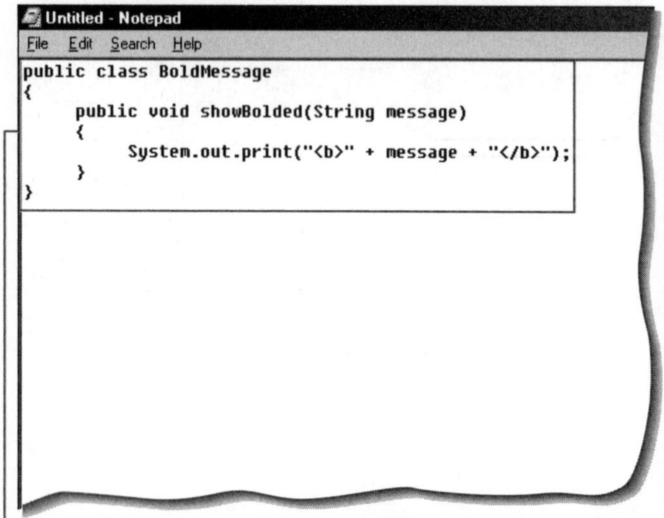

Untitled - Notepad
File Edit Search Help
public class BoldMessage
{
public void showBolded(String message)
{
System.out.print("<b>" + message + "</b>");
}
}

CREATE THE SUPER-CLASS

1 Type the code that defines a class you want to be able to extend to another class.

2 Compile the Java code for the class.

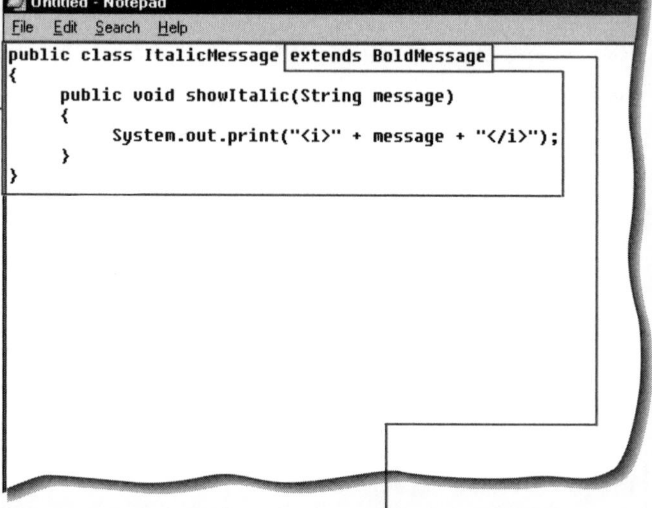

CREATE THE SUB-CLASS

1 Type the code that defines a class you want to use as an extension of another class.

2 In the method declaration, type **extends** followed by the name of the class you want to use as the super-class.

3 Compile the Java code for the class.

Extra

As with methods, fields within a super-class will also be available to a sub-class, depending on the access modifier a field uses. A field that uses the `private` access modifier will not be accessible to any sub-classes, while a field that uses the `public` access modifier will be available to all sub-classes.

When creating a sub-class, you can override a method in the super-class that you do not want to be available when the sub-class is accessed. To override a method in the super-class, create a method in the sub-class that has the same name as the method you want to override. The access modifier of the method in the sub-class must be the same or less restrictive than the access modifier of the method in the super-class. When an object is created using the sub-class, the method in the sub-class will be available instead of the method in the super-class.

A class you created as a sub-class can be used as the super-class of another class. This allows you to create a chain of sub-classes and super-classes. A class that extends directly from a super-class is called a direct sub-class of the super-class. A class that is an extension of another sub-class is called a non-direct sub-class of the super-class. There is no limit to the number of sub-classes that can be created from other sub-classes.

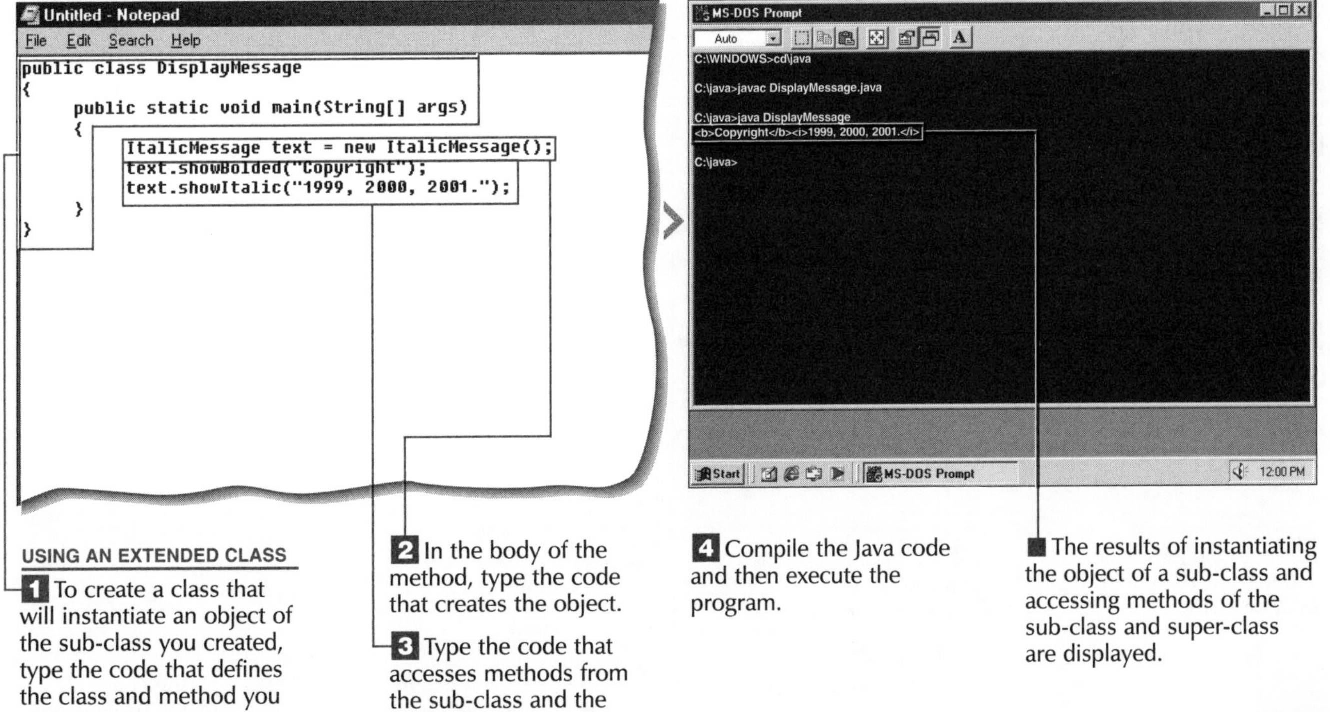

USING AN EXTENDED CLASS

1 To create a class that will instantiate an object of the sub-class you created, type the code that defines the class and method you want to use.

2 In the body of the method, type the code that creates the object.

3 Type the code that accesses methods from the sub-class and the super-class.

4 Compile the Java code and then execute the program.

■ The results of instantiating the object of a sub-class and accessing methods of the sub-class and super-class are displayed.

UNDERSTANDING VARIABLE SCOPE

The scope of a variable determines the part of a program that can access the variable and use its value. In Java, there are strict guidelines governing variable scope. These guidelines are referred to as scoping rules.

The scope of a variable is determined by the position of the variable declaration within a block of code. An opening brace and a closing brace denote a block of code. The scope of a variable is from the line of code containing the variable declaration to the closing brace of the block.

If you declare a variable in the body of a class, outside of any method, the variable will be accessible to all the methods in the class. A variable declared in a class body is referred to as a member variable.

When using the Java interpreter to execute a class file, methods and variables created in the body of the class file must be declared using the `static` access modifier.

A variable declared within a method is referred to as a local variable. A local variable is accessible only within the method in which it was declared. Other blocks of code created within the method can access the local variable.

You can use the same name to declare a member variable and a local variable in one class. When you use the same name to declare two variables of different scope, Java treats the variables as distinct. Although variables with different scopes can have the same name, using unique variable names will make your code easier to understand. For example, instead of using a variable named counter for all your counting functions, you should use variations of the name, such as loopCounter for counting loop iterations or processCounter for counting the number of times a particular process is executed.

UNDERSTANDING VARIABLE SCOPE

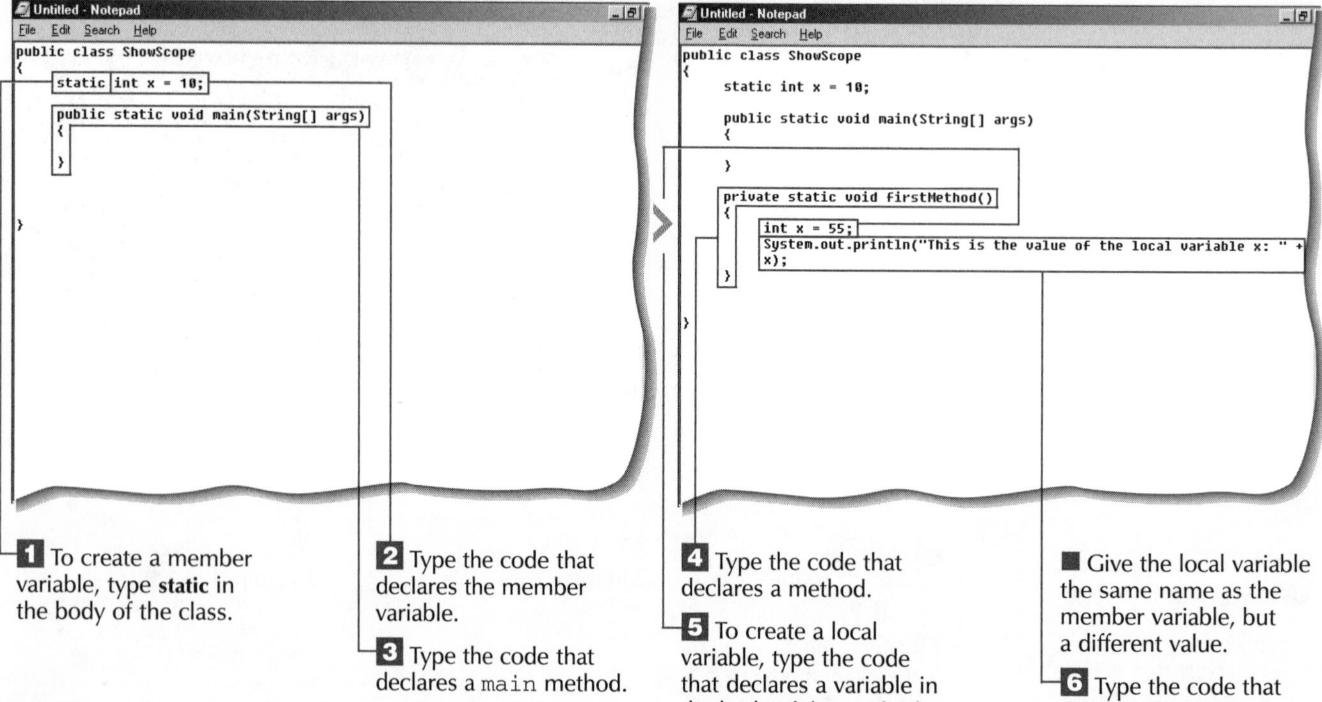

1 To create a member variable, type **static** in the body of the class.

2 Type the code that declares the member variable.

3 Type the code that declares a `main` method.

4 Type the code that declares a method.

5 To create a local variable, type the code that declares a variable in the body of the method.

■ Give the local variable the same name as the member variable, but a different value.

6 Type the code that displays the value of the local variable.

Extra

The scope of a variable is restricted to the block of code that contains the variable declaration. If you declare a variable in a block of code created by an `if` statement or a statement that produces a loop, the variable will be a local variable.

Example:

```
boolean go = true;

if (go)
{
      int x = 3;
}

System.out.print(x);
```

Produces this error message when compiled:

```
Scope.java:12: cannot resolve symbol
symbol  : variable x
location: class Scope
          System.out.print(x);
                           ^
1 error
```

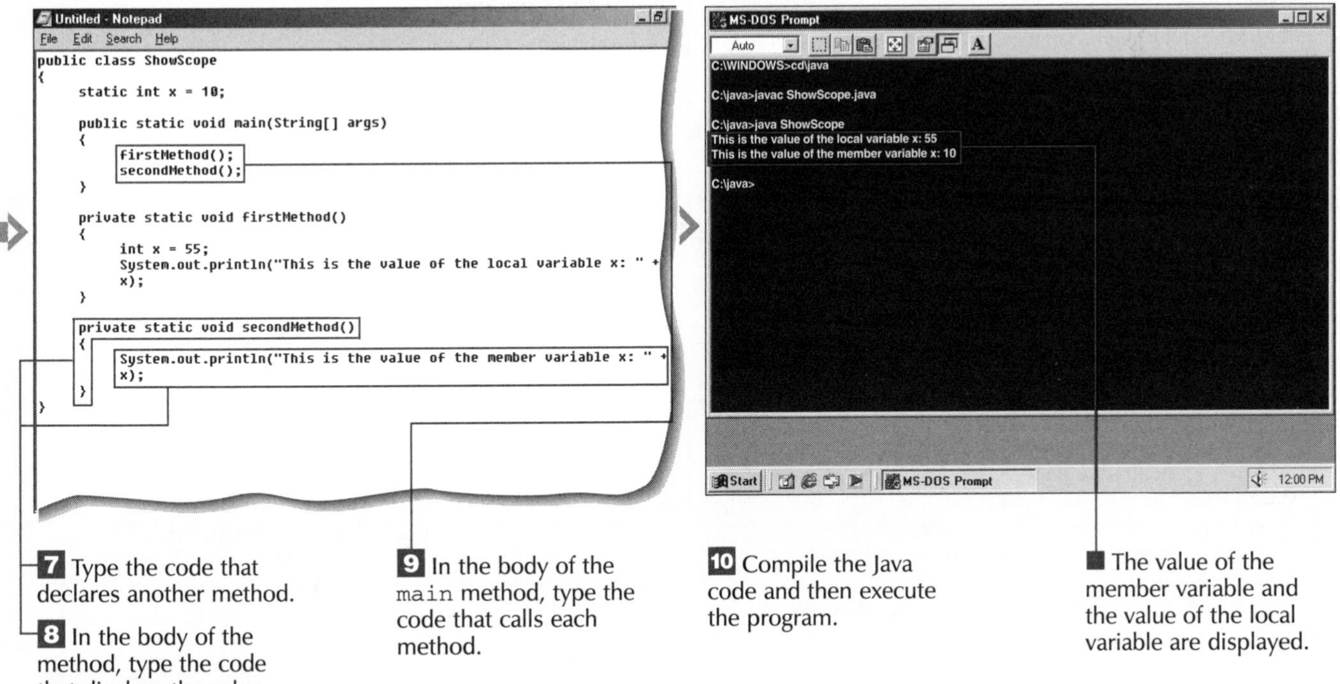

7 Type the code that declares another method.

8 In the body of the method, type the code that displays the value of the member variable.

9 In the body of the `main` method, type the code that calls each method.

10 Compile the Java code and then execute the program.

■ The value of the member variable and the value of the local variable are displayed.

JSP-COMPATIBLE WEB SERVERS

You must have access to a JSP-compatible Web server before beginning to develop JavaServer Pages code. There are several JSP-compatible Web servers to choose from and most of the server software is available in both Windows and UNIX versions. Some of the available Web servers are written in the Java programming language and can be installed on any computer that has a Java Runtime Environment installed.

A computer running a Windows operating system with the Tomcat Web server installed was used to process the JSP pages created in this book.

CHOOSING A WEB SERVER

When choosing a Web server, you should evaluate the strengths and weaknesses of several Web servers to determine which server best suits your needs and meets your level of expertise. For example, while a Web server may be capable of processing thousands of JSP pages per hour, the server may be very complicated to set up.

Feature List

Some Web servers support a wider range of features than other Web servers. For example, some Web servers support detailed logging and error reporting, while others do not. You should examine the feature list for a Web server to determine whether the server meets your current and future needs.

Cost

Web server software is often available free of charge for development purposes, but you may have to pay for the software if it will be used in a commercial application. Some Web servers can be used free of charge for a specific period of time, after which a fee must be paid to continue using the Web server.

Terms and Conditions

Each Web server has its own specific terms and conditions of use. Prior to using any Web server software, you should carefully review the terms and conditions to ensure that the way you intend to use the software complies with the conditions of use.

POPULAR JSP-COMPATIBLE WEB SERVERS

The following are examples of JSP-compatible Web servers.

Jigsaw

Jigsaw is a Java-based Web server developed by the World Wide Web Consortium (W3C), which is the body responsible for many Web standards. The Jigsaw Web server is better suited to development than deployment. For more information about the Jigsaw Web server, visit the www.w3c.org/Jigsaw Web site.

LiteWebServer

LiteWebServer is a small, robust Web server developed by Gefion Software. This Web server is suitable for developing JSP pages and for making pages available on an intranet. For more information about LiteWebServer, visit the www.gefionsoftware.com Web site.

POPULAR JSP-COMPATIBLE WEB SERVERS (Continued)

Nexus

Nexus is written entirely in Java and can be used either as a stand-alone Web server or as part of a larger application. To download the Nexus Web server, visit the www-uk.hpl.hp.com/people/ak/java/nexus Web site.

Orion Application Server

Orion Application Server is a popular JSP-compatible Web server that is suitable for most commercial needs. Orion Application Server supports clustering, which allows a large Web site to be stored on multiple Web servers. To learn more about Orion Application Server, visit the www.orionserver.com Web site.

Servertec Internet Server

Servertec Internet Server is an easy-to-use Web server that can be used as a stand-alone Web server or can be integrated with the Apache Web server. Apache is the most popular Web server on the Internet. Servertec Internet Server is written entirely in the Java programming language. For more information about Servertec Internet Server, visit the www.servertec.com Web site.

Tomcat

The Tomcat Web server can be used as a stand-alone Web server or can be integrated with the Apache Web server. The Tomcat Web server is available at the jakarta.apache.org Web site. For information about installing the Tomcat Web server, see page 60.

WebSphere Application Server

WebSphere Application Server is a Java-based Web server developed by IBM that can be used to develop JSP pages and deploy large-scale e-business applications. For more information about WebSphere Application Server, visit the www-4.ibm.com/software/webservers Web site.

WEB HOSTING SERVICES

If you do not want to install your own Web server software to develop JSP pages, you can use a Web hosting service that offers JSP-compatible Web servers. A Web hosting service is a company that allows individuals to store Web sites they create on the hosting service's Web servers. A Web hosting service may also offer access to other technologies related to JSP, such as JDBC, the Java technology used to enable JSP pages to retrieve information from a database.

Web hosting fees are typically inexpensive, making a Web hosting service an affordable alternative to installing a Web server on your own computer. A Web hosting service usually charges a monthly fee for their services. The fees vary depending on the amount of space, bandwidth and other resources required by the Web site.

When developing JSP pages using a Web hosting service, you will need a text editor to write the code and an ftp program to transfer your pages to the Web hosting service's Web servers.

Examples of Web hosting services that offer JSP-compatible Web servers include:

SpinWeb
www.spinweb.net

iMagine Internet Services
www.imagineis.com

MyServletHosting.com
www.myservlethosting.com

Reinvent Technologies, Inc.
www.reinventinc.com

Colossus, Inc.
www.colossus.net

INSTALL THE TOMCAT WEB SERVER

Before you can create interactive and dynamic JSP pages, you must install a Web server that can interpret and process JavaServer Pages code. Tomcat is a fully-functional Web server that you can install on your computer to create and test JSP pages.

You need to install the Java Software Development Kit before installing the Tomcat Web server. You may need to change certain Tomcat settings to specify the location of the Java SDK. Consult the documentation included with Tomcat for information about changing these settings.

Tomcat is constantly being updated. A recent release of the Tomcat Web server is included on the CD-ROM disc that accompanies this book, but you should make sure you install the latest version of the server. The latest version of Tomcat is available at the jakarta.apache.org/tomcat Web site.

The version of Tomcat you install may be an unfinished, or beta, version. Although Tomcat is a very stable application, some difficulties, such as system crashes, should be expected when using any beta software.

To install Tomcat, you simply copy the Tomcat Web server files to your computer. Once Tomcat is installed, it can be started using a program called startup, which is located in the bin directory. The bin directory also stores the shutdown program, which you can execute to stop Tomcat when you have finished displaying Web and JSP pages.

To confirm that Tomcat has been installed and started properly, you can have the server display a page in a Web browser. After starting the Web browser you want to use, you enter the name or IP number of your computer, as well as the port number used by Tomcat. The default port number used by Tomcat is 8080. If you do not know the IP number of your computer, you can use 127.0.0.1, which is the IP number that computers running TCP/IP use to refer to themselves.

A Web hosting service may also allow you to access their Web server to test your JSP pages. For a list of Web hosting services, see page 59.

INSTALL THE TOMCAT WEB SERVER

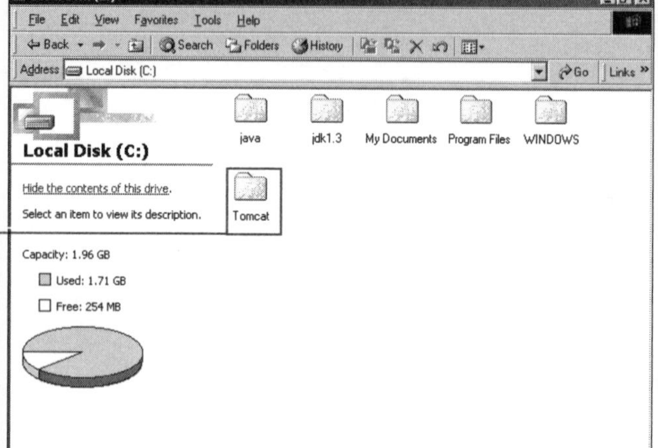

INSTALL TOMCAT

1 Copy the Tomcat Web server files to your computer.

■ In this example, we copy the Tomcat Web server files to the C: drive. The files are stored in a directory called Tomcat.

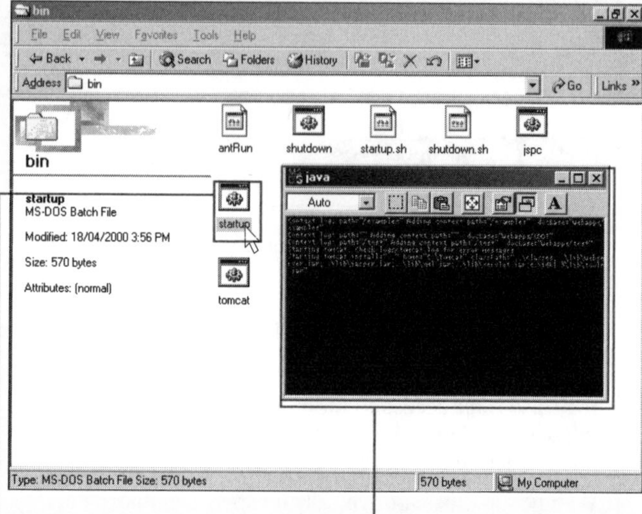

START TOMCAT

1 Display the contents of the bin directory, which is located in the Tomcat directory.

2 Double-click the appropriate startup file to start the Tomcat Web server.

Note: The startup.bat file is used to start Tomcat on Windows platforms. The startup.sh file is used to start Tomcat on non-Windows platforms.

■ A command prompt window appears.

Extra

When the Tomcat Web server is installed, several directories are automatically created. These directories can be found in the main Tomcat directory.

DIRECTORY NAME:	DESCRIPTION:
bin	Stores programs for starting and shutting down the Tomcat Web server.
conf	Stores configuration files for the Tomcat Web server.
doc	Stores miscellaneous documents.
lib	Stores JAR (Java ARchive) files. The JAR file format is used to compress all the components of a Java program into a single file.
logs	Stores log files.
src	Stores the servlet Application Program Interface (API) source files used by the Tomcat Web server.
webapps	Stores sample Web applications.
work	Stores intermediate files, such as compiled JSP files. This directory may not have been created when you installed the Tomcat Web server.

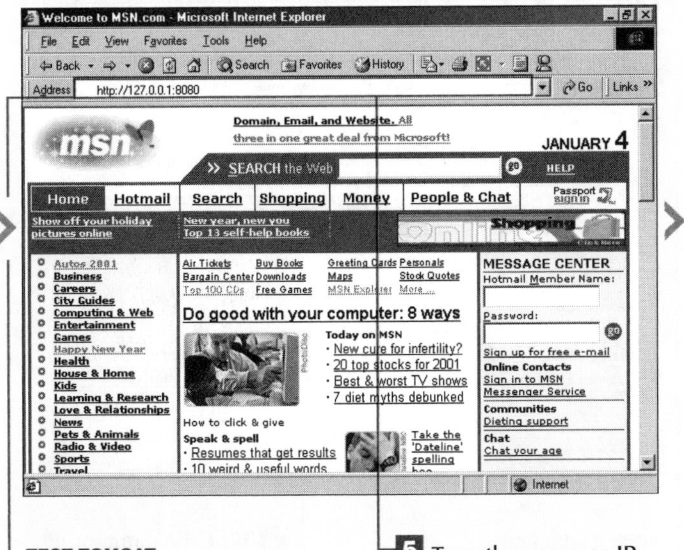

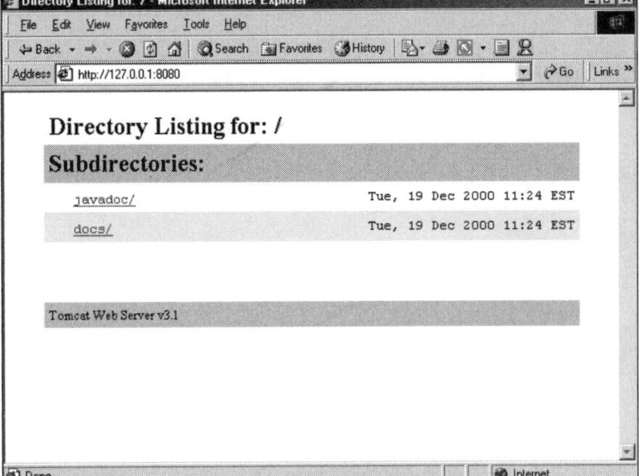

TEST TOMCAT

3 Start the Web browser you want to use to test the Tomcat Web server.

4 Click this area to highlight the current Web page address and then type **http://**.

5 Type the name or IP number of your computer followed by a colon.

6 Type the Tomcat port number and then press Enter.

■ The Web browser displays a Web page generated by the Tomcat Web server.

■ If the Tomcat Web server is not working properly, the Web browser will display an error message.

DISPLAY A WEB PAGE USING TOMCAT

After installing the Tomcat Web server, you can create a Web page and store the page on the server. You can then use a Web browser to display the Web page. Displaying a Web page allows you to confirm that Tomcat is installed properly and that you are storing pages in the correct directory.

Make sure you add the .html extension to the name of a Web page you save. Some text editors do not recognize the .html extension, so you may have to enclose the Web page name in quotation marks, such as "index.html".

When installed on a Windows platform, Tomcat uses the webapps directory as the root directory. All of the Web and JSP pages you want to display must be stored in the root directory or its subdirectories. When a Web server receives a request for a Web page, the server looks for the page in the root directory if no other directory is specified in the request. If another directory is specified, the Web server expects it to be a subdirectory of the root directory. For example, when a Web server with a root directory named docs receives the request www.server.com/work/sale.html, the server displays the document sale.html stored in the C:\docs\work directory.

If Tomcat is installed on a computer running a non-Windows operating system, such as Linux, the root directory may be different. The root directory could also change with newer versions of Tomcat. Always check the documentation included with Tomcat to verify the name and location of the root directory.

The webapps directory contains a number of directories that can be used to store your Web pages. If you are only using the Tomcat Web server to test Web and JSP pages, you may want to store the pages in the examples directory.

Before displaying Web pages, you must ensure that the Tomcat Web server is running. To start the Tomcat Web server, see page 60.

DISPLAY A WEB PAGE USING TOMCAT

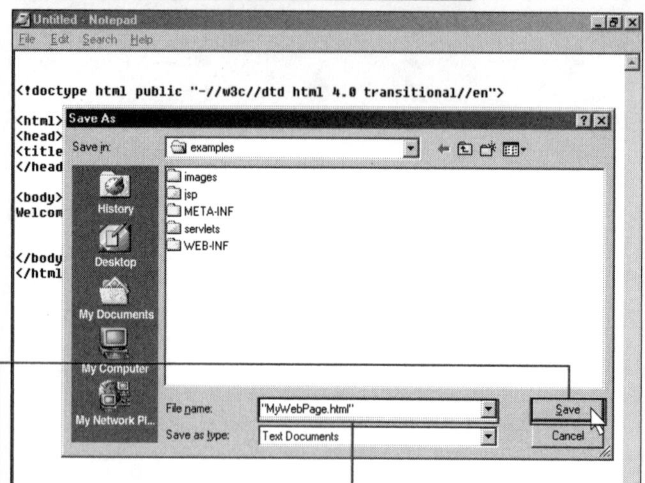

CREATE A WEB PAGE

1 In a text editor, create a Web page.

2 Save the Web page in the Tomcat root directory or one of its subdirectories.

Note: In this example, we save the Web page in the C:\Tomcat\webapps\examples directory.

■ The filename must have the .html extension and may need to be enclosed in quotation marks.

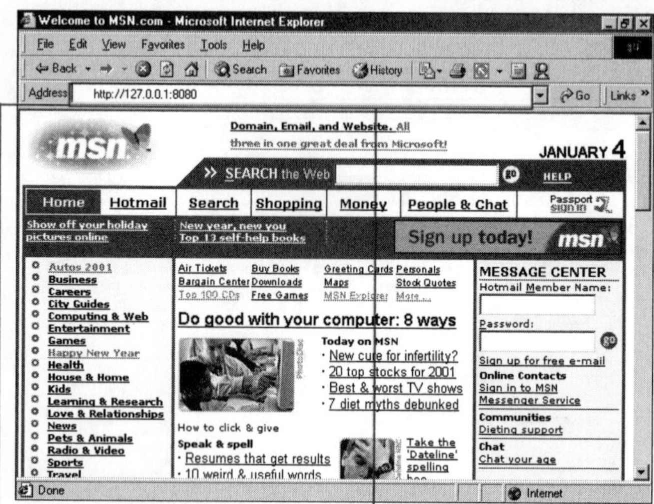

VIEW A WEB PAGE

1 Start the Web browser you want to use to display a Web page.

2 Click this area to highlight the current Web page address and then type **http://**.

3 Type the name or IP number of your computer followed by a colon.

4 Type the Tomcat port number.

Extra

You can create your own directory within the webapps directory and then store pages you want to display in that directory. Creating your own directories is useful when you want to use Tomcat to make your pages available to others. Before you can display pages saved in a directory you created, you must change settings in the server.xml file. For example, if you created a directory named pages, you would add the following code to the server.xml file between the `<ContextManager>` tags:

```
<Context path="/pages" docBase="/pages" debug="0"
reloadable="true" >
</Context>
```

The configuration settings for the Tomcat Web server are stored in the server.xml file located in the conf subdirectory of the main Tomcat directory. You can adjust the settings for Tomcat by changing or adding information to the server.xml file. To edit the file, you can open the file in a text editor. You should consult the user documentation included with Tomcat before changing any settings in the server.xml file.

By default, the port number used by Tomcat is 8080. You must specify this number in the addresses you type when accessing pages generated by Tomcat. To change the port number used by Tomcat, open the server.xml file and look for the following section of code:

```
<Connector className="org.apache.tomcat.service.SimpleTcpConnector">
  <Parameter name="handler"
  value="org.apache.tomcat.service.http.HttpConnectionHandler"/>
  <Parameter name="port" value="8080"/>
</Connector>
```

In the line that specifies the port number, replace the existing port number with the port number you want to use. After you change the port number, you must specify the new number in Web page addresses.

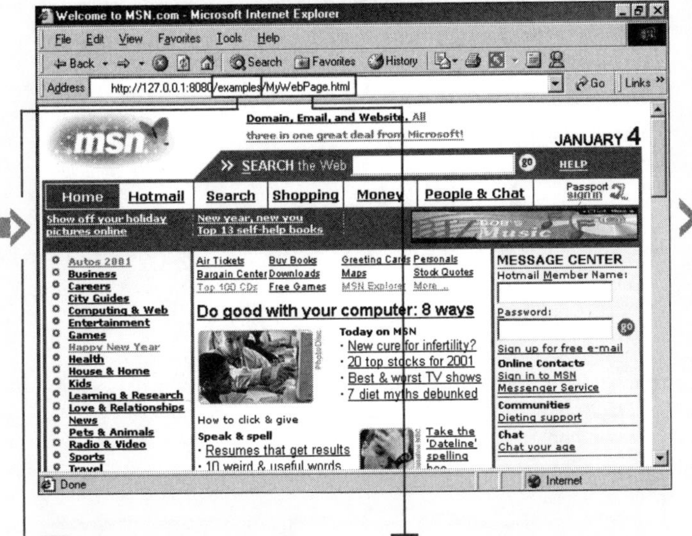

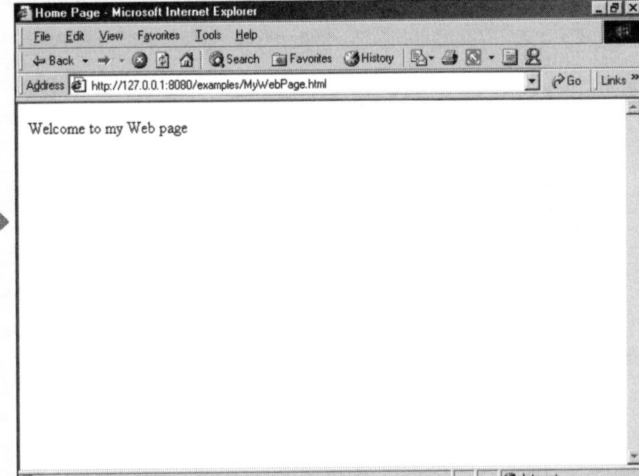

5 If the Web page is stored in a subdirectory of the root directory, type / followed by the name of the subdirectory that stores the page.

6 Type / followed by the filename of the Web page and then press Enter.

■ The Web page appears in the Web browser.

ADD A COMMENT TO A JSP PAGE

Adding comments to your HTML or JSP code is good programming practice and can help clarify the code. For example, you may use a variable named totalCost in your code. You could use a comment to explain whether the variable stores the total cost of all the products in a database or only some of the products. Comments can also contain information such as the author's name or the date the code was created. You can also use comments for debugging a program or as reminders to remove or update sections of code.

You can include HTML comments within the HTML code of a JSP page by enclosing the comments between the <!-- and --> delimiters. Any text enclosed in these delimiters will be sent to the Web browser, but will not be displayed on the page. The information may be displayed by users who view the HTML source code however.

You can also add comments within the HTML code of a JSP page using the hidden comment tags, <%-- and --%>. Any code or information within the hidden comment tags will be discarded before any processing of the JSP page takes place on the Web server and will not be sent to the Web browser.

You can add comments to JSP code the same way you add comments to a Java application. The // notation can be used to create single-line comments and the /* and */ delimiters can be used to create multi-line comments. For information about adding comments to Java code, see page 15.

You should be very careful about where you place comments in a JSP page, especially when the comments are placed within the JSP code. The Web server expects to find only valid Java code within your JSP expressions, scriptlets and declarations. Any HTML comments or hidden comments in the JSP code will cause an error to occur.

ADD A COMMENT TO A JSP PAGE

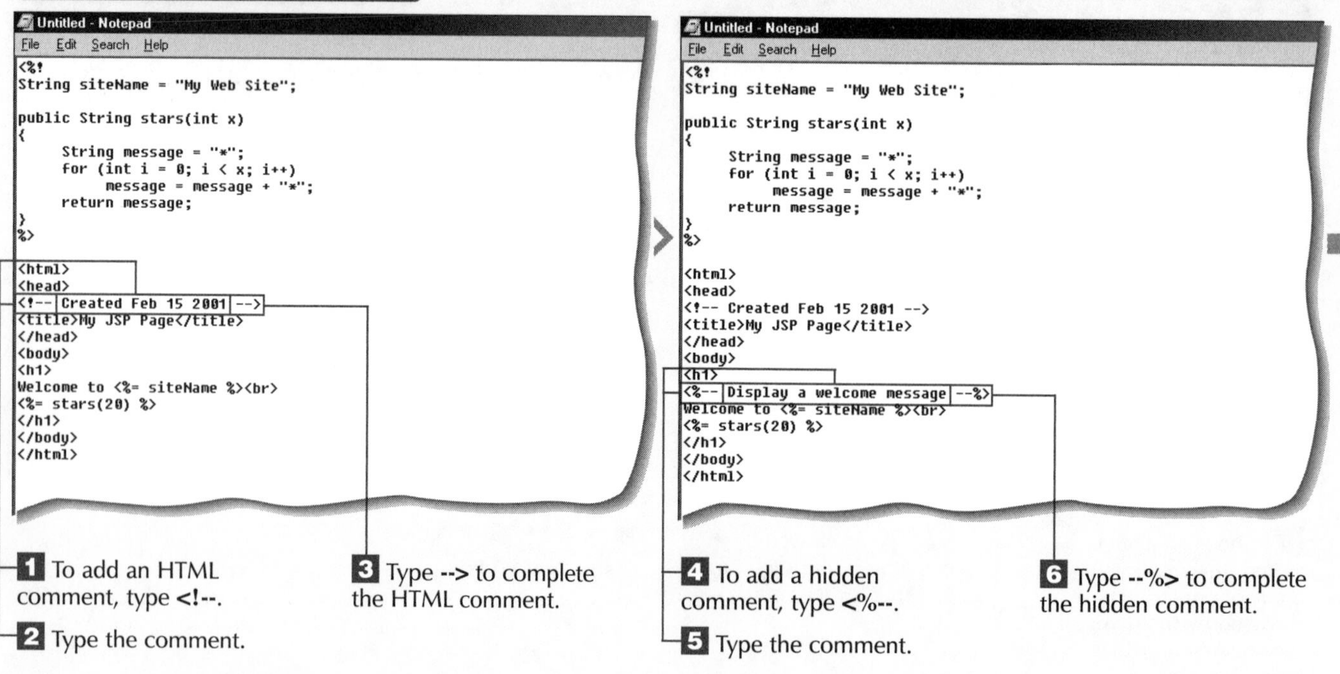

Apply It

You may include JSP code within an HTML comment. This allows you to include dynamically generated comments in your JSP page. Embedding JSP code within HTML comments can help you to determine the state of various aspects of your JSP code without affecting the display of the Web page and can be a useful troubleshooting technique.

TYPE THIS:

```
<%! String siteName = "My Web Site"; %>
<html>
<head>
<!-- The variable siteName has a value of
"<%= siteName %>" -->
<title>My JSP Page</title>
</head>
<body>
<% siteName = "* " + siteName + " *"; %>
<!-- The variable siteName has a value of
"<%= siteName %>" -->
Welcome to <%= siteName %><br>
</body>
</html>
```

HTML SOURCE CODE:

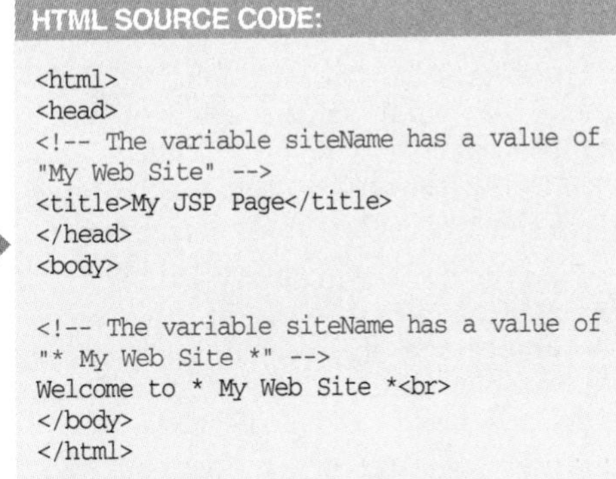

```
<html>
<head>
<!-- The variable siteName has a value of
"My Web Site" -->
<title>My JSP Page</title>
</head>
<body>

<!-- The variable siteName has a value of
"* My Web Site *" -->
Welcome to * My Web Site *<br>
</body>
</html>
```

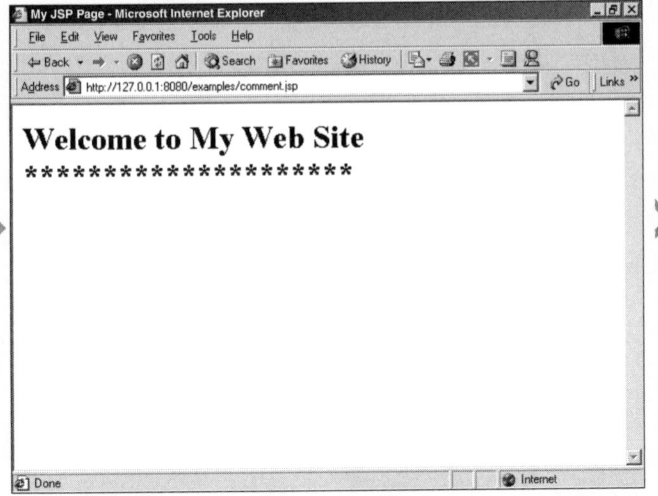

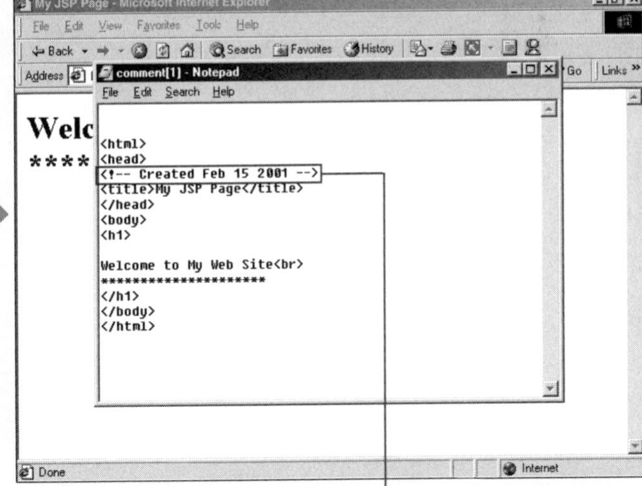

7 Save the page with the .jsp extension and then display the page in a Web browser.

■ The comments do not affect the display of the JSP page.

8 Display the source code of the JSP page.

■ The HTML comment is included in the HTML source code, but the hidden comment does not appear.

CREATE AN EXPRESSION

An expression is a scripting element that allows you to generate output on a JSP page. You can use expressions to insert information into a Web page rather than using scriptlets with `out.print()` or `out.println()` statements. This reduces the amount of code you have to type and can make your scripts easier to read.

The Web server processes the code within the expression and converts the results to a string. The results of the expression are then inserted into the HTML code in the same manner as the result of `out.print()` and `out.println()` statements in scriptlets.

A simple expression can be used to display a string enclosed in quotation marks or the value of a variable. The Web server simply inserts the string or value into the HTML code. Variables must be declared and initialized in scriptlets or declarations in the same JSP page.

You can also use calculations and method calls in your expressions. The expression processes the calculation or method and inserts the result into the HTML code. Methods used in expressions must be declared in the same JSP page and return a printable value. If a method does not return a value, the Web server displays an error message.

You can use string concatenation to join different types of information in a single expression. For example, you can create an expression such as <%= "Date of Birth: " + getDOB() %>, which generates a string followed by the value returned by a method.

An expression cannot end with a semicolon, as is customary with most Java statements. If a semicolon is included in an expression, an error will occur.

Users viewing the source code of the Web page from within a Web browser will not be able to view the contents of the expression. They will see only the information generated by the expression.

CREATE AN EXPRESSION

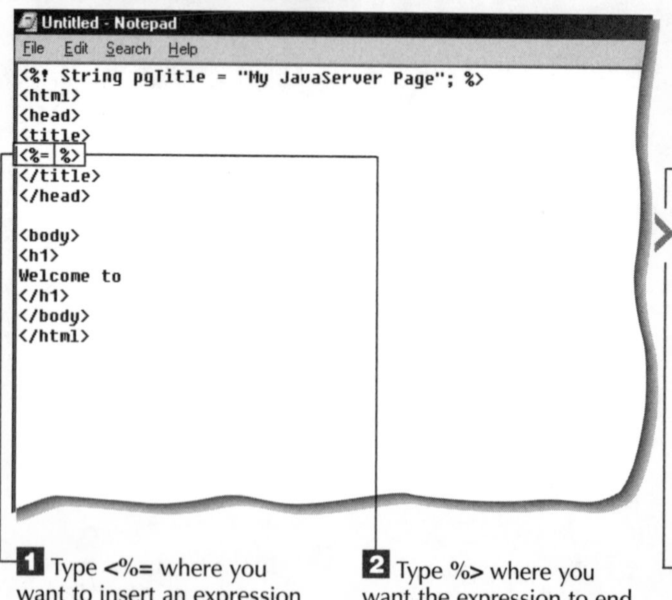

1 Type **<%=** where you want to insert an expression in the JSP page.

2 Type %> where you want the expression to end.

```
<%! String pgTitle = "My JavaServer Page"; %>
<html>
<head>
<title>
<%= pgTitle %>
</title>
</head>

<body>
<h1>
Welcome to
</h1>
</body>
</html>
```

3 Between the opening and closing delimiters (<%= and %>), type the code to be evaluated and included in the HTML code.

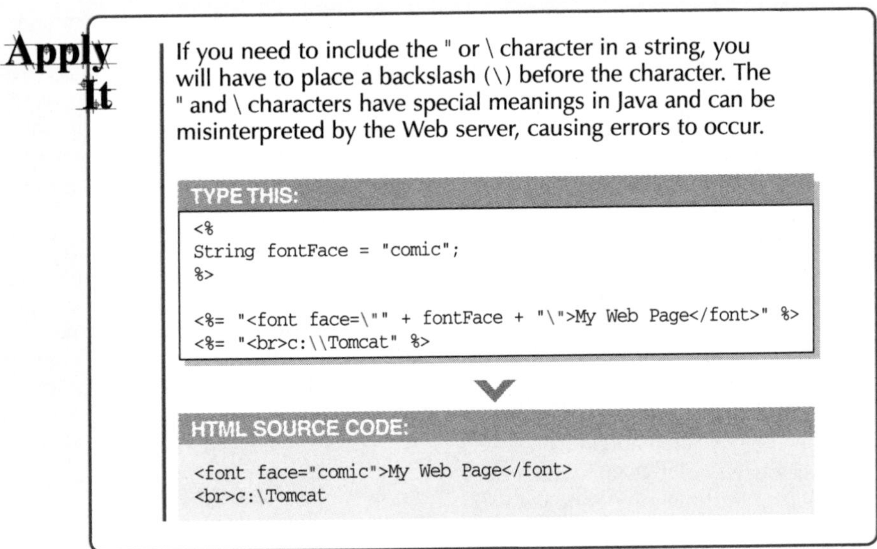

Apply It

If you need to include the " or \ character in a string, you will have to place a backslash (\) before the character. The " and \ characters have special meanings in Java and can be misinterpreted by the Web server, causing errors to occur.

TYPE THIS:

```
<%
String fontFace = "comic";
%>

<%= "<font face=\"" + fontFace + "\">My Web Page</font>" %>
<%= "<br>c:\\Tomcat" %>
```

HTML SOURCE CODE:

```
<font face="comic">My Web Page</font>
<br>c:\Tomcat
```

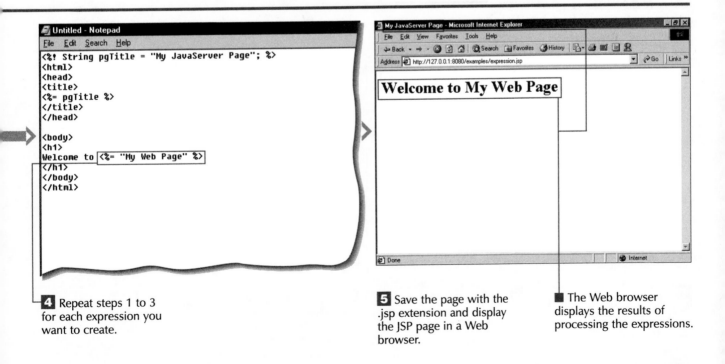

4 Repeat steps 1 to 3 for each expression you want to create.

5 Save the page with the .jsp extension and display the JSP page in a Web browser.

■ The Web browser displays the results of processing the expressions.

CREATE A DECLARATION

A declaration is a scripting element that allows you to define variables and methods that will be used throughout a JSP page. You must define variables and methods in a JSP page before you can use the variables and methods in the page. Although variables can also be defined within a scriptlet, using a declaration is the preferred method for defining variables.

To create a declaration, you place the code for the declaration between the `<%!` opening delimiter and the `%>` closing delimiter. Although a JSP page can include multiple declarations, this is not typically required. There is no limit to the amount of code you can include in a declaration, so you can define multiple variables and methods within the same declaration. Each line of code in a declaration must end with a semicolon, if a semicolon is required according to Java programming syntax.

Since declarations do not generate any output, they can be placed anywhere on a JSP page without interfering with the HTML code. Declarations are typically placed at the top of a page.

When defining a method in a declaration, you can use the `public`, `private` or `protected` access modifier to specify how the method will be accessed. For more information about access modifiers, see page 17. The access modifier you use becomes important when you import class files and other JSP pages into your code. For more information about including external files in a JSP page, see page 76.

If a declaration you want to add to a JSP page will contain many variables and methods, you may want to use another method of including the code, such as JavaBeans. JavaBeans allow you to store code in an external file so the source code of your JSP page is easier to understand and manage. For information on JavaBeans, see page 122.

CREATE A DECLARATION

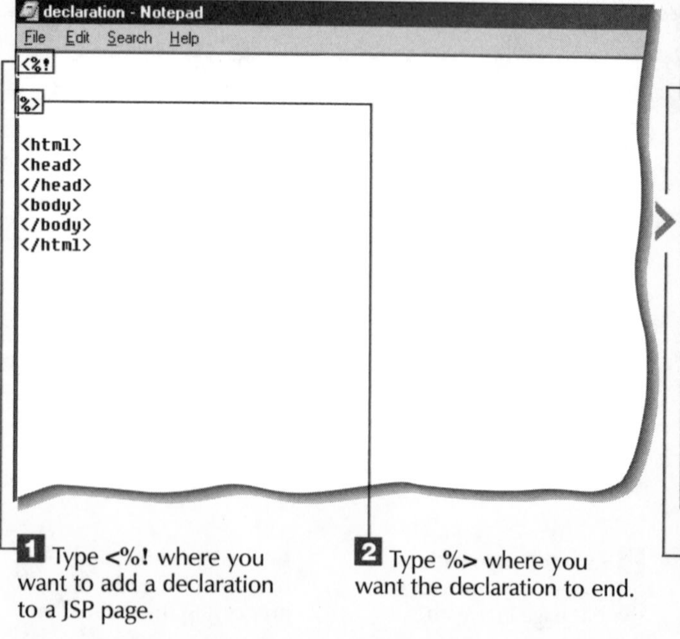

1 Type **<%!** where you want to add a declaration to a JSP page.

2 Type **%>** where you want the declaration to end.

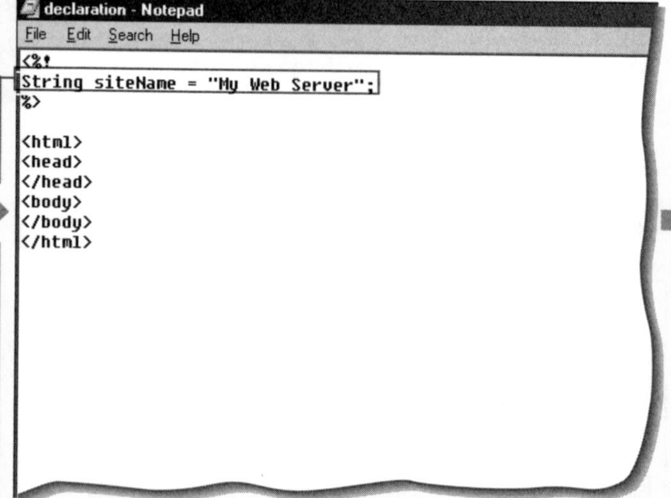

3 Between the opening and closing delimiters (`<%!` and `%>`), type the code that defines a variable or method.

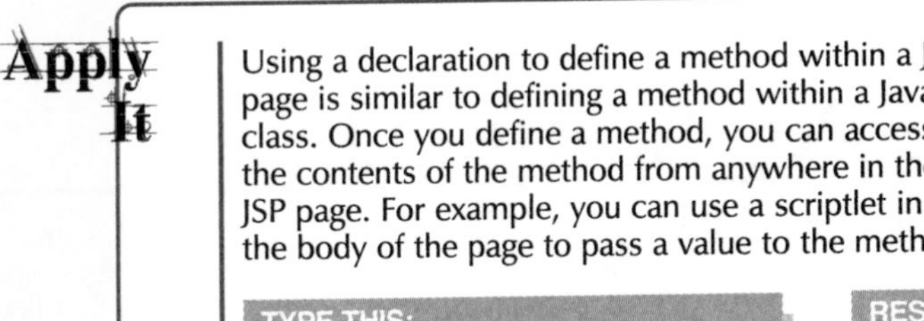

Apply It

Using a declaration to define a method within a JSP page is similar to defining a method within a Java class. Once you define a method, you can access the contents of the method from anywhere in the JSP page. For example, you can use a scriptlet in the body of the page to pass a value to the method.

TYPE THIS:

```
<%!
String siteName = "My Web Server";
public String stars(int x)
{
      String message = "*";
      for (int i = 0; i < x; i++)
            message = message + "*";
      return message;
}
%>

<html>
<body>
Welcome to <%= siteName %><br>
<%= stars(22) %>
</body>
</html>
```

RESULT:

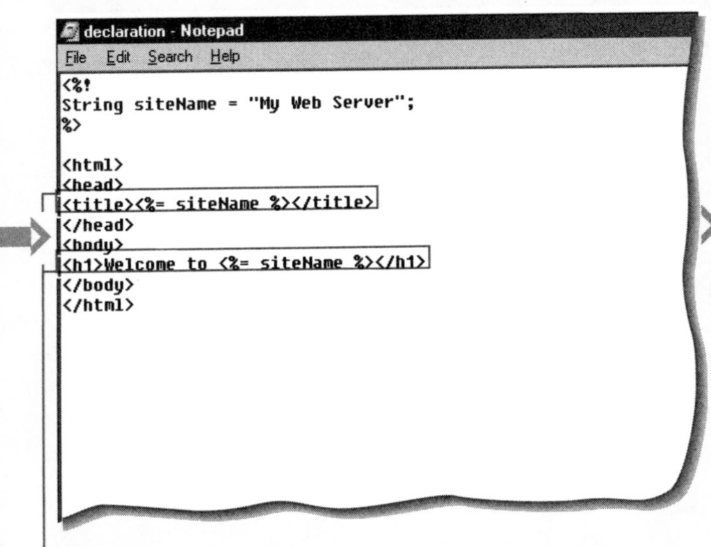

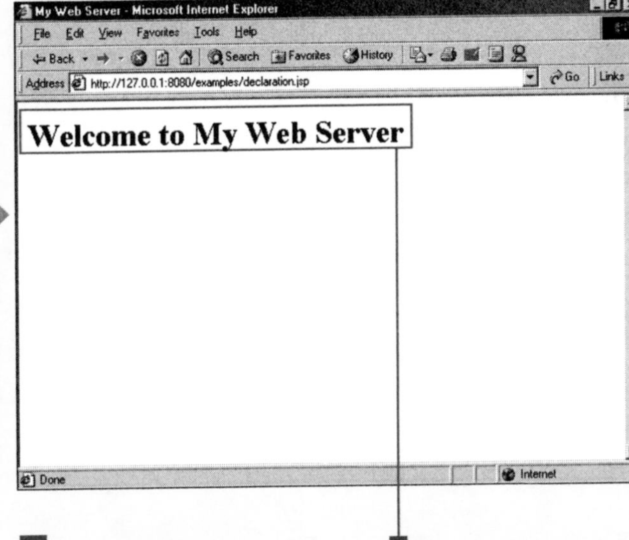

4 Type the code that uses the variable or method.

5 Save the page with the .jsp extension and then display the JSP page in a Web browser.

■ The Web browser displays the result of using the variable or method you defined in the declaration.

GENERATE TEXT USING SCRIPTLETS

You can use scriptlets to generate text on a JSP page. A scriptlet is a block of code embedded within a page. The code for a scriptlet is almost always written in the Java programming language, though some Web servers support scriptlets written in other languages. A page containing a scriptlet is often referred to as a template.

To add a scriptlet to a page, you place the code you want to embed in the page between the `<%` opening delimiter and the `%>` closing delimiter. A scriptlet can be used to generate text ranging from a simple message to the entire content of a JSP page.

Within a scriptlet, you can use the `out` object with the `print` or `println` member to generate text for a JSP page. The `out` object sends output to a Web browser, while the `print` and `println` members generate the text that is to be inserted into the page.

The placement of a scriptlet within a JSP page is important. If a scriptlet is used to generate output, it must be placed in the body of the page rather than in an area that does not display content, such as between the `<head>` and `</head>` tags.

Before a JSP page containing scriptlets is generated, a Web server processes the code in the scriptlets. The information generated by the code is inserted into the page before the page is displayed. Users who visit the JSP page will not be able to see the code for a scriptlet, even if they display the source code for the page, since the source code will contain only the output generated by the scriptlet. Although scriptlets are relatively secure, you should avoid including sensitive information, such as passwords, in the code.

GENERATE TEXT USING SCRIPTLETS

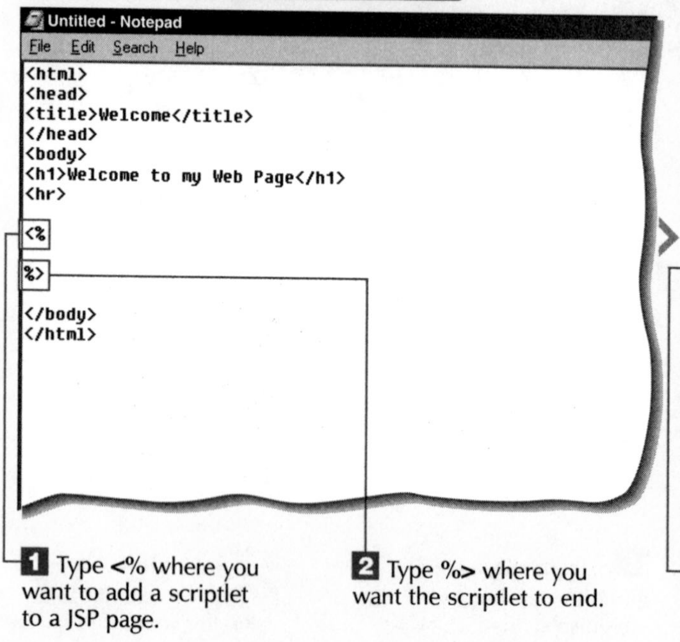

1 Type **<%** where you want to add a scriptlet to a JSP page.

2 Type **%>** where you want the scriptlet to end.

Untitled - Notepad

File Edit Search Help

```
<html>
<head>
<title>Welcome</title>
</head>
<body>
<h1>Welcome to my Web Page</h1>
<hr>

<%
out.print();
%>

</body>
</html>
```

3 Between the opening and closing delimiters (`<%` and `%>`), type **out.print( )** or **out.println( )** to generate text on the page.

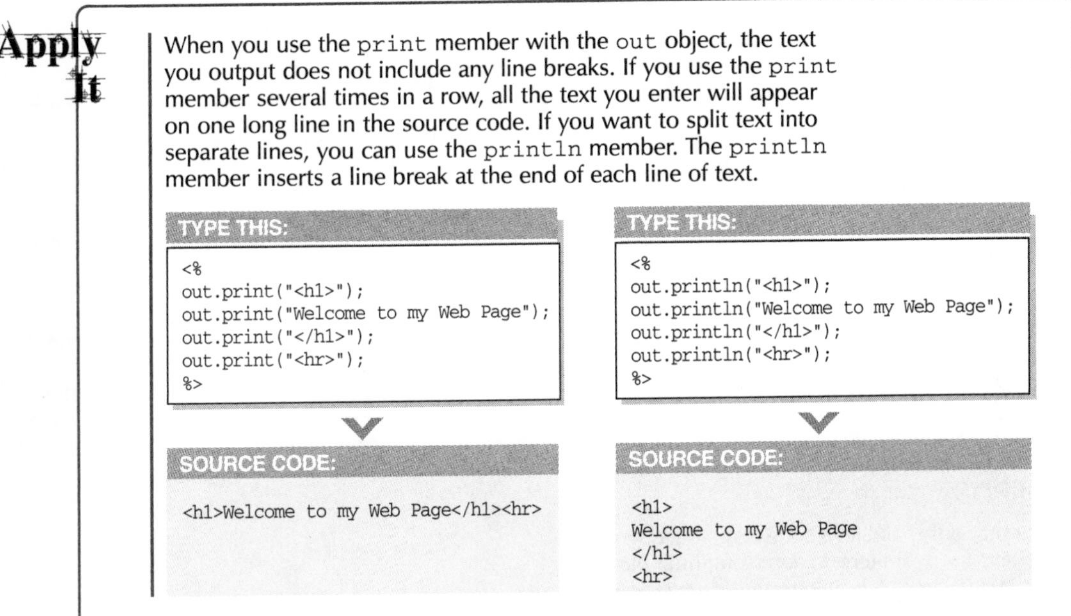

Apply It

When you use the `print` member with the `out` object, the text you output does not include any line breaks. If you use the `print` member several times in a row, all the text you enter will appear on one long line in the source code. If you want to split text into separate lines, you can use the `println` member. The `println` member inserts a line break at the end of each line of text.

TYPE THIS:

```
<%
out.print("<h1>");
out.print("Welcome to my Web Page");
out.print("</h1>");
out.print("<hr>");
%>
```

SOURCE CODE:

```
<h1>Welcome to my Web Page</h1><hr>
```

TYPE THIS:

```
<%
out.println("<h1>");
out.println("Welcome to my Web Page");
out.println("</h1>");
out.println("<hr>");
%>
```

SOURCE CODE:

```
<h1>
Welcome to my Web Page
</h1>
<hr>
```

```
<html>
<head>
<title>Welcome</title>
</head>
<body>
<h1>Welcome to my Web Page</h1>
<hr>

<%
out.print("This is a JSP page");
%>

</body>
</html>
```

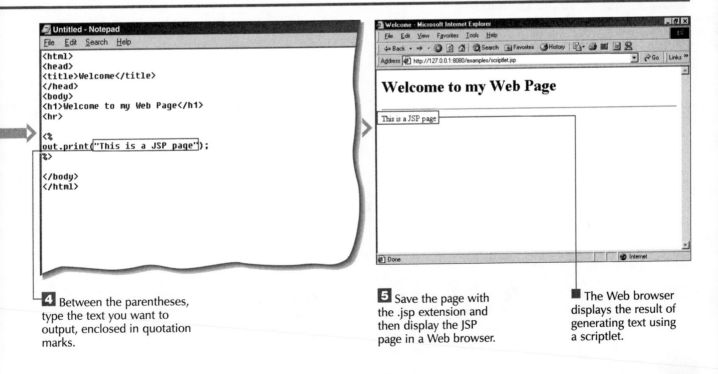

4 Between the parentheses, type the text you want to output, enclosed in quotation marks.

Welcome to my Web Page

This is a JSP page

5 Save the page with the .jsp extension and then display the JSP page in a Web browser.

■ The Web browser displays the result of generating text using a scriptlet.

WORK WITH MULTIPLE SCRIPTLETS

You can use multiple scriptlets within a single JSP page. This enables you to place dynamically created information in multiple locations throughout your Web page.

Any code used in one scriptlet can be accessed by other scriptlets in the same JSP page. For example, you can declare a variable in one scriptlet and then access the variable in another scriptlet that is in the same JSP page. Scriptlets will be processed in the order they appear on the JSP page, so you should consider the order of processing when creating scriptlets that use information from other scriptlets. For example, a scriptlet at the top of a JSP page will not be able to access variables declared in a scriptlet further down the page.

You must ensure that only valid Java code is included between the `<%` and `%>` delimiters. When using multiple scriptlets within HTML code, it is a common mistake to leave some HTML code between the scriptlet delimiters. HTML code included between the scriptlet delimiters must be included in valid Java statements so the Web server can dynamically generate the HTML code. If the Web server finds any raw HTML code in a scriptlet, an error will occur.

Using many large scriptlets in a JSP page can cause your code to be difficult to read and troubleshoot, should an error occur. Scriptlets are suitable for small amounts of code and for development and learning purposes. For other purposes, you should convert your scriptlets into a more manageable format, such as JavaBeans. For information about creating JavaBeans, see page 122.

WORK WITH MULTIPLE SCRIPTLETS

Untitled - Notepad

File Edit Search Help

```
<%

%>
<html>
<head>
<title>

</title>
</head>
<body>
<h1>

Welcome to


</h1>
</body>
</html>
```

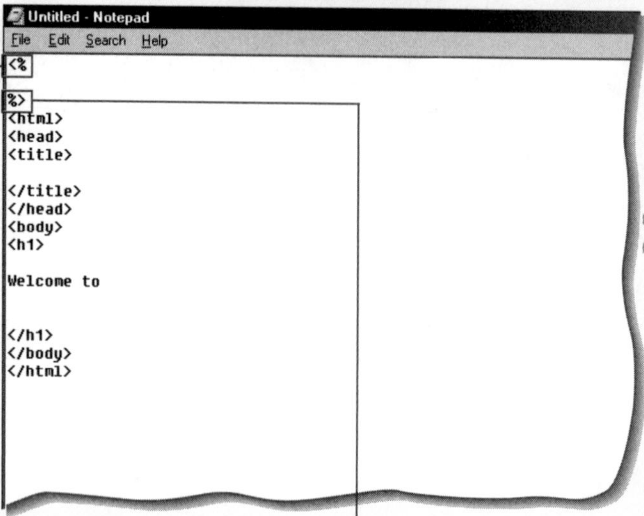

1 Type **<%** where you want to add a scriptlet to a JSP page.

2 Type **%>** where you want the scriptlet to end.

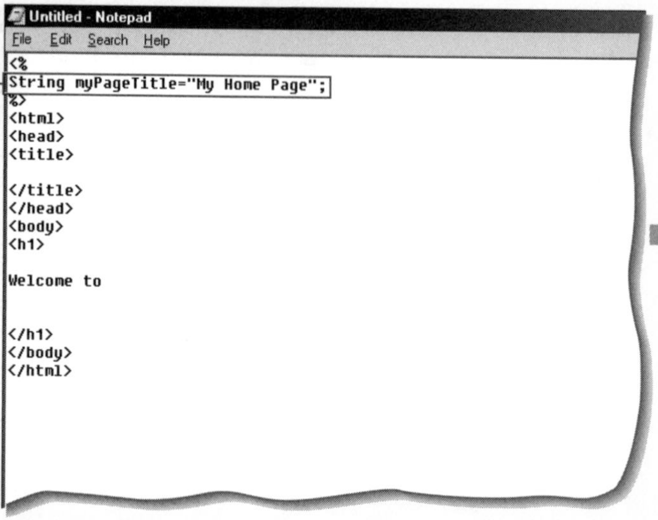

Untitled - Notepad

File Edit Search Help

```
<%
String myPageTitle="My Home Page";
%>
<html>
<head>
<title>

</title>
</head>
<body>
<h1>

Welcome to


</h1>
</body>
</html>
```

3 Between the opening and closing delimiters (`<%` and `%>`), type the code for the scriptlet.

■ In this example, code that assigns a value to a variable is inserted.

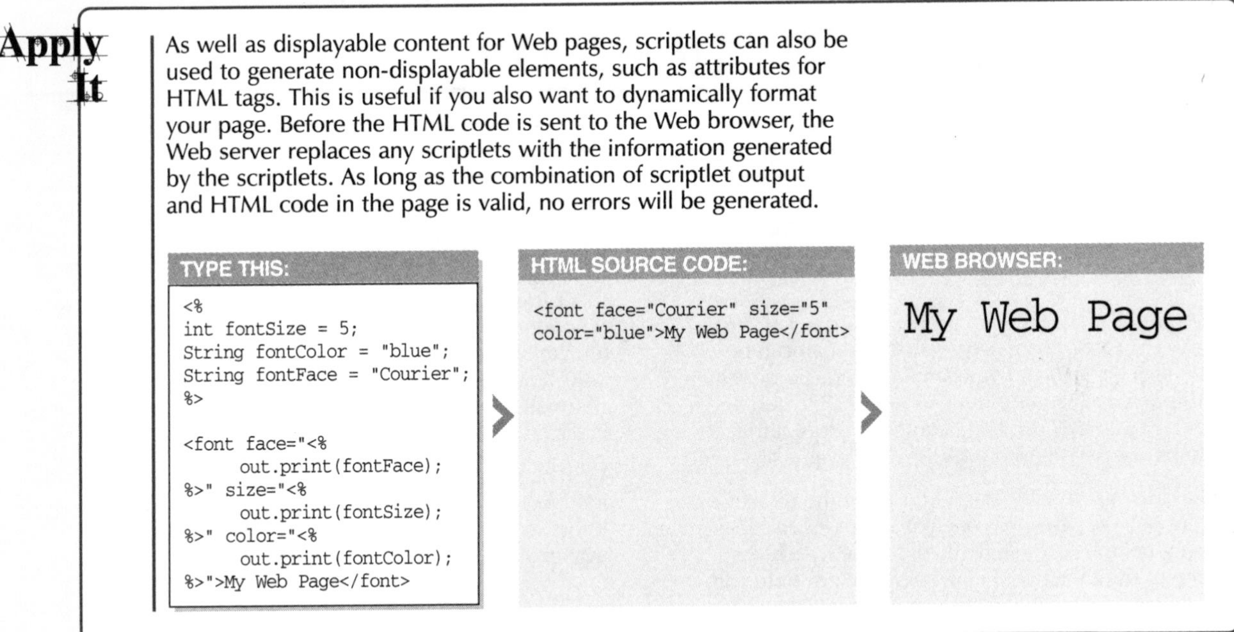

Apply It

As well as displayable content for Web pages, scriptlets can also be used to generate non-displayable elements, such as attributes for HTML tags. This is useful if you also want to dynamically format your page. Before the HTML code is sent to the Web browser, the Web server replaces any scriptlets with the information generated by the scriptlets. As long as the combination of scriptlet output and HTML code in the page is valid, no errors will be generated.

TYPE THIS:

```
<%
int fontSize = 5;
String fontColor = "blue";
String fontFace = "Courier";
%>

<font face="<%
      out.print(fontFace);
%>" size="<%
      out.print(fontSize);
%>" color="<%
      out.print(fontColor);
%>">My Web Page</font>
```

HTML SOURCE CODE:

```
<font face="Courier" size="5"
color="blue">My Web Page</font>
```

WEB BROWSER:

My Web Page

```
<%
String myPageTitle="My Home Page";
%>
<html>
<head>
<title>
<%
out.print(myPageTitle);
%>
</title>
</head>
<body>
<h1>

Welcome to

<%
out.print(myPageTitle);
%>

</h1>
</body>
</html>
```

Welcome to My Home Page

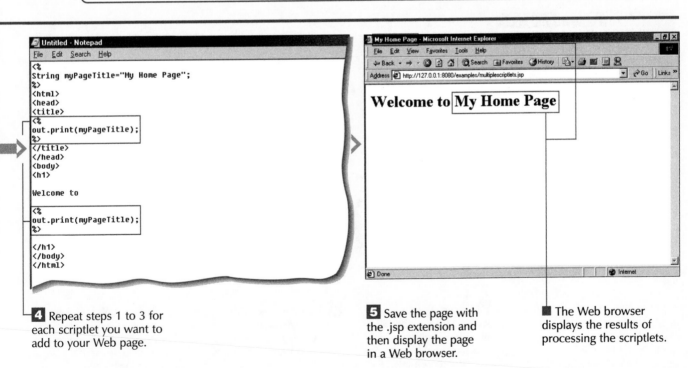

4 Repeat steps 1 to 3 for each scriptlet you want to add to your Web page.

5 Save the page with the .jsp extension and then display the page in a Web browser.

■ The Web browser displays the results of processing the scriptlets.

USING THE PAGE DIRECTIVE

Directives provide information about a JSP page to the software that processes the page. This software is often referred to as a *JSP engine* and is part of a Web server. Directives are sometimes called *JSP engine directives*. Directives do not produce visible output, but rather provide instructions and settings that determine how a JSP page is processed.

There are three JSP directives available–`page`, `include` and `taglib`. Each directive has attributes that can be assigned specific values. For example, the `page` directive offers the `autoFlush` attribute, which can be assigned a value of `true` or `false`. For a complete list of attributes that can be used with each directive, see page 241.

To add a directive to a JSP page, you place the directive statement between the `<%@` opening delimiter and the `%>` closing delimiter. The directive statement includes the name of the directive, followed by the attribute and value pairs you want to use. An attribute and its corresponding value are separated by an equal sign. A directive will only affect the JSP page containing the directive.

The `page` directive is the most commonly used directive. The `page` directive allows you to specify information about the configuration of a JSP page, such as the type of content you want the page to display. For example, you can use the `contentType` attribute with the `text/plain` value to specify that you want the information generated by a JSP page to be displayed as plain text.

A JSP page can contain multiple `page` directives. It is good programming practice to place `page` directives at the beginning of a JSP page, before any HTML or JavaServer Pages code on the page.

USING THE PAGE DIRECTIVE

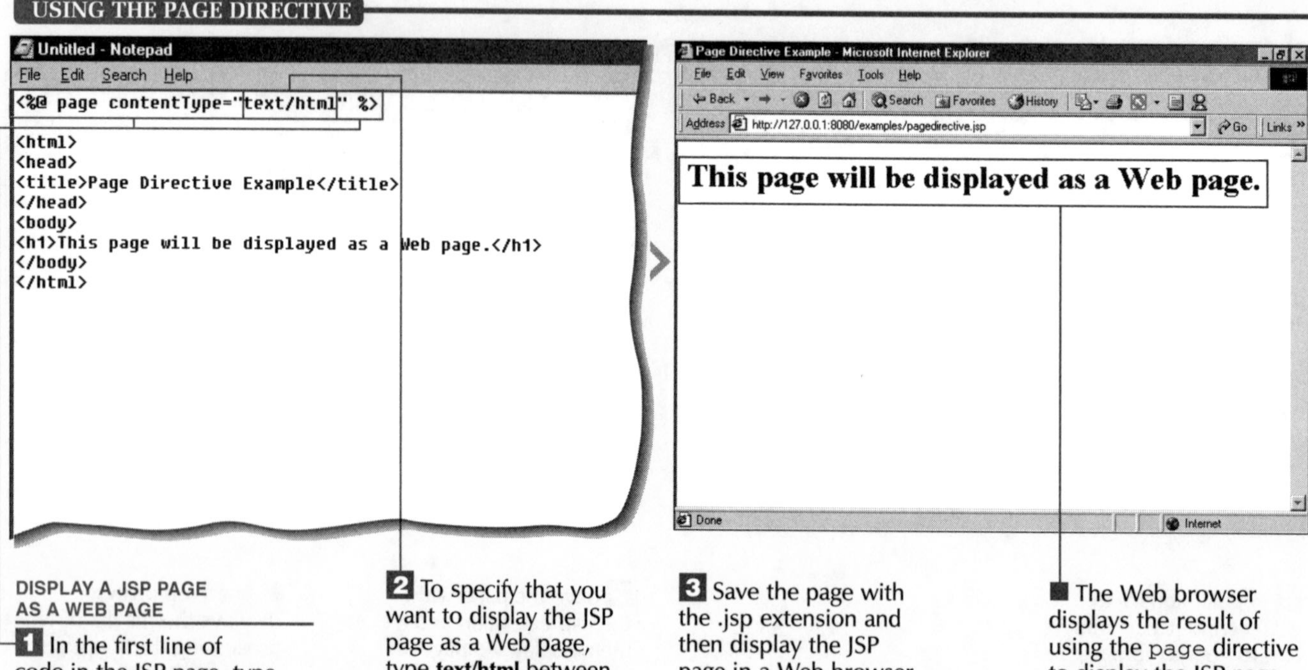

DISPLAY A JSP PAGE AS A WEB PAGE

1 In the first line of code in the JSP page, type **<%@ page contentType="" %>**.

2 To specify that you want to display the JSP page as a Web page, type **text/html** between the quotation marks.

3 Save the page with the .jsp extension and then display the JSP page in a Web browser.

■ The Web browser displays the result of using the `page` directive to display the JSP page as a Web page.

Extra

If you do not use any directives in a JSP page, the Web server's JSP engine will use its own default settings when processing the page. For example, if you do not use the `page` directive with the `contentType` attribute to specify how you want the information in a JSP page to be generated, a JSP engine will automatically display the information as a Web page.

Although you can add more than one `page` directive to a JSP page and each directive can contain more than one attribute, you usually cannot use the same attribute more than once on a page. For example, you cannot use the `contentType` attribute several times on a JSP page, since the information in the JSP page can only be generated one way at a time.

Some JSP engines do not support all of the attributes and values offered by the `page` directive. Before using the `page` directive, you should view the latest documentation for your Web server to determine whether the JSP engine will support the attributes and values you want to use.

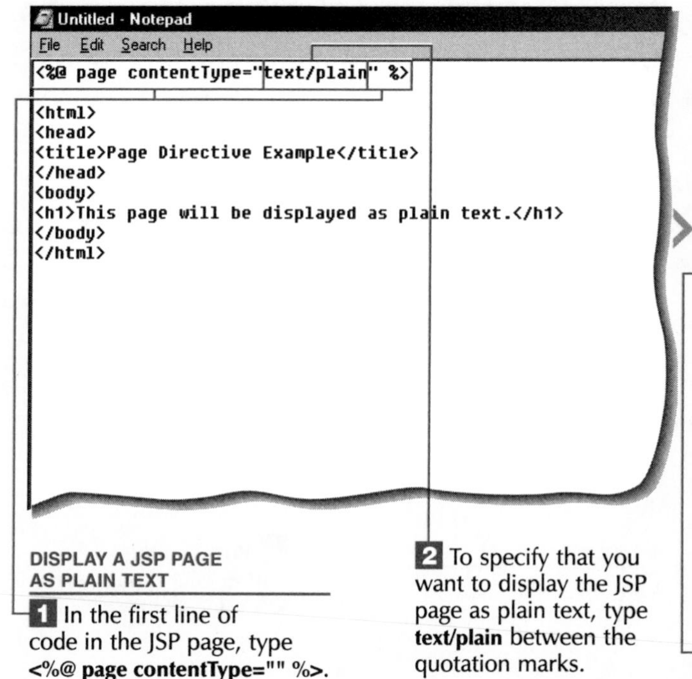

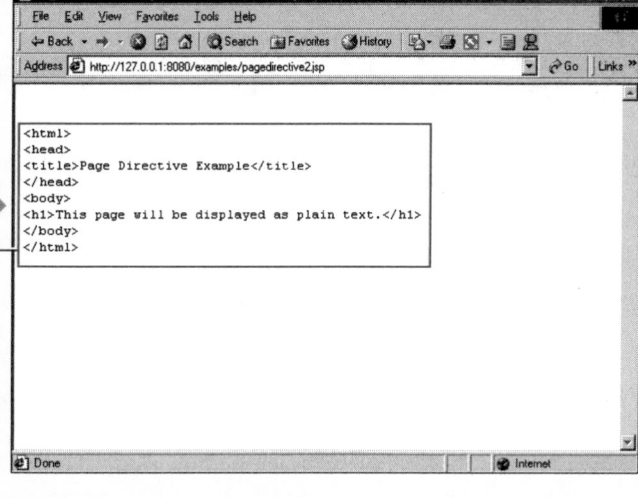

DISPLAY A JSP PAGE AS PLAIN TEXT

1 In the first line of code in the JSP page, type **<%@ page contentType="" %>**.

2 To specify that you want to display the JSP page as plain text, type **text/plain** between the quotation marks.

3 Save the page with the .jsp extension and then display the JSP page in a Web browser.

■ The Web browser displays the result of using the `page` directive to display the JSP page as plain text.

Note: Some Web browsers may automatically display a plain-text JSP page as a Web page.

USING THE INCLUDE DIRECTIVE

The `include` directive allows you to use one file in several different JSP pages. This can save you time when you need to include the same information in multiple pages. For example, if you have a copyright notice you want to display on all your JSP pages, you can create a file that contains the copyright notice and then use the `include` directive to include the information on all your pages. The file must be stored on the Web server and be accessible from all the JSP pages that you want to include the file.

You must first create the file you want to include. The file can contain plain text or HTML code, such as a table, header or footer. If the file contains plain text, you can save the file with the .txt extension. If the file contains HTML code, you can save it with the .html extension. The include file should not contain any JavaServer Pages code. The Web server will ignore any JavaServer Pages code included in the file.

To include a file in a JSP page, you add an `include` statement to the page. The `include` statement must be enclosed between the `<%@` opening delimiter and the `%>` closing delimiter. The filename specified in the `include` statement must be enclosed in quotation marks. The filename must be a fixed value, such as "footer.html". You cannot use a variable that represents the name of a file in an `include` statement.

If you change the code in the file, all of the JSP pages that include the file will be updated. You may have to clear the Web server's buffer before your JSP pages will display the changes made to the file. For information about clearing the Web server's buffer, see page 92.

USING THE INCLUDE DIRECTIVE

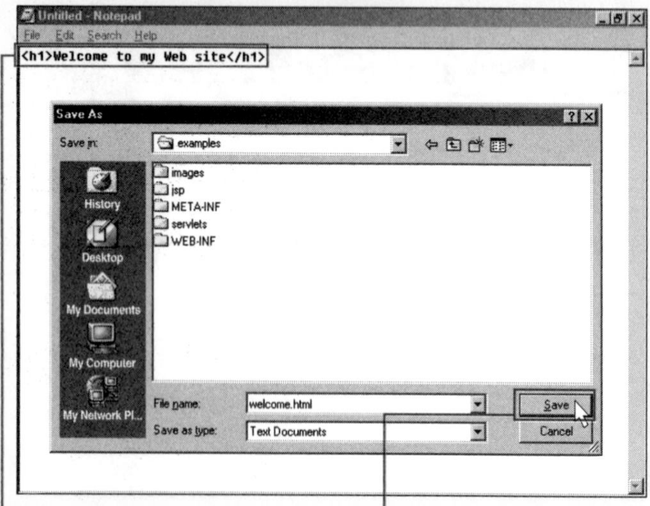

CREATE A FILE TO INCLUDE

1 In a text editor, create the file you want to include in several JSP pages.

2 Save the file.

Note: If the file contains plain text, save the file with the .txt extension. If the file contains HTML code, save the file with the .html extension.

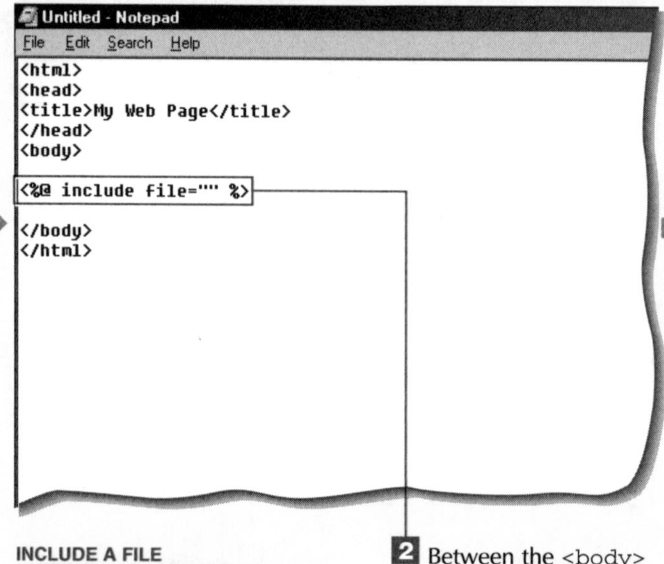

INCLUDE A FILE

1 Display the code for the JSP page in which you want to include a file.

2 Between the `<body>` and `</body>` tags, type **<%@ include file="" %>**.

Extra

The include directive allows you to include a file that is stored in the same directory as the JSP page that includes the file or in a subdirectory of that directory. In this example, the JSP page is stored in a directory called test and the footer.html file is stored in a subdirectory called test/pages.

Example:

```
<%@ include file="pages/footer.html" %>
```

You can also include a file that is located in the parent directory of the directory that stores the JSP page. To do so, you use the double dot notation to represent the name of the parent directory. In this example, the JSP page is instructed to look for the welcome.html file in the parent directory.

Example:

```
<%@ include file="../welcome.html" %>
```

Using the include directive allows you to break code into manageable sections and then include the code in JSP pages as needed. Each include file should contain code specific to only one task. If you create a file that contains code for many tasks, the JSP pages may not use all the code and the Web server's resources will be wasted.

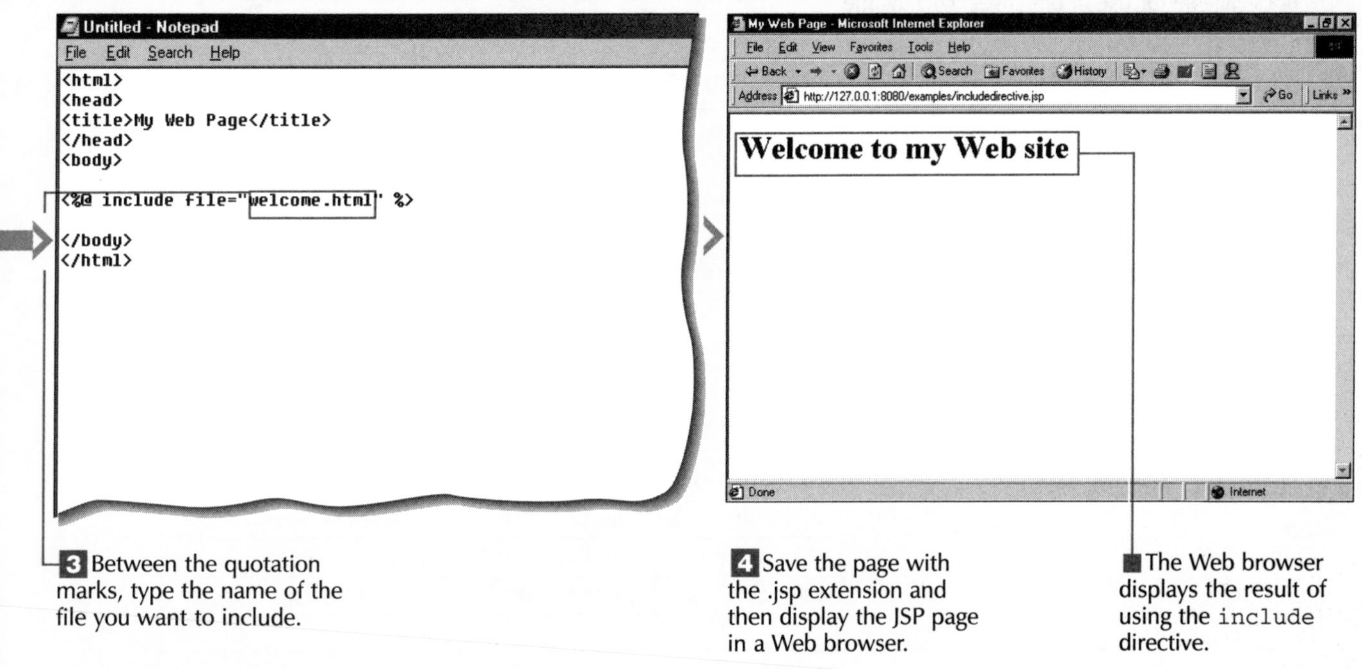

3 Between the quotation marks, type the name of the file you want to include.

4 Save the page with the .jsp extension and then display the JSP page in a Web browser.

■ The Web browser displays the result of using the include directive.

INTRODUCTION TO IMPLICIT OBJECTS

Implicit objects are created automatically when a Web server processes a JSP page. The available implicit objects include `application`, `config`, `exception`, `out`, `page`, `pageContext`, `request`, `response` and `session`. Each object is used to perform a specific task, such as handling errors, sending text generated by a JSP page to a Web browser or interpreting information submitted by a form on a Web page.

Implicit objects are available for use in every JSP page you create. You do not have to write code that imports or instantiates an implicit object.

Object Scope

The scope of an object determines where the object can be accessed in an application. For example, the `session` object has session scope, which means that the object can be accessed by any JSP page processed during a session. Most implicit objects have page scope. When an object has page scope, the object can be accessed only in the JSP page in which the object was created. You can access implicit objects only from within scriptlets or expressions on a JSP page. Implicit objects are not available for use in directives, such as the `page` directive.

OBJECT:	SCOPE:
`application`	application
`config`	page
`exception`	page
`out`	page
`page`	page
`pageContext`	page
`request`	request
`response`	page
`session`	session

Class Files

Since JSP pages use the underlying servlet technology of the Web server, implicit objects are usually derived from class files that are part of the servlet packages. For more information about implicit objects and the servlet packages, you can consult the Java SDK documentation.

OBJECT:	CLASS:
`application`	`javax.servlet.ServletContext`
`config`	`javax.servlet.ServletConfig`
`exception`	`java.lang.Throwable`
`out`	`javax.servlet.jsp.JspWriter`
`page`	`java.lang.Object`
`pageContext`	`javax.servlet.jsp.PageContext`
`request`	`javax.servlet.ServletRequest`
`response`	`javax.servlet.ServletResponse`
`session`	`javax.servlet.http.HttpSession`

IMPLICIT OBJECTS

`application`

The `application` object is used to store information about an application. An application is a collection of JSP pages stored in a specific directory and its subdirectories on a Web server.

`pageContext`

The `pageContext` object is used to access the characteristics of a JSP page that are specific to the Web server processing the page.

`config`

The `config` object is used to store information about the configuration of the environment in which a JSP page is processed on a Web server.

`request`

The `request` object is used to store information supplied by a client, such as data submitted in a form or the IP number and name of the client computer.

`exception`

The `exception` object is used to handle errors that may occur when a JSP page is processed. The `exception` object also stores error information.

`response`

The `response` object is used to store information generated by a Web server before the information is sent to a client.

`out`

The `out` object is used to send output generated by a JSP page to a client's Web browser.

`page`

The `page` object is used to store information about a JSP page while the page is being processed. The `page` object is not typically accessed from within a JSP page.

`session`

The `session` object is used to store information associated with a session. A sessions starts when a client requests a JSP page from a Web site and ends when the client does not request another page for a specific period of time or the session is abandoned.

CREATE A FORM

Adding a form to a Web page allows you to gather data from users who visit the page. A form can be placed anywhere between the <body> and </body> tags in an HTML document. The body of your Web page can include as many forms as you need.

You use the <form> tag to create a form and the action attribute to specify the location and name of the JSP page that will process the data entered into the form. If the JSP page is stored in the same directory as the Web page containing the form, you only have to specify the name of the JSP page. If the JSP page is not stored on the same Web server as the Web page containing the form, you must specify the full URL of the JSP page.

You must also specify which method the form will use to pass data to the JSP page. There are two methods the form can use–get and post. The method you should use depends on the amount of data that will be passed. The get method sends data to the JSP page by appending the data to the URL of the page. The post method sends the data and the URL separately. The get method is faster than the post method and is suitable for small forms. The post method is suitable for large forms that will send more than 2000 characters to the JSP page.

Unlike other technologies used to process form information, JavaServer Pages can automatically determine whether a form is submitting data using the get or post method and then retrieve the information.

For information about creating a JSP page that processes data from a form, see page 84.

CREATE A FORM

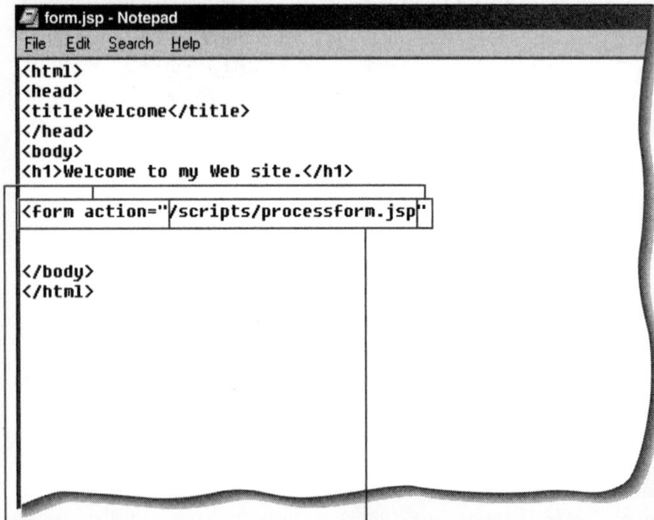

form.jsp - Notepad

File Edit Search Help

```
<html>
<head>
<title>Welcome</title>
</head>
<body>
<h1>Welcome to my Web site.</h1>

<form action="/scripts/processform.jsp"


</body>
</html>
```

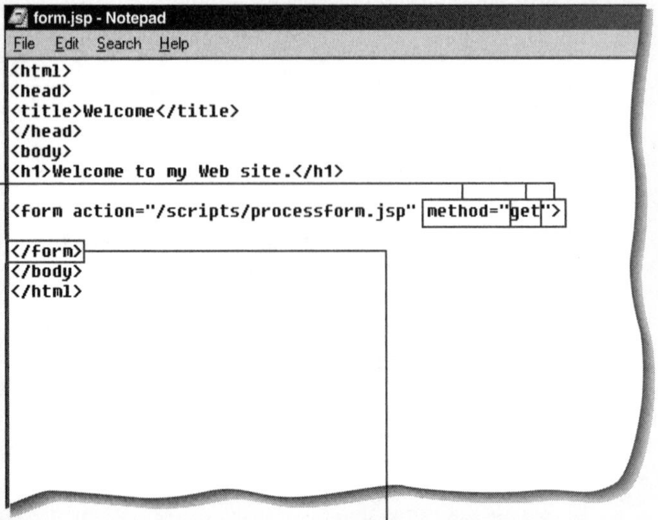

1 Type **<form action=""** where you want to add a form to a Web page.

2 Between the quotation marks, type the location and name of the JSP page that will process the data entered into the form.

form.jsp - Notepad

File Edit Search Help

```
<html>
<head>
<title>Welcome</title>
</head>
<body>
<h1>Welcome to my Web site.</h1>

<form action="/scripts/processform.jsp" method="get">

</form>
</body>
</html>
```

3 Type **method="">**.

4 Between the quotation marks, type the method the form will use to pass data to the JSP page.

5 Type **</form>** where you want to end the form.

■ You can now add elements to the form.

ADD ELEMENTS TO A FORM

Elements are areas in a form where users can enter data and select options. The most commonly used element is a text box, which allows users to enter a single line of data into a form. Text boxes are often used for entering names, addresses and other short responses.

Elements you add to a form must be placed between the <form> and </form> tags. A form can contain as many elements as you need.

There are many different types of elements you can add to a form, such as text areas and check boxes. Text areas allow users to enter several lines or paragraphs of text, while check boxes let users select options on a form. For information about commonly used elements, see page 82.

Each form element has attributes, such as `name`, `type` and `size`, which offer options for the element. The `name` attribute allows you to provide a name for an element. The name you specify is used by the JSP page that processes the form to identify the element and access the information in the element. A name can contain letters and numbers, but should not contain spaces or punctuation. If you want to include spaces in a name, use an underscore character (_) instead.

You must add a submit button to every form you create. The submit button allows users to send the data they entered into the form to the Web server. When the Web server receives data from a form, the server transfers the data to the JSP page that will process the data. The JSP page can then perform an action with the data, such as storing the data in a database or displaying the information in a Web browser.

ADD ELEMENTS TO A FORM

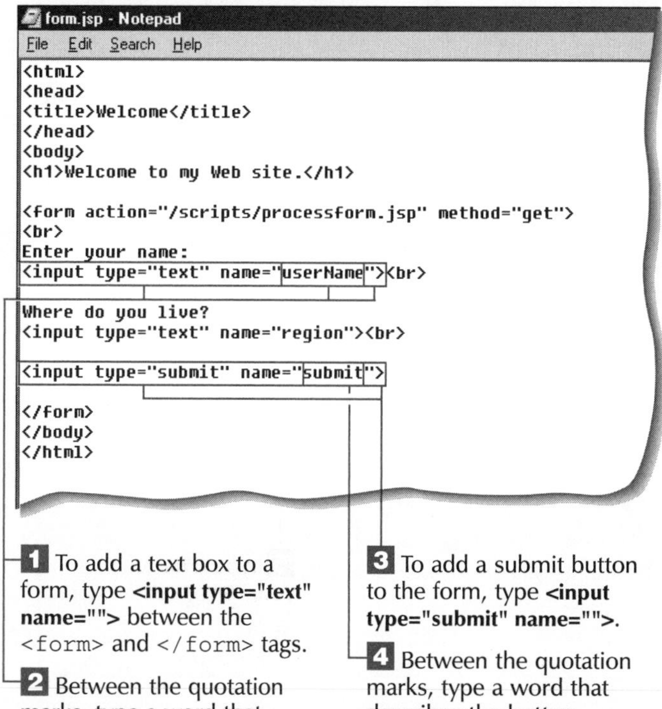

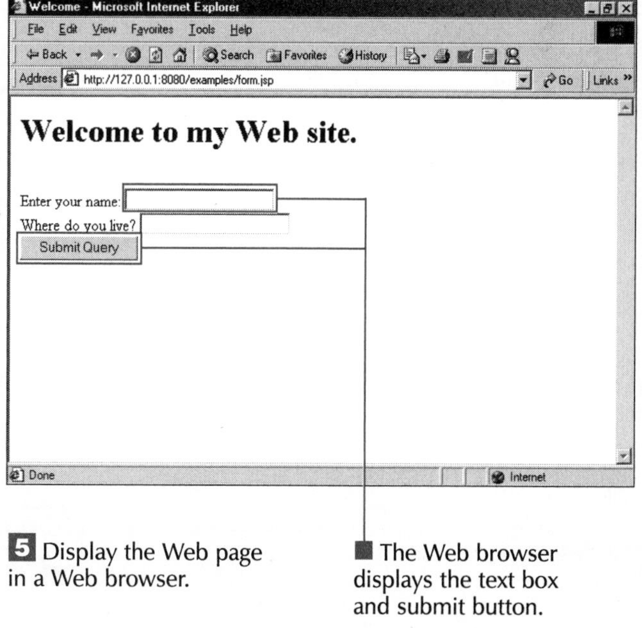

1 To add a text box to a form, type **<input type="text" name="">** between the <form> and </form> tags.

2 Between the quotation marks, type a word that describes the text box.

3 To add a submit button to the form, type **<input type="submit" name="">**.

4 Between the quotation marks, type a word that describes the button.

5 Display the Web page in a Web browser.

■ The Web browser displays the text box and submit button.

FORM ELEMENTS

An element is an area in a form where users can enter data or select options. There are several different types of elements you can add to a form.

Most elements require you to specify attributes that determine how the element will appear on a Web page.

You can find more information about form elements and attributes at the www.w3.org/TR/1999/REC-html401-19991224/interact/forms Web site.

COMMONLY USED ATTRIBUTES

Type	Name	Value
The `type` attribute allows you to specify the kind of element you want to use.	The `name` attribute allows you to specify a name for an element. The JSP page that will process data from the element uses the `name` attribute to identify the data. Element names can contain more than one word, but should not contain spaces or special characters.	The `value` attribute allows you to specify a value for an element. If an element displays a button, you can use the `value` attribute to specify the text that will appear on the button.
Maxlength	**Size**	**Checked**
The `maxlength` attribute allows you to restrict the number of characters a user can enter into an element.	The `size` attribute allows you to specify the width of an element.	The `checked` attribute allows an element to display a selected option by default.

COMMONLY USED ELEMENTS

Password Box

A password box allows users to enter private data. When a user types data into a password box, an asterisk (*) appears for each character, which prevents others from viewing the data on the screen. A password box does not protect the data from being accessed as it is transferred over the Internet. You must set the `type` attribute to `password` and use the `name` attribute to create a password box. You may also want to use the `value`, `maxlength` and `size` attributes.

```
Password Please <input type="password"
name="secretWord" value="password" maxlength="20">
```

Password Please ********

Drop-Down List

The `select` element displays a drop-down list that allows users to select an option from a list of several options. For example, a drop-down list can be used to allow users to select one of three shipping methods. You must use the `name` attribute to create a drop-down list. You use the `<option>` tag with the `value` attribute to add options to the list.

```
How would you like your products shipped?
<select name="shipMethod">
<option value="air">Air</option>
<option value="land">Land</option>
<option value="sea">Sea</option>
</select>
```

How would you like your products shipped? Air

COMMONLY USED ELEMENTS

Text Box

A text box allows users to enter a single line of text, such as a name or telephone number. You must set the `type` attribute to `text` and use the `name` attribute to create a text box. You may also want to use the `maxlength` and `size` attributes.

```
First Name <input type="text" name="firstName" maxlength="20">
```

First Name

Text Area

The `textarea` element displays a large text area that allows users to enter several lines or paragraphs of text. A large text area is ideal for gathering comments or questions from users. You must use the `name` attribute to create a text area.

```
Questions? <textarea name="userQuestions"></textarea>
```

Questions?

Check Box

Check boxes allow users to select one or more options. For example, check boxes can be used to allow users to specify which states they have visited. You must set the `type` attribute to `checkbox` and use the `name` and `value` attributes to create a check box. You may also want to use the `checked` attribute.

```
Which states have you visited in the past year?<br>
New York <input type="checkbox" name="states" value="New York" checked>
California <input type="checkbox" name="states" value="California">
Texas <input type="checkbox" name="states" value="Texas">
```

Which states have you visited in the past year?
New York ☑ California ☐ Texas ☐

Radio Button

Radio buttons allow users to select only one of several options. For example, radio buttons can be used to allow users to specify if they are male or female. You must set the `type` attribute to `radio` and use the `name` and `value` attributes to create a radio button. You may also want to use the `checked` attribute.

```
What is your gender?<br>
Female <input type="radio" name="gender" value="female" checked>
Male <input type="radio" name="gender" value="male">
```

What is your gender?
Female ⦿ Male ○

Submit Button

A submit button allows users to send data in the form to the JSP page that will process the data. You must add a submit button to each form you create. You must set the `type` attribute to `submit` to create a submit button. You may also want to use the `name` and `value` attributes.

```
<input type="submit" name="submit" value="Submit Now">
```

Submit Now

Reset Button

A reset button allows users to clear the data they entered into a form. A user cannot redisplay data that has been cleared. Reset buttons are commonly used in forms that have many text boxes. You must set the `type` attribute to `reset` to create a reset button. You may also want to use the `value` attribute.

```
<input type="reset" value="Click to Reset">
```

Click to Reset

PROCESS DATA FROM A FORM
Using the getParameter Method

After creating a form on a Web page, you can create a JSP page that will process data submitted in the form. The `getParameter` method of the `request` object allows a JSP page to access form data.

You must specify the name of the form element you want to access using the `getParameter` method. The name you specify must be exactly the same as the name that was assigned to the element when it was created. If the element name you specify does not exist in the form, the `getParameter` method will return a null value.

Once a JSP page has accessed data from a form element, the page can perform a task, such as storing the data in a file or a database. While JSP pages that process data from forms do not need to generate any output, these pages typically produce an acknowledgement message or redirect a client to another page.

Some Web servers require JSP pages that process data from a form to be saved in a specific directory. You should check the latest documentation for your Web server to determine where you should save a JSP page that processes form information. If your Web server does not require the JSP page to be saved in a specific directory, you may want to save the page in the same directory as the form it processes.

After saving the JSP page, you should review the code for the Web page that contains the form to verify that the `action` attribute displays the correct filename and location for the JSP page.

Although the `getParameter` method is still commonly used, the method is deprecated. This means that the `getParameter` method is no longer recommended and will eventually become obsolete. The `getParameterValues` method is now the preferred method for accessing information in a form element. For more information about the `getParameterValues` method, see page 86.

USING THE GETPARAMETER METHOD

Untitled - Notepad

File Edit Search Help

```
<html>
<head>
<title>Thank You</title>
</head>
<body>

Your information has been processed.
<hr>

Thank You  request.getParameter("userName")

<br>

You live in

</body>
</html>
```

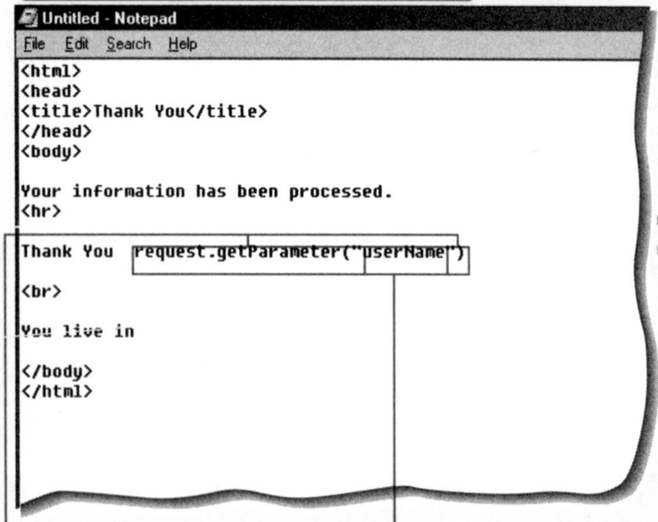

1 In the JSP page you want to process data from a form, type **request.getParameter("")**.

2 Between the quotation marks, type the name of the form element you want to access.

Untitled - Notepad

File Edit Search Help

```
<html>
<head>
<title>Thank You</title>
</head>
<body>

Your information has been processed.
<hr>

Thank You <%= request.getParameter("userName") %>
<br>

You live in <%= request.getParameter("region") %>

</body>
</html>
```

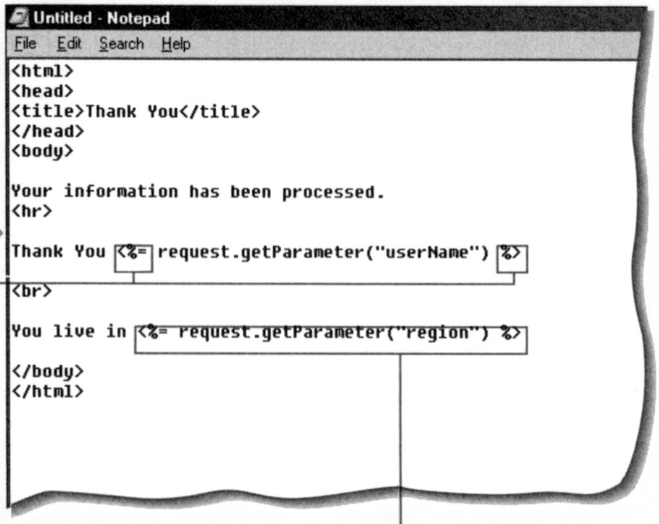

3 Type the code that uses the data from the form element.

4 Repeat steps 1 to 3 for each form element you want to process.

5 Save the page with the .jsp extension.

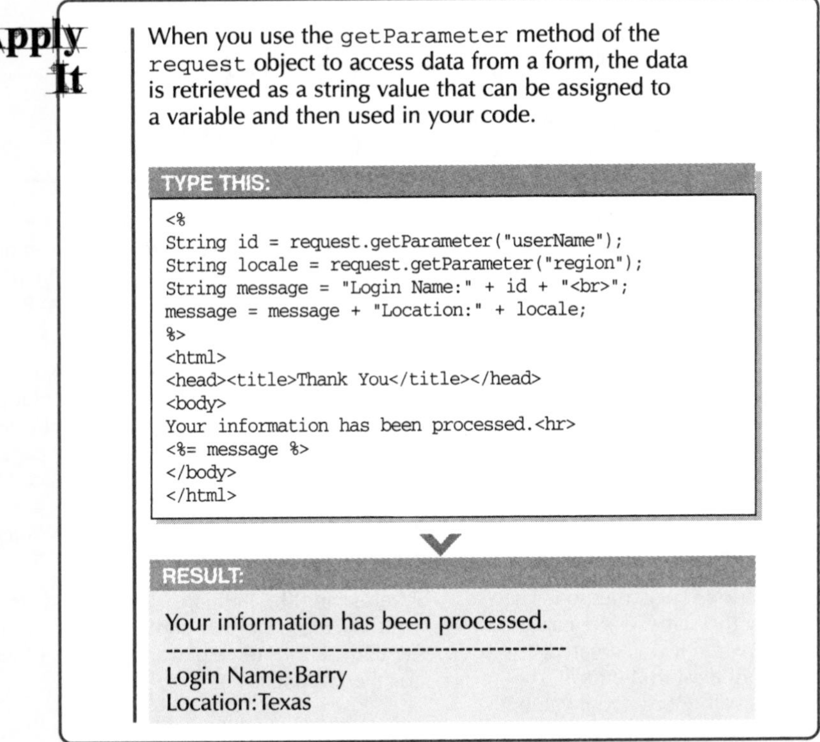

Apply It

When you use the `getParameter` method of the `request` object to access data from a form, the data is retrieved as a string value that can be assigned to a variable and then used in your code.

TYPE THIS:

```
<%
String id = request.getParameter("userName");
String locale = request.getParameter("region");
String message = "Login Name:" + id + "<br>";
message = message + "Location:" + locale;
%>
<html>
<head><title>Thank You</title></head>
<body>
Your information has been processed.<hr>
<%= message %>
</body>
</html>
```

RESULT:

Your information has been processed.

Login Name:Barry
Location:Texas

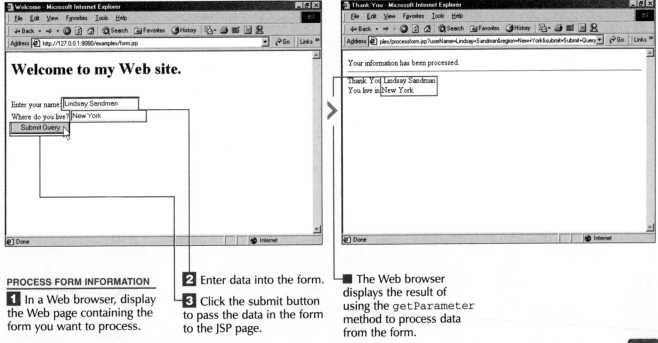

PROCESS FORM INFORMATION

1. In a Web browser, display the Web page containing the form you want to process.
2. Enter data into the form.
3. Click the submit button to pass the data in the form to the JSP page.

■ The Web browser displays the result of using the `getParameter` method to process data from the form.

PROCESS DATA FROM A FORM
Using the getParameterValues Method

The `getParameterValues` method of the `request` object can be used to access the data passed by a form. The `getParameterValues` method is the preferred method for accessing form data, although the `getParameter` method can also be used. For information about the `getParameter` method, see page 84.

The `getParameterValues` method is particularly useful for accessing a form element that can contain multiple values. For example, some drop-down lists allow users to select more than one option. The `getParameterValues` method returns the data in a form element as an array of string values.

You must specify the name of the form element you want to access using the `getParameterValues` method. The name you specify must be exactly the same as the name that was assigned to the element when it was created. If the element name you specify does not exist in the form, the `getParameterValues` method will return a null value.

You can assign the data returned by the `getParameterValues` method to an array variable. This allows you to work with the data in the form element. For example, you can use a `for` loop to display each value stored in the element.

When saving a JSP page that processes data from a form, you should check the latest documentation for your Web server to determine where you should save the page. Some Web servers require you to save JSP pages that process form data in a specific directory. If your Web server does not specify the directory you should use, you may want to save the JSP page in the same directory as the form it processes.

After saving the JSP page, you should review the code for the Web page that contains the form to verify that the `action` attribute displays the correct filename and location for the JSP page.

USING THE GETPARAMETERVALUES METHOD

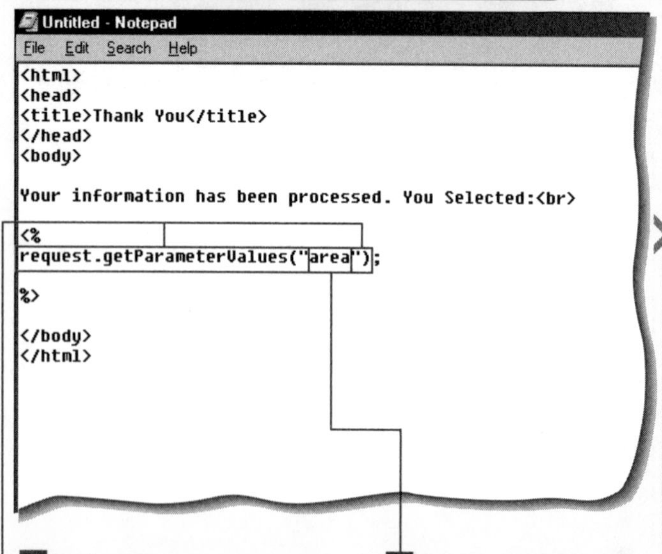

```
Untitled - Notepad
File Edit Search Help
<html>
<head>
<title>Thank You</title>
</head>
<body>

Your information has been processed. You Selected:<br>

<%
request.getParameterValues("area");

%>

</body>
</html>
```

1 In the JSP page you want to process data from a form, type **request.getParameterValues("")**.

2 Between the quotation marks, type the name of the form element you want to access.

```
Untitled - Notepad
File Edit Search Help
<html>
<head>
<title>Thank You</title>
</head>
<body>

Your information has been processed. You Selected:<br>

<%
String[] names = request.getParameterValues("area");

for (int x = 0 ; x < names.length ; x++)
     out.print(names[x] + "<br>");
%>

</body>
</html>
```

3 Type the code that assigns the data from the form element to an array variable.

4 Type the code that uses the data from the form element.

5 Save the page with the .jsp extension.

When processing data from a form, you should include code in your JSP page that checks the validity of data a user submits in the form. For example, if you want users to select at least two options from a drop-down list, you can add error-checking code that ensures two selections were made.

FORM:

Please select at least two catergories you would like more information about:

Products
Order Information
Contact Information
Shipping Information
Employment

Submit

IN THE JSP PAGE, TYPE:

```
<%
String[] names = request.getParameterValues("info");
if (names.length > 1)
{
      for (int x = 0; x < names.length; x++)
            out.print(names[x] + "<br>");
}
else
{
      out.print("Please select at least 2 items");
}
%>
```

RESULT:

Please select at least 2 items.

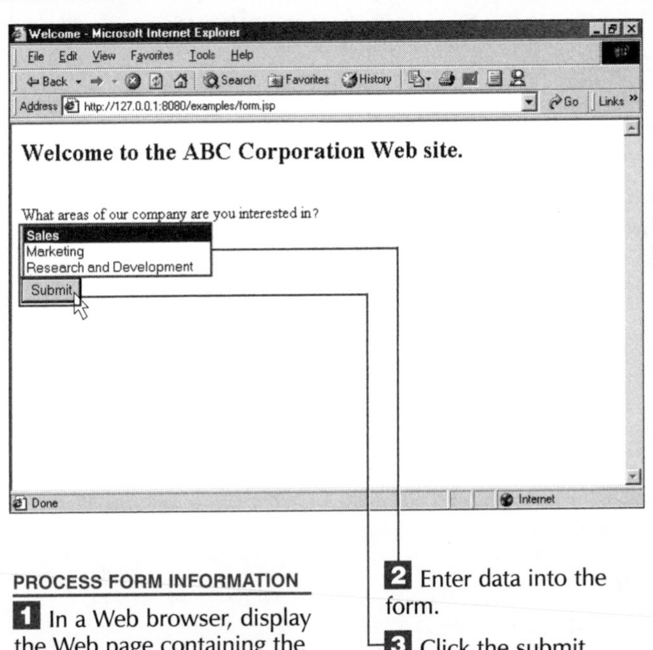

Thank You - Microsoft Internet Explorer

Address http://127.0.0.1:8080/examples/processform.jsp?area=Sales&submit=Submit

Your information has been processed. You Selected:

Sales

PROCESS FORM INFORMATION

1 In a Web browser, display the Web page containing the form you want to process.

2 Enter data into the form.

3 Click the submit button to pass the data in the form to the JSP page.

■ The Web browser displays the result of using the `getParameterValues` method to process data from the form.

DETERMINE THE ELEMENTS IN A FORM

The getParameterNames method of the request object can be used to retrieve the name of each element a form contains. You may want to determine the names of elements in a form to verify that the form contains the correct elements. Being able to determine the names of form elements also allows you to create a single JSP page that can process data from several different forms.

Form elements do not have to contain data in order to be included in the list retrieved by the getParameterNames method. If you gave the submit button on your form a name, the name will be included in the list of element names.

An efficient way to work with the element names retrieved by the getParameterNames method is to cast the names as a collection, or iteration, that can be used by the Iterator interface. An interface is a set of method declarations that offers the same functionality as a class.

You must use the page directive with the import attribute to import the Iterator interface from the java.util package. For more information about the page directive, see page 74. For more information about the Iterator interface and the java.util package, you can refer to the Java SDK documentation.

A for statement can be used to create a loop that will process each element name in the collection. The next method of the Iterator interface controls the loop, so a re-initialization expression is not required in the for statement.

When you create the code for the form whose elements you want to determine, the action attribute of the <form> tag must specify the name and location of the JSP page you set up to process form information.

DETERMINE THE ELEMENTS IN A FORM

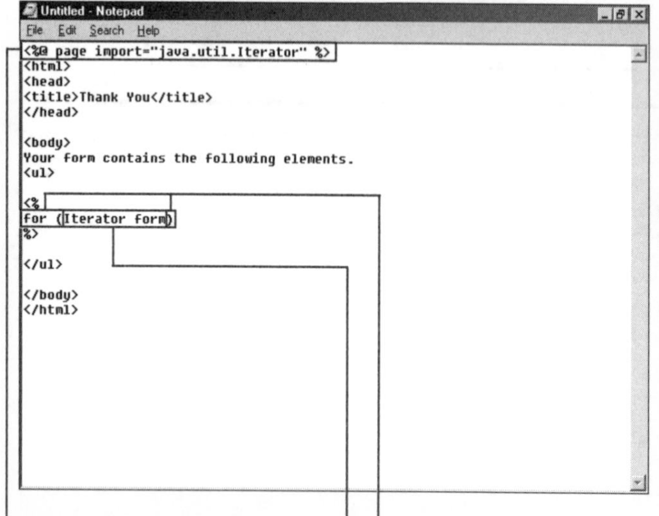

1 In the first line of code in the JSP page, type **<%@ page import="java.util.Iterator" %>** to import the Iterator interface from the java.util package.

2 To create a loop that will process each element name in a form, type **for ()**.

3 To create the initialization expression for the for statement, type **Iterator** followed by a name for the element names in a form.

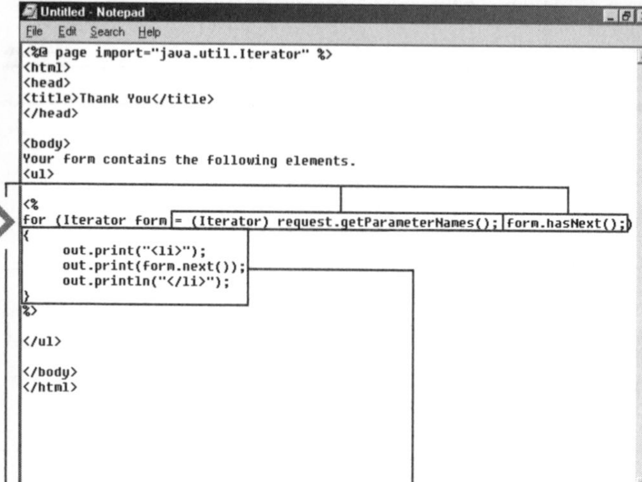

4 Type = followed by **(Iterator) request.getParameterNames();** to cast the element names retrieved by the getParameterNames method as a collection.

5 To create a condition for the for statement, type the name of the collection followed by **.hasNext();**.

6 Type the code that will process each element in the collection. Enclose the code in braces.

7 Save the page with the .jsp extension.

Extra

The `Iterator` interface includes three methods that can be used to work with a collection of elements.

NAME:	DESCRIPTION:
`hasNext`	This method is used to determine if there are any elements left to process in the collection. The `hasNext` method returns a boolean value of true if the collection has another element that can be accessed. If there are no more elements in the collection, a value of false is returned.
`next`	This method returns the next element in the collection. If there are no more elements in the collection, an error is generated.
`remove`	This method discards the last element returned by the `next` method. If the `next` method is not used before the `remove` method, an error is generated.

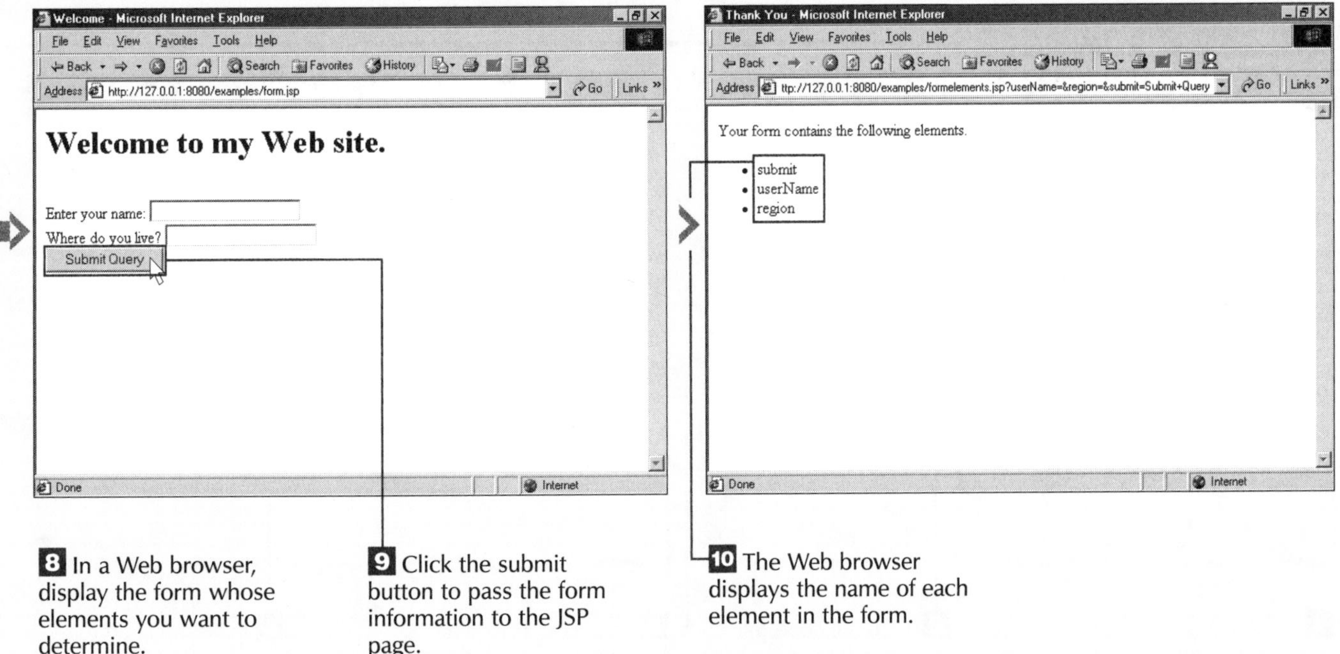

8 In a Web browser, display the form whose elements you want to determine.

9 Click the submit button to pass the form information to the JSP page.

10 The Web browser displays the name of each element in the form.

ACCESS CLIENT INFORMATION

A JSP page can access information about a client computer, such as the IP address and name of the computer. Accessing information about a client computer is useful if you want to verify the identity of a client or perform an administrative task, such as creating a log that documents Web site usage.

Every computer connected to a network using the TCP/IP protocol has a unique IP address. The `getRemoteAddr` method of the `request` object is used to access a client computer's IP address and return the IP address as a string value.

The `getRemoteHost` method of the `request` object allows a JSP page to access the name of a client computer. This method returns a string value containing the full domain name of the client, such as computer2.abccorp.com. The `getRemoteHost` method retrieves the name of a client from your Web server, which uses a Domain Name System (DNS) server to determine the name based on the client computer's IP address. This means that your Web server must be able to communicate with a DNS server before the `getRemoteHost` method can access the name of a client. If the method cannot access the name of a client, it will return the client's IP address.

A JSP page can use the `getServerPort` method of the `request` object to access the port number a client is using for a request. This method returns an integer that indicates which server port received the request. Using the `getServerPort` method is useful when your server uses different ports for different types of programs. For example, if administrative programs use a specific port on your server, accessing the port number lets you determine whether a client is an administrator or a regular user. This allows you to customize the content of a JSP page depending on the type of client accessing the page.

ACCESS CLIENT INFORMATION

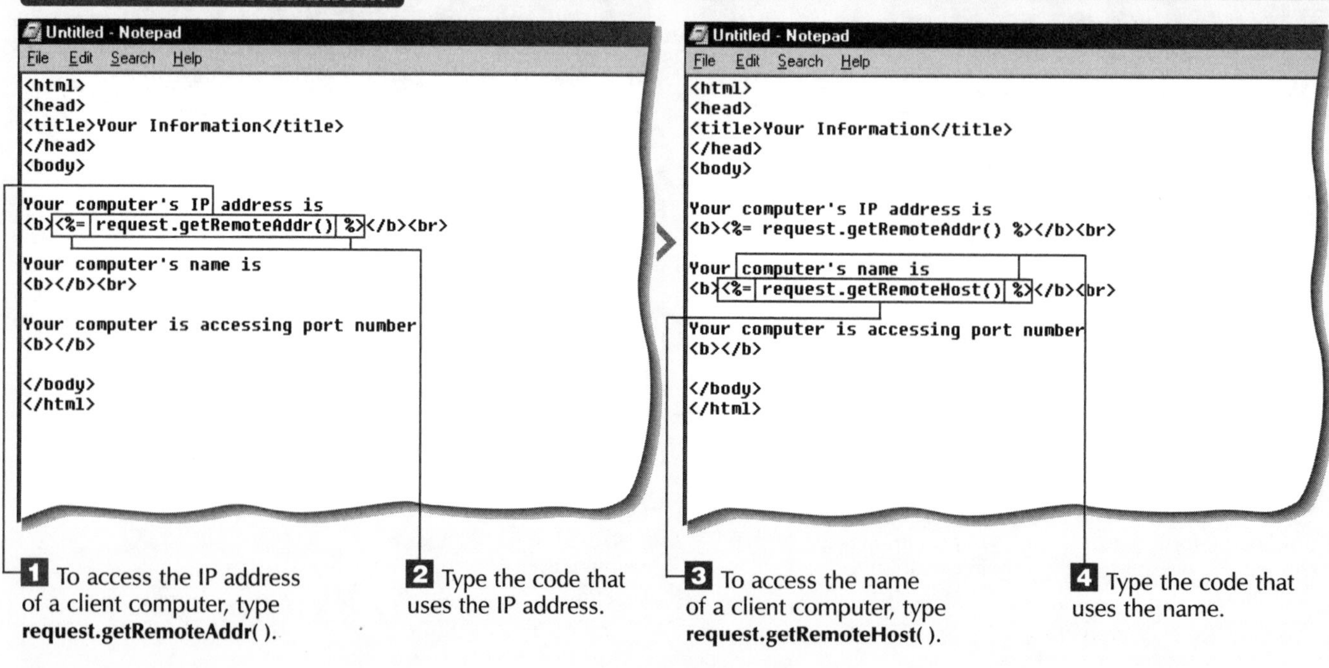

1 To access the IP address of a client computer, type **request.getRemoteAddr( )**.

2 Type the code that uses the IP address.

3 To access the name of a client computer, type **request.getRemoteHost( )**.

4 Type the code that uses the name.

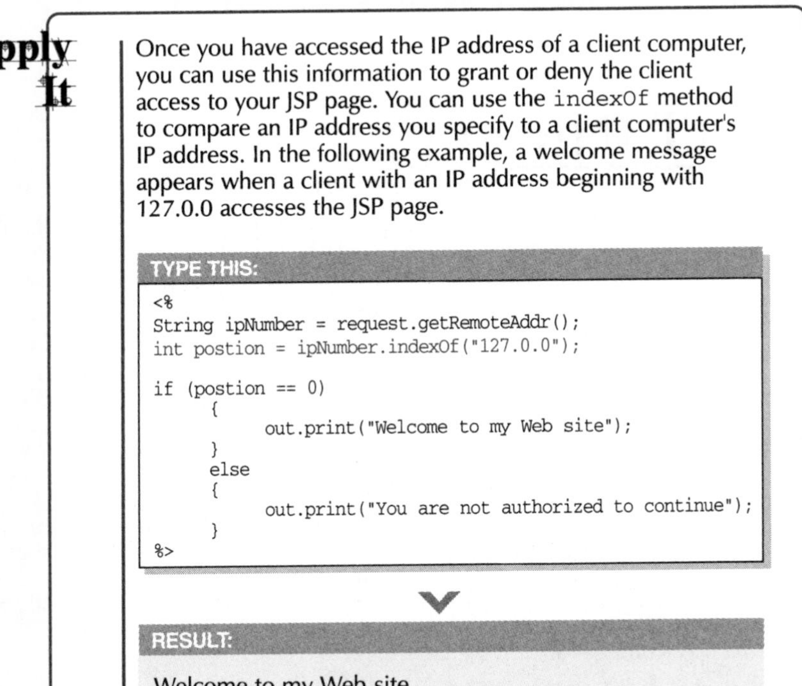

Apply It

Once you have accessed the IP address of a client computer, you can use this information to grant or deny the client access to your JSP page. You can use the `indexOf` method to compare an IP address you specify to a client computer's IP address. In the following example, a welcome message appears when a client with an IP address beginning with 127.0.0 accesses the JSP page.

TYPE THIS:

```
<%
String ipNumber = request.getRemoteAddr();
int postion = ipNumber.indexOf("127.0.0");

if (postion == 0)
      {
            out.print("Welcome to my Web site");
      }
      else
      {
            out.print("You are not authorized to continue");
      }
%>
```

RESULT:

Welcome to my Web site

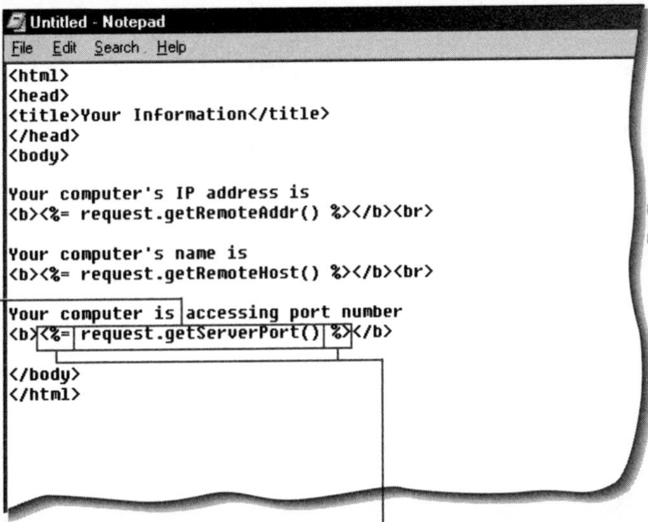

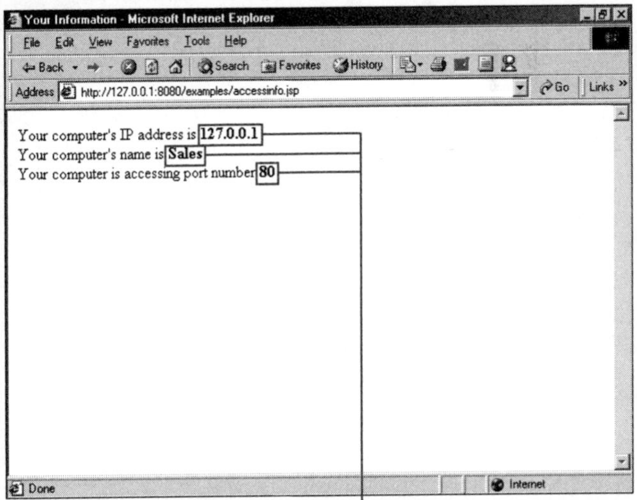

```
<html>
<head>
<title>Your Information</title>
</head>
<body>

Your computer's IP address is
<b><%= request.getRemoteAddr() %></b><br>

Your computer's name is
<b><%= request.getRemoteHost() %></b><br>

Your computer is accessing port number
<b><%= request.getServerPort() %></b>

</body>
</html>
```

Your computer's IP address is **127.0.0.1**
Your computer's name is **Sales**
Your computer is accessing port number **80**

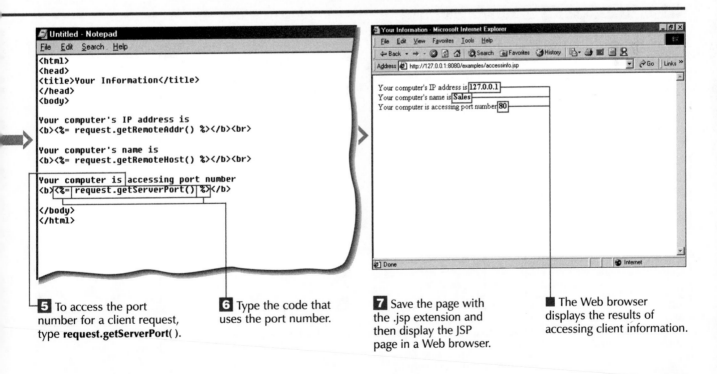

5 To access the port number for a client request, type **request.getServerPort( )**.

6 Type the code that uses the port number.

7 Save the page with the .jsp extension and then display the JSP page in a Web browser.

■ The Web browser displays the results of accessing client information.

WORK WITH THE BUFFER

The buffer is a section of the Web server's memory where a JSP page can be stored temporarily. When a JSP page is being processed, the data for the page is stored in the buffer instead of being sent directly to a user's Web browser. When the buffer is full or the entire JSP page has been generated, the Web server automatically sends the contents of the buffer to the Web browser.

The `flush` method of the `out` object forces the Web server to send the contents of the buffer to the Web browser. This allows you to control when a user will see information from your JSP page. For example, if your JSP page displays a banner image followed by a large amount of data from a database, you can use the `flush` method to force the JSP page to display the banner first.

When you use the `flush` method, all the information in the buffer is immediately sent to the user's browser and the buffer is emptied. The next time the `flush` method is called, the contents of the buffer will include only the information processed since the `flush` method was last used.

You can use the `clearBuffer` method of the `out` object to clear information from the buffer before the information is sent to a user's Web browser. The Web server deletes any information that was processed and added to the buffer since the `clearBuffer` method was last called or since the beginning of the JSP page.

Deleting the contents of the buffer is useful when an error occurs in a JSP page. For example, if there is information in the buffer and the JSP page detects an error, you can clear the information in the buffer and display an error message in the user's Web browser.

SEND CONTENTS OF BUFFER TO WEB BROWSER

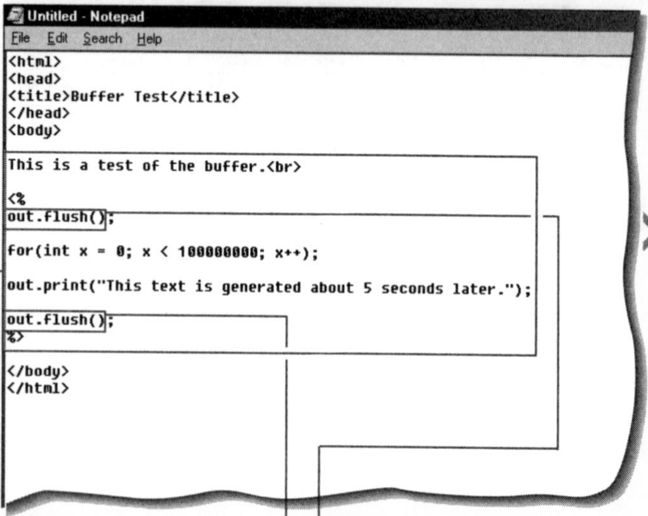

```
<html>
<head>
<title>Buffer Test</title>
</head>
<body>

This is a test of the buffer.<br>

<%
out.flush();

for(int x = 0; x < 100000000; x++);

out.print("This text is generated about 5 seconds later.");

out.flush();
%>

</body>
</html>
```

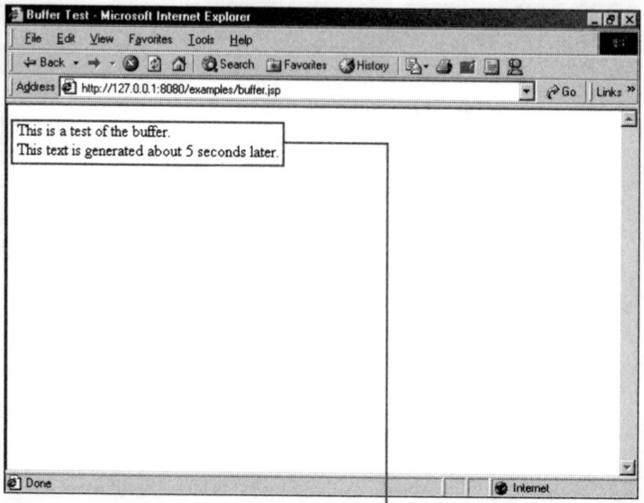

This is a test of the buffer.
This text is generated about 5 seconds later.

1 Type the code you want to execute to display information in a user's Web browser.

2 Type **out.flush()** directly below the information you want to send to a user's Web browser.

3 Repeat step 2 for each section of code you want to send to a user's Web browser at a time.

4 Save the page with the .jsp extension and then display the JSP page in a Web browser.

■ The result of sending the contents of the buffer to the Web browser is displayed.

The size allocated for the buffer on the Web server depends on a number of parameters, such as the type of Web server you are using. On Windows platforms, the default size of the Tomcat Web server's buffer is 8 KB, or 8192 bytes. You can verify the size of the buffer on your Web server using the `getBufferSize` method of the `response` object.

TYPE THIS:

```
The current size of the buffer, in bytes, is:
<%= response.getBufferSize() %>
```

RESULT:

The current size of the buffer, in bytes, is: 8192

You can turn off buffering for specific JSP pages using the `page` directive. This is useful for JSP pages that require a small amount of processing. When the buffer is turned off, the Web server will send information to a user's Web browser as the information is generated from the JSP code. The `page` directive should be placed before any HTML code in a JSP page. You may not be able to turn off buffering for some Web servers, such as the Tomcat Web server.

TYPE THIS:

```
<%@ page buffer = "none" %>
```

DELETE BUFFER CONTENTS

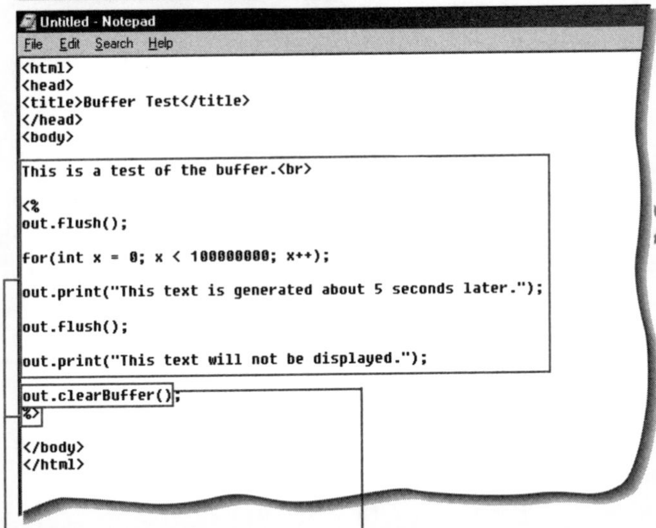

Untitled - Notepad

```
<html>
<head>
<title>Buffer Test</title>
</head>
<body>

This is a test of the buffer.<br>

<%
out.flush();

for(int x = 0; x < 100000000; x++);

out.print("This text is generated about 5 seconds later.");

out.flush();

out.print("This text will not be displayed.");

out.clearBuffer();
%>

</body>
</html>
```

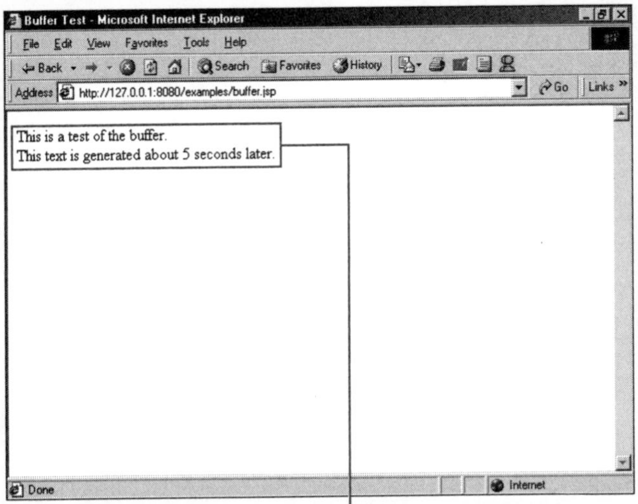

Buffer Test - Microsoft Internet Explorer

Address http://127.0.0.1:8080/examples/buffer.jsp

This is a test of the buffer.
This text is generated about 5 seconds later.

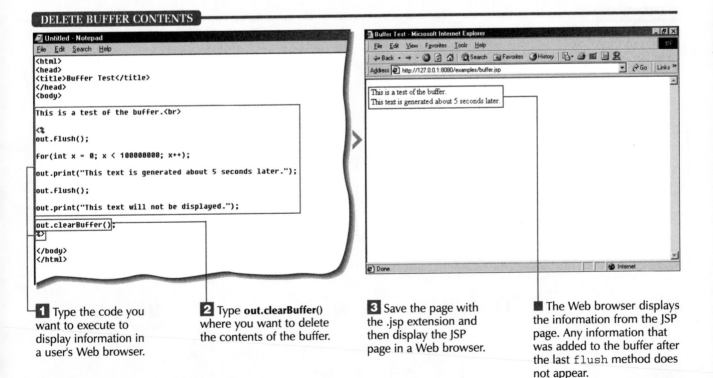

1 Type the code you want to execute to display information in a user's Web browser.

2 Type **out.clearBuffer()** where you want to delete the contents of the buffer.

3 Save the page with the .jsp extension and then display the JSP page in a Web browser.

■ The Web browser displays the information from the JSP page. Any information that was added to the buffer after the last `flush` method does not appear.

ENCODE A URL

A session is started for each user who requests a JSP page from your Web site. When a session is created, a session ID is assigned to identify each user. By default, the session ID is stored on the user's computer using a cookie. Unfortunately, many users disable the Web browser's cookie features or use Web browsers that do not support cookie technology. Filtering software can also prevent the exchange of cookie information between clients and servers.

URL encoding, or rewriting, is the process of adding the session ID to a URL in a JSP page. This process allows the Web server to keep track of a client session when cookie technology is not supported. You use the `encodeURL` method of the `response` object to modify a URL in a page.

The `encodeURL` method first determines if the client supports the use of cookies. If the client does not support the use of cookies, the `encodeURL` method adds the session ID to the end of the URL that is passed to the method as an argument. If the encodeURL method determines that the client supports the use of cookies, the URL that is passed to the method is inserted into the HTML code without any modifications.

You should use the `encodeURL` method to generate any URL in the HTML code. If a client that does not support cookies accesses a URL that has not been rewritten, a new session will be created and the information from the previous session will be lost.

You can easily verify that URL encoding is being performed by viewing the URL of the Web page, which is typically displayed in the location or address box of the Web browser.

ENCODE A URL

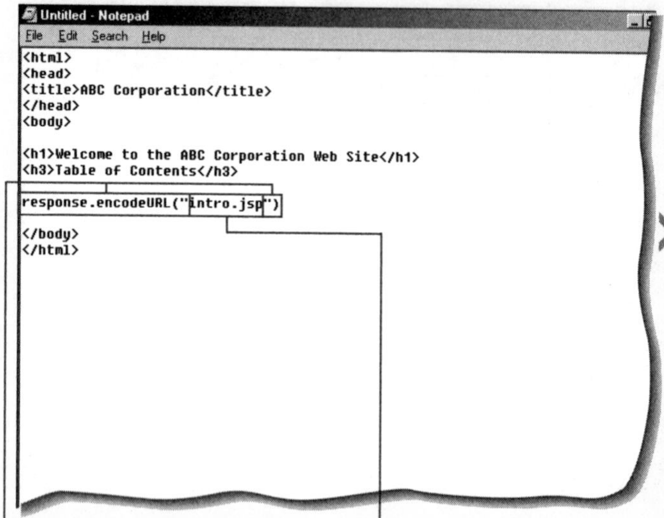

```
<html>
<head>
<title>ABC Corporation</title>
</head>
<body>

<h1>Welcome to the ABC Corporation Web Site</h1>
<h3>Table of Contents</h3>

response.encodeURL("intro.jsp")

</body>
</html>
```

1 To encode a URL, type **response.encodeURL("")**.

2 Between the quotation marks, type the URL you want to be rewritten when cookie technology is not supported.

```
<html>
<head>
<title>ABC Corporation</title>
</head>
<body>

<h1>Welcome to the ABC Corporation Web Site</h1>
<h3>Table of Contents</h3>

<a href="<%= response.encodeURL("intro.jsp") %>">Introduction</a>
<br><a href="<%= response.encodeURL("history.jsp") %>">Company History</a>
<br><a href="<%= response.encodeURL("catalog.jsp") %>">Catalog</a>
<br><a href="<%= response.encodeURL("phonelist.jsp") %>">Employee Phone
Listing</a>

</body>
</html>
```

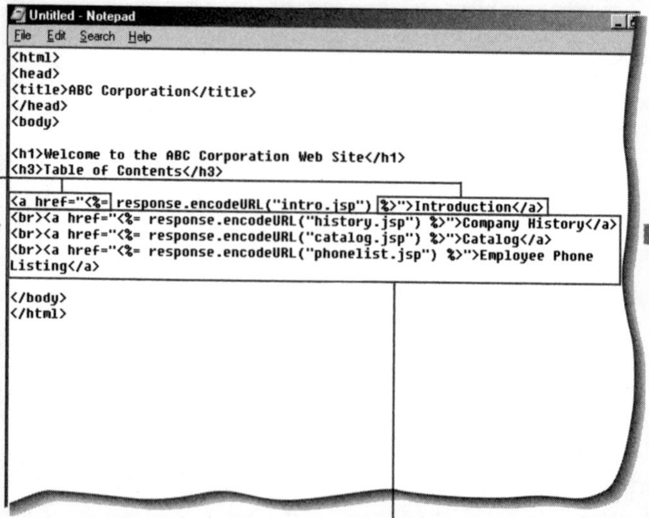

3 Type the code that uses the encoded URL.

4 Repeat steps 1 to 3 for each URL you want to encode in the HTML code.

Extra

Cookies can be disabled in most browsers by modifying the Web browser security or file settings. Many Web sites offer reduced features and functionality if cookies are not supported by the client Web browser.

The `sendRedirect` method of the `response` object is used to redirect users to another Web page automatically. If you need to keep track of a client session when redirecting the user to another Web page, you should use the `sendRedirect` method in conjunction with the `encodeRedirectURL` method of the `response` object. The `encodeRedirectURL` method appends the session ID to the redirect URL when necessary, ensuring that session information is maintained even for users with browsers that do not support cookie technology.

Example:

```
response.sendRedirect(response.encodeRedirectURL("errorPage.jsp"));
```

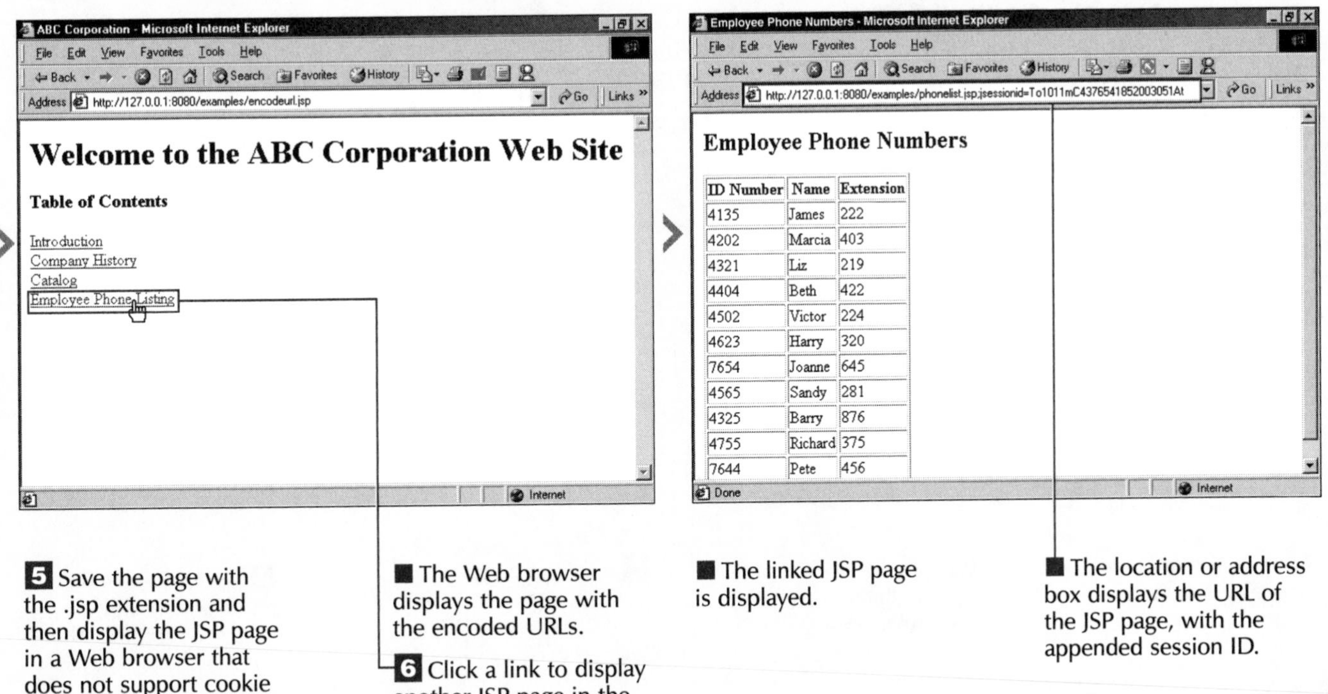

5 Save the page with the .jsp extension and then display the JSP page in a Web browser that does not support cookie technology.

■ The Web browser displays the page with the encoded URLs.

6 Click a link to display another JSP page in the Web site.

■ The linked JSP page is displayed.

■ The location or address box displays the URL of the JSP page, with the appended session ID.

ACCESS THE SESSION ID

A session is started for each user who requests a JSP page from your Web site. Sessions enable a Web server to collect and use information entered by a user while the user accesses different resources on the Web server. For example, if a user specifies a user name on the main page of a Web site, this user name can be used by the Web server to personalize any other Web pages the user requests during that session. The Web server keeps track of each session by assigning a session ID that identifies each current user.

To access the session ID number, you can use the `getId` method of the `session` object. You cannot change a session ID you access. The format of the session ID will be different depending on the Web server you are using.

When a user requests a JSP page from your Web site, the Web server stores a session ID as a *cookie* on the user's computer. When the user requests another page from the site, the user's Web browser sends the session ID to the Web server to identify the user. If the user's Web browser or computer does not support cookies, you can use URL encoding to append the session ID to the URLs accessed by the user. For information about encoding URLs, see page 94.

A session ends when the user does not request another JSP page for a specific amount of time or when the session is *abandoned*. Any information that the Web server collected from the user during a session will be discarded when the session ends.

You should not use the session ID as the *primary key* in a database, as the session ID may not always be unique. For example, if the Web server is restarted, the server may assign a user a session ID that was previously assigned to a different user.

ACCESS THE SESSION ID

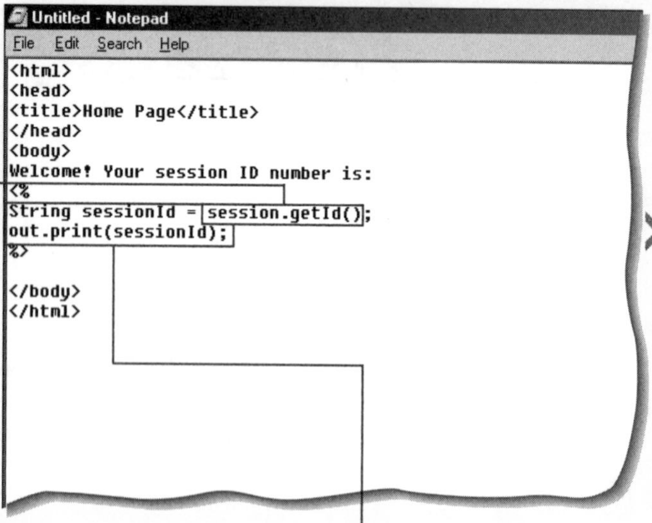
Untitled - Notepad
File Edit Search Help
<html>
<head>
<title>Home Page</title>
</head>
<body>
Welcome! Your session ID number is:
<%
String sessionId = session.getId();
out.print(sessionId);
%>
</body>
</html>

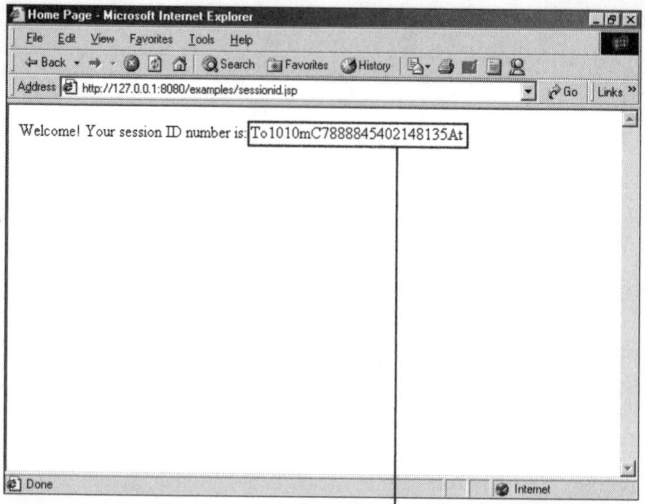
Home Page - Microsoft Internet Explorer
File Edit View Favorites Tools Help
Back Search Favorites History
Address http://127.0.0.1:8080/examples/sessionid.jsp
Go Links
Welcome! Your session ID number is: To1010mC7888845402148135At
Done
Internet

1 Type **session.getId()** where you want to access a session ID.

2 Type the code that will display the session ID in a Web browser.

3 Save the page with the .jsp extension and then display the JSP page in a Web browser.

■ The Web browser displays the result of accessing the session ID.

ABANDON A SESSION

During a session, information is saved on the Web server and the client computer. As a result, each session requires the use of Web server resources, such as computer memory. If information for a session is no longer required, the session can be abandoned to free up resources on the Web server. This can improve the efficiency of a busy Web server.

The `invalidate` method of the `session` object allows you to immediately end a session for one user and erase the information associated with the session. The information for the session will be permanently removed from the Web server. If you want to be able to later access the session information, you should write the information to a file or store the information in a database before abandoning the session.

Abandoning a session is useful when an error occurs or when a user performs an action that indicates they no longer need the session information, such as logging out of the Web site. If the session was not abandoned, the Web server would keep the session information in memory until the session timed out. Abandoning a session also allows users to perform tasks such as clearing their Web site preferences or logging into your Web site using a different user name.

Abandoning a session does not stop the Web server from processing the JSP page, but does make session information generated before the session was abandoned unavailable to the page. An attempt to access session information after the session has been abandoned may generate an error.

Abandoning a session does not usually remove the cookie that stores session information on the client computer. The cookie will usually remain on the client until it is deleted by the Web browser, which typically occurs after the cookie expires or when a new session is started between the client and the Web server.

ABANDON A SESSION

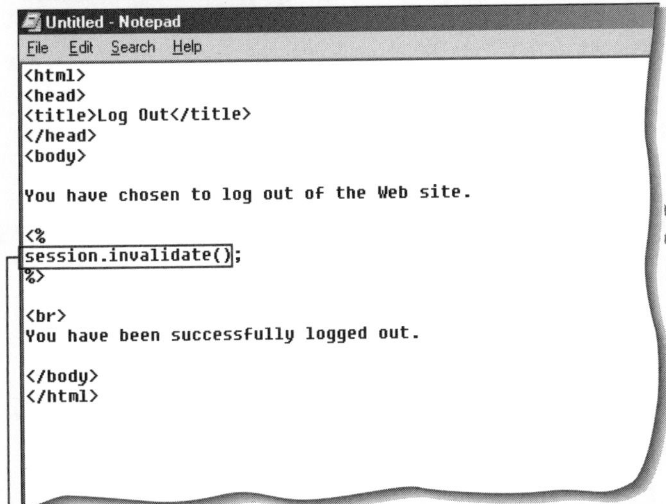

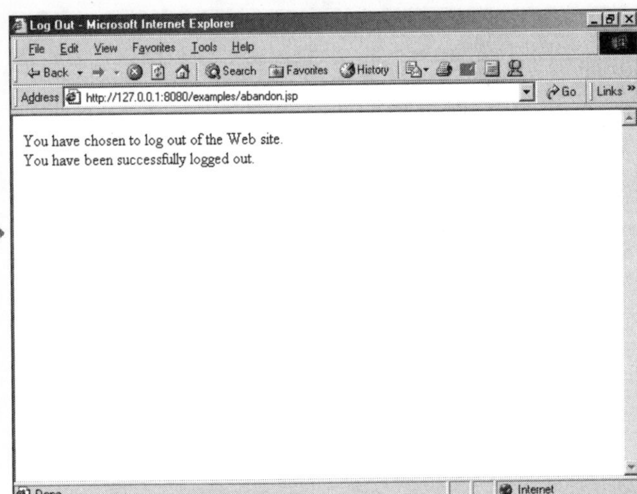

1 Type **session.invalidate()** where you want to abandon a session.

2 Save the page with the .jsp extension and then display the JSP page in a Web browser.

■ The Web server abandons the session.

CREATE SESSION VALUES

As a user moves through the pages in your Web site, the user may be asked to enter information such as a user name, password or preferences to display each page. Creating session values allows you to store this information and make the information available to all the pages viewed by the user in your Web site. This saves the user from having to repeatedly enter the same information to display each page during a session.

You use the `setAttribute` method of the `session` object to create a session value. When creating a session value, you need to specify the name of the value and the information to be stored. A `null` value will be assigned if you do not specify any information for the session value. The information stored in a session value cannot be a primitive data type, such as `boolean` or `int`. For information on primitive data types, see page 30.

The information stored in a session value can come from sources such as forms, databases and cookies. The use of session values is an effective way of collecting and accessing information across multiple pages on a Web site and is more secure and easier to maintain than hidden fields or cookies.

All session values and the information stored in them will be discarded when the session ends or is terminated. If necessary, you can use cookies or a database to save the information stored in a session value.

After creating session values, the information stored in the session values can be accessed using the `getAttribute` method. For information about the `getAttribute` method, see page 100.

CREATE SESSION VALUES

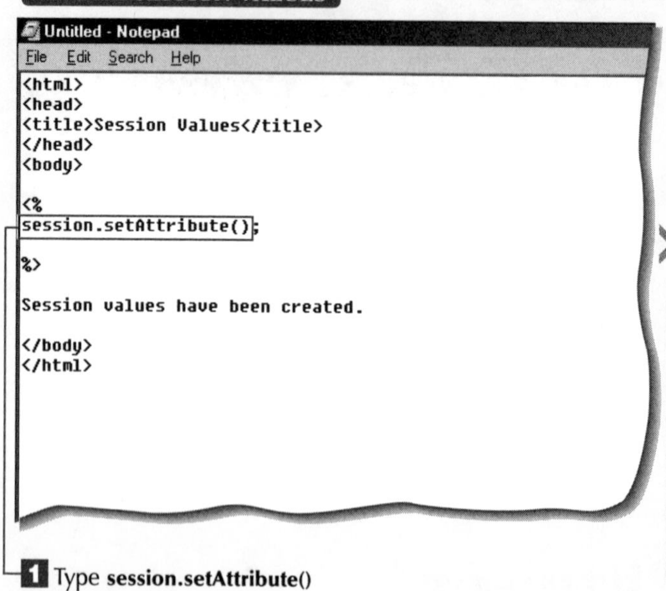

1 Type **session.setAttribute()** where you want to create a session value.

Untitled - Notepad

File Edit Search Help

```
<html>
<head>
<title>Session Values</title>
</head>
<body>

<%
session.setAttribute("userName",);

%>

Session values have been created.

</body>
</html>
```

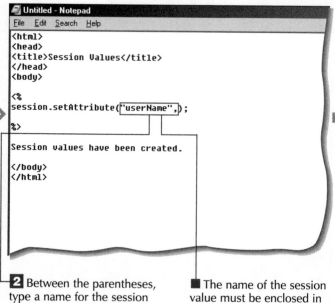

2 Between the parentheses, type a name for the session value followed by a comma.

■ The name of the session value must be enclosed in quotation marks.

Extra

You can turn off the use of session information for a JSP page by using the `page` directive. Turning off the use of session information does not produce any noticeable improvement in speed on the Web server, but it may offer increased security to JSP pages that do not use session information. If you try to use session values when session handling is turned off, an error will occur when the JSP page is viewed.

The `page` directive should be placed before any HTML code in a JSP page. To once again allow the use of session information in the JSP page, simply remove the `page` directive from the code.

Example:

```
<%@ page session = "false" %>
<html>
<head>
<title>Home Page</title>
</head>
<body>
<%
session.setAttribute("userName", "Tim");
session.setAttribute("preferredColor", "blue");
%>
</body>
</html>
```

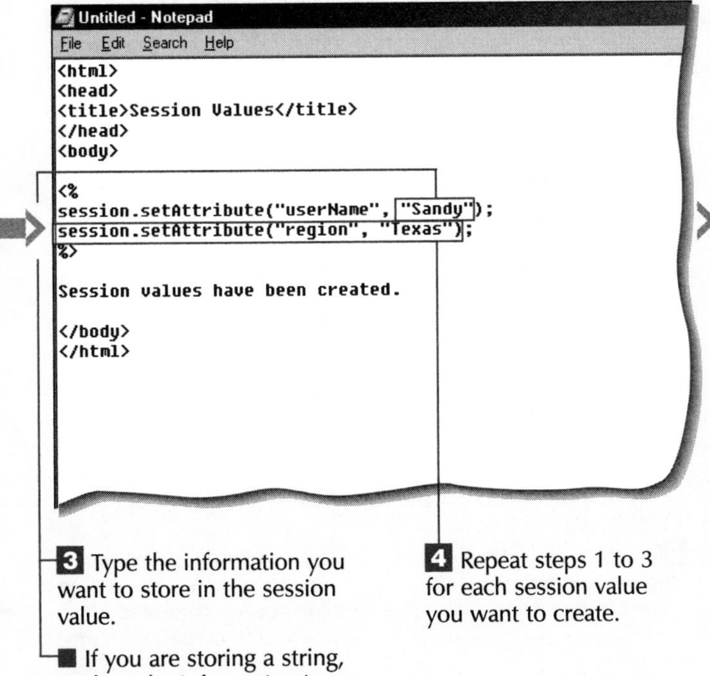

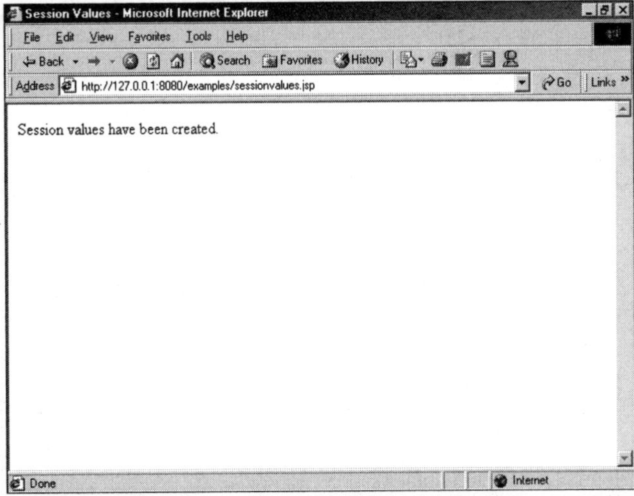

3 Type the information you want to store in the session value.

■ If you are storing a string, enclose the information in quotation marks.

4 Repeat steps 1 to 3 for each session value you want to create.

5 Save the page with the .jsp extension and then display the JSP page in a Web browser.

■ You can now read the information stored in the session values. See page 100 to read session values.

READ SESSION VALUES

If a JSP page in your Web site creates session values for a user, other JSP pages viewed by the user in the Web site can read and process the information stored in the session values until the session times out or is terminated. For information about creating session values, see page 98.

A Web server can personalize each JSP page in a Web site according to the user information saved in session values. For example, if a user prefers not to view images on Web pages, each page that the user visits in the Web site will read the session information for the user and display only text.

A JSP page reads the information stored in a session value using the `getAttribute` method of the `session` object. The JSP page that reads the information stored in a session value does not usually modify the information.

In most cases, the information stored in a session value is assigned to a variable. You can then use the variable to display the session information on the screen or to perform a more complex action, such as locating information in a database. You may have to `cast` the information stored in a session value as a data type that is compatible with the variable to which it is assigned. For information about casting, see page 30.

It is also important to note that variables can be accessed only by the JSP page on which they are created. If you want to use the same variable on another JSP page, you will have to recreate the variable and re-assign the information stored in the session value to the variable.

READ SESSION VALUES

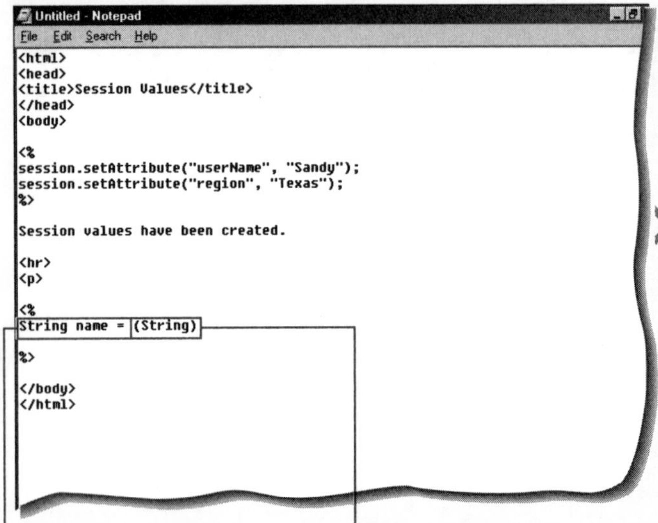

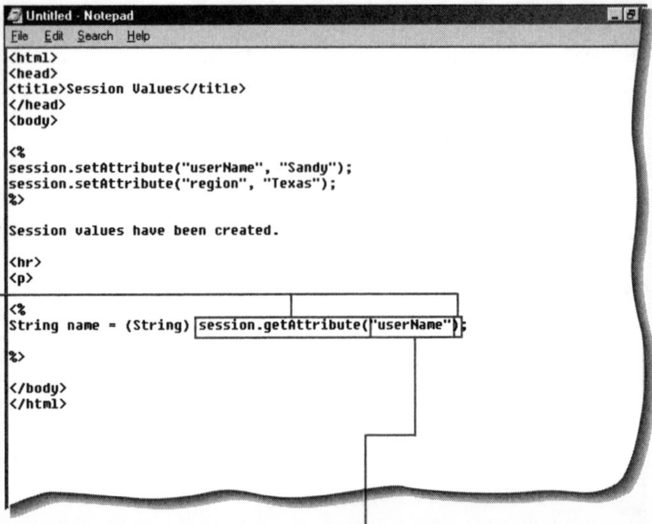

```
<html>
<head>
<title>Session Values</title>
</head>
<body>

<%
session.setAttribute("userName", "Sandy");
session.setAttribute("region", "Texas");
%>

Session values have been created.

<hr>
<p>

<%
String name = (String)

%>

</body>
</html>
```

1 Type the code that declares a variable you want to store the information in a session value.

2 To cast the information in the session value as a specific data type, enter the data type you want to use, enclosed in parentheses.

```
<html>
<head>
<title>Session Values</title>
</head>
<body>

<%
session.setAttribute("userName", "Sandy");
session.setAttribute("region", "Texas");
%>

Session values have been created.

<hr>
<p>

<%
String name = (String) session.getAttribute("userName");

%>

</body>
</html>
```

3 To read a session variable, type **session.getAttribute()**.

4 Between the parentheses, type the name of the session value you want to read, enclosed in quotation marks.

Extra

In most cases, you know which session value you want to retrieve information from, but there may be times when you are required to find out which session values are available. You can use the `getAttributeNames` method of the `session` object to generate a list of the names of all the session values that are available during a session. You must cast the names as a collection that can be used by the `Iterator` interface. To use the `Iterator` interface, you must first import the interface from the `java.util` package.

TYPE THIS:

```
<body>
<%@ page import="java.util.Iterator" %>
Session values for this session:
<ul>
<%
Iterator sessionValues = (Iterator) session.getAttributeNames();

while (sessionValues.hasNext())
     out.print("<li>" + sessionValues.next() + "</li>");
%>
</ul>
</body>
```

RESULT:

Session values for this session:

- login
- memberLevel
- region

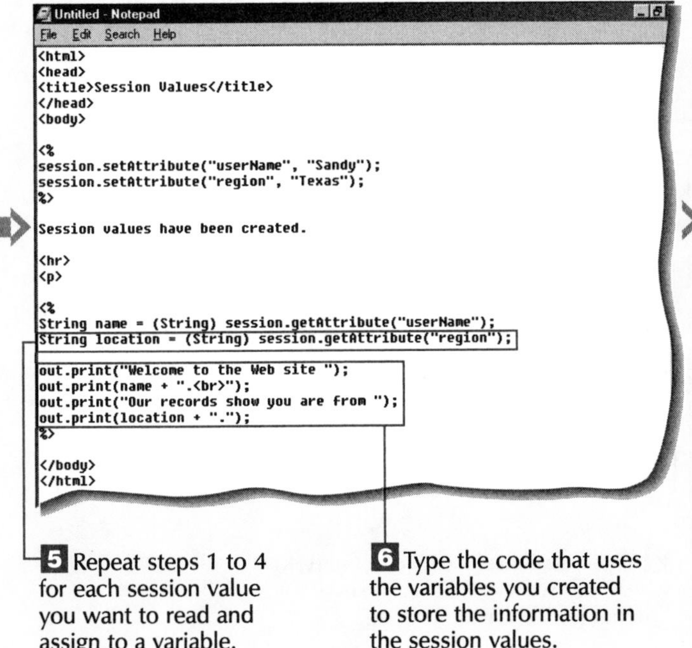

```
<html>
<head>
<title>Session Values</title>
</head>
<body>

<%
session.setAttribute("userName", "Sandy");
session.setAttribute("region", "Texas");
%>

Session values have been created.

<hr>
<p>

<%
String name = (String) session.getAttribute("userName");
String location = (String) session.getAttribute("region");

out.print("Welcome to the Web site ");
out.print(name + ".<br>");
out.print("Our records show you are from ");
out.print(location + ".");
%>

</body>
</html>
```

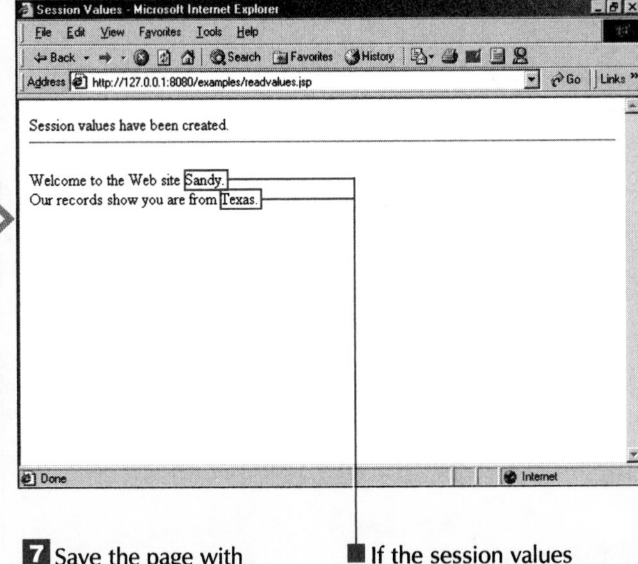

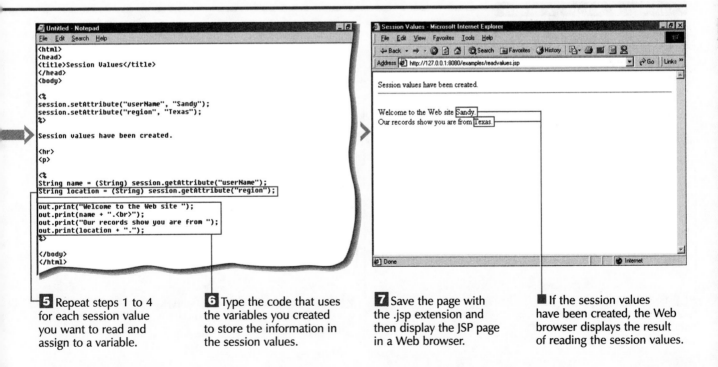

5 Repeat steps 1 to 4 for each session value you want to read and assign to a variable.

6 Type the code that uses the variables you created to store the information in the session values.

7 Save the page with the .jsp extension and then display the JSP page in a Web browser.

■ If the session values have been created, the Web browser displays the result of reading the session values.

ADJUST THE SESSION TIMEOUT

The `setMaxInactiveInterval` method of the `session` object allows you to set the session timeout for a JSP page, in seconds. The session timeout determines how long a user's session information is stored on the Web server after the user last refreshes a page or requests a page in the Web site.

A session allows the Web server to identify a client computer as the user moves from page to page within a Web site. This is useful for applications such as shopping carts, when you need to be able to track the items a user has selected throughout your Web site. For more information about session information, see pages 96 to 101.

Typically, a user's session information is stored on the Web server for 30 minutes and is available to the JSP pages that the user views in your Web site. The session information created for a user will be available to the JSP pages in the Web site even if the user visits another Web site and then returns to your site within the timeout period. If the user returns to your Web site after the timeout period, the session information for the client will no longer be available.

The session timeout that you set for a JSP page applies to every client that accesses the JSP page.

Adjusting the session timeout period can help make your Web site more secure. For example, if you have a Web site that requires a user to log in, a short timeout period will help to prevent other users from accessing your site if the user leaves the computer while logged in. Keep in mind, however, that setting the session timeout too short may lead to the inadvertent loss of session information.

ADJUST THE SESSION TIMEOUT

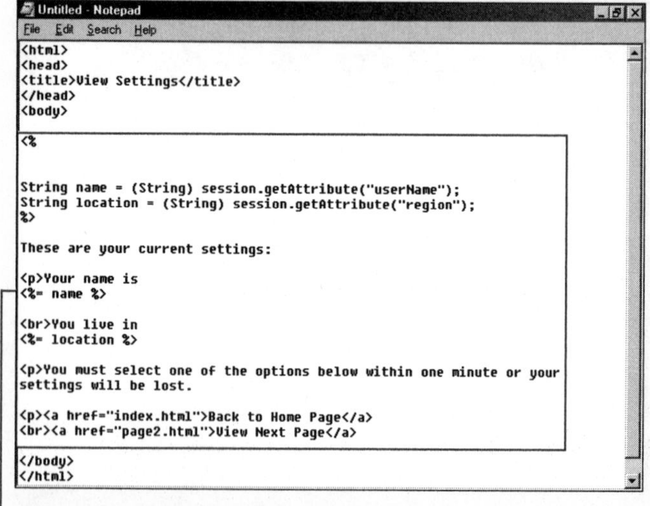

1 Type the code you want to execute to display information in a Web browser.

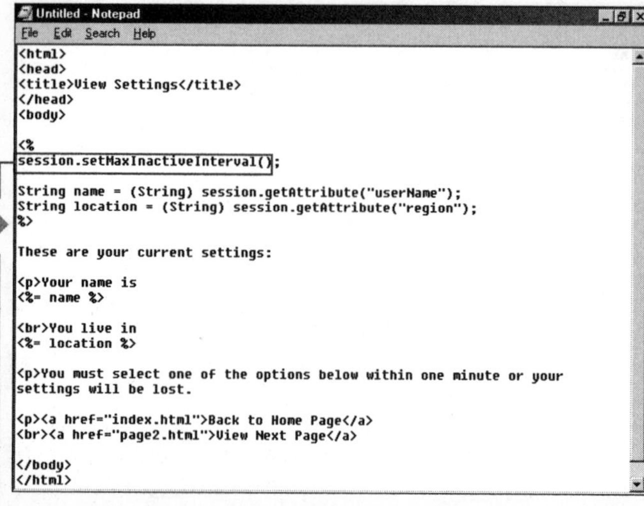

2 Type **session.setMaxInactiveInterval()** where you want to adjust the session timeout period for the JSP page.

Extra

The `session` object has many methods that can be used to alter or obtain information about the current session. Some methods and values of the `session` object can be accessed only during the session in which they were created. When the session ends, the items no longer exist. When another session starts, the items are recreated for that session.

Popular Session Object Methods

METHOD:	DESCRIPTION:
`getCreationTime`	Returns the time the session started, measured in milliseconds since January 1, 1970.
`getId`	Returns the session ID.
`getLastAccessedTime`	Returns the last time the client sent a request during the session, measured in milliseconds since January 1, 1970.
`setMaxInactiveInterval(interval)`	Sets the session timeout, in seconds.
`getMaxInactiveInterval`	Returns the session timeout, in seconds.
`invalidate`	Closes the session.
`isNew`	Returns `true` if the Web server has created a session, but the client computer has not yet accepted a session ID.
`getAttribute(name)`	Returns the information stored in a session value.
`getAttributeNames`	Returns a list of all session values.
`setAttribute(name, value)`	Creates a session value.
`removeAttribute(name)`	Removes a session value.

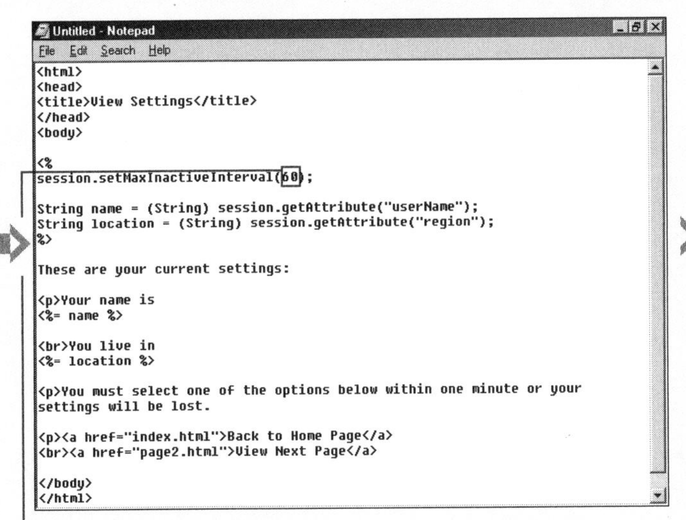

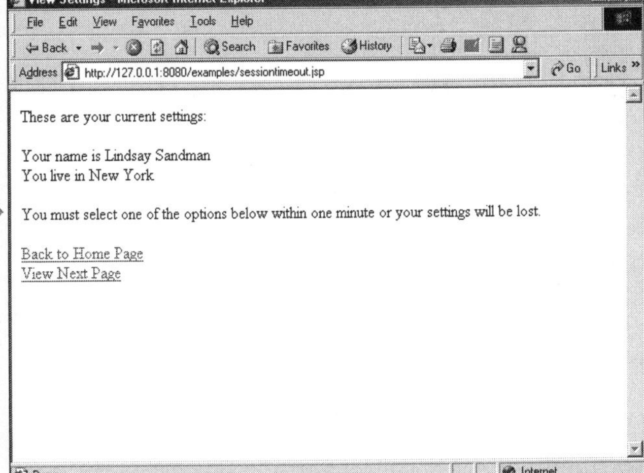

3 Between the parentheses, type the number of seconds you want the Web server to wait for activity before closing the session.

4 Save the page with the .jsp extension and then display the JSP page in a Web browser.

■ The Web browser displays the JSP page in which the session timeout is adjusted.

■ If you do not request a new page in the Web site or refresh the page within the new timeout period, the Web server will erase your session information.

USING APPLICATION VALUES

JavaServer Pages allows you to define a Web site or part of a Web site as an application. An application is a collection of JSP pages stored in a specific directory and its subdirectories on the Web server. For example, if you have 10 JSP pages stored in the same directory, those pages would make up an application.

All the JSP pages in an application typically must be stored in the same *virtual* directory on the Web server. The type of Web server you use will determine how the virtual directory and applications are created. For more information about creating virtual directories, refer to your Web server documentation.

You use the `setAttribute` method of the `application` object to create an application value. When using the `setAttribute` method, you must specify the name of the application value and the information the value will contain. The information stored in an application value cannot be a primitive data type, such as `boolean` or `int`. For information about primitive data types, see page 30.

All the JSP pages in an application can access the information stored in an application value. For example, if you create an application value that stores a counter, the number of people who have used your application could be displayed at the bottom of each page in the application.

You access an application value in your JSP pages using the `getAttribute` method of the `application` object. If a JSP page tries to access an application value that does not exist, the `getAttribute` method will return a value of null.

An application starts when the first user requests a JSP page from the application and ends when the Web server shuts down or restarts. Application values are discarded when the application ends.

CREATE AN APPLICATION VALUE

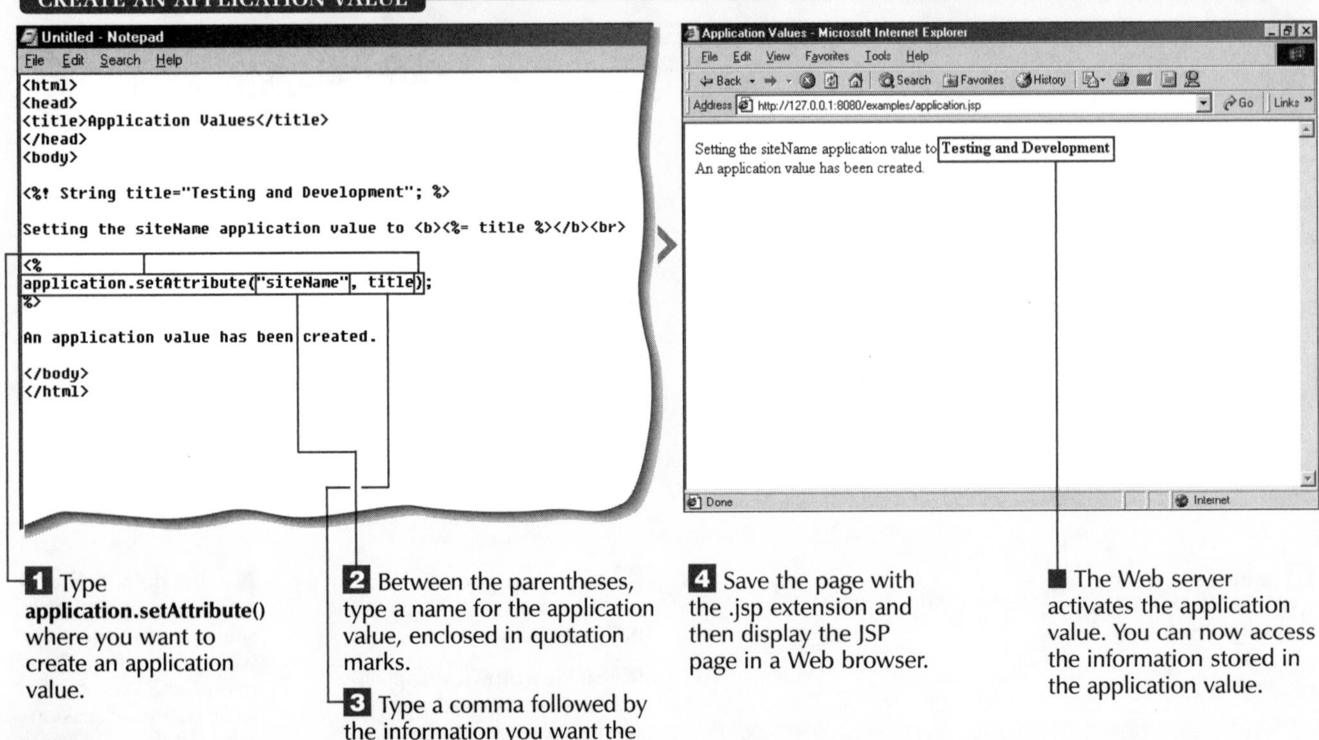
Untitled - Notepad
File Edit Search Help
<html>
<head>
<title>Application Values</title>
</head>
<body>
<%! String title="Testing and Development"; %>
Setting the siteName application value to <b><%= title %></b>
<%
application.setAttribute("siteName", title);
%>
An application value has been created.
</body>
</html>
Application Values - Microsoft Internet Explorer
File Edit View Favorites Tools Help
Back Search Favorites History
Address http://127.0.0.1:8080/examples/application.jsp
Go Links
Setting the siteName application value to **Testing and Development**
An application value has been created.
Done
Internet

1 Type **application.setAttribute()** where you want to create an application value.

2 Between the parentheses, type a name for the application value, enclosed in quotation marks.

3 Type a comma followed by the information you want the application value to use.

4 Save the page with the .jsp extension and then display the JSP page in a Web browser.

■ The Web server activates the application value. You can now access the information stored in the application value.

Extra

You can delete an existing application value using the `removeAttribute` method. You should delete any application values that you no longer need. If a JSP page tries to access an application value that has been removed, a null value will be generated.

TYPE THIS:

```
Welcome to the <b>
<%= application.getAttribute("siteName") %>
</b> Web site. <br>
<% application.removeAttribute("siteName"); %>
Application value deleted. <br>
Welcome to the <b>
<%= application.getAttribute("siteName") %>
</b> Web site.
```

RESULT:

Welcome to the **Testing and Development** Web site.
Application value deleted.
Welcome to the **null** Web site.

You can change the information stored in an application value. If the application value has not yet been created, changing the information stored in the value will create the value.

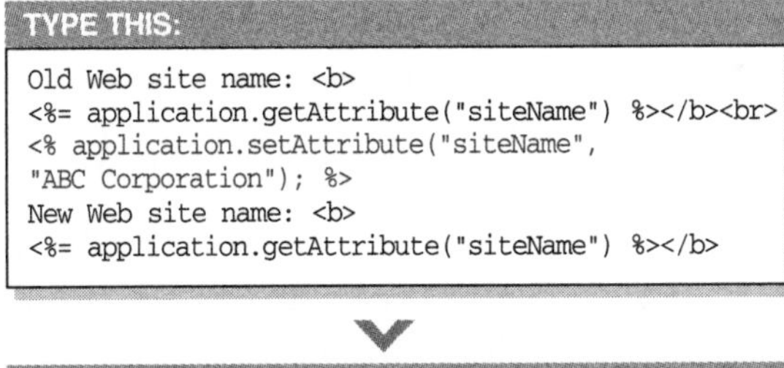

TYPE THIS:

```
Old Web site name: <b>
<%= application.getAttribute("siteName") %></b><br>
<% application.setAttribute("siteName",
"ABC Corporation"); %>
New Web site name: <b>
<%= application.getAttribute("siteName") %></b>
```

RESULT:

Old Web site name: **Testing and Development**
New Web site name: **ABC Corporation**

ACCESS AN APPLICATION VALUE

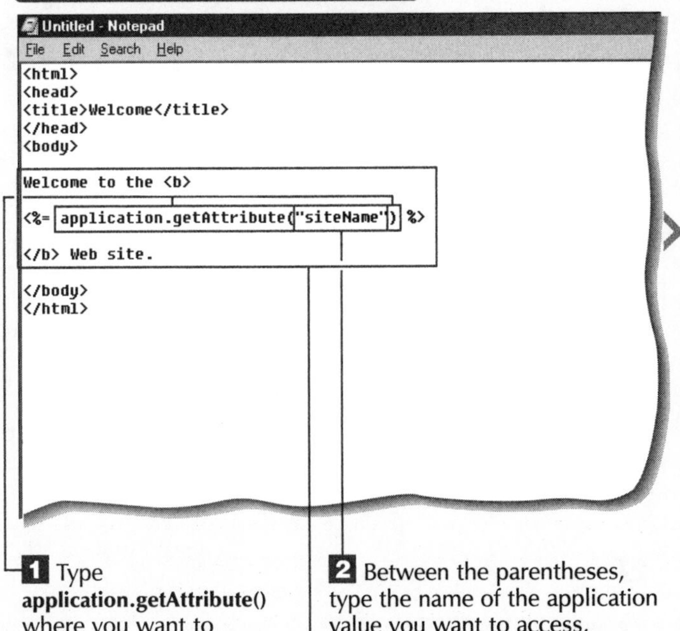

```
<html>
<head>
<title>Welcome</title>
</head>
<body>

Welcome to the <b>
<%= application.getAttribute("siteName") %>
</b> Web site.

</body>
</html>
```

1 Type **application.getAttribute()** where you want to access an application value.

2 Between the parentheses, type the name of the application value you want to access, enclosed in quotation marks.

3 Type the code that uses the application value.

4 Save the page with the .jsp extension and then display the JSP page in a Web browser.

Note: You must save the page in the same directory that stores the JSP page in which the application value was created.

■ The Web browser displays the result of accessing the application value.

DETERMINE THE PATH OF A FILE

The getRealPath method of the application object allows you to identify where a file, such as a Web page or JSP page, is stored on the Web server.

A Web server can store files in many different directories. The directory that stores a page is not always apparent in the URL of the page. For example, a JSP page named login.jsp stored in the directory C:\Tomcat\webapps\public\sign_in could have the URL http://www.abccorp.com/sign_in/login.jsp. When a JSP page needs to access a page on the Web server, such as when using the include directive to access information from a Web page, the JSP page may need to know the exact location of the page, not the URL of the page.

To identify the path of a page, you must know the filename of the page. The getRealPath method uses the filename of the page, enclosed in quotation marks, as its argument.

Regardless of the operating system you use, you should use slashes (/) within the path of the page you want to locate. When the path to the page starts with a slash (/), the path will be determined starting at the document root directory of the current Web application. The document root directory is the parent directory that contains all the documents and applications on a Web server. The location of the document root directory depends on the configuration of the Web server. On Web servers that host multiple Web sites, the document root directory will be different for each Web site.

The result returned by the getRealPath method is a string value. You can assign this value to a variable and then use the variable in your code.

The getRealPath method shows where a page is located on the Web server but does not verify that the page or the directories actually exist.

DETERMINE THE PATH OF A FILE

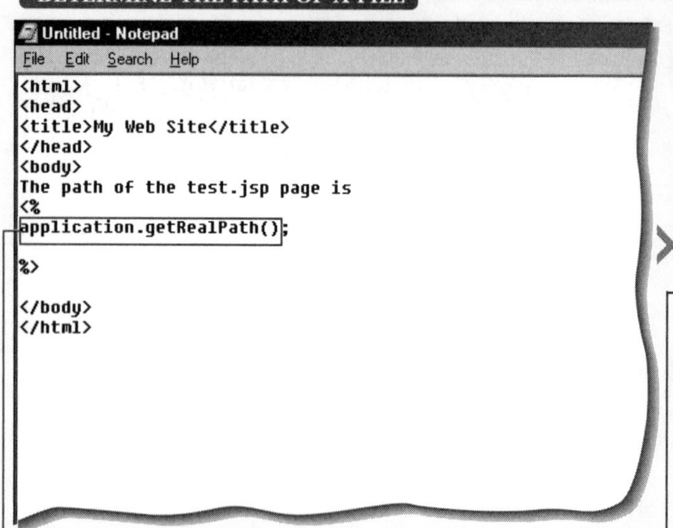

1 Type **application.getRealPath()** where you want to find the path of a file.

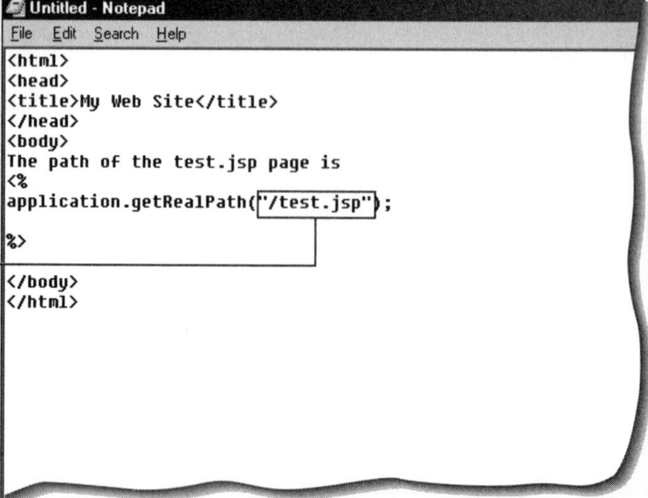

2 Between the parentheses, type a slash (/) followed by the name of the file whose path you want to determine, enclosed in quotation marks.

You can determine the path of the current JSP page by using a single slash enclosed in quotation marks as the argument for the `getRealPath` method. Identifying the path of the current page is useful when you are creating a JSP page for different Web applications and you need to make sure the directory structure is the same for each application.

TYPE THIS:

```
<html>
<head>
<title>My Web Site</title>
</head>
<body>
This JSP page is stored in
<%
String docPath = application.getRealPath("/");
out.print(docPath);
%>

</body>
</html>
```

RESULT:

This JSP page is stored in C:\Tomcat\webapps\examples\

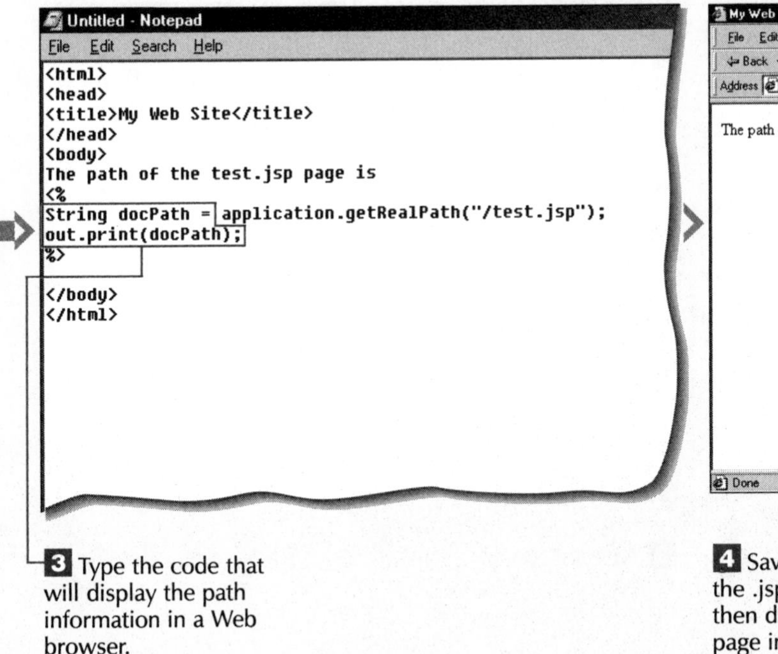

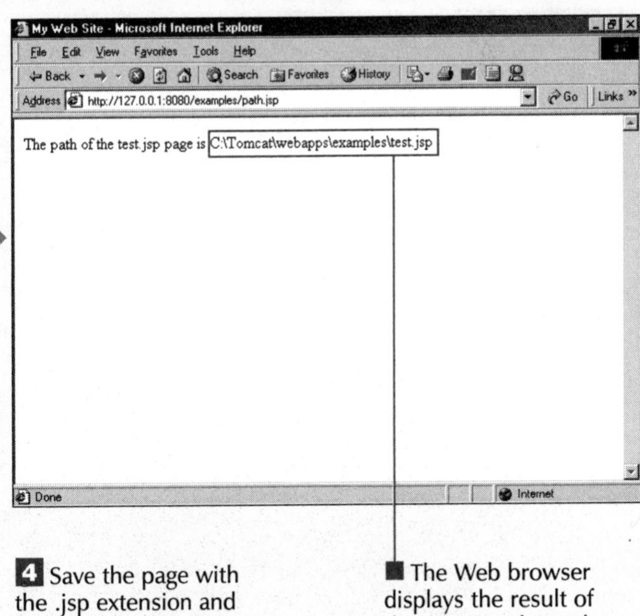

3 Type the code that will display the path information in a Web browser.

4 Save the page with the .jsp extension and then display the JSP page in a Web browser.

■ The Web browser displays the result of determining the path of a file.

GENERATE A NEWLINE CHARACTER

A newline character instructs a processing program to stop placing output on the current line and begin a new line. The `newLine` method of the `out` object can be used in a JSP page to generate a newline character. Newline characters are sometimes called line separators.

To generate a newline character, you create a scriptlet that contains the `out.newLine` statement. Scriptlets are processed by the Web server and a newline character generated by a scriptlet is inserted into the source code for a JSP page before the page is displayed.

Since Web browsers ignore extra spaces and new lines in source code, the line break you add using a newline character will not appear on a JSP page when the page is displayed in a Web browser. To view the results of generating a newline character, you must display the source code for your JSP page. Most Web browsers allow users to easily view the source code for a page. A new line will begin in the source code where you added the newline character. To have a new line appear on your JSP page when it is displayed in a Web browser, use the HTML tag `<br>`.

Using newline characters is particularly useful when a JSP page generates HTML source code. HTML code that does not contain any new lines can be difficult to read and troubleshoot. By inserting new lines into the code, you can separate the various elements on the page, making the page easier to understand. For example, a page containing images and text can have newline characters after each paragraph and image. Newline characters are typically inserted after closing HTML tags, such as the `</p>` and `</img>` tags.

GENERATE A NEWLINE CHARACTER

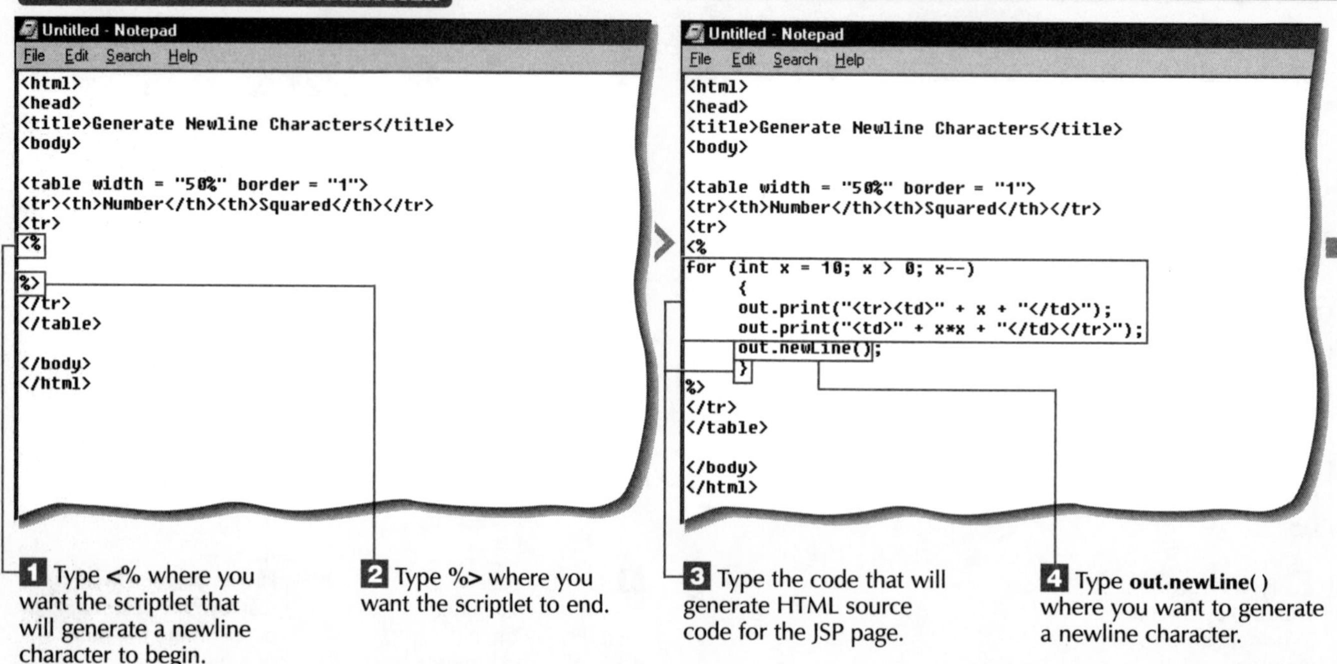

1 Type **<%** where you want the scriptlet that will generate a newline character to begin.

2 Type **%>** where you want the scriptlet to end.

3 Type the code that will generate HTML source code for the JSP page.

4 Type **out.newLine( )** where you want to generate a newline character.

Apply It

The actual character or characters a computer uses for a new line depends on the operating system installed on the computer. For example, a new line may be created by a carriage return, a newline character or both. Because these characters are not displayable, you cannot view them. You can, however, use the Java `getBytes` method to view the ASCII code for the characters.

TYPE THIS:

```
The ASCII codes for the characters used to create new lines on this computer are: <br>
<%
String lineSeparator = System.getProperties().getProperty("line.separator");
byte[] array = lineSeparator.getBytes();

for (int x = 0; x < array.length; x++)
     out.print(array[x] + "<br>");
%>
```

RESULT:

The ASCII codes for the characters used to create new lines on this computer are:
13
10

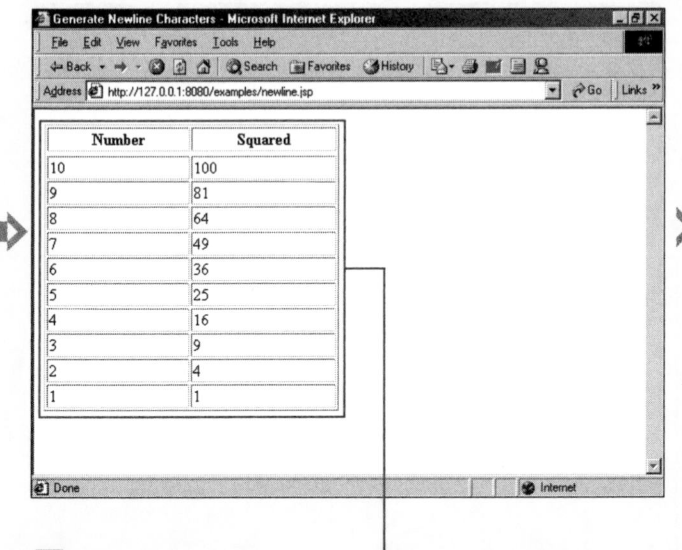

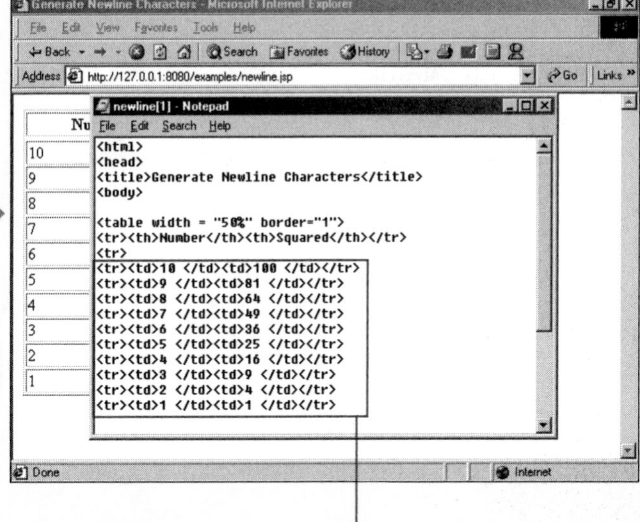

5 Save the page with the .jsp extension and then display the JSP page in a Web browser.

■ Generating newline characters does not affect the way a JSP page appears in a Web browser.

6 Display the source code for the JSP page.

■ The source code displays the result of generating newline characters.

DETERMINE THE OPERATING SYSTEM

You can use the getProperties and getProperty methods of the System object to determine the operating system being used on the computer running your JSP pages.

JSP code should not have problems running on different operating systems, but the way JSP interacts with the computer may differ depending on the operating system. For example, you may develop JSP pages on a computer using a Windows operating system and then transfer the JSP pages to an Internet Web server that uses the Linux operating system. When JSP pages run on a computer using a Windows operating system, the JSP pages will attempt to find files, such as include files, in a specific directory. When the JSP pages run on a computer using the Linux operating system, errors may occur because the required files may be located in a different directory. Instead of creating two sets of JSP pages, you could simply set the JSP page to determine which operating system is running on the computer and then automatically alter the path required to access the files.

The getProperties method returns all of the system properties that are specific to the computer running the JSP pages. The system properties that are available depend on the operating system running on the computer.

You use the getProperty method to specify the name of a specific property you wish to access. The property name used to identify the current operating system is os.name.

The value returned by the getProperties and getProperty methods is a String data type and can be assigned to a variable, which can then be used in your code. You can use the indexOf method to match the content of the variable with the name of a specific operating system. Refer to the Java SDK documentation for more information about using the indexOf method.

DETERMINE THE OPERATING SYSTEM

Untitled - Notepad

File Edit Search Help

```
<html>
<head>
<title>Operating System</title>
</head>
<body>

<%
String oprSystemName = System.getProperties().getProperty("os.name");
%>

</body>
</html>
```

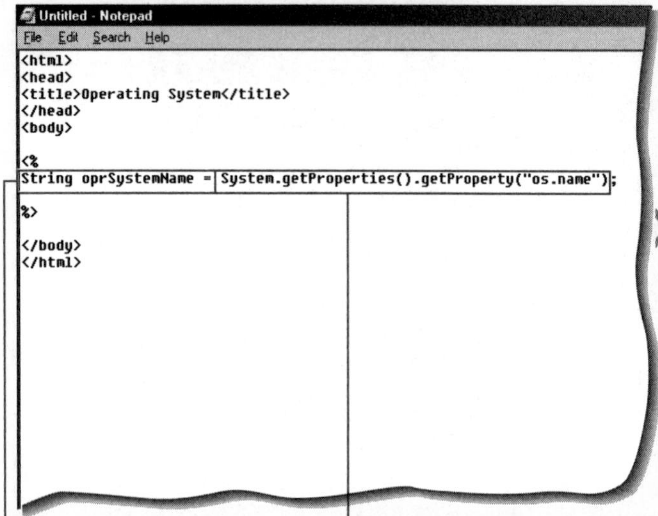

1 Type the code that declares a variable you want to store the name of the operating system.

2 Type **System.getProperties().getProperty("os.name")** to determine the name of the operating system.

Untitled - Notepad

File Edit Search Help

```
<html>
<head>
<title>Operating System</title>
</head>
<body>

<%
String oprSystemName = System.getProperties().getProperty("os.name");

oprSystemName.indexOf() == 0
%>

</body>
</html>
```

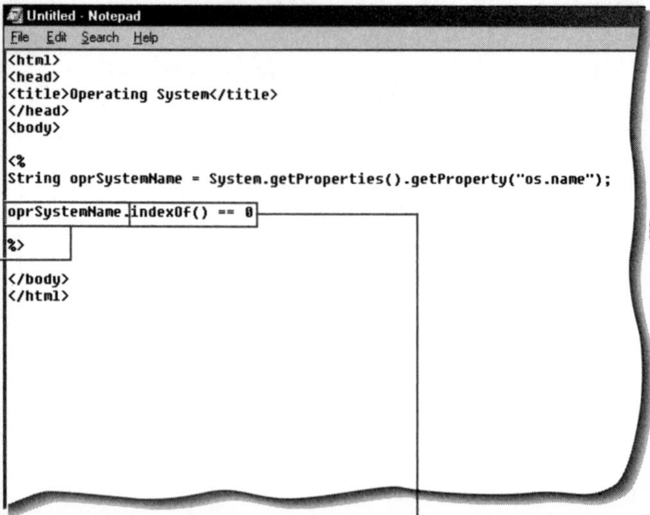

3 To match the content of the variable that stores the name of the operating system with the name of a specific operating system, type the name of the variable followed by a dot.

4 Type **indexOf() == 0**.

Extra

The following is a list of some of the other system properties you may determine using the `getProperty` method:

PROPERTY NAME:	RETURNS:
java.home	The directory where Java is installed
java.class.path	The path where the classes are loaded from
java.version	The version of the Java API implementation
java.vendor	The vendor of the Java API implementation
java.class.version	The version of the Java class file format
os.arch	The architecture of the operating system
os.version	The version of the operating system
user.name	The account name of the current user
user.home	The home directory of the current user
user.dir	The current working directory

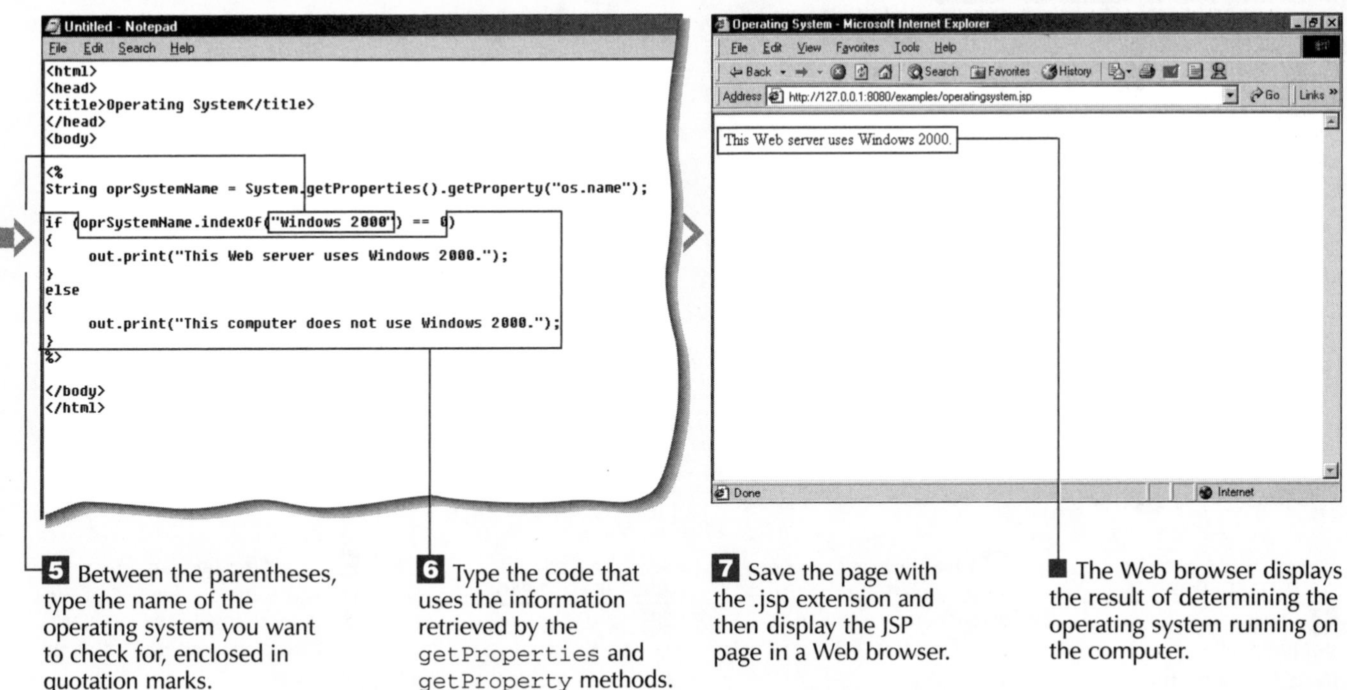

5 Between the parentheses, type the name of the operating system you want to check for, enclosed in quotation marks.

6 Type the code that uses the information retrieved by the `getProperties` and `getProperty` methods.

7 Save the page with the .jsp extension and then display the JSP page in a Web browser.

■ The Web browser displays the result of determining the operating system running on the computer.

FORWARD TO ANOTHER JSP PAGE

The <jsp:forward> tag is used to instruct a Web server to stop processing the current JSP page and start processing another page. For example, when an error occurs during the processing of a JSP page, you can use the <jsp:forward> tag to transfer control to another JSP page that handles errors and displays help information for the user. The <jsp:forward> tag is also useful for transferring control to a different JSP page depending on the value of a variable, such as a user name or the time of day.

When using the <jsp:forward> tag, you assign a value to the `page` attribute. The value can be a string literal, a value generated by an expression or the relative path of the JSP page that control will be transferred to.

When the Web server processes a JSP page that contains a <jsp:forward> tag, the server stops processing the page and executes the code in the JSP page specified in the tag. The Web server does not return to the original page.

You should use the <jsp:forward> tag early in your code. No information should be sent to the client before the <jsp:forward> tag is executed or an error will be generated. Any data currently in the buffer when the <jsp:forward> tag is encountered will be deleted.

Any information available to the original JSP page will also be available to the JSP page that control is transferred to. Information available to the controlling JSP page includes application values, session values and any data stored in a `request` object, such as values submitted to a form. The JSP page control is transferred to can access this information even if the page is not part of the same application as the original JSP page.

FORWARD TO ANOTHER JSP PAGE

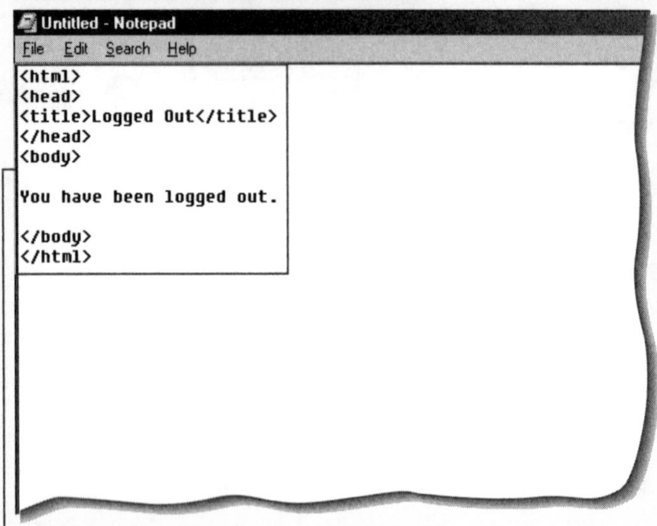

CREATE A JSP PAGE YOU WANT TO FORWARD TO

1 In a text editor, create the JSP page you want to transfer control to.

2 Save the page on the Web server with the .jsp extension.

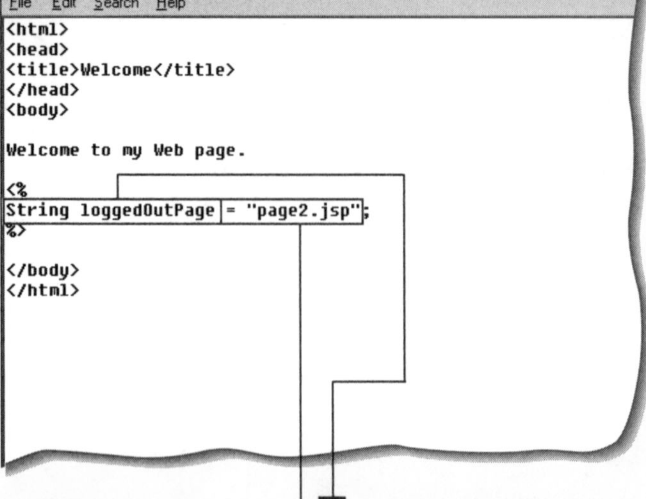

FORWARD TO ANOTHER JSP PAGE

1 Display the page in which you want to transfer control to another JSP page.

2 To create a variable that will store the parameter for the JSP page you want to transfer control to, type **String**, followed by a name for the variable.

3 Type = followed by a value for the variable, enclosed in quotation marks.

Extra

The <jsp:param> tag can be used to pass additional information to the request object before transferring control to the other JSP page. For example, you can use the <jsp:param> tag to create a parameter that stores the name of the page that forwarded the request object. This allows the page that will receive control to use the getParameter method of the request object to determine where the request object originated. The <jsp:param> tag is placed between the <jsp:forward> and the </jsp:forward> tags.

Type this in the original JSP page:

```
<jsp:forward page="logout.jsp">
<jsp:param name="callingPage" value="index.jsp"/>
</jsp:forward>
```

Type this in the page control is being transferred to:

```
You are now logged out.<br>
You have been forwarded to this page from the JSP page:<br>
<%= request.getParameter("callingPage") %>
```

Result:

You are now logged out.
You have been forwarded to this page from the JSP page:
index.jsp

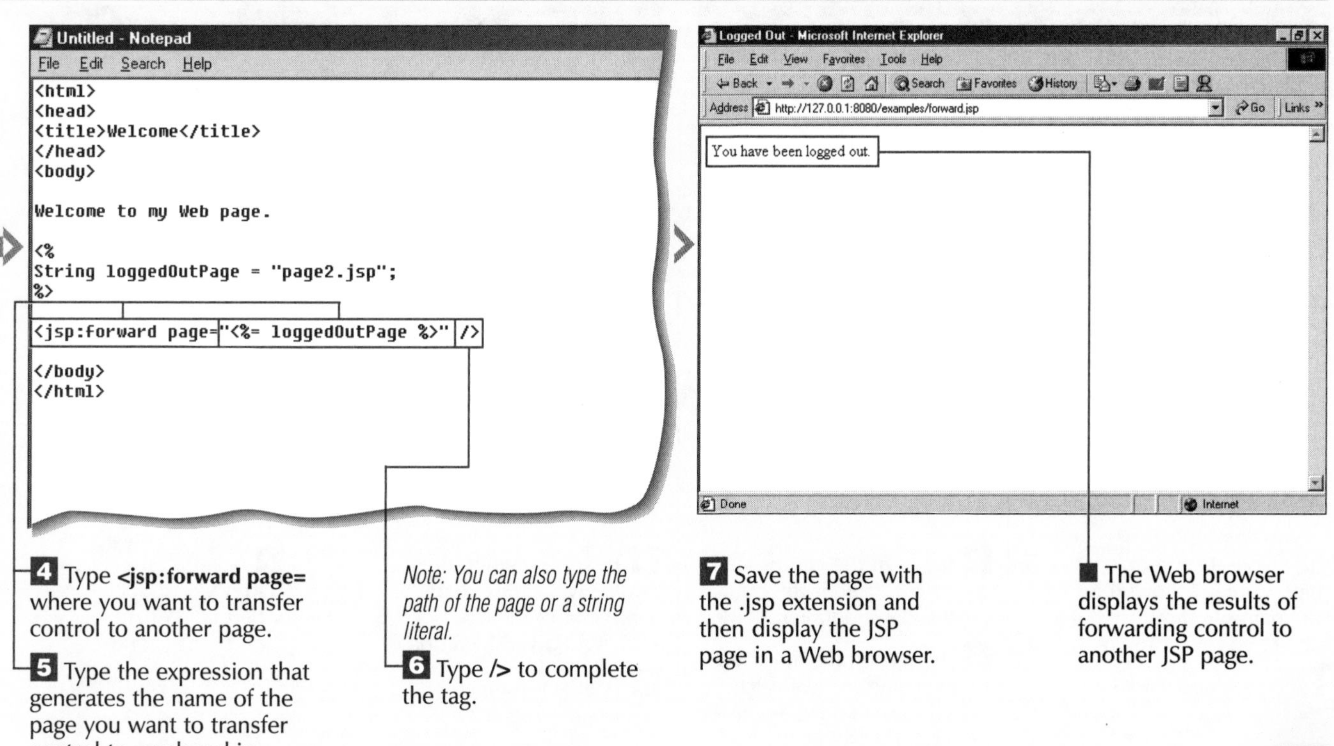

4 Type **<jsp:forward page=** where you want to transfer control to another page.

5 Type the expression that generates the name of the page you want to transfer control to, enclosed in quotation marks.

Note: You can also type the path of the page or a string literal.

6 Type **/>** to complete the tag.

7 Save the page with the .jsp extension and then display the JSP page in a Web browser.

■ The Web browser displays the results of forwarding control to another JSP page.

CREATE A COOKIE

You can create a cookie with your JSP page. When a user views the page, the cookie is stored as a small text file on the user's computer. Cookies are often used to personalize a JSP page. For example, a cookie can store a user's name. The next time the user accesses the JSP page, the page can use the value stored in the cookie to display the user's name.

A cookie consists of a key, which indicates the name of the cookie, and a value, which is the information stored in the cookie. To create a cookie, you must create a `Cookie` object and then assign the key and value of the cookie to the object.

You should also specify when the cookie will expire. By default, a cookie will be deleted when the user closes their Web browser. Setting an expiry time for a cookie allows the cookie to store information for longer periods of time. The `setMaxAge` method of the `Cookie` object is used to set the expiry time, in seconds, for a cookie.

The `setPath` method of the `Cookie` object allows you to specify a path for the cookie. Only the pages stored in the specified directory will be able to read the cookie.

When all of the cookie information has been set, the `addCookie` method of the `response` object is used to send the cookie information to a user's computer.

The scriptlet containing the code that creates the cookie should be placed before any other code on the JSP page. If HTML code is sent before the scriptlet, an error may occur.

After creating a cookie, you can have a JSP page read the cookie. For information about reading a cookie, see page 116.

CREATE A COOKIE

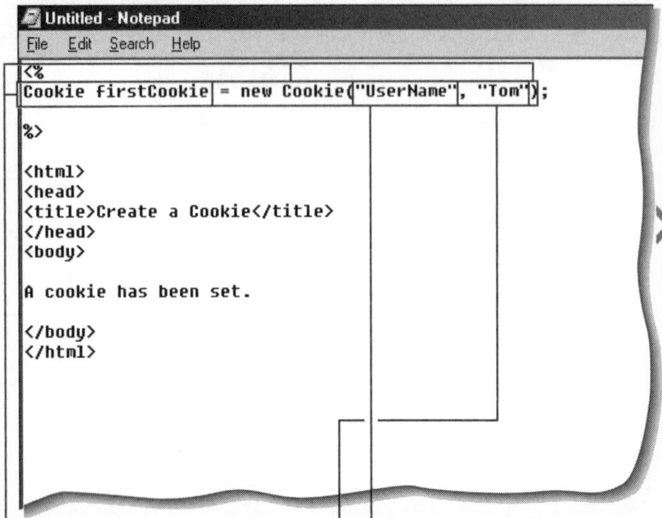

Untitled - Notepad

File Edit Search Help

```
<%
Cookie firstCookie = new Cookie("UserName", "Tom");

%>

<html>
<head>
<title>Create a Cookie</title>
</head>
<body>

A cookie has been set.

</body>
</html>
```

1 To create a cookie, type **Cookie** followed by the name of the `Cookie` object you want to create.

2 Type **= new Cookie()**.

3 Between the parentheses, type the name for the cookie enclosed in quotation marks.

4 Type a comma followed by the value you want to assign to the cookie enclosed in quotation marks.

Untitled - Notepad

File Edit Search Help

```
<%
Cookie firstCookie = new Cookie("UserName", "Tom");
firstCookie.setMaxAge(3600);

%>

<html>
<head>
<title>Create a Cookie</title>
</head>
<body>

A cookie has been set.

</body>
</html>
```

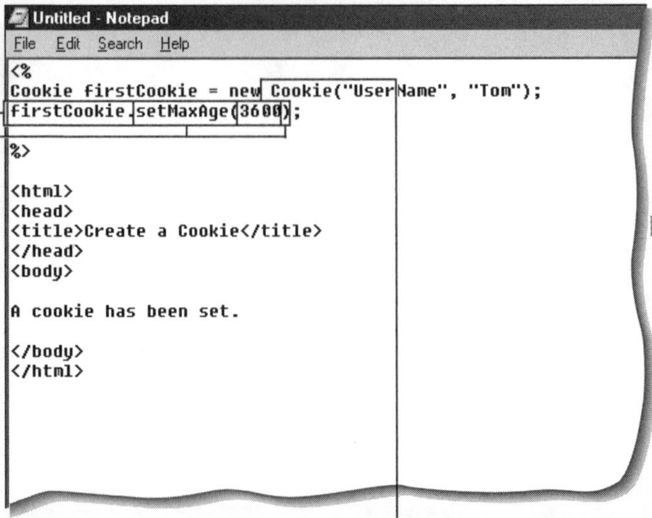

5 To specify when the cookie will expire, type the name of the `Cookie` object followed by a dot.

6 Type **setMaxAge()**.

7 Between the parentheses, specify when the cookie will expire, in seconds.

Extra

Although some people consider cookies to be a security risk, there has never been a report of a virus being transmitted by creating or reading a cookie. Cookies are text files, so unlike executable programs, they do not transmit viruses.

You can create many cookies to store information about a user, but keep in mind that Web browsers limit the number of cookies a Web site can store on a user's computer. Most Web browsers allow each domain to store a maximum of 20 cookies. Cookies created by your Web site should not exceed 4 KB in size.

The `setDomain` method of the `Cookie` object lets you specify the domain name that the cookies you create belong to. When used with the `setPath` method, the `setDomain` method increases the security of cookies you create by preventing unauthorized JSP pages from accessing the cookies.

Example:

```
myCookie.setDomain("www.abccorp.com");
myCookie.setPath("/jsppages");
```

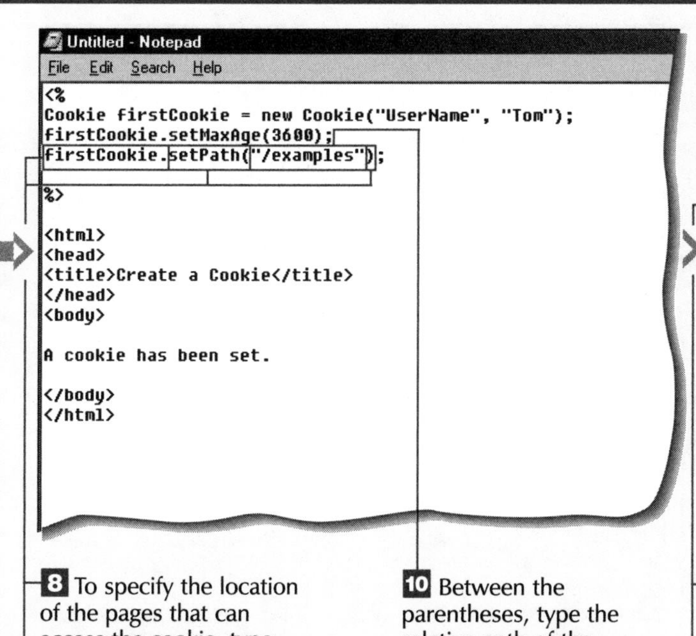

8 To specify the location of the pages that can access the cookie, type the name of the `Cookie` object followed by a dot.

9 Type **setPath()**.

10 Between the parentheses, type the relative path of the JSP pages enclosed in quotation marks.

```
<%
Cookie firstCookie = new Cookie("UserName", "Tom");
firstCookie.setMaxAge(3600);
firstCookie.setPath("/examples");
response.addCookie(firstCookie);
%>

<html>
<head>
<title>Create a Cookie</title>
</head>
<body>

A cookie has been set.

</body>
</html>
```

11 To send the cookie to a user's computer, type **response.addCookie()**.

12 Between the parentheses, type the name of the `Cookie` object.

13 Save the page with the .jsp extension.

■ When a user accesses the JSP page, the cookie will be stored on the user's computer. To read the cookie information, see page 116.

READ A COOKIE

A JSP page can read a cookie stored on a user's computer. Reading a cookie allows the page to access the information in the cookie, such as the user's name or location.

When a user visits a JSP page that sets a cookie, the cookie is stored as a small text file on the user's computer. The location where a cookie is stored depends on the type of Web browser being used.

The `getCookies` method of the `request` object is used to read all the cookies that can be accessed by your JSP page. You can create an array to store all the cookie information retrieved from a user's computer and then access the specific cookie information you want.

The array element with an index number of 0 contains the information for the first cookie stored on a user's computer. If the server has session tracking enabled, the first cookie in the array may contain information about the session ID. You may need to access the next array element to read the other cookie values. For information about reading multiple cookies, see page 118.

Once the cookies have been retrieved from a user's computer, you use the `getName` and `getValue` methods to retrieve the name and value stored in a cookie. The `getName` and `getValue` methods return string values. You can use an expression to display the name and value returned by the methods in the JSP page.

When working with cookies, keep in mind that a Web browser may be configured to reject cookies or may be located behind a security firewall that filters out cookie information. In such cases, you will not be able to read a cookie on a user's computer.

READ A COOKIE

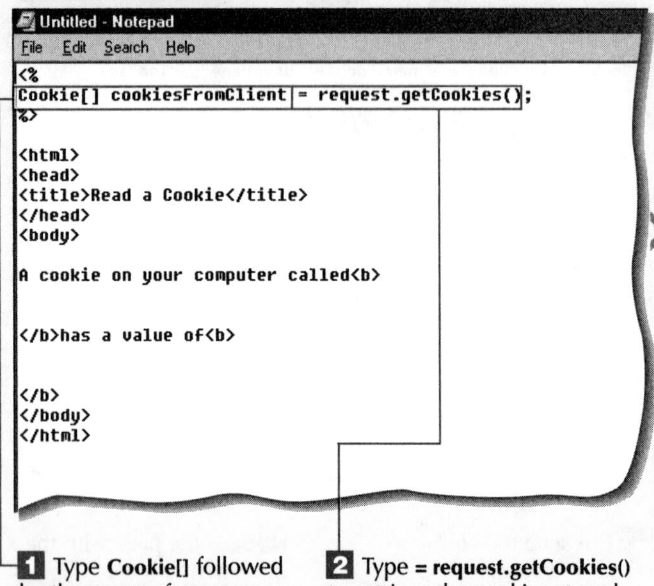

1 Type **Cookie[]** followed by the name of an array you want to use to store all the cookies on a user's computer.

2 Type **= request.getCookies()** to retrieve the cookies stored on a user's computer and place the values in the array.

Untitled - Notepad

File Edit Search Help

```
<%
Cookie[] cookiesFromClient = request.getCookies();
%>

<html>
<head>
<title>Read a Cookie</title>
</head>
<body>

A cookie on your computer called<b>
<%= cookiesFromClient[0].getName() %>
</b>has a value of<b>


</b>
</body>
</html>
```

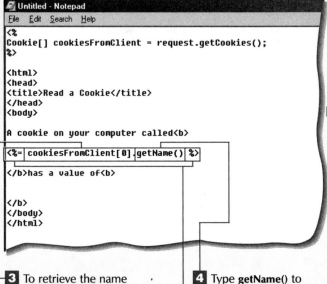

3 To retrieve the name of the cookie stored in the first element of the array, type the name of the array followed by **[0]** and a dot.

4 Type **getName()** to retrieve the name.

5 Type the code that uses the name of the cookie.

Extra

To verify that at least one cookie exists, you can use the `length` method to check if the array of `Cookie` objects contains any information. An error may occur if you attempt to access elements of an array that do not exist.

Example:

```
<%
if (cookiesFromClient.length > 0)
{
      out.print("Name:");
      out.print(cookiesFromClient[0].getName());
      out.print("<br>Value:");
      out.print(cookiesFromClient[0].getValue());
}
%>
```

The `equals` method allows you to evaluate a string value so you can then perform an action based on the evaluation. This is useful for working with the names and values of cookies returned by the `getName` and `getValue` methods. For example, you can compare the value of a cookie returned from a user's computer to a string you specify and display a customized message depending on the value.

Example:

```
<%
if (cookiesFromClient[0].getName().equals("beenHere") &&
          cookiesFromClient[0].getValue().equals("yes"))
    out.print("Welcome Back!");
else
    out.print("Welcome to my Web site.");
%>
```

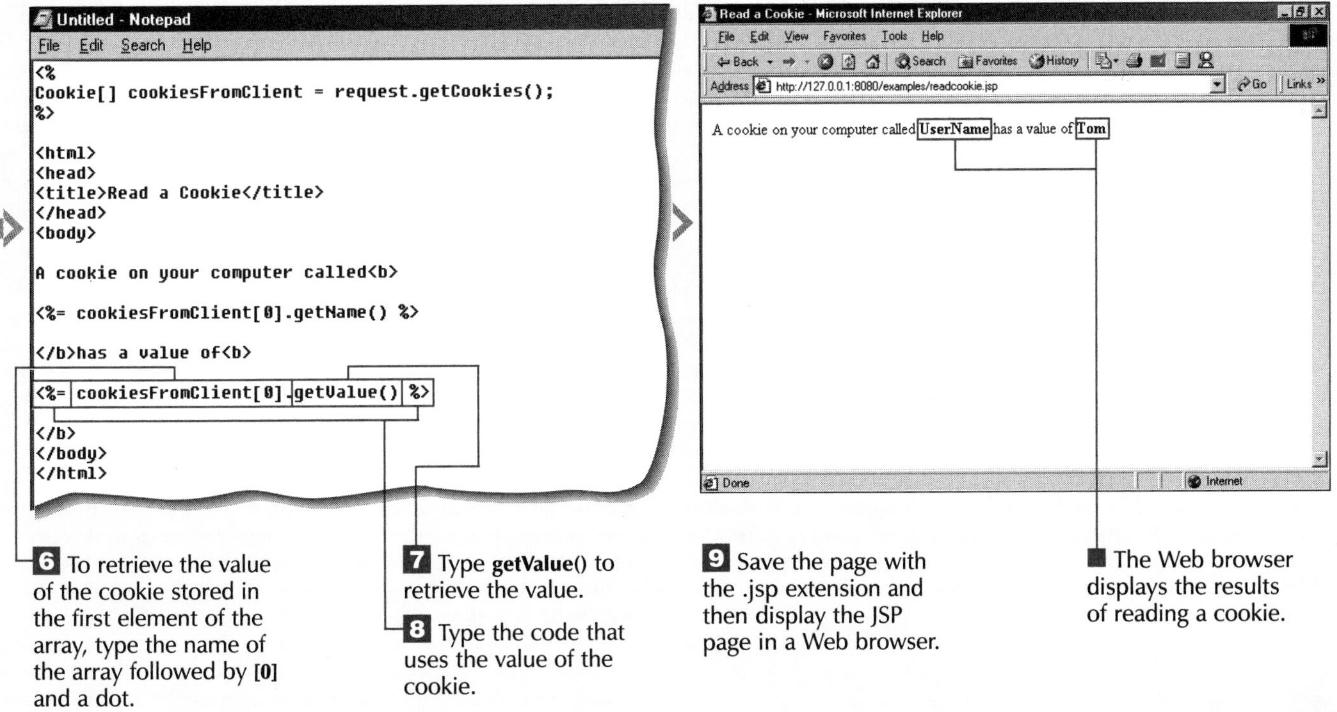

6 To retrieve the value of the cookie stored in the first element of the array, type the name of the array followed by **[0]** and a dot.

7 Type **getValue()** to retrieve the value.

8 Type the code that uses the value of the cookie.

9 Save the page with the .jsp extension and then display the JSP page in a Web browser.

■ The Web browser displays the results of reading a cookie.

READ MULTIPLE VALUES FROM A COOKIE

The getCookies method of the request object is used to retrieve all the cookies stored on a user's computer and returns an array of Cookie objects. After the cookies have been assigned to an array, the length method can be used to determine the number of elements in the array, which allows you to determine the number of cookies retrieved from the user's computer.

Keep in mind that some users may have disabled the exchange of cookies on their Web browsers. This is often done out of concern for privacy. Since no cookies can be stored on the user's computer, any attempt to read a cookie will indicate that no cookies exist and may result in an error. You should also keep in mind that you will not be able to retrieve a cookie from a user's computer if the cookie has reached its expiry time. If no cookies exist on the user's computer, the value returned by the length method will be 0.

Once it has been determined that cookies exist, a loop can then be used to examine each cookie and retrieve the names and values of the cookies.

Even if no cookies have been explicitly stored on a user's computer from a JSP page, there may still be cookies available to read, such as the cookie that stores the session ID. For information about the session ID, see page 96.

If your Web server uses JSP in combination with other technologies, such as ASP and PHP, your JSP pages will also be able to read the cookies created by ASP and PHP pages.

READ MULTIPLE VALUES FROM A COOKIE

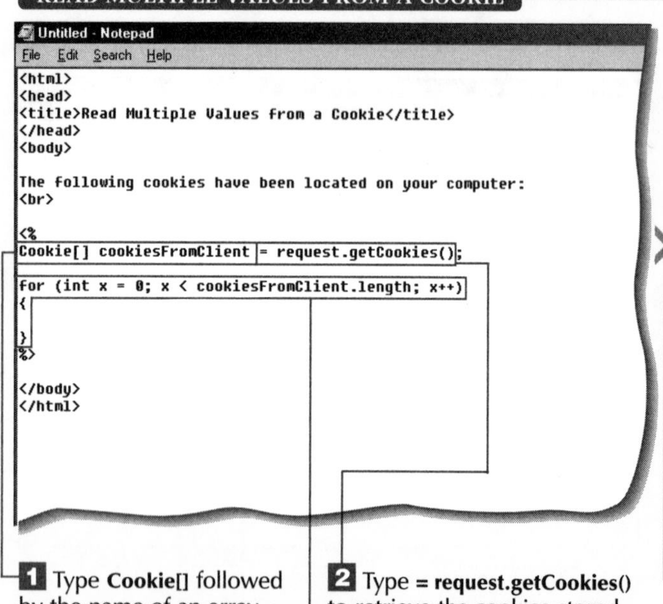

1 Type **Cookie[]** followed by the name of an array you want to use to store all the cookies on a user's computer.

2 Type **= request.getCookies()** to retrieve the cookies stored on a user's computer and place the values in the array.

3 Type the code to create a loop that will cycle through all the elements in the array. For information about creating a for loop, see page 42.

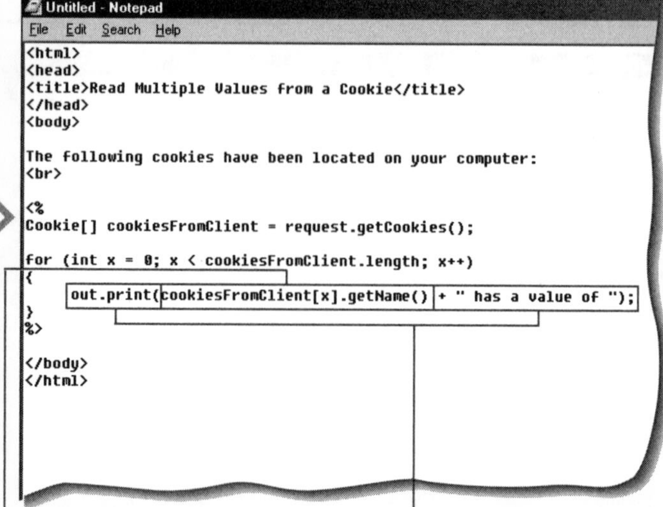

4 To retrieve the name of a cookie stored in an element of the array, type the name of the array followed by **[x].getName()**.

5 Type the code that uses the name of the cookie.

Extra

Any information retrieved from a cookie should be validated before it is used. For example, if you are reading a ZIP code from a cookie, you may want to check that the ZIP code contains the proper number of digits and does not contain any letters. Since invalid data may cause an error during the processing of the JSP page, you may want to add code to handle invalid cookie values passed to your JSP page.

When creating multiple cookies, you need to create a new `Cookie` object for each cookie you want to set. Even though multiple cookies are being created, only one cookie file will be created on the user's computer.

Example:

```
<%
Cookie firstCookie  = new Cookie("UserName", "Tom");
firstCookie.setMaxAge(3600);
firstCookie.setPath("/examples");
response.addCookie(firstCookie);

Cookie secondCookie  = new Cookie("UserAge", "26");
secondCookie.setMaxAge(3600);
secondCookie.setPath("/examples");
response.addCookie(secondCookie);
%>
```

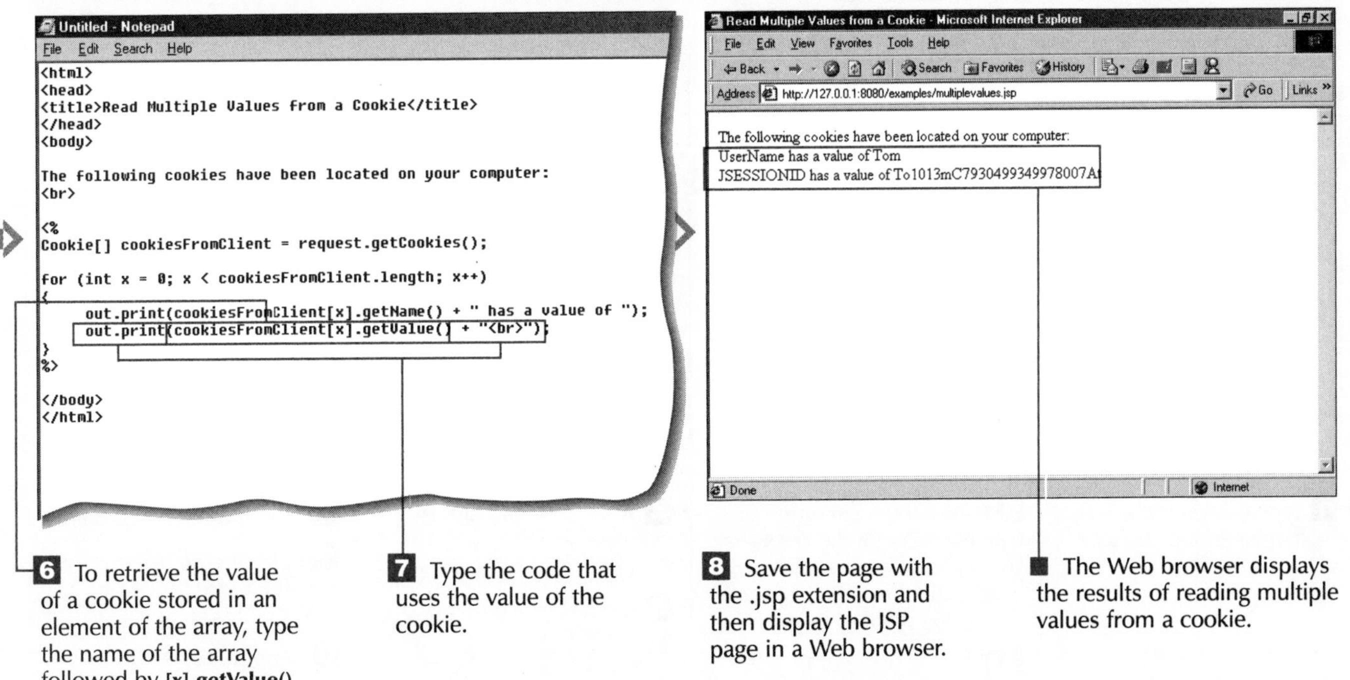

6 To retrieve the value of a cookie stored in an element of the array, type the name of the array followed by **[x].getValue()**.

7 Type the code that uses the value of the cookie.

8 Save the page with the .jsp extension and then display the JSP page in a Web browser.

■ The Web browser displays the results of reading multiple values from a cookie.

REMOVE A COOKIE

JavaServer Pages allows you to delete a cookie before it expires. This is useful if you no longer need the information in the cookie. For example, you may want to delete a cookie that contains user registration information if the user cancels their registration to your Web site. It may also be necessary to remove cookies if the size of your cookies exceeds the size limit for cookies in your Web site, which is usually 4 KB.

To remove a cookie, you create a new cookie with the same name as the cookie you want to remove, except you set the expiry time for the new cookie to zero seconds. This will cause the cookie to expire immediately. The value you assign to the cookie can be an empty string. If you specified a path when you created the original cookie, you should also specify the same path when deleting the cookie to ensure that the correct cookie is removed. For more information about creating a cookie, see page 114.

Working with cookies is not always a simple task. While almost all Web browsers accept cookies, many Web browsers may return different information about cookies, such as different version numbers. Web servers and JSP engines also do not always work with cookies in the same way. For example, some Web servers will not allow a cookie to be removed from the client computer until the cookie reaches its original expiry time. When creating JSP code to work with cookies, you should thoroughly test your code on all Web browsers and client software you expect to access your JSP page.

REMOVE A COOKIE

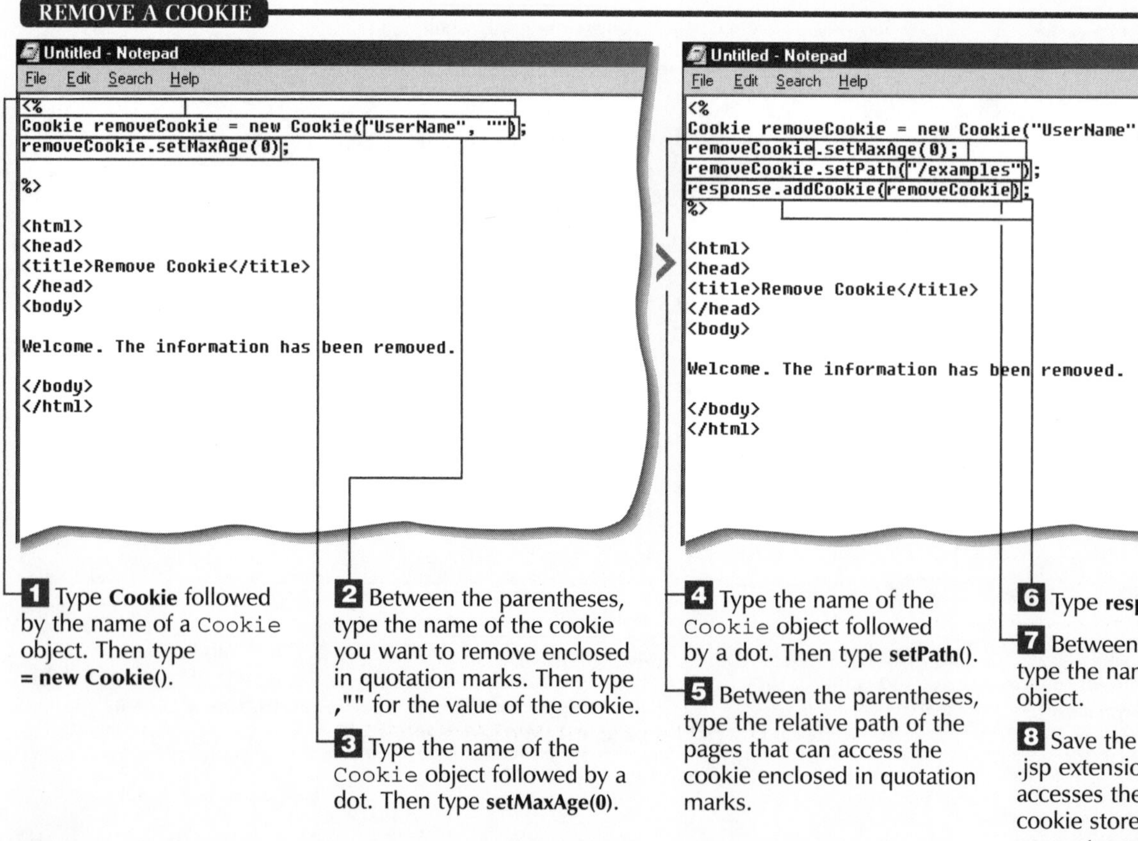

1 Type **Cookie** followed by the name of a `Cookie` object. Then type **= new Cookie()**.

2 Between the parentheses, type the name of the cookie you want to remove enclosed in quotation marks. Then type ,"" for the value of the cookie.

3 Type the name of the `Cookie` object followed by a dot. Then type **setMaxAge(0)**.

4 Type the name of the `Cookie` object followed by a dot. Then type **setPath()**.

5 Between the parentheses, type the relative path of the pages that can access the cookie enclosed in quotation marks.

6 Type **response.addCookie()**.

7 Between the parentheses, type the name of the `Cookie` object.

8 Save the page with the .jsp extension. When a user accesses the JSP page, the cookie stored on the user's computer will be deleted.

COOKIE METHODS

There are several useful methods of the `Cookie` object that you can use to manipulate and examine the contents of a cookie. Before using any of the following methods in your JSP code, you should check your Web server documentation to verify whether the Web server supports the method you want to use.

Method	Description
`Object` **`clone()`**	Overrides the standard `java.lang.Object.clone()` method to create a copy of the cookie.
`void` **`setComment`** `(String purpose)`	Includes a comment that describes the purpose of the cookie.
`String` **`getComment()`**	Returns a comment. Returns `null` if there is no comment.
`void` **`setDomain`** `(String pattern)`	Specifies the domain or server that the cookie belongs to.
`String` **`getDomain()`**	Returns the domain name for the cookie.
`void` **`setMaxAge`** `(int expiry)`	Specifies the expiry time of the cookie, in seconds. By default, a cookie will expire when the Web browser shuts down.
`int` **`getMaxAge()`**	Returns the expiry time of the cookie, in seconds. Returns `-1` if no expiry time was specified.
`String` **`getName()`**	Returns the name assigned to the cookie.
`void` **`setPath`** `(String uri)`	Specifies the location of the pages on the Web server that can access the cookie.
`String` **`getPath()`**	Returns the location of the pages on the Web server that can access the cookie.
`void` **`setSecure`** `(boolean flag)`	Specifies whether the Web browser needs to send the cookie using a secure protocol, such as HTTPS or SSL.
`boolean` **`getSecure()`**	Returns `true` if the Web browser must send the cookie over a secure protocol.
`void` **`setValue`** `(String newValue)`	Sets or changes the value for the cookie.
`String` **`getValue()`**	Returns the value assigned to the cookie.
`void` **`setVersion`** `(int v)`	Specifies the version number of the cookie protocol.
`int` **`getVersion()`**	Returns the version number of the protocol the cookie can use.

CREATE A JAVABEAN

A JavaBean is a class file that stores Java code for a JSP page. Although you can use a scriptlet to place Java code directly into a JSP page, it is considered better programming practice to store the code in a JavaBean.

JavaBeans offer several advantages. Using a JavaBean allows you to keep the Java code for a JSP page separate from the HTML code for the page, which can help keep the code from becoming long and difficult to work with. In addition, one JavaBean can be used with multiple JSP pages, which saves you from having to retype the same Java code in several pages.

JavaBeans also enable specialization when developing a Web site. For example, experts in Web page design can work with the HTML content of a JSP page, while programmers develop the Java code that will make the page dynamic. This allows both types of professionals to concentrate on their own areas of expertise.

You create a JavaBean as you would create any class file. JavaBeans can contain one or more methods. After creating the Java source code for a JavaBean, you must compile the code.

Once the JavaBean code has been compiled, you must copy the JavaBean to the appropriate directory on your Web server. On the Tomcat Web server, JavaBeans are usually stored in a directory named classes. Consult the documentation for your Web server to determine which directory you should use to store your JavaBeans.

You can organize your JavaBeans by storing them in packages. A package is a set of related class files stored together in a directory. To create a package for your JavaBeans, create a subdirectory within the directory that stores JavaBeans on your Web server and then store your JavaBeans in that subdirectory. Packages you create for JavaBeans are similar to packages that store class files in the Java SDK. For information about creating packages in the Java SDK, see page 50.

CREATE A JAVABEAN

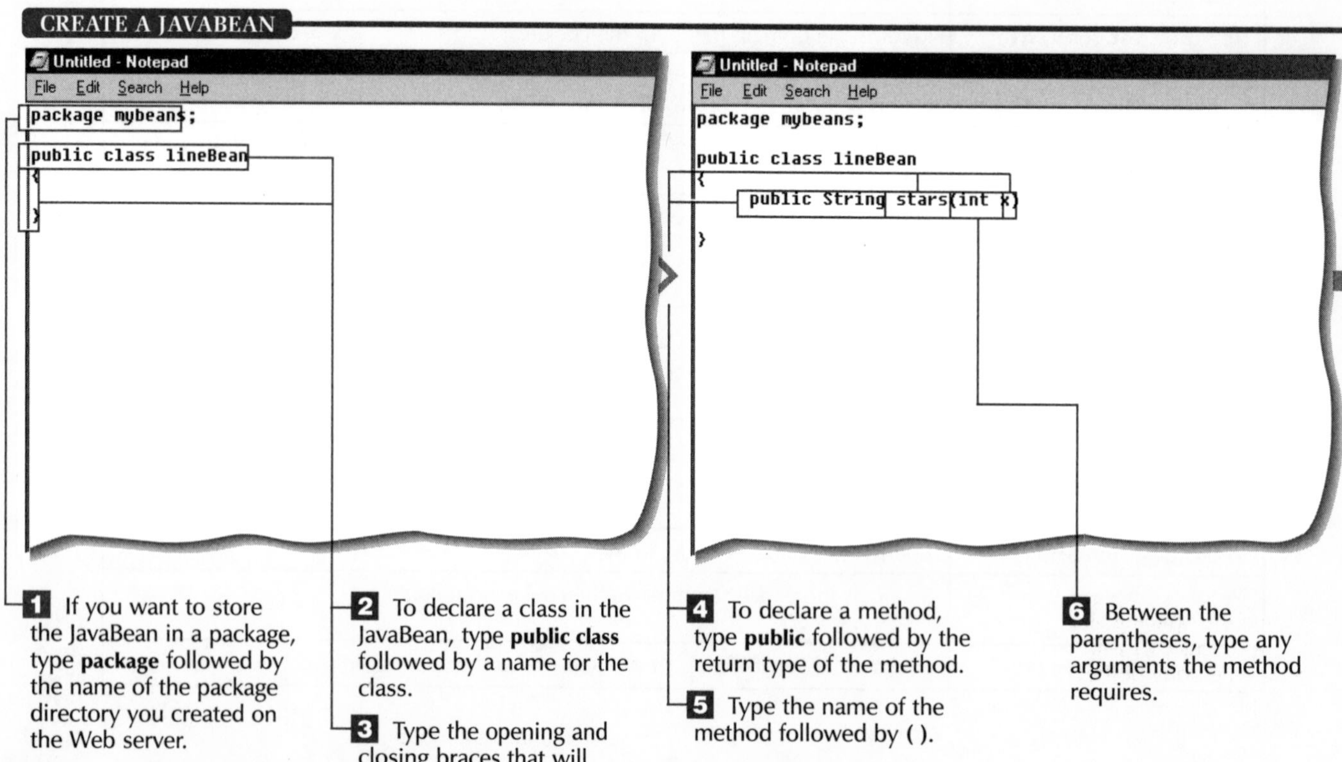

Untitled - Notepad
File Edit Search Help
package mybeans;
public class lineBean
{
}
Untitled - Notepad
File Edit Search Help
package mybeans;
public class lineBean
{
public String stars(int x)
}

1 If you want to store the JavaBean in a package, type **package** followed by the name of the package directory you created on the Web server.

2 To declare a class in the JavaBean, type **public class** followed by a name for the class.

3 Type the opening and closing braces that will contain the body of the class.

4 To declare a method, type **public** followed by the return type of the method.

5 Type the name of the method followed by **( )**.

6 Between the parentheses, type any arguments the method requires.

Extra

The JavaBeans you create for your JSP pages are platform independent. This means that a JavaBean created on a computer with a UNIX-based operating system, such as Linux, can be used on a computer running a different operating system, such as Windows.

There are many JavaBeans available on the Internet that you can use with your JSP pages. If you need a JavaBean to perform a specific task but do not want to create the JavaBean yourself, you may be able to purchase a ready-made JavaBean or have a programmer create a custom JavaBean according to your specifications.

JavaBeans were originally developed as a way for Java programmers to easily create and share re-usable portions of code for Java programs. If you want to create JavaBeans for use with your own stand-alone Java applications, you should obtain the Beans Development Kit (BDK). The BDK is available for download free of charge at the java.sun.com/products/javabeans Web site.

Integrated Development Environments (IDEs) are specialized programs used to create Java applications. Most Java IDEs can also be used to create JSP pages and JavaBeans. If you intend to create many JavaBeans for use with your JSP pages, you should consider purchasing an IDE.

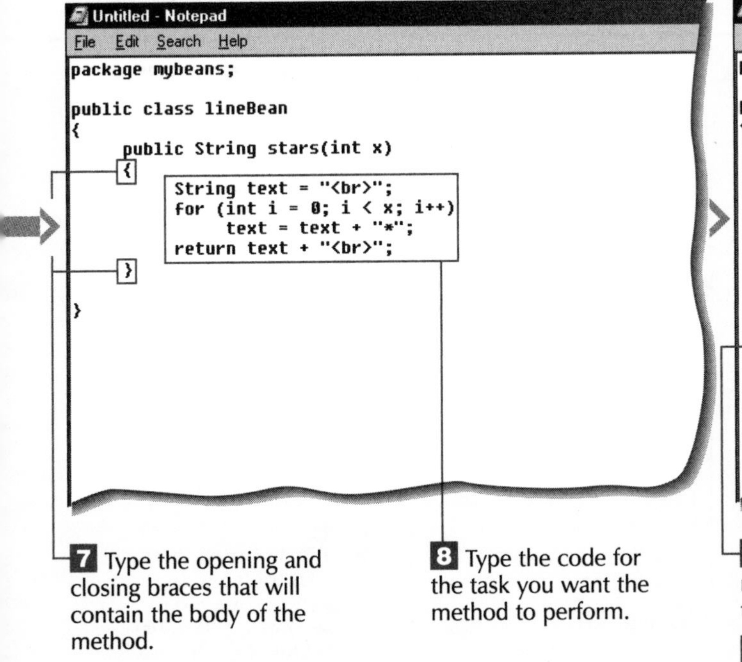
Untitled - Notepad
File Edit Search Help
package mybeans;
public class lineBean
{
public String stars(int x)
{
String text = "<br>";
for (int i = 0; i < x; i++)
text = text + "*";
return text + "<br>";
}
}

7 Type the opening and closing braces that will contain the body of the method.

8 Type the code for the task you want the method to perform.

Untitled - Notepad

File Edit Search Help

```
package mybeans;

public class lineBean
{
      public String stars(int x)
      {
            String text = "<br>";
            for (int i = 0; i < x; i++)
                  text = text + "*";
            return text + "<br>";
      }
      public String doubleLine(int x)
      {
            String text = "<br>";
            for (int i = 0; i < x; i++)
                  text = text + "=";
            return text + "<br>";
      }
}
```

9 Repeat steps 4 to 8 for each method you want the JavaBean to contain.

10 Save the file with the .java extension and then compile the source code for the file. For information about compiling Java code, see page 20.

11 Copy the compiled class file to the appropriate directory on your Web server.

■ You can now set up a JSP page to use the JavaBean.

SET UP A JSP PAGE TO USE A JAVABEAN

Once you have created a JavaBean, you can use the `<jsp:useBean>` tag to set up a JSP page to access the JavaBean.

The `<jsp:useBean>` tag associates the JSP page with a specific JavaBean. This tag has several attributes that you must use in order to ensure that the correct JavaBean is used and that the JSP page can access the JavaBean. The `class` attribute allows you to specify the full class name of the JavaBean you want the JSP page to use. If the JavaBean is stored in a package, the full name will consist of the name of the package and the name of the class, separated by a dot.

The `id` attribute allows you to specify a case-sensitive name that identifies the JavaBean instance. If an instance of the JavaBean already exists, the `id` attribute identifies the instance. If the JavaBean does not already exist, a new instance is created.

The `scope` attribute allows you to specify when the JavaBean instance will be available. If you want the JavaBean instance to be available to a client only on the page in which the instance is created, you can specify the `page` value. This is the default value of the `scope` attribute. The `request` value allows you to make the JavaBean instance accessible to a client during a single request.

The `session` and `application` values of the `scope` attribute allow you to make a JavaBean available within any JSP page in the application. The `session` attribute makes the JavaBean available to a single client for the duration of the session, while the `application` attribute makes the JavaBean available to multiple clients for the duration of the application.

SET UP A JSP PAGE TO USE A JAVABEAN

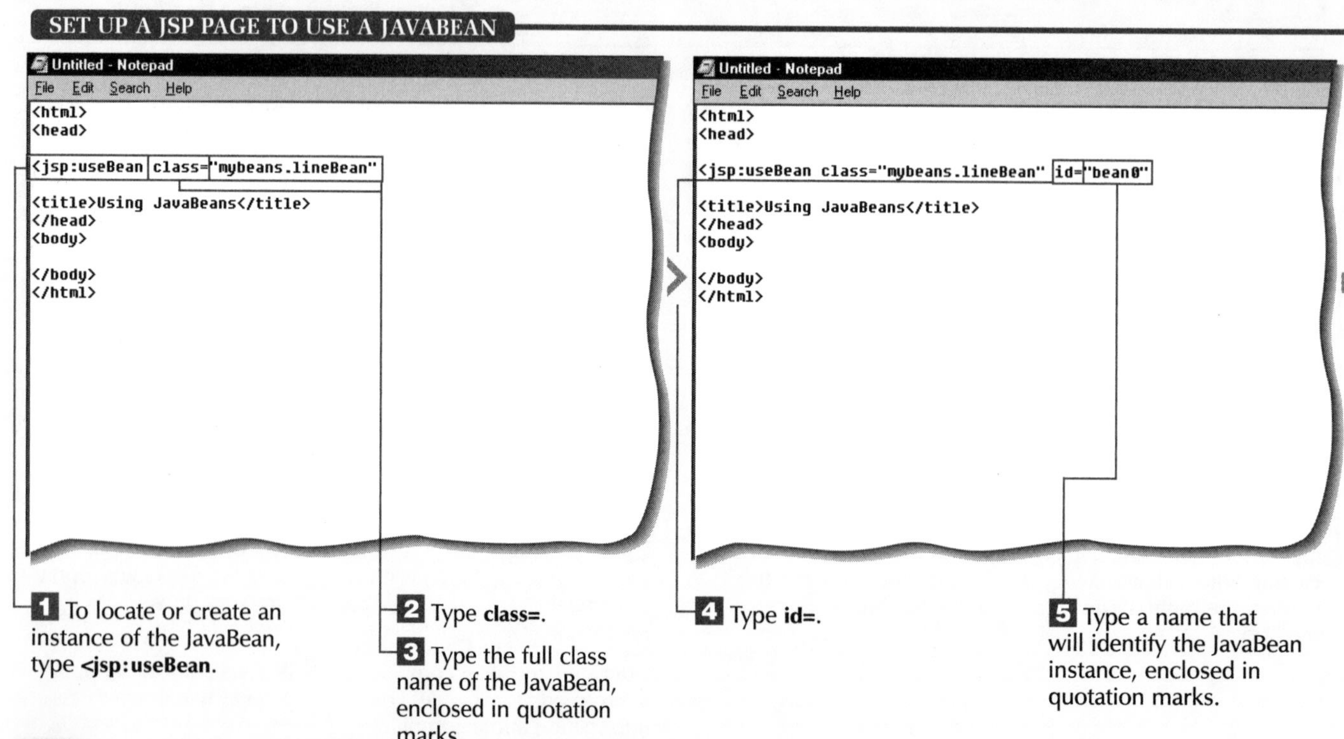

Untitled - Notepad
File Edit Search Help
<html>
<head>
<jsp:useBean class="mybeans.lineBean"
<title>Using JavaBeans</title>
</head>
<body>
</body>
</html>
Untitled - Notepad
File Edit Search Help
<html>
<head>
<jsp:useBean class="mybeans.lineBean" id="bean0"
<title>Using JavaBeans</title>
</head>
<body>
</body>
</html>

1 To locate or create an instance of the JavaBean, type **<jsp:useBean**.

2 Type **class=**.

3 Type the full class name of the JavaBean, enclosed in quotation marks.

4 Type **id=**.

5 Type a name that will identify the JavaBean instance, enclosed in quotation marks.

Extra

When the JSP engine encounters the <jsp:useBean> tag, it uses the information specified in the tag to locate or create an instance of the JavaBean. If an instance already exists, the <jsp:useBean> tag is not processed. To ensure that code is processed only if a new instance of a JavaBean is created, you can place the code between an opening <jsp:useBean> tag and a closing </jsp:useBean> tag. For example, using the <jsp:setProperty> tag between the <jsp:useBean> tags allows you to initialize properties only when a new instance of the JavaBean is created.

Example:

```
<jsp:useBean class="mybeans.lineBean" id="lineBeanId" scope="session">
     <jsp:setProperty name="lineBeanId" property="counter" value="0" />
</jsp:useBean>
```

When creating an instance of a JavaBean, the <jsp:useBean> tag may insert an additional method into the JavaBean instance that does not exist in the original JavaBean. This method, called a constructor, is a special method that has the same name as the class and is processed when the JavaBean instance is first created. Constructors are often used to initialize values. It is good programming practice to include a constructor in your JavaBean code, even if you do not plan to use the constructor. If a JavaBean does not include a constructor, the <jsp:useBean> tag will automatically create an empty constructor for you.

Example:

```
public void lineBean
{
}
```

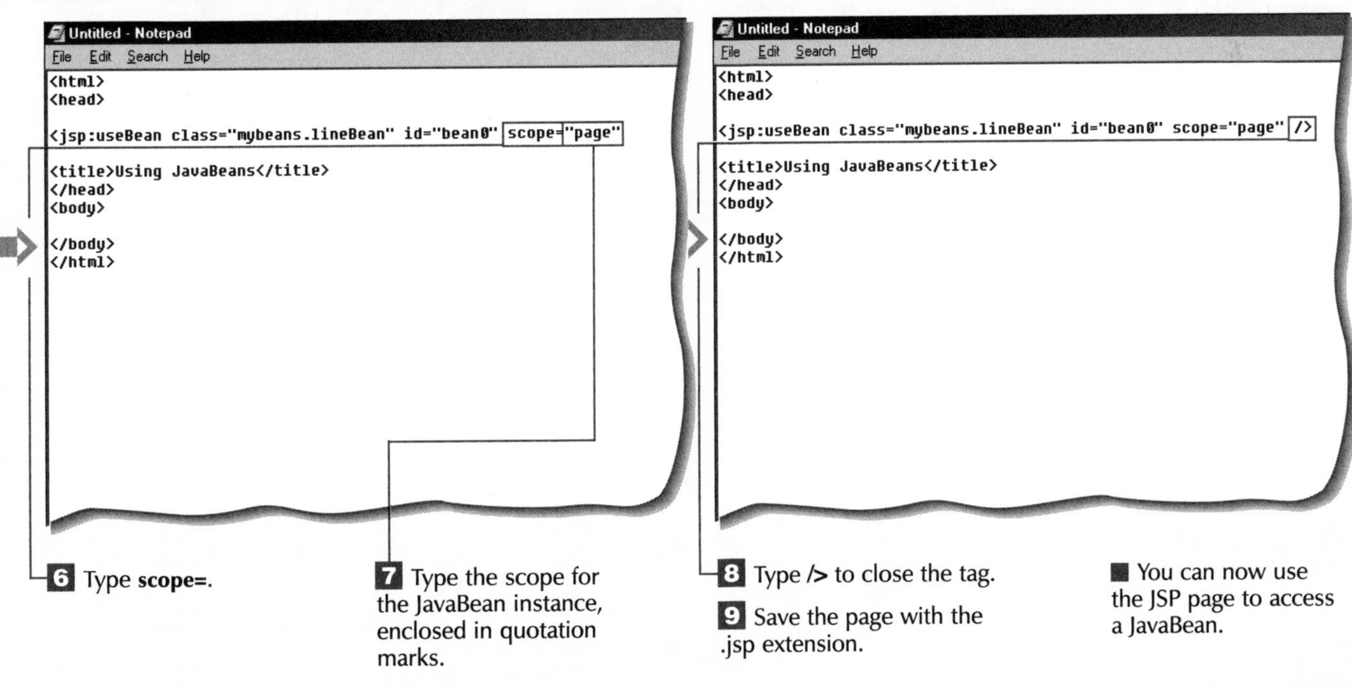
Untitled - Notepad
File Edit Search Help
<html>
<head>
<jsp:useBean class="mybeans.lineBean" id="bean0" scope="page"
<title>Using JavaBeans</title>
</head>
<body>
</body>
</html>
Untitled - Notepad
File Edit Search Help
<html>
<head>
<jsp:useBean class="mybeans.lineBean" id="bean0" scope="page" />
<title>Using JavaBeans</title>
</head>
<body>
</body>
</html>

6 Type **scope=**.

7 Type the scope for the JavaBean instance, enclosed in quotation marks.

8 Type **/>** to close the tag.

9 Save the page with the .jsp extension.

■ You can now use the JSP page to access a JavaBean.

ACCESS A JAVABEAN METHOD

Once you have created a JavaBean, you can add the code that will access the methods in the JavaBean to your JSP page.

Before accessing a JavaBean method, you must add the `<jsp:useBean>` tag to the JSP page. This tag and its attributes ensure that the correct JavaBean will be used and that the JSP page has access to the JavaBean. For more information about setting up a JSP page to use a JavaBean, see page 124.

To access a method in a JavaBean, you create a scriptlet that includes the name of the JavaBean, followed by the name of the method you want to call. The name of the JavaBean is specified in the `id` attribute of the `<jsp:useBean>` tag. The name is case-sensitive and must be typed in the code that calls the method exactly as it was typed in the tag.

You can also include any arguments that the method may require in the scriptlet. If a method returns a result that can be displayed on a JSP page, you can use an expression to display the returned value.

Prior to accessing a method in a JavaBean, you should make sure that the JavaBean source code you created has been compiled and that the Web server has access to the JavaBean class files. JavaBeans are usually stored in a directory called classes on the server. For example, when using a Tomcat Web server, you must save the class files in the classes subdirectory of the main Tomcat directory. If the classes subdirectory does not exist, you should create the subdirectory. To determine which directory you should use to store your JavaBeans, consult the documentation for your Web server.

ACCESS A JAVABEAN METHOD

Untitled - Notepad

File Edit Search Help

```
<html>
<head>

<jsp:useBean class="mybeans.lineBean" id="bean0" scope="page" />

<title>Access JavaBean Methods</title>
</head>
<body>

Welcome to my Web page

<%= bean0.doubleLine(30) %>

</body>
</html>
```

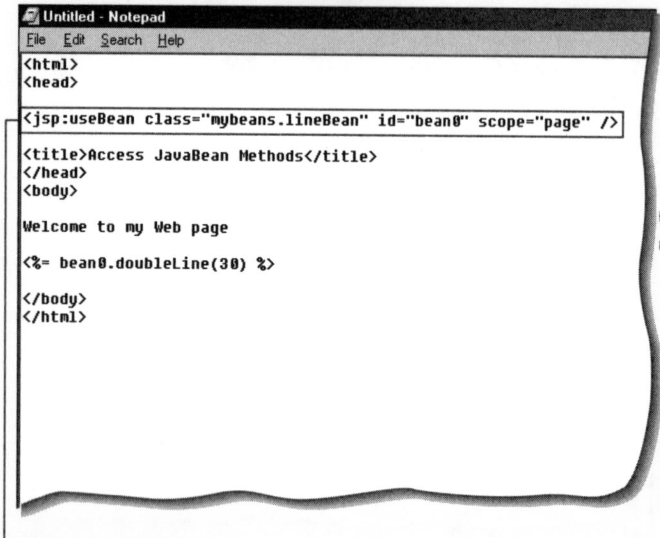

1 Type the code that sets up the JSP page to use a JavaBean.

Untitled - Notepad

File Edit Search Help

```
<html>
<head>

<jsp:useBean class="mybeans.lineBean" id="bean0" scope="page" />

<title>Access JavaBean Methods</title>
</head>
<body>

bean0.stars()

Welcome to my Web page

<%= bean0.doubleLine(30) %>

</body>
</html>
```

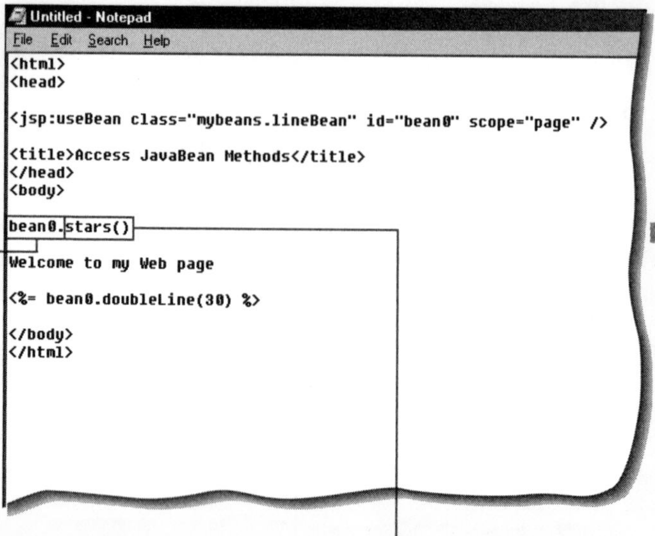

2 To access a method in the JavaBean, type the name of the JavaBean followed by a dot.

■ The name of the JavaBean must be the same as the value assigned to the `id` attribute of the `<jsp:useBean>` tag in step 1.

3 Type the name of the method you want to access, followed by a set of parentheses.

One of the features of JavaBeans is its ability to access methods that share the same name but accept different data types as arguments, referred to as method overloading. For example, you can create two methods with the same name, but one method may use an `int` data type as an argument and the other method may use a `String` data type.

To create a JavaBean, type:

```
public String stars(int x)
{
     String text = "<br>";
     for (int i = 0; i < x; i++)
          text = text + "*";
     return text + "<br>";
}
public String stars(String x)
{
     return "<br>* * " + x +  " * *<br>";
}
```

To use the methods declared in the JavaBean, type:

```
<%= lineBeanId.stars(30) %>
<%= lineBeanId.stars("Welcome") %>
```

Result:

```
******************************

* * Welcome * *
```

```
<html>
<head>

<jsp:useBean class="mybeans.lineBean" id="bean0" scope="page" />

<title>Access JavaBean Methods</title>
</head>
<body>

<%= bean0.stars(20) %>

Welcome to my Web page

<%= bean0.doubleLine(30) %>

</body>
</html>
```

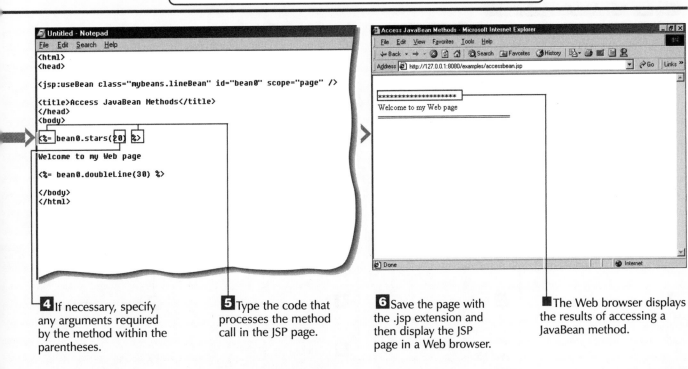

4 If necessary, specify any arguments required by the method within the parentheses.

5 Type the code that processes the method call in the JSP page.

6 Save the page with the .jsp extension and then display the JSP page in a Web browser.

■ The Web browser displays the results of accessing a JavaBean method.

CREATE A JAVABEAN PROPERTY

You can create a property to store information about a JavaBean. Properties are fields that define the behavior of a JavaBean.

After creating the code for a JavaBean, you can specify a property you want the JavaBean to contain. To do so, you specify the data type of the value the property will store and a name for the property. You can then create a method that assigns the property an initial value.

JavaBean properties are private or protected fields, which means they cannot be directly accessed by a JSP page. In order to access the value of a property, you must create a special method, called a getter method. A getter method, also referred to as an accessor method, returns the value of a property.

There are specific rules that must be followed when declaring a getter method. The access modifier of the method must be set to `public` and the data type of the value to be returned must be specified. The name of the method is the same as the name of the property, but begins with a capital letter and is prefixed by the word `get`. For example, if you want to return the value of the loginTime property, you would create a getter method called getLoginTime. The name of a getter method is followed by parentheses.

The body of a getter method includes a `return` statement that specifies the name of the property whose value you want to return.

When you finish creating the JavaBean source code, you must compile the code and store the resulting class file in the appropriate directory on your Web server. If you are using the Tomcat Web server, the class file should be saved in the classes directory located in the main Tomcat directory. If the JavaBean is part of a package, the class file would be stored in the appropriate package directory within the classes directory.

CREATE A JAVABEAN PROPERTY

Untitled - Notepad

File Edit Search Help

```
package mybeans;

public class lineBean
{

     private byte lineRepeat;

     public String dividers()
     {
          String htmlCode = "";

          for (int x = 0; x < lineRepeat; x++)
          htmlCode = htmlCode + "<hr>";

          return htmlCode;
     }

}
```

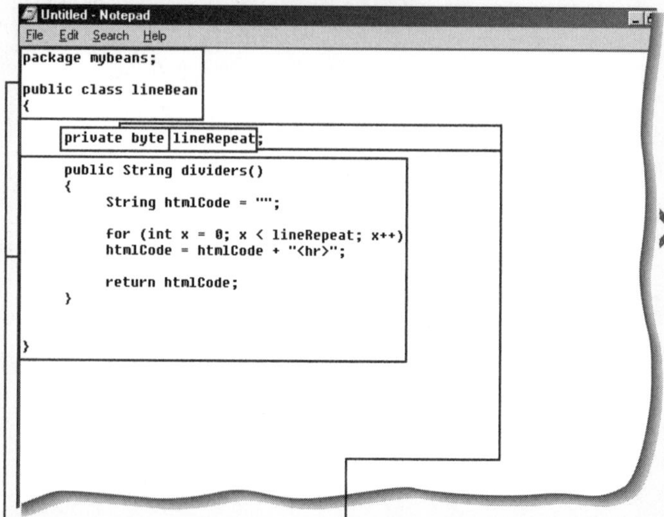

1 Type the code that creates a JavaBean. For information about creating a JavaBean, see page 122.

2 To create a property for the JavaBean, type **private** followed by the data type of the value the property will store.

3 Type a name for the property.

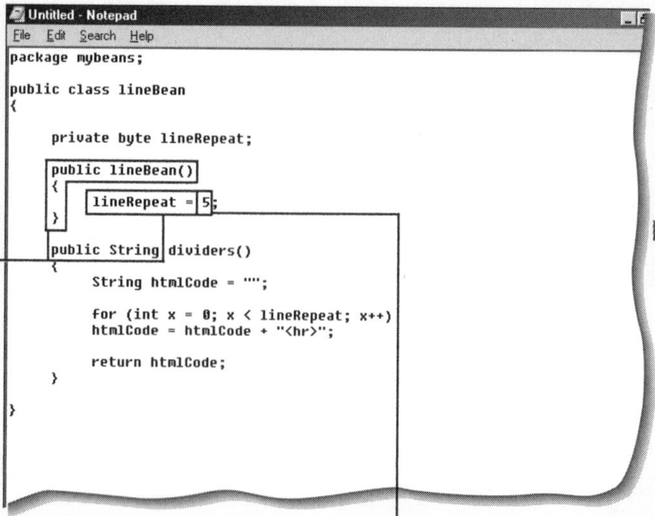

Untitled - Notepad

File Edit Search Help

```
package mybeans;

public class lineBean
{

     private byte lineRepeat;

     public lineBean()
     {
          lineRepeat = 5;
     }

     public String dividers()
     {
          String htmlCode = "";

          for (int x = 0; x < lineRepeat; x++)
          htmlCode = htmlCode + "<hr>";

          return htmlCode;
     }

}
```

4 Declare a method to assign the property an initial value.

5 In the body of the method, type the name of the property followed by **=**.

6 Type an initial value for the property.

Extra

A getter method can be used to return various types of data, including a boolean value of true or false. When declaring a getter method that returns a boolean value, the method name can be prefixed by `is` instead of `get`. This can help make your code easier to read and understand. If you choose to use `is` when returning a boolean value, you should do so consistently throughout your code.

For example:

```
public boolean getJobStatus()
    {
        return jobStatus;
    }
```

Can be typed as:

```
public boolean isJobStatus()
    {
        return jobStatus;
    }
```

You should declare the method that assigns a property an initial value in the body of the class. If you declare the method elsewhere, such as in another method, the getter method may not be able to access the value.

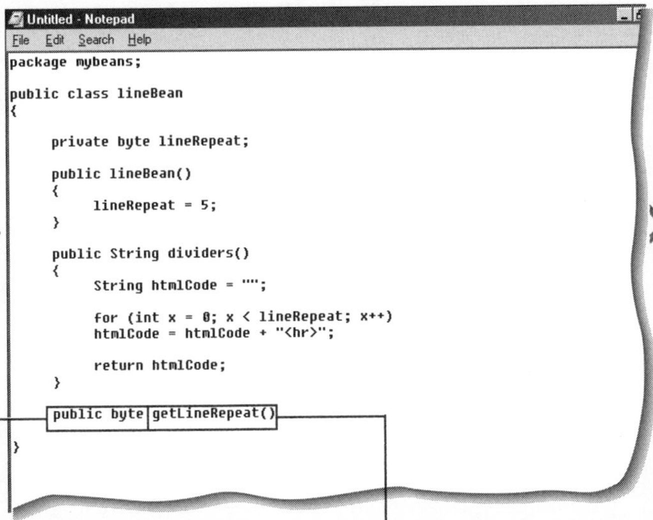

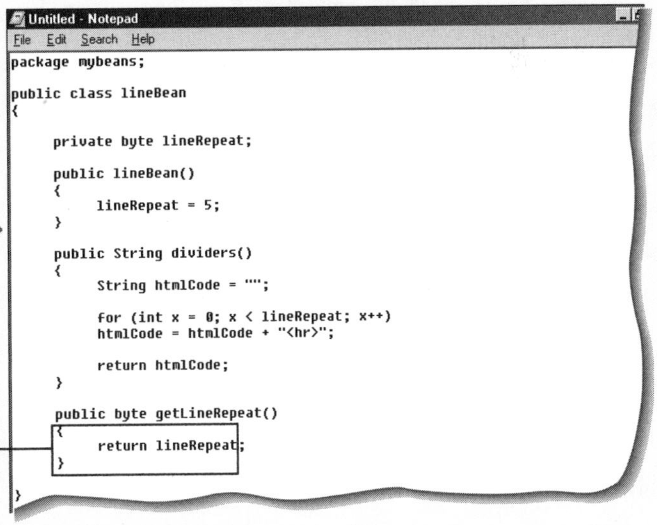

```
package mybeans;

public class lineBean
{
    private byte lineRepeat;

    public lineBean()
    {
        lineRepeat = 5;
    }

    public String dividers()
    {
        String htmlCode = "";

        for (int x = 0; x < lineRepeat; x++)
        htmlCode = htmlCode + "<hr>";

        return htmlCode;
    }

    public byte getLineRepeat()

}
```

7 To declare a getter method that will return the value of the property, type **public** followed by the data type of the value.

8 To name the method, type **get** immediately followed by the name of the property, beginning with a capital letter. Then type ().

```
package mybeans;

public class lineBean
{
    private byte lineRepeat;

    public lineBean()
    {
        lineRepeat = 5;
    }

    public String dividers()
    {
        String htmlCode = "";

        for (int x = 0; x < lineRepeat; x++)
        htmlCode = htmlCode + "<hr>";

        return htmlCode;
    }

    public byte getLineRepeat()
    {
        return lineRepeat;
    }
}
```

9 Type **return** followed by the name of the property. Enclose the code in braces.

10 Save the file with the .java extension and then compile the source code for the file.

11 Copy the compiled class file to the appropriate directory on your Web server.

■ You can now access the JavaBean property in a JSP page.

ACCESS A JAVABEAN PROPERTY

The <jsp:getProperty> tag can be used in a JSP page to access a property of a JavaBean. When the <jsp:getProperty> tag retrieves the value of a property, the tag converts the value to a string and then inserts the value into the JSP page output.

Before accessing a JavaBean property, you must add the <jsp:useBean> tag to the JSP page. This tag and its attributes ensure that the correct JavaBean is used and that the JSP page has access to the JavaBean.

The <jsp:getProperty> tag must be embedded in the HTML code of a JSP page. You cannot place the <jsp:getProperty> tag in Java code that generates HTML code. The tag must also be placed in an area of a page that can be displayed in a Web browser, such as within the <body> tag.

The <jsp:getProperty> tag has two required attributes. The name attribute allows you to specify the name of the JavaBean that contains the property you want to access. The value you assign to the name attribute must be the same as the value you assigned to the id attribute of the <jsp:useBean> tag.

You use the property attribute to specify the name of the property you want to access. You should be careful to use the correct uppercase and lowercase letters when typing the name of the property you want to access. If you do not enter the name of the property correctly, the <jsp:getProperty> tag will not be able to locate the property in the JavaBean and will return an error message.

ACCESS A JAVABEAN PROPERTY

```
Untitled - Notepad
File  Edit  Search  Help
<html>
<head>
<title>Using JavaBeans</title>
</head>
<body>

<jsp:useBean id="lineBeanId" scope="session" class="mybeans.lineBean" />

Welcome to my Web site. <br>

The default number of horizontal lines that will be displayed using this
JavaBean is:
<jsp:getProperty

</body>
</html>
```

1 Type the code that sets up the JSP page to use a JavaBean. For information about setting up a JSP page, see page 124.

2 To access a property in the JavaBean, type **<jsp:getProperty**.

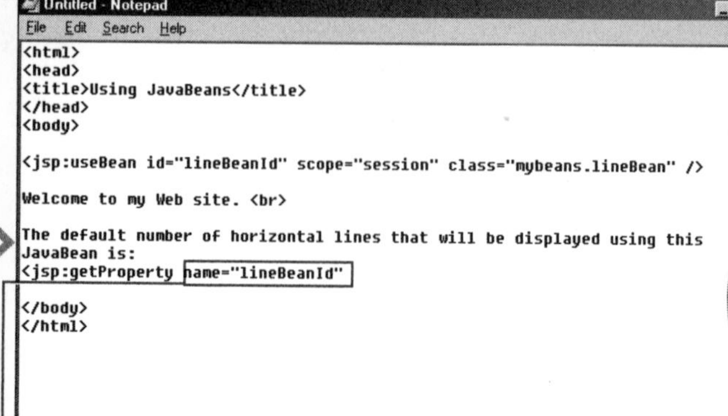

```
Untitled - Notepad
File  Edit  Search  Help
<html>
<head>
<title>Using JavaBeans</title>
</head>
<body>

<jsp:useBean id="lineBeanId" scope="session" class="mybeans.lineBean" />

Welcome to my Web site. <br>

The default number of horizontal lines that will be displayed using this
JavaBean is:
<jsp:getProperty name="lineBeanId"

</body>
</html>
```

3 Type **name=** followed by the name of the JavaBean that contains the property you want to access, enclosed in quotation marks.

■ The value you assign to the name attribute must be the same as the value you assigned to the id attribute of the <jsp:useBean> tag in step 1.

Extra

JavaServer Pages code is processed by the Web server and then sent to the Web browser as HTML code. People can view the HTML source code for a JSP page, but they will not be able to view the JavaServer Pages code. This means that users viewing the source code for a JSP page that contains the `<jsp:getProperty>` tag will not see the actual tag. Instead, they will see the value returned by the tag.

The source code viewed in a Web browser:

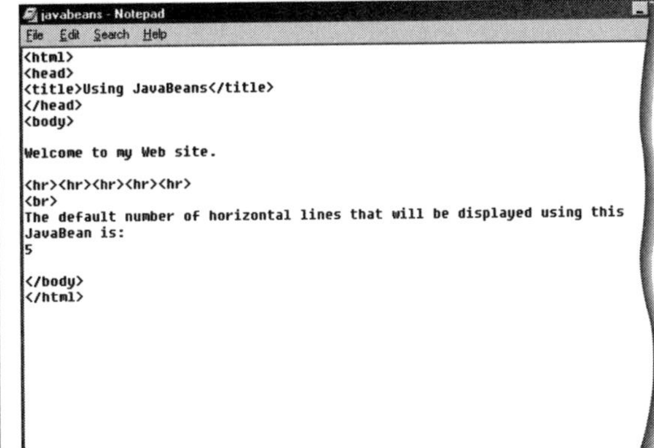

```
<html>
<head>
<title>Using JavaBeans</title>
</head>
<body>

Welcome to my Web site.

<hr><hr><hr><hr><hr>
<br>
The default number of horizontal lines that will be displayed using this
JavaBean is:
5

</body>
</html>
```

The actual code of the JSP page:

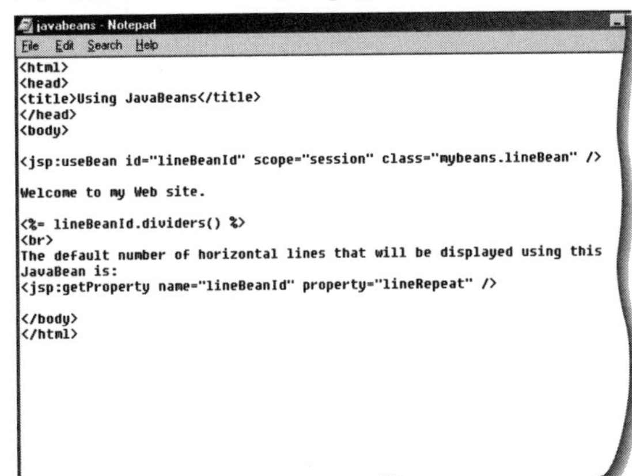

```
<html>
<head>
<title>Using JavaBeans</title>
</head>
<body>

<jsp:useBean id="lineBeanId" scope="session" class="mybeans.lineBean" />

Welcome to my Web site.

<%= lineBeanId.dividers() %>
<br>
The default number of horizontal lines that will be displayed using this
JavaBean is:
<jsp:getProperty name="lineBeanId" property="lineRepeat" />

</body>
</html>
```

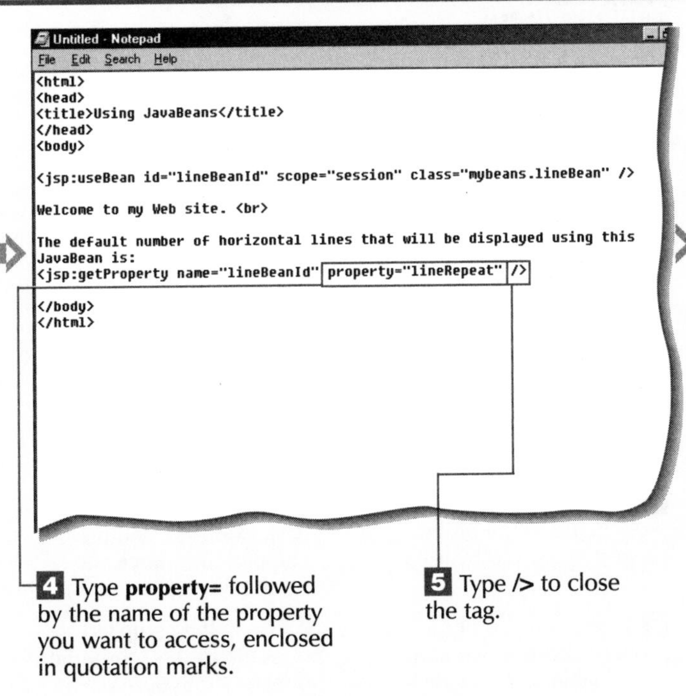

```
<html>
<head>
<title>Using JavaBeans</title>
</head>
<body>

<jsp:useBean id="lineBeanId" scope="session" class="mybeans.lineBean" />

Welcome to my Web site. <br>

The default number of horizontal lines that will be displayed using this
JavaBean is:
<jsp:getProperty name="lineBeanId" property="lineRepeat" />

</body>
</html>
```

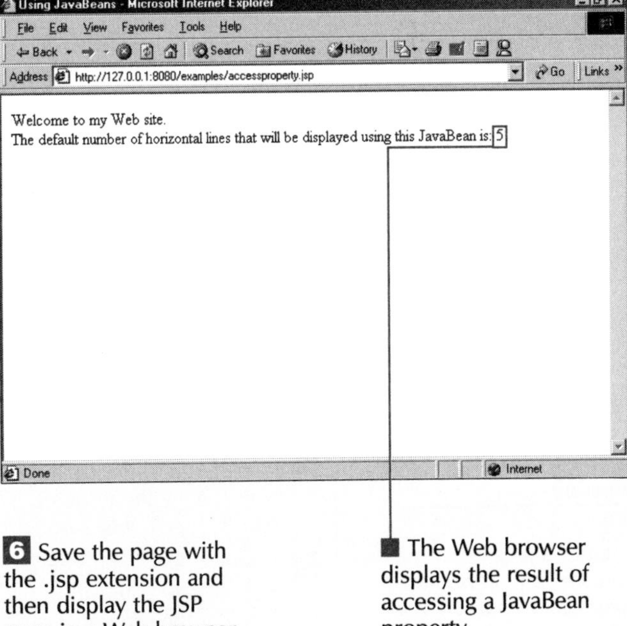

4 Type **property=** followed by the name of the property you want to access, enclosed in quotation marks.

5 Type **/>** to close the tag.

6 Save the page with the .jsp extension and then display the JSP page in a Web browser.

■ The Web browser displays the result of accessing a JavaBean property.

SET A JAVABEAN PROPERTY

A JSP page can be used to change the initial value of a JavaBean property. Changing the value of a property will affect how the JavaBean works.

To change the value of a JavaBean property, you must declare a setter method in the code for the JavaBean. Setter methods are often referred to as accessor methods. A setter method can work with a getter method. When used together, they allow a JSP page to write and read the value of a JavaBean property. For more information about getter methods, see page 128.

The access modifier of a setter method must be set to `public` and the return type set to `void`, since the method does not return a value. The name of the method is the same as the name of the property to be changed, but begins with a capital letter and is prefixed by the word `set`. The parentheses at the end of the setter method name enclose the data type of the property and a variable to store the value passed by a JSP page.

The `<jsp:useBean>` tag must be included in the JSP page you want to use to access a JavaBean. For information about this tag, see page 124. The `<jsp:setProperty>` tag and its attributes can then be used to change the value of a JavaBean property.

The `name` attribute allows you to specify the name of the JavaBean that contains the property you want to set. The value you assign to the `name` attribute must be the same as the value you assigned to the `id` attribute of the `<jsp:useBean>` tag. The `property` attribute specifies the name of the property whose value you want to set. The `value` attribute specifies the value for the property.

SET A JAVABEAN PROPERTY

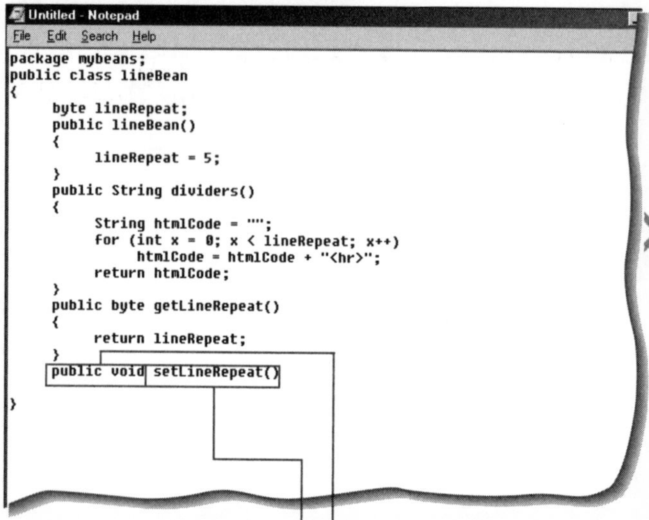

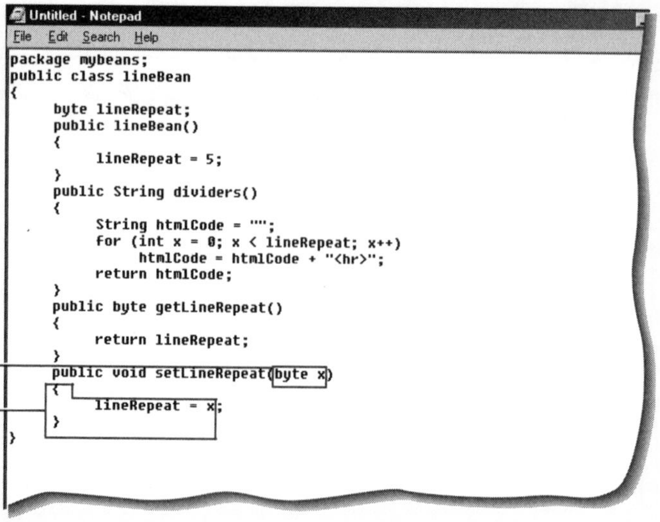

Untitled - Notepad

File Edit Search Help

```
package mybeans;
public class lineBean
{
	byte lineRepeat;
	public lineBean()
	{
		lineRepeat = 5;
	}
	public String dividers()
	{
		String htmlCode = "";
		for (int x = 0; x < lineRepeat; x++)
			htmlCode = htmlCode + "<hr>";
		return htmlCode;
	}
	public byte getLineRepeat()
	{
		return lineRepeat;
	}
	public void setLineRepeat()
}
```

Untitled - Notepad

File Edit Search Help

```
package mybeans;
public class lineBean
{
	byte lineRepeat;
	public lineBean()
	{
		lineRepeat = 5;
	}
	public String dividers()
	{
		String htmlCode = "";
		for (int x = 0; x < lineRepeat; x++)
			htmlCode = htmlCode + "<hr>";
		return htmlCode;
	}
	public byte getLineRepeat()
	{
		return lineRepeat;
	}
	public void setLineRepeat(byte x)
	{
		lineRepeat = x;
	}
}
```

DECLARE A SETTER METHOD

1 Type the code that creates a JavaBean and include any properties you want the JavaBean to contain.

2 To declare a setter method that will change the value of a property, type **public void**.

3 To name the method, type **set** immediately followed by the name of the property you want to change, beginning with a capital letter. Then type ().

4 Between the parentheses, type the data type of the property followed by a variable.

5 Type the name of the property followed by = and the variable. Enclose the code in braces.

6 Save the file with the .java extension and then compile the source code for the file.

7 Copy the compiled class file to the appropriate directory on your Web server.

Extra

Before you can change or retrieve a JavaBean property, the JSP engine must examine the JavaBean to determine if the property exists. A JSP engine is Web server software that processes JSP pages. When a JSP page attempts to access a JavaBean property, the JSP engine uses a process called *introspection* to examine the JavaBean. If the JSP engine finds a getter method, setter method or both for the property, then the property exits and can be accessed. A property without an accessor method does not exist. This is why the naming conventions for accessor methods are so rigid.

When the `<jsp:getProperty>` tag retrieves the value of a property, the value is converted to a string and then inserted into the JSP page output. If the value retrieved is a string, then no data conversion is required. Otherwise, the JSP engine will automatically convert the data using the appropriate class of the `java.lang` package.

VALUE DATA TYPE:	DATA CONVERSION CLASS:
boolean	`java.lang.Boolean.valueOf(string)`
byte	`java.lang.Byte.valueOf(string)`
char	`java.lang.Character.valueOf(string)`
double	`java.lang.Double.valueOf(string)`
int	`java.lang.Integer.valueOf(string)`
float	`java.lang.Float.valueOf(string)`
long	`java.lang.Long.valueOf(string)`

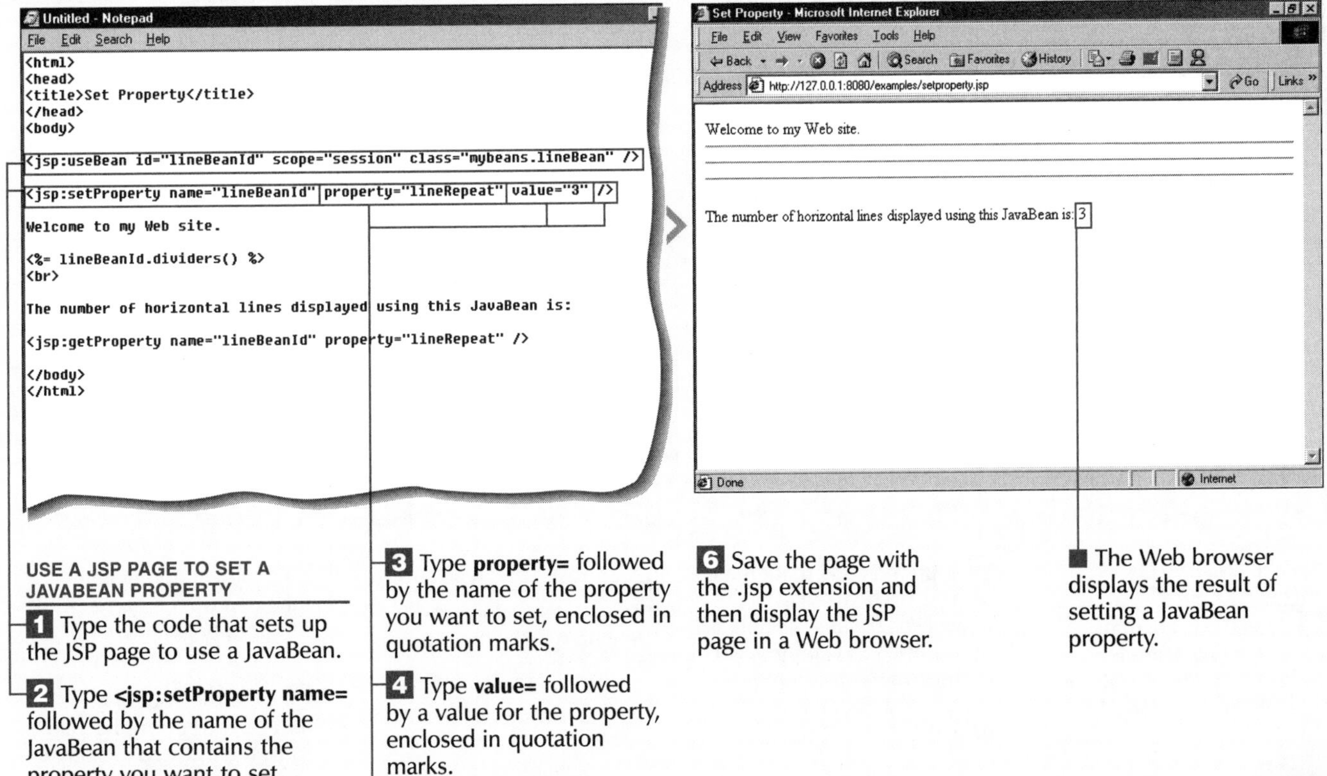

USE A JSP PAGE TO SET A JAVABEAN PROPERTY

1. Type the code that sets up the JSP page to use a JavaBean.
2. Type **<jsp:setProperty name=** followed by the name of the JavaBean that contains the property you want to set, enclosed in quotation marks.
3. Type **property=** followed by the name of the property you want to set, enclosed in quotation marks.
4. Type **value=** followed by a value for the property, enclosed in quotation marks.
5. Type **/>** to close the tag.
6. Save the page with the .jsp extension and then display the JSP page in a Web browser.

■ The Web browser displays the result of setting a JavaBean property.

CREATE AN INDEXED JAVABEAN PROPERTY

You can create an indexed property to store a collection of related information about a JavaBean. To create an indexed property, you first specify an array of values the indexed property will store. For information about creating arrays, see page 48.

In order to allow a JSP page to access the values of an indexed property, you must declare a getter method in the JavaBean. The access modifier of the getter method must be set to `public` and the data type of the return value must be specified. The name of the method is the same as the name of the indexed property, but begins with a capital letter and is prefixed by the word `get`. The body of a getter method includes a `return` statement that returns the values stored in the indexed property.

To allow a JSP page to change the values stored in an indexed property, you must declare a setter method in the JavaBean. The access modifier of a setter method must be set to `public` and the return value set to `void`. The name of the method is the same as the name of the indexed property but begins with a capital letter and is prefixed by the word `set`. The parentheses at the end of the setter method name must contain two arguments. The first argument represents the index of the element that is to be changed in an indexed property, while the second argument represents the new value to be placed in the element.

When you finish creating the JavaBean source code, you must compile the code and store the resulting class file in the appropriate directory on your Web server. If the JavaBean is part of a package, the class file must be stored in the appropriate package directory within the class file directory.

WORK WITH AN INDEXED JAVABEAN PROPERTY

Untitled - Notepad

```
package mybeans;

public class officeBean
{

     String[] sections = {"Sales", "Service", "Shipping"};

}
```

CREATE AN INDEXED JAVABEAN PROPERTY

1 Type the code that creates a JavaBean. For information about creating a JavaBean, see page 122.

2 Type the code that creates an array to be used as an index property and specifies the values you want to store in the array. For information about creating an array, see page 48.

Untitled - Notepad

```
package mybeans;

public class officeBean
{

     String[] sections = {"Sales", "Service", "Shipping"};

     public String getSections()
     {
          String htmlCode = "";
          for (int x = 0; x < sections.length; x++)
               htmlCode = htmlCode + "<li>" + sections[x];
          return "<ul>" + htmlCode + "</ul>";
     }

}
```

DECLARE A GETTER METHOD

3 Type **public** followed by the data type of the return value of the method.

4 Type **get** immediately followed by the name of the method, beginning with a capital letter. Then type **()**.

5 Type the code that will access and return the values from the indexed property.

Extra

In a JavaBean, you may want to declare a getter method that allows the JSP page to retrieve the value of a single element of an indexed property. You can use this getter method to display the value of a single element from an indexed property instead of having to display all the values of an indexed property at one time. You can have more than one getter method with the same name in a JavaBean.

Example:

```
public String getSections(int x)
{
      return sections[x];
}
```

You can declare a setter method that allows the JSP page to change all the values stored in an indexed property in a JavaBean. Changing all the values stored in an indexed property at once is more efficient that using a setter method to change the value of each element of an indexed property individually.

Example:

```
public void setSections(String[] i)
{
      for (int x = 0; x < i.length; x++)
            sections[x] = i[x];
}
```

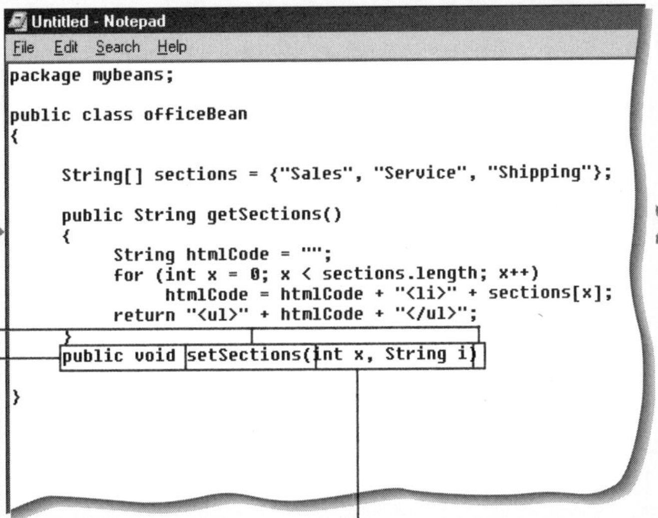

Untitled - Notepad

File Edit Search Help

```
package mybeans;

public class officeBean
{

    String[] sections = {"Sales", "Service", "Shipping"};

    public String getSections()
    {
        String htmlCode = "";
        for (int x = 0; x < sections.length; x++)
            htmlCode = htmlCode + "<li>" + sections[x];
        return "<ul>" + htmlCode + "</ul>";
    }
    public void setSections(int x, String i)

}
```

Untitled - Notepad

File Edit Search Help

```
package mybeans;

public class officeBean
{

    String[] sections = {"Sales", "Service", "Shipping"};

    public String getSections()
    {
        String htmlCode = "";
        for (int x = 0; x < sections.length; x++)
            htmlCode = htmlCode + "<li>" + sections[x];
        return "<ul>" + htmlCode + "</ul>";
    }
    public void setSections(int x, String i)
    {
        sections[x] = i;
    }

}
```

DECLARE A SETTER METHOD

6 Type **public void**.

7 Type **set** immediately followed by the name of the indexed property, beginning with a capital letter. Then type ().

8 Between the parentheses, type **int x**, followed by the data type of the indexed property and a variable name.

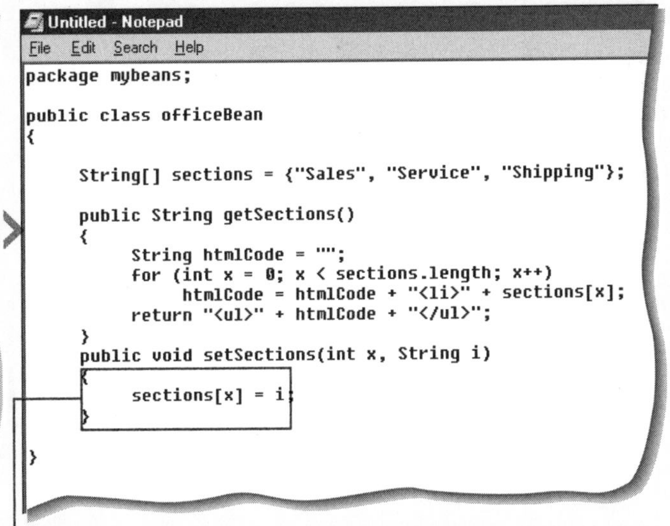

9 Type the name of the indexed property followed by **[x] =**. Then type the variable and enclose the code in braces.

10 Save the file with the .java extension and compile the source code. Then copy the compiled class file to the appropriate directory on your Web server.

■ You can now access the indexed JavaBean property in a JSP page.

ACCESS AN INDEXED JAVABEAN PROPERTY

After creating a JavaBean that has an indexed property, you can access the values stored in the indexed property from your JSP page.

First, you must set up the JSP page to use a JavaBean. To set up a JSP page, you must add the `<jsp:useBean>` tag to the page. This tag and its attributes ensure that the correct JavaBean is used and that the JSP page has access to the JavaBean. See page 124 for more information about setting up a JSP page to use a JavaBean.

You should make sure that the name of the JavaBean you specify in the `<jsp:useBean>` tag is the JavaBean that contains the indexed property you want to access. A JavaBean must also contain the accessor methods that allow the JSP page to retrieve and alter the values of the indexed property.

To display the values of an indexed property, you add code that calls a getter method to your JSP page. Since a getter method usually returns a value, you can use an expression to display the returned value.

You can change the value of an element of an indexed property by calling a setter method declared in the JavaBean. A setter method is called from within a scriplet in your JSP page and usually does not return any value. To change the value of an element using the setter method, you must pass the index number of the element and the new value to the method as arguments.

After changing the value of an element of an indexed property, you may want to once again call the getter method to display the values. This is an easy way to confirm that the setter method is working properly.

ACCESS AN INDEXED JAVABEAN PROPERTY

Untitled - Notepad

File Edit Search Help

```
<html>
<head>

<jsp:useBean id="myBeanId" scope="page" class="mybeans.officeBean" />

<title>Using an Indexed Property</title>
</head>
<body>

The sections list has been changed from<br>



<br>to<br>

<%

%>

</body>
</html>
```

1 Type the code that sets up the JSP page to use a JavaBean. For information about setting up a JSP page to use a JavaBean, see page 124.

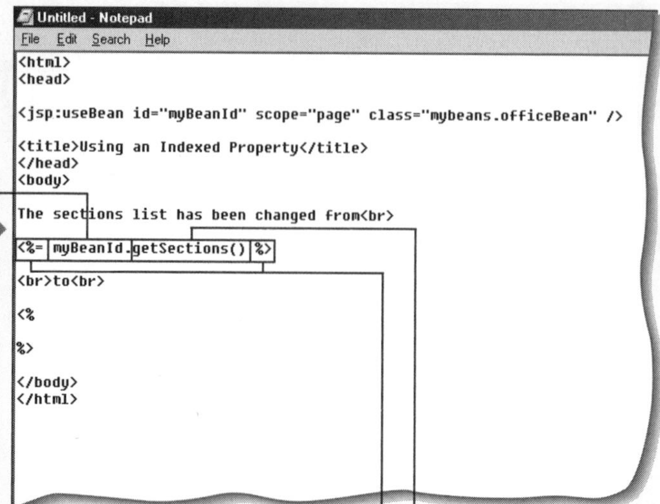

CALL A GETTER METHOD

2 Type the name of the JavaBean that contains the indexed property you want to access followed by a dot.

■ The name of the JavaBean must be the same as the value assigned to the `id` attribute of the `<jsp:useBean>` tag in step 1.

3 Type the name of the getter method followed by a set of parentheses.

4 Type the code that uses the method call.

Extra

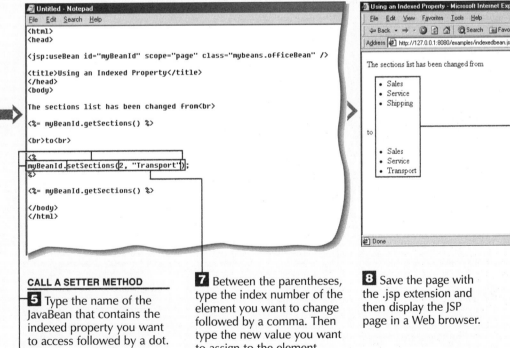

If you declared a getter method in your JavaBean that allows you to retrieve the value of a single element of an indexed property, you can call the method in your JSP page. When retrieving all the values of an indexed property, you usually do not need to pass any arguments to the getter method, however, if you want to retrieve the value of a single element, you must pass the index number of the element. Keep in mind that the first element of an indexed property has an index number of 0. This means that if you want to retrieve the third element of an indexed property, you must pass an index number of 2.

Example:

```
<%= myBeanId.getSections(2) %>
```

If you declared a setter method in your JavaBean that allows you to change all the values stored in an indexed property, you can call the method in your JSP page. When changing all the values of an indexed property, you pass an array containing all the new values to be stored in the indexed property as an argument.

Example:

```
<%
String[] t = {"Accounting", "Operations", "Transport"};
myBeanId.setSections(t);
%>
```

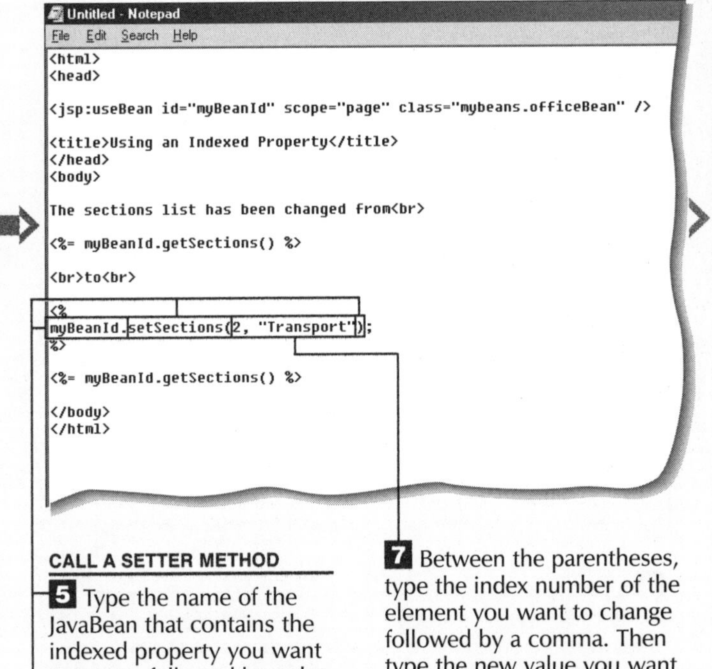

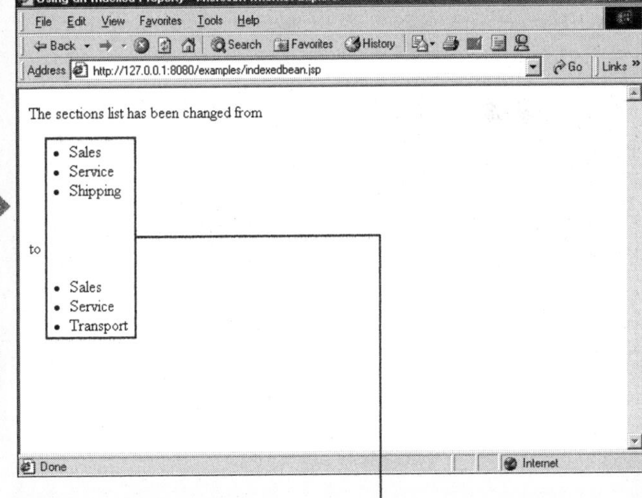

CALL A SETTER METHOD

5 Type the name of the JavaBean that contains the indexed property you want to access followed by a dot.

6 Type the name of the setter method followed by a set of parentheses.

7 Between the parentheses, type the index number of the element you want to change followed by a comma. Then type the new value you want to assign to the element.

8 Save the page with the .jsp extension and then display the JSP page in a Web browser.

■ The Web browser displays the results of using the getter and setter methods to access an indexed property in a JavaBean.

PROCESS FORM DATA USING A JAVABEAN

JavaBeans can be used to help a JSP page process data submitted by a form. For example, a JavaBean can store the values submitted by a form and allow the JSP page to retrieve and manipulate the values. Using a JavaBean to manage the data submitted by a form can make the data easier to work with.

While simple forms can be processed entirely by scriptlets within a JSP page, complex forms that contain many elements are best handled using JavaBeans. Using JavaBeans helps make the code that processes a form easier to manage, maintain and modify.

A JavaBean that will manage data submitted by a form should contain a property for each element in the form. The properties will store the values from the form elements. The names of the JavaBean properties should match the names of the form elements. For example, a property that will store the value of a text box named username should be called username.

You must declare a setter method for each property you create. If you want the JSP page to be able to retrieve the values stored in the properties, you must also declare a getter method for each property. These methods are often referred to as accessor methods. A setter method allows you to assign a value from a form to a JavaBean property. A getter method returns the value of a property. The conventions you must use when declaring setter and getter methods are very strict. For information about declaring a setter method, see page 135. For information about declaring a getter method, see page 134.

Once you have created the JavaBean source code, you must compile the code and store the resulting class file in the appropriate directory on your Web server.

CREATE A JAVABEAN TO STORE FORM DATA

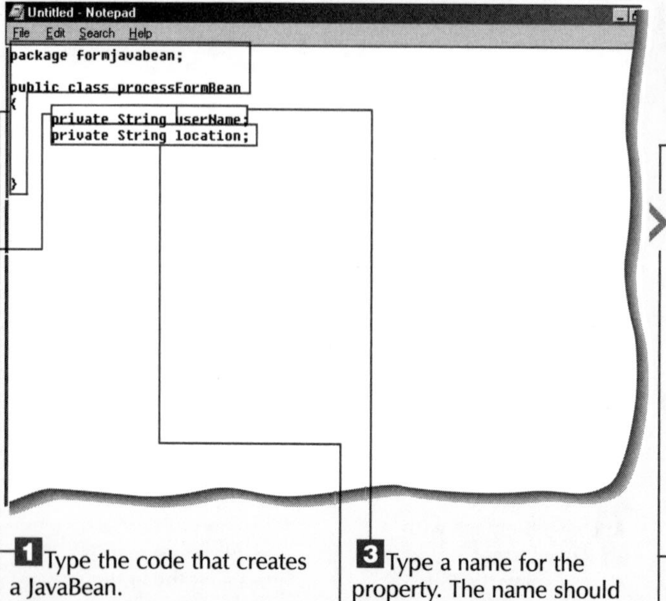

1 Type the code that creates a JavaBean.

2 To create a property that will store a value from a form element, type **private** followed by the data type of the value the property will store.

3 Type a name for the property. The name should match the name of the corresponding form element.

4 Repeat steps 2 and 3 for each property you want to create.

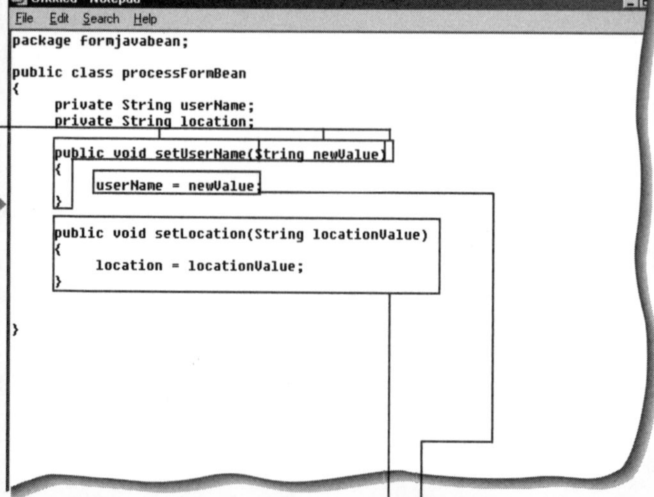

5 Type the code that declares a setter method. The setter method will assign a form value to the specified property.

6 Between the parentheses at the end of the setter method name, type the data type of the property followed by a variable.

7 In the body of the setter method, type the name of the property followed by = and the variable.

8 Repeat steps 5 to 7 for each setter method you want to declare.

Extra

Data can also be passed to a JSP page by a query string. A query string is one or more name and value pairs appended to the URL of a page. To create a query string, you enter the URL of the JSP page in a Web browser, followed by a question mark. You then enter a name followed by an equal sign and a value for the name. To enter multiple name and value pairs, separate each pair with an ampersand (&). A query string should not exceed 2000 characters and should not contain spaces.

Example:

```
http://www.abccorp.com/processform.jsp?userName=Ernest&location=USA
```

You can create a JavaBean that will store data submitted by a query string just as you would create a JavaBean to store data from a form. The JavaBean should contain a property for each name and value pair that will be submitted. The property names should match the names submitted by the query string. For example, if the name and value pair userName=Ernest will be submitted by a query string, the JavaBean should contain a property called userName.

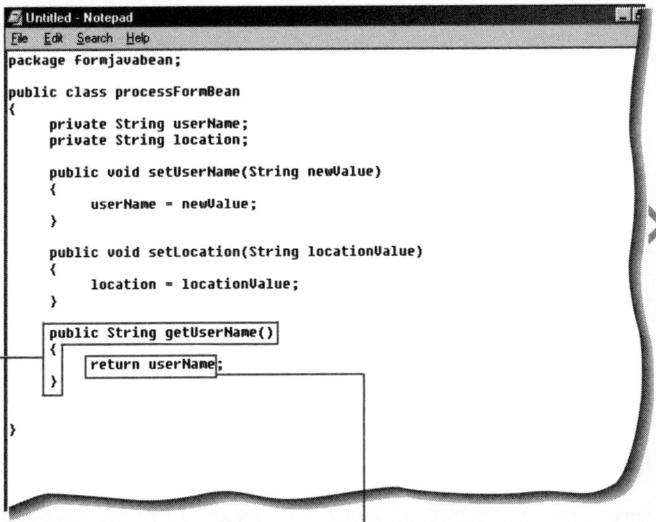

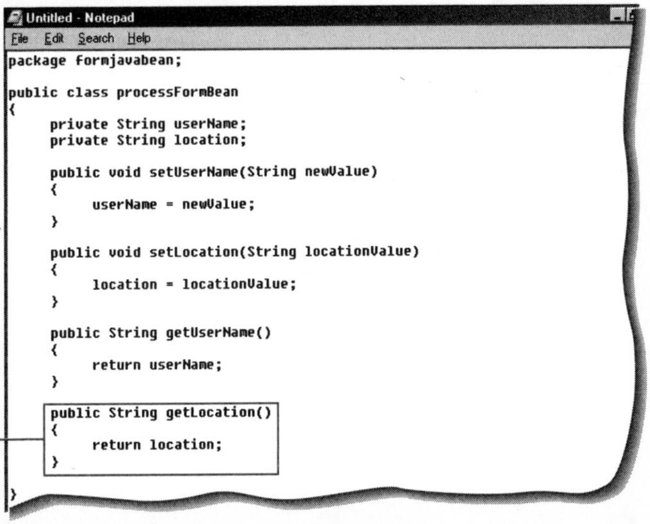

```
package formjavabean;

public class processFormBean
{
     private String userName;
     private String location;

     public void setUserName(String newValue)
     {
          userName = newValue;
     }

     public void setLocation(String locationValue)
     {
          location = locationValue;
     }

     public String getUserName()
     {
          return userName;
     }

}
```

9 Type the code that declares a getter method. The getter method will return the value of the specified property.

10 In the body of the getter method, type **return** followed by the name of the property.

```
package formjavabean;

public class processFormBean
{
     private String userName;
     private String location;

     public void setUserName(String newValue)
     {
          userName = newValue;
     }

     public void setLocation(String locationValue)
     {
          location = locationValue;
     }

     public String getUserName()
     {
          return userName;
     }

     public String getLocation()
     {
          return location;
     }
}
```

11 Repeat steps 9 and 10 for each getter method you want to declare.

12 Save the file with the .java extension and then compile the source code for the file.

13 Copy the compiled class file to the appropriate directory on your Web server.

■ You can now set up a JSP page to use the JavaBean when processing form data.

CONTINUED

PROCESS FORM DATA USING A JAVABEAN

The JSP page you want to process form data using a JavaBean must be set up to use the JavaBean. The JSP page can simply pass form data to the JavaBean and then retrieve and display the data. A JSP page and JavaBean can also be used to perform a more complicated task, such as storing the data in a database.

The `<jsp:useBean>` tag allows you to associate the JSP page with the JavaBean you created to manage form data. This tag must appear in the JSP page before the `<jsp:setProperty>` tag, which is used to set JavaBean properties. The `property` attribute of the `<jsp:setProperty>` tag allows you to specify the properties you want to set. If the names of the properties match the names of the elements in the form, you can quickly set all the properties in the JavaBean using the * wildcard character.

When a form is submitted to the JSP page, the `<jsp:setProperty>` tag will pass the form values from the JSP page to the JavaBean, assigning the values to the appropriate properties. The values are assigned during the process of *introspection*, in which the JavaBean is examined and its properties detected.

The `<jsp:getProperty>` tag allows the JSP page to access a property of the JavaBean. This tag retrieves the value of a property and automatically inserts the value into the output of the JSP page. You must use a `<jsp:getProperty>` tag for each property you want to access.

In the code for the form the JSP page will process, the `action` attribute of the `<form>` tag must specify the correct filename and location of the JSP page. The `method` attribute can specify either `get` or `post`. The JSP page will be able to process the form regardless of the method used to pass information to the page.

SET UP A JSP PAGE TO PROCESS FORM DATA

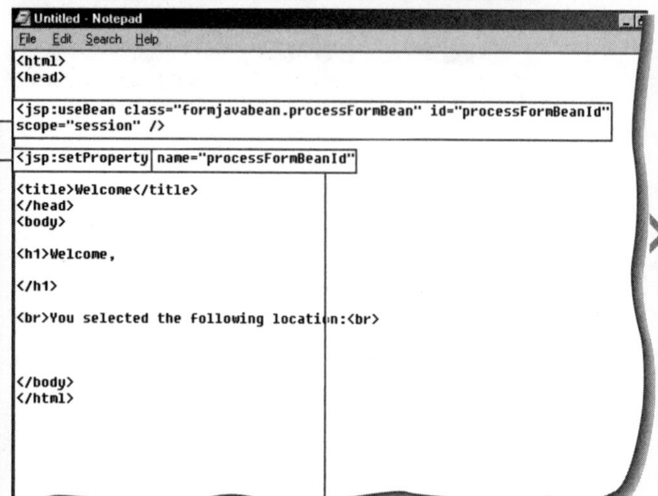

1 Type the code that sets up the JSP page to use a JavaBean.

2 To set the JavaBean properties with values from a form, type **<jsp:setProperty**.

3 Type **name=** followed by the name of the JavaBean that contains the properties you want to set, enclosed in quotation marks.

■ The value you assign to the `name` attribute must be the same as the value you assigned to the `id` attribute of the `<jsp:useBean>` tag in step 1.

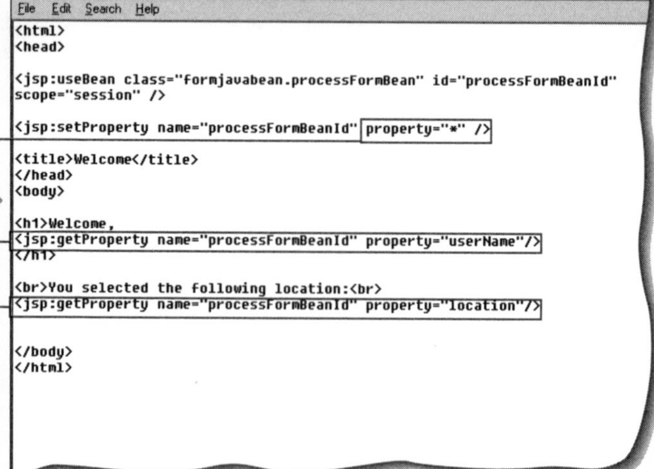

4 Type **property="*" />**.

5 Type the code that will access the JavaBean properties.

6 Save the page with the .jsp extension.

Extra

If the names of the properties in the JavaBean do not match the names of the elements in the form, you must set the value of each property individually. To set the value of a property, use the `property` attribute to specify the name of the property and the `param` attribute to specify the name of its corresponding form element. For example, the following line of code assigns the value of a form element named clientName to a property called userName.

Example:

```
<jsp:setProperty name="processFormBean"
property="userName" param="clientName"/>
```

A form does not have to be submitted directly to the JSP page that will process the form data. The form can be submitted to a JSP page and then forwarded to another JSP page. For example, form data can be submitted to a JSP page that verifies data before being forwarded to the JSP page that will process the data. The `<jsp:forward>` tag can be used to pass form data from one JSP page to another.

Example:

```
<jsp:forward page="process.jsp"/>
```

PROCESS FORM INFORMATION

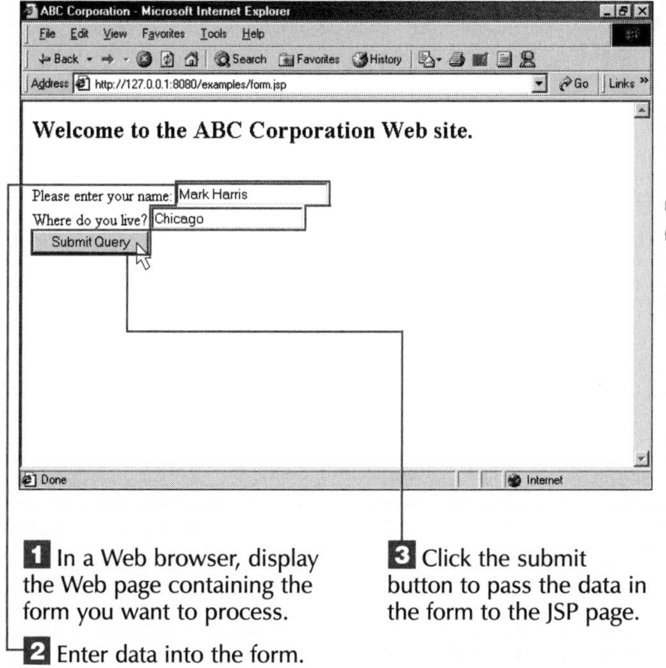

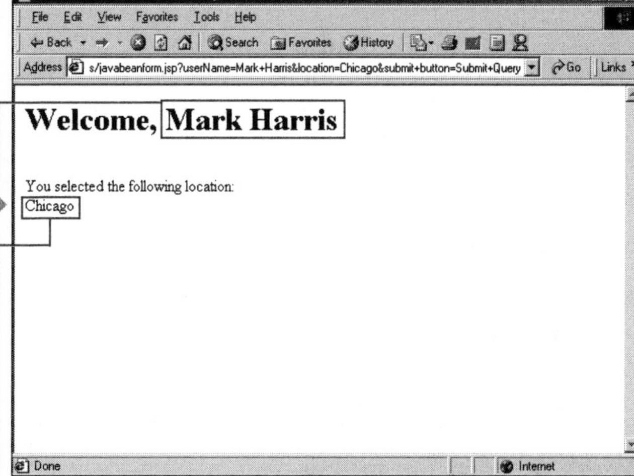

1 In a Web browser, display the Web page containing the form you want to process.

2 Enter data into the form.

3 Click the submit button to pass the data in the form to the JSP page.

■ The Web browser displays the result of using a JavaBean to process data from the form.

INTRODUCTION TO DATABASES

One of the most important features of JavaServer Pages technology is the ability to connect to a database. Databases store and efficiently manage large collections of information. JSP pages can be used to make this information available to the users who visit your Web site or to store information submitted by users.

Instead of storing information in text files or static Web pages, a JSP page can be set up to retrieve, format and display data from a database. When a user accesses the JSP page, the information displayed by the page will be created from the current information in the database. A JSP page can also allow users to manipulate the data in a database.

Using databases to store information and using JSP pages to access the information is an efficient method of displaying up-to-date information in a Web site.

DATABASE PROGRAMS

There are several different programs available that you can use to create a database. The two most popular database programs used when working with Windows-based systems are Microsoft Access and Microsoft SQL Server. Microsoft Access is useful for creating relatively small databases, while Microsoft SQL Server is useful for creating large databases, such as a database used to provide information to a busy e-commerce Web site.

For information about Microsoft Access and Microsoft SQL Server, you can visit the www.microsoft.com/office/access and www.microsoft.com/sql Web sites.

Two popular database programs used when working with UNIX-based systems are MySQL and PostgreSQL. Information about these database programs is available at the www.mysql.com and www.postgresql.org Web sites.

DATABASE STRUCTURE

A database is made up of one or more tables. A table contains records that store the information entered into the table. For example, a record could store the information for one customer. Each record is divided into fields. A field is a specific piece of information in a record, such as the first name of a customer.

Great care should be taken when initially planning and designing the structure of a database. A well-planned database ensures that tasks, such as adding or deleting records, can be performed efficiently and accurately. Poor database design may cause problems if the database needs to be changed in the future.

CONNECT TO A DATABASE

Before a JSP page can access a database, you must create a connection to the database. On Windows-based systems, you can first create a Data Source Name (DSN) for the database to tell your JSP pages what kind of database you want to connect to and where the database is located. You can then use the DSN with the `java.sql` package in a JSP page to connect the page to the database.

Once connected, you can easily access the database to add, modify and delete records, as well as administer the database.

STRUCTURED QUERY LANGUAGE

In order for a JSP page to work with the records in a database, the page must be able to communicate with the database. You use the Structured Query Language (SQL) in a JSP page you want to communicate with a database.

SQL FEATURES

Standardized

SQL is the industry standard language for managing and manipulating data in a database. SQL can be used to work with many types of databases, which makes it easy to upgrade from one database program to another. For example, a small Web site might start out using a Microsoft Access database, but then grow large enough to require a database created using Microsoft SQL Server. You need to learn only one language to have your JSP pages communicate with both types of databases.

Easy to Use

SQL is a very simple language to work with and uses many easy-to-understand commands. For example, SQL uses the `INSERT` statement to add information to a database. These plain-language commands make it easy for you to read code created using SQL and determine the purpose of the code.

Powerful

Although SQL is easy to use, it is a very powerful language. As well as being suitable for retrieving data from a database and performing simple tasks such as adding and deleting records, SQL can be used to perform complicated procedures, such as compiling different types of data from multiple data sources.

SQL STATEMENTS

Although SQL is made up of many statements and clauses, you will need to be familiar with only a few to perform the examples in this chapter.

SELECT

The `SELECT` statement specifies the data you want to retrieve from a database. The `SELECT` statement uses the `FROM` clause to specify the name of the table that stores the data you want to retrieve. The `WHERE` clause specifies exactly which data you want to retrieve.

Example:

```
SELECT Total
FROM invoiceNumbers
WHERE Total > '$100'
```

INSERT

The `INSERT` statement allows you to add data to a database. The `INSERT` statement uses the `INTO` clause to specify the name of the table to which you want to add data and the names of the fields that store the data in the table. The `VALUES` clause specifies the values that you are adding.

Example:

```
INSERT INTO invoiceNumbers (INVOICE, TOTAL)
VALUES (12843, '$34.56')
```

DELETE

The `DELETE` statement is used to remove data from a database. The `DELETE` statement uses the `FROM` clause to specify the name of the table that stores the data you want to delete. The `WHERE` clause contains information that uniquely identifies the data you want to delete.

Example:

```
DELETE FROM invoiceNumbers
WHERE year < 1996
```

CREATE A DATA SOURCE NAME

If a Web server running a Windows operating system will be used to access a database you created, you must assign a Data Source Name (DSN) to the database.

A DSN stores information that tells Web applications how to access a specific database. You include the data source name in the JSP pages you want to connect to the database.

You only have to create a DSN once for a database. You do not have to create a new data source name when you change or update the structure of the database.

The data source name must be created on the Web server that will access both the database and the JSP pages that use the database. If a Web hosting service is storing your database and JSP pages, the Web hosting service will usually create the DSN for you.

To create a data source name, you specify the driver for the program you used to create the database, such as Microsoft Access or SQL Server. You then specify the DSN you want to use and the location of the database. The data source name does not have to be the same as the name of the database. You should use a short, descriptive DSN.

The steps below create a system DSN for a Microsoft Access database that will be accessed by a Web Server running the Windows 2000 operating system. Windows 2000 computers use a program labeled Data Sources to control DSN configuration. The name and location of the program used to create a DSN on your computer may be different, depending on the operating system you are using. For more information about how to create a DSN on your computer, refer to the computer's operating system documentation.

CREATE A DATA SOURCE NAME

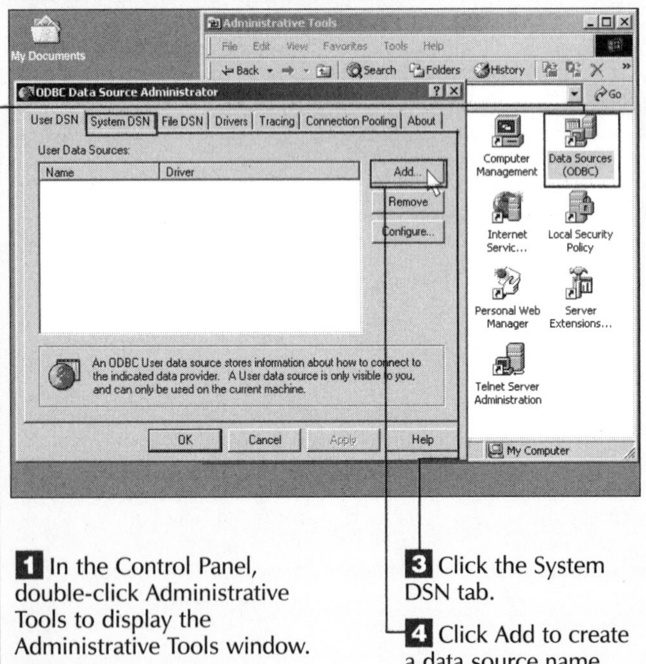

1 In the Control Panel, double-click Administrative Tools to display the Administrative Tools window.

2 Double-click Data Sources.

■ The ODBC Data Source Administrator dialog box appears.

3 Click the System DSN tab.

4 Click Add to create a data source name.

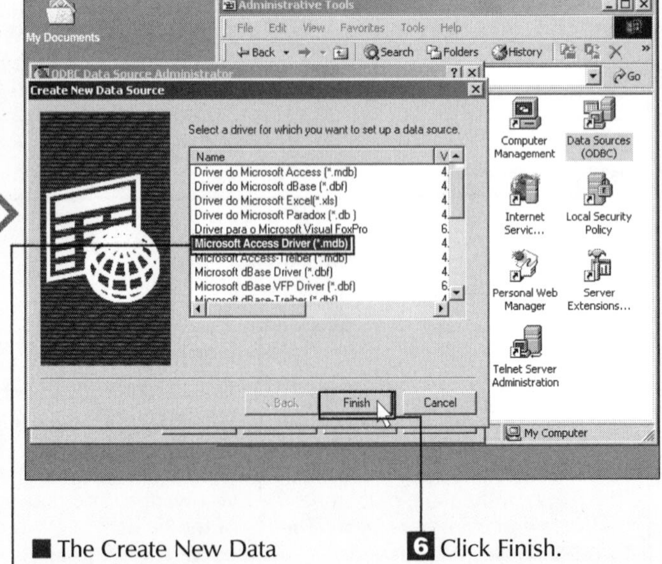

■ The Create New Data Source dialog box appears.

5 Click Microsoft Access Driver.

6 Click Finish.

■ The ODBC Microsoft Access Setup dialog box appears.

Extra

TYPES OF DATA SOURCE NAMES

There are three main types of data source names available on computers running a Windows operating system. The types of data source names differ in where the information about a database is stored and who can use the DSN. The administrator of the Web server usually specifies the type of DSN that must be used.

System DSN

The information in a system DSN is stored in the registry of the Web server. Any user that has access to the server will be able to use a system DSN to access the database.

User DSN

The information in a user DSN is stored in the registry of the Web server, but only a specific user account can use the DSN. User data source names are often used when developing intranet Web applications that require secure access to a database.

File DSN

The information in a file DSN is stored in a text file on the Web server. File data source names make it easy to transfer databases and data source names between different Web servers. Any user who has access to the Web server will be able to use a file DSN to access the database.

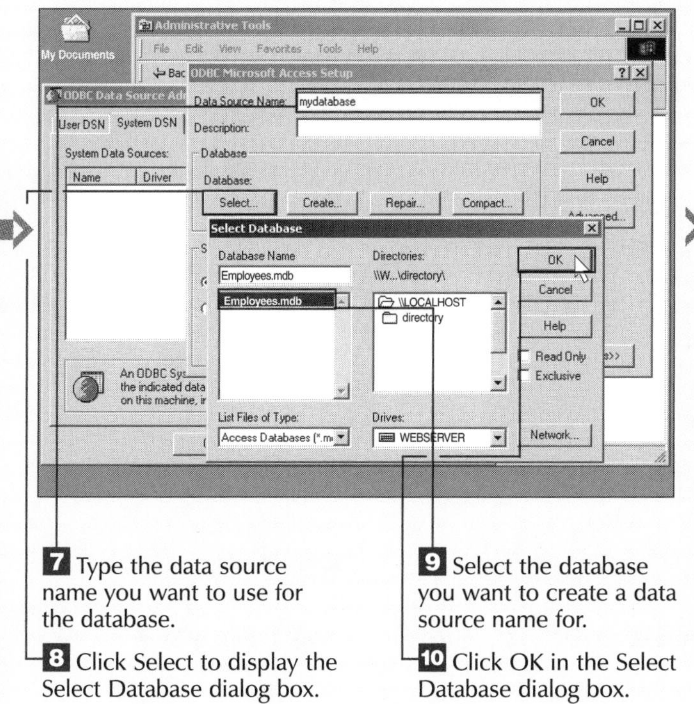

7 Type the data source name you want to use for the database.

8 Click Select to display the Select Database dialog box.

9 Select the database you want to create a data source name for.

10 Click OK in the Select Database dialog box.

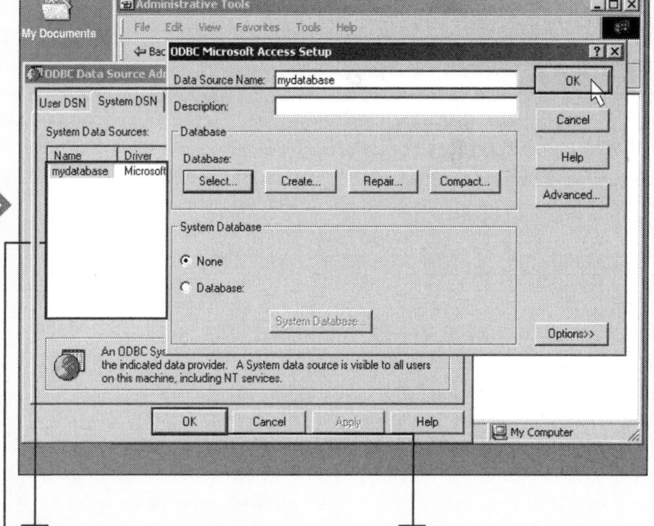

11 Click OK in the ODBC Microsoft Access Setup dialog box.

■ The new data source name appears in this area.

12 Click OK to close the ODBC Data Source Administrator dialog box.

CONNECT TO A DATABASE

Once a Data Source Name (DSN) has been created for a database, you can set up a connection to the database in a JSP page. You can then use the JSP page to access the database. For example, the JSP page can be used to retrieve information from the database.

In order to set up a connection to a database, a driver that enables the JSP page to communicate with the database must be loaded. JavaServer Pages technology uses the Java DataBase Connectivity (JDBC) specification to access databases, while most databases created on computers using the Windows platform use the Open DataBase Connectivity (ODBC) specification. The Java SDK includes a JDBC-ODBC bridge driver that allows JSP pages to communicate with these Windows databases.

To load a driver in a JSP page, you use the `Class.forName` statement to specify the name of the driver. The name of the JDBC-ODBC bridge driver is `sun.jdbc.odbc.JdbcOdbcDriver`.

Once the driver has been loaded, a `Connection` object can be created that will allow the JSP page to connect to the database. Before a `Connection` object can be created, you must use the `page` directive to import the `java.sql` package. The `java.sql` package contains the `Connection` interface and is part of the Java class library. For more information about the `page` directive, see page 74.

The `DriverManager.getConnection` statement is used to specify the location of the database you want the JSP page to connect to. For connections created using the JDBC-ODBC bridge driver, the location will begin with `jdbc:odbc:` and be immediately followed by the DSN of the database. The `DriverManager.getConnection` statement also allows you to specify a login name and password if this information is required to establish a connection to the database.

The `close` method of the `Connection` object should be used to close a database connection when the connection is no longer needed.

CONNECT TO A DATABASE

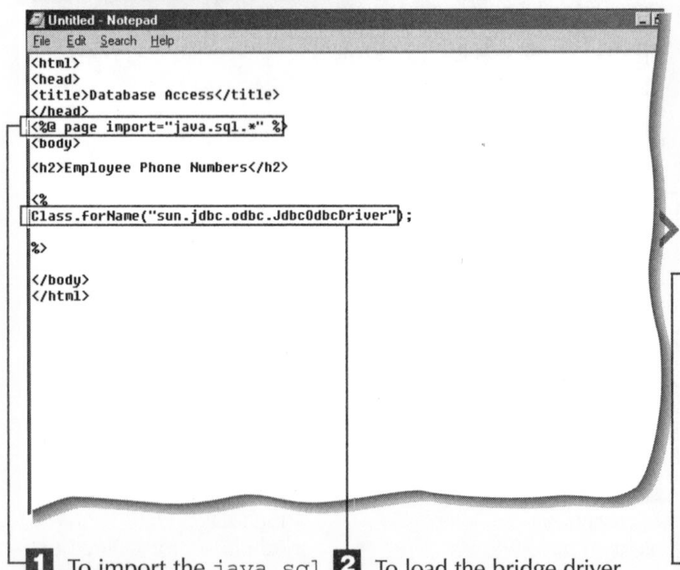


```
<html>
<head>
<title>Database Access</title>
</head>
<%@ page import="java.sql.*" %>
<body>

<h2>Employee Phone Numbers</h2>

<%
Class.forName("sun.jdbc.odbc.JdbcOdbcDriver");
Connection con =
%>

</body>
</html>
```

1 To import the `java.sql` package, type **<%@ page import="java.sql.*" %>**.

■ The `java.sql` package contains the `Connection` interface.

2 To load the bridge driver that allows the JSP page to communicate with a Windows database, type **Class.forName ("sun.jdbc.odbc.JdbcOdbcDriver")**.

3 To create a `Connection` object that allows the JSP page to connect to a Windows database, type **Connection**.

4 Type a name for the `Connection` object followed by **=**.

Extra

You must load a driver to connect a JSP page to a database even if the database uses the JDBC specification and does not require the use of the JDBC-ODBC bridge driver. Many database programs come with their own JDBC drivers. You may be able to load a database program's driver simply by specifying the name of the driver in the `Class.forName` statement. You should consult the documentation for the database program to determine which drivers are offered and how to load and use the drivers.

There is more than one version of the JDBC specification available. Version 2.0 is the latest version and includes features that are not found in older versions. You must ensure that your database is compatible with the JDBC version you intend to use. The Java SDK includes JDBC version 2.0.

Specifying a login name and password in a JSP page for a database connection can present a security risk, since anyone who has access to the JSP code will be able to determine this sensitive information. You may be able to use security features provided by your database program to minimize the security risk. For example, if the information in a database will only be retrieved, you may want to set up read-only access to the database. Consult the documentation for your database program for information on the available security features.

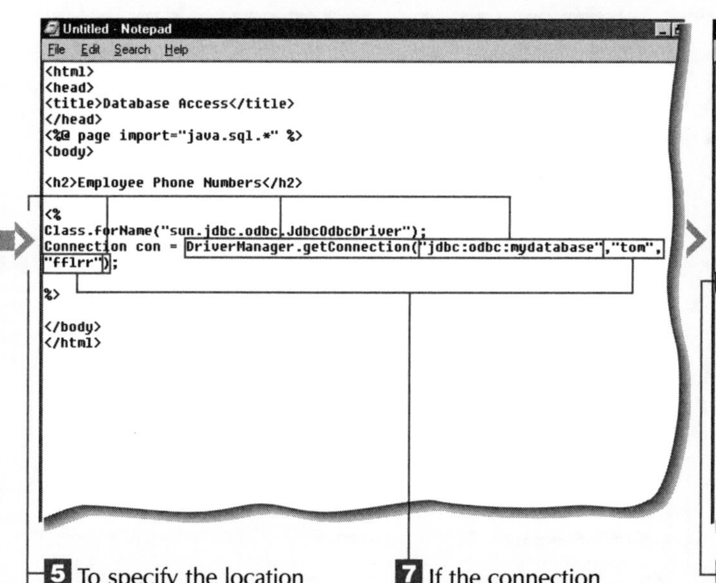

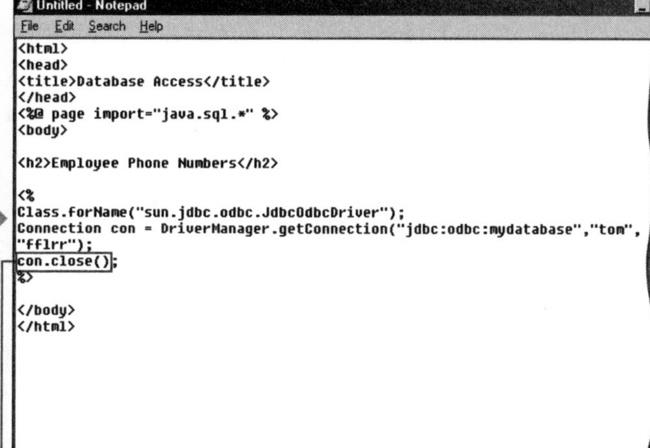

5 To specify the location of the database you want the JSP page to connect to, type **DriverManager.getConnection()**.

6 Between the parentheses, type **"jdbc:odbc:** immediately followed by the DSN of the database. Then type ".

7 If the connection requires a login name and password, type a comma followed by the login name enclosed in quotation marks. Then type a comma followed by the password enclosed in quotation marks.

8 To close the conection to the database, type the name of the `Connection` object followed by a dot. Then type **close()**.

9 Save the page with the .jsp extension.

■ You can now use the JSP page to access a Windows database.

CREATE A RESULT SET

After setting up a connection to a database in a JSP page, you can create a result set to store information you retrieve from the database.

Before a JSP page can retrieve data from a database, the page must have permission to access the database. Permission to access a database from a JSP page is usually controlled by your operating system or database program. For information about access permissions, you should consult the documentation included with your software.

Before creating a result set, you must first create a `Statement` object that will retrieve information from a database. To create a `Statement` object, you use the `createStatement` method of the `Connection` object created when the database connection was set up. The `Statement` interface that is used to create the `Statement` object is part of the `java.sql` package.

Once the `Statement` object has been created, the results retrieved by the object must then be assigned to a `ResultSet` object. This object will be used to store the results returned from the database in a result set. To use the `ResultSet` object, you must create an instance of the object and assign it a name.

When the `ResultSet` object has been created, you can specify the information you want to place in the result set. To do this, you use the `executeQuery` method of the `Statement` object to issue a `SELECT` statement to the database. The `SELECT` statement allows you to specify the data you want to retrieve from a table in the database. You can specify the data you want to retrieve by name or use an asterisk (`*`) to retrieve all the data in the table. The `SELECT` statement uses the `FROM` clause to specify the name of the table that stores the information you want to retrieve.

CREATE A RESULT SET

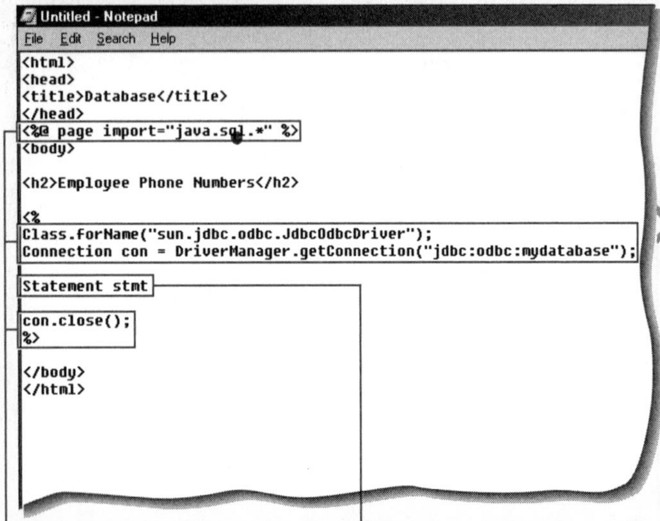

Untitled - Notepad

```
<html>
<head>
<title>Database</title>
</head>
<%@ page import="java.sql.*" %>
<body>

<h2>Employee Phone Numbers</h2>

<%
Class.forName("sun.jdbc.odbc.JdbcOdbcDriver");
Connection con = DriverManager.getConnection("jdbc:odbc:mydatabase");

Statement stmt

con.close();
%>

</body>
</html>
```

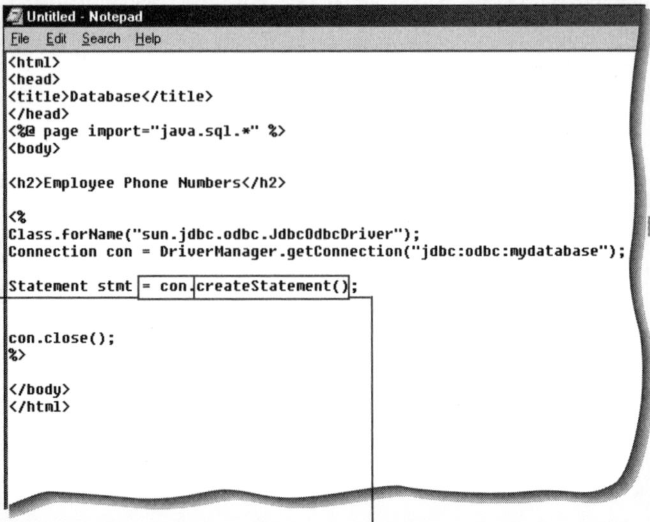

1 Type the code that creates a connection to the database from which you want to retrieve information.

2 To create the `Statement` object that will retrieve information from the database, type **Statement** followed by a name for the `Statement` object.

Untitled - Notepad

```
<html>
<head>
<title>Database</title>
</head>
<%@ page import="java.sql.*" %>
<body>

<h2>Employee Phone Numbers</h2>

<%
Class.forName("sun.jdbc.odbc.JdbcOdbcDriver");
Connection con = DriverManager.getConnection("jdbc:odbc:mydatabase");

Statement stmt = con.createStatement();


con.close();
%>

</body>
</html>
```

3 Type = and the name for the `Connection` object followed by a dot.

4 Type **createStatement()**.

Extra

You can use any name you want for your database objects. However, there are some names that are usually used for certain common objects. For example, the `Connection` object is often named con and the name stmt is often used for the `Statement` object. The `ResultSet` object is usually named rs.

Depending on the size, speed and location of the database, it may take a long time for a JSP page to pass a `SELECT` statement to the database, process the statement and then retrieve the results generated from the database. You should take this time into account when designing your JSP pages. For example, if your JSP page displays a banner image followed by a large amount of data from a database, you can use the `flush` method of the `out` object to force the JSP page to display the banner first, while the database information is being retrieved.

In order to minimize delays when communicating with a database, you should design your SQL statements to be efficient. For example, if you require data only from a particular field in a database, the `SELECT` statement should retrieve only the relevant information. It is much more efficient to retrieve only the data you need from the database than to retrieve unnecessary information and then filter the results.

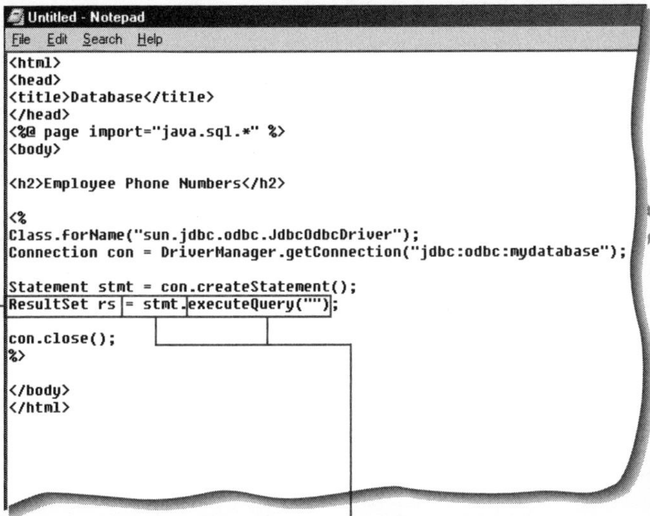

```
<html>
<head>
<title>Database</title>
</head>
<%@ page import="java.sql.*" %>
<body>

<h2>Employee Phone Numbers</h2>

<%
Class.forName("sun.jdbc.odbc.JdbcOdbcDriver");
Connection con = DriverManager.getConnection("jdbc:odbc:mydatabase");

Statement stmt = con.createStatement();
ResultSet rs = stmt.executeQuery("");

con.close();
%>

</body>
</html>
```

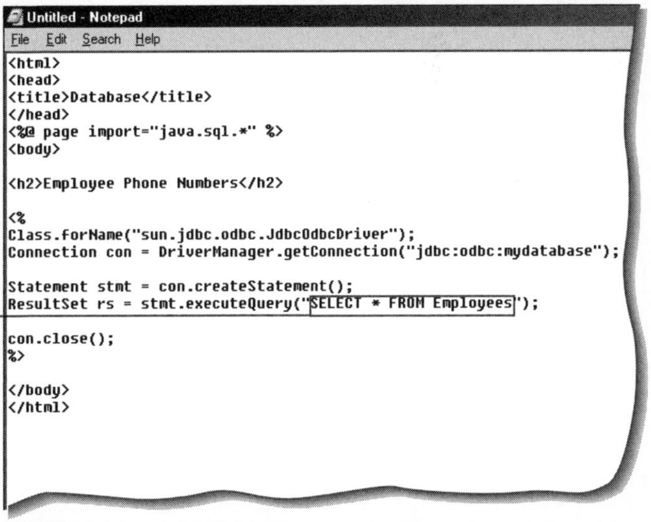

5 To create a `ResultSet` object to store the results returned from the database, type **ResultSet** followed by a name for the `ResultSet` object.

6 Type = and the name for the `Statement` object followed by dot.

7 Type **executeQuery**("").

```
<html>
<head>
<title>Database</title>
</head>
<%@ page import="java.sql.*" %>
<body>

<h2>Employee Phone Numbers</h2>

<%
Class.forName("sun.jdbc.odbc.JdbcOdbcDriver");
Connection con = DriverManager.getConnection("jdbc:odbc:mydatabase");

Statement stmt = con.createStatement();
ResultSet rs = stmt.executeQuery("SELECT * FROM Employees");

con.close();
%>

</body>
</html>
```

8 Between the quotation marks, type **SELECT * FROM** followed by the name of the table in the database from which you want to retrieve information.

9 Save the page with the .jsp extension.

■ To retrieve the data from the result set, see page 150.

RETRIEVE DATA FROM A RESULT SET

Once information has been retrieved from a database and placed in a result set, you can retrieve the data from the result set. A result set consists of rows which store information generated by the database when an SQL statement is processed.

Information may be accessed in the result set one row at a time. An imaginary indicator, called a cursor, is used to identify which row can currently be accessed. When the rows of data are initially placed in a result set, the cursor is placed just above the first row of data. To access the first row of data in a result set, you must call the `next` method of the `ResultSet` object to move the cursor to the first row.

If a result set contains multiple rows, a loop is typically used to retrieve information from each row. The `next` method of the `ResultSet` object is usually used in conjunction with a `while` loop to move the cursor through the rows of data in the result set, one at a time. The `next` method returns a boolean value which indicates if another row to which the cursor can be moved to exists. If the `next` method returns a `true` value, the loop continues and the next row of data is processed.

When the cursor is positioned in a particular row of data, a method of the `ResultSet` object can be used to retrieve information from that row. For example, the `getString` method can be used to retrieve string information from a row of data. When using the `getString` method, you must specify the name of the field from which you want to retrieve data. You can assign the value returned by the `getString` method to a variable, which allows you to use the value in a process or to display the value in a Web browser.

RETRIEVE DATA FROM A RESULT SET

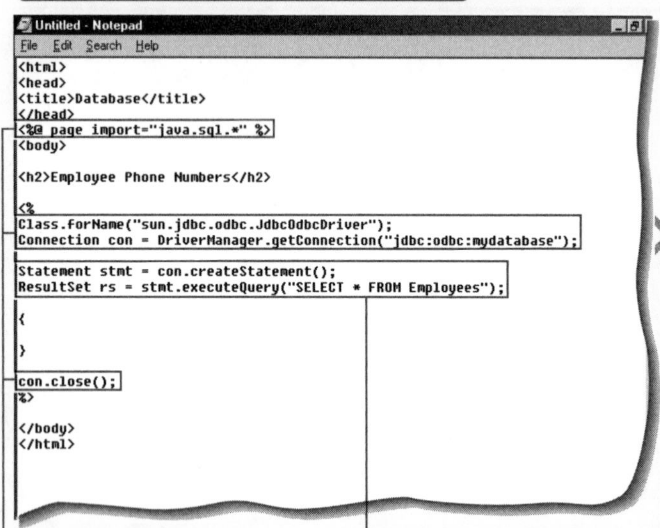

1 Type the code that creates a connection to the database from which you want to retrieve information.

2 Type the code to create a `Statement` object that retrieves information from a database and to create a result set that stores the results returned from the database.

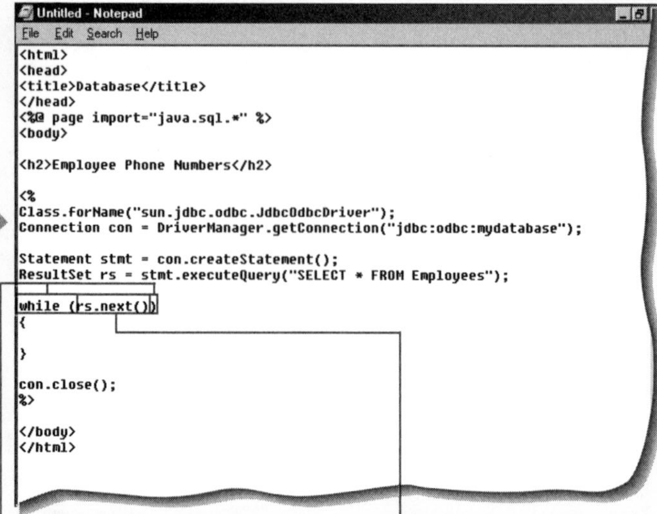

3 To create a `while` loop to cycle through the rows of data in the result set, type **while ()**.

4 Between the parentheses, type the name of the `ResultSet` object followed by **.next()**.

Extra

In addition to string data, a result set can also contain other types of data such as objects and primitive data types. Different methods of the `ResultSet` object are used to access different data types.

Example:

```
int numberOfItems = rs.getInt("quantity");
double itemPrice = rs.getDouble("price");
```

If multiple columns in the same result set have the same name, the method used to retrieve the data from the result set will retrieve the data from the first column that has the common name. Although it is not recommended, it is possible to have multiple columns with the same name in a database.

You can also use a column number instead of a field name to retrieve information from a row of data. In a result set, the first column of information has a column number of 1, not 0 as some programmers might expect.

Example:

```
while (rs.next())
{
      String employeeId = rs.getString(1);
      String employeeName = rs.getString(2);
      String employeeExt = rs.getString(3);
}
```

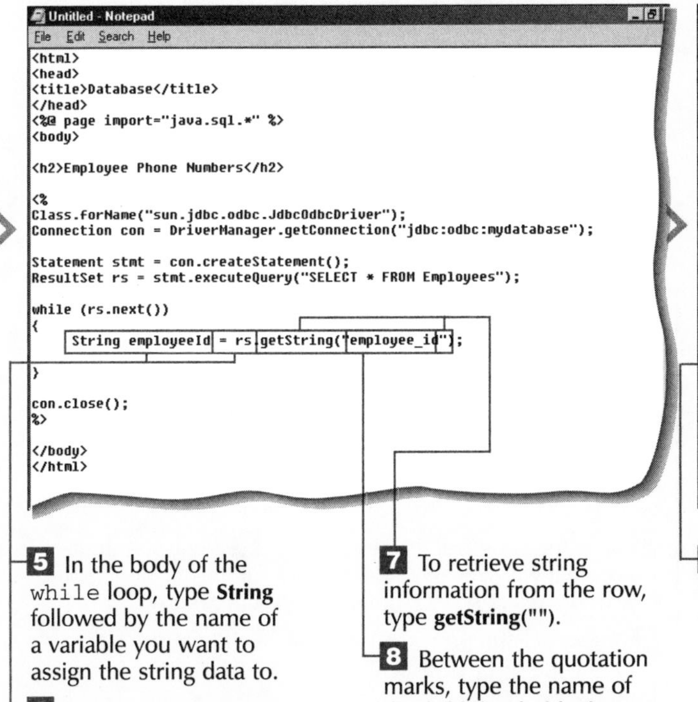

5 In the body of the `while` loop, type **String** followed by the name of a variable you want to assign the string data to.

6 Type = and the name of the `ResultSet` object followed by a dot.

7 To retrieve string information from the row, type **getString("")**.

8 Between the quotation marks, type the name of the field that holds the information you want to retrieve.

```
<html>
<head>
<title>Database</title>
</head>
<%@ page import="java.sql.*" %>
<body>

<h2>Employee Phone Numbers</h2>

<%
Class.forName("sun.jdbc.odbc.JdbcOdbcDriver");
Connection con = DriverManager.getConnection("jdbc:odbc:mydatabase");

Statement stmt = con.createStatement();
ResultSet rs = stmt.executeQuery("SELECT * FROM Employees");

while (rs.next())
{
     String employeeId = rs.getString("employee_id");
     String employeeName = rs.getString("name");
     String employeeExt = rs.getString("extension");
}

con.close();
%>

</body>
</html>
```

9 Repeat steps 5 to 8 to retrieve the information you want from the result set.

10 Save the page with the .jsp extension.

■ To format the retrieved data for display in a Web browser, see page 152.

FORMAT DATA FOR DISPLAY

Once information has been retrieved from a database and accessed from the result set, the information can be formatted for display on a JSP page. When displaying information retrieved from a database, you can use HTML tags to format the information. For example, HTML tags can be used to place the information in a list or table.

If a result set contains multiple rows, a loop is typically used to retrieve information from each row, one at a time. The `next` method of the `ResultSet` object is usually used in conjunction with a `while` loop to move the cursor through the rows of data.

When the cursor is positioned in a particular row of data, a method of the `ResultSet` object can be used to retrieve information from that row. For example, the `getString` method can be used to retrieve string information from a field you specify in the current row.

Assigning the value of the `getString` method to a variable can make it easier to work with the data. You can use the `print` method of the `out` object to display the contents of the variable on a JSP page. When using the `print` method, different types of data, such as variables and string literals, can be joined together using the concatenation operator, +.

You can incorporate any HMTL code you want to use into the loop that accesses each row of data so that with each iteration of the loop, a row of data and the HTML code used to format the data will be sent to the client.

FORMAT DATA FOR DISPLAY

Untitled - Notepad

File Edit Search Help

```
<html>
<head>
<title>Database</title>
</head>
<%@ page import="java.sql.*" %>
<body>

<h2>Employee Phone Numbers</h2>
<table border="1">
<tr><th>ID Number<th>Name<th>Extension</tr>
<%
Class.forName("sun.jdbc.odbc.JdbcOdbcDriver");
Connection con = DriverManager.getConnection("jdbc:odbc:mydatabase");

Statement stmt = con.createStatement();
ResultSet rs = stmt.executeQuery("SELECT * FROM Employees");

con.close();
%>

</table>
</body>
</html>
```

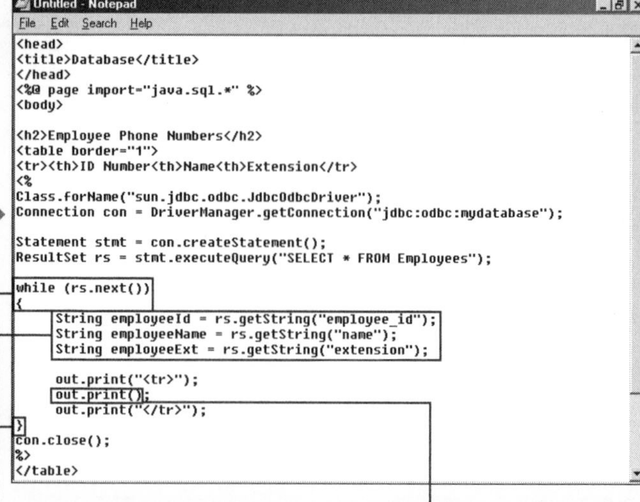

Untitled - Notepad

File Edit Search Help

```
<head>
<title>Database</title>
</head>
<%@ page import="java.sql.*" %>
<body>

<h2>Employee Phone Numbers</h2>
<table border="1">
<tr><th>ID Number<th>Name<th>Extension</tr>
<%
Class.forName("sun.jdbc.odbc.JdbcOdbcDriver");
Connection con = DriverManager.getConnection("jdbc:odbc:mydatabase");

Statement stmt = con.createStatement();
ResultSet rs = stmt.executeQuery("SELECT * FROM Employees");

while (rs.next())
{
        String employeeId = rs.getString("employee_id");
        String employeeName = rs.getString("name");
        String employeeExt = rs.getString("extension");

        out.print("<tr>");
        out.print();
        out.print("</tr>");
}
con.close();
%>
</table>
```

1 Type the code that creates a connection to a database and retrieves information from the database.

2 To display the information you retrieve from the result set in a table, type the HTML code that sets up the table.

3 Type the code that creates a loop that will process one row of the result set at a time.

4 Type the code that retrieves the data you want to display from the result set.

5 To display an item of information, type **out.print()**.

Extra

Many Web pages on the Internet are not static pages, but rather are made up of information retrieved from databases. This information is assembled on a page each time a client views the page. For example, the home page of a news organization may contain information retrieved from a news database, a weather database and an advertising database. The information from each database is formatted with HTML tags and the separate sections are all joined together to create a single, seamless page.

When formatting information retrieved from a database for display on a JSP page, you should first sketch out the desired layout of the page to ensure proper placement of information. If the amount of information retrieved from the database will vary with each query, you must take this into account when laying out the page.

If the information you want to display from a database is relatively simple, you can use an expression to display the information directly from the result set, without first assigning the information to variables.

Example:

```
<table>
<tr>
<td><%= rs.getString("employee_id") %></td>
<td><%= rs.getString("name") %></td>
<td><%= rs.getString("extension") %></td>
</tr>
</table>
```

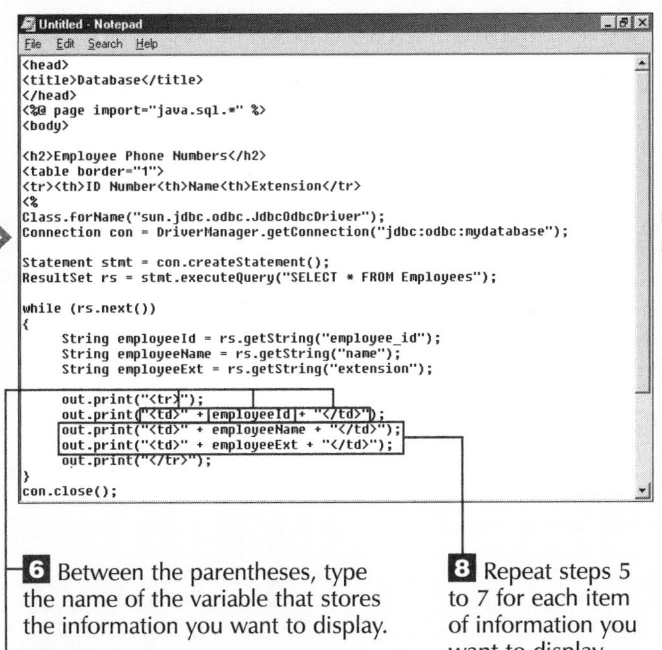

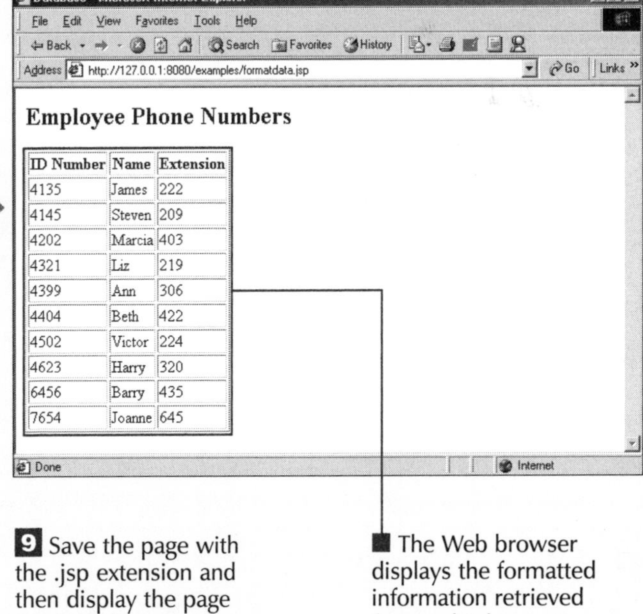

6 Between the parentheses, type the name of the variable that stores the information you want to display.

7 To generate a cell in the table, type the required HTML tags, enclosed in quotation marks. Separate each tag and variable with the concatenation operator.

8 Repeat steps 5 to 7 for each item of information you want to display.

9 Save the page with the .jsp extension and then display the page in a Web browser.

■ The Web browser displays the formatted information retrieved from a database.

POSITION THE CURSOR IN A RESULT SET

The `ResultSet` object provides several methods that can be used to move the cursor to a particular row in a result set.

Initially, the cursor is positioned above the first row in a result set, so there is no current row. You must call a method of the `ResultSet` object to move the cursor to the row you want to make current. The values in the current row are affected by any methods that are called.

If the `next` method of the `ResultSet` object is used to move the cursor forward through each row in a result set, a new result set would have to be created to revisit a row or iterate through the entire result set a second time. Most new JDBC drivers allow you to create a scrollable result set. You can move the cursor forward, backward and to a specific row in a scrollable result set.

To make a result set scrollable, you must specify the result set type as `TYPE_SCROLL_INSENSITIVE` or `TYPE_SCROLL_SENSITIVE`. If you want to be able to change information in the result set, you must also specify the concurrency type as `CONCUR_UPDATABLE`. The result set type and concurrency type are specified as arguments of the `createStatement` method. The values available for both of these types are constants determined by the `ResultSet` interface.

After setting the result set type and concurrency type, you can call a `ResultSet` method to position the cursor at the row you want to make the current row. Calling the `first` method moves the cursor to the first row in the result set. Calling the `last` method moves the cursor to the last row. To position the cursor at a specific row, you use the `absolute` method to specify the number of the row you want to make current.

POSITION THE CURSOR IN A RESULT SET

Untitled - Notepad

File Edit Search Help

```
<html>
<head>
<title>Result Set</title>
</head>
<%@ page import="java.sql.*" %>
<body>

<h2>Employee Phone Numbers</h2>
<table border="1">
<tr><th>ID Number<th>Name<th>Extension</tr>
<%
Class.forName("sun.jdbc.odbc.JdbcOdbcDriver");
Connection con = DriverManager.getConnection("jdbc:odbc:mydatabase");

Statement stmt = con.createStatement(ResultSet.TYPE_SCROLL_SENSITIVE,
      ResultSet.CONCUR_UPDATABLE);
ResultSet rs = stmt.executeQuery("SELECT * FROM Employees");

con.close();
%>

</table>
</body>
</html>
```

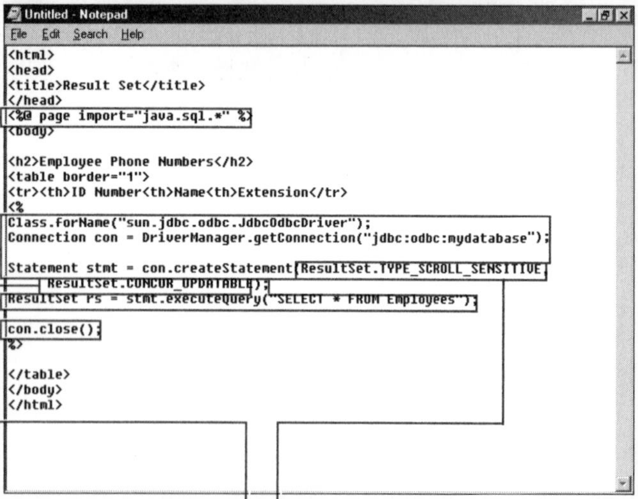

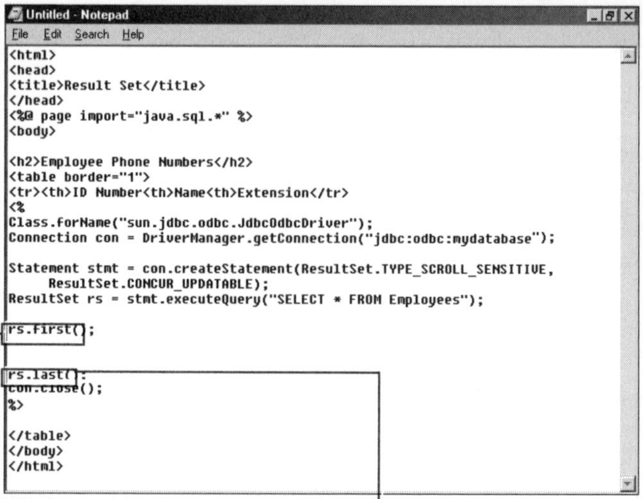

1 Type the code that creates a connection to a database and retrieves information from the database.

2 Between the parentheses for the `createStatement` method of the `Connection` object, type **ResultSet.TYPE_SCROLL_SENSITIVE** followed by a comma to specify the result set type.

3 Type **ResultSet.CONCUR_UPDATABLE** to specify the concurrency type.

Untitled - Notepad

File Edit Search Help

```
<html>
<head>
<title>Result Set</title>
</head>
<%@ page import="java.sql.*" %>
<body>

<h2>Employee Phone Numbers</h2>
<table border="1">
<tr><th>ID Number<th>Name<th>Extension</tr>
<%
Class.forName("sun.jdbc.odbc.JdbcOdbcDriver");
Connection con = DriverManager.getConnection("jdbc:odbc:mydatabase");

Statement stmt = con.createStatement(ResultSet.TYPE_SCROLL_SENSITIVE,
      ResultSet.CONCUR_UPDATABLE);
ResultSet rs = stmt.executeQuery("SELECT * FROM Employees");

rs.first();

rs.last();
con.close();
%>

</table>
</body>
</html>
```

4 To create a method that moves the cursor to the first row in the result set, type the name of the `ResultSet` object followed by a dot. Then type **first()**.

5 To create a method that moves the cursor to the last row in the result set, type the name of the `ResultSet` object followed by a dot. Then type **last()**.

Extra

You can display the result set type and concurrency type of a result set in a JSP page. To do so, use the `getType` and `getConcurrency` methods of the `ResultSet` object in the JSP page, such as `<%= rs.getType() %>` and `<%= rs.getConcurrency() %>`. When the JSP page is displayed in a Web browser, a numerical value appears, representing the result set type and concurrency type.

Result Set Types

VALUE:		DESCRIPTION:
1003	TYPE_FORWARD_ONLY	The result set is not scrollable. The cursor can move forward from top to bottom only.
1004	TYPE_SCROLL_INSENSITIVE	The result set is scrollable. Any changes made to the database while the result set is open are not reflected in the result set.
1005	TYPE_SCROLL_SENSITIVE	The result set is scrollable. Any changes made to the database are immediately reflected in the result set.

Concurrency Types

VALUE:		DESCRIPTION:
1007	CONCUR_READ_ONLY	The information in the result set cannot be modified.
1008	CONCUR_UPDATABLE	The information in the result set can be updated.

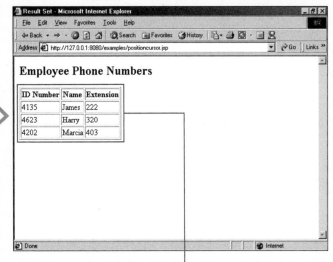

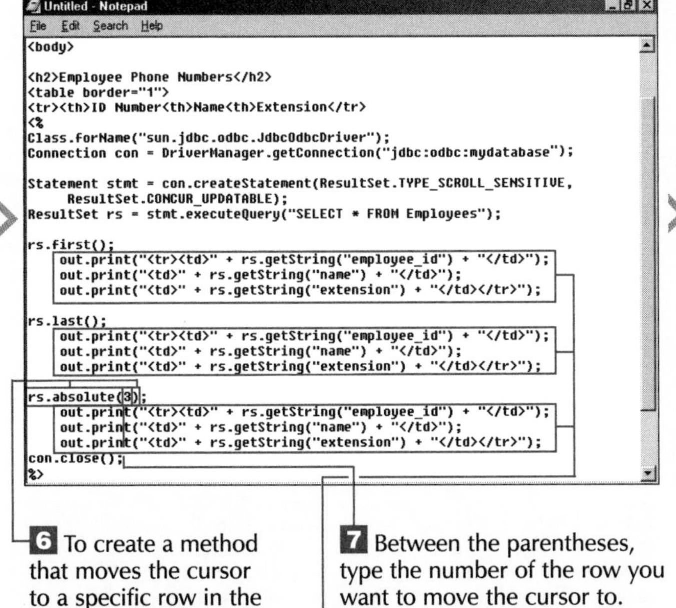

```
<body>

<h2>Employee Phone Numbers</h2>
<table border="1">
<tr><th>ID Number<th>Name<th>Extension</tr>
<%
Class.forName("sun.jdbc.odbc.JdbcOdbcDriver");
Connection con = DriverManager.getConnection("jdbc:odbc:mydatabase");

Statement stmt = con.createStatement(ResultSet.TYPE_SCROLL_SENSITIVE,
      ResultSet.CONCUR_UPDATABLE);
ResultSet rs = stmt.executeQuery("SELECT * FROM Employees");

rs.first();
    out.print("<tr><td>" + rs.getString("employee_id") + "</td>");
    out.print("<td>" + rs.getString("name") + "</td>");
    out.print("<td>" + rs.getString("extension") + "</td></tr>");

rs.last();
    out.print("<tr><td>" + rs.getString("employee_id") + "</td>");
    out.print("<td>" + rs.getString("name") + "</td>");
    out.print("<td>" + rs.getString("extension") + "</td></tr>");

rs.absolute(3);
    out.print("<tr><td>" + rs.getString("employee_id") + "</td>");
    out.print("<td>" + rs.getString("name") + "</td>");
    out.print("<td>" + rs.getString("extension") + "</td></tr>");
con.close();
%>
```

6 To create a method that moves the cursor to a specific row in the result set, type the name of the `ResultSet` object followed by a dot. Then type **absolute()**.

7 Between the parentheses, type the number of the row you want to move the cursor to.

8 Type the code that retrieves and displays information from each row you specified in the result set.

Employee Phone Numbers

ID Number	Name	Extension
4135	James	222
4623	Harry	320
4202	Marcia	403

9 Save the page with the .jsp extension and then display the JSP page in a Web browser.

■ The Web browser displays the result of positioning the cursor in a result set. The first, last and third rows in the result set are displayed.

ADD A RECORD

The ResultSet object provides methods you can use to insert records into a table in a database.

You insert a record into a table by inserting a new row into the result set that contains information retrieved from the database. The result set must contain all the columns in the table that are to be given values for a record. A column that is not included in the result set will be given a null value when the record is inserted into the table. If the column does not accept null values, an error will occur.

Before you can add a record, you must first use the moveToInsertRow method of the ResultSet object to position the cursor at the insert row. The insert row allows you to create a new row in a result set.

Once the cursor is positioned at the insert row, you can specify the values you want to add to each column in the row using special update methods of the ResultSet object. The method name you use depends on the type of data to be used for the value. For example, if you want to specify a string value for a column, you use the updateString method. To specify an integer value, you use the updateInt method.

Each update method requires two arguments. The first argument specifies the name or number of the column you want to contain the data. The number of the first column in the table is 1. The second argument specifies the value that will be inserted into the column. The data type of the value must match the update method you specified.

Once the values have been specified for each column in the table, you can call the insertRow method of the ResultSet object to add the new record to the result set and to the table in the database.

ADD A RECORD

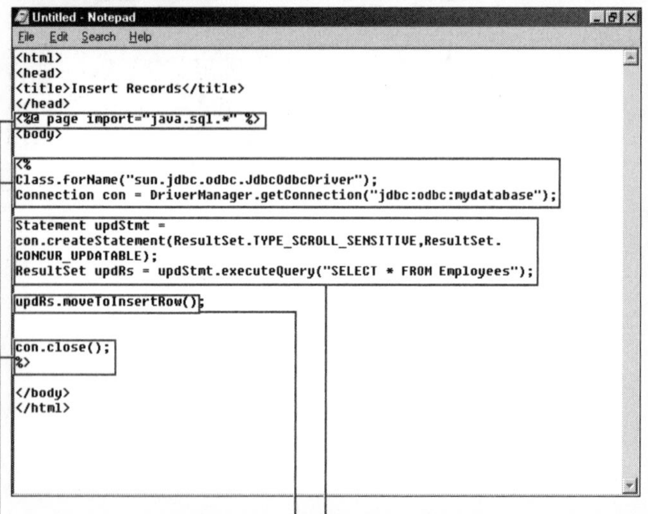

```
<html>
<head>
<title>Insert Records</title>
</head>
<%@ page import="java.sql.*" %>
<body>

<%
Class.forName("sun.jdbc.odbc.JdbcOdbcDriver");
Connection con = DriverManager.getConnection("jdbc:odbc:mydatabase");

Statement updStmt =
con.createStatement(ResultSet.TYPE_SCROLL_SENSITIVE,ResultSet.
CONCUR_UPDATABLE);
ResultSet updRs = updStmt.executeQuery("SELECT * FROM Employees");

updRs.moveToInsertRow();

con.close();
%>

</body>
</html>
```

1 Type the code that creates a connection to a database to which you want to add a record.

2 Type the code that retrieves information from the table where you want to add a record and allows you to update the database.

3 To position the cursor at the insert row, type the name of the ResultSet object followed by **.moveToInsertRow()**.

```
<html>
<head>
<title>Insert Records</title>
</head>
<%@ page import="java.sql.*" %>
<body>

<h2>Employee Phone Numbers</h2>
<table border="1">
<tr><th>ID Number<th>Name<th>Extension</tr>

<%
Class.forName("sun.jdbc.odbc.JdbcOdbcDriver");
Connection con = DriverManager.getConnection("jdbc:odbc:mydatabase");

Statement updStmt = con.createStatement(ResultSet.TYPE_SCROLL_SENSITIVE,
ResultSet.CONCUR_UPDATABLE);
ResultSet updRs = updStmt.executeQuery("SELECT * FROM Employees");

updRs.moveToInsertRow();
updRs.updateInt("employee_id", 4347);
con.close();
%>

</table>
</body>
```

4 To specify a value for a column in the new record, type the name of the ResultSet object followed by a dot. Then type the update method you want to use followed by ().

5 Between the parentheses, type the name or number of the column to which you want to add data followed by a comma. Then type the value you want the column to contain.

■ String arguments must be enclosed in quotation marks.

Extra

In order to add a record to a table in a database, the database driver must support the `insertRow` method. If errors occur when calling the `insertRow` method, you should check whether a version of the database driver that supports the method is available for your database program.

If you do not want to use the update methods of the `ResultSet` object to add a record, you can use the SQL `INSERT` command instead. You issue the `INSERT` command to a database using the `executeUpdate` method of the `Statement` object.

Example:

```
stmt.executeUpdate("INSERT INTO employees VALUES(4347, 'Peter', 456)");
```

You can access other rows in a result set to which you are adding a new row. When you finish inserting a row, you can move the cursor to any row in the result set. For example, you can use the `moveToCurrentRow` method of the `ResultSet` object to reposition the cursor at the last row accessed before you inserted the new record. To avoid losing the information you added to the insert row, you should move the cursor only after calling the `insertRow` method.

Example:

```
updRs.insertRow();
updRs.moveToCurrentRow();
```

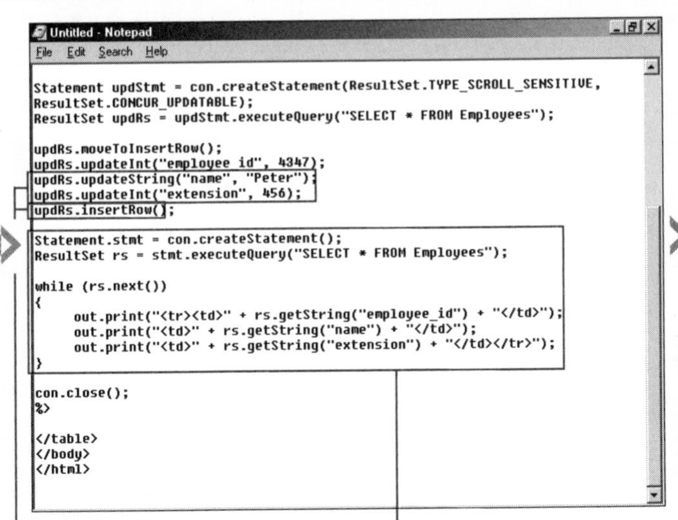

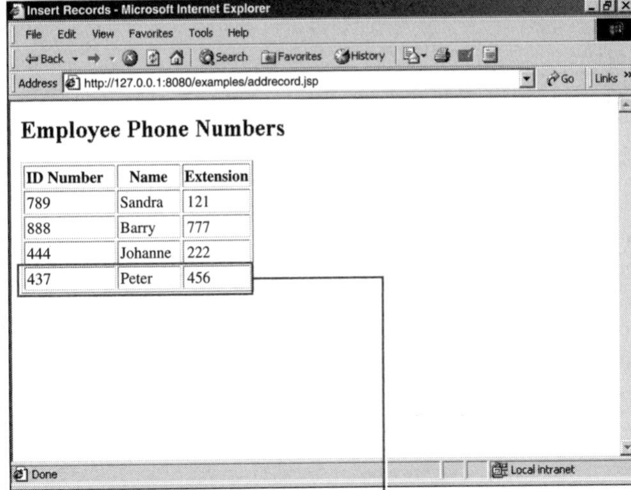

6 Repeat steps 4 and 5 for each value you want to insert for the record.

7 To insert the record into the result set and the database, type the name of the `ResultSet` object followed by **.insertRow()**.

8 Type the code that displays the information from the database.

9 Save the page with the .jsp extension and then display the JSP page in a Web browser.

■ The Web browser displays the results of adding a record to a table in a database.

ADD FORM DATA TO A DATABASE

A JSP page that contains a connection to a database can be used to add records to the database. Records are commonly added using data submitted by forms. Forms provide an easy-to-use interface for working with a database.

The `getParameter` method of the `request` object can be used in a JSP page to access data passed by a form. For more information about the `getParameter` method, see page 84.

When creating a result set to add a record to a database, you must set the result set type and concurrency type. For information about setting the result set type and concurrency type, see page 154.

The SQL `INSERT` statement allows you to add a record to a database. The `INSERT` statement uses the `INTO` clause to specify the name of the database table you want to add a record to and the names of the fields that store information in the table. The `VALUES` clause specifies the field values that make up the record you are adding to the database. You may have to enclose the field values in single or double quotation marks, depending on your database program.

It is common programming practice to store an SQL `INSERT` statement in a variable. Using variables can help make your code easier to read and update.

The SQL `INSERT` statement is executed by the `executeUpdate` method of the `Statement` object to add data to the database.

When creating the code for a form that will be used to add records to a database, you must specify the name of the JSP page that connects to the database in the `action` attribute of the `<form>` tag.

ADD FORM DATA TO A DATABASE

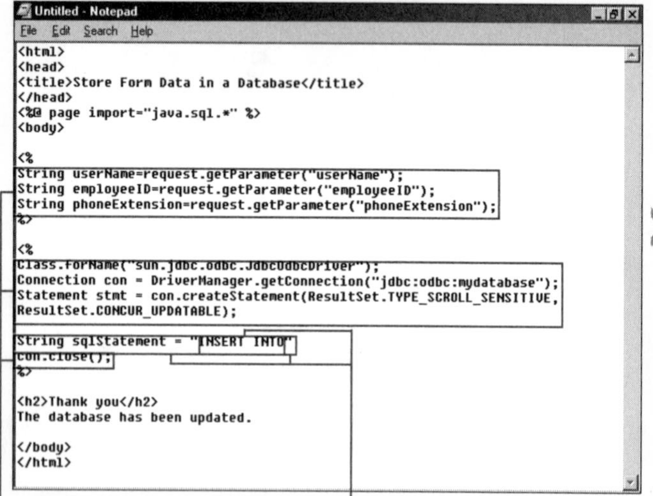

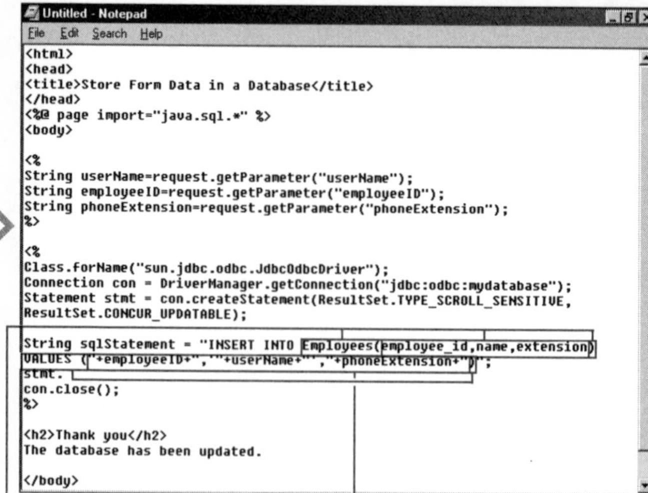

1 Type the code that accesses information passed to the JSP page by a form.

2 Type the code that creates a connection to the database you want to add records to and creates a result set.

3 Type the code that creates a variable to store the SQL `INSERT` statement followed by **=""**.

4 Between the quotation marks, type **INSERT INTO**.

5 Type the name of the table in the database that you want to add records to followed by ().

6 Between the parentheses, type the name of each field in the table, separated by a comma.

7 Type **VALUES()**.

8 Between the parentheses, type the code that uses the information passed by the form.

Using an `if` statement allows you to confirm that information has been submitted by a form before the JSP page connects to the database that stores the form data. For example, you can ensure that a user name entered into a form contains at least one character before the JSP page sends any information to the database.

TYPE THIS:

```
if (userName.length()>0)
{
Class.forName("sun.jdbc.odbc.JdbcOdbcDriver");
Connection con = DriverManager.getConnection("jdbc:odbc:mydatabase");
Statement stmt = con.createStatement(ResultSet.TYPE_SCROLL_SENSITIVE,ResultSet.CONCUR_UPDATABLE);

String sqlStatement = "INSERT INTO Employees(employee_id,name,extension) VALUES
("+employeeID+",'"+userName+"',"+phoneExtension+")";
stmt.executeUpdate(sqlStatement);
}
else
{
out.print("Please enter a user name.");
}
```

RESULT:

Please enter a user name.

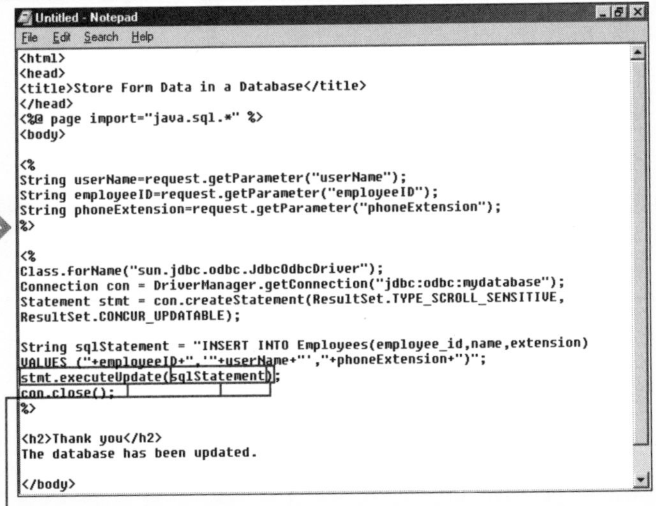

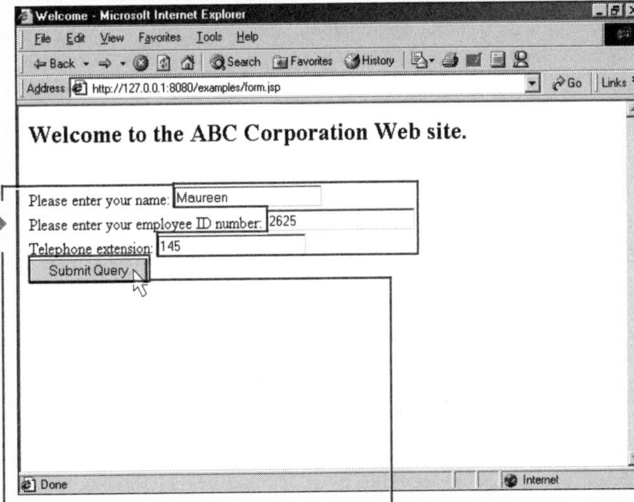

9 Type the name of the `Statement` object followed by a dot. Then type **executeUpdate()**.

10 Between the parentheses, type the variable name that stores the SQL `INSERT` statement.

11 Save the page with the .jsp extension.

12 In a Web browser, display the form you created to add records to the database.

13 Enter data into the form.

14 Click the submit button to pass the data in the form to the JSP page.

■ The JSP page that adds the record will appear and the record will be added to the database.

UPDATE A RECORD

Once you establish a connection with a database, you can edit the information contained in the database. Editing the information in a database allows you to keep the information up-to-date.

If you want to update a single record, you can use the `WHERE` clause with the SQL `SELECT` command to create a result set that stores only the row of data you want to update.

When a result set is created, the cursor is positioned above the first row of data. Before information in the result set can be modified, you must use the `next` method of the `ResultSet` object to move the cursor to the row that is to be updated, even if the result set contains only a single row.

You can specify the values you want to change for the current row using special update methods of the `ResultSet` object. The method name you use depends on the type of data to be used for the value. For example, if you want to specify a string value, you use the `updateString` method. To specify an integer value, you use the `updateInt` method.

Each update method requires two arguments. The first argument specifies the name of the column you want to contain the data. The second argument specifies the value that will be inserted into the column. The data type of the value must match the update method you specified.

Once the update methods have been used to specify the data you want to change in the current record, you can call the `updateRow` method of the `ResultSet` object to update the information in the database.

UPDATE A RECORD

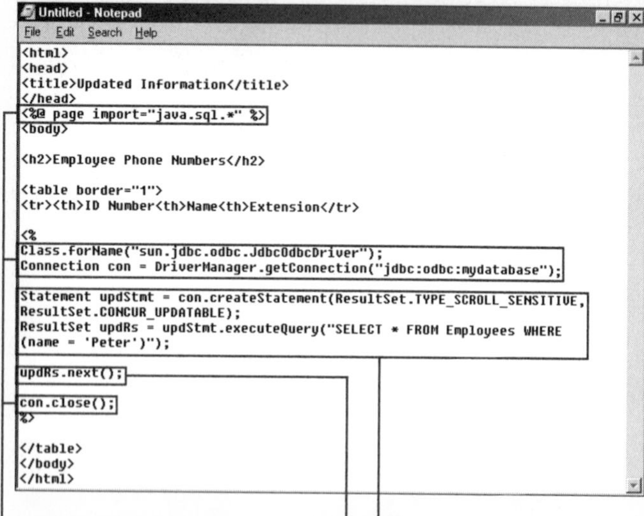

Untitled - Notepad

```
<html>
<head>
<title>Updated Information</title>
</head>
<%@ page import="java.sql.*" %>
<body>

<h2>Employee Phone Numbers</h2>

<table border="1">
<tr><th>ID Number<th>Name<th>Extension</tr>

<%
Class.forName("sun.jdbc.odbc.JdbcOdbcDriver");
Connection con = DriverManager.getConnection("jdbc:odbc:mydatabase");

Statement updStmt = con.createStatement(ResultSet.TYPE_SCROLL_SENSITIVE,
ResultSet.CONCUR_UPDATABLE);
ResultSet updRs = updStmt.executeQuery("SELECT * FROM Employees WHERE
(name = 'Peter')");

updRs.next();

con.close();
%>

</table>
</body>
</html>
```

Untitled - Notepad

```
<head>
<title>Updated Information</title>
</head>
<%@ page import="java.sql.*" %>
<body>

<h2>Employee Phone Numbers</h2>

<table border="1">
<tr><th>ID Number<th>Name<th>Extension</tr>

<%
Class.forName("sun.jdbc.odbc.JdbcOdbcDriver");
Connection con = DriverManager.getConnection("jdbc:odbc:mydatabase");

Statement updStmt = con.createStatement(ResultSet.TYPE_SCROLL_SENSITIVE,
ResultSet.CONCUR_UPDATABLE);
ResultSet updRs = updStmt.executeQuery("SELECT * FROM Employees WHERE
(name = 'Peter')");

updRs.next();
updRs.updateString("name", "Pete");

con.close();
%>

</table>
</body>
</html>
```

1 Type the code that creates a connection to a database in which you want to update records.

2 Type the code that retrieves a record from the table you want to update and allows you to update the database.

3 Type the code that moves the cursor to the row you want to update.

4 To specify a new value for a column in the record you want to update, type the name of the `ResultSet` object followed by a dot. Then type the update method you want to use followed by ().

5 Between the parentheses, type the name of the column you want to update followed by a comma. Then type the new value you want the column to contain.

■ String arguments must be enclosed in quotation marks.

Extra

If you do not want to use the update methods of the `ResultSet` object to update a record, you can use the SQL `UPDATE` statement instead. You issue the `UPDATE` command to a database using the `executeUpdate` method of the `Statement` object.

Example:

```
stmt.executeUpdate("UPDATE Employees SET
name = 'Pete' WHERE (name = 'Peter')");
```

You can cancel updates to a database by using the `cancelRowUpdates` method. The `cancelRowUpdates` method can be called after any update methods are used, but before the `updateRow` method is called. Canceling updates is useful if the JSP code detects invalid data or a database access error.

Example:

```
updRs.updateString("name", "Pete");
updRs.cancelRowUpdates();
```

You can also use column numbers instead of column names to specify the columns you want to update in a record. In SQL, column numbers start at column 1, not 0 like many other indexing systems used in programming.

Example:

```
updRs.next();
updRs.updateString(2, "Pete");
updRs.updateInt(3, 456);
updRs.updateRow();
```

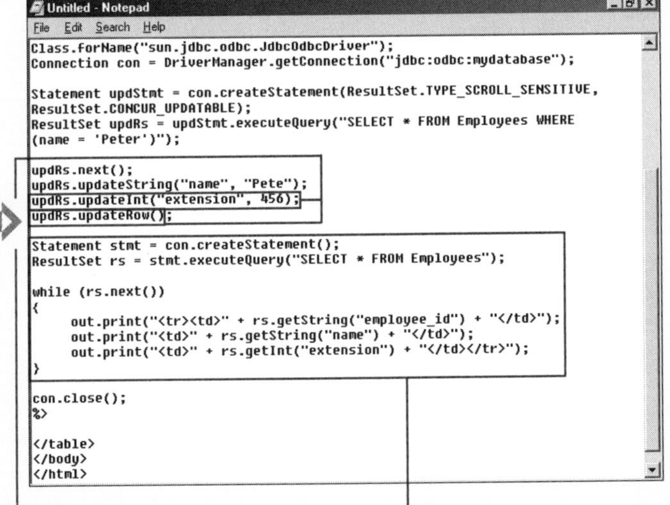

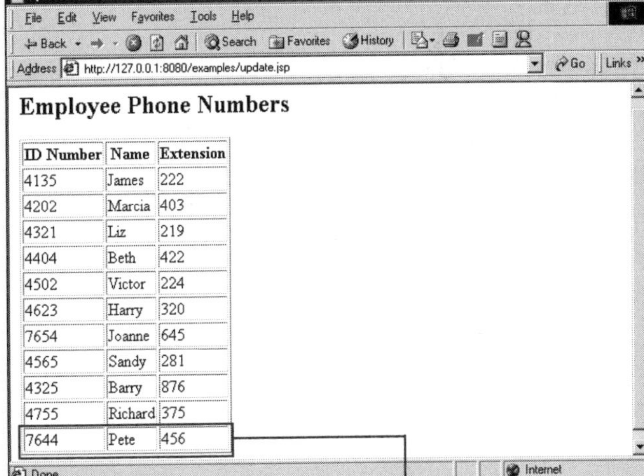

6 Repeat steps 4 and 5 for each column you want to update.

7 To change the information in the database, type the name of the `ResultSet` object followed by **.updateRow()**.

8 Type the code that displays the information in the database.

9 Save the page with the .jsp extension and then display the JSP page in a Web browser.

■ The Web browser displays the result of updating a row in a database.

MAKE A BATCH UPDATE

SQL statements are usually sent to a database program one at a time and the program processes each SQL statement as it is received. In most cases, this is an acceptable way of processing SQL statements. However, for some larger databases, it may be more efficient to combine individual SQL statements together in a batch that is sent at one time. This is especially useful when sending multiple update statements to a database program.

When a connection to a database is established, the connection is usually configured to send each SQL statement to the database program as it is created. To make batch updates, you must set up the `Connection` object so the connection will wait for a specific instruction before sending the SQL statements to the database program. To do this, you must set the parameter of the `setAutoCommit` method of the `Connection` object to `false`.

An SQL statement is added to a batch using the `addBatch` method of the `Statement` object. The argument of the `addBatch` method must be a valid SQL statement, although the statement cannot return a result set. Once all the SQL statements you want to send to the database program have been added to the batch, the batch can be sent to the database program using the `executeBatch` method of the `Connection` object.

After the `executeBatch` method is called, you must also call the `commit` method of the `Connection` object to make any changes to the database permanent. If the `commit` method is not called, the changes made by the batch update will still be reflected in the result set, but the changes will not be permanently written to the database.

MAKE A BATCH UPDATE

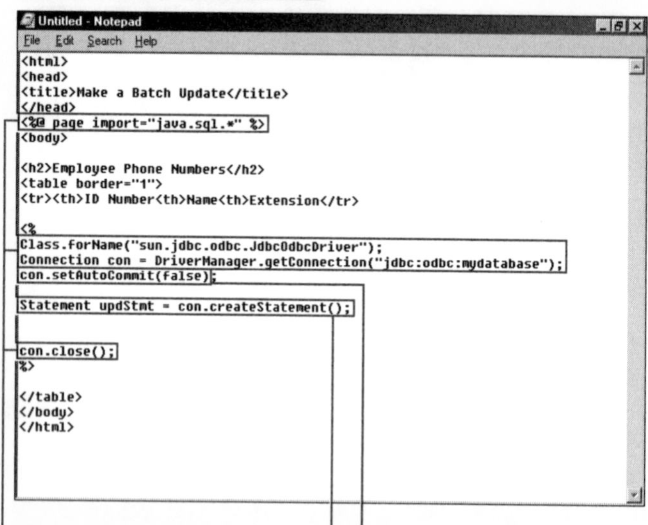

```
<html>
<head>
<title>Make a Batch Update</title>
</head>
<%@ page import="java.sql.*" %>
<body>

<h2>Employee Phone Numbers</h2>
<table border="1">
<tr><th>ID Number<th>Name<th>Extension</tr>

<%
Class.forName("sun.jdbc.odbc.JdbcOdbcDriver");
Connection con = DriverManager.getConnection("jdbc:odbc:mydatabase");
con.setAutoCommit(false);

Statement updStmt = con.createStatement();


con.close();
%>

</table>
</body>
</html>
```

1 Type the code that creates a connection to the database to which you want to make a batch update.

2 To disable the auto-commit mode of the `Connection` object, type **con.setAutoCommit(false)**.

3 Type the code that creates a `Statement` object for the batch.

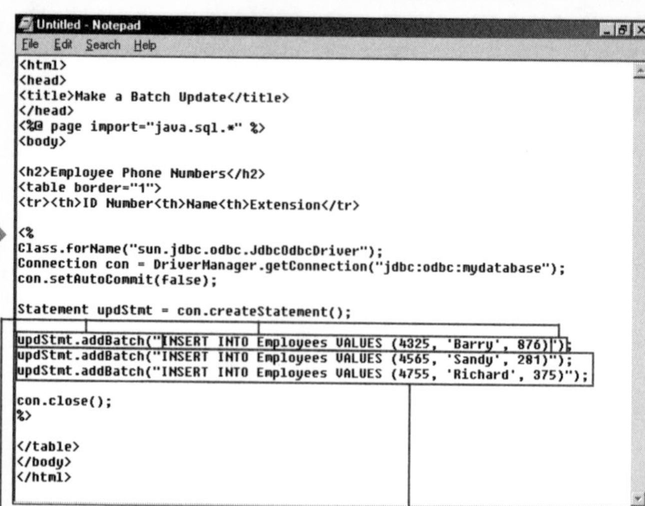

```
<html>
<head>
<title>Make a Batch Update</title>
</head>
<%@ page import="java.sql.*" %>
<body>

<h2>Employee Phone Numbers</h2>
<table border="1">
<tr><th>ID Number<th>Name<th>Extension</tr>

<%
Class.forName("sun.jdbc.odbc.JdbcOdbcDriver");
Connection con = DriverManager.getConnection("jdbc:odbc:mydatabase");
con.setAutoCommit(false);

Statement updStmt = con.createStatement();

updStmt.addBatch("INSERT INTO Employees VALUES (4325, 'Barry', 876)");
updStmt.addBatch("INSERT INTO Employees VALUES (4565, 'Sandy', 281)");
updStmt.addBatch("INSERT INTO Employees VALUES (4755, 'Richard', 375)");

con.close();
%>

</table>
</body>
</html>
```

4 To add an SQL statement to the batch, type the name of the `Statement` object followed by **.addBatch("")**.

5 Between the quotation marks, type a valid SQL statement.

6 Repeat steps 4 and 5 for each SQL statement you want to add to the batch.

Extra

You should make sure that the database driver used to communicate with the database program is able to perform batch operations before using the `executeBatch` method. If the database driver does not support batch operations, you should check if a newer version of the driver is available.

After using the `commit` method of the `Connection` object to make your changes to a database permanent, you may need to re-enable the auto-commit mode of the `Connection` object. To do so, you must set the parameter of the `setAutoCommit` method of the `Connection` object to `true`.

Example:

```
updStmt.executeBatch();
con.commit();
con.setAutoCommit(true);
```

The `executeBatch` method returns an array of integers that indicates the number of records affected by each SQL statement in a batch. The value of the first element in the array corresponds to the first SQL statement in the batch, and so forth.

TYPE THIS:

```
updStmt.addBatch("DELETE FROM Employees WHERE name='Martine'");
updStmt.addBatch("DELETE FROM Employees WHERE name='Tom'");
int[] returnValues = updStmt.executeBatch();
for (int x = 0; x < returnValues.length; x++)
{
     out.print("SQL statement #" + (x+1) + " deleted ");
     out.print(returnValues[x] + " record(s)");
}
```

RESULT:

SQL statement #1 deleted 1 record(s)
SQL statement #2 deleted 1 record(s)

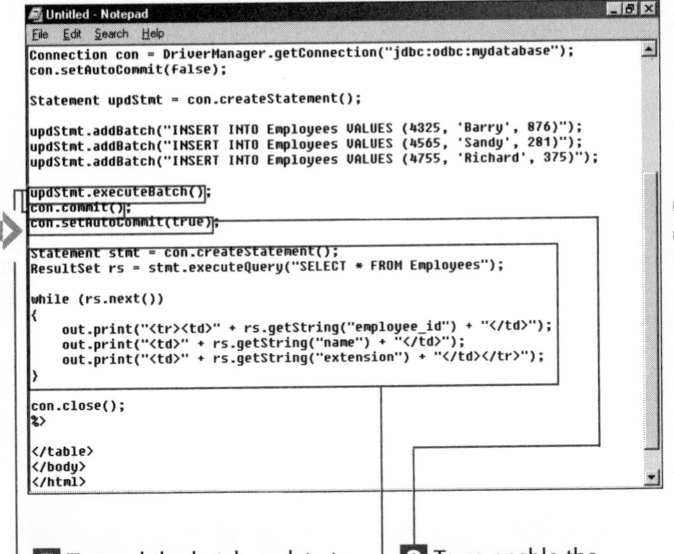
```
Connection con = DriverManager.getConnection("jdbc:odbc:mydatabase");
con.setAutoCommit(false);

Statement updStmt = con.createStatement();

updStmt.addBatch("INSERT INTO Employees VALUES (4325, 'Barry', 876)");
updStmt.addBatch("INSERT INTO Employees VALUES (4565, 'Sandy', 281)");
updStmt.addBatch("INSERT INTO Employees VALUES (4755, 'Richard', 375)");

updStmt.executeBatch();
con.commit();
con.setAutoCommit(true);

Statement stmt = con.createStatement();
ResultSet rs = stmt.executeQuery("SELECT * FROM Employees");

while (rs.next())
{
    out.print("<tr><td>" + rs.getString("employee_id") + "</td>");
    out.print("<td>" + rs.getString("name") + "</td>");
    out.print("<td>" + rs.getString("extension") + "</td></tr>");
}

con.close();
%>

</table>
</body>
</html>
```

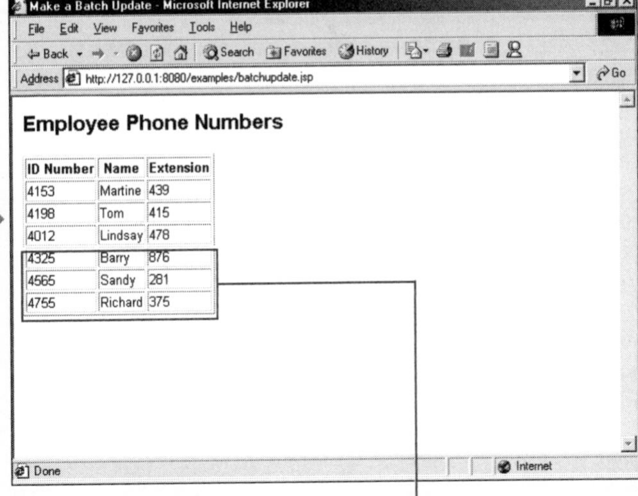

ID Number	Name	Extension
4153	Martine	439
4198	Tom	415
4012	Lindsay	478
4325	Barry	876
4565	Sandy	281
4755	Richard	375

7 To send the batch update to the database program, type the name of the `Statement` object followed by **.executeBatch()**.

8 To make any changes to the database permanent, type the name of the `Connection` object followed by **.commit()**.

9 To re-enable the auto-commit mode of the `Connection` object, type **con.setAutoCommit(true)**.

10 Type the code that retrieves information from the updated database and displays the information on the JSP page.

11 Save the page with the .jsp extension and then display the JSP page in a Web browser.

■ The Web browser displays the result of making a batch update.

CREATE A PREPARED STATEMENT

Before a database program can execute an SQL statement sent from a JSP page, the SQL statement is compiled into a form that is understood by the inner workings of the database program. Compiling an SQL statement can be a relatively lengthy process, but you can create a prepared statement to save time in accessing the database after the initial query is processed.

A prepared statement is an SQL statement that is precompiled by a database program. A prepared statement needs to be compiled only once, so it is very useful in cases where the same SQL statement will be sent to the database program numerous times.

You use a `PreparedStatement` object to send an SQL statement that you want to precompile to a database program. A `PreparedStatement` object is created using the `prepareStatement` method of the `Connection` object. The `prepareStatement` method takes the SQL statement you want to precompile as an argument.

You use the `executeQuery` method of the `PreparedStatement` object to instruct the database program to process the SQL statement that has been precompiled. The result generated when a prepared statement is processed is usually assigned to a `ResultSet` object.

Depending on the SQL statement you are precompiling, you may need to specify the result set type and concurrency type of the result set in the `prepareStatement` method. For information about specifying result set and concurrency types, see page 154.

If the SQL statement you want to precompile requires parameters, you must set up the prepared statement to accept parameters. For information about using parameters in a prepared statement, see page 166.

CREATE A PREPARED STATEMENT

```
<html>
<head>
<title>Create a Prepared Statement</title>
</head>
<%@ page import="java.sql.*" %>
<body>

<h2>Employee Phone Numbers</h2>
<table border="1">
<tr><th>ID Number<th>Name<th>Extension</tr>

<%
Class.forName("sun.jdbc.odbc.JdbcOdbcDriver");
Connection con = DriverManager.getConnection("jdbc:odbc:mydatabase");

PreparedStatement pstmt = con.prepareStatement("");
con.close();
%>

</table>
</body>
</html>
```

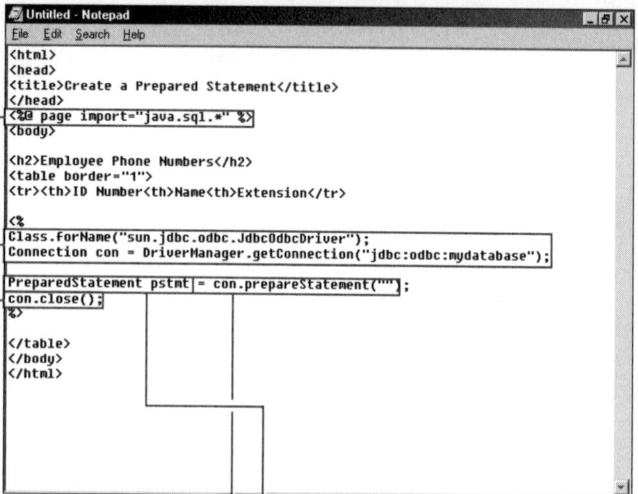

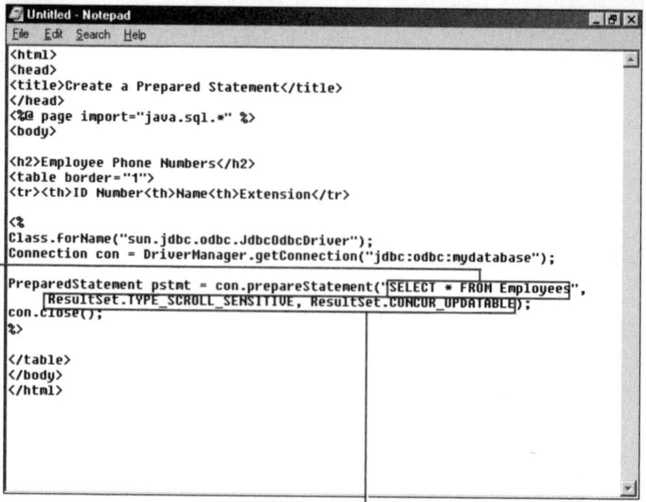

1 Type the code that creates a connection to the database to which you want to send a prepared statement.

2 To create a `PreparedStatement` object, type **PreparedStatement** followed by a name for the `PreparedStatement` object.

3 Type = and the name of the `Connection` object followed by **.prepareStatement("")**.

```
<html>
<head>
<title>Create a Prepared Statement</title>
</head>
<%@ page import="java.sql.*" %>
<body>

<h2>Employee Phone Numbers</h2>
<table border="1">
<tr><th>ID Number<th>Name<th>Extension</tr>

<%
Class.forName("sun.jdbc.odbc.JdbcOdbcDriver");
Connection con = DriverManager.getConnection("jdbc:odbc:mydatabase");

PreparedStatement pstmt = con.prepareStatement("SELECT * FROM Employees",
    ResultSet.TYPE_SCROLL_SENSITIVE, ResultSet.CONCUR_UPDATABLE);
con.close();
%>

</table>
</body>
</html>
```

4 Between the quotation marks, type the SQL statement to be precompiled.

5 If necessary, type the code that specifies the result set type and concurrency type for the `ResultSet` object that will store the results returned from the database.

Extra

When using the `executeQuery` method, a result set is generated to store the results of the query. The `execute` method of the `PreparedStatement` object can be used instead of the `executeQuery` method to execute a prepared statement that does not return a result. For example, you may use the `execute` method for an SQL statement that removes a table from a database.

Example:

```
PreparedStatement pstmt = con.prepareStatement("DROP TABLE Employee");
pstmt.execute();
```

Like the `Statement` object, the `PreparedStatement` object can use the `execute`, `executeQuery` and `executeUpdate` methods to execute SQL statements. These methods do not require any arguments when used with a `PreparedStatement` object because the SQL statement is specified when the `PreparedStatement` object is created. When the same methods are used with a `Statement` object however, an SQL statement is usually passed to the methods as an argument. For more information about the methods supported by the `Statement` and `PreparedStatement` objects, refer to the `java.sql` package documentation.

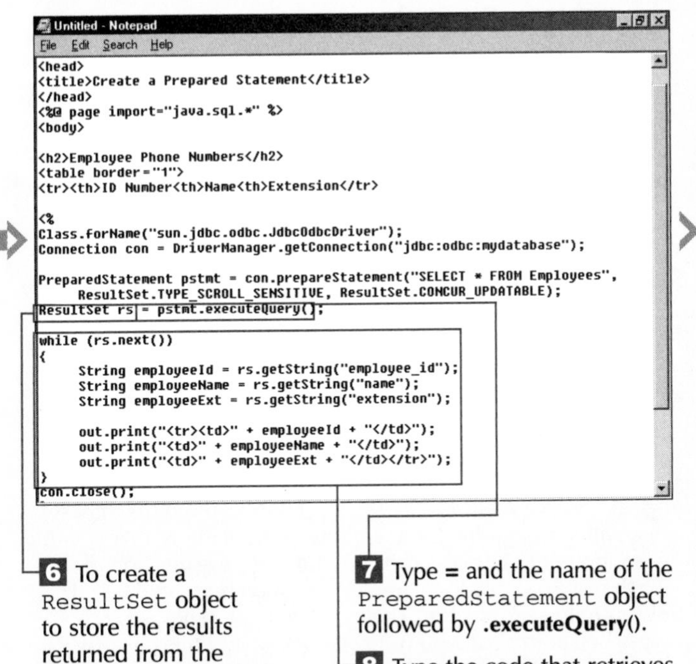

```
<head>
<title>Create a Prepared Statement</title>
</head>
<%@ page import="java.sql.*" %>
<body>

<h2>Employee Phone Numbers</h2>
<table border="1">
<tr><th>ID Number<th>Name<th>Extension</tr>

<%
Class.forName("sun.jdbc.odbc.JdbcOdbcDriver");
Connection con = DriverManager.getConnection("jdbc:odbc:mydatabase");

PreparedStatement pstmt = con.prepareStatement("SELECT * FROM Employees",
     ResultSet.TYPE_SCROLL_SENSITIVE, ResultSet.CONCUR_UPDATABLE);
ResultSet rs = pstmt.executeQuery();

while (rs.next())
{
     String employeeId = rs.getString("employee_id");
     String employeeName = rs.getString("name");
     String employeeExt = rs.getString("extension");

     out.print("<tr><td>" + employeeId + "</td>");
     out.print("<td>" + employeeName + "</td>");
     out.print("<td>" + employeeExt + "</td></tr>");
}
con.close();
```

Employee Phone Numbers

ID Number	Name	Extension
4135	James	222
4145	Steven	209
4202	Marcia	403
4321	Liz	219
4399	Ann	306
4404	Beth	422
4502	Victor	224
4623	Harry	320

6 To create a `ResultSet` object to store the results returned from the database, type **ResultSet** followed by a name for the `ResultSet` object.

7 Type **=** and the name of the `PreparedStatement` object followed by **.executeQuery()**.

8 Type the code that retrieves the data from each row of the result set and formats the data for display.

9 Save the page with the .jsp extension and then display the JSP page in a Web browser.

■ The Web browser displays the results of using a prepared statement to send SQL statements to a database.

USING PARAMETERS IN A PREPARED STATEMENT

Prepared statements are ideal for repeatedly sending the same SQL statements to a database. Typically, prepared statements are used with SQL statements that have parameters. For example, an SQL statement can be used to add records to a database. The structure of the SQL statement remains the same for each record that is added, but the values of the parameters change each time the statement is executed.

The `PreparedStatement` object is used to issue an SQL statement that contains one or more parameters to a database. When creating a prepared statement that uses parameters, you use question marks to indicate where you want to place parameter values in the SQL statement. There is no limit to the number of question marks you can use in an SQL statement.

Before the SQL statement can be executed, the values for the question marks must be specified using special set methods of the `PreparedStatement` object. The method name you use depends on the type of data to be used for the value. For example, if you want to specify a string value for a question mark, you use the `setString` method. To specify an integer value, you use the `setInt` method.

Each set method requires two arguments. The first argument specifies the position of the question mark in the SQL statement. The position of the first question mark in an SQL statement is 1. The second argument specifies the value that will replace the question mark in the SQL statement. The data type of the value must match the set method you specified.

Once the values have been specified for the SQL statement, you can use the `execute` method of the `PreparedStatement` object to process the SQL statement using the parameters you set.

USING PARAMETERS IN A PREPARED STATEMENT

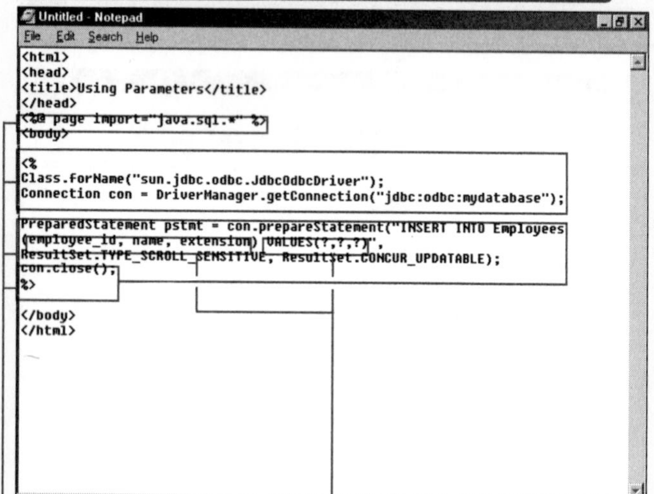

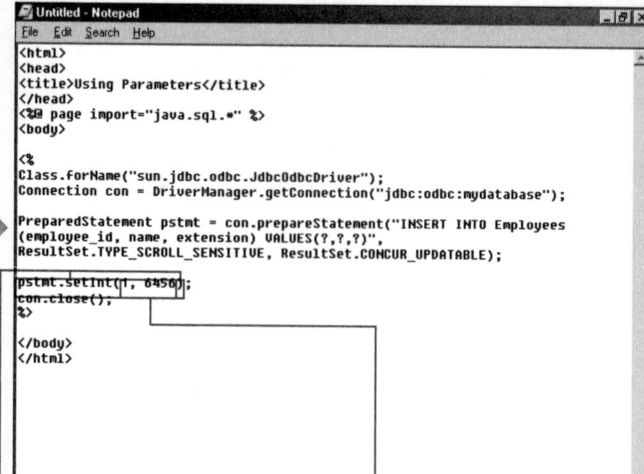

1 Type the code that connects the JSP page to the database to which you want to send a prepared statement.

2 Type the code that creates the `PreparedStatement` object and allows you to update the database.

3 Between the parentheses of the `prepareStatement` method, type the names of the fields in the table to which you want to add information. Separate each name with a comma.

4 Type **VALUES(?, ?, ?)**.

5 To create a method that will store a value for a question mark, type the name for the `PreparedStatement` object followed by a dot. Then type the set method you want to use followed by ().

6 Between the parentheses, type the number that indicates the position of the question mark in the SQL statement, followed by a comma and the value for the question mark.

■ String values must be enclosed in quotation marks.

Extra

The following table displays the set methods commonly used to specify parameter values for specific data types. For a complete list of set methods and data types that can be used with prepared statements, refer to the `java.sql` package documentation.

METHOD:	DATA TYPE:	METHOD:	DATA TYPE:
`setArray`	Array	`setFloat`	Float value
`setBigDecimal`	Large decimal number	`setInt`	Integer value
`setBlob`	Database blob type	`setLong`	Long value
`setBoolean`	Boolean value	`setNull`	Null value
`setByte`	Byte value	`setObject`	Object
`setBytes`	Array of bytes	`setShort`	Short value
`setDate`	Date	`setString`	String value
`setDouble`	Double value	`setTime`	Time

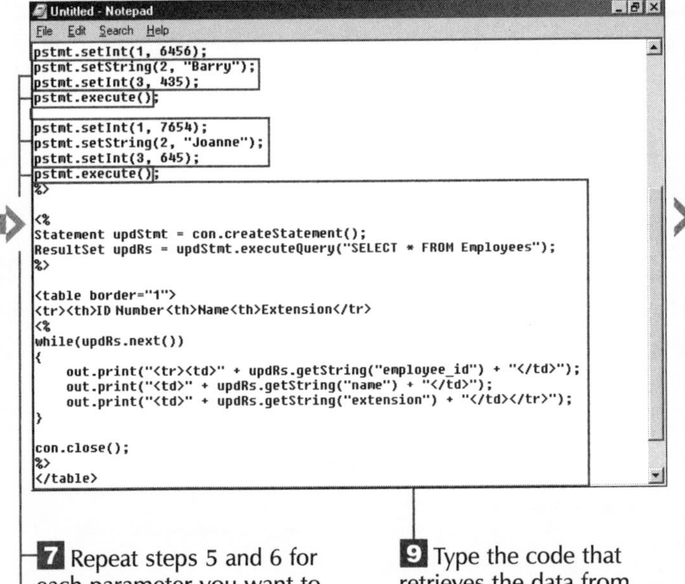

Untitled - Notepad
File Edit Search Help
pstmt.setInt(1, 6456);
pstmt.setString(2, "Barry");
pstmt.setInt(3, 435);
pstmt.execute();
pstmt.setInt(1, 7654);
pstmt.setString(2, "Joanne");
pstmt.setInt(3, 645);
pstmt.execute();
%>
<%
Statement updStmt = con.createStatement();
ResultSet updRs = updStmt.executeQuery("SELECT * FROM Employees");
%>
<table border="1">
<tr><th>ID Number<th>Name<th>Extension</tr>
<%
while(updRs.next())
{
out.print("<tr><td>" + updRs.getString("employee_id") + "</td>");
out.print("<td>" + updRs.getString("name") + "</td>");
out.print("<td>" + updRs.getString("extension") + "</td></tr>");
}
con.close();
%>
</table>

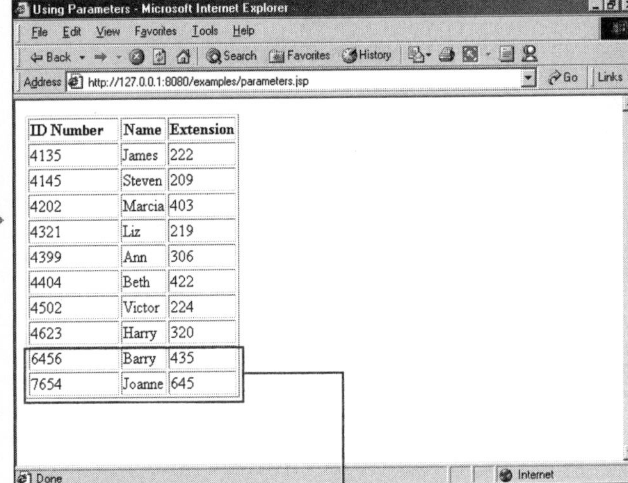

ID Number	Name	Extension
4135	James	222
4145	Steven	209
4202	Marcia	403
4321	Liz	219
4399	Ann	306
4404	Beth	422
4502	Victor	224
4623	Harry	320
6456	Barry	435
7654	Joanne	645

7 Repeat steps 5 and 6 for each parameter you want to specify.

8 To execute the prepared statement, type the name for the `PreparedStatement` object followed by **.execute()**.

9 Type the code that retrieves the data from the database and formats the data for display.

10 Save the page with the .jsp extension and then display the JSP page in a Web browser.

■ The Web browser displays the results of using parameters in a prepared statement. The information in the database is also updated.

CALL A STORED PROCEDURE

A stored procedure is a set of instructions that are stored on a database server. A stored procedure can be as simple as an SQL statement that returns all the information in a table, but stored procedures are most often used to increase the efficiency of performing complex queries on a database. For example, stored procedures are ideal for tasks such as retrieving information based on a number of parameters. Using stored procedures tends to be more efficient than repeatedly using complex SQL statements because the stored procedures are compiled and executed within the database engine itself.

In order to use a stored procedure, the database program must support stored procedures and the stored procedure must be saved on the database server. Stored procedures are usually supported by large database programs such as Microsoft SQL Server and Oracle. Smaller database programs such as Microsoft Access often do not support stored procedures. You should consult the documentation included with your software to determine whether your database program supports stored procedures.

Before calling a stored procedure, you must first create a `CallableStatement` object that will retrieve the stored procedure from the database server. `CallableStatement` objects are commonly named cstmt. To create a `CallableStatement` object, you use the `prepareCall` method of the `Connection` object created when the database connection was set up. When using the `prepareCall` method, you use the `call` keyword followed by the name of the stored procedure you want to call. The name must match the name of a stored procedure already saved on the database server.

Once the `CallableStatement` object is created, the `executeQuery` method is used to generate a `ResultSet` object that will contain the results generated by the database using the stored procedure.

CALL A STORED PROCEDURE

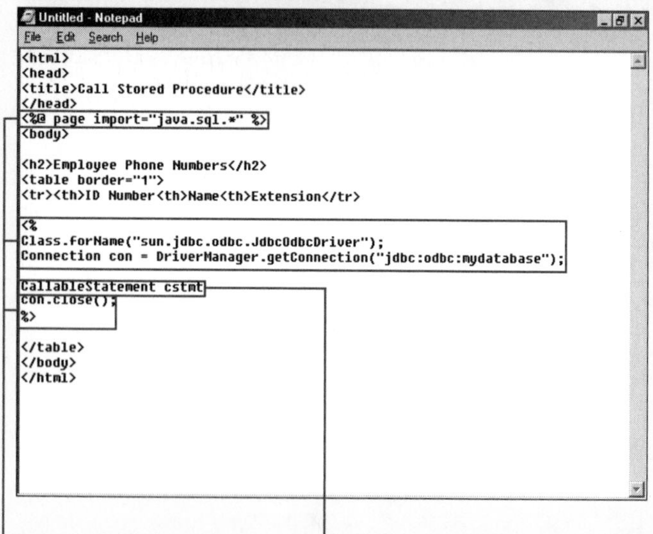


```
<html>
<head>
<title>Call Stored Procedure</title>
</head>
<%@ page import="java.sql.*" %>
<body>

<h2>Employee Phone Numbers</h2>
<table border="1">
<tr><th>ID Number<th>Name<th>Extension</tr>

<%
Class.forName("sun.jdbc.odbc.JdbcOdbcDriver");
Connection con = DriverManager.getConnection("jdbc:odbc:mydatabase");

CallableStatement cstmt
con.close();
%>

</table>
</body>
</html>
```

1 Type the code that creates the connection to the database that contains the stored procedure.

2 To create the `CallableStatement` object that will allow you to call a stored procedure, type **CallableStatement** followed by a name for the `CallableStatement` object.

Untitled - Notepad

```
<html>
<head>
<title>Call Stored Procedure</title>
</head>
<%@ page import="java.sql.*" %>
<body>

<h2>Employee Phone Numbers</h2>
<table border="1">
<tr><th>ID Number<th>Name<th>Extension</tr>

<%
Class.forName("sun.jdbc.odbc.JdbcOdbcDriver");
Connection con = DriverManager.getConnection("jdbc:odbc:mydatabase");

CallableStatement cstmt = con.prepareCall("{call getLargeExt}");
con.close();
%>

</table>
</body>
</html>
```

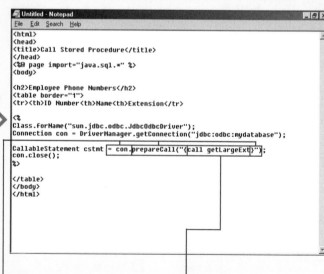

3 Type = and the name of the `Connection` object followed by a dot.

4 Type **prepareCall**("{}").

5 Between the braces, type **call** followed by the name of the stored procedure you want to use.

Extra

You can create a stored procedure by using a JSP page to issue SQL commands to the database server. You use the `execute` method of the `Statement` object to issue the SQL statements to the database server. When naming a stored procedure, you can use a lowercase first letter and then capitalize the first letter of each of the following words to make the name easy to read. For example, a stored procedure used to retrieve records in an employee database with extension numbers of more than three digits may be called getLargeExt.

Example:

```
Statement stmt = con.createStatement();
stmt.execute("CREATE PROCEDURE getLargeExt AS
SELECT * FROM Employees WHERE extension > 999")
```

You can create a stored procedure directly on your database server. The SQL statements and methods you use to create a stored procedure on a database server depend on the database program you are using. You should consult your database program's documentation for information.

Example:

```
CREATE PROCEDURE getLargeExt AS SELECT * FROM Employees
WHERE extension > 999
```

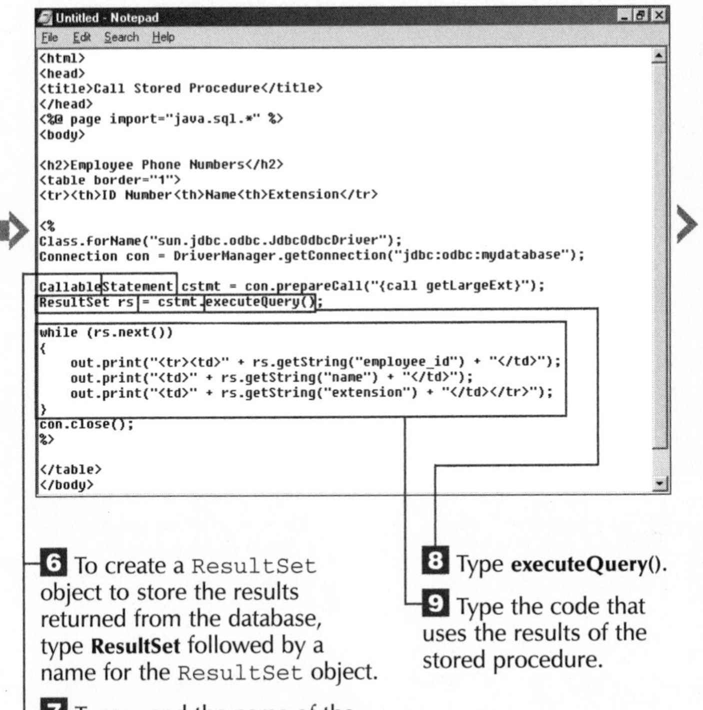

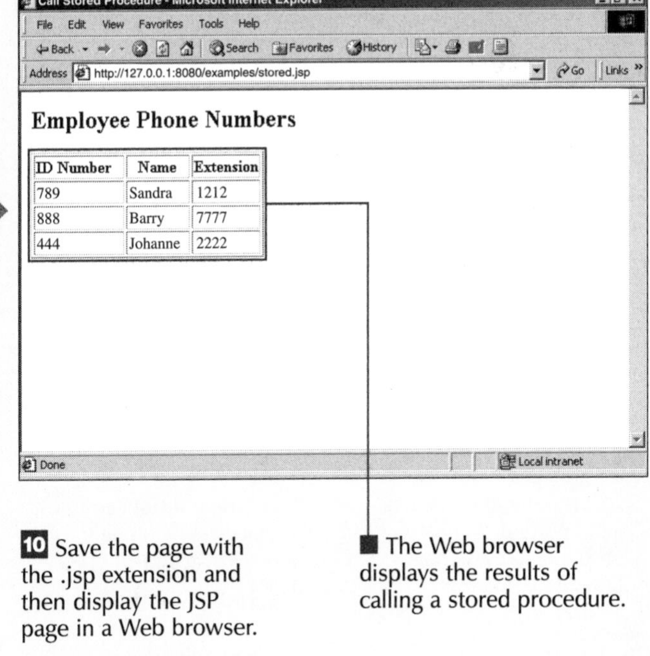

6 To create a `ResultSet` object to store the results returned from the database, type **ResultSet** followed by a name for the `ResultSet` object.

7 Type = and the name of the `CallableStatement` object followed by dot.

8 Type **executeQuery()**.

9 Type the code that uses the results of the stored procedure.

10 Save the page with the .jsp extension and then display the JSP page in a Web browser.

■ The Web browser displays the results of calling a stored procedure.

GET DATABASE INFORMATION

The DatabaseMetaData object allows you to determine information about a database. Information you can determine using the DatabaseMetaData object includes a database program's configuration, the features the database supports and information about data stored in the database.

To determine information about a database, you first create a DatabaseMetaData object using the getMetaData method of the Connection object created when the connection was set up.

Once you create a DatabaseMetaData object, there are several methods of the object that you can use to determine specific information about the database to which you are connected.

One common use of the DatabaseMetaData object is to determine if a specific stored procedure exists on a database server. Stored procedures allow you to perform efficient queries on a database by storing and executing the instructions for the queries on the database server itself. You use the getProcedures method of the DatabaseMetaData object to retrieve the names of stored procedures available to the JSP page connected to the database. Using three null values as the arguments of the getProcedures method will retrieve a list of all the available stored procedures.

The information returned from the database using the DatabaseMetaData object is usually stored in a result set. Once information has been retrieved from a database and placed in a result set, you can retrieve the data from the result set. For information about retrieving information from a result set, see page 150.

Not all databases or database drivers will support all of the methods available to the DatabaseMetaData object. Typically, if a database or a database driver does not support a method implemented by the DatabaseMetaData object, an exception error will be generated. For information about error handling, see page 174.

GET DATABASE INFORMATION

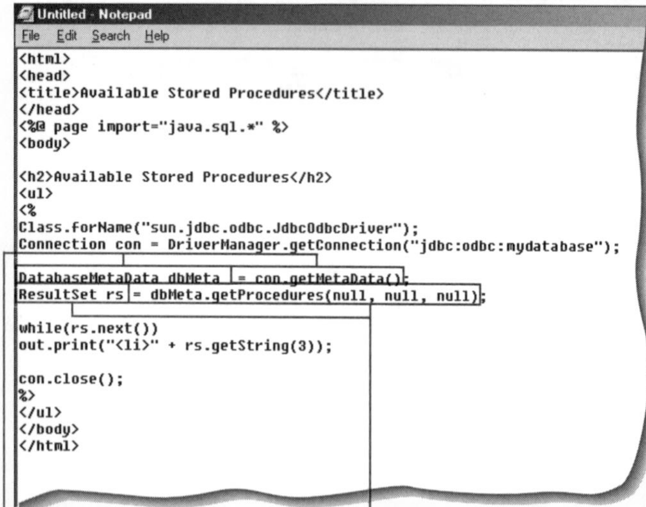

1 To retrieve information about the database to which a connection has been created, type **DatabaseMetaData** followed by a name for the DatabaseMetaData object.

2 Type = and the name of the Connection object followed by **.getMetaData()**.

3 To create a result set, type **ResultSet** followed by a name for the ResultSet object.

4 Type = and the name of the DatabaseMetaData object followed by **.getProcedures()**. Between the parentheses, type the arguments for the method.

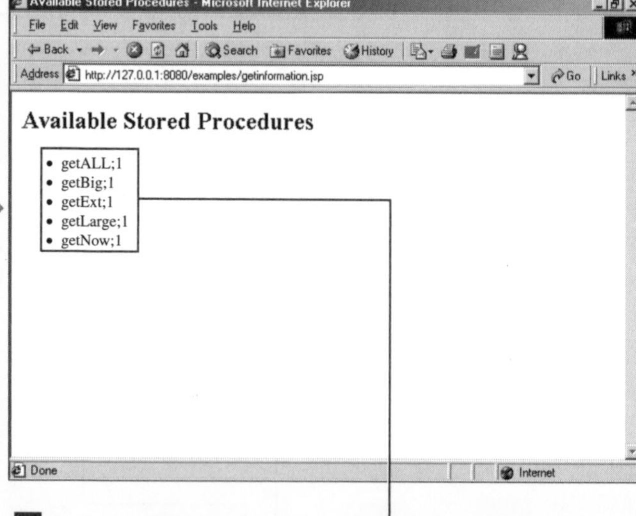

5 Save the page with the .jsp extension and then display the JSP page in a Web browser.

■ The Web browser displays the result of retrieving information about a database.

COMMONLY USED METHODS OF THE DatabaseMetaData OBJECT

There are several methods of the `DatabaseMetaData` object that you can use to determine information about a database. For a complete list of the methods supported by the `DatabaseMetaData` object, consult the `java.sql` package documentation. Before using any of the following methods in your JSP code, you should check your database program's documentation to verify whether the program supports the method you want to use.

METHOD:	DATA TYPE:
`boolean` **`allProceduresAreCallable()`**	Determines whether a user can call all the procedures returned by the `getProcedures` method.
`ResultSet` **`getCatalogs()`**	Returns the catalog names that the database contains.
`Connection` **`getConnection()`**	Returns the ID of the connection that produced the `DatabaseMetaData` object.
`String` **`getDatabaseProductName()`**	Returns the name of the database program.
`String` **`getDatabaseProductVersion()`**	Returns the version number of the database program.
`String` **`getDriverVersion()`**	Returns the version number of the JDBC driver.
`int` **`getMaxColumnNameLength()`**	Returns the maximum length allowed for column headings.
`int` **`getMaxConnections()`**	Returns the maximum number of active connections the database can support at one time.
`int` **`getMaxRowSize()`**	Returns the maximum length allowed for a row.
`int` **`getMaxStatementLength()`**	Returns the maximum length allowed for an SQL statement.
`ResultSet` **`getProcedures`**`(String catalog, String schemaPattern, String procedureNamePattern)`	Returns the stored procedures available in the database.
`String` **`getSQLKeywords()`**	Returns a comma-separated list of all the SQL keywords from the database.
`ResultSet` **`getTableTypes()`**	Returns the table types available in the database.
`String` **`getUserName()`**	Returns the user name used to access the database.
`boolean` **`isReadOnly()`**	Indicates whether the database is in read-only mode.
`boolean` **`supportsBatchUpdates()`**	Indicates whether the driver supports batch updates.
`boolean` **`supportsMultipleResultSets()`**	Indicates whether you can create multiple result sets at once.
`boolean` **`supportsNonNullableColumns()`**	Indicates whether you can specify that columns must contain data.
`boolean` **`supportsOuterJoins()`**	Indicates whether outer joins are supported.
`boolean` **`supportsStoredProcedures()`**	Indicates whether you can use stored procedures with the database.
`boolean` **`usesLocalFiles()`**	Indicates whether the database stores tables in a local file.

USING A JAVABEAN TO ACCESS A DATABASE

Accessing a database from a JSP page requires large amounts of Java code. You can use a JavaBean to separate the code that performs this task from the HTML code in the JSP page.

The code required to create a JavaBean that accesses a database is similar to that used to access a database directly from a JSP page. To retrieve information from a database, you must set up a connection to the database and then create a result set to store the retrieved information.

You can create a constructor method to perform initialization tasks in the JavaBean. A constructor method has the same name as the class and is executed when the JavaBean is instantiated. The constructor method for a JavaBean that accesses a database may load the appropriate drivers and connect to the database. You use the `Class.forName` statement to specify the name of the driver you want to load. A `Connection` object in the constructor method allows the JavaBean to connect to the database. The constructor method should also include the code to retrieve information from the database and store the information in a result set.

Retrieving information from a result set must be done using JavaBean properties. You can create a property and getter method for each column in the database you want to be made available through the JavaBean. For more information about getter methods, see page 128. You should declare the `ResultSet` object and properties in the body of the class. If you declare the object and properties elsewhere, such as within a method of the class, the getter methods may not be able to access the result set or the properties.

When using a JavaBean to access a database, errors may occur. You should ensure that the JavaBean includes `try` blocks and `catch` blocks to handle any errors.

USING A JAVABEAN TO ACCESS A DATABASE

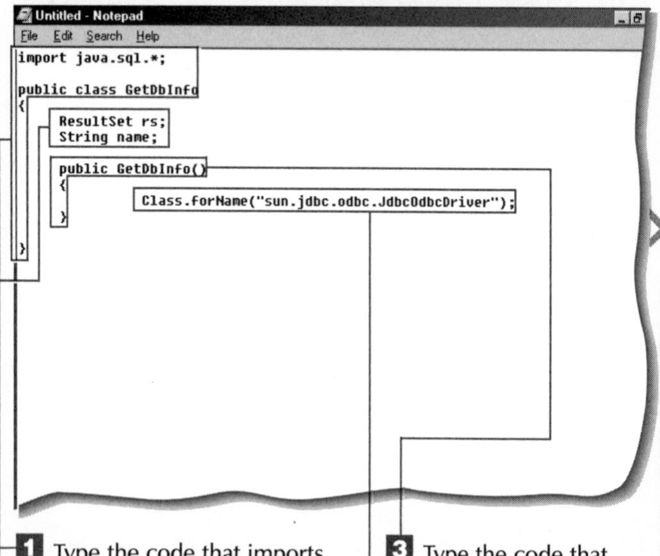

1 Type the code that imports the `java.sql` package and creates a JavaBean class.

2 Type the code that declares a `ResultSet` object and declares a property for each column in the database you want to be able to access from a JSP page.

3 Type the code that creates the constructor method for the JavaBean.

4 Type the code that loads the bridge driver.

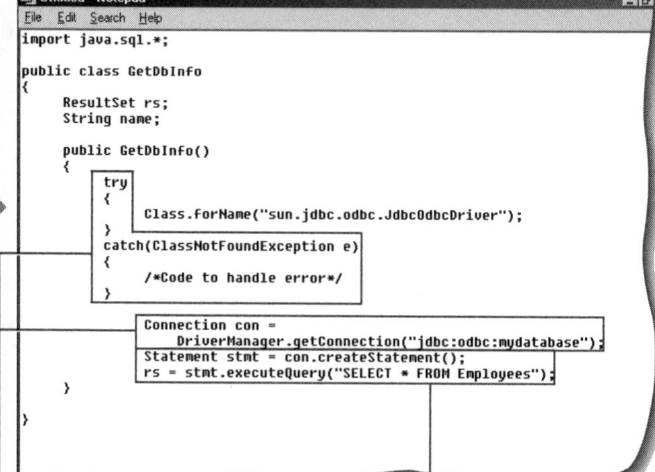

5 Create a `try` block and a `catch` block that will handle any exceptions that may be thrown when loading the bridge driver.

6 Type the code that creates a `Connection` object that specifies the location of the database you want to connect to.

7 Type the code that retrieves information from the database and stores it in a result set.

Apply It

To use a JavaBean you created to access a database, you use the `property` attribute of the `<jsp:getProperty>` tag to specify which column in the database you want to access. The JavaBean will then make the connection to the database and use the appropriate getter method of the JavaBean required to retrieve the information.

TYPE THIS:

```
<html>
<head>
<jsp:useBean id="DbBean" scope="session" class="GetDbInfo" />
<jsp:setProperty name="DbBean" property="*" />
</head>
<body>
The first three names in the database are:
<ul>
<%
for (int x = 0; x < 3; x++)
{
%>
     <li><jsp:getProperty name="DbBean" property="name" /></li>
<%
}
%>
</ul>
</body>
</html>
```

RESULT:

The first three names in the database are:

- James
- Steven
- Marcia

```
Class.forName("sun.jdbc.odbc.JdbcOdbcDriver");
        }
        catch(ClassNotFoundException e)
        {
            /*Code to handle error*/
        }

        try
        {
            Connection con =
                DriverManager.getConnection("jdbc:odbc:mydatabase");
            Statement stmt = con.createStatement();
            rs = stmt.executeQuery("SELECT * FROM Employees");
        }
        catch(SQLException e)
        {
            /*Code to handle error*/
        }
    }

    public String getName()
    {
            rs.next();
            name = rs.getString(2);

        return name;
    }
}
```

8 Create a `try` block and a `catch` block that will handle any exceptions that may be thrown when retrieving information from the database.

9 Type the code that creates the getter method that will retrieve information from the record set and return the value of a property specified in step 2.

```
        try
        {
            Connection con =
                DriverManager.getConnection("jdbc:odbc:mydatabase");
            Statement stmt = con.createStatement();
            rs = stmt.executeQuery("SELECT * FROM Employees");
        }
        catch(SQLException e)
        {
            /*Code to handle error*/
        }
    }

    public String getName()
    {
        try
        {
            rs.next();
            name = rs.getString(2);
        }
        catch(SQLException e)
        {
            /*Code to handle error*/
        }

        return name;
    }
}
```

10 Create a `try` block and a `catch` block that will handle any exceptions that may be thrown while accessing the database.

11 Save the file with the .java extension and then compile the source code for the file.

12 Copy the compiled class file to the appropriate directory on your Web server.

■ You can now use the JavaBean to access a database in your JSP pages.

INTRODUCTION TO EXCEPTION ERRORS

An exception error occurs when a problem is encountered during the processing of a JSP page. When an exception error occurs, an object that stores information about the error is created. Error handling is achieved by accessing the properties of this object.

The two main types of exception errors are RuntimeException errors and Error exception errors. `RuntimeException` and `Error` are the names of the classes that create objects when one of these types of errors is encountered.

RuntimeException errors are the most common type of exception error. These errors can arise from a variety of problems ranging from simple mathematical errors, such as dividing a number by zero, to more complex programming errors, such as specifying an incorrect type when attempting to cast an object.

Error exception errors occur when a problem related to the processing environment arises. For example, a problem with the Java Virtual Machine or a problem with a supporting file that is required by a JSP page will generate an Error exception.

Encountering an exception error does not necessarily mean that the processing of a JSP page must stop. Some errors can be handled within the code for the page. For example, you can create a `try` block and a `catch` block to handle exception errors that could potentially arise when a section of code is processed. This allows your code to recover from an exception error. For information about creating a `try` block and `catch` block, see page 176.

Some exception errors cannot be recovered from. For example, an Error exception error generated by a problem with the Java Virtual Machine cannot be fixed within the code for a JSP page. In such cases, the object can be accessed to determine valuable information about the error and how it may have been caused.

RUNTIMEEXCEPTION ERRORS

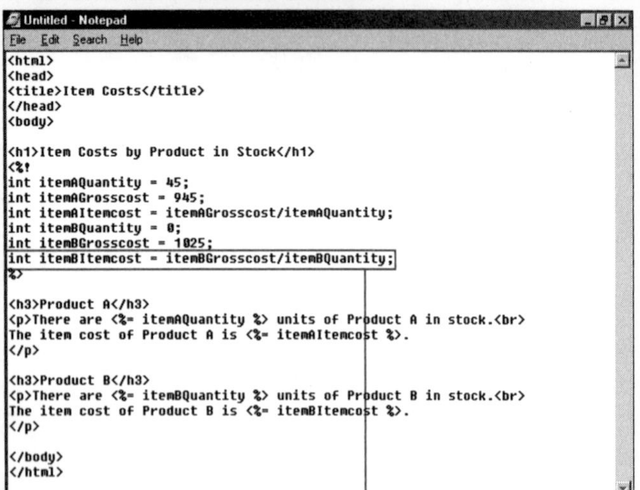

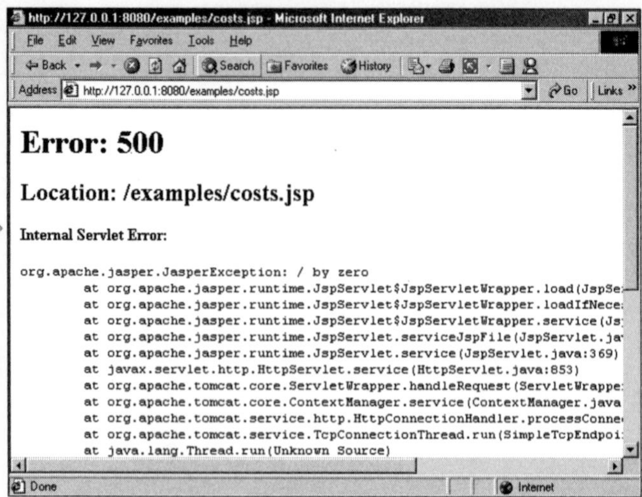

■ A RuntimeException error is typically generated by an error in the code for a JSP page.

■ In this example, the JSP page contains code that divides a number by zero.

■ When the JSP page is displayed in a Web browser, a message appears displaying information about the RuntimeException error.

Extra

Although exception errors can arise from a wide variety of situations, the situations can be grouped into three general categories.

Logical Errors

Logical errors are the most common type of errors and usually result when a programmer has not validated parameters or values before performing an action. An example of a common logical error is dividing a number by zero.

Standard Errors

Most of the methods that make up the Java class library contain code that will generate errors when certain situations arise. For example, an error will result if you use a number where a string is expected or assign a value to an array element that does not exist.

Program Errors

Problems with the Java Virtual Machine or a Web server that processes Java code can cause errors to occur. Applications that are not yet stable, such as beta releases, are more likely to generate errors.

ERROR EXCEPTION ERRORS

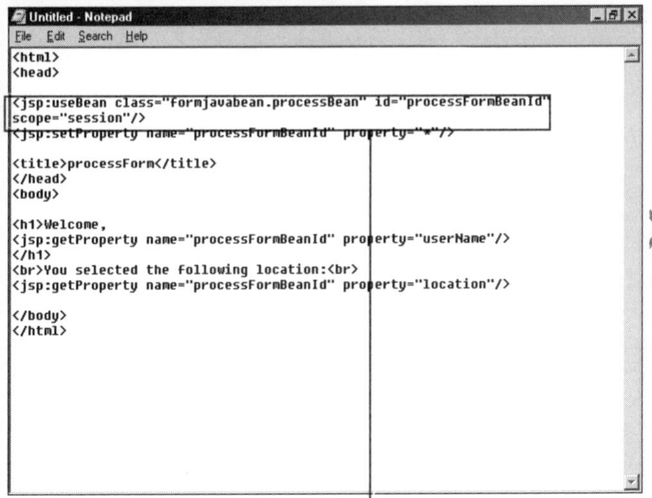

http://127.0.0.1:8080/examples/process.jsp - Microsoft Internet Explorer

Address http://127.0.0.1:8080/examples/process.jsp

Error: 500

Location: /examples/process.jsp

Internal Servlet Error:

```
org.apache.jasper.JasperException: Unable to load class formjavabean.process
        at org.apache.jasper.compiler.BeanRepository.getBeanType(BeanReposit
        at org.apache.jasper.compiler.GetPropertyGenerator.generate(GetPrope
        at org.apache.jasper.compiler.JspParseEventListener$GeneratorWrapper
        at org.apache.jasper.compiler.JspParseEventListener.generateAll(JspP
        at org.apache.jasper.compiler.JspParseEventListener.endPageProcessin
        at org.apache.jasper.compiler.Compiler.compile(Compiler.java:183)
        at org.apache.jasper.runtime.JspServlet.loadJSP(JspServlet.java:413)
        at org.apache.jasper.runtime.JspServlet$JspServletWrapper.loadIfNece
        at org.apache.jasper.runtime.JspServlet$JspServletWrapper.service(Js
        at org.apache.jasper.runtime.JspServlet.serviceJspFile(JspServlet.ja
        at org.apache.jasper.runtime.JspServlet.service(JspServlet.java:369)
```

■ An Error exception error is typically generated by a problem with the environment that processes a JSP page.

■ In this example, the JSP page contains code that attempts to access a JavaBean that does not exist.

■ When the JSP page is displayed in a Web browser, a message appears displaying information about the Error exception error.

CREATE A TRY BLOCK AND CATCH BLOCK

If a section of code in a JSP page may generate an exception error, you can create a `try` block and a `catch` block to handle the error.

A `try` block detects if an exception error has occurred in a section of code. To create a `try` block, use the keyword `try` and surround the code that may cause an exception error in braces.

A `catch` block contains the code that is executed when the `try` block detects an error. The `catch` block must immediately follow the `try` block. To create a `catch` block, use the keyword `catch` and enclose the code you want to execute in braces. The `catch` keyword is followed by a parameter enclosed in parentheses. The parameter specifies the class of the exception error and a name for the object that is created when the error occurs.

A `catch` block can only catch the type of exception error specified by the parameter. If the `try` block generates a different type of exception error, the code in the `catch` block will not be executed.

When an exception error occurs in a line of code, the line of code is said to throw an error. When a line of code in a `try` block throws an error, the processing of code in the `try` block stops immediately and any remaining statements in the `try` block are not executed. The `catch` block catches the error thrown by the `try` block and processing continues on the first line of code in the `catch` block.

The code in a `catch` block can display a customized error message to notify a user that an error has occurred. The customized error message should be specific to the error and easy to understand. When a `try` block and `catch` block are not used to handle errors, Java generates cryptic error messages that can be difficult to comprehend.

CREATE A TRY BLOCK AND CATCH BLOCK

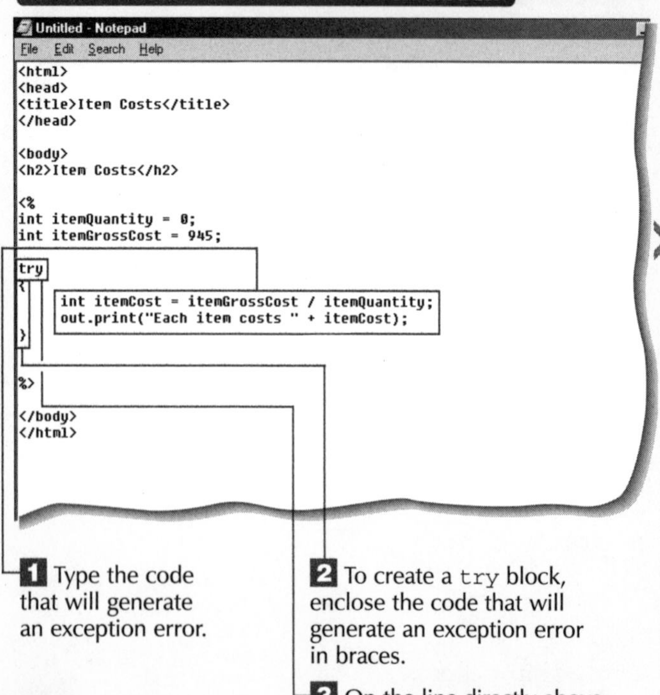

1 Type the code that will generate an exception error.

2 To create a `try` block, enclose the code that will generate an exception error in braces.

3 On the line directly above the opening brace, type **try**.

```
Untitled - Notepad
File  Edit  Search  Help
<html>
<head>
<title>Item Costs</title>
</head>

<body>
<h2>Item Costs</h2>

<%
int itemQuantity = 0;
int itemGrossCost = 945;

try
{
     int itemCost = itemGrossCost / itemQuantity;
     out.print("Each item costs " + itemCost);
}
catch(ArithmeticException e)

%>

</body>
</html>
```

4 To create a `catch` block, type **catch()** on the line immediately following the `try` block.

5 Between the parentheses, type the class of the exception error that will be thrown by the `try` block.

6 Type a name for the object that will be created when an exception error is thrown.

Extra

As with any Java code, there are strict rules governing the scope of variables used in `try` and `catch` blocks. Variables declared in a `try` block are not available for use in the `catch` block. In the following example, the locationMessage variable is not available in the `catch` block.

Example:

```
try
{
     String locationMessage = "determining item cost";
     int itemCost = itemGrossCost / itemQuantity;
     out.print("Each item costs " + itemCost);
}
catch(ArithmeticException e)
{
     out.print("Error has occurred at " + locationMessage);
}
```

The above code can easily be rewritten to change the scope of the locationMessage variable so that it is available to both the `try` and `catch` blocks.

```
String locationMessage = "";
try
{
     locationMessage = "determining item cost";
     int itemCost = itemGrossCost / itemQuantity;
     out.print("Each item costs " + itemCost);
}
catch(ArithmeticException e)
{
     out.print("Error has occurred at " + locationMessage);
}
```

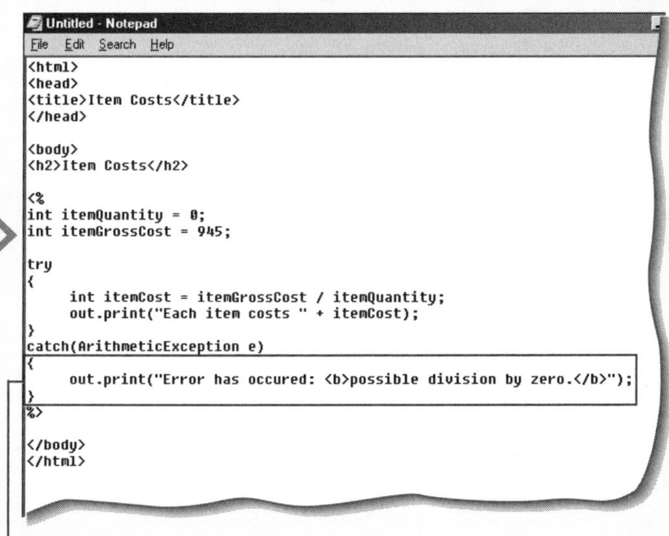

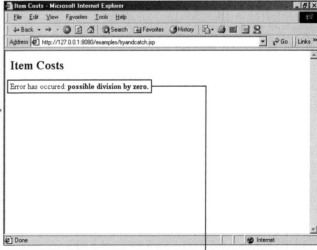

Item Costs - Microsoft Internet Explorer

Address http://127.0.0.1:8080/examples/tryandcatch.jsp

Item Costs

Error has occured: **possible division by zero.**

7 Type the code you want to execute when the `catch` block is processed. Enclose the code in braces.

8 Save the page with the .jsp extension and then display the JSP page in a Web browser.

■ The Web browser displays the result of creating a `try` block and `catch` block.

CATCH MULTIPLE EXCEPTION ERRORS

Although a try block may be capable of throwing different types of exception errors, a catch block can catch only one specific type of exception error. You can create multiple catch blocks to catch different types of exception errors.

When a catch block is created, the exception error class the block can handle is specified. If the try block throws an exception error of a different class, the code in the catch block will not be executed. A try block that contains a complex section of code may throw different types of exception errors. Creating multiple catch blocks allows a section of code to be executed for each type of exception error the try block throws.

The first catch block must immediately follow the try block and each subsequent catch block must be placed one right after the other. There cannot be any lines of code between the try block and the first catch block. You also cannot place lines of code between any of the subsequent catch blocks.

When using multiple catch blocks, the order of the catch blocks is important. For example, since the Exception class is a superclass of the RuntimeException class, a catch block that uses the Exception class will catch most of the exception errors thrown by a try block. If you place a catch block that uses the Exception class before other catch blocks in your code, the code in the other catch blocks may never be executed. As a rule, you should place catch blocks that handle exception error subclasses before catch blocks that have a broader scope.

CATCH MULTIPLE EXCEPTION ERRORS

```
<html>
<head>
<title>Catch Multiple Exception Errors</title>
</head>
<body>

<b>Item Costs</b><br>

<%
int[] itemGrossCost = {280, 42, 44, 156};
int[] itemQuanity = {20, 0, 4, 12};
int[] itemCost = new int[3];

for(int x = 0; x < itemQuanity.length; x++)
{
      try
      {
            itemCost[x] = itemGrossCost[x] / itemQuanity[x];
            out.print("<br>Item " + x + " costs " + itemCost[x]);
      }
}
%>

</body>
</html>
```

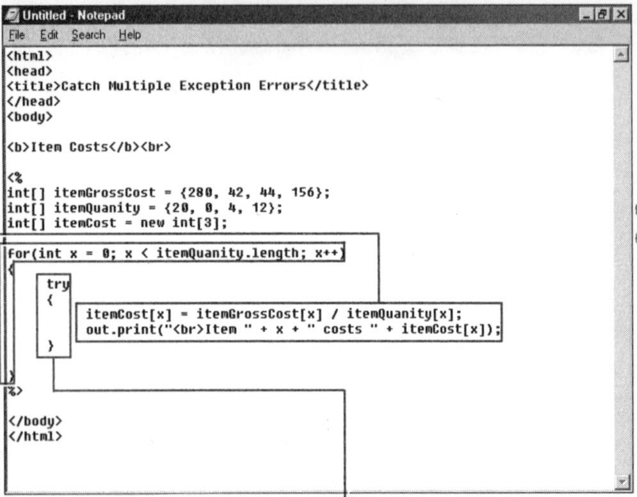

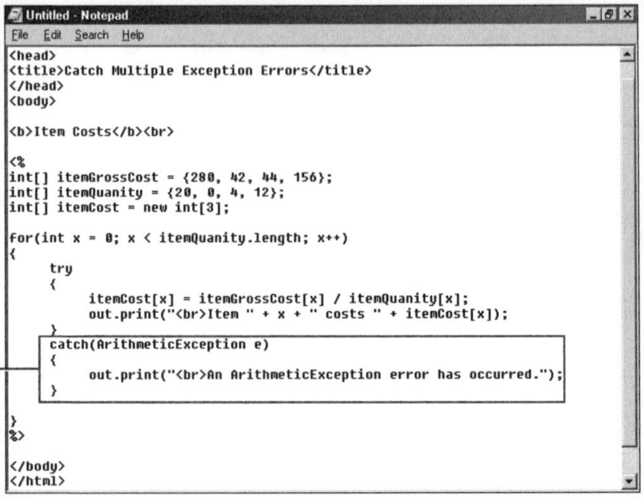

1 Type the code that will generate multiple exception errors.

2 Type the code that creates a try block.

```
<head>
<title>Catch Multiple Exception Errors</title>
</head>
<body>

<b>Item Costs</b><br>

<%
int[] itemGrossCost = {280, 42, 44, 156};
int[] itemQuanity = {20, 0, 4, 12};
int[] itemCost = new int[3];

for(int x = 0; x < itemQuanity.length; x++)
{
      try
      {
            itemCost[x] = itemGrossCost[x] / itemQuanity[x];
            out.print("<br>Item " + x + " costs " + itemCost[x]);
      }
      catch(ArithmeticException e)
      {
            out.print("<br>An ArithmeticException error has occurred.");
      }
}
%>

</body>
</html>
```

3 Type the code that creates a catch block to handle exception errors of the ArithmeticException class.

Extra

When using multiple `catch` blocks, you may want to add a `finally` block to your code. A `finally` block executes a section of code regardless of which `catch` block is processed. The `finally` block must immediately follow the last `catch` block.

Example:

```
for(int x = 0; x < itemQuanity.length; x++)
{
      try
      {
            itemCost[x] = itemGrossCost[x] / itemQuanity[x];
            out.print("<br>Item " + x + " costs " + itemCost[x]);
      }
      catch(ArithmeticException e)
      {
            out.print("<br>An ArithmeticException error has occurred.");
      }
      catch(ArrayIndexOutOfBoundsException e)
      {
            out.print("<br>An ArrayIndexOutOfBoundsException error");
            out.print(" has occurred.");
      }
      finally
      {
            out.print("<hr>");
      }
}
```

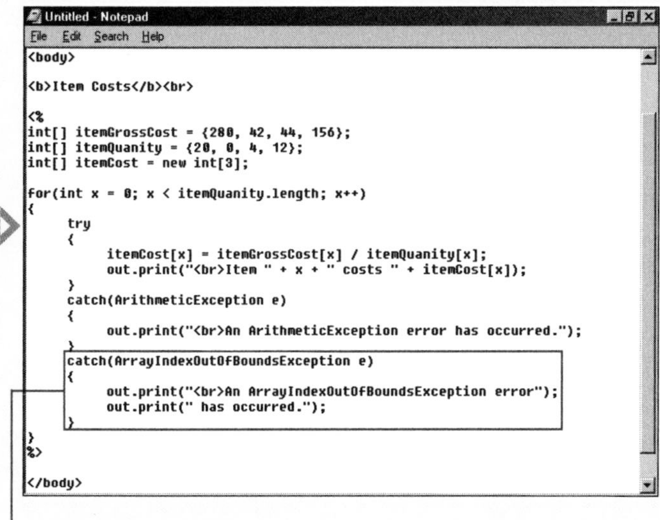

4 Type the code that creates a `catch` block to handle exception errors of the `ArrayIndexOutOfBounds Exception` class.

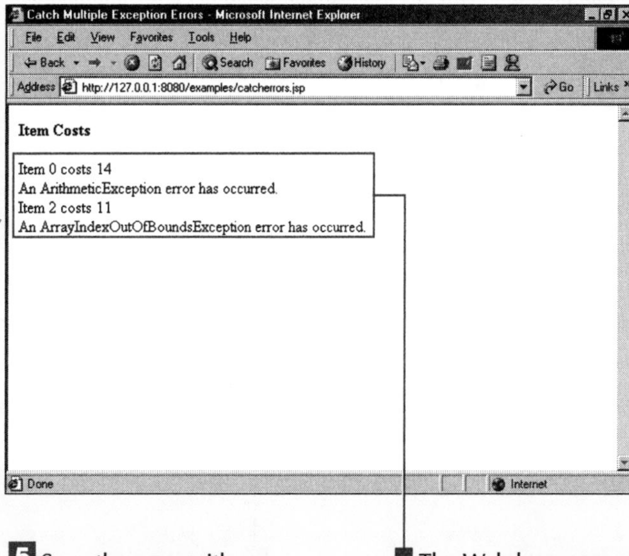

5 Save the page with the .jsp extension and then display the JSP page in a Web browser.

■ The Web browser displays the result of catching multiple exception errors.

CREATE A FINALLY BLOCK

When a `try` block throws an exception error, the processing of code in the `try` block stops and any remaining statements in the `try` block are not executed. This can cause problems if the `try` block contains code that is important to the execution of your JSP page. To ensure important code is executed regardless of whether an exception error is thrown, you can place the code in a `finally` block.

To create a `finally` block, use the keyword `finally` and enclose the code you want to execute in braces. A `finally` block is useful for performing tasks that 'tidy up' a JSP page. For example, it is common for a `finally` block to contain code that closes a connection to a database or finishes writing data to a file.

There are strict rules governing the scope of variables used in `try`, `catch` and `finally` blocks. Variables declared in a `try` or `catch` block are not available for use in a `finally` block.

When a `try` block uses a `finally` block, a `catch` block is not required. If a `catch` block is used, the `finally` block must immediately follow the `catch` block. If a `catch` block is not used, the `finally` block must immediately follow the `try` block. There can be no lines of code between a `finally` block and a `catch` or `try` block.

When a JSP page containing a `finally` block is processed, the code in the `try` block is executed first. If an error is thrown, the code in the appropriate `catch` block is then executed. The code in the `finally` block is executed last. The `finally` block is executed whether or not an exception error occurs and regardless of the type of exception error thrown.

CREATE A FINALLY BLOCK

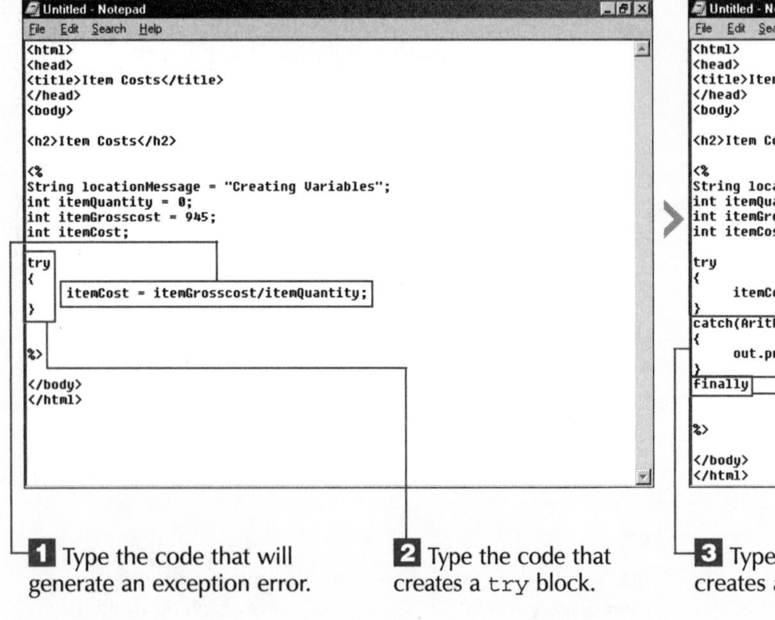

1 Type the code that will generate an exception error.

2 Type the code that creates a `try` block.

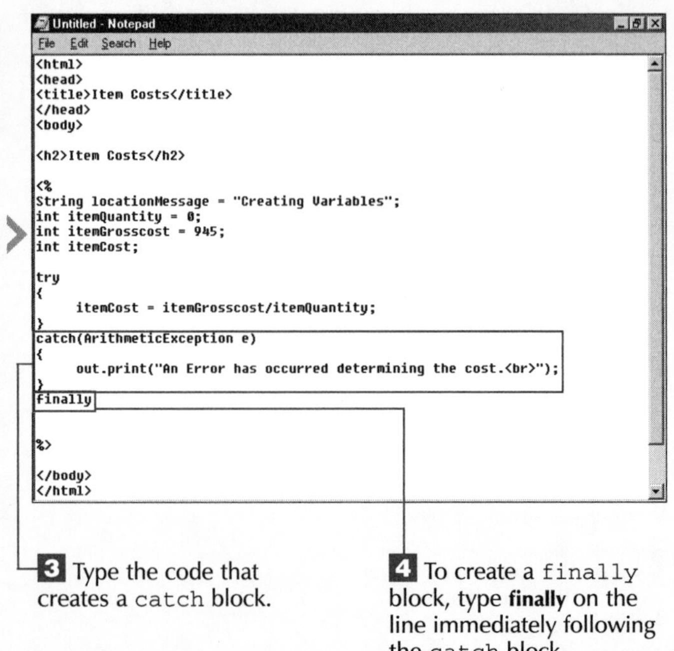

3 Type the code that creates a `catch` block.

4 To create a `finally` block, type **finally** on the line immediately following the `catch` block.

Apply It

Although the main purpose of a `try` block is to identify code that may generate an exception error, a `try` block can also be used with a `finally` block to save you time when typing code. For example, if a series of `if` statements will all have the same result, you can place the `if` statements in a `try` block and the result in a `finally` block. This saves you from having to type the same result for each `if` statement.

TYPE THIS:

```
try
{
      if (winningScore > 10)
            return 10;
      if (winningScore > 20)
            return 20;
      if (winningScore > 30)
            return 30;
}
finally
{
      out.print("The winning number has been determined.");
}
```

RESULT:

The winning number has been determined.

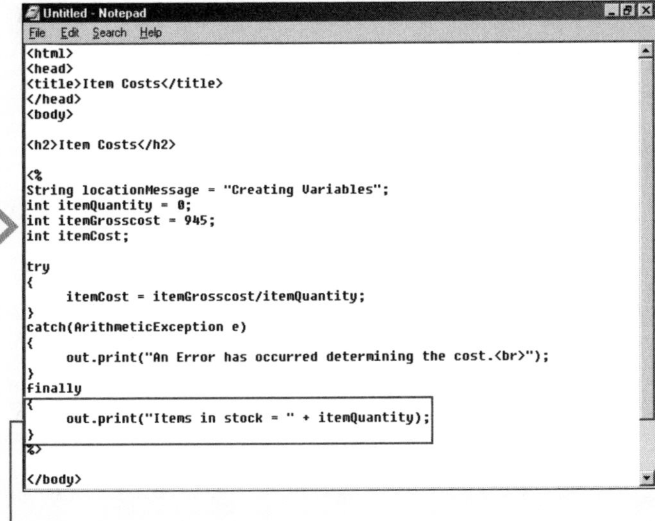

```
<html>
<head>
<title>Item Costs</title>
</head>
<body>

<h2>Item Costs</h2>

<%
String locationMessage = "Creating Variables";
int itemQuantity = 0;
int itemGrosscost = 945;
int itemCost;

try
{
     itemCost = itemGrosscost/itemQuantity;
}
catch(ArithmeticException e)
{
     out.print("An Error has occurred determining the cost.<br>");
}
finally
{
     out.print("Items in stock = " + itemQuantity);
}
%>

</body>
```

5 Type the code you want to execute when the `finally` block is processed. Enclose the code in braces.

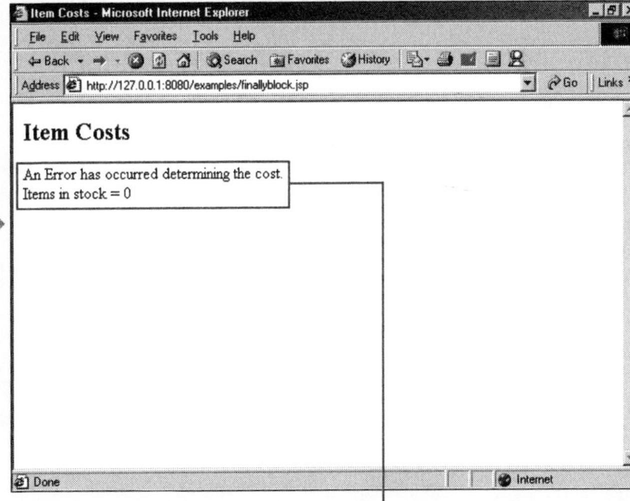

6 Save the page with the .jsp extension and then display the JSP page in a Web browser.

■ The Web browser displays the result of using a `finally` block.

REDIRECT TO AN ERROR PAGE

There are many types of exception errors that can be generated by the JSP pages in a Web site. Instead of trying to catch each specific type of exception error that could occur, you can configure the JSP pages to redirect to another page when an error occurs. The error page can be a JSP page or other type of Web document, such as an HTML document.

When an exception error occurs in a JSP page, the Web server stops processing the page and sends an error message to the Web browser to notify the client about the error. The type of exception error that occurs determines the information displayed in the error message. While the error information generated by the server may be useful to someone troubleshooting the JSP page, the information is usually not helpful to clients. Creating an error page allows you to determine the information that a client sees when an exception error occurs. For example, you may want to display a user-friendly page that provides clients with helpful instructions.

To redirect a JSP page to another page in the event of an exception error, you use the `errorPage` attribute of the `page` directive. For more information about the `page` directive, see page 74. The `errorPage` attribute takes the URL of the error page, enclosed in quotation marks, as its value. The URL of the error page must be a relative URL. This means that the JSP page and error page must be stored on the same Web server.

Multiple JSP pages can use the same error page. You must include the redirection instructions on each JSP page you want to use the error page.

REDIRECT TO AN ERROR PAGE

Untitled - Notepad

File Edit Search Help

```
<html>
<head>
<title>Error Message</title>
</head>
<body>

The JSP page you were viewing has generated an error.

</body>
</html>
```

CREATE AN ERROR PAGE

1 In a text editor, create the page you want to display when an error occurs.

2 Save the page on the Web server.

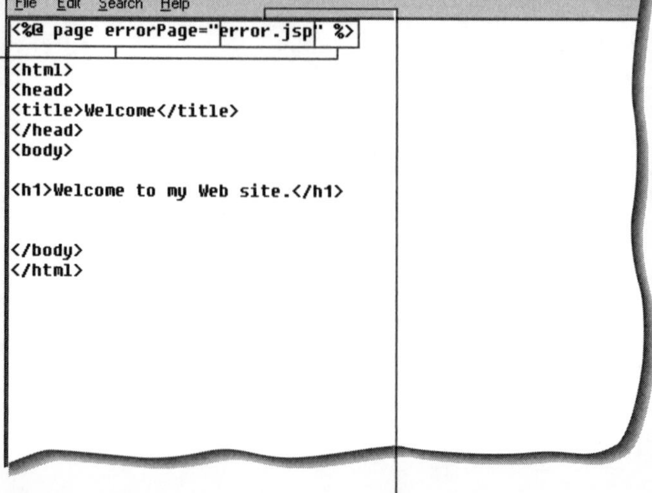
Untitled - Notepad
File Edit Search Help
<%@ page errorPage="error.jsp" %>
<html>
<head>
<title>Welcome</title>
</head>
<body>
<h1>Welcome to my Web site.</h1>
</body>
</html>

REDIRECT A JSP PAGE TO AN ERROR PAGE

1 On the first line of code in a JSP page you want to redirect to an error page, type **<%@ page errorPage="" %>**.

2 Between the quotation marks, type the URL of the error page.

Extra

On most Web servers, the default value for the `autoFlush` attribute of the `page` directive is `true`, which means that the buffer is set to automatically flush when it is full. When the buffer is flushed, information in the buffer is sent to a client's Web browser. If the buffer is flushed before a JSP page is redirected to the error page, an additional error will be generated. To avoid this, you can set the value of the `autoFlush` attribute to `false` when using the `errorPage` attribute.

Example:

```
<@ page autoFlush="false" errorPage="error.jsp" %>
```

Information available to the JSP page, such as application values, session values and data stored in a `request` object, will not be available to the error page. For example, if the JSP page processes data from a form, the error page will not be able to access the form information.

When an exception error occurs in a JSP page that uses an error page, the Web server stops processing the JSP page, executes the `page` directive and processes the code in the error page. The Web server does not return to the JSP page.

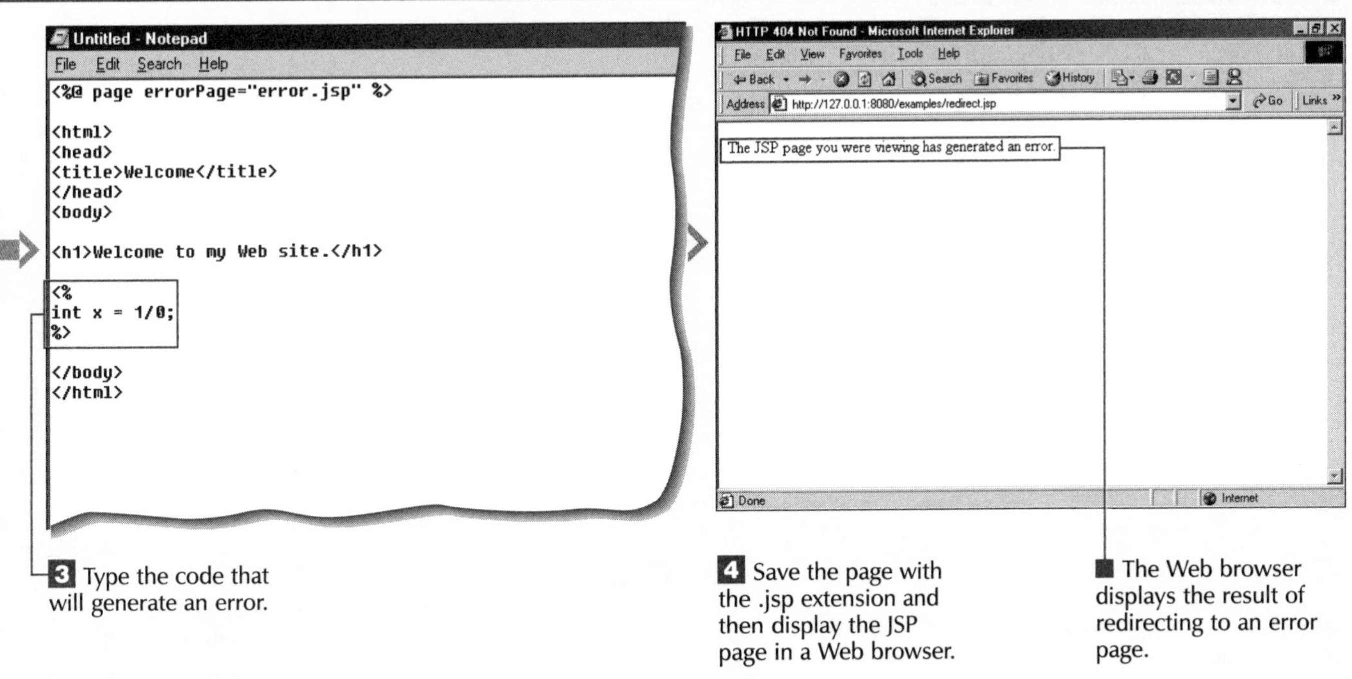

3 Type the code that will generate an error.

4 Save the page with the .jsp extension and then display the JSP page in a Web browser.

■ The Web browser displays the result of redirecting to an error page.

CREATE A DETAILED ERROR PAGE

You can create an error page that accesses detailed information about an exception error that has occurred in a JSP page. Accessing detailed information can help you troubleshoot the page. You can choose to simply display the detailed information about an exception error or you can log the information in a file or database.

When a JSP page generates an exception error of the `Exception` class, an `exception` object is created. The object holds information about the exception error. You can access the `exception` object in an error page to find detailed information about the error that occurred.

To make the `exception` object available to an error page, you use the `isErrorPage` attribute of the `page` directive. For more information about the `page` directive, see page 74. The `isErrorPage` attribute can have a value of either true or false. A value of true will make the `exception` object available to an error page. False is the default value of the `isErrorPage` attribute.

The `getMessage` method of the `exception` object can be called to access an error message that describes the type of error that has occurred. You can use an expression to display the information returned by the `getMessage` method. Some exception errors do not have an error message associated with them. In this case, the `getMessage` method will return a null value. For more information about the methods of the `exception` object, refer to the Java SDK documentation.

To redirect a JSP page to a detailed error page in the event of an error, you use the `errorPage` attribute of the `page` directive. The `errorPage` attribute takes the URL of the detailed error page, enclosed in quotation marks, as its value. The URL of the detailed error page must be a relative URL.

CREATE A DETAILED ERROR PAGE

Untitled - Notepad

```
<%@ page isErrorPage="true" %>
<html>
<head>
<title>A Detailed Error Page</title>
</head>
<body>

The JSP page you were viewing generated an error.
<p>The type of error appears to be:<br>



</body>
</html>
```

Untitled - Notepad

```
<%@ page isErrorPage="true" %>
<html>
<head>
<title>A Detailed Error Page</title>
</head>
<body>

The JSP page you were viewing generated an error.
<p>The type of error appears to be:<br>

<%= exception.getMessage() %>

</body>
</html>
```

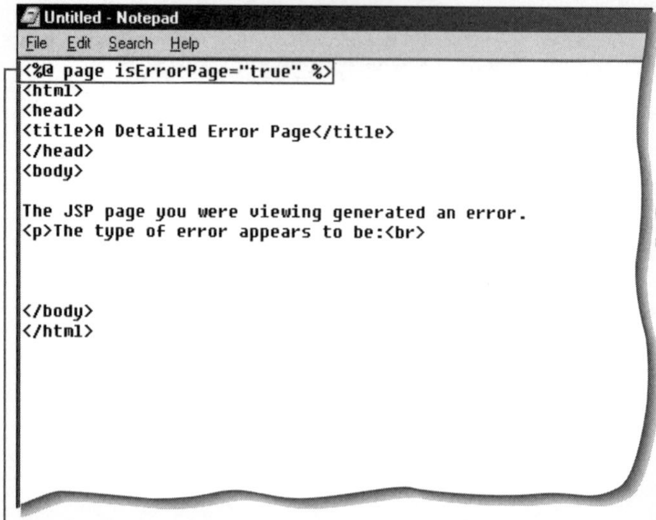

1 On the first line of code in the error page, type **<%@ page isErrorPage="true" %>** to access the `exception` object.

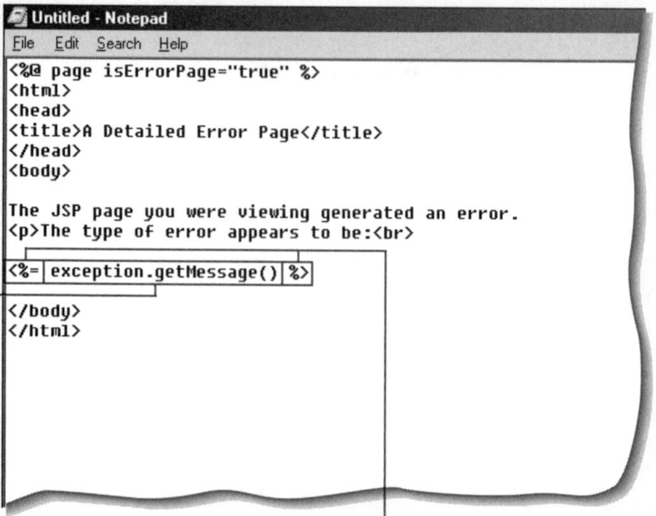

2 Type **exception.getMessage()** where you want to access an error message.

3 Type the code that displays the error message on the detailed error page.

4 Save the page on the Web server with the .jsp extension.

Extra

The `exception` object is only available to the detailed error page. However, there are techniques you can use to make the information in the `exception` object available to other JSP pages. For example, in the detailed error page, you can use the `setAttribute` method of the `session` object to store the error message as a session value.

Example:

```
<%
session.setAttribute("errorMessage", exception.getMessage());
%>
```

You may be able to use the `getLocalizedMessage` method of the `exception` object to access even more detailed information about an exception error. However, in most cases, the `getLocalizedMessage` method returns the same information as the `getMessage` method.

Example:

```
<%= exception.getLocalizedMessage() %>
```

The `toString` method of the `exception` object can be used to display the class name of an exception error. The result of the `toString` method may also contain the information returned by the `getMessage` method.

Example:

```
<%= exception.toString() %>
```

Returns:

java.lang.ArithmeticException: / by zero

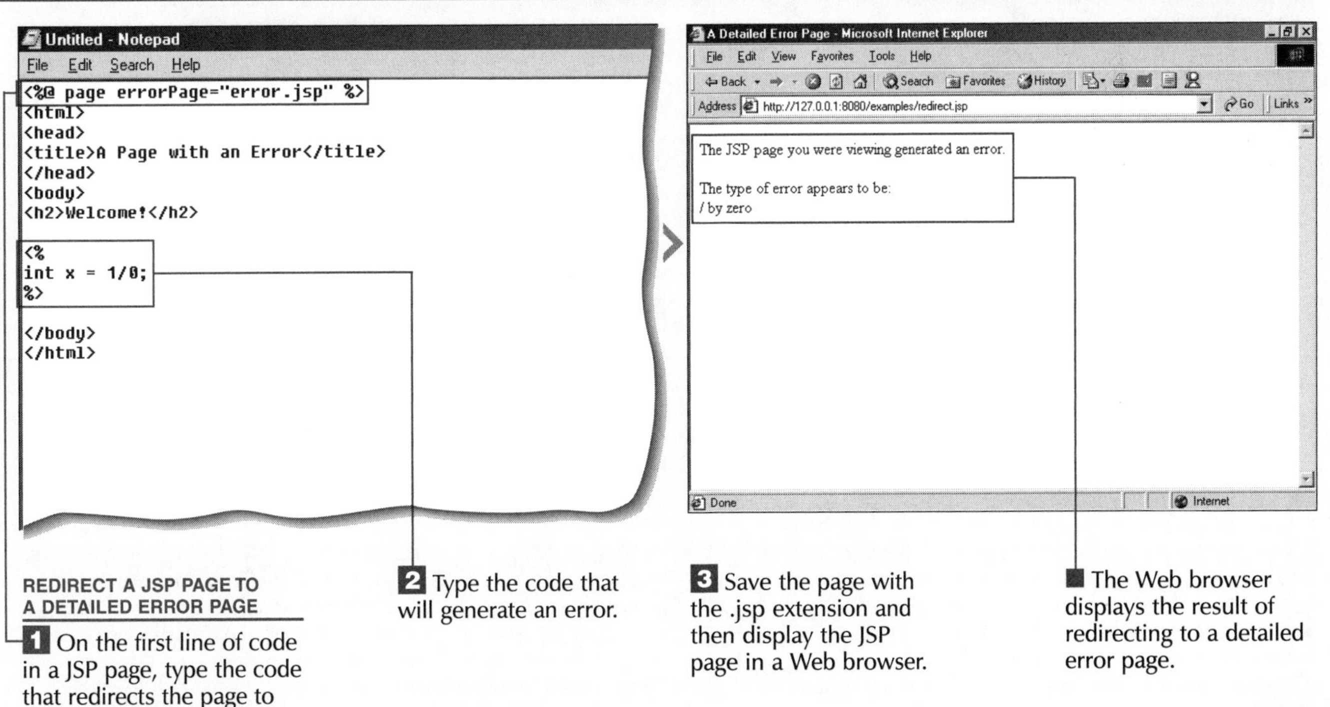

REDIRECT A JSP PAGE TO A DETAILED ERROR PAGE

1 On the first line of code in a JSP page, type the code that redirects the page to the detailed error page.

2 Type the code that will generate an error.

3 Save the page with the .jsp extension and then display the JSP page in a Web browser.

■ The Web browser displays the result of redirecting to a detailed error page.

VERIFY THAT A FILE OR DIRECTORY EXISTS

When working with files and directories, it is often necessary to verify that a file or directory exists before performing an action. For example, you should verify that a file exists before deleting the file. This is particularly important when working with files and directories located on a network, since events beyond your control can make the files and directories unavailable.

To verify that a file or directory exists, you create a `File` object that uses the path of the file or directory as its argument. The class that is used to create a `File` object is located in the `java.io` package. You must use the `page` directive to import the `java.io` package before you can create a `File` object.

You may want to store the path of the file or directory you want to check in a variable and then use the variable as the argument for the `File` object. A path can also be submitted by a form or retrieved from a database. When specifying the path of a file or directory, you should use slashes (/).

Once you have created a `File` object for a file or directory, you can use methods of the object to determine information about the file or directory. You use the `exists` method to determine if the file or directory exists on the current system. The `exists` method returns a value of `true` if the file or directory exists and a value of `false` if the file or directory does not exist.

The `isFile` method of the `File` object allows you to verify whether a file or directory represented by a `File` object is a file, while the `isDirectory` method lets you verify whether the item is a directory. These methods return a value of `true` or `false`, depending upon the type of the item.

VERIFY THAT A FILE OR DIRECTORY EXISTS

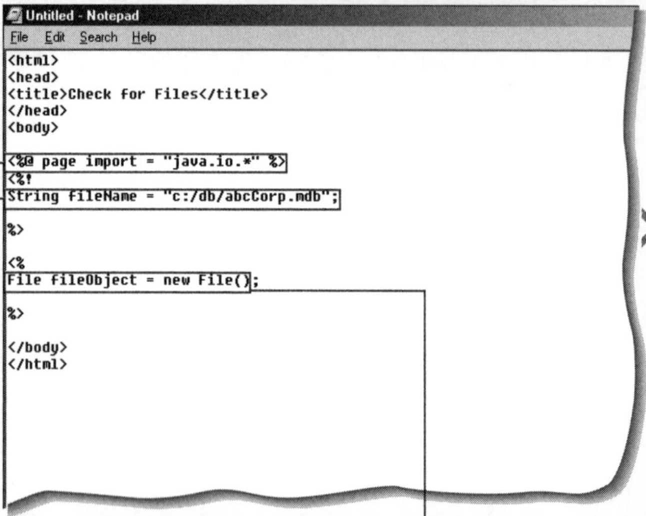

```
Untitled - Notepad
File Edit Search Help
<html>
<head>
<title>Check for Files</title>
</head>
<body>

<%@ page import = "java.io.*" %>
<%!
String fileName = "c:/db/abcCorp.mdb";

%>

<%
File fileObject = new File();

%>

</body>
</html>
```

1 To import the `java.io` package, type **<%@ page import = "java.io.*" %>**.

2 To store the path of a file you want to check in a variable, type the code that assigns the path to the variable.

3 To create a `File` object for the file, type **File** followed by a name for the `File` object. Then type **= new File()**.

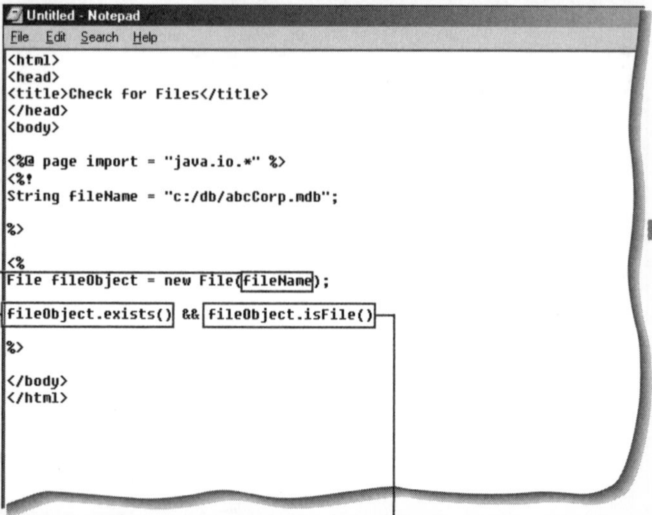

```
Untitled - Notepad
File Edit Search Help
<html>
<head>
<title>Check for Files</title>
</head>
<body>

<%@ page import = "java.io.*" %>
<%!
String fileName = "c:/db/abcCorp.mdb";

%>

<%
File fileObject = new File(fileName);

fileObject.exists() && fileObject.isFile()

%>

</body>
</html>
```

4 Between the parentheses, type the name of the variable that stores the path of the file you want to check.

5 To determine whether the file exists, type the name of the `File` object, immediately followed by **.exists()**.

6 To determine whether the file is a file, type the name of the `File` object, immediately followed by **.isFile()**.

Extra

Permissions may have been set for a file, affecting the types of tasks you can perform while working with the file. For example, a file's permissions can regulate whether you will be able to read or write to the file. To determine whether you have permission to read a file, use the `canRead` method of the `File` object. To determine whether you have permission to write to a file, use the `canWrite` method of the `File` object. If you attempt to read or write to a file that you do not have permission to work with, an error will usually be generated.

Example:

```
if (fileObject.canRead())
     out.print("You can read the file " + fileName);

if (fileObject.canWrite())
     out.print("You can write to the file " + fileName);
```

When specifying the path to a file or directory for the argument of a `File` object, you can use a relative or absolute path. A relative path specifies the location of the file or directory relative to the current directory. For example, the relative path `../file.txt` refers to a file named file that is located in the parent directory of the current directory. An absolute path specifies the location of a file or directory in relation to the root directory of the storage system in which the file is stored, such as `c:/data/examples/file.txt`.

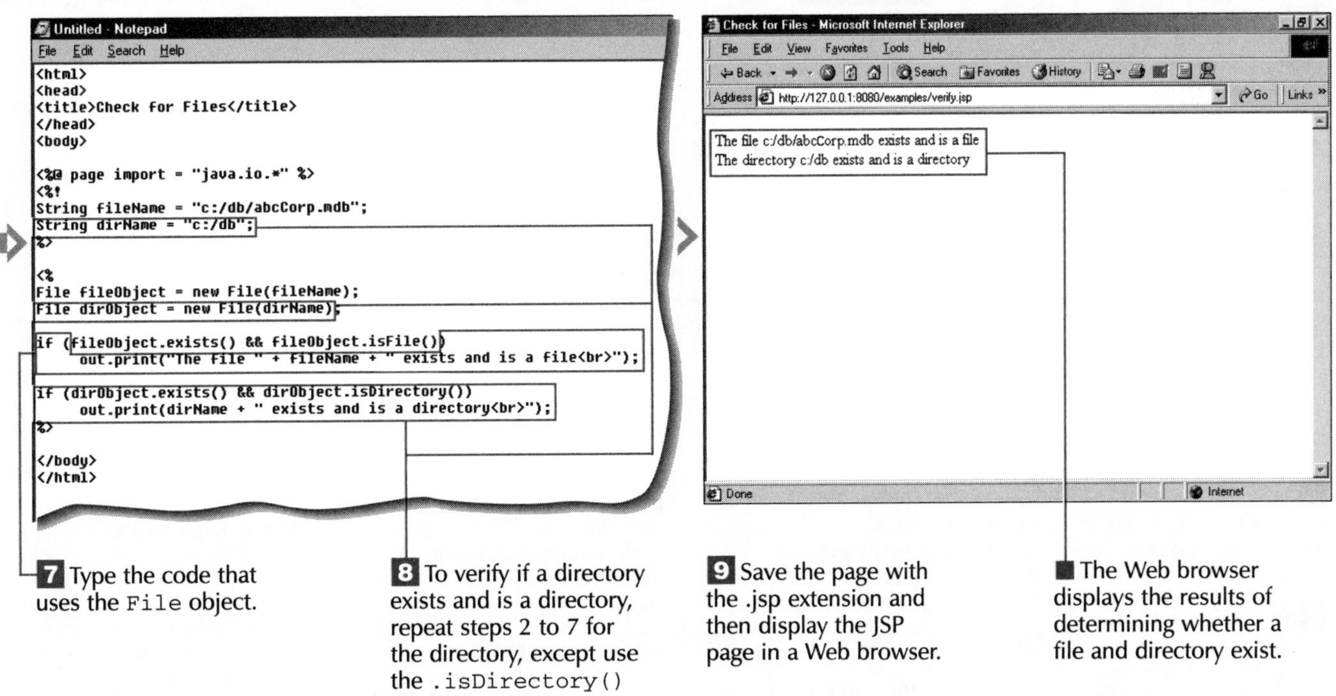

7 Type the code that uses the `File` object.

8 To verify if a directory exists and is a directory, repeat steps 2 to 7 for the directory, except use the `.isDirectory()` method in step 6.

9 Save the page with the .jsp extension and then display the JSP page in a Web browser.

■ The Web browser displays the results of determining whether a file and directory exist.

CREATE AND WRITE TO A FILE

A JSP page can be used to create a new file and then write information to the file. A file could be created to track how many times the JSP page has been accessed or store data retrieved from a database. You can also use a JSP page to create and write other JSP files.

You create a `File` object to specify a name and location for the new file. You can then use the `createNewFile` method of the `File` object to create the new file. You must use the `page` directive to import the `java.io` package from the Java class library before creating a new file.

Information is written to a file using an output stream. Stream is the term typically used to describe one continuous line of data. You use a `FileOutputStream` object to create an output stream and specify the name of the `File` object that represents the file you want to write to.

In order to write primitive data types to the output stream, a `DataOutputStream` object must be created. You then associate the `DataOutputStream` object with the `FileOutputStream` object.

You use a write method of the `DataOutputStream` object to write information to the file. The method you should use depends on the type of data you want to write to the file. For example, if you want to write an integer value, you would use the `writeInt` method.

After all the information has been written to the file, you can use the `close` method of the `DataOutputStream` object to close the output stream.

When you display the JSP page in a Web browser, the file will be created and the information you specified will be written to the file. You can open the file with the appropriate program or use a JSP page to read the file.

CREATE AND WRITE TO A FILE

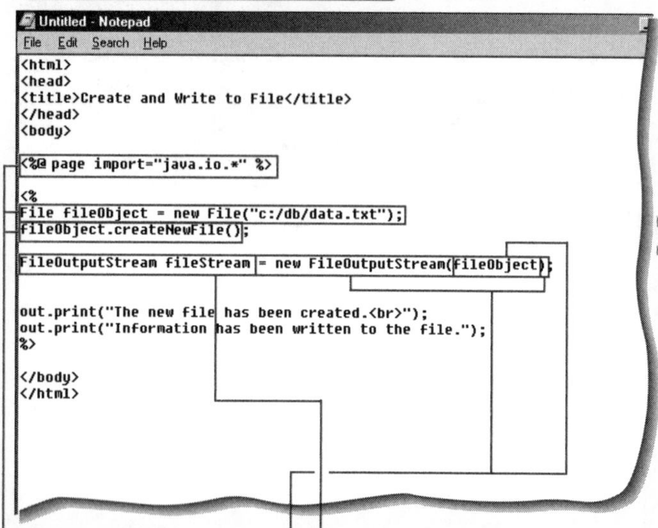

Untitled - Notepad
File Edit Search Help
<html>
<head>
<title>Create and Write to File</title>
</head>
<body>
<%@ page import="java.io.*" %>
<%
File fileObject = new File("c:/db/data.txt");
fileObject.createNewFile();
FileOutputStream fileStream = new FileOutputStream(fileObject);
out.print("The new file has been created.
");
out.print("Information has been written to the file.");
%>
</body>
</html>

1 Type the code that imports the `java.io` package and creates a `File` object.

2 To create the new file, type the name of the `File` object followed by a dot. Then type **createNewFile()**.

3 To create an output stream to write to the file, type **FileOutputStream** followed by a name for the `FileOutputStream` object.

4 Type **= new FileOutputStream()**.

5 Between the parentheses, type the name of the `File` object.

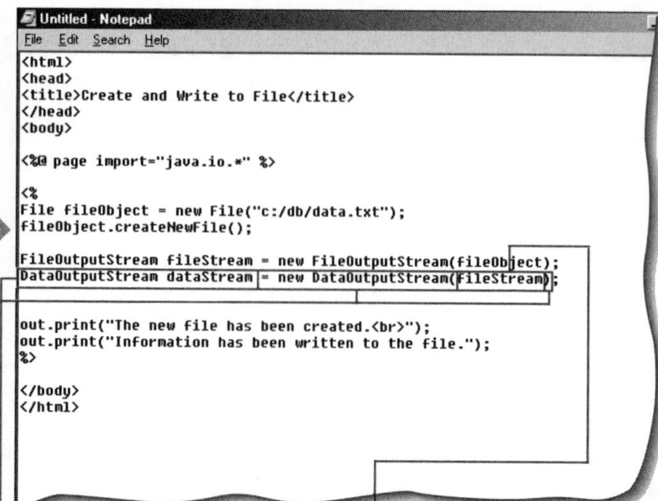

Untitled - Notepad
File Edit Search Help
<html>
<head>
<title>Create and Write to File</title>
</head>
<body>
<%@ page import="java.io.*" %>
<%
File fileObject = new File("c:/db/data.txt");
fileObject.createNewFile();
FileOutputStream fileStream = new FileOutputStream(fileObject);
DataOutputStream dataStream = new DataOutputStream(fileStream);
out.print("The new file has been created.
");
out.print("Information has been written to the file.");
%>
</body>
</html>

6 To write primitive data types to the file, type **DataOutputStream** followed by a name for the `DataOutputStream` object.

7 To associate the `DataOutputStream` object with the `FileOutputStream` object, type **= new DataOutputStream()**.

8 Between the parentheses, type the name of the `FileOutputStream` object.

Extra

The `DataOutputStream` object offers several methods that can be used to write information to a file. Each method writes a different primitive data type or string value to the output stream.

WRITE METHOD:	DESCRIPTION:
`writeBoolean(boolean value)`	Writes a `boolean` value to the output stream.
`writeByte(int value)`	Writes a `byte` value to the output stream.
`writeBytes(String value)`	Writes a string of `byte` values to the output stream.
`writeChar(int value)`	Writes a `char` value to the output stream.
`writeChars(String value)`	Writes a string of `char` values to the output stream.
`writeDouble(double value)`	Converts the `double` argument to a `long` value and writes the `long` value to the output stream.
`writeFloat(float value)`	Converts the `float` argument to an `int` value and writes the `int` value to the output stream.
`writeInt(int value)`	Writes an `int` value to the output stream.
`writeLong(long value)`	Writes a `long` value to the output stream.
`writeShort(int value)`	Writes a `short` value to the output stream.

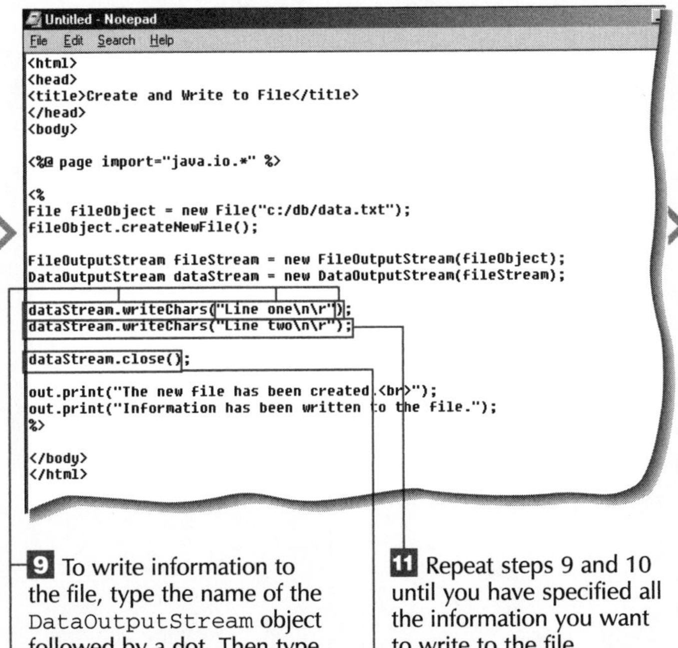

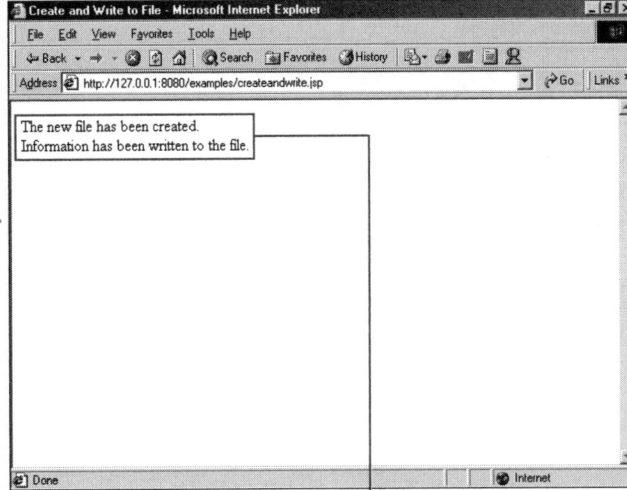

9 To write information to the file, type the name of the `DataOutputStream` object followed by a dot. Then type the write method you want to use followed by ().

10 Between the parentheses, type the information you want to write to the file.

11 Repeat steps 9 and 10 until you have specified all the information you want to write to the file.

12 To close the output stream, type the name of the `DataOutputStream` object followed by a dot. Then type **close()**.

13 Save the page with the .jsp extension and then display the JSP page in a Web browser.

■ The new file is created in the specified directory. You can open the file with the appropriate program to view its contents or use a JSP page to read the file.

READ A FILE

A JSP page can be used to read information from a specific file. The first step in reading information from a file is to create a `File` object that is used to specify the path and the name of the file to be read. Once a `File` object has been created, a `FileReader` object that works with the `File` object must be created. The `FileReader` object is used to convert the information in the file and make it available to the JSP page.

When reading information from a file using a `FileReader` object, the information should be buffered so that it can be read more efficiently. A `BufferedReader` object is used to buffer the information read from a file. For more information about the `BufferedReader` and `FileReader` objects, refer to the `java.io` package information in the Java API specification.

The `readLine` method of the `BufferedReader` object is used to read a single line from a file. The newline character usually indicates the end of a line in a file. A loop is often used to process each line in a file. With each iteration of the loop, the information retrieved from the file using the `readLine` method can be assigned to a variable and displayed to the client using the `print` method of the `out` object.

After reading information from a file, you should close the file using the `close` method of the `FileReader` object.

As with other operations involving accessing a file, the proper permissions must be in place that allows the file to be read. Permissions are typically controlled by the operating system. For information about permissions, you should consult your operating system's documentation.

READ A FILE

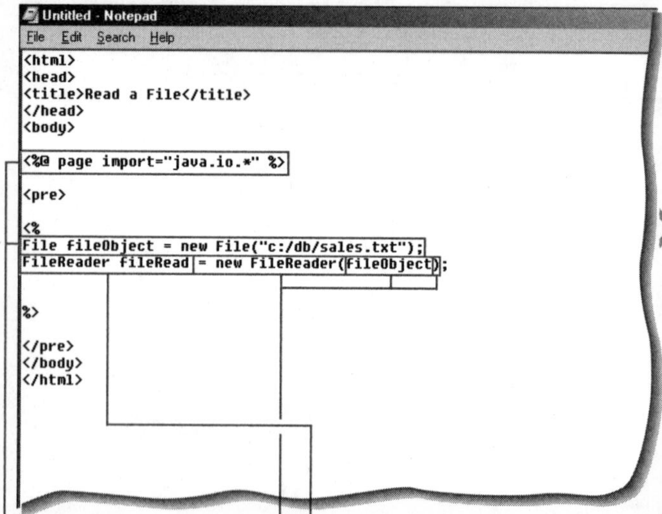

Untitled - Notepad

```
<html>
<head>
<title>Read a File</title>
</head>
<body>

<%@ page import="java.io.*" %>

<pre>

<%
File fileObject = new File("c:/db/sales.txt");
FileReader fileRead = new FileReader(fileObject);

%>

</pre>
</body>
</html>
```

1 Type the code that imports the `java.io` package and creates a `File` object.

2 To create a `FileReader` object to make the information in the file available to the JSP page, type **FileReader** followed by a name for the `FileReader` object.

3 Type **= new FileReader()**.

4 Between the parentheses, type the name of the `File` object.

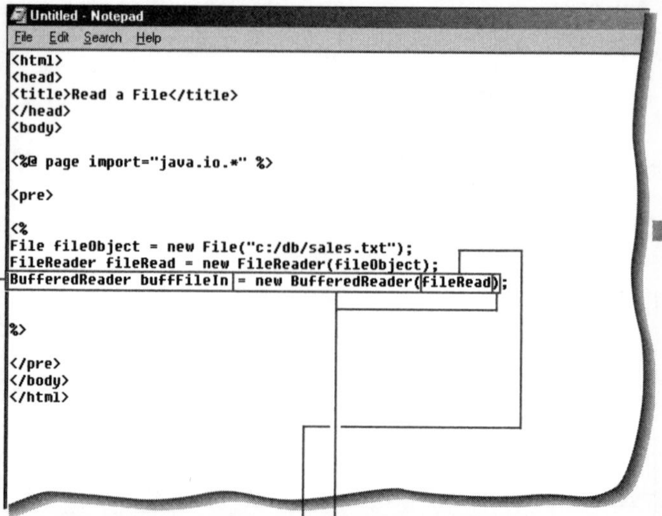

Untitled - Notepad

```
<html>
<head>
<title>Read a File</title>
</head>
<body>

<%@ page import="java.io.*" %>

<pre>

<%
File fileObject = new File("c:/db/sales.txt");
FileReader fileRead = new FileReader(fileObject);
BufferedReader buffFileIn = new BufferedReader(fileRead);

%>

</pre>
</body>
</html>
```

5 To create a `BufferedReader` object to buffer the information read from the file, type **BufferedReader** followed by a name for the `BufferedReader` object.

6 Type **= new BufferedReader()**.

7 Between the parentheses, type the name of the `FileReader` object.

Extra

You can adjust the size of the input buffer used to process the character stream that is read from a file. The default input buffer size is determined by the Web server and may differ from one system to another. For example, on a Windows platform using the Tomcat Web server, the default input buffer size is typically 512 KB, which is adequate for most needs. However, depending on the size and configuration of the files that are being read, adjusting the size of the input buffer may improve efficiency.

Example:

```
File fileObject = new File("c:/db/data.txt");
FileReader fileRead = new FileReader(fileObject);
BufferedReader buffFileIn = new BufferedReader(fileRead, 1024);
```

If the `FileReader` object does not already exist, you can pass the object creation code for the `FileReader` object as an argument when creating the `BufferedReader` object.

Example:

```
File fileObject = new File("c:/db/data.txt");
FileReader fileRead = new FileReader(fileObject);
BufferedReader buffFileIn = new BufferedReader(fileRead);
```

Can be typed as:

```
File fileObject = new File("c:/db/data.txt");
BufferedReader buffFileIn = new BufferedReader(new FileReader(fileObject));
```

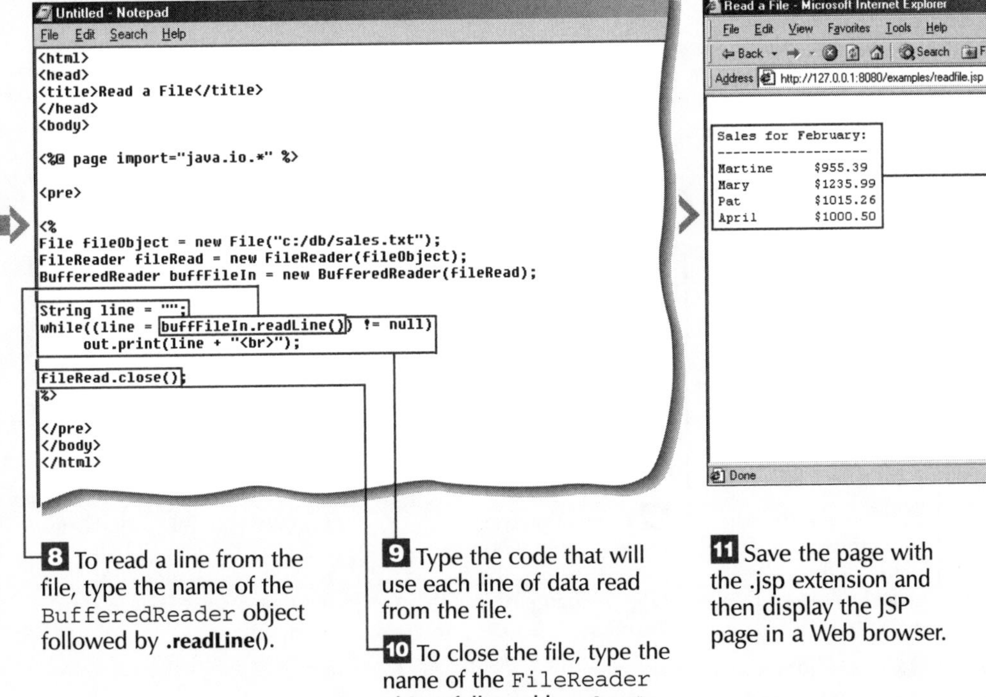

```
<html>
<head>
<title>Read a File</title>
</head>
<body>

<%@ page import="java.io.*" %>

<pre>

<%
File fileObject = new File("c:/db/sales.txt");
FileReader fileRead = new FileReader(fileObject);
BufferedReader buffFileIn = new BufferedReader(fileRead);

String line = "";
while((line = buffFileIn.readLine()) != null)
     out.print(line + "<br>");

fileRead.close();
%>

</pre>
</body>
</html>
```

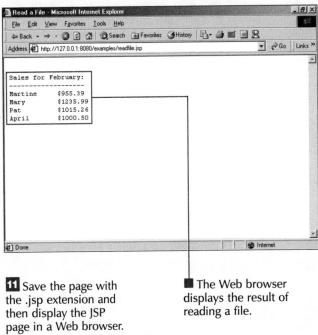

8 To read a line from the file, type the name of the `BufferedReader` object followed by **.readLine()**.

9 Type the code that will use each line of data read from the file.

10 To close the file, type the name of the `FileReader` object followed by **.close()**.

11 Save the page with the .jsp extension and then display the JSP page in a Web browser.

■ The Web browser displays the result of reading a file.

READ A FILE RANDOMLY

A JSP page typically reads and processes a file one line at a time until the entire file is processed. This method of reading a file is referred to as sequential access and is an effective way of working with small text files, but can be inefficient when working with larger files.

You can access a specific area of a file without having to start at the beginning and read each line in the file. Accessing a file at a specific location is referred to as random access. Random access is useful for working with large files that have a set structure, such as files that have the same number of characters in every line.

Once a `File` object that specifies the path and the name of the file to be accessed randomly has been created, a `RandomAccessFile` object must be created. A `RandomAccessFile` object is used to read a file randomly and requires two arguments. The first argument is the name of the `File` object. The second argument is the access mode. Specifying a value of `r` for the access mode indicates the file is read only.

Random access is achieved by positioning an imaginary pointer in the file. The pointer location is measured by the number of bytes the pointer is from the beginning of the file. This distance is known as the offset. The `seek` method of the `RandomAccessFile` object is used to position the pointer. Using the `seek` method, the pointer can be moved forward or backward through a file. When positioning the pointer, you should keep in mind that the carriage return character and the newline character each count as one byte.

When using random access to read data from a file, information is read starting from the location of the pointer. For example, if the `seek` method is set to 13, the data starting at the 13th byte in the file will be read. You can use the `readLine` method to read data up to the next newline character.

READ A FILE RANDOMLY

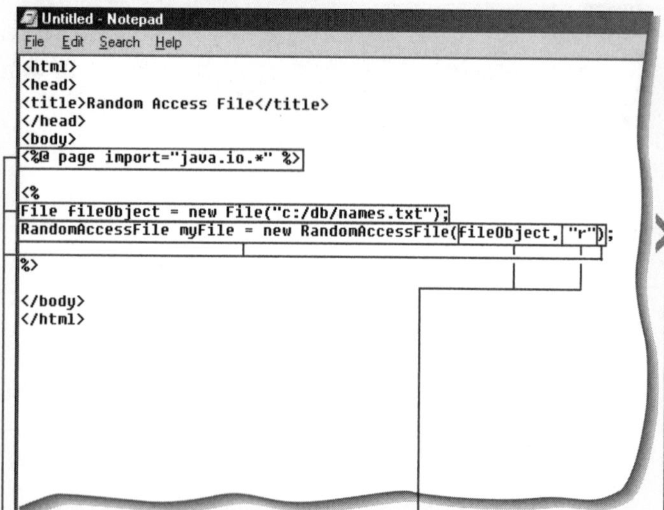

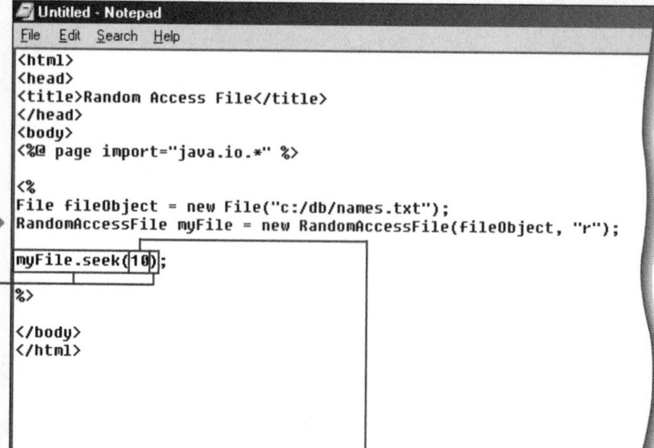

1 Type the code that imports the `java.io` package and creates a `File` object.

2 To create a `RandomAccessFile` object to read the file randomly, type **RandomAccessFile** followed by a name for the `RandomAccessFile` object. Then type **= new RandomAccessFile()**.

3 Between the parentheses, type the name of the `File` object followed by a comma.

4 To specify the access mode is read only, type **r** enclosed in quotation marks.

5 To position the pointer where you want to start reading the file, type the name of the `RandomAccessFile` object followed by a dot. Then type **seek()**.

6 Between the parentheses, type the number of bytes from the beginning of the file where you want to start reading.

Extra

Before you start accessing a file randomly, you may want to determine the length of the file. You can determine the length of a file by using the `length` method of the `RandomAccessFile` object.

Example:

```
The length of the file is 
<%
File fileObject = new File("c:/db/names.txt");
RandomAccessFile myFile = new RandomAccessFile(fileObject, "r");
out.print(myFile.length());
%>
 bytes.
```

You can also use the `RandomAccessFile` object to write data to a file. To be able to read and write to a file, you must specify an access mode of `rw` when creating the `RandomAccessFile` object.

Example:

```
<%
File fileObject = new File("c:/db/names.txt");
RandomAccessFile myFile = new RandomAccessFile(fileObject, "rw");
myFile.seek(40);
myFile.writeBytes("Barry...");
%>
```

The `RandomAccessFile` class is part of the `java.io` package. You can refer to the Java SDK documentation for more information about the `java.io` package and the methods of the `RandomAccessFile` object.

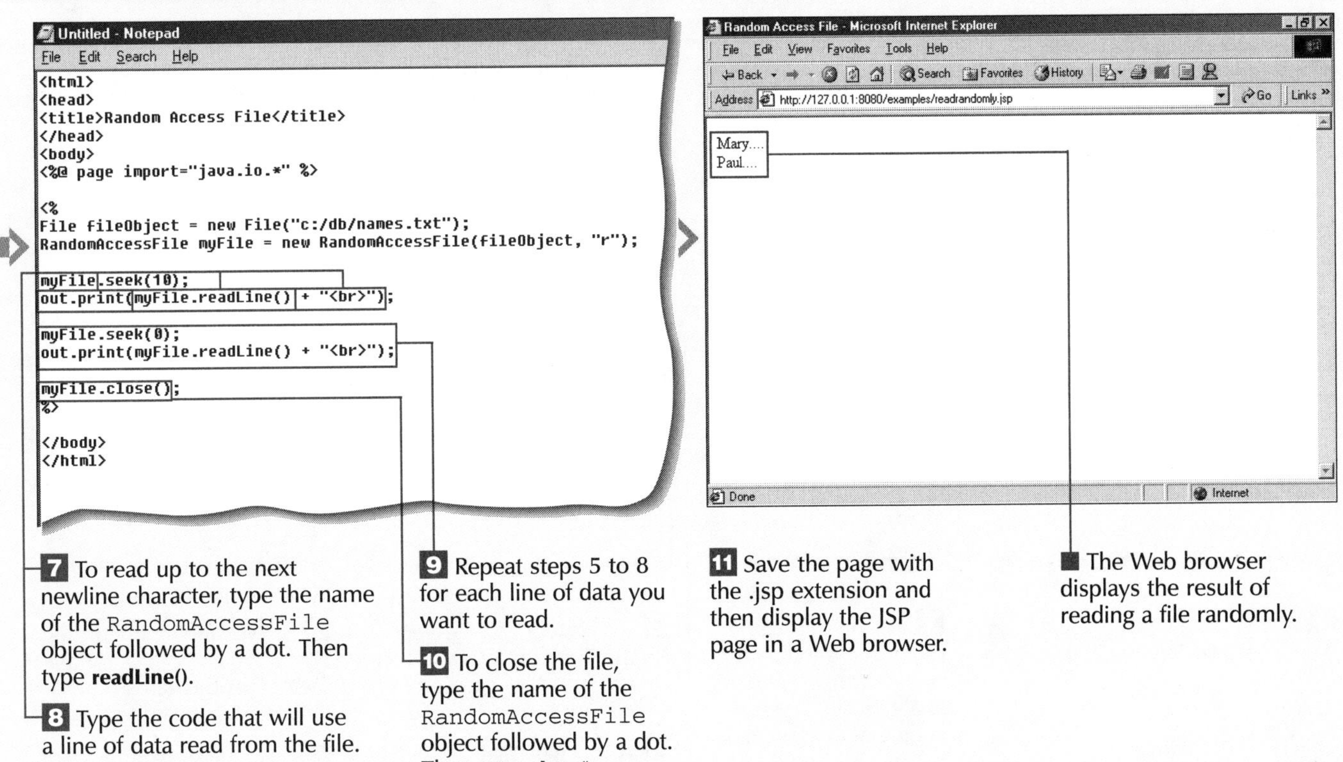

7 To read up to the next newline character, type the name of the `RandomAccessFile` object followed by a dot. Then type **readLine**().

8 Type the code that will use a line of data read from the file.

9 Repeat steps 5 to 8 for each line of data you want to read.

10 To close the file, type the name of the `RandomAccessFile` object followed by a dot. Then type **close**().

11 Save the page with the .jsp extension and then display the JSP page in a Web browser.

■ The Web browser displays the result of reading a file randomly.

CREATE A DIRECTORY

JavaServer Pages allows you to create a directory from within a JSP page. You may want to create a directory in a JSP page to help organize files or to store temporary files that will be used by the JSP page.

To create a directory, you must create a `File` object that specifies the name of the directory you want to create. In this case, the `File` object represents a directory, not a file. The name of the new directory is included as the argument of the `File` object. You may want to store the name of the directory in a variable and then use the variable as the argument for the `File` object.

Once the `File` object has been created, you use the `mkdir` method to create the directory. The `mkdir` method will return a `boolean` value of `true` or `false`, depending on whether or not the command to create the directory was successful. You may not be able to use the `mkdir` command to create directories if proper permissions are not in place.

You must have permission to access the parent directory in which you want to create the new directory. You must also have permission to create directories in the JSP page. Permission to create directories is usually controlled by the operating system. For information about access permissions, you should consult your operating system's documentation.

After you create a directory, you can create files and store them in the new directory. For information about creating files, see page 188.

It is good programming practice to verify that a directory was created successfully before using the directory. For information about verifying that a directory exists, see page 186.

CREATE A DIRECTORY

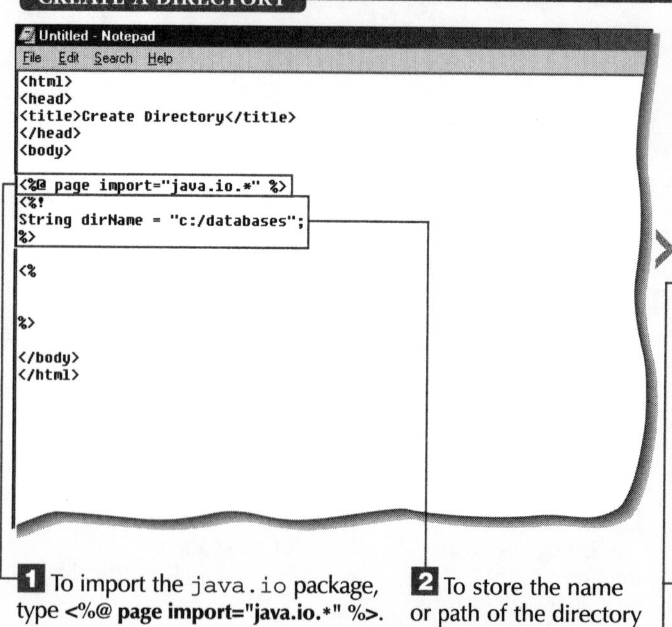

1 To import the `java.io` package, type **<%@ page import="java.io.*" %>**.

2 To store the name or path of the directory you want to create in a variable, type the code that assigns the information to the variable.

```
<html>
<head>
<title>Create Directory</title>
</head>
<body>

<%@ page import="java.io.*" %>
<%!
String dirName = "c:/databases";
%>

<%
File dirObject = new File(dirName);
%>

</body>
</html>
```

3 To create a `File` object for the directory you want to create, type **File** followed by a name for the `File` object.

4 Type **= new File()**.

5 Between the parentheses, type the name of the variable that stores the name of the directory you want to create.

■ You can also type the path or name of the directory, enclosed in quotation marks.

Apply It

You can delete a directory you no longer need. This is useful if you frequently create and use temporary directories within your JSP pages. You cannot delete a directory from within a JSP page if the directory contains files. Before deleting a directory, you should remove all the files in the directory.

TYPE THIS:

```
<%!
String dirName = "c:/databases";
%>
<%
File dirObject = new File(dirName);
dirObject.delete();

if (!dirObject.exists())
    out.print("The directory " + dirName
    + " has been deleted.");
%>
```

RESULT:

The directory c:/databases has been deleted.

Using the `mkdirs` method instead of the `mkdir` method allows you to create multiple directories at the same time. When you use the `mkdirs` method to create a directory, any directories you specify in the path will also be created if they do not currently exist. For example, if the path specified for the directory is /temp/data and the temp directory does not exist, the Web server will create the temp directory and then the data subdirectory.

TYPE THIS:

```
File dirObject= new File("/temp/data");
dirObject.mkdirs();
```

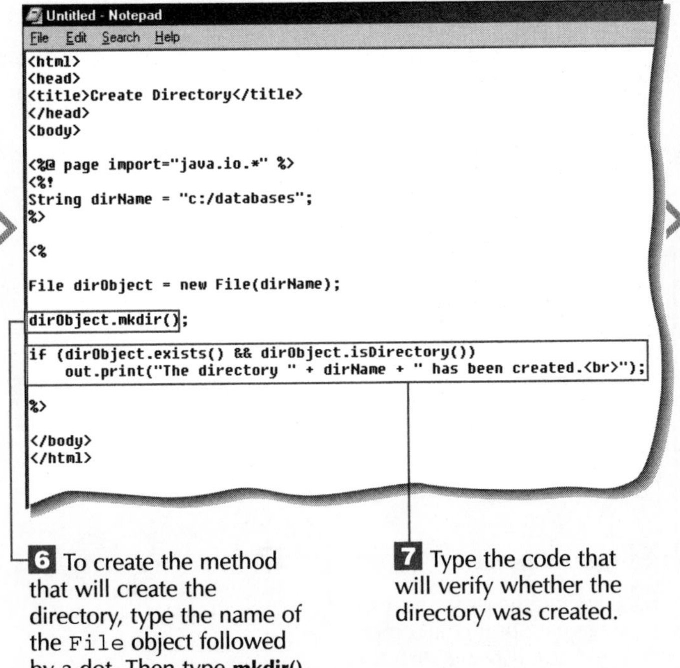

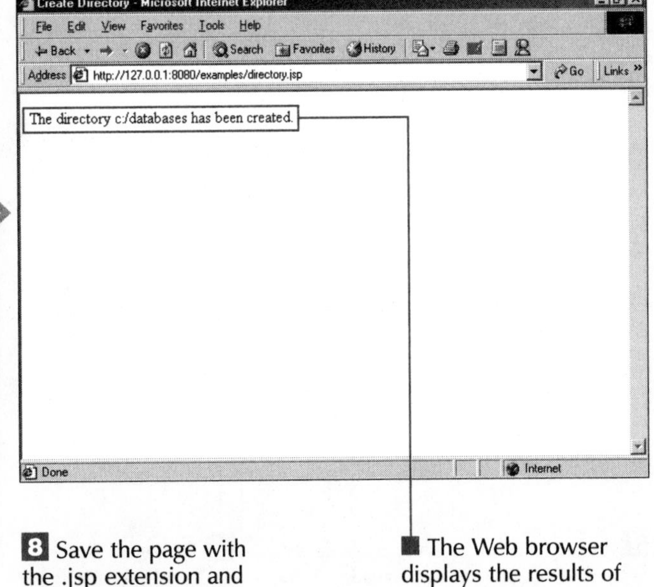

6 To create the method that will create the directory, type the name of the `File` object followed by a dot. Then type **mkdir()**.

7 Type the code that will verify whether the directory was created.

8 Save the page with the .jsp extension and then display the JSP page in a Web browser.

■ The Web browser displays the results of creating a directory.

DISPLAY A DIRECTORY LISTING

A JSP page can be used to examine a directory and retrieve the names of the files and subdirectories stored in the directory. Displaying a directory listing is useful when you want to verify that certain support files, such as database files, exist before a JSP page continues processing.

To retrieve the names of the files and subdirectories in a directory, you first create a `File` object that represents the directory. The directory must be accessible from the computer you use to create the `File` object.

The directory you specify as the argument for the `File` object must be a valid directory. If the directory does not exist, an error may be generated when the JSP page is displayed. You may want to use the `exists` method of the `File` object to verify that a directory exists before attempting to display the contents of the directory. For more information about the `exists` method, see page 186.

To retrieve the names of the files and subdirectories stored in the directory, you use the `listFiles` method of the `File` object. The `listFiles` method returns an array of `File` objects that represent the files and subdirectories in the directory. You can then use a `for` loop to display the contents of each `File` object on the JSP page. The path for the files and subdirectories in the directory will be displayed.

The directory listing you display may not contain all the files in the directory, since the `listFiles` method will not return files that the JSP page does not have permission to access. If permissions have been set that prevent the JSP page from reading or listing a file, the file will not appear in the directory listing.

DISPLAY A DIRECTORY LISTING

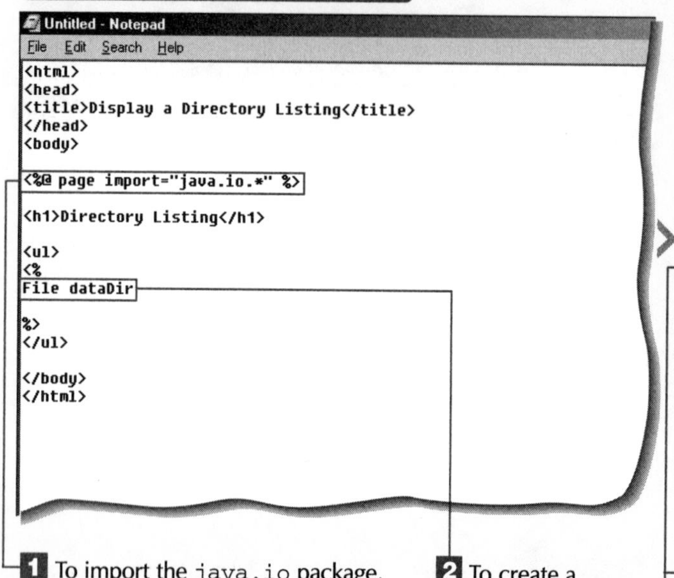

1 To import the `java.io` package, type **<%@ page import = "java.io.*" %>**.

2 To create a `File` object for the directory you want to display a directory listing for, type **File** followed by a name for the `File` object.

```
Untitled - Notepad
File Edit Search Help
<html>
<head>
<title>Display a Directory Listing</title>
</head>
<body>

<%@ page import="java.io.*" %>

<h1>Directory Listing</h1>

<ul>
<%
File dataDir = new File("c:/Data");
File[] listing =

%>
</ul>

</body>
</html>
```

3 Type **= new File()**.

4 Between the parentheses, type the path of the directory you want to display a directory listing for, enclosed in quotation marks.

5 To create an array that will store the files and subdirectories in the directory as an array of `File` objects, type **File[]** followed by a name for the array. Then type **=**.

Extra

While working on a computer connected to a network, you may want to access a directory located on another computer on the network and display the contents of the directory in a directory listing. On a Microsoft Windows network, the convention for indicating a computer within a path is to prefix the computer name with two backslashes (\\). Since you must escape backslashes you use in the argument of a `File` object, you must use four backslashes when specifying the computer name. You must also escape backslashes you use before directory names on a Windows network.

Example:

```
File dataDir = new File("\\\\Server\\data");
```

You can delete a file you no longer need from a directory. Deleting files allows you to free up resources on a computer and is useful when you want to delete a directory, since all the files in a directory must be deleted before the directory can be removed. To delete a file, create a `File` object for the file and then use the `delete` method of the `File` object to delete the file.

Example:

```
File fileObject = new File("c:/Data/file.txt);
fileObject.delete();
```

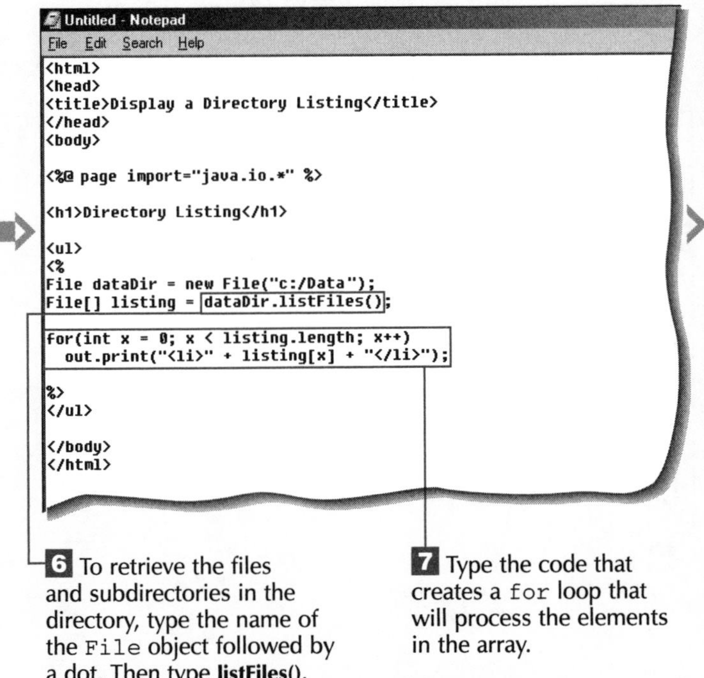

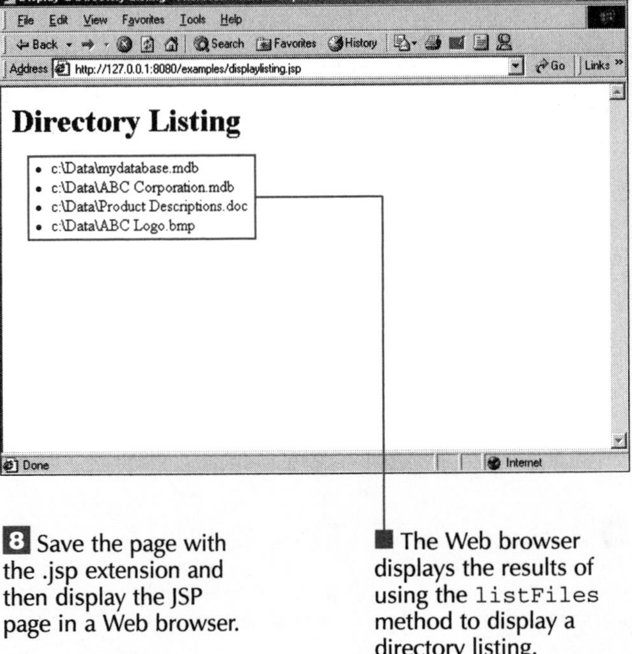

6 To retrieve the files and subdirectories in the directory, type the name of the `File` object followed by a dot. Then type **listFiles()**.

7 Type the code that creates a `for` loop that will process the elements in the array.

8 Save the page with the .jsp extension and then display the JSP page in a Web browser.

■ The Web browser displays the results of using the `listFiles` method to display a directory listing.

CREATE THE TAG HANDLER

Similar to JavaBeans, custom tags provide a way for you to easily work with complex Java code in your JSP pages. You can create your own custom tags to suit your needs.

Using custom tags can help make the code in a JSP page easier to work with by allowing you to separate the Java code from the HTML code. Since custom tags can be used in multiple JSP pages, using custom tags also saves you from having to retype the same Java code over and over.

The first step in creating a custom tag is to create a tag handler class file, which stores the methods that perform specific actions when the custom tags are processed. A tag handler must import the `javax.servlet.jsp` and `javax.servlet.jsp.tagext` packages in order to access the classes found in these packages. You can refer to the Java SDK documentation for more information about these packages. A tag handler may need to extend the classes found in these packages, such as the `TagSupport` class of the `javax.servlet.jsp.tagext` package. For information about extending a class, see page 54.

A simple tag handler must have a `doStartTag` method that contains the code to be executed when the start tag of the custom tag is processed. The access modifier of the `doStartTag` method must be specified as `public` in order for the method to be accessed as part of a tag handler.

The `doStartTag` method must return a value to indicate whether the custom tag will include information that must be processed between the start and end tags, called a body. A body is not required for a simple tag handler, so the `doStartTag` method returns the value `SKIP_BODY`. `SKIP_BODY` is a constant and is defined in the imported `javax` packages. `SKIP_BODY` contains an integer value so the return type of the `doStartTag` method must be specified as `int`.

CREATE THE TAG HANDLER

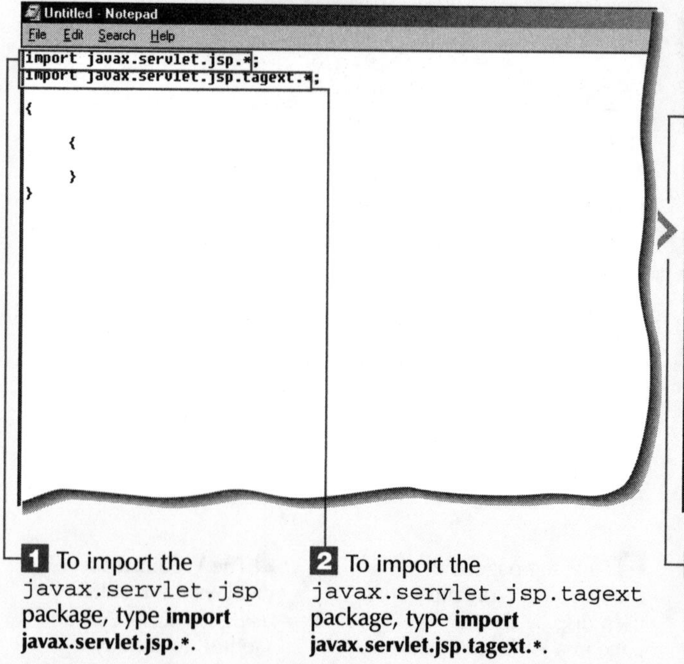


```
Untitled - Notepad
File  Edit  Search  Help
import javax.servlet.jsp.*;
import javax.servlet.jsp.tagext.*;

public class SimpleTag
{
      {
      }
}
```

1 To import the `javax.servlet.jsp` package, type **import javax.servlet.jsp.***.

2 To import the `javax.servlet.jsp.tagext` package, type **import javax.servlet.jsp.tagext.***.

3 To create a class for the custom tag, type **public class** followed by a name for the class.

Extra

Before creating tag handlers, you need to install the Java Servlet API class files, which contain the packages that must be imported when you compile the Java code used to create tag handlers. The Java Servlet API class files are available at the java.sun.com/products/servlet Web site. Make sure you store the Java Servlet API class files in the appropriate directory on your computer. For example, on the Windows platform, the Java Servlet API class files are stored in the c:\jdk1.3\jre\lib\ext directory. You should check the Java Servlet API specification documentation for installation instructions specific to your operating system.

Custom tags can enable specialization when developing a Web site. For example, Web page designers can work with the HTML content of a JSP page, while programmers develop the Java code that will make the Web page dynamic. This allows both types of professionals to concentrate on their own areas of expertise.

In addition to the value `SKIP_BODY`, the `doStartTag` method may return two other values. The value `EVAL_BODY_INCLUDE` is returned when the body of the custom tag needs to be processed. If the body of the custom tag must be processed using a `BodyContent` object, the value `EVAL_BODY_TAG` is returned.

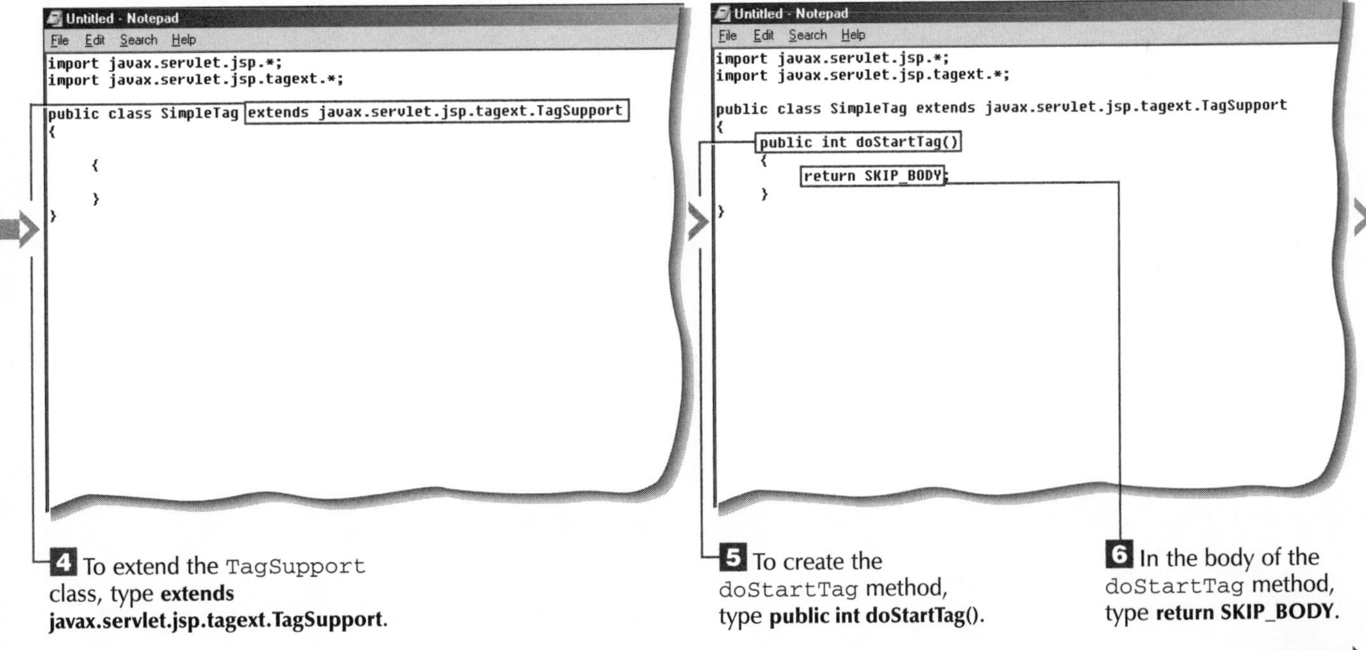

4 To extend the `TagSupport` class, type **extends javax.servlet.jsp.tagext.TagSupport**.

5 To create the `doStartTag` method, type **public int doStartTag()**.

6 In the body of the `doStartTag` method, type **return SKIP_BODY**.

CONTINUED

CREATE THE TAG HANDLER

A simple tag handler can be created to generate a message, such as copyright information or a greeting, which you want to display on several JSP pages in your Web site. You can then simply insert a custom tag into each JSP page where you want to display the message. Using a custom tag can make it easier to update the message in each JSP page where it is used.

After you create the tag handler class and declare the `doStartTag` method, you can use methods of the `PageContext` object to generate output for the tag. The `PageContext` object is used by an object to determine the kind of environment in which the object is contained. Once the object's environment is determined, the tag handler will use the `PageContext` object to help perform the requested actions.

The `getOut` method of the `PageContext` object determines the method being used to send information to a client. For a tag handler that displays a message, you can use the `print` method of the `PageContext` object to generate a text message that the JSP page will send to a Web browser when the custom tag is processed. To display the information for the tag, you use the `print` method and the `getOut` method of the `PageContext` object together.

Using the `print` method of the `PageContext` object may throw an IOException error. To handle any errors that occur, you should enclose the code that generates a message in a `try` block and create a `catch` block to catch any exception errors. For more information about error handling, see pages 174 to 185.

CREATE THE TAG HANDLER (CONTINUED)

Untitled - Notepad

File Edit Search Help

```
import javax.servlet.jsp.*;
import javax.servlet.jsp.tagext.*;

public class SimpleTag extends javax.servlet.jsp.tagext.TagSupport
{
     public int doStartTag() throws JspException
     {

          return SKIP_BODY;
     }
}
```

7 To specify that the `doStartTag` method may throw a JSP related exception error, type **throws JspException** on the same line as the method declaration.

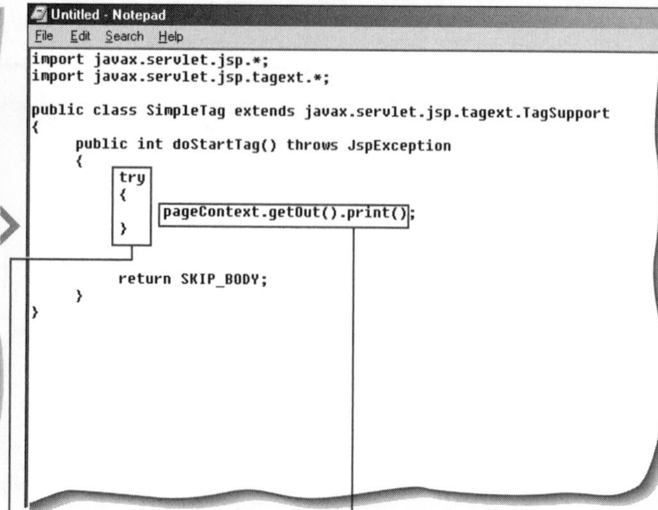

8 Type the code that creates a `try` block in the body of the `doStartTag` method.

9 In the body of the `try` block, type **pageContext.getOut().print()**.

Extra

The tag handler class file you create must be stored in a specific directory on your Web server. For example, if you are using the c:\tomcat\webapps\examples directory to store your JSP pages on a Windows platform using the Tomcat Web server, you would store your tag handler class files in the c:\tomcat\webapps\examples\WEB-INF\classes directory. You can refer to your Web server documentation to determine the proper directory to store your tag handler class files.

The `doStartTag` method is called when the start tag of a custom tag is processed. The start tag is the opening tag. For example, in the HTML code <title>My Web Page</title>, the start tag is <title> and the end tag is </title>. The phrase "My Web Page" is the body of the tag.

When a tag does not require a body, the start and end tags can be combined into one tag in a JSP page.

Example:

```
<mytag></mytag>
```

Can be written as:

```
<mytag />
```

Untitled - Notepad

File Edit Search Help

```
import javax.servlet.jsp.*;
import javax.servlet.jsp.tagext.*;

public class SimpleTag extends javax.servlet.jsp.tagext.TagSupport
{
     public int doStartTag() throws JspException
     {
          try
          {
               pageContext.getOut().print("Welcome to my Web site.");
          }

          return SKIP_BODY;
     }
}
```

10 Between the second set of parentheses, type the message you want the tag to display, enclosed in quotation marks.

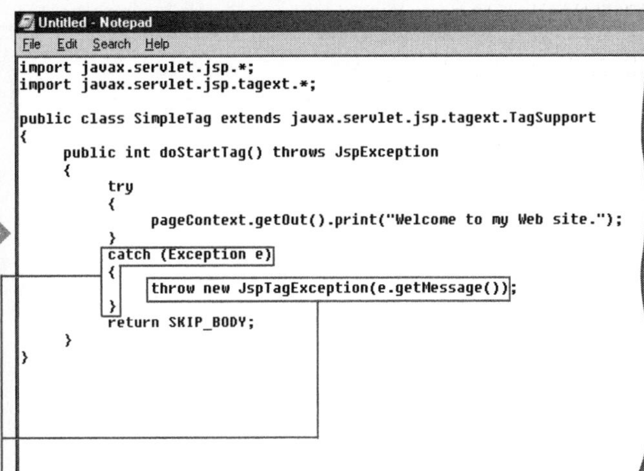

11 On the line immediately following the `try` block, type the code that creates a `catch` block.

12 In the body of the `catch` block, type **throw new JspTagException(e.getMessage())**.

13 Save the file with the .java extension and then compile the source code for the file.

14 Copy the compiled class file to the appropriate directory on your Web server.

■ You can now add the tag handler class to a tag library descriptor file.

CREATE THE TAG LIBRARY DESCRIPTOR FILE

Once you have created a tag handler for a custom tag, you must create a Tag Library Descriptor (TLD) file that will tell the Web server where to locate the tag handler when the custom tag is used in a JSP page. Tag library descriptor files are XML documents that can be created and edited using a simple text editor.

When creating a tag library descriptor file, you must begin the file with an XML header that specifies information about the file. The XML header consists of the `<?xml?>` tag and the `<!DOCTYPE>` tag. The information in the XML header is a standard requirement of XML documents and will be the same for every tag library descriptor file you create. For more information about XML documents, visit the www.xml.org Web site.

The `<taglib>` and `</taglib>` tags are used to enclose the main body of a tag library descriptor file. There are several tags you must use in the main body of the file. For example, you must use the `<jspversion>` tag to specify the version of JavaServer Pages that the tag library descriptor file uses.

A tag library descriptor file can contain information about multiple custom tags. To provide information about a custom tag you are creating, use the `<tag>` and `</tag>` tags to enclose the information. To specify the name of a custom tag, use the `<name>` tag. The name you specify must be the same as the name you will use for the tag in a JSP page. To specify the name of the tag handler class file for a custom tag, use the `<tagclass>` tag. You do not need to include the .class extension when specifying the name.

Tag library descriptor files should be saved with the .tld extension. When using version 3.1 of the Tomcat Web server, the name and location of the tag library descriptor file must be specified in the web.xml configuration file. To configure the web.xml configuration file, see page 204.

CREATE THE TAG LIBRARY DESCRIPTOR FILE

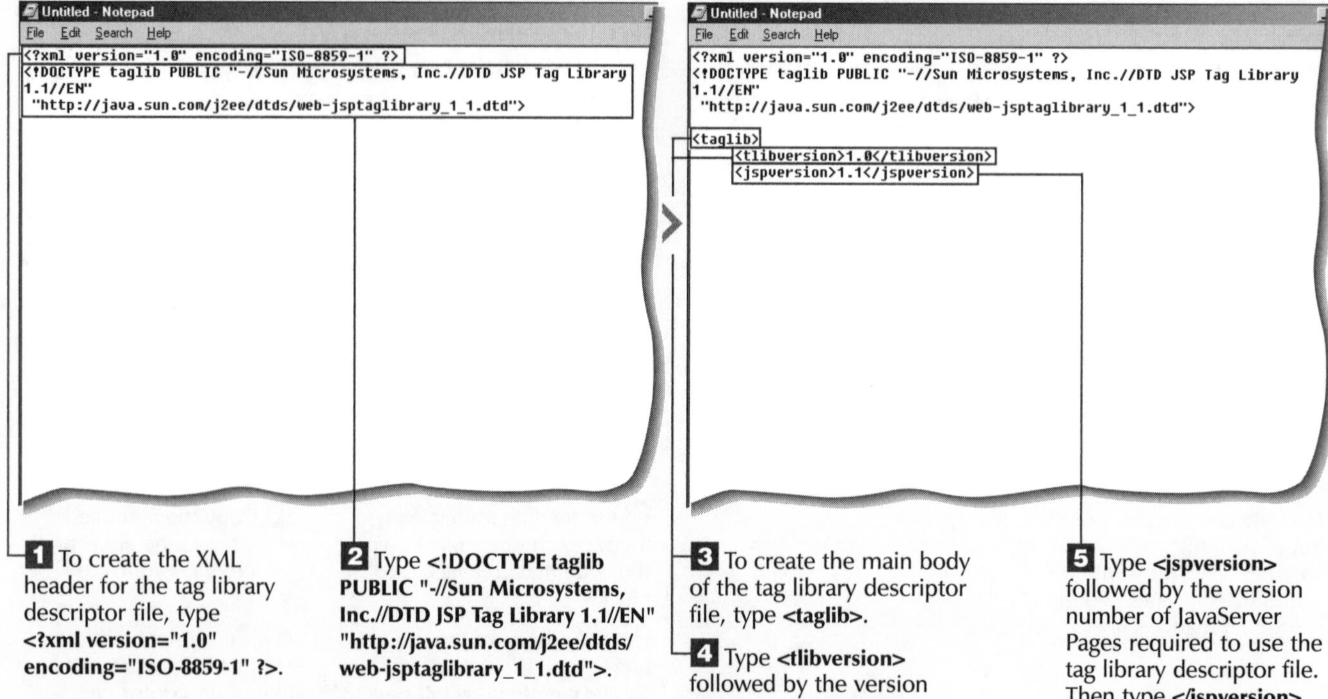

1 To create the XML header for the tag library descriptor file, type **<?xml version="1.0" encoding="ISO-8859-1" ?>**.

2 Type **<!DOCTYPE taglib PUBLIC "-//Sun Microsystems, Inc.//DTD JSP Tag Library 1.1//EN" "http://java.sun.com/j2ee/dtds/web-jsptaglibrary_1_1.dtd">**.

3 To create the main body of the tag library descriptor file, type **<taglib>**.

4 Type **<tlibversion>** followed by the version number of the tag library descriptor file. Then type **</tlibversion>**.

5 Type **<jspversion>** followed by the version number of JavaServer Pages required to use the tag library descriptor file. Then type **</jspversion>**.

Extra

The following tags must also be included in the main body of all the tag library descriptor files you create.

TAG:	DESCRIPTION:
`<tlibversion>`	The version of the tag library descriptor file.
`<shortname>`	A name that will be used to reference the tag library descriptor file from a JSP page.
`<info>`	A description of the tag library descriptor file.

The tag handler class file for a custom tag may be stored in a package. Grouping tags into packages is a common practice that allows you to easily organize and work with a large number of tags. When using the `<tagclass>` tag to specify the name of a tag handler class file that is stored in a package, prefix the name of the class file with the name of the package, separating the names with a dot. For example, a tag handler class file called SimpleTag.class that is part of the mytags.web.text package can be indicated in the tag descriptor file using the code `<tagclass>mytags.web.text.SimpleTag</tagclass>`.

If you are not using version 3.1 of the Tomcat Web server, you should use the `<uri>` tag in the main body of the tag library descriptor file to provide a unique identifier for the file, such as `<uri>www.maran.com/taglib</uri>` or `<uri>MyTagLibrary</uri>`. A JSP page that uses the tag library will contain the same identifier, linking the JSP page to the tag library descriptor file. In this situation, you do not need to configure the web.xml file.

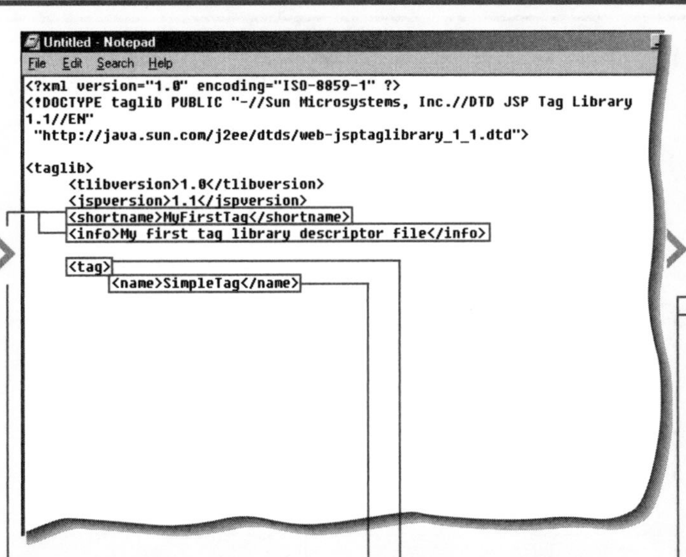

6 Type **<shortname>** followed by a name that will reference the tag library descriptor file from a JSP page. Then type **</shortname>**.

7 Type **<info>** followed by a description of the tag library descriptor file. Then type **</info>**.

8 Type **<tag>** to begin specifying information about a custom tag you are creating.

9 Type **<name>** followed by the name of the custom tag. Then type **</name>**.

```
Untitled - Notepad
File Edit Search Help
<?xml version="1.0" encoding="ISO-8859-1" ?>
<!DOCTYPE taglib PUBLIC "-//Sun Microsystems, Inc.//DTD JSP Tag Library
1.1//EN"
 "http://java.sun.com/j2ee/dtds/web-jsptaglibrary_1_1.dtd">

<taglib>
     <tlibversion>1.0</tlibversion>
     <jspversion>1.1</jspversion>
     <shortname>MyFirstTag</shortname>
     <info>My first tag library descriptor file</info>

     <tag>
          <name>SimpleTag</name>
          <tagclass>SimpleTag</tagclass>
     </tag>
</taglib>
```

10 Type **<tagclass>** followed by the name of the tag handler class file. Then type **</tagclass>**.

11 Type **</tag>** to complete the information about the custom tag.

12 Type **</taglib>** to complete the main body of the tag library descriptor file.

13 Save the file with the .tld extension.

■ You can now configure the web.xml file to work with your tag library descriptor file.

CONFIGURE THE WEB.XML FILE

If you are using version 3.1 of the Tomcat Web server, you must configure a Web application's web.xml file before using custom tags in the application. This task can be completed once you have created the tag handler class and the tag library descriptor file.

Each Web application on your Web server may have its own web.xml file. The web.xml files may be automatically created by the Web server. If you are storing your JSP pages in the \webapps\examples directory under the main Tomcat directory, then the web.xml file you should configure is located in the \webapps\examples\WEB-INF directory under the main Tomcat directory.

The web.xml file defines the setup of certain features of your Web application, such as session tracking and the file name of the default home page. To enable JSP pages in your Web application to use custom tags, you must use the `<taglib>` tag to configure the web.xml file. If the web.xml file already contains `<taglib>` tags, you can add a new `<taglib>` tag immediately following the existing `<taglib>` tags. If there are currently no `<taglib>` tags in the web.xml file, the new `<taglib>` tag can be inserted anywhere between the `<web-app>` and `</web-app>` tags. You can consult the Web server documentation for more information about the web.xml file.

Within the `<taglib>` and `</taglib>` tags, you must include the `<taglib-uri>` and `<taglib-location>` tags. The `<taglib-uri>` tag specifies a label, which will be used in your JSP pages to refer to the tag library descriptor file. The label can be an address, such as www.xyzcorp.com, or a word, such as mytags. The `<taglib-location>` tag specifies the location of the tag library descriptor file on the Web server.

CONFIGURE THE WEB.XML FILE

1 Open the web.xml file you want to configure in a text editor.

2 To enable the Web application to use custom tags, type **<taglib>**.

■ If the web.xml file already contains `<taglib>` tags, place the new `<taglib>` tag on the line immediately following the existing `<taglib>` tags.

```
web - Notepad
File Edit Search Help
<taglib>
    <taglib-uri>
       http://java.apache.org/tomcat/examples-taglib
    </taglib-uri>
    <taglib-location>
       /WEB-INF/jsp/example-taglib.tld
    </taglib-location>
</taglib>
<taglib>
    <taglib-uri>
       http://www.maran.com/taglib
    </taglib-uri>

<security-constraint>
  <web-resource-collection>
     <web-resource-name>Protected Area</web-resource-name>
     <!-- Define the context-relative URL(s) to be protected -->
     <url-pattern>/jsp/security/protected/*</url-pattern>
     <!-- If you list http methods, only those methods are protected -->
     <http-method>DELETE</http-method>
     <http-method>GET</http-method>
     <http-method>POST</http-method>
     <http-method>PUT</http-method>
  </web-resource-collection>
  <auth-constraint>
```

3 To create a label for the tag library descriptor file, type **<taglib-uri>**.

4 Type the label for the tag library descriptor file.

5 Type **</taglib-uri>** to close the `<taglib-uri>` tag.

Extra

You must configure the appropriate web.xml file in order to use custom tags with version 3.1 of the Tomcat Web server. Other Web servers, as well as other versions of the Tomcat Web server, may not require any alteration of the configuration file. Carefully consult your Web server documentation to determine what, if any, changes need to be made to the server's configuration files prior to using custom tags.

The web.xml file conforms to the XML specification for document structure and, therefore, should be very easy to read and edit. Text information, such as the label and location of the tag descriptor file, does not have to be enclosed in quotation marks.

In addition to the specific web.xml files for each application on your Web server, there is also a default web.xml file located in the \conf directory within the main Tomcat directory. This default web.xml file stores information such as the server's basic configuration. If you want all your JSP pages in any Web application to have access to a custom tag, you can add the `<taglib>` tag for the custom tag to the default web.xml file. Both the default web.xml file and the application-specific web.xml file will be accessed by a JSP page that uses a custom tag.

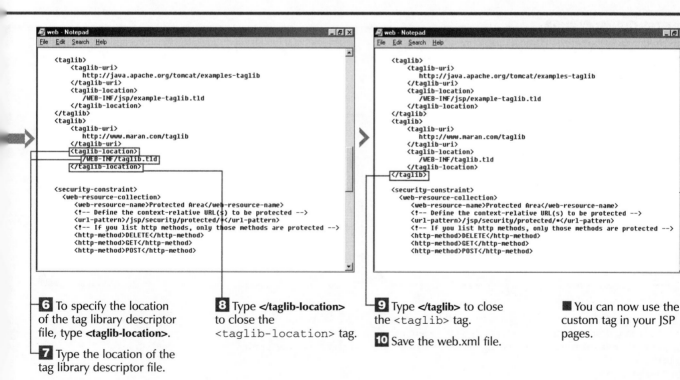

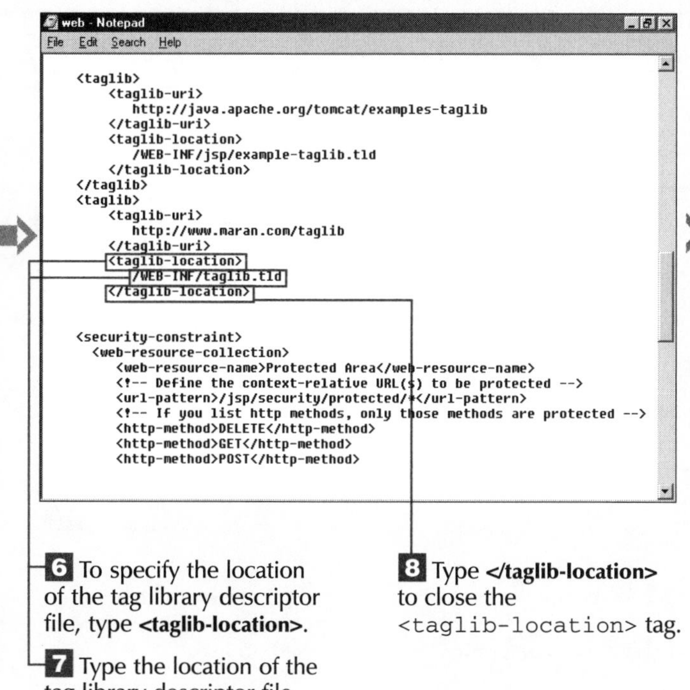


```
web - Notepad
File Edit Search Help

    <taglib>
        <taglib-uri>
            http://java.apache.org/tomcat/examples-taglib
        </taglib-uri>
        <taglib-location>
            /WEB-INF/jsp/example-taglib.tld
        </taglib-location>
    </taglib>
    <taglib>
        <taglib-uri>
            http://www.maran.com/taglib
        </taglib-uri>
        <taglib-location>
            /WEB-INF/taglib.tld
        </taglib-location>
    </taglib>

    <security-constraint>
      <web-resource-collection>
         <web-resource-name>Protected Area</web-resource-name>
         <!-- Define the context-relative URL(s) to be protected -->
         <url-pattern>/jsp/security/protected/*</url-pattern>
         <!-- If you list http methods, only those methods are protected -->
         <http-method>DELETE</http-method>
         <http-method>GET</http-method>
         <http-method>POST</http-method>
```

6 To specify the location of the tag library descriptor file, type **<taglib-location>**.

7 Type the location of the tag library descriptor file.

8 Type **</taglib-location>** to close the `<taglib-location>` tag.

9 Type **</taglib>** to close the `<taglib>` tag.

10 Save the web.xml file.

■ You can now use the custom tag in your JSP pages.

USING A CUSTOM TAG

Once you have compiled the tag handler class file, created the tag library descriptor file and configured the web.xml file for a custom tag, you can use the custom tag in a JSP page.

You must first include the `taglib` directive in the JSP page to identify the tag library descriptor file that contains the tag you want to use. To add the `taglib` directive to a JSP page, you place the directive statement between the `<%@` opening delimiter and the `%>` closing delimiter.

The `taglib` directive uses the `uri` attribute to specify an identifier for the tag library descriptor file. The identifier must be the same identifier specified for the tag library descriptor file in the web.xml file.

Within the `taglib` directive, you must also specify a prefix you want to use to reference the tag library that contains the custom tag information. Each tag library requires a different prefix, so you can use different prefixes to work with custom tags that have the same name but are stored in different tag libraries.

To use a custom tag in a JSP page, you type the prefix and the name you assigned to the tag in the tag library descriptor file, separated by a colon. Like HTML tags, the start tag is enclosed in angle brackets. The end tag is also enclosed in angle brackets and begins with a forward slash. For simple tags that do not contain a body, or information between the start and end tags, the start and end tags can be combined into one tag, such as `<myTags:SimpleTag />`.

USING A CUSTOM TAG

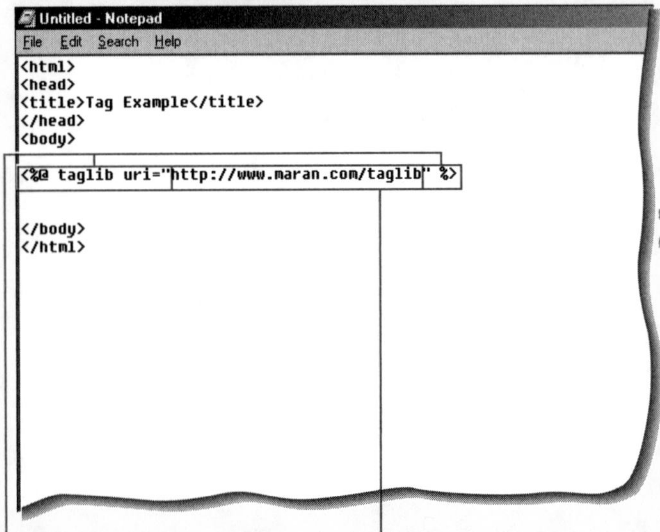

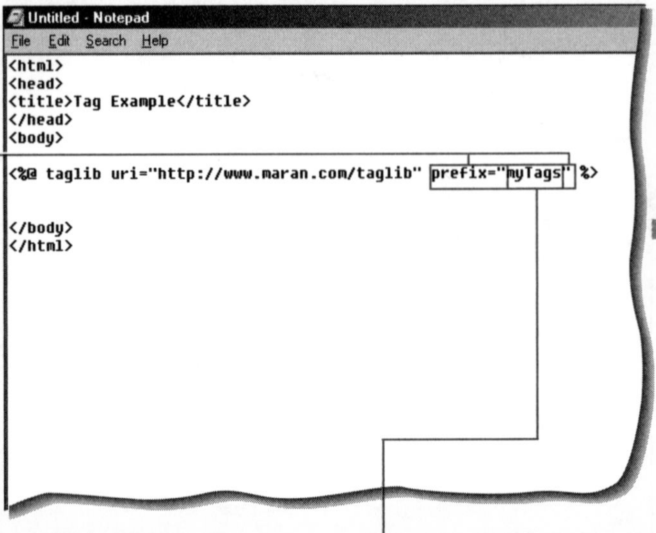

```
Untitled - Notepad
File  Edit  Search  Help
<html>
<head>
<title>Tag Example</title>
</head>
<body>

<%@ taglib uri="http://www.maran.com/taglib" %>

</body>
</html>
```

1 To specify the location of the tag library descriptor file for the custom tag you want to use in the JSP page, type **<%@ taglib uri="" %>**.

2 Between the quotation marks, type the identifier of the tag library descriptor file.

```
Untitled - Notepad
File  Edit  Search  Help
<html>
<head>
<title>Tag Example</title>
</head>
<body>

<%@ taglib uri="http://www.maran.com/taglib" prefix="myTags" %>

</body>
</html>
```

3 To specify the prefix you want to use for the tag library, type **prefix=""**.

4 Between the quotation marks, type the prefix you want to use.

Extra

The custom tag examples in this chapter were created using Tomcat Web server version 3.1. This version of Tomcat uses a label, known as the URI, to map to the tag library descriptor file. Other Web servers, as well as other versions of the Tomcat Web server, may require a different format when using the `taglib` directive. You should consult your Web server documentation for information about using the `taglib` directive.

Custom tags that display information can be enclosed within HTML tags or other custom tags that will format or organize the information the tag will display.

Example:

```
<b><myTags:SimpleTag /></b>
```

Result:

Welcome to my Web site.

If any information in the required supporting files for the custom tag, such as the web.xml file, is incorrect, an error may be generated when the `taglib` directive or the custom tag is processed by the Web server. To prevent problems with the JSP page, you should ensure that the tag handler class file includes error handling processes, such as a `try` block and a `catch` block.

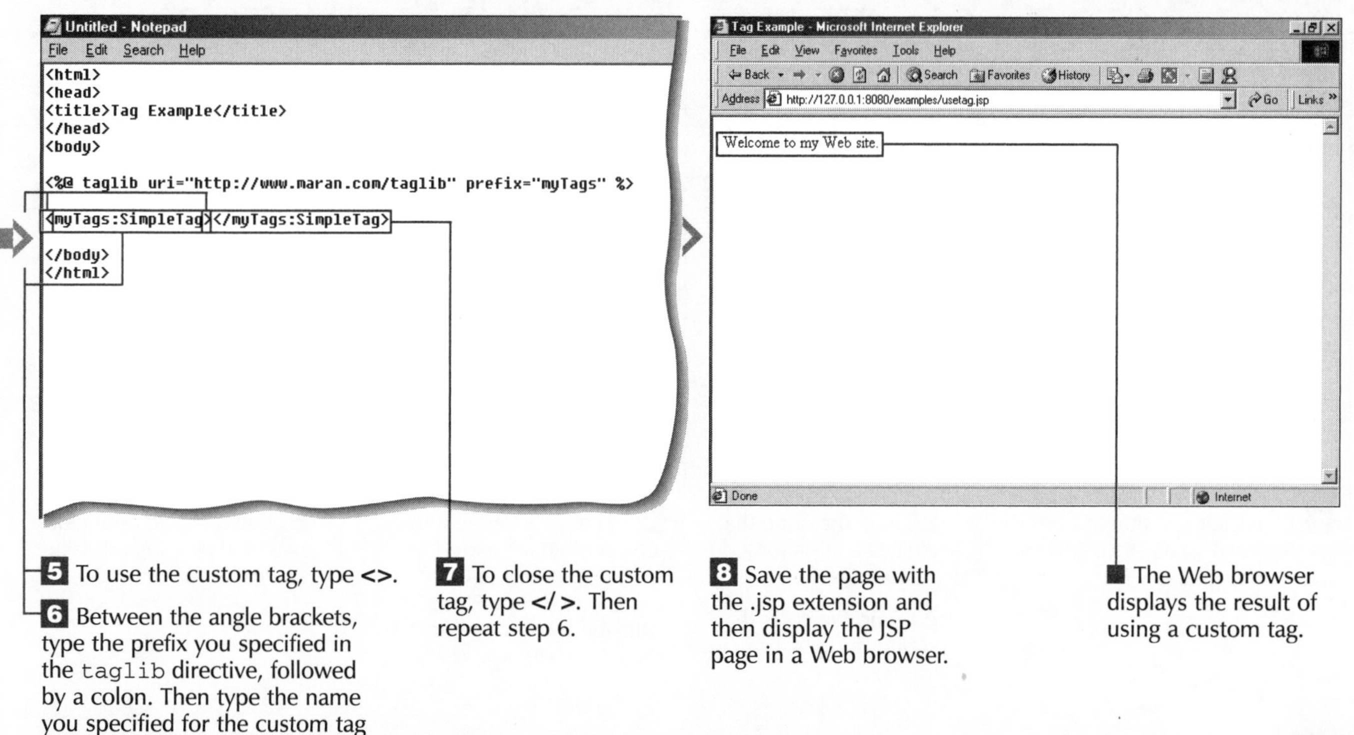

5 To use the custom tag, type **<>**.

6 Between the angle brackets, type the prefix you specified in the `taglib` directive, followed by a colon. Then type the name you specified for the custom tag in the tag library descriptor file.

7 To close the custom tag, type **</ >**. Then repeat step 6.

8 Save the page with the .jsp extension and then display the JSP page in a Web browser.

■ The Web browser displays the result of using a custom tag.

CREATE THE TAG HANDLER FOR A TAG WITH AN ATTRIBUTE

A custom tag can be set up to support attributes that are specified when the tag is used in a JSP page. This adds flexibility to the tag and allows you to customize the tag's behavior. For example, you can have a tag that displays a heading accept an attribute that specifies the color of the heading.

An attribute for a custom tag is represented by a variable in a tag handler class file. When you create the variable that will represent an attribute, you can assign a default value to the variable. The tag handler will use this value for the attribute if a value is not specified when the custom tag is used.

When the custom tag is used with an attribute in the JSP page, the value specified for the attribute is passed to the tag handler as a variable. In order to convert a value specified for an attribute in a JSP page to a variable, you must use a setter method. The access modifier of a setter method must be set to `public` and the return type set to `void`, since the method does not return a value. The name of the method is the same as the name of the variable that stores the value for the attribute, but begins with a capital letter and is prefixed by the word `set`. The parentheses at the end of the setter method name enclose the data type of the variable and the variable used to pass the value to the method. The argument is then assigned to the variable used to store the attribute value.

The variable that represents the attribute value is typically declared in the class body of the tag handler. This allows the variable to be accessed by any method in the tag handler class file.

CREATE THE TAG HANDLER FOR A TAG WITH AN ATTRIBUTE

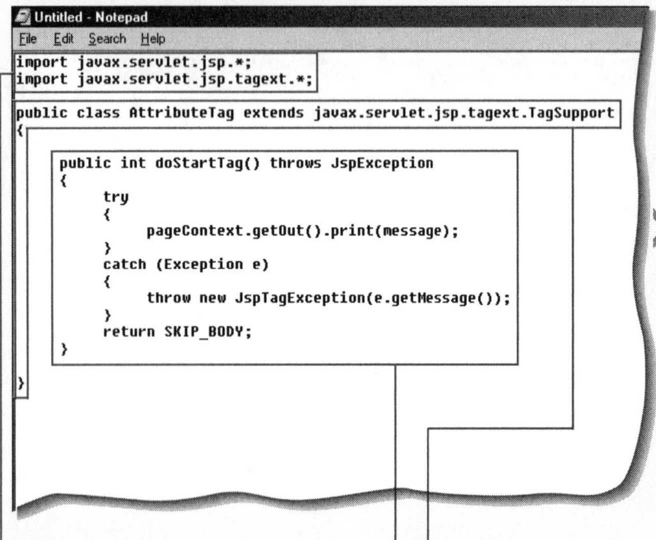

1 Type the code that imports the `javax.servlet.jsp` and the `javax.servlet.jsp.tagext` packages.

2 Type the code that creates a class for a custom tag.

3 Type the code that creates a `doStartTag` method.

```
import javax.servlet.jsp.*;
import javax.servlet.jsp.tagext.*;

public class AttributeTag extends javax.servlet.jsp.tagext.TagSupport
{
    private String message = "No message specified.";

    public int doStartTag() throws JspException
    {
        try
        {
            pageContext.getOut().print(message);
        }
        catch (Exception e)
        {
            throw new JspTagException(e.getMessage());
        }
        return SKIP_BODY;
    }
}
```

4 To create a variable to represent an attribute that will be specified in a JSP page, type **private String** followed by a name for the variable. Then type = `""`.

5 Between the quotation marks, type a default value for the variable.

Apply It

You can create multiple attributes for each tag. You must create a variable and a setter method for each attribute.

Example:

```
private String message = "No message specified.";
private String boldText = "b";
public int doStartTag() throws JspException
{
      try
      {
            String output="<" + boldText + ">" + message + "</" +
            boldText + ">";
            pageContext.getOut().print(output);
      }
      catch(Exception e)
      {
            throw new JspTagException(e.getMessage());
      }
      return SKIP_BODY;
}
public void setMessage(String text)
{
      message = text;
}
public void setBoldText(String text)
{
      boldText = text;
}
```

```
import javax.servlet.jsp.*;
import javax.servlet.jsp.tagext.*;

public class AttributeTag extends javax.servlet.jsp.tagext.TagSupport
{
     private String message = "No message specified.";

     public int doStartTag() throws JspException
     {
          try
          {
               pageContext.getOut().print(message);
          }
          catch (Exception e)
          {
               throw new JspTagException(e.getMessage());
          }
          return SKIP_BODY;
     }
     public void setMessage(String text)

}
```

6 To declare a setter method that will convert the value of the attribute to the variable you created in step 4, type **public void**.

7 To name the method, type **set** immediately followed by the name of the variable, beginning with a capital letter. Then type **()**.

8 Between the parentheses, type the data type of the variable followed by a name for the variable that will pass the value to the setter method.

```
import javax.servlet.jsp.*;
import javax.servlet.jsp.tagext.*;

public class AttributeTag extends javax.servlet.jsp.tagext.TagSupport
{
     private String message = "No message specified.";

     public int doStartTag() throws JspException
     {
          try
          {
               pageContext.getOut().print(message);
          }
          catch (Exception e)
          {
               throw new JspTagException(e.getMessage());
          }
          return SKIP_BODY;
     }
     public void setMessage(String text)
     {
          message = text;
     }
}
```

9 Type the name of the variable that represents the attribute followed by **=** and the variable you specified in step 8. Enclose the code in braces.

10 Save the file with the .java extension and then compile the source code for the file.

11 Copy the compiled class file to the appropriate directory on your Web server.

■ You can now add the tag handler class to a tag library descriptor file.

CREATE THE TAG LIBRARY DESCRIPTOR FILE FOR A TAG WITH AN ATTRIBUTE

You need to add an `<attribute>` tag to a tag library descriptor file for each attribute of a custom tag. An `<attribute>` tag allows you to specify details about an attribute of a custom tag and is placed following the `<tagclass>` tag in a tag library descriptor file.

The name of the attribute is specified using the `<name>` tag, which is placed following the `<attribute>` tag. The name specified with the `<name>` tag must match the name that will be used when the custom tag is used on a JSP page. The name of the attribute specified with the `<name>` tag is case sensitive. Most attribute names use only lower case letters.

After the name of the attribute is specified, a `<required>` tag is used to specify if the attribute is required when the custom tag is used on a JSP page. If a value of `false` is specified for a `<required>` tag, the use of the attribute is optional when the custom tag is used. If a value of `true` is specified, the attribute must be included each time the custom tag is used.

When you specify that an attribute is not required, you should ensure that the tag handler class file for the custom tag contains the code that specifies a default value for the attribute in the event that the attribute is left out when the custom tag is used. This code can be part of the method in the tag handler that is used to set the value of the attribute when the attribute is included when the custom tag is used. For more information about creating a tag handler for a tag with an attribute, see page 208.

CREATE THE TAG LIBRARY DESCRIPTOR FILE FOR A TAG WITH AN ATTRIBUTE

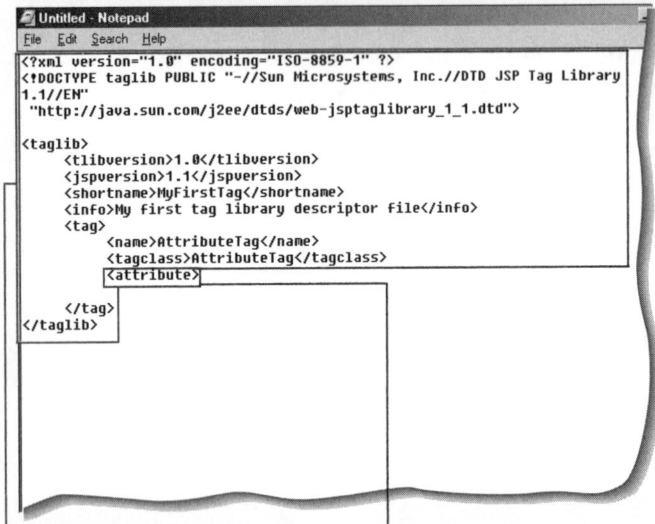

Untitled - Notepad

File Edit Search Help

```
<?xml version="1.0" encoding="ISO-8859-1" ?>
<!DOCTYPE taglib PUBLIC "-//Sun Microsystems, Inc.//DTD JSP Tag Library
1.1//EN"
 "http://java.sun.com/j2ee/dtds/web-jsptaglibrary_1_1.dtd">

<taglib>
     <tlibversion>1.0</tlibversion>
     <jspversion>1.1</jspversion>
     <shortname>MyFirstTag</shortname>
     <info>My first tag library descriptor file</info>
     <tag>
          <name>AttributeTag</name>
          <tagclass>AttributeTag</tagclass>
          <attribute>

     </tag>
</taglib>
```

Untitled - Notepad

File Edit Search Help

```
<?xml version="1.0" encoding="ISO-8859-1" ?>
<!DOCTYPE taglib PUBLIC "-//Sun Microsystems, Inc.//DTD JSP Tag Library
1.1//EN"
 "http://java.sun.com/j2ee/dtds/web-jsptaglibrary_1_1.dtd">

<taglib>
     <tlibversion>1.0</tlibversion>
     <jspversion>1.1</jspversion>
     <shortname>MyFirstTag</shortname>
     <info>My first tag library descriptor file</info>
     <tag>
          <name>AttributeTag</name>
          <tagclass>AttributeTag</tagclass>
          <attribute>
               <name>message</name>

     </tag>
</taglib>
```

1 Type code that creates a tag library descriptor file. See page 202 for information about creating a tag library descriptor file.

2 To specify an attribute for a custom tag, type **<attribute>** following the `<tagclass>` tag.

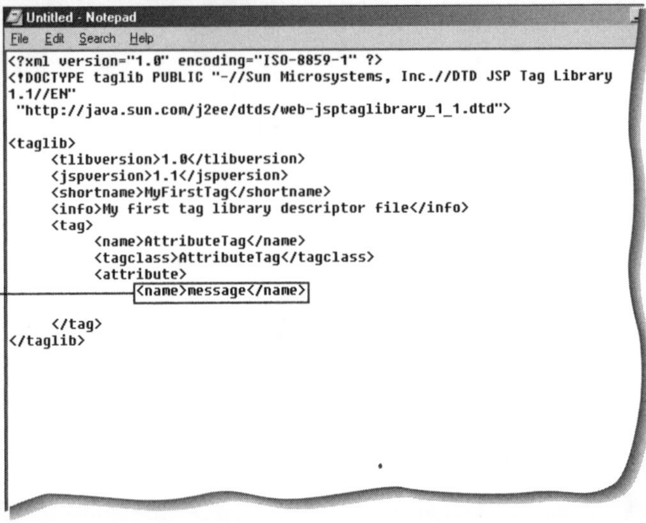

3 To specify the name of the attribute, type **<name>** followed by the name of the attribute. Then type **</name>**.

Extra

You can specify as many attributes as required by your custom tag. To add an additional attribute, you can simply use another set of `<attribute>` tags.

Example:

```
<tag>
      <name>AttributeTag</name>
      <tagclass>AttributeTag</tagclass>
      <attribute>
            <name>message</name>
            <required>false</required>
      </attribute>
      <attribute>
            <name>length</name>
            <required>true</required>
      </attribute>
</tag>
```

When using a custom tag with an attribute, you can have the value of the attribute be determined at runtime by a section of JSP code, such as an expression, by adding an `<rtexprvalue>` tag and assigning it a value of `true`.

Example:

```
<tag>
      <name>AttributeTag</name>
      <tagclass>AttributeTag</tagclass>
      <attribute>
            <name>message</name>
            <required>false</required>
            <rtexprvalue>true</rtexprvalue>
      </attribute>
</tag>
```

Untitled - Notepad

File Edit Search Help

```
<?xml version="1.0" encoding="ISO-8859-1" ?>
<!DOCTYPE taglib PUBLIC "-//Sun Microsystems, Inc.//DTD JSP Tag Library
1.1//EN"
 "http://java.sun.com/j2ee/dtds/web-jsptaglibrary_1_1.dtd">

<taglib>
      <tlibversion>1.0</tlibversion>
      <jspversion>1.1</jspversion>
      <shortname>MyFirstTag</shortname>
      <info>My first tag library descriptor file</info>
      <tag>
            <name>AttributeTag</name>
            <tagclass>AttributeTag</tagclass>
            <attribute>
                  <name>message</name>
                  <required>false</required>

      </tag>
</taglib>
```

4 To specify if the attribute is required when the custom tag is used, type **<required>** followed by true or false. Then type **</required>**.

Untitled - Notepad

File Edit Search Help

```
<?xml version="1.0" encoding="ISO-8859-1" ?>
<!DOCTYPE taglib PUBLIC "-//Sun Microsystems, Inc.//DTD JSP Tag Library
1.1//EN"
 "http://java.sun.com/j2ee/dtds/web-jsptaglibrary_1_1.dtd">

<taglib>
      <tlibversion>1.0</tlibversion>
      <jspversion>1.1</jspversion>
      <shortname>MyFirstTag</shortname>
      <info>My first tag library descriptor file</info>
      <tag>
            <name>AttributeTag</name>
            <tagclass>AttributeTag</tagclass>
            <attribute>
                  <name>message</name>
                  <required>false</required>
            </attribute>
      </tag>
</taglib>
```

5 Type **</attribute>** to end the attribute specification.

6 Save the tag library descriptor file with a .tld extension.

■ You can now use the custom tag with an attribute.

USING A CUSTOM TAG WITH AN ATTRIBUTE

To use a custom tag with an attribute, you must include a `taglib` directive in the JSP page to identify the tag library descriptor file that contains the tag you want to use.

As with any other custom tag that you wish to use in a JSP page, you must specify the prefix and the name you assigned to the tag in the tag library descriptor file, separated by a colon. To add an attribute to the custom tag, you type the name of the attribute and a value to be assigned to the attribute, separated by an equal sign. The value of the attribute must be enclosed in quotation marks.

When using custom tags with an attribute, you can use the common notation, which uses both an start and a end tag, or the shortened notation, which combines the start and end tags into one tag. When using the common notation, the attribute must be specified in the start tag of the custom tag. When using the shortened notation, the attribute should be specified within the tag, such as <mt:AttributeTag message="Welcome to my Web page." />.

The tag library descriptor file indicates whether an attribute is required or not. For information about specifying required attributes in the tag library descriptor file, see page 210. If an attribute is optional, you should ensure that the tag handler class file can process the custom tag when an attribute is not specified. This may be done by assigning a default value to be used in case the attribute is not specified in the custom tag. For information about assigning default attribute values in the tag handler class file, see page 208.

USING A CUSTOM TAG WITH AN ATTRIBUTE

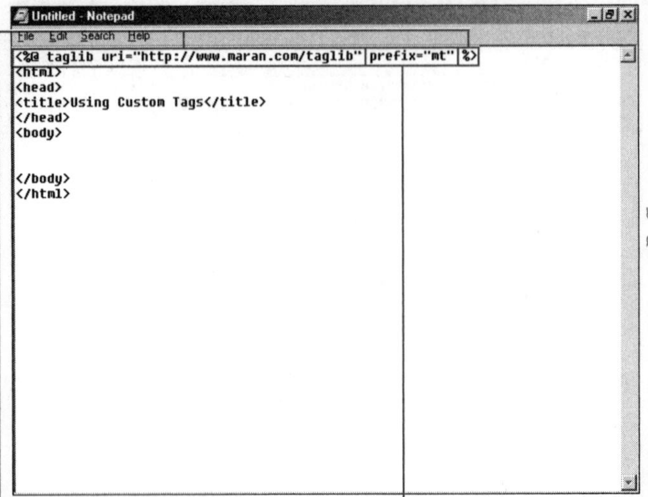

1 Create the `taglib` directive that specifies the location of the tag library descriptor file for the custom tag you want to use in the JSP page.

2 In the `taglib` directive, type the code that specifies the prefix you want to use for the tag library.

3 To use the custom tag, type **<>**.

4 Between the angle brackets, type the prefix you specified in the `taglib` directive, followed by a colon. Then type the name of the custom tag.

Extra

Attribute values can be enclosed within single or double quotation marks.

Example:
```
<mt:AttributeTag message="This is a tag with an attribute" />
```

Can be typed as:
```
<mt:AttributeTag message='This is a tag with an attribute' />
```

If the `<rtexprvalue>` tag is set to `true` in the tag library descriptor file, you can use a JSP expression in the JSP page to determine the value of an attribute. This allows you to include dynamically generated attribute values in your custom tags. If the `<rtexprvalue>` tag is not specified or is set to `false`, then the attribute value must be a string.

Example:
```
<mt:AttributeTag message="<%= Session.getAttribute.("userName") %>" />
```

You can use more than one attribute in a tag if the tag handler class file and the tag library descriptor file support multiple attributes.

Example:
```
<mt:AttributeTag message="Welcome to my Web page" encloseText="h1" />
```

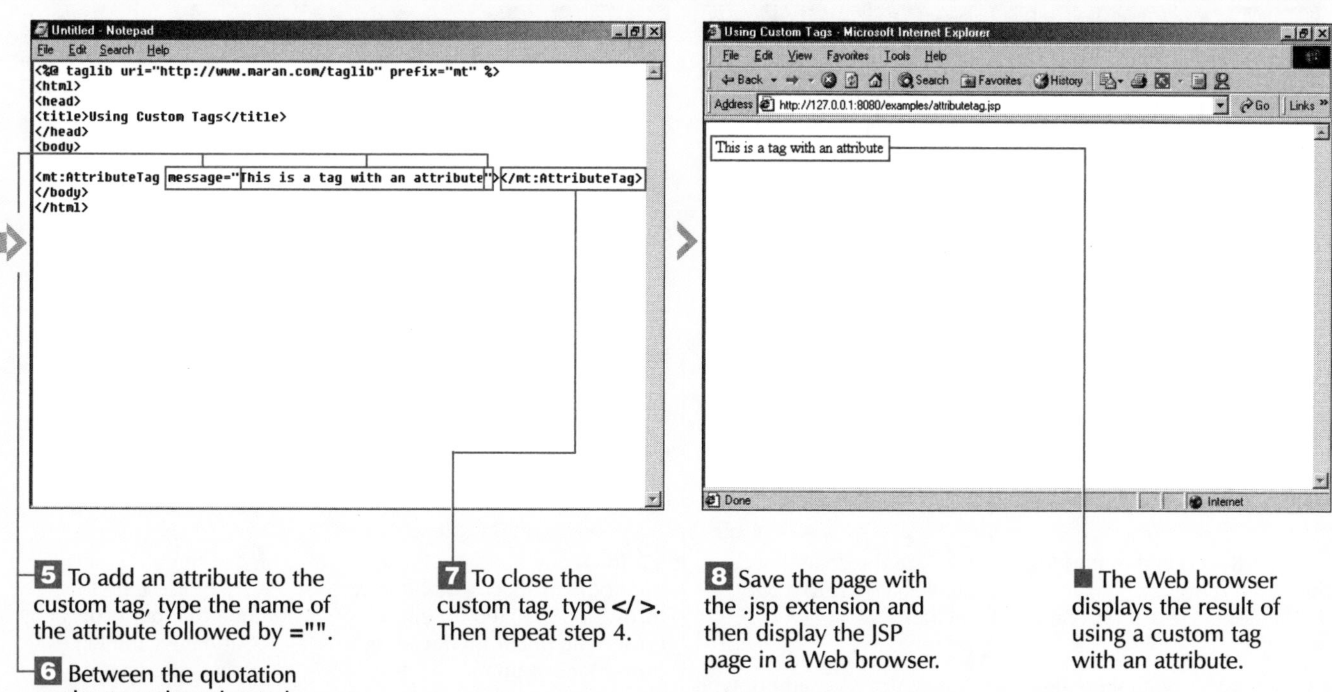

5 To add an attribute to the custom tag, type the name of the attribute followed by **=""**.

6 Between the quotation marks, type the value to be assigned to the attribute.

7 To close the custom tag, type **</ >**. Then repeat step 4.

8 Save the page with the .jsp extension and then display the JSP page in a Web browser.

■ The Web browser displays the result of using a custom tag with an attribute.

CREATE THE TAG HANDLER FOR A TAG WITH A BODY

The body of a tag is the information enclosed within the start and end tags. The tag body can consist of plain text or any JSP code, including scriptlets, expressions and directives. You can create a tag handler class file to use the information contained in the body of a custom tag. The tag handler class file required for a custom tag with a body is similar to that of a simple custom tag.

As with a tag handler class for a simple tag, a `doStartTag` method must be included. The `doStartTag` method is processed when the start tag of a custom tag is encountered in a JSP page. The `doStartTag` method of a tag handler for a tag with a body must return the value `EVAL_BODY_INCLUDE`, which instructs the Web server to process the information contained in the tag body. When the `doStartTag` method has finished processing and the `EVAL_BODY_INCLUDE` value has been returned, the Web server includes the information in the tag body in the results that are sent to the client.

The tag handler class file for a custom tag with a body should also include a method called `doEndTag`. The `doEndTag` method contains the code to be executed after the body is processed. This method is executed when the end tag of the custom tag is encountered in the JSP page. The `doEndTag` method must also return a value. The return value determines whether or not the remainder of the JSP page must be processed. In most cases, you will use the `EVAL_PAGE` return value, which indicates to the Web server that the rest of the JSP page should be processed. If you want the Web server to stop processing the JSP page and ignore the remainder of the code in the JSP page, use the `SKIP_PAGE` return value.

CREATE THE TAG HANDLER FOR A TAG WITH A BODY

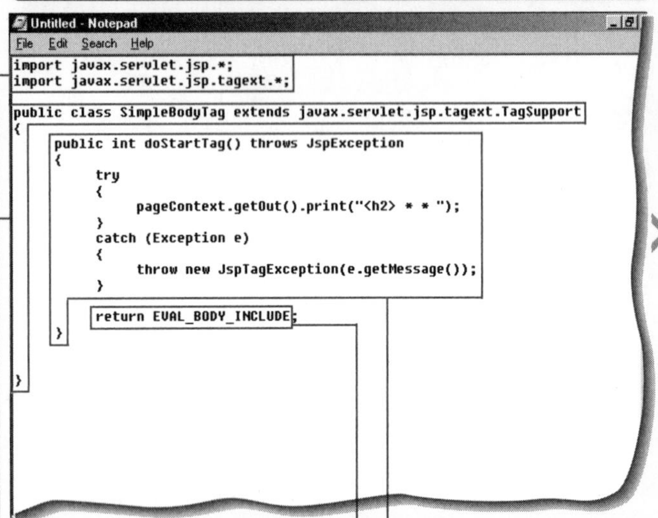

1 Type the code that imports the `javax.servlet.jsp` and the `javax.servlet.jsp.tagext` packages.

2 Type the code that creates a class for a custom tag.

3 Type the code that creates a `doStartTag` method.

4 In the body of the `doStartTag` method, type **return EVAL_BODY_INCLUDE** to allow the tag to process the information in the tag body.

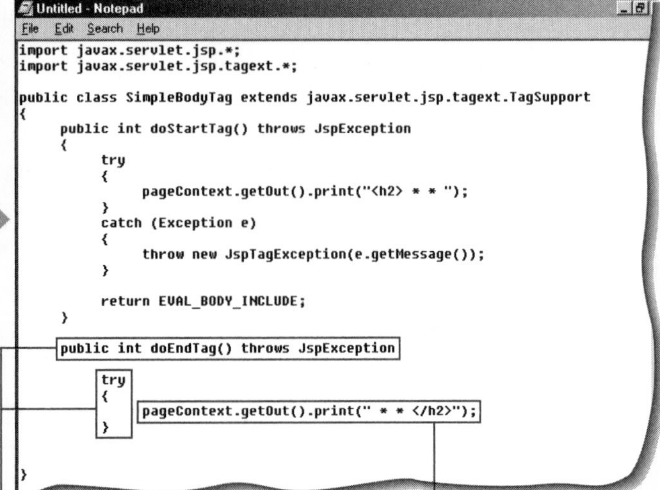

5 To create the `doEndTag` method and specify that it may throw a JSP related exception error, type **public int doEndTag() throws JspException**.

6 Type the code that creates a `try` block in the body of the `doEndTag` method.

7 In the body of the `try` block, type the code that performs an action after the tag body is processed.

Apply It

You can create versatile custom tags that can use attributes and the information in the tag body at the same time. For example, you can modify a custom tag to apply a header level specified by an attribute of the tag to the information in the body of the tag.

Example:

```
private String level = "2";
public int doStartTag() throws JspException
{
      try
      {
            pageContext.getOut().print("<h" + level + "> * * ");
      }
      catch (Exception e)
      {
            throw new JspTagException(e.getMessage());
      }
      return EVAL_BODY_INCLUDE;
}
public int doEndTag() throws JspException
{
      try
      {
            pageContext.getOut().print(" * * </h" + level + ">");
      }
      catch (Exception e)
      {
            throw new JspTagException(e.getMessage());
      }
      return EVAL_PAGE;
}
public void setLevel(String text)
{
      level = text;
}
```

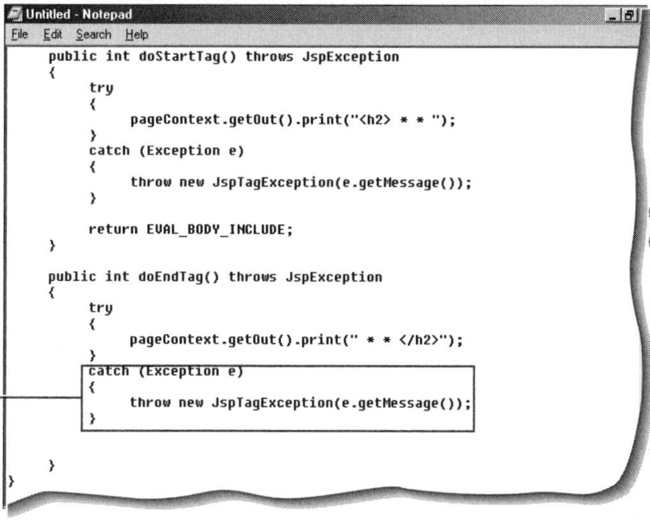

```
    public int doStartTag() throws JspException
    {
        try
        {
            pageContext.getOut().print("<h2> * * ");
        }
        catch (Exception e)
        {
            throw new JspTagException(e.getMessage());
        }

        return EVAL_BODY_INCLUDE;
    }

    public int doEndTag() throws JspException
    {
        try
        {
            pageContext.getOut().print(" * * </h2>");
        }
        catch (Exception e)
        {
            throw new JspTagException(e.getMessage());
        }


    }
}
```

8 On the line immediately following the `try` block, type the code that creates a `catch` block that throws a `JspTagException` exception.

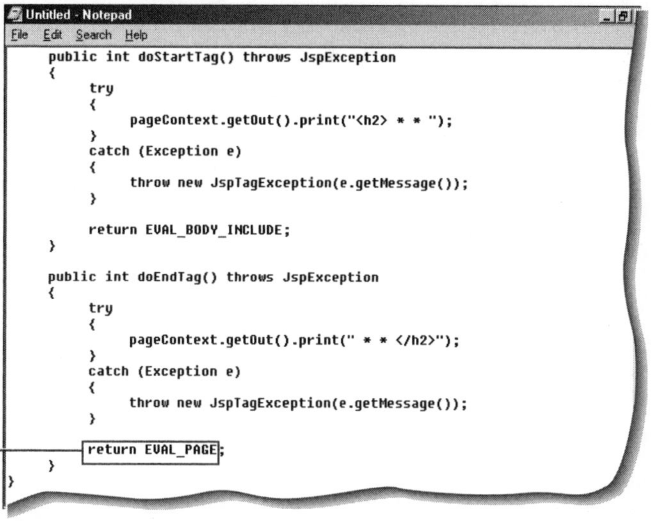

```
    public int doStartTag() throws JspException
    {
        try
        {
            pageContext.getOut().print("<h2> * * ");
        }
        catch (Exception e)
        {
            throw new JspTagException(e.getMessage());
        }

        return EVAL_BODY_INCLUDE;
    }

    public int doEndTag() throws JspException
    {
        try
        {
            pageContext.getOut().print(" * * </h2>");
        }
        catch (Exception e)
        {
            throw new JspTagException(e.getMessage());
        }

        return EVAL_PAGE;
    }
}
```

9 In the body of the `doEndTag` method, type **return** followed by the return value that specifies if the Web server should process the remainder of the JSP page.

10 Save the file with the .java extension and then compile the source code for the file.

11 Copy the compiled class file to the appropriate directory on your Web server.

■ You can now add the tag handler class to a tag library descriptor file.

CREATE THE TAG LIBRARY DESCRIPTOR FILE FOR A TAG WITH A BODY

After you create a tag handler class file for a custom tag, you should include an entry in the tag library descriptor file that indicates whether the tag will include a body. The body of a custom tag is the information that is enclosed by the start and end tags of the custom tag.

You use the `<bodycontent>` tag in the tag library descriptor file to indicate that a custom tag will contain a body. Using the `<bodycontent>` tag does not usually affect how a custom tag operates, since the processing of the tag is performed mainly by the tag handler. The `<bodycontent>` tag is used primarily for providing information about the custom tag itself. You should always include a `<bodycontent>` tag, especially if you are creating tag libraries that you intend to share with other people.

In the tag library descriptor file, the `<bodycontent>` tag must be located between the `<tag>` and `</tag>` tags that contain detailed information about the custom tag. Only one body content entry can exist for each custom tag.

You specify the content type of the custom tag by inserting a value between the `<bodycontent>` and `</bodycontent>` tags. If no content type is specified, the custom tag will assume the default value of `JSP`, which allows the custom tag to use JSP code as the body of the tag. It is good programming practice to specify `JSP` as the content type for any custom tag that will use a body.

If you are using version 3.1 of the Tomcat Web server, you must specify the name and location of the tag library descriptor file for a custom tag with a body in the web.xml configuration file. For more information, see page 204.

CREATE THE TAG LIBRARY DESCRIPTOR FILE FOR A TAG WITH A BODY

```
<?xml version="1.0" encoding="ISO-8859-1" ?>
<!DOCTYPE taglib PUBLIC "-//Sun Microsystems, Inc.//DTD JSP Tag Library
1.1//EN"
 "http://java.sun.com/j2ee/dtds/web-jsptaglibrary_1_1.dtd">

<taglib>
     <tlibversion>1.0</tlibversion>
     <jspversion>1.1</jspversion>
     <shortname>MyFirstTag</shortname>
     <info>My first tag library descriptor file</info>
     <tag>
          <name>SimpleBodyTag</name>
          <tagclass>SimpleBodyTag</tagclass>
          <bodycontent>
     </tag>
</taglib>
```

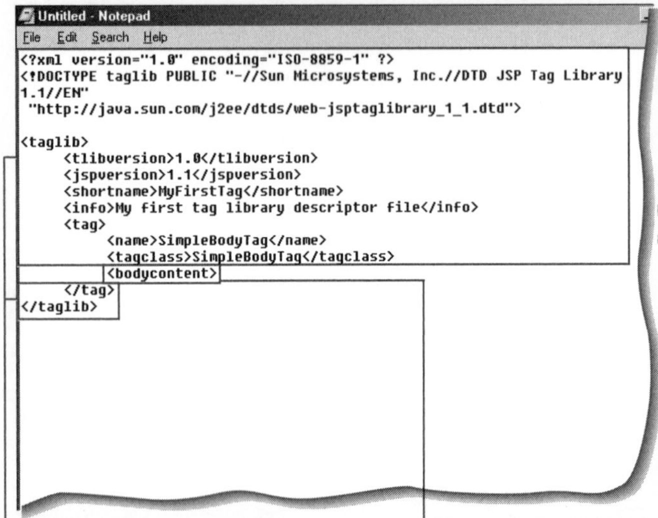

1 Type the code that creates a tag library descriptor file. See page 202 for information about creating a tag library descriptor file.

2 To specify that the custom tag will include a body, type **<bodycontent>** following the `<tagclass>` tag.

```
<?xml version="1.0" encoding="ISO-8859-1" ?>
<!DOCTYPE taglib PUBLIC "-//Sun Microsystems, Inc.//DTD JSP Tag Library
1.1//EN"
 "http://java.sun.com/j2ee/dtds/web-jsptaglibrary_1_1.dtd">

<taglib>
     <tlibversion>1.0</tlibversion>
     <jspversion>1.1</jspversion>
     <shortname>MyFirstTag</shortname>
     <info>My first tag library descriptor file</info>
     <tag>
          <name>SimpleBodyTag</name>
          <tagclass>SimpleBodyTag</tagclass>
          <bodycontent>JSP
     </tag>
</taglib>
```

3 To specify the content type of the tag body, enter the content type the tag will use.

Extra

To be consistent in your code, you should include a <bodycontent> tag in the tag library descriptor file even for custom tags you create or update that do not include a body. You can specify that a tag does not use a body by indicating the value `empty` as the content type of the tag.

Example:
```
<bodycontent>empty</bodycontent>
```

When you specify `JSP` as the content type of the <bodycontent> tag, you are not restricted to using only JSP code in the body of the tag. You can also use HTML tags, plain text, other custom tags and any other valid Web page content in the body of your custom tag.

If you want to use non-JSP information, such as an SQL statement, as the body of your custom tag, you should specify the value `tagdependent` as the content type of the tag. When using the `tagdependent` content type, you must ensure that the code in the tag handler class file is capable of properly interpreting the body content specified in the custom tag.

Example:
```
<bodycontent>tagdependent</bodycontent>
```

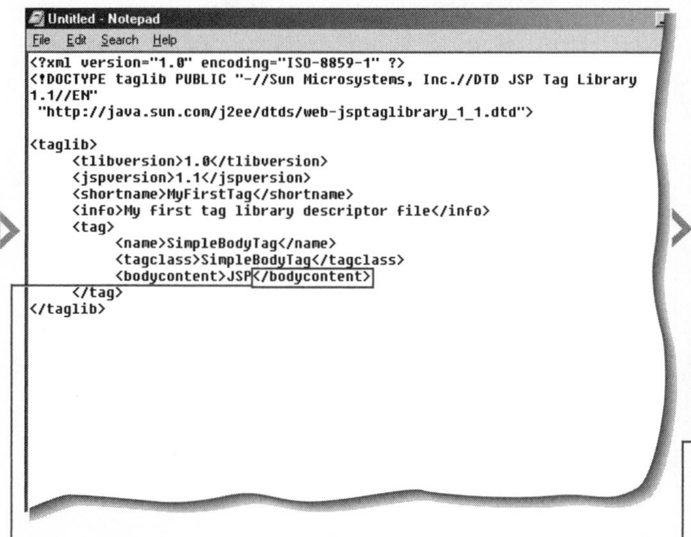

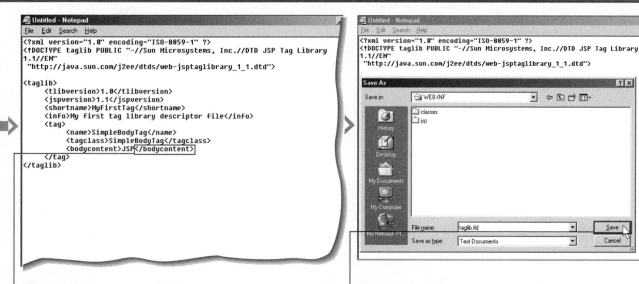

4 Type **</bodycontent>** to end the body content specification.

Untitled - Notepad
File Edit Search Help
<?xml version="1.0" encoding="ISO-8859-1" ?>
<!DOCTYPE taglib PUBLIC "-//Sun Microsystems, Inc.//DTD JSP Tag Library 1.1//EN"
"http://java.sun.com/j2ee/dtds/web-jsptaglibrary_1_1.dtd">
Save As
Save in: WEB-INF
classes
jsp
History
Desktop
My Documents
My Computer
My Network Pl...
File name: taglib.tld
Save as type: Text Documents
Save
Cancel

5 Save the tag library descriptor file with the .tld extension.

■ You can now use the custom tag with a body.

USING A CUSTOM TAG WITH A BODY

After a tag handler that uses information contained in the body of a tag has been created, the tag library descriptor file has been configured to indicate that the custom tag will process the body and the web.xml file has been configured for the Tomcat Web server if necessary, the custom tag that makes use of a body can be employed on a JSP page.

As with all custom tags, the `taglib` directive must be placed in the JSP page before the custom tag can be used. The `uri` attribute and a prefix you want to use to reference the custom tag that uses a body must be specified in the `taglib` directive.

Using a custom tag with a body makes it easy to generate data that will surround the information found in the body. For example, a custom tag can create specific HTML tags to enclose the body of the tag specified in the JSP page. You can use a custom tag to apply simple formatting options, such as bolding or changing the font of text, to text supplied in the body of the tag. A custom tag can also be used to place the information in the body within more complex HTML structures, such as tables or lists.

You should not use the short form of writing a tag for a tag that processes a body, since the tag must use start and end tags to denote the start and end of the body content. If the short form of writing a tag is used for a custom tag that uses a body, an empty body will be passed to the tag handler.

USING A CUSTOM TAG WITH A BODY

Untitled - Notepad

File Edit Search Help

```
<%@ taglib uri="http://www.maran.com/taglib" prefix="myTag" %>
<html>
<head>
<title>Using a Custom Tag with a Body</title>
</head>
<body>


</body>
</html>
```

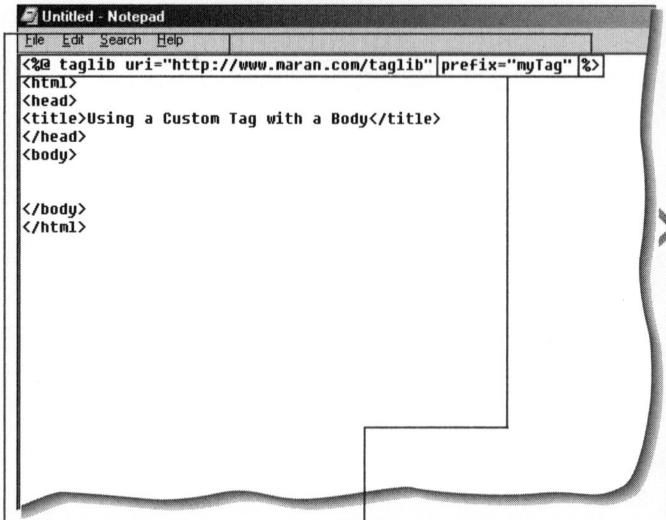

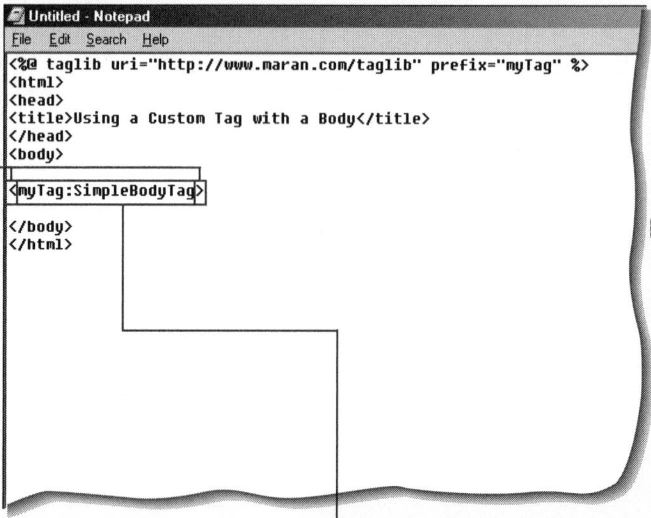

1 Create the `taglib` directive that specifies the location of the tag library descriptor file for the custom tag you want to use in the JSP page.

2 In the `taglib` directive, type the code that specifies the prefix you want to use for the tag library.

Untitled - Notepad

File Edit Search Help

```
<%@ taglib uri="http://www.maran.com/taglib" prefix="myTag" %>
<html>
<head>
<title>Using a Custom Tag with a Body</title>
</head>
<body>

<myTag:SimpleBodyTag>

</body>
</html>
```

3 To use the custom tag, type **<>**.

4 Between the angle brackets, type the prefix you specified in the `taglib` directive, followed by a colon. Then type the name of the custom tag.

Extra

The information that is placed in the body of a custom tag does not have to be on one line. If the tag handler is simply returning the body of the custom tag to the JSP page, the information in the source code of the JSP page will have the same format as the information in the body of the tag.

Example:

```
<pre>
<myTag:SimpleBodyTag>
Welcome
       To
           My
               Web Page
</myTag:SimpleBodyTag>
</pre>
```

Since the body is returned directly to the JSP page by the tag handler, the body of a custom tag can also include valid HTML code.

TYPE THIS:

```
<myTag:SimpleBodyTag><i>Welcome To My Web Page</i></myTag:SimpleBodyTag>
```

RESULT:

* * *Welcome to My Web Page* * *

JSP expressions and scriptlets can also be placed in the body of a custom tag. The JSP code will be evaluated and the information generated by the JSP code will be passed to the tag handler.

TYPE THIS:

```
<myTag:SimpleBodyTag><%= new java.util.Date() %></myTag:SimpleBodyTag>
```

RESULT:

* * Wed Apr 18 12:00:00 EST 2001 * *

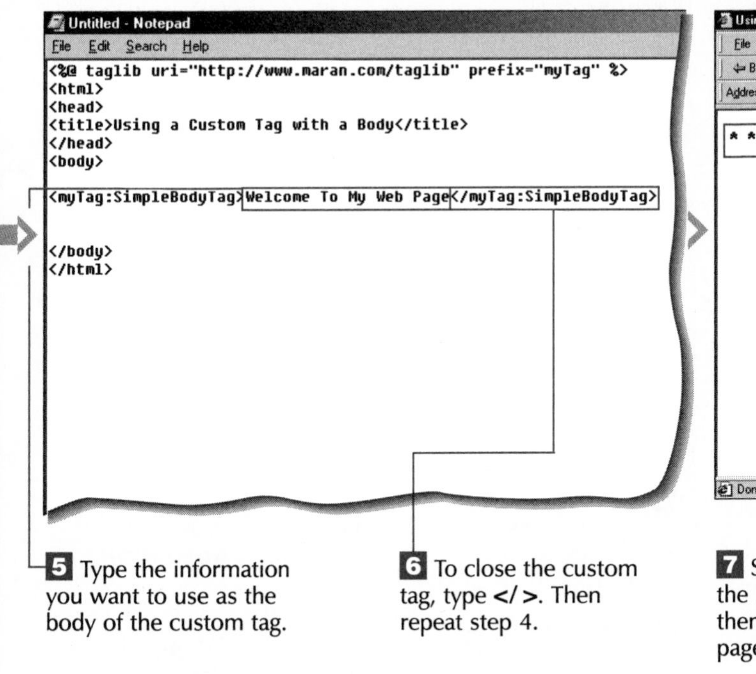

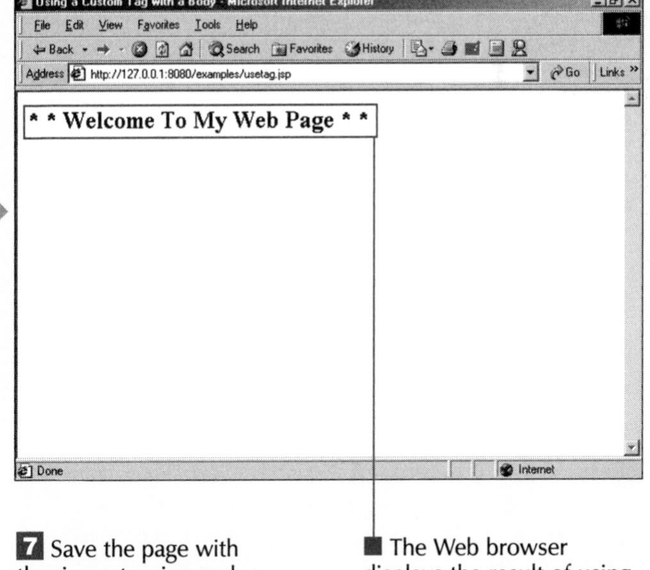

5 Type the information you want to use as the body of the custom tag.

6 To close the custom tag, type **</ >**. Then repeat step 4.

7 Save the page with the .jsp extension and then display the JSP page in a Web browser.

■ The Web browser displays the result of using a custom tag with a body.

CREATE THE TAG HANDLER FOR A TAG THAT MANIPULATES A BODY

A tag handler that receives a body passed from a custom tag may simply return the body back to a JSP page without making any changes. You can, however, create a tag handler for a custom tag that can manipulate a body and then return the manipulated body back to a JSP page. For example, a tag handler may change the formatting of the text within the body or use the information in a body to perform other tasks, such as retrieving information from a database.

A tag handler used to manipulate the body of a custom tag must extend the `BodyTagSupport` class, which in turn extends the `TagSupport` class and contains special methods used for processing the body of a custom tag.

A `doAfterBody` method must be used to process the body of a custom tag. Within the `doAfterBody` method, the `getBodyContent` method is used to create a `BodyContent` object. This object stores information about the body of the custom tag passed to the tag handler.

The `getString` method of the `BodyContent` object is used to retrieve the body and returns a string that can be assigned to a variable. The string variable can then be manipulated. For example, you can use the `toUpperCase` method of the `String` object to convert all the text in the string to uppercase. When generating output to be passed back to a JSP page, the `getEnclosingWriter` method of the `BodyContent` object is used.

You should include a `try` block and `catch` block in the `doAfterBody` method to catch any exception errors that may occur. After the `doAfterBody` method has finished manipulating the body of a custom tag, the method should return the value `SKIP_BODY`.

CREATE THE TAG HANDLER FOR A TAG THAT MANIPULATES A BODY

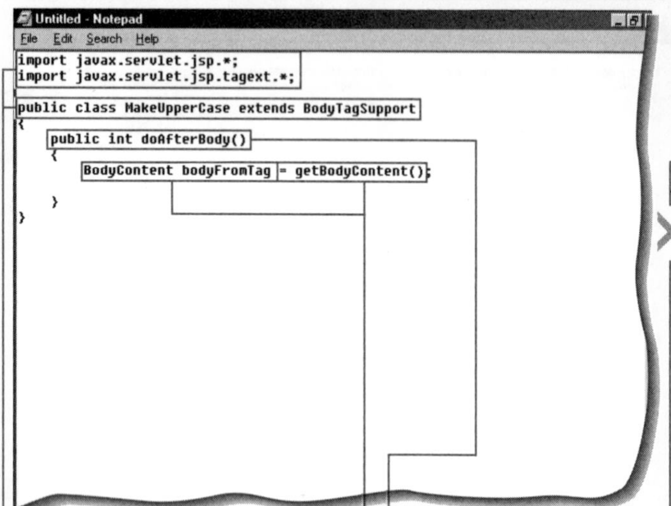

1 Type the code that imports the `javax.servlet.jsp` and the `javax.servlet.jsp.tagext` packages.

2 Type the code that creates a class for a custom tag, followed by **extends BodyTagSupport**.

3 To create the `doAfterBody` method, type **public int doAfterBody()**.

4 To create a `BodyContent` object that will store information about the body, type **BodyContent** followed by a name for the `BodyContent` object.

5 Type **= getBodyContent()**.

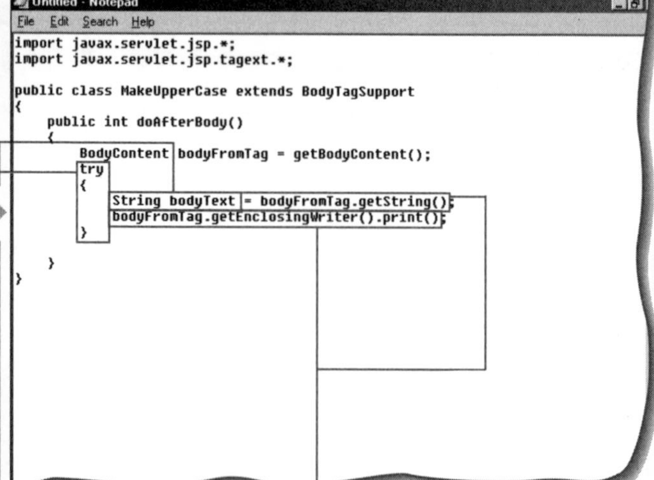

6 Type the code that creates a `try` block in the body of the `doAfterBody` method.

7 Type the code that creates a string variable that will store the content of the body.

8 Type = followed by the name of the `BodyContent` object. Then type **.getString()**.

9 To display the result of manipulating the body, type the name of the `BodyContent` object followed by **.getEnclosingWriter().print()**.

Extra

In addition to the `doAfterBody` method, other methods, such as the `doStartTag` and `doEndtag` methods, can be used to perform certain actions, such as producing HTML code that is processed before and after the body is manipulated. Since the body of the custom tag is processed using a `BodyContent` object, the return value of the `doStartTag` method should be `EVAL_BODY_TAG`.

Example:

```
public int doStartTag() throws JspException
{
      try
      {
            pageContext.getOut().print("The following text" +
                  " will be in uppercase.<br>");
      }
      catch (Exception e)
      {
            throw new JspTagException(e.getMessage());
      }
      return EVAL_BODY_TAG;
}
public int doEndTag() throws JspException
{
      try
      {
            pageContext.getOut().print("<hr>Thank You");
      }
      catch (Exception e)
      {
            throw new JspTagException(e.getMessage());
      }
      return EVAL_PAGE;
}
```

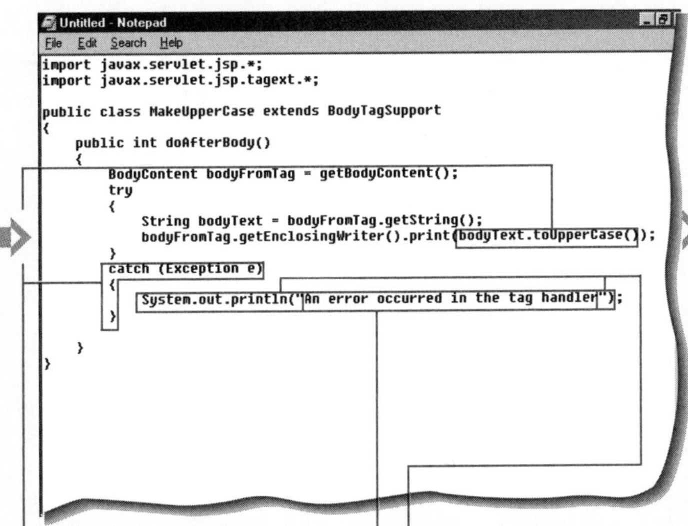

```
import javax.servlet.jsp.*;
import javax.servlet.jsp.tagext.*;

public class MakeUpperCase extends BodyTagSupport
{
    public int doAfterBody()
    {
        BodyContent bodyFromTag = getBodyContent();
        try
        {
            String bodyText = bodyFromTag.getString();
            bodyFromTag.getEnclosingWriter().print(bodyText.toUpperCase());
        }
        catch (Exception e)
        {
            System.out.println("An error occurred in the tag handler");
        }

    }
}
```

10 Between the second set of parentheses, type the code that manipulates the body.

11 On the line immediately following the `try` block, type the code that creates a `catch` block.

12 In the body of the `catch` block, type **System.out.println("")**.

13 Between the quotation marks, type the information you want to display if an error occurs.

```
import javax.servlet.jsp.*;
import javax.servlet.jsp.tagext.*;

public class MakeUpperCase extends BodyTagSupport
{
    public int doAfterBody()
    {
        BodyContent bodyFromTag = getBodyContent();
        try
        {
            String bodyText = bodyFromTag.getString();
            bodyFromTag.getEnclosingWriter().print(bodyText.toUpperCase());
        }
        catch (Exception e)
        {
            System.out.println("An error occurred in the tag handler");
        }
        return SKIP_BODY;
    }
}
```

14 On the line immediately following the `catch` block, type **return SKIP_BODY**.

15 Save the file with the .java extension and then compile the source code for the file.

16 Copy the compiled class file to the appropriate directory on your Web server.

■ You can now add the tag handler class to a tag library descriptor file. For more information see page 216.

USING A CUSTOM TAG THAT MANIPULATES A BODY

Using a custom tag that manipulates the content of a body is similar to using any other custom tag that contains information between the start and end tags. The difference is that the tag handler can modify the body before it is returned to the JSP page. The information returned to a JSP page depends on the process contained in the tag handler class itself. A tag handler may simply change the formatting of the text within the body or may take the information in a body and use it to perform other tasks, such as retrieving information from a database or sending an e-mail message.

It may take some time for a tag handler that manipulates the body of a custom tag to process the information, such as when using a tag handler to retrieve information from a database. If you are using a custom tag that may take some time to process, it is important to thoroughly test the tag to evaluate how the tag will perform when used on a Web site under real-world conditions. While a custom tag may perform well under developmental conditions, it may easily malfunction when multiple users of a Web site use the custom tag, as is common when different users are trying to access the same database. If an error occurs within a tag handler while it processes the body content, a server error may be generated and the remainder of the JSP page may not be processed.

The body of a custom tag can be either plain text or be generated by other methods, such as Java code contained within a scriptlet or an expression.

As with other custom tags and tag handlers, changes to the tag library descriptor file and the web.xml file may need to be made before the custom tag can be used.

USING A CUSTOM TAG THAT MANIPULATES A BODY

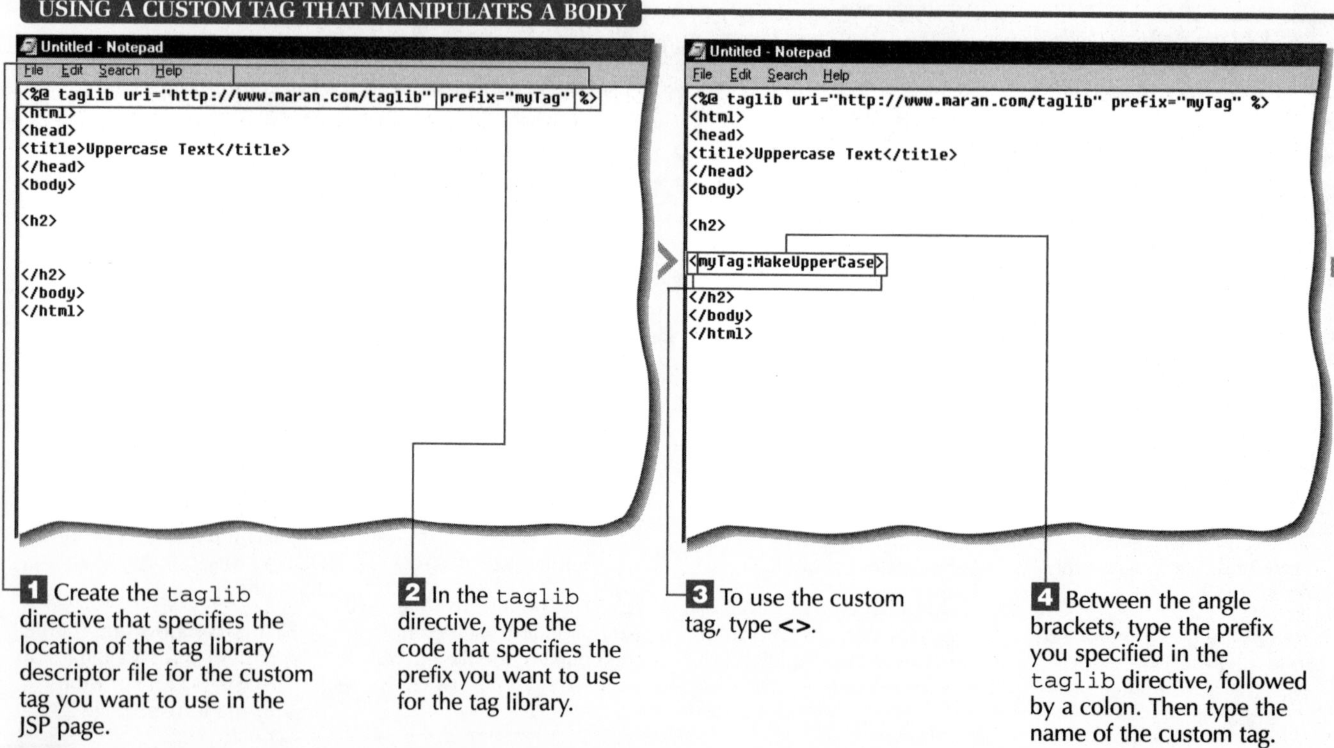

1 Create the `taglib` directive that specifies the location of the tag library descriptor file for the custom tag you want to use in the JSP page.

2 In the `taglib` directive, type the code that specifies the prefix you want to use for the tag library.

3 To use the custom tag, type **<>**.

4 Between the angle brackets, type the prefix you specified in the `taglib` directive, followed by a colon. Then type the name of the custom tag.

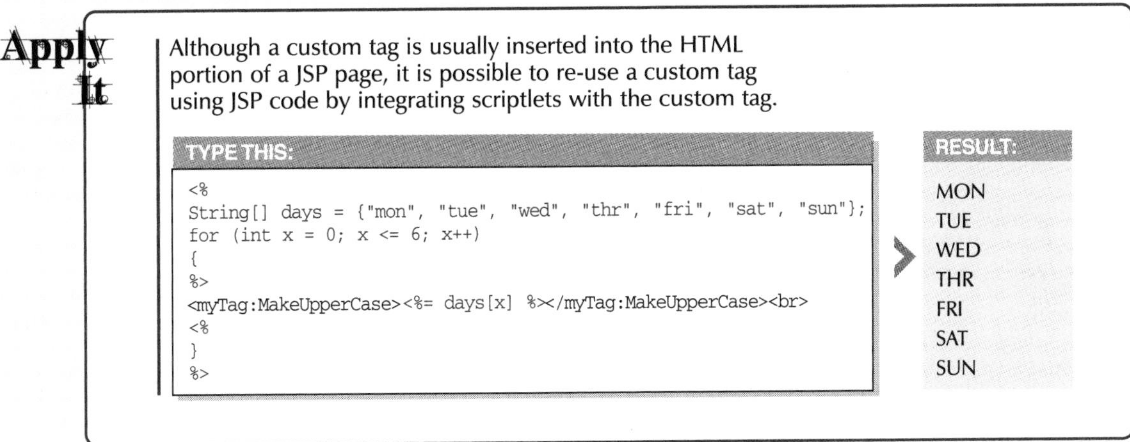

Apply It

Although a custom tag is usually inserted into the HTML portion of a JSP page, it is possible to re-use a custom tag using JSP code by integrating scriptlets with the custom tag.

TYPE THIS:

```
<%
String[] days = {"mon", "tue", "wed", "thr", "fri", "sat", "sun"};
for (int x = 0; x <= 6; x++)
{
%>
<myTag:MakeUpperCase><%= days[x] %></myTag:MakeUpperCase><br>
<%
}
%>
```

RESULT:

MON
TUE
WED
THR
FRI
SAT
SUN

```
<%@ taglib uri="http://www.maran.com/taglib" prefix="myTag" %>
<html>
<head>
<title>Uppercase Text</title>
</head>
<body>

<h2>

<myTag:MakeUpperCase>welcome to my web site</myTag:MakeUpperCase>

</h2>
</body>
</html>
```

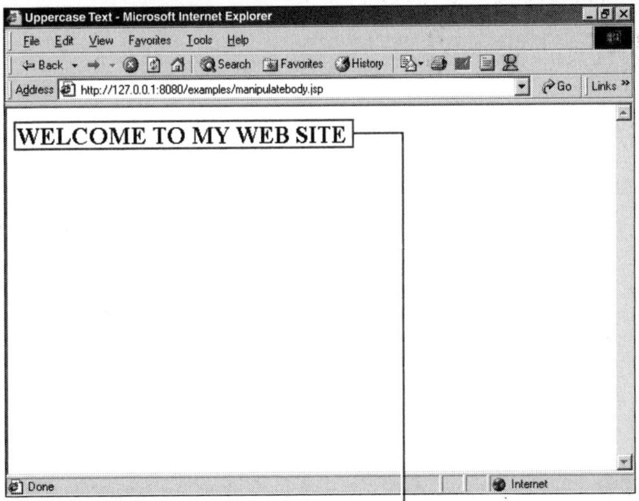

WELCOME TO MY WEB SITE

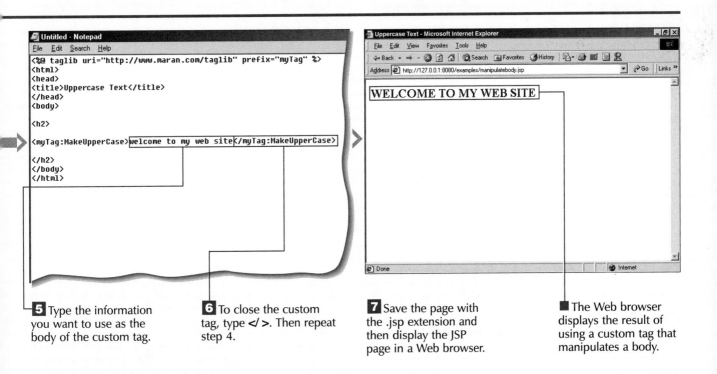

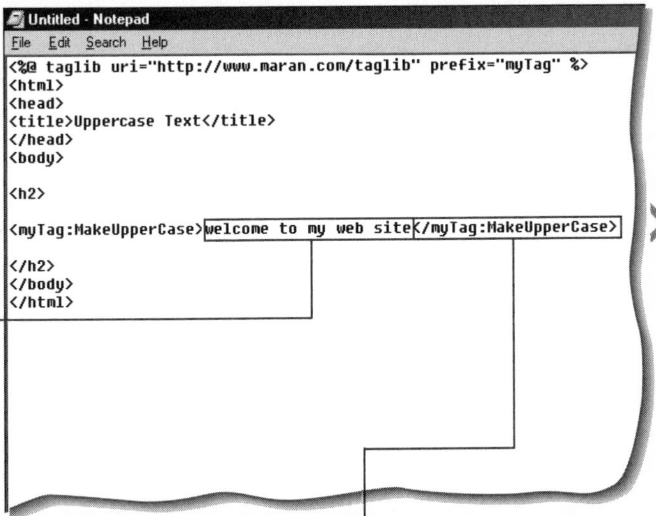

5 Type the information you want to use as the body of the custom tag.

6 To close the custom tag, type **</ >**. Then repeat step 4.

7 Save the page with the .jsp extension and then display the JSP page in a Web browser.

■ The Web browser displays the result of using a custom tag that manipulates a body.

USING A CUSTOM TAG TO ACCESS A DATABASE

While custom tags are often used for relatively simple tasks, such as formatting text, they are also ideally suited for performing more complex tasks, such as retrieving information from a database.

You must first create a tag handler for the custom tag. The tag handler for a tag that accesses a database is very similar to the tag handler for a custom tag that manipulates a body. For more information, see page 220. To use the body of a custom tag to locate information in a database, you include the same Java code used to work with databases from within a JSP page in the tag handler class file. For information about working with databases, see pages 142 to 153.

You must load the driver for the database, create a connection to the database and create a result set that stores the information you will access in the database. When you use the custom tag in a JSP page, the tag handler retrieves the information from the database and then uses the `getEnclosingWriter` method of the `BodyContent` object to send the retrieved information back to the JSP page.

When using a tag handler to work with a database, you can place most of your code in the body of the `doAfterBody` method that processes the body of the custom tag. If you are using other methods in the custom tag, you can place parts of the code in the body of the other methods. For example, you can place the code that opens a connection to the database in the body of the `doStartTag` method.

To prevent problems when the JSP page is processed, you need to include `try` and `catch` blocks to handle any errors that may occur.

USING A CUSTOM TAG TO ACCESS A DATABASE

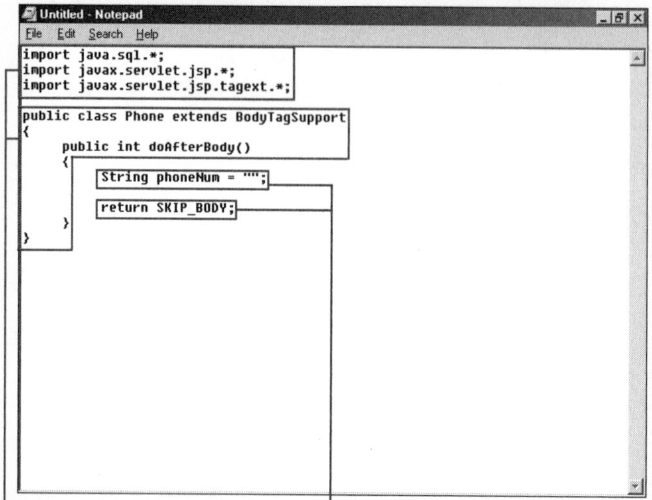
Untitled - Notepad
File Edit Search Help
import java.sql.*;
import javax.servlet.jsp.*;
import javax.servlet.jsp.tagext.*;
public class Phone extends BodyTagSupport
{
public int doAfterBody()
{
String phoneNum = "";
return SKIP_BODY;
}
}

1 Type the code that imports the packages required by the custom tag.

2 Type the code that creates the tag handler class and the `doAfterBody` method.

3 In the body of the method, type **return SKIP_BODY**.

4 Type the code that creates a variable that will store the value you want to retrieve from the database.

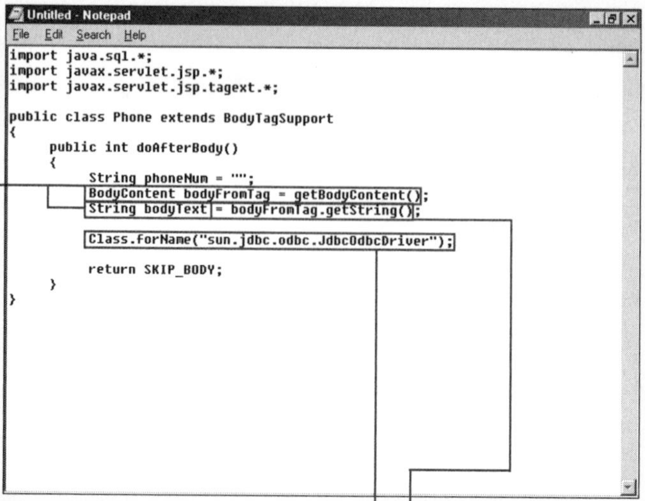
Untitled - Notepad
File Edit Search Help
import java.sql.*;
import javax.servlet.jsp.*;
import javax.servlet.jsp.tagext.*;
public class Phone extends BodyTagSupport
{
public int doAfterBody()
{
String phoneNum = "";
BodyContent bodyFromTag = getBodyContent();
String bodyText = bodyFromTag.getString();
Class.forName("sun.jdbc.odbc.JdbcOdbcDriver");
return SKIP_BODY;
}
}

5 To create a `BodyContent` object, type **BodyContent** followed by a name for the object. Then type **= getBodyContent()**.

6 Type the code that creates a string variable that will store the content of the body.

7 To retrieve the content of the body, type = followed by the name of the `BodyContent` object. Then type **.getString()**.

8 Type the code that loads the bridge driver.

Apply It

You can use a custom tag that accesses a database as you would use a custom tag that manipulates a body. In your JSP page, you must include the `taglib` directive to specify the `uri` attribute and the prefix you want to use to reference the custom tag. In the body of the tag, you should include the information that specifies the data you want to retrieve from the database.

TYPE THIS:

```
<%@ taglib uri="http://www.maran.com/taglib" prefix="myTag" %>
<html>
<head>
<title>Phone Numbers</title>
</head>
<body bgcolor="#FFFFFF">
<b>Phone Numbers</b><br>
<myTag:Phone>Hannah</myTag:Phone>
<br>
<myTag:Phone>Paul</myTag:Phone>
</body>
</htmL>
```

RESULT:

Phone Numbers
Hannah is at extension 678
Paul is at extension 456

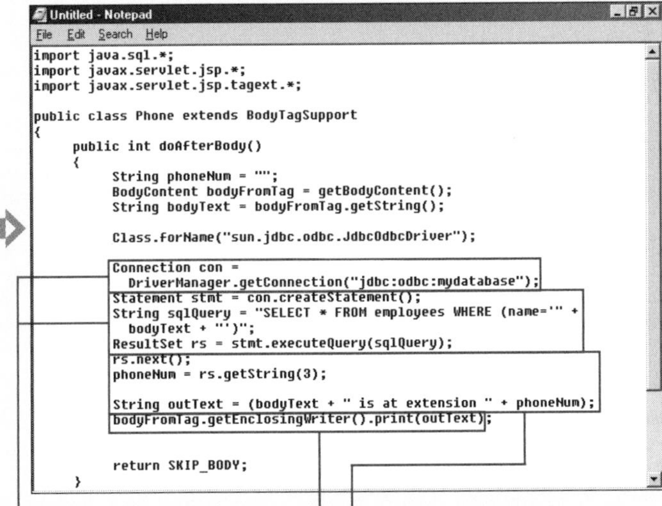

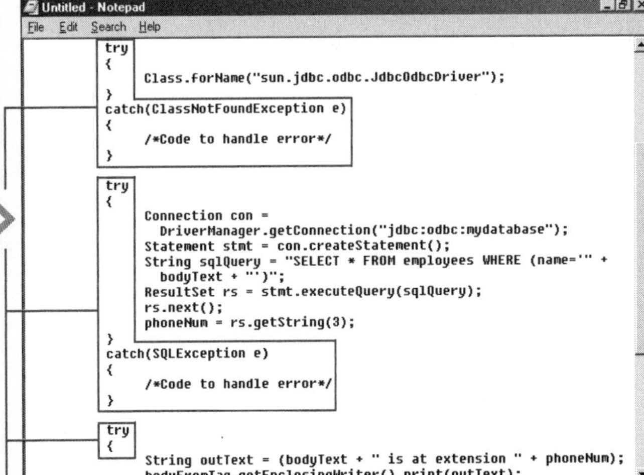

9 Type the code that creates a connection to the database.

10 Type the code that retrieves information from the database and stores it in a result set.

11 Type the code that retrieves the information from the result set and then type the code that uses the retrieved information.

12 Type the name of the `BodyContent` object followed by **.getEnclosingWriter().print()**. Between the second set of parentheses, type any arguments the method requires.

13 Create `try` and `catch` blocks that will handle any exceptions thrown while accessing the information from the database.

14 Save the file with the .java extension and then compile the source code for the file.

15 Copy the compiled class file to the appropriate directory on your Web server.

■ You can now add the tag handler class to a tag library descriptor file as you would for any custom tag with a body.

INTRODUCTION TO SERVLETS

A servlet is a module of Java code that adds functionality to a Web server. Servlets use text to communicate with a Web server and have no graphical user interface.

The Java Servlet API

The construction of servlets is governed by a rigid specification. This specification is known as the Java Servlet Application Programming Interface, or more simply, the Java Servlet API. Detailed information about the Java Servlet API can be found at the java.sun.com Web site.

The Java Class Library

Servlets have access to all the class files that make up the Java class library, which is also called the Java API. This enables servlets to perform a wide variety of complex tasks, such as working with databases, reading and writing to files on local and remote computers and manipulating data passed by forms.

Object-Oriented Programming

Servlets make use of the object-oriented approach to programming. Object-oriented programming provides increased flexibility when maintaining and modifying code. While beginners may not benefit greatly from the object-oriented approach, this style of programming is vital to developers of large, complex Web sites.

Portable

Since servlets have to conform to the rigid Java Servlet API, a Web server that supports this specification will be able to run any servlet, regardless of the platform the servlet was developed on. This allows the same servlet to run on a Web server that uses the Windows operating system and a Web server that uses the UNIX operating system.

Efficient

When a servlet is used for the first time, the servlet is compiled into bytecode. Bytecode is a set of instructions that a Web server can use to perform the tasks specified in the servlet. Once a servlet is compiled into bytecode, the bytecode is retained in the Web server's memory. When the servlet is requested again, the Web server can use the bytecode stored in memory, without having to recompile the servlet. This dramatically speeds up the processing of servlets. A servlet will only need to be recompiled if it is modified.

Dynamic Content

Servlets can be used to enable a Web server to generate dynamic content. Dynamic content is Web page content that is generated depending on a set of changing parameters. For example, a servlet can generate a Web page that displays weather information obtained from a database. Each time the Web page is requested by a client, the servlet instructs the Web server to retrieve the latest weather information from the database and place the information in the Web page.

Multitasking

Servlets are able to handle multiple processes at once. As a result, servlets are useful for creating complex multi-user applications, such as chat room programs and file swapping programs. Besides handling multiple instructions at once, servlets can, when necessary, locate and use other servlets to share the workload.

SERVLETS AND CGI PROGRAMMING

Servlets provide an alternative to more traditional Common Gateway Interface (CGI) programming. While both servlets and CGI programs add functionality to a Web server, servlets give a Web server more control over the processing of information.

With CGI programming, a Web server does not have control over the way a CGI program processes information. When information is passed to the Web server, the server simply passes the information on to the CGI program and then waits for the program to finish processing the information. When the CGI program completes its tasks, the program passes the information back to the Web server, typically in the form of HTML code that is then sent to the client.

Servlets are more tightly integrated with a Web server than CGI programs, allowing more communication between the Web server and a servlet. This gives a Web server more control over the processing of information and allows for more advanced processing features, such as maintaining session information across multiple servlets.

SERVLETS AND JSP PAGES

Since JavaServer Pages technology is built on servlet technology, JSP pages and servlets are closely related. When a JSP page is processed, the page is converted into a servlet by the JSP engine on the Web server. The Web server can use the servlet generated from the JSP page as it would use any servlet. A Web server must support servlets before it can process JSP pages.

The translation of a JSP page into a servlet is transparent to the developer. Although it is an asset, developers do not need to understand servlet programming in order to work with JSP pages.

The relationship between JSP pages and servlets:

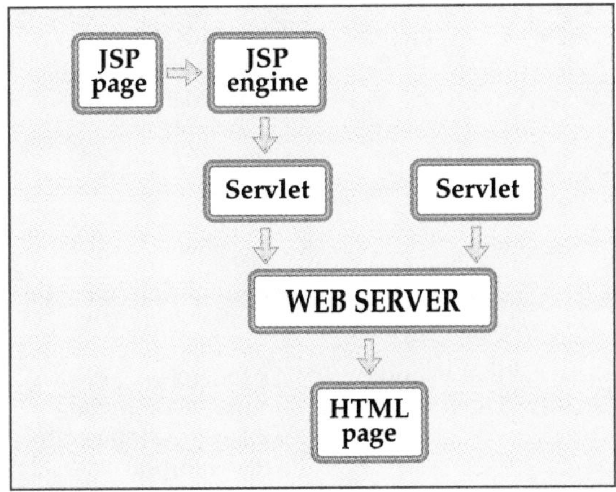

CREATE A SERVLET

You can create a simple servlet that uses Java to generate text that will be displayed in a Web browser.

To create a servlet, you must first import the `javax.servlet` and `javax.servlet.http` servlet packages. Before the servlet packages can be imported, they must be installed on your computer and accessible to your Web server software. The packages are located in the Java Servlet API class files, which are available at the java.sun.com/products/servlet Web site. For more information about obtaining and installing the Java Servlet API class files, see the top of page 199.

You will also need to import any additional packages needed by the servlet you want to create. For example, a servlet that will output text requires the `java.io` package.

You can make a servlet you create a sub-class of the `HttpServlet` class, which contains the code a Web server needs to run servlets. This saves you from having to type all the code needed by a Web server in each servlet. The `HttpServlet` class is part of the `javax.servlet` package.

The `doGet` method is the main method of a servlet. This method is processed each time a client uses a Web browser to connect to a servlet. The `doGet` method takes two arguments. The first argument is an `HttpServletRequest` object, which will contain information passed from the client. The second argument is an `HttpServletResponse` object, which will contain information to be sent to the client. The `doGet` method may also throw two errors—`ServletException` and `IOException`.

To generate text that will be sent to the client, you must create a `PrintWriter` object using the `getWriter` method of the `HttpServletResponse` object. The methods of the `PrintWriter` object can then be used to generate output.

CREATE A SERVLET

Untitled - Notepad

File Edit Search Help

```
import javax.servlet.*;
import javax.servlet.http.*;
import java.io.*;

public class SimpleServlet extends HttpServlet
```

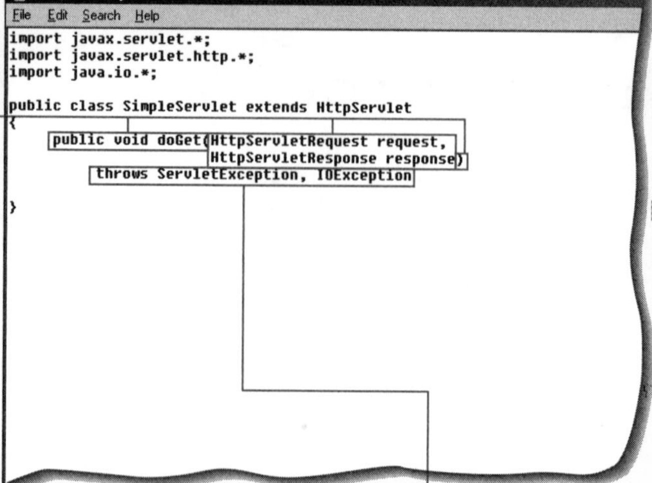

1 Type the code that imports the `javax.servlet` and `javax.servlet.http` packages.

2 Type the code that imports any additional packages needed by the servlet.

3 To declare the class for the servlet, type **public class** followed by a name for the class.

4 To make the class a sub-class of the `HttpServlet` class, type **extends HttpServlet**.

5 To create a `doGet` method, type **public void doGet()**.

6 Between the parentheses, type **HttpServletRequest** followed by a name for the `HttpServletRequest` object. Then type **HttpServletResponse** followed by a name for the `HttpServletResponse` object.

7 To specify the exception errors that may be thrown by the method, type **throws ServletException, IOException**.

Extra

Servlets are platform independent. This means that a servlet you create can be stored and processed by any Web server that supports servlets, regardless of the platform on which you developed the servlet. Most Web servers that are capable of running Java programs are also able to run servlets.

The first time you attempt to display the results of using a servlet you created, the results may take a few moments to appear in the Web browser. This delay will occur only the first time the servlet is accessed. When a client requests a servlet for the first time, the Web server processes the servlet and then stores the servlet in memory. Subsequent requests for the servlet will be much faster, since the servlet will not need to be processed each time.

JavaServer Pages technology is built on servlet technology. JSP pages you create are converted into servlet code by the JSP engine on a Web browser when the pages are processed. A familiarity with servlet programming can help improve your ability to develop JSP pages, since you will have an increased understanding of how JSP pages are processed by a Web server.

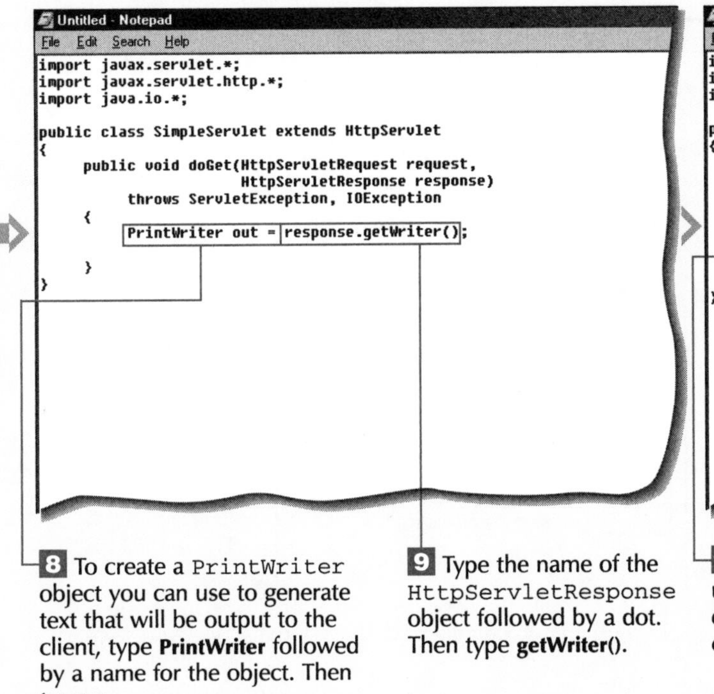


```
Untitled - Notepad
File Edit Search Help
import javax.servlet.*;
import javax.servlet.http.*;
import java.io.*;

public class SimpleServlet extends HttpServlet
{
     public void doGet(HttpServletRequest request,
                       HttpServletResponse response)
          throws ServletException, IOException
     {
          PrintWriter out = response.getWriter();
          out.println("This is a Servlet");
          out.close();
     }
}
```

8 To create a `PrintWriter` object you can use to generate text that will be output to the client, type **PrintWriter** followed by a name for the object. Then type **=**.

9 Type the name of the `HttpServletResponse` object followed by a dot. Then type **getWriter()**.

10 Type the code that uses the `PrintWriter` object to generate text output.

11 Save the servlet with the .java extension.

■ You can now compile and execute the servlet.

COMPILE AND EXECUTE A SERVLET

Once you have created a servlet, you can compile the Java code for the servlet. A servlet must be compiled before it can be executed.

A Java compiler is required to compile a servlet. The Java SDK includes a Java compiler called javac. The javac compiler can only be executed from the command prompt. If you are using a Windows operating system, you will need to open an MS-DOS Prompt or Command Prompt window to use javac. For more information about using javac, see page 20.

Before a servlet is compiled, the Java compiler checks the servlet code for errors. If an error is found, an error message will be generated. If no errors are found, the code will be successfully compiled and stored in a class file. The class file will have the same name as the source file, but will use the .class extension.

Once a servlet has been compiled, the resulting class file must be copied to the appropriate directory on the Web server. Consult the documentation for your Web server to determine where to save servlets. Most Web servers require executable files to be stored in a specific directory. For example, if you are using the Tomcat Web server version 3.1 and you use the examples directory for development, you should store your servlets in the examples/WEB-INF/classes directory.

Depending on the configuration of your Web server and the operating system you use, you may need to modify the permissions for a servlet class file. Refer to your Web server and operating system documentation for information about setting servlet permissions.

To execute a servlet, enter the URL of the servlet in a Web browser window.

COMPILE AND EXECUTE A SERVLET

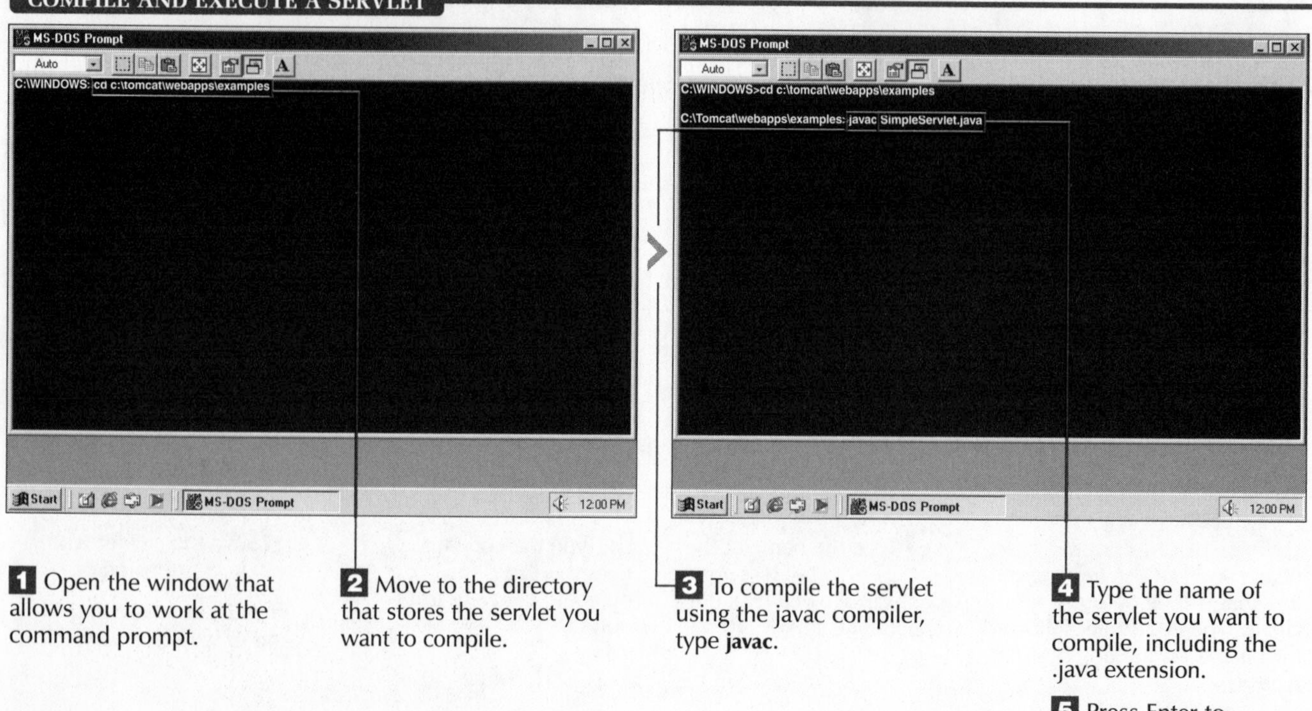

1 Open the window that allows you to work at the command prompt.

2 Move to the directory that stores the servlet you want to compile.

3 To compile the servlet using the javac compiler, type **javac**.

4 Type the name of the servlet you want to compile, including the .java extension.

5 Press Enter to compile the Java code.

Extra

If you use the Tomcat Web server version 3.1, the URL you enter to execute a servlet will be determined by the settings in the web.xml file. You must edit the web.xml configuration file to specify information about a servlet you want to execute. If you use the examples directory for development, the web.xml file you must edit is located in the examples/WEB-INF directory.

To edit the web.xml file, you enter tags that specify information about the servlet between the `<web-app>` and `</web-app>` tags. The `<servlet>` tag allows you to specify the class name of the servlet, while the `<servlet-mapping>` tag lets you specify the URL that will be used to execute the servlet. For example, to edit the web.xml file for a servlet named SimpleServlet that you want to access by typing **/SimpleServlet** in the URL, enter the following code after the `<web-app>` tag in the web.xml file.

Example:

```
<servlet>
     <servlet-name>SimpleServlet</servlet-name>
     <servlet-class>SimpleServlet</servlet-class>
</servlet>
<servlet-mapping>
     <servlet-name>SimpleServlet</servlet-name>
     <url-pattern>/SimpleServlet</url-pattern>
</servlet-mapping>
```

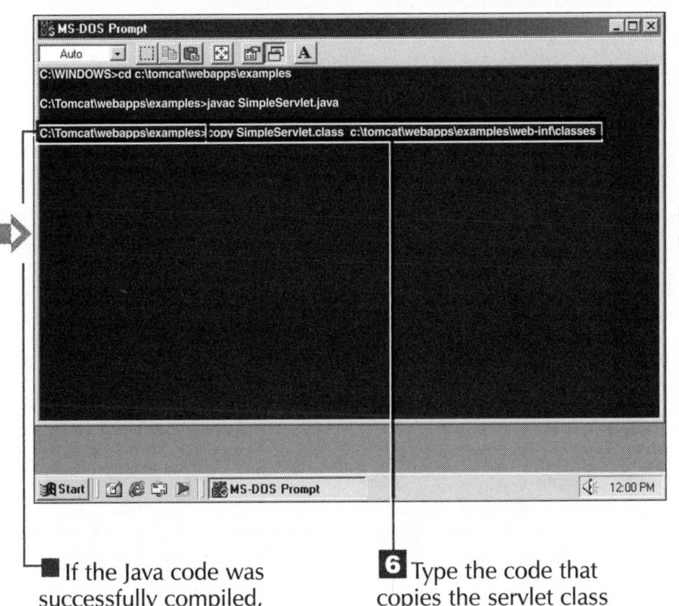

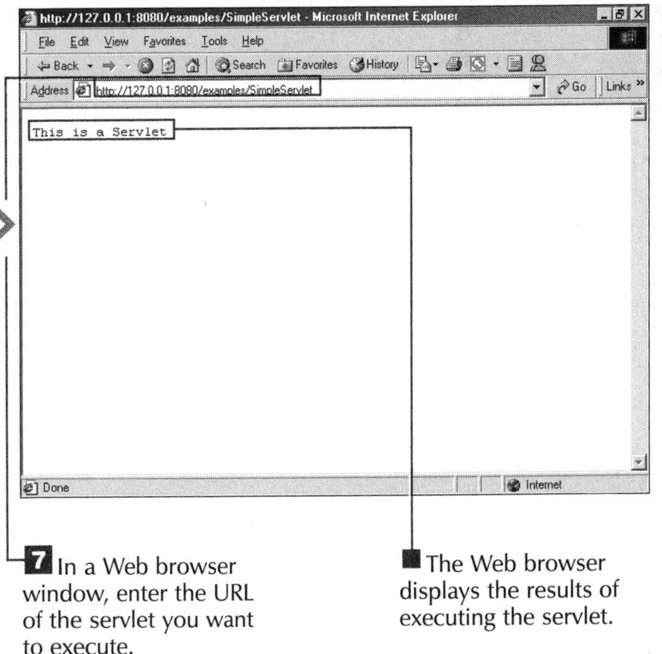

■ If the Java code was successfully compiled, the command prompt re-appears.

6 Type the code that copies the servlet class file to the appropriate directory on your Web server.

7 In a Web browser window, enter the URL of the servlet you want to execute.

■ The Web browser displays the results of executing the servlet.

GENERATE A WEB PAGE USING A SERVLET

A servlet can be used to generate HTML code that is rendered as a Web page when viewed in a Web browser. Generating HTML code from a servlet allows you to use features of the Java programming language, such as variables, methods and objects to create Web pages. Information for the Web pages can be retrieved from files, databases or other Web pages. To generate Web pages from a servlet, you simply send strings of data containing valid HTML code to the client using the `print` method of the `out` object.

Before sending HTML data to a client, the `response` object can be instructed to send an HTTP header. HTTP headers provide instructions and information to the client application, usually a Web browser. For example, the `setContentType` method of the `response` object can be used to specify the content type of information to be sent to the client. The `"text/html"` argument can be passed to the `setContentType` method to inform the client to expect HTML information.

HTML pages typically start with a document type declaration. The document type declaration allows the Web browser to determine what type of document is being viewed by specifying which version of the HTML specification the Web browser should use to render the Web page. While most browsers will display Web pages that do not have a document type declaration, some applications, such as search engines, rely on the document type declaration to better classify Web pages. You can find information about the document type declaration for the version of HTML you use at the www.w3.org Web site.

When generating a Web page using a servlet, the `setContentType` method and the document type declaration should be sent before any other HTML code is sent to the client.

GENERATE A WEB PAGE USING A SERVLET

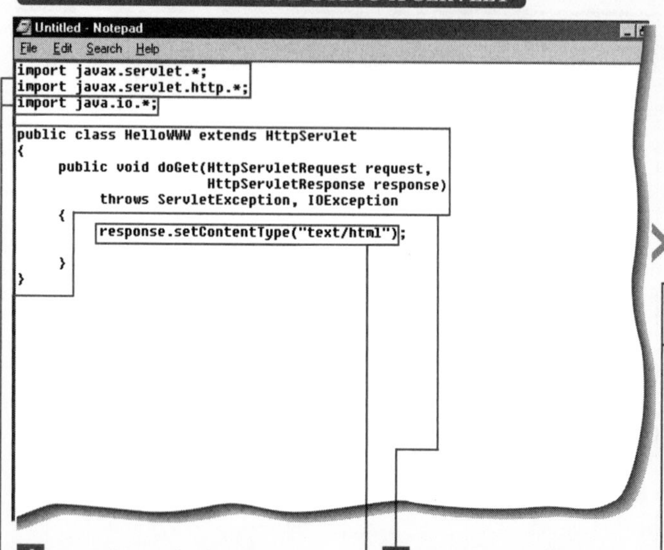

1 Type the code that imports the `javax.servlet` and the `javax.servlet.http` packages.

2 Type the code that imports any additional packages needed by the servlet.

3 Type the code that creates the servlet class and the `doGet` method.

4 To specify that the document will contain HTML information, type **response.setContentType ("text/html")**.

```
import javax.servlet.*;
import javax.servlet.http.*;
import java.io.*;

public class HelloWWW extends HttpServlet
{
    public void doGet(HttpServletRequest request,
                      HttpServletResponse response)
        throws ServletException, IOException
    {
        response.setContentType("text/html");
        PrintWriter out = response.getWriter();

        out.print("<!doctype html public \"-//w3c//dtd html 4.0 " +
                  "transitional//en\">");
    }
}
```

5 Type the code that creates a `PrintWriter` object from the `getWriter` method of the `response` object.

6 To send a document type declaration to the client application, type **out.print("")**.

7 Between the quotation marks, type the appropriate document type declaration for the version of the HTML specification the Web browser should use to render the Web page.

You can split long strings of data over multiple lines by using the concatenation operator (+) to break up the strings into multiple parts.

Example:

```
out.print("<!doctype html public" +
          " \"-//w3c//dtd html 4.0 " +
          "transitional//en\">" +
          "<html><head>" +
          "<title>Servlet Generated Web Page</title>" +
          "</head><body>" +
          "<h1>Servlet Generated Web Page</h1>" +
          "</body></html>");
```

You can use the `setContentType` method to indicate that a page contains other types of content besides HTML information. This chart displays the most common content types.

CONTENT TYPE:	DESCRIPTION:
`text/html`	Page contains HTML code.
`text/plain`	Page contains only plain text.
`audio/basic`	Page contains an audio file.
`video/mpeg`	Page contains a video file.
`image/gif`	Page contains a GIF image.
`image/jpeg`	Page contains a JPEG image.
`application/pdf`	Page contains a PDF file.
`application/msword`	Page contains a Word document.

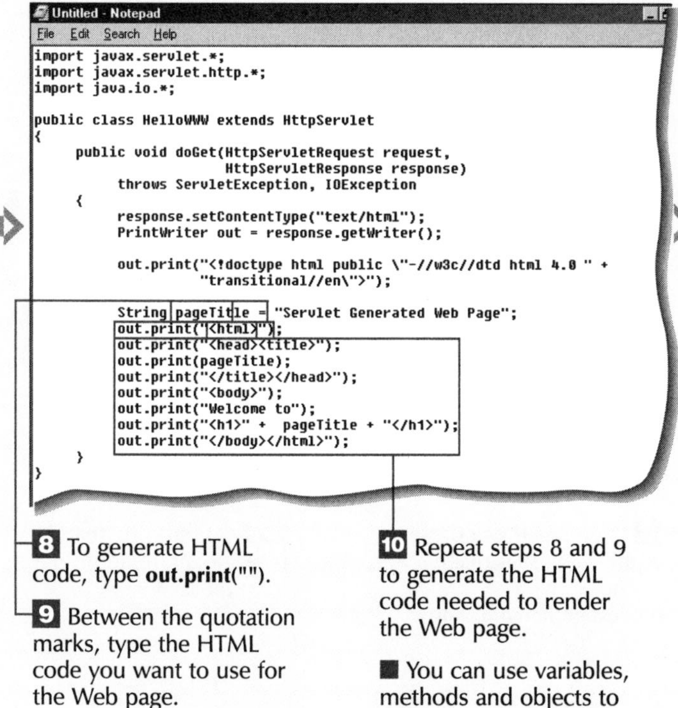

```
import javax.servlet.*;
import javax.servlet.http.*;
import java.io.*;

public class HelloWWW extends HttpServlet
{
    public void doGet(HttpServletRequest request,
                      HttpServletResponse response)
        throws ServletException, IOException
    {
        response.setContentType("text/html");
        PrintWriter out = response.getWriter();

        out.print("<!doctype html public \"-//w3c//dtd html 4.0 " +
                  "transitional//en\">");

        String pageTitle = "Servlet Generated Web Page";
        out.print("<html>");
        out.print("<head><title>");
        out.print(pageTitle);
        out.print("</title></head>");
        out.print("<body>");
        out.print("Welcome to");
        out.print("<h1>" + pageTitle + "</h1>");
        out.print("</body></html>");
    }
}
```

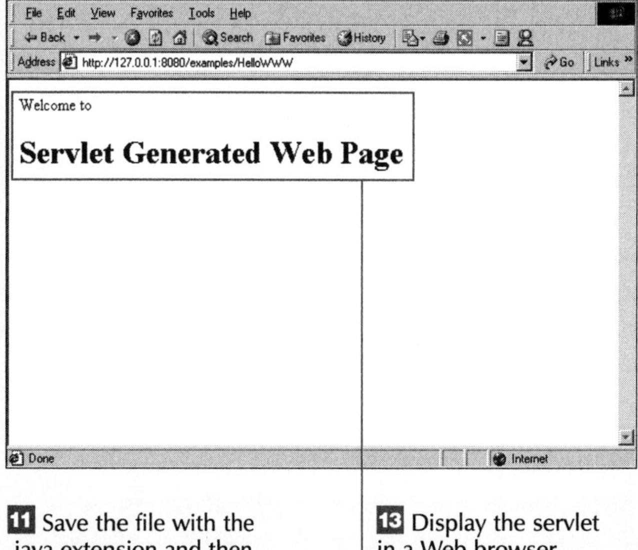

8 To generate HTML code, type **out.print("")**.

9 Between the quotation marks, type the HTML code you want to use for the Web page.

10 Repeat steps 8 and 9 to generate the HTML code needed to render the Web page.

■ You can use variables, methods and objects to generate dynamic HTML code.

11 Save the file with the .java extension and then compile the source code for the file.

12 Copy the compiled class file to the appropriate directory on your Web server.

13 Display the servlet in a Web browser.

■ The Web browser displays the Web page generated by the servlet.

CREATE A SERVLET THAT ACCESSES CGI VARIABLES

The Common Gateway Interface (CGI) is a standard used to create interactive Web sites. Servlets are often used to replace CGI applications on a Web server.

Like the CGI applications they replace, servlets often need to determine information about the environment in which the servlet is running. For example, a servlet may need to determine the type of Web server on which it is running before performing an action such as writing to a database. Information about the environment is typically stored in CGI, or environment, variables, which store information about the computer, Web server and operating system that is running the servlet.

When you create servlets to replace CGI applications, the servlets will need to access the CGI variables. Because servlets are created using the Java programming language, which was not developed specifically for use on Web servers, servlets do not contain a built-in method for accessing CGI variables. Servlets can access CGI variables only by using objects, such as the `HttpServletRequest` object, to retrieve information.

Methods of the `HttpServletRequest` object, which handles the request information passed between a client and a servlet, are the most common methods used to access CGI variable information. For example, to access the address of the client that made a request, you use the `getRemoteAddr()` method of the `HttpServletRequest` object.

Methods of the `ServletContext` object, such as the `getServerInfo()` method, can be used to obtain information about the Web server on which the servlet is running, such as the name and version of the Web server software and the operating system running on the server.

CREATE A SERVLET THAT ACCESSES CGI VARIABLES

Untitled - Notepad

File Edit Search Help

```
import javax.servlet.*;
import javax.servlet.http.*;
import java.io.*;

public class SimpleServlet extends HttpServlet
{
     public void doGet(HttpServletRequest request,HttpServletResponse
          response)
     throws ServletException, IOException
     {
          PrintWriter out = response.getWriter();
          response.setContentType("text/html");
          out.print("<!doctype html public \"-//w3c//dtd html 4.0 ");
          out.print("transitional//en\">");
          out.print("<html>");
          out.print("<head><title>CGI Variables</title></head>");
          out.print("<body>");

          out.print("</b><body></html>");
     }
}
```

1 Type the code that imports the `javax.servlet` and `javax.servlet.http` packages.

2 Type the code that imports any additional packages needed by the servlet.

3 Type the code that creates the servlet class and the `doGet` method.

4 Type the code that sends HTML data to the client. For information about generating a Web page, see page 232.

Untitled - Notepad

File Edit Search Help

```
import javax.servlet.*;
import javax.servlet.http.*;
import java.io.*;

public class SimpleServlet extends HttpServlet
{
     public void doGet(HttpServletRequest request,HttpServletResponse
          response)
     throws ServletException, IOException
     {
          PrintWriter out = response.getWriter();
          response.setContentType("text/html");
          out.print("<!doctype html public \"-//w3c//dtd html 4.0 ");
          out.print("transitional//en\">");
          out.print("<html>");
          out.print("<head><title>CGI Variables</title></head>");
          out.print("<body>");

          out.print("<p>The address of the client is: <b>");
          out.print(request.getRemoteAddr());

          out.print("</b><body></html>");
     }
}
```

5 To access the address of the client that made a request, type **request.getRemoteAddr()**.

6 Type the code that uses the information from the CGI variable.

Extra

The following is a list of some commonly used CGI variables and the methods used to access the variables in a servlet.

CGI VARIABLE:	METHOD REQUIRED:
AUTH_TYPE	request.getAuthType()
CONTENT_TYPE	request.getContentType()
DOCUMENT_ROOT	getServletContext().getRealPath("/")
PATH_INFO	request.getPathInfo()
QUERY_STRING	request.getQueryString()
REMOTE_ADDR	request.getRemoteAddr()
REMOTE_HOST	request.getRemoteHost()
REMOTE_USER	request.getRemoteUser()
SCRIPT_NAME	request.getServletPath()
SERVER_NAME	request.getServerName()
SERVER_PORT	request.getServerPort()
SERVER_SOFTWARE	getServletContext().getServerInfo()

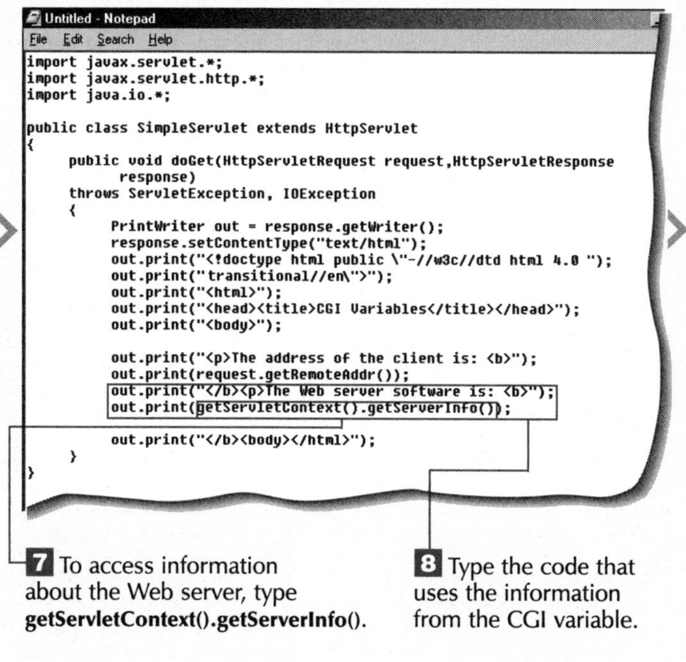

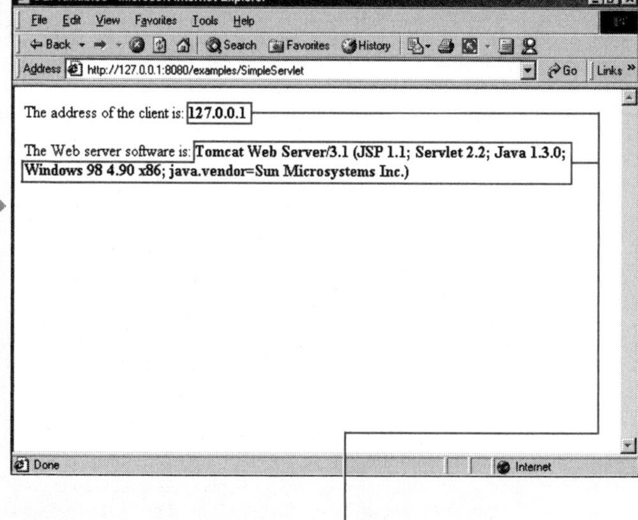

7 To access information about the Web server, type **getServletContext().getServerInfo()**.

8 Type the code that uses the information from the CGI variable.

9 Save the file with the .java extension and then compile the source code for the file.

10 Copy the compiled class file to the appropriate directory on your Web server.

11 Display the servlet in a Web browser.

■ The Web browser displays the result of accessing CGI variable information using the servlet.

PROCESS FORM DATA USING A SERVLET

Using a servlet is a very effective method of processing data passed by a form. Servlets process data faster and are more efficient than CGI applications.

In addition to data passed by a form, a servlet can also be used to process data submitted by a query string. A query string is one or more name and value pairs appended to a URL. To submit a query string to a servlet, you enter the URL of the servlet in a Web browser, followed by a question mark. You then enter a name followed by an equal sign and a value for the name. To enter multiple name and value pairs, separate each pair with an ampersand (&), such as ?userName=Martine&id=123. A query string should not contain spaces.

In order for a servlet to process data passed by a form using the `get` method or a query string, a `doGet` method must be created in the servlet. The `getParameter` method of the `HttpServletRequest` object can be used in the `doGet` method to access form or query string data. The argument for the `getParameter` method is the name of the form element you want to access or a name specified in the query string.

Once the servlet has retrieved the data from a form or a query string, the data can be displayed in a Web browser or stored in a variable for later use. A servlet may also perform a more complex task, such as placing the data in a database or writing the data to file.

Before the servlet file can be used to process form data, the file must be saved with the .java extension and then compiled. After saving the servlet, you should review the code for the form to verify that the `action` attribute of the `<form>` tag displays the correct filename and location of the servlet.

PROCESS FORM DATA USING A SERVLET

Untitled - Notepad

```
import javax.servlet.*;
import javax.servlet.http.*;
import java.io.*;
import java.util.*;

public class ProcessForm extends HttpServlet
{
    public void doGet(HttpServletRequest request,
        HttpServletResponse response) throws ServletException, IOException
    {

    }
}
```

Untitled - Notepad

```
import javax.servlet.*;
import javax.servlet.http.*;
import java.io.*;
import java.util.*;

public class ProcessForm extends HttpServlet
{
    public void doGet(HttpServletRequest request,
        HttpServletResponse response) throws ServletException, IOException
    {
        response.setContentType("text/html");
        PrintWriter out = response.getWriter();

        out.print("<!doctype html public \"-//w3c//dtd html 4.0 ");
        out.print("transitional//en\">");
        out.print("<html>");
        out.print("<head><title>Process Form Data</title></head>");
        out.print("<body>");
        out.print("<h2>");
        out.print("Welcome to my Web page ");
        out.print(request.getParameter("userName"));
        out.print("</h2>");
        out.print("</body></html>");
    }
}
```

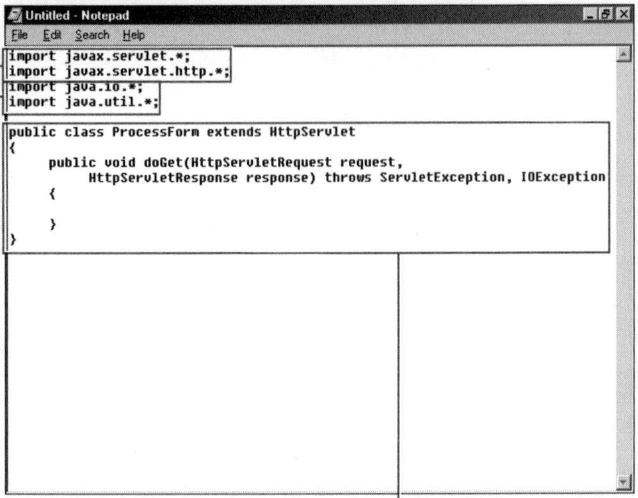

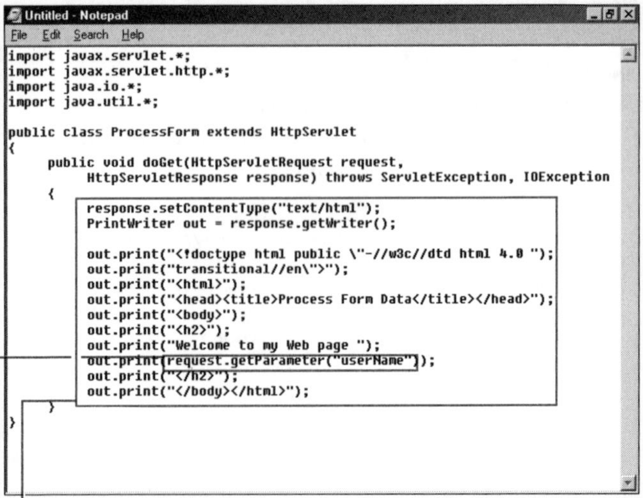

1 Type the code that imports the `javax.servlet` and `javax.servlet.http` packages.

2 Type the code that imports any additional packages needed by the servlet.

3 Type the code that creates the servlet class and the `doGet` method.

4 Type the code that sends HTML data to the client. For information about generating a Web page, see page 232.

5 Type the code that accesses data passed by a form.

6 Save the file with the .java extension and then compile the source code for the file.

7 Copy the compiled class file to the appropriate directory on your Web server.

Extra

There are two methods a form can use to pass information to a servlet—`get` and `post`. The `get` method is faster than the `post` method and is suitable for small forms. The `post` method is suitable for large forms that will send more than 2000 characters to the servlet. When the `post` method is used by a form, a `doPost` method must be created in the servlet. You can then pass the information from the `doPost` method to the `doGet` method. This creates a servlet that can handle information passed using either the `post` or `get` method.

Example:

```
public void doGet(HttpServletRequest request,
     HttpServletResponse response) throws ServletException, IOException
{
     response.setContentType("text/html");
     PrintWriter out = response.getWriter();

     out.print("<!doctype html public \"-//w3c//dtd html 4.0 ");
     out.print("transitional//en\">");
     out.print("<html>");
     out.print("<head><title>Process Form Data</title></head>");
     out.print("<body>");
     out.print("Welcome to my Web page");
     out.print(request.getParameter("userName"));
     out.print("</body></html>");
}
public void doPost(HttpServletRequest request, HttpServletResponse response)
     throws ServletException, IOException
{
     doGet(request, response);
}
```

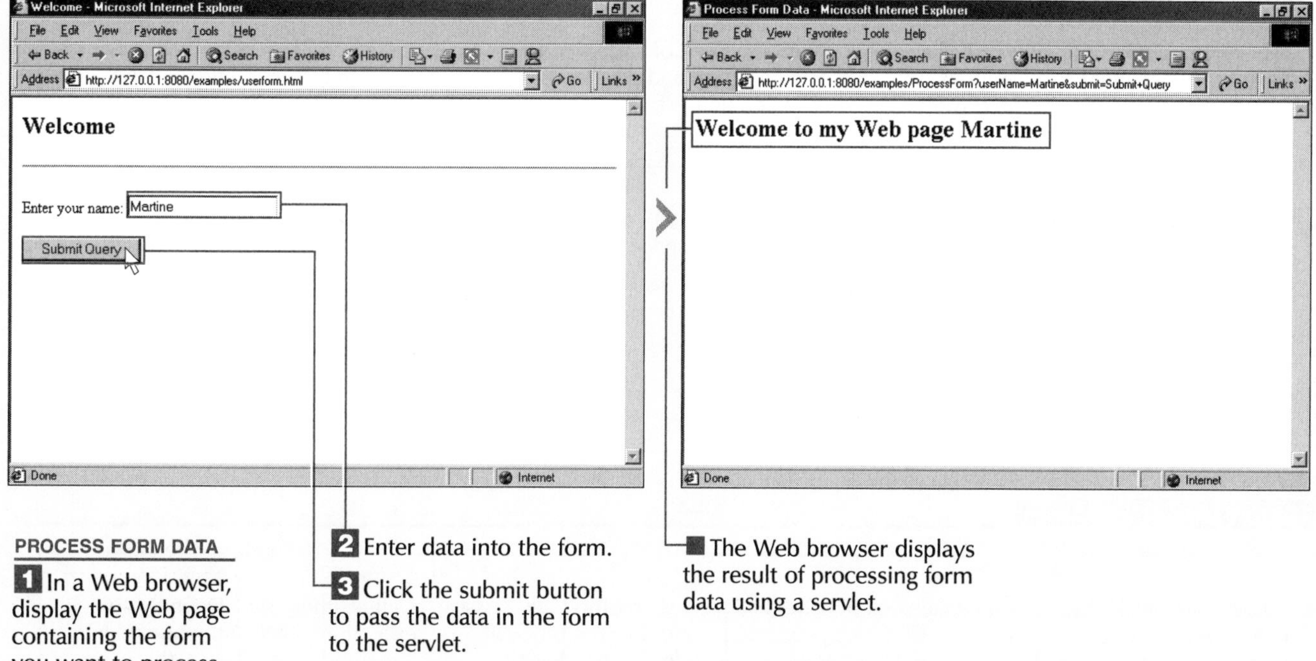

PROCESS FORM DATA

1 In a Web browser, display the Web page containing the form you want to process.

2 Enter data into the form.

3 Click the submit button to pass the data in the form to the servlet.

■ The Web browser displays the result of processing form data using a servlet.

JAVA ESSENTIALS

The Java programming language includes many keywords reserved for use only by Java. You cannot use keywords as variable names or values in your code. If you use a Java keyword inappropriately, the Java compiler will usually detect the error and stop compiling the code. The following is a list of Java reserved keywords.

PRIMITIVE DATA TYPES

`boolean`	`byte`	`char`	`double`
Holds the value `true` or `false`.	Holds an integer value ranging from -128 to 127.	Holds a single Unicode character.	Holds a 64-bit floating-point value ranging from ±4.9E-324 to ±1.7976931348623157E+308.

`float`	`int`	`long`	`short`
Holds a 32-bit floating-point value ranging from ±1.4E-45 to ±3.4028235E+38.	Holds a 32-bit integer value ranging from -2,147,483,648 to 2,147,483,647.	Holds a 64-bit integer value ranging from -9,223,372,036,854,775,808 to 9,223,372,036,854,775,807.	Holds a 16-bit integer value ranging from -32,768 to 32,767.

FLOW CONTROL

`break`	`case`	`continue`
Exits the flow of a loop or switch and continues execution from the line following the loop or switch.	Defines an option within a `switch` statement and the block of code that should be executed for that option.	Exits the flow of a loop and re-evaluates the loop condition.
`default` Defines a default option within a `switch` statement and the block of code that should be executed when there is no matching `case` statement.	`do` Defines a block of code that is executed once and repeats as long as a condition is true.	`else` Defines a block of code that is executed if a condition is false in an `if` statement.
`for` Defines a block of code that repeats depending on the value of a counter.	`if` Defines a block of code that is executed if a condition is true.	`return` Exits a method and returns control to the calling method, possibly returning a value.

`switch`	`while`
Defines a variable or field whose current value may induce the execution of the block of code defined by a matching `case` statement.	Defines a block of code that repeats as long as a condition is true.

EXCEPTION HANDLING

`catch`	`finally`	`throw`	`throws`	`try`
Defines a block of code that handles exceptions thrown by a `try` block of code.	Defines a block of code that is executed in a `try-catch` structure whether an exception is thrown or not.	Exits a method and passes control to the block of code that handles the thrown exception.	Defines the exceptions that a method may throw.	Defines a block of code that may throw an exception.

MODIFIERS

`abstract` Indicates that a method's functionality should be implemented by a subclass of the class that contains the method. Also, indicates that a class has such methods.	`final` Indicates that a class, method or field cannot be modified.	`native` Declares a Java method which is written in another language.	`private` Indicates that a method or field can be accessed only by the class that contains it.
`protected` Indicates that a method or field can be accessed only by the class that contains it or by a subclass of the class that contains it.	`public` Indicates that a method or field can be accessed by any class.	`static` Indicates that a method or field is a class member and can be instantiated only in the class that contains it.	`strictfp` Indicates that a method or class stores intermediate results using strict floating-point guidelines set by the IEEE 754 standard.
`synchronized` Indicates that a method cannot be executed by two threads at the same time and cannot be interrupted during execution. Also, indicates an object that can be accessed by only one synchronized block of code at a time.		`void` Indicates a method that does not return a value.	`volatile` Indicates that a field may be changed by multiple threads.

OBJECTS

`class` Defines a block of code that outlines the methods and fields of a class.	`extends` Specifies which class a subclass inherits methods and fields from.
`implements` Specifies interfaces from which a class implements methods and fields.	`interface` Indicates a block of code that defines an interface.

REFERENCE TYPES

`instanceof` Tests an object to determine if the object is an instance of a particular data type or class.	`new` Creates a new object in memory and calls the constructor method.
`super` Refers to the parent class of an object.	`this` Refers to the current object.

PACKAGES

`import` Specifies packages to be used by the source file.	`package` Specifies which package the classes of a source file belong to.

MISCELLANEOUS RESERVED WORDS

In addition to the keywords above, you also may not use `const`, `false`, `goto`, `null`, `transient` and `true` as names in your JSP code.

JAVASERVER PAGES ESSENTIALS

Legend: plain text = required
italics = user-defined
[] = optional
... = list of items
bold = default
| = or
{} = required choice
+ = can repeat

COMMENTS

HTML Comment

An HTML comment is sent to the Web browser, but is not displayed. The information may be viewed by users who view the HTML source code.

Syntax:

```
<!-- comment [<%= expression %>] -->
```

Example:

```
<!-- Session ID: <%= session.getId() %> -->
```

Hidden Comment

A hidden comment is discarded before any processing of the JSP page takes place and is not sent to the Web browser.

Syntax:

```
<%-- comment --%>
```

Example:

```
<%-- Page created by: Jade Williams --%>
```

SCRIPTING ELEMENTS

Declaration

A declaration allows you to define variables and methods that will be used throughout a JSP page.

Syntax:

```
<%! declaration; [declaration;]+ ... %>
```

Example:

```
<%! String siteName = "ABC Corporation"; %>
```

Expression

An expression allows you to generate output on a JSP page.

Syntax:

```
<%= expression %>
```

Example:

```
<%= request.getAttribute("firstName") %>
```

SCRIPTING ELEMENTS (CONTINUED)

Scriptlet

A scriptlet is a block of code embedded within a JSP page, which performs tasks such as generating output.

Syntax:

```
<% code_fragment %>
```

Example:

```
<% out.println("ABC Corporation Web site") %>
```

DIRECTIVES

Include Directive

The `include` directive allows you to use one file in several different JSP pages.

Syntax:

```
<%@ include file="relativeURL" %>
```

Example:

```
<%@ include file="pages/footer.html" %>
```

Taglib Directive

The `taglib` directive allows you to define a tag library and a prefix that can be used to reference the custom tags.

Syntax:

```
<%@ taglib uri="tagLibURI" prefix="tagPrefix" %>
```

Example:

```
<%@ taglib uri="http://www.mysite.com/chart"
  prefix="barchart" %>
```

Page Directive

The `page` directive allows you to specify information about the configuration of a JSP page.

Syntax:

```
<%@ page [language="java"] [extends="package.class"]
  [import="{package.class|package.*}, ..."]
  [isThreadSafe="true|false"]
  [session="true|false"] [info="text"]
  [buffer="none|8kb|sizekb"] [autoFlush="true|false"]
  [errorPage="relativeURL"] [isErrorPage="true|false"]
  [contentType="{mimeType[; charset=characterSet]
               |text/html; charset=iso-8859-1}"] %>
```

Example:

```
<%@ page isErrorPage="true" contentType="text/plain" %>
```

JAVASERVER PAGES ESSENTIALS

CUSTOM TAGS

Custom Tag

A custom tag invokes custom actions included in a tag library. Custom actions are re-usable modules that may create and access objects and affect the output stream.

Syntax:

```
<tagPrefix:name attribute="value"+ ... />
```

or

```
<tagPrefix:name attribute="value"+ ... >
JSPContent
</tagPrefix:name>
```

Example:

```
<barchart:Vertical values="1, 4, 3" />
```

ACTIONS

<jsp:forward> Action

The `<jsp:forward>` action instructs a Web server to stop processing the current JSP page and start processing another.

Syntax:

```
<jsp:forward page="{relativeURL|<%= expression %>}" />
```

or

```
<jsp:forward page="{relativeURL|<%= expression %>}" >
     <jsp:param name="parameterName"
       value="{parameterValue|<%= expression %>}" />+
</jsp:forward>
```

Example:

```
<jsp:forward page="/search" />
```

<jsp:setProperty> Action

The `<jsp:setProperty>` action sets the value or values of a property in a JavaBean.

Syntax:

```
<jsp:setProperty name="beanID"
   {property="*"
   |property="propertyName" [param="parameterName"]
   |property="propertyName"
     value="{string|<%= expression %>}"} />
```

Example:

```
<jsp:setProperty name="lineBean" property="color"
  value="red" />
```

ACTIONS (CONTINUED)

<jsp:getProperty> Action

The <jsp:getProperty> action accesses a property of a JavaBean and can display the property in a JSP page.

Syntax:

```
<jsp:getProperty name="beanID" property="propertyName" />
```

Example:

```
<jsp:getProperty name="movieBean" property="title" />
```

<jsp:plugin> Action

The <jsp:plugin> action generates HTML code to display an applet or JavaBean using a Java plug-in in a Web browser. The plug-in is downloaded from a specified location if the Web browser is not capable of displaying the applet or JavaBean.

Syntax:

```
<jsp:plugin type="bean|applet" code="fileName.class"
  codebase="classURL"
  [name="instanceName"] [archive="archiveURI, ..."]
  [align="bottom|top|middle|left|right"]
  [height="hPixels"] [width="wPixels"]
  [hspace="horPixels"] [vspace="verPixels"]
  [jreversion="JREVersionNumber|1.1"]
  [nspluginurl="PluginURL"] [iepluginurl="PluginURL"] >
    [<jsp:params>
      [<jsp:param name="parameterName"
        value="{parameterValue|<%= expression %>}" />]+
    </jsp:params>]
    [<jsp:fallback> alternateText </jsp:fallback>]
</jsp:plugin>
```

Example:

```
<jsp:plugin type="applet" code="fireworks.class"
  codebase="/java" height=250 width=187>
    <jsp:fallback> Unable to load applet </jsp:fallback>
</jsp:plugin>
```

<jsp:include> Action

The <jsp:include> action includes a file, such as an HTML or JSP page, in the current JSP page.

Syntax:

```
<jsp:include page="{relativeURL|<%= expression %>}"
  flush="true" />
```

or

```
<jsp:include page="{relativeURL|<%= expression %>}"
  flush="true" >
    <jsp:param name="parameterName"
      value="{parameterValue|<%= expression %>}" />+
</jsp:include>
```

Example:

```
<jsp:include page="welcome.jsp" flush="true" />
```

<jsp:useBean> Action

The <jsp:useBean> action associates a JSP page with a specific JavaBean.

Syntax:

```
<jsp:useBean id="beanID"
  scope="page|request|session|application"
  {class="package.class" [type="package.class"]
  |[beanName="{package.class|<%= expression %>}"]
  type="package.class"}/>
```

or

```
<jsp:useBean id="beanID"
  scope="page|request|session|application"
  {class="package.class" [type="package.class"]
  |[beanName="{package.class|<%= expression %>}"]
  type="package.class"} >
otherElements
</jsp:useBean>
```

Example:

```
<jsp:useBean id="lineBean" scope="session"
  class="myBeans.lnBean" />
```

JSP IMPLICIT OBJECTS QUICK REFERENCE

REQUEST OBJECT

The `request` object retrieves and controls information sent from a client to the Web server. The `request` object is a subclass of the `javax.servlet.ServletRequest` class.

METHODS

`Object` **`getAttribute(`**`String name)` Returns the value of an attribute of the `request` object.	`String` **`getParameter(`**`String name)` Returns the value of a parameter in the `request` object.
`Enumeration` **`getAttributeNames()`** Returns a list of names of available attributes in the `request` object.	`Enumeration` **`getParameterNames()`** Returns a list of names of parameters contained in the `request` object.
`String` **`getCharacterEncoding()`** Returns the name of the character set used by the `request` object.	`String[]` **`getParameterValues(`**`String name)` Returns an array containing all the values of a parameter.
`int` **`getContentLength()`** Returns the length of the content body for the `request` object, in bytes.	`String` **`getProtocol()`** Returns the name and version of the protocol used by the `request` object.
`String` **`getContentType()`** Returns the content type of the `request` object.	`BufferedReader` **`getReader()`** Uses a `BufferedReader` object to retrieve a request as character data.
`ServletInputStream` **`getInputStream()`** Uses a `ServletInputStream` object to retrieve a request as binary data.	`String` **`getRealPath(`**`String virtualPath)` Returns the real path that corresponds to a virtual path. Deprecated. Use `String ServletContext.getRealPath(String virtualPath)` instead.
`Locale` **`getLocale()`** Returns the preferred regional setting in which the client computer accepts information.	`String` **`getRemoteAddr()`** Returns the Internet Protocol (IP) address of the client computer that made the request.
`Enumeration` **`getLocales()`** Returns a list of regional settings in which the client computer accepts information, in decreasing order of preference.	`String` **`getRemoteHost()`** Returns the name or IP address of the client computer that made the request.

METHODS (Continued)

RequestDispatcher **getRequestDispatcher**(String path) Returns a RequestDispatcher object to be used with the resource located at the specified path.	int **getServerPort**() Returns the number of the server port the request was received on.
String **getScheme**() Returns the scheme used to make the request, such as http, https or ftp.	boolean **isSecure**() Returns a boolean value indicating whether the request was made through a secure channel.
String **getServerName**() Returns the name of the server that received the request.	void **removeAttribute**(String name) Removes an attribute from the request object.
	void **setAttribute**(String name, Object attribute) Adds an attribute to the request object.

RESPONSE OBJECT

The response object sends and controls information from the Web server to a client. The response object is a subclass of the javax.servlet.ServletResponse class.

METHODS

void **flushBuffer**() Sends information stored in the buffer to a client immediately.	ServletOutputStream **getOutputStream**() Returns a ServletOutputStream object that allows the response object to write binary data to the client.
int **getBufferSize**() Returns the buffer size of the response object, in bytes.	PrintWriter **getWriter**() Returns a PrintWriter object that allows the response object to write character data to the client.
String **getCharacterEncoding**() Returns the name of the character set used by the response object.	boolean **isCommitted**() Returns a boolean value indicating if the response object has written the status code and headers.
Locale **getLocale**() Returns the regional setting assigned to the response object.	void **reset**() Clears information, status code and headers from the buffer.

JSP IMPLICIT OBJECTS QUICK REFERENCE

RESPONSE OBJECT (CONTINUED)

METHODS (Continued)

void **setBufferSize**(int size) Sets the buffer size for the `response` object, in bytes.	void **setContentType**(String type) Sets the content type of the `response` object.
void **setContentLength**(int len) Sets the length of the content body for the `response` object, in bytes.	void **setLocale**(Locale loc) Sets the regional setting for the `response` object.

PAGECONTEXT OBJECT

A `pageContext` object provides access to the namespaces associated with a JSP page, page attributes and implementation details. The `pageContext` object is a subclass of the `javax.servlet.jsp.PageContext` class.

FIELDS

String **APPLICATION** Stores the `application` object in the name table of the `pageContext` object.	String **EXCEPTION** Stores an uncaught exception in the attribute list of the `request` object and in the name table of the `pageContext` object.
int **APPLICATION_SCOPE** Indicates that a reference has application scope.	String **OUT** Stores the `out` object in the name table of the `pageContext` object.
String **CONFIG** Stores the `config` object in the name table of the `pageContext` object.	String **PAGE** Stores the `Servlet` object in the name table of the `pageContext` object.

FIELDS (Continued)

`int` **`PAGE_SCOPE`** Indicates that a reference has page scope.	`String` **`RESPONSE`** Stores the `response` object in the name table of the `pageContext` object.
`String` **`PAGECONTEXT`** Stores the `pageContext` object in its own name table.	`String` **`SESSION`** Stores the `session` object in the name table of the `pageContext` object.
`String` **`REQUEST`** Stores the `request` object in the name table of the `pageContext` object.	`int` **`SESSION_SCOPE`** Indicates that a reference has session scope.
`int` **`REQUEST_SCOPE`** Indicates that a reference has request scope.	

METHODS

`Object` **`findAttribute(`**`String name`**`)`** Searches for an attribute in all valid scopes and returns the value.	`Enumeration` **`getAttributeNamesInScope(`**`int scope`**`)`** Returns a list of names of the available attributes in the specified scope.
`void` **`forward(`**`String relativeUrlPath`**`)`** Forwards the current `request` and `response` objects to another resource found at the specified path.	`int` **`getAttributesScope(`**`String name`**`)`** Returns the scope of an attribute.
`Object` **`getAttribute(`**`String name`**`)`** Returns the value of an attribute in the page scope.	`Exception` **`getException()`** Returns any `exception` object that was passed to the JSP page.
`Object` **`getAttribute(`**`String name, int scope`**`)`** Returns the value of an attribute in the specified scope.	`JspWriter` **`getOut()`** Returns the `out` object that is being used for client response.

JSP IMPLICIT OBJECTS QUICK REFERENCE

PAGECONTEXT OBJECT (CONTINUED)

METHODS (Continued)

`Object` **`getPage()`** Returns the `Servlet` associated with the `pageContext` object.	`void` **`initialize(`**`Servlet servlet, ServletRequest request, ServletResponse response, String errorPageURL, boolean needsSession, int bufferSize, boolean autoFlush`**`)`** Initializes a `pageContext` object.
`ServletRequest` **`getRequest()`** Returns the `request` object associated with the `pageContext` object.	`JspWriter` **`popBody()`** Returns the previous `out` object saved by the previous call of the `pushBody` method and updates the value of the `OUT` attribute in the page scope of the `pageContext` object.
`ServletResponse` **`getResponse()`** Returns the `response` object associated with the `pageContext` object.	`BodyContent` **`pushBody()`** Returns a new `BodyContent` object, saves the current `out` object and updates the value of the `OUT` attribute in the page scope of the `pageContext` object.
`ServletConfig` **`getServletConfig()`** Returns the `config` object associated with the `pageContext` object.	`void` **`release()`** Resets the `pageContext` object.
`ServletContext` **`getServletContext()`** Returns the `application` object associated with the `pageContext` object.	`void` **`removeAttribute(`**`String name`**`)`** Removes an attribute.
`HttpSession` **`getSession()`** Returns the `session` object associated with the `pageContext` object.	`void` **`removeAttribute(`**`String name, int scope`**`)`** Removes an attribute in the specified scope.
`void` **`handlePageException(`**`Exception exception`**`)`** Executes code when a specific error is encountered.	`void` **`setAttribute(`**`String name, Object attribute`**`)`** Adds an attribute with page scope.
`void` **`include(`**`String relativeUrlPath`**`)`** Processes the resource found at the specified path as part of the `request` and `response` objects currently being processed.	`void` **`setAttribute(`**`String name, Object attribute, int scope`**`)`** Adds an attribute with the specified scope.

SESSION OBJECT

The `session` object stores session information about a client computer as the client navigates a Web site. The `session` object is a subclass of the `javax.servlet.http.HttpSession` class.

METHODS

Method	Description
`Object` **`getAttribute(String name)`**	Returns the information stored in a session value of the `session` object.
`Enumeration` **`getAttributeNames()`**	Returns a list of all session values available in the `session` object.
`long` **`getCreationTime()`**	Returns the time the session started, measured in milliseconds since January 1, 1970.
`String` **`getId()`**	Returns the session ID.
`long` **`getLastAccessedTime()`**	Returns the last time the client sent a request during the session, measured in milliseconds since January 1, 1970.
`int` **`getMaxInactiveInterval()`**	Returns the session timeout, in seconds.
`HttpSessionContext` **`getSessionContext()`**	Deprecated. This method will be removed in a future version of the Java Servlet API.
`Object` **`getValue(String name)`**	Returns the information stored in a session value of the `session` object. Deprecated. Use `Object getAttribute(String name)` instead.
`String[]` **`getValueNames()`**	Returns a list of all session values available in the `session` object. Deprecated. Use `Enumeration getAttributeNames()` instead.
`void` **`invalidate()`**	Terminates the current session.
`boolean` **`isNew()`**	Returns `true` if the client computer has not yet joined the session.
`void` **`putValue(String name, Object value)`**	Creates a session value for the `session` object. Deprecated. Use `void setAttribute(String name, Object attribute)` instead.
`void` **`removeAttribute(String name)`**	Removes a session value from the `session` object.
`void` **`removeValue(String name)`**	Removes a session value from the `session` object. Deprecated. Use `void removeAttribute(String name)` instead.
`void` **`setAttribute(String name, Object attribute)`**	Creates a session value for the `session` object.
`void` **`setMaxInactiveInterval(int interval)`**	Sets the session timeout, in seconds.

JSP IMPLICIT OBJECTS QUICK REFERENCE

APPLICATION OBJECT

The `application` object stores and shares information for use during an active application. The `application` object is a subclass of the `javax.servlet.ServletContext` class.

METHODS

`Object` **`getAttribute`**`(String name)` Returns the value of an attribute of the `application` object.	`int` **`getMinorVersion`**`()` Returns the minor version of the Java Servlet API that the server supports.
`Enumeration` **`getAttributeNames`**`()` Returns a list of names of available attributes in the `application` object.	`RequestDispatcher` **`getNamedDispatcher`**`(String name)` Returns a `RequestDispatcher` object to be used by the named `application` object.
`ServletContext` **`getContext`**`(String path)` Returns a `ServletContext` object to be used with the resource located at the specified path.	`String` **`getRealPath`**`(String virtualPath)` Returns the real path that corresponds to the specified virtual path.
`String` **`getInitParameter`**`(String name)` Returns the value of an initialization parameter of the `application` object.	`RequestDispatcher` **`getRequestDispatcher`**`(String path)` Returns a `RequestDispatcher` object to be used with the resource located at the specified path.
`Enumeration` **`getInitParameterNames`**`()` Returns a list of names of available initialization parameters in the `application` object.	`URL` **`getResource`**`(String path)` Returns a URL to the resource that is mapped to the specified path.
`int` **`getMajorVersion`**`()` Returns the major version of the Java Servlet API that the server supports.	`InputStream` **`getResourceAsStream`**`(String path)` Returns the resource located at the specified path as an `InputStream` object.
`String` **`getMimeType`**`(String file)` Returns the MIME type of a file.	`String` **`getServerInfo`**`()` Returns information about the server on which the servlet is running.

METHODS (Continued)

Servlet **getServlet**(String name) Deprecated. This method will be removed in a future version of the Java Servlet API.	void **log**(String msg) Writes a message to a servlet log file.
Enumeration **getServletNames**() Deprecated. This method will be removed in a future version of the Java Servlet API.	void **log**(String msg, Throwable throwable) Writes an explanatory message and a stack trace to the servlet log file for a given error.
Enumeration **getServlets**() Deprecated. This method will be removed in a future version of the Java Servlet API.	void **removeAttribute**(String name) Removes an attribute from the `application` object.
void **log**(Exception exception, String msg) Writes an explanatory error message to the servlet log file. Deprecated. Use `void log(String msg, Throwable throwable)` instead.	void **setAttribute**(String name, Object attribute) Creates an attribute for the `application` object.

OUT OBJECT

The `out` object is a buffered output stream that sends output to the client. The `out` object is a subclass of the `javax.servlet.jsp.JspWriter` class.

FIELDS

boolean **autoFlush** Indicates whether the buffer flushes automatically.	int **NO_BUFFER** Indicates that the `out` object is not buffered.
int **bufferSize** Stores the buffer size used by the `out` object, in bytes.	int **UNBOUNDED_BUFFER** Indicates that the `out` object is buffered and is using an unlimited buffer size.
int **DEFAULT_BUFFER** Indicates that the `out` object is buffered and is using the default buffer size.	

JSP IMPLICIT OBJECTS QUICK REFERENCE

OUT OBJECT (CONTINUED)

METHODS

void **clear()**
Clears the buffer. If the buffer has been flushed, this method causes an error to occur.

void **clearBuffer()**
Clears the buffer. This method does not cause an error if the buffer has been flushed.

void **close()**
Flushes the buffer and closes the output stream.

void **flush()**
Flushes the buffer.

int **getBufferSize()**
Returns the buffer size used by the `out` object, in bytes.

int **getRemaining()**
Returns the size of the unused area in the buffer, in bytes.

boolean **isAutoFlush()**
Returns `true` if the buffer flushes automatically.

void **newLine()**
Writes the line separator string to start a new line in the output stream.

void **print**(boolean b)
Prints a boolean value.

void **print**(char c)
Prints a character.

void **print**(char[] s)
Prints an array of characters.

void **print**(double d)
Prints a double-precision floating-point number.

void **print**(float f)
Prints a floating-point number.

void **print**(int i)
Prints an integer.

METHODS (Continued)

void **print**(long l) Prints a long integer.	void **println**(double d) Prints a double-precision floating-point number and then terminates the line.
void **print**(Object obj) Prints an object.	void **println**(float f) Prints a floating-point number and then terminates the line.
void **print**(String s) Prints a string.	void **println**(int i) Prints an integer and then terminates the line.
void **println**() Writes the line separator string to terminate the current line.	void **println**(long l) Prints a long integer and then terminates the line.
void **println**(boolean b) Prints a boolean value and then terminates the line.	void **println**(Object obj) Prints an object and then terminates the line.
void **println**(char c) Prints a character and then terminates the line.	void **println**(String s) Prints a string and then terminates the line.
void **println**(char[] s) Prints an array of characters and then terminates the line.	

JSP IMPLICIT OBJECTS QUICK REFERENCE

CONFIG OBJECT

The `config` object contains information about the servlet configuration. The `config` object is a subclass of the `javax.servlet.ServletConfig` class.

METHODS

String **getInitParameter**(String name) Returns the value of the initialization parameter of the servlet.	ServletContext **getServletContext**() Returns a reference to the `application` object in which the servlet is executing.
Enumeration **getInitParameterNames**() Returns a list of names of the servlet's initialization parameters.	String **getServletName**() Returns the name of the current servlet.

PAGE OBJECT

The `page` object refers to the JSP page itself. The `page` object is a subclass of the `java.lang.Object` class.

METHODS

Object **clone**() Creates and returns a copy of the `page` object.	Class **getClass**() Returns the runtime class of the `page` object.
boolean **equals**(Object obj) Indicates whether another object is the same as the `page` object.	int **hashCode**() Returns a hash code value for the `page` object.
void **finalize**() Performs cleanup tasks when there are no more references to the `page` object.	void **notify**() Wakes up a single thread that is waiting on the `page` object's monitor.

METHODS (Continued)

void **notifyAll()** Wakes up all threads that are waiting on the page object's monitor.	void **wait(**long timeout**)** Causes the current thread to wait until another thread awakens the page object or the specified amount of time, measured in milliseconds, has elapsed.
String **toString()** Returns a string representation of the page object.	void **wait(**long timeout, int nanos**)** Causes the current thread to wait until another thread awakens the page object, another thread interrupts the current thread or the specified amount of time, measured in nanoseconds, has elapsed.
void **wait()** Causes the current thread to wait until another thread awakens the page object.	

EXCEPTION OBJECT

The exception object contains information about a runtime error and is available only in an error page. An error page must contain the isErrorPage=true attribute in the page directive. The exception object is a subclass of the java.lang.Throwable class.

METHODS

Throwable **fillInStackTrace()** Fills the exception object with current error information.	void **printStackTrace(**PrintStream s**)** Prints information about the exception object to the specified print stream.
String **getLocalizedMessage()** Returns an error message according to regional settings.	void **printStackTrace(**PrintWriter s**)** Prints information about the exception object to the specified print writer.
String **getMessage()** Returns the error message describing the exception.	String **toString()** Returns a short description of this exception object.
void **printStackTrace()** Prints information about the exception object to the standard error stream.	

JAVA.SQL QUICK REFERENCE

The `java.sql` package provides interfaces and classes that allow Java programs to access and manipulate information in a database. The `java.sql` package is also known as the Java DataBase Connectivity 2.0 core Application Program Interface, or JDBC 2.0 core API.

INTERFACES

`Array` Provides methods for handling data in an SQL `ARRAY` type.	`Driver` This interface must be implemented by every driver class.
`Blob` Provides methods for handling data in an SQL `BLOB` type.	`PreparedStatement` Provides methods for handling precompiled SQL statements.
`CallableStatement` Provides methods for executing SQL stored procedures.	`Ref` Provides a method for retrieving the SQL name of a data structure type referenced by the `Ref` object and SQL `REF`.
`Clob` Provides methods for handling data in an SQL `CLOB` type.	`ResultSet` Provides methods for handling the information generated by the execution of a statement that queries a database.
`Connection` Provides methods for controlling a connection to a database.	`ResultSetMetaData` Provides methods for obtaining information about the columns in a `ResultSet` object.
`DatabaseMetaData` Provides comprehensive information about a database.	`SQLData` Provides methods for manipulating SQL user-defined types.

INTERFACES (Continued)

`SQLInput` Provides methods for manipulating data in an input stream.	`Statement` Provides methods for executing an SQL statement and obtaining the results.
`SQLOutput` Provides methods for writing data back to a database.	`Struct` Provides methods for retrieving information about an SQL structured type.

CLASSES

`Date` Provides methods for manipulating an SQL `DATE`, which is measured in milliseconds since January 1, 1970.	`Time` Provides methods for manipulating an SQL `TIME` value, which is the time of day, based on the number of milliseconds since January 1, 1970.
`DriverManager` Provides methods for managing a set of JDBC drivers.	`Timestamp` Provides methods for manipulating an SQL `TIMESTAMP` value, which is the time of day and a nanosecond component. The time of day is based on the number of milliseconds since January 1, 1970.
`DriverPropertyInfo` Provides methods for discovering and supplying properties for database connections.	`Types` Defines the constants that represent generic SQL types.
`SQLPermission` Holds the name of the permission that is checked by the `SecurityManager` when there is a call to one of the `setLogWriter` methods.	

JAVASERVER PAGES AND ACTIVE SERVER PAGES

Active Server Pages (ASP) is an alternative technology for generating dynamic Web pages. ASP, developed by Microsoft, and JSP have many similarities. Both technologies allow programmers to insert dynamic Web content into HTML pages using special tags, access information in databases, store information about a client computer throughout a session and use encapsulated components, such as ActiveX in ASP and JavaBeans in JSP.

There are many differences between the two technologies as well. ASP pages are processed almost exclusively by Microsoft Web servers—Internet Information Server (IIS) or Personal Web Server, while JSP pages can be processed by any server that supports Java servlets.

ASP code is usually written using VBScript or JScript, which are Microsoft proprietary scripting languages. JSP code, however, is written using Java, which is platform independent and can run on any computer that has a Java virtual machine. Java has more flexibility and fewer limitations than the scripting languages used in ASP.

There are also differences in the way JSP and ASP pages are processed by Web servers. Every time an ASP page is requested by a client, the code in the ASP page is interpreted by the Web server and the results are then sent to the Web browser. The first time a JSP page is requested, the code in the JSP page is compiled into a servlet by the Web server. The server then processes the servlet to generate the HTML code which is sent to the Web browser. The Web server keeps a copy of the servlet for future requests. The next time the page is requested, the precompiled servlet can simply be processed. Processing precompiled servlets is faster than re-interpreting the code in ASP pages each time a page is requested.

The following pages illustrate the differences between JSP and ASP implicit objects and their most common functions, as well as other JSP and ASP features, such as scripting elements and comments.

REQUEST OBJECT

Function	JSP	ASP
Object name	`request`	`Request`
Retrieve certification information	N/A	`ClientCertificate (String key[String field])`
Retrieve cookies	`getCookies()`	`Cookies(String name) [(String key)]`
Retrieve form data	`getParameter(String name)`, `getParameterNames()` and `getParameterValues(String name)`	`Form(String element) [(int index)]`
Retrieve query data	`getParameter(String name)` and `getQueryString()`	`QueryString(String element) [(int index)]`
Retrieve HTTP headers	`getHeaderNames()`, `getHeader(String name)`, `getIntHeader(String name)` and `getDateHeader(String name)`	`ServerVariables(String serverVar)`

RESPONSE OBJECT

Function	JSP	ASP
Object name	`response`	`Response`
Enable or disable buffering	The JSP `response` object does not support this function, but this can be done using the `<%@ page buffer="sizekb|none" %>` directive.	`Buffer = True|False`
Enable or disable proxy server caching	`setHeader("Cache-Control", "no-cache")`	`CacheControl = Public|Private`
Create a cookie	`addCookie(Cookie name)`	`Cookies(String name)[(String key).attribute] = value`
Add an HTTP header	`setHeader(String name, String value)`	`AddHeader String Name, String Value`
Load a new page	`sendRedirect(String AbsURL)` This function needs an encoded URL from `encodeRedirectURL(String url)` if URL rewriting is being used to track a session.	`Redirect String url`
Send an error to client	`sendError(int code, String msg)`	N/A
Encode a URL	`encodeURL(String url)` This function appends the session ID to the URL if URL rewriting is being used to track a session.	The ASP `Response` object does not support this function, but this can be done using the `Server.URLencode(String url)` method.
Set the MIME type	`setContentType(String mimeType)`	`ContentType = String mimeType`

PAGECONTEXT OBJECT

Function	JSP	ASP
Object name	`pageContext`	No similar object

JAVASERVER PAGES AND ACTIVE SERVER PAGES

SESSION OBJECT

Function	JSP	ASP
Object name	session	Session
Terminate a session	invalidate()	Abandon
Create a session variable	setAttribute(String name, Object attribute)	Session(String name) = "Variable Data"
Create a session object	setAttribute(String name, Object attribute)	Set Session(String name) = Server.CreateObject(String name)
Retrieve a session variable	getAttribute(String name)	My_Variable = Session(String name)
Retrieve a session object	getAttribute(String name)	Set My_Object = Session(String name)
Remove a session variable or object	removeAttribute(String name)	Contents.Remove(String name)
Retrieve session variable or object names	getAttributeNames()	For Each Key in Session.Contents Response.Write(Key & " : " & Session(Key) & " ") Next
Retrieve the session ID	getId()	SessionID
Set the session timeout	setMaxInactiveInterval(int seconds)	Timeout(int Minutes)
Retrieve the session timeout	getMaxInactiveInterval()	N/A
Retrieve the preferred regional setting in which the client computer accepts information	The JSP session object does not support this function, but this can be done using the request.getLocale() method.	LCID
Disable the session	This function can be done using the <%@ page session="false" %> directive.	This function can be done using the <%@ EnableSessionState=False %> directive.

APPLICATION OBJECT

Function	JSP	ASP
Object name	application	Application
Create a variable	setAttribute(String name, Object object)	Application(String name) = "Variable Data"
Create an object	setAttribute(String name, Object object)	Set Application(String name) = Server.CreateObject(String name)
Retrieve a variable	getAttribute(String name)	My_Variable = Application(String name)
Retrieve an object	getAttribute(String name)	Set My_Object = Application(String name)
Remove a variable or object	removeAttribute(String name)	Contents.Remove(String name)
Retrieve variable or object names	getAttributeNames()	For Each Key in Application.Contents Response.Write(Key & " : " & Application(Key) & " ") Next
Lock and unlock variables	The JSP application object does not support this function, but this can be done using thread control.	Lock and Unlock
Retrieve information about the server	getServerInfo()	N/A
Determine the servlet API version	getMajorVersion() and getMinorVersion()	N/A
Write to the servlet log file	log(String msg)	The ASP Application object does not support this function, but this can be done using the Response.AppendToLog(String msg) method.
Determine the MIME type of a file	getMimeType(String file)	N/A
Find a virtual path's corresponding real path	getRealPath(String virtualpath)	The ASP Application object does not support this function, but this can be done using the Server.MapPath(String path) method.
Find the URL to a resource	getResource(String path)	N/A

JAVASERVER PAGES AND ACTIVE SERVER PAGES

OUT OBJECT

Function	JSP	ASP
Object name	`out`	`Response`
Write to the output buffer	`print(data)`	`Write(data)`
Write binary data	The JSP `out` object does not support this function, but this can be done using the `OutputStream.write (Byte[] buffer)` method.	`BinaryWrite(data)`
Clear the buffer	`clearBuffer()`	`Clear()`
Flush the buffer	`flush()`	`Flush()`
Close the output stream	`close()`	`End()` This method stops the processing of the current page.

CONFIG OBJECT

Function	JSP	ASP
Object name	`config`	No similar object
Determine the name of the current servlet	`getServletName()`	N/A
Return a reference to the application object	`getServletContext()`	N/A
Retrieve the names of the servlet's initialization parameters	`getInitParameterNames()`	N/A
Retrieve the value of an initialization parameter	`getInitParameter(String name)`	N/A

PAGE OBJECT

Function	JSP	ASP
Object name	`page`	No similar object

ERROR OBJECT

Function	JSP	ASP
Object name	`exception`	`ASPError`
Retrieve an error message	`getMessage()`	`Description()`
Retrieve a detailed error description	`toString()`	`ASPDescription()`
Print information about an error	`printStackTrace(PrintStream s)` or `printStackTrace(PrintWriter s)`	N/A
Determine the position of an error in the source file	N/A	`Line` and `Column`

SERVER OBJECT

Function	JSP	ASP
Object name	No similar object, but other JSP implicit objects have methods that support most functions of the ASP `Server` object.	`Server`
Create an object	To create an object, use standard Java syntax.	`CreateObject(Object id)`
Apply HTML encoding to a string	N/A	`HTMLEncode(String s)`
Find a virtual path's corresponding real path	This function can be done using the `application.getRealPath(String virtualPath)` method.	`MapPath(String virtualPath)`
Encode a URL	This function can be done using the `response.encodeURL(String url)` method.	`URLEncode(String url)`
Forward control to a new page	This function can be done using the `<jsp:forward page="String path" />` action.	`Transfer(String path)`
Set the amount of time a script can run on the server before it is terminated	N/A	`ScriptTimeout = int Seconds`

JAVASERVER PAGES AND ACTIVE SERVER PAGES

SCRIPTING ELEMENTS

Element	JSP	ASP

Declarations: define functions, methods and variables that will be used by the scriptlets in a Web page.	`<%!`
	`Method and variable declarations`
	`%>`
		`<%`
		`Function and variable declarations`
		`%>`

Expressions: generate output directly to a Web page.	`<%=`
	`Variable name or call to a method`
	`%>`
		`<%=`
		`Variable name or call to a function`
		`%>`

Scriptlets: embed blocks of code within a Web page to perform tasks such as generating output.	`<%`
	`JSP code`
	`%>`
		`<%`
		`ASP code`
		`%>`

SCRIPTING COMMENTS

Comment Type	JSP	ASP

Scriptlet comments: add information to the scriptlet code.	`// a single-line comment`
	or
	`/* a multiple-line comment */`
		`' a single-line comment`

Hidden comments: add information to the server-side file and are not sent to the Web browser.	`<%-- a hidden comment --%>`	N/A

INCLUDE COMMANDS

Include Type	JSP	ASP

Static includes: include files before the processing of a page.	`<%@ include file="String url" %>`
	or
	`<jsp:include file="String url" flush="true" >`
	`<jsp:param name="String name" value="String value" />`
	`</jsp:include>`
		`<!--#include file="String relativePath"-->`
		or
		`<!--#include virtual="String virtualPath"-->`

Dynamic includes: include a file during the processing of a page.	`<%@ include page="String url" %>`
	or
	`<jsp:include page="String url" flush="true" >`
	`<jsp:param name="String name" value="String value" />`
	`</jsp:include>`
		`Server.Execute("String url")`

FILE REDIRECTION

Redirection Type	JSP	ASP

Server redirection: stops the execution of the current page and transfers control to a new page.	`<jsp:forward page="String path" />`
	or
	`<jsp:forward page="String path" >`
	`<jsp:param name="String name" value="String value" />`
	`</jsp:forward>`
		`Server.Transfer(String path)`

WHAT'S ON THE CD-ROM

The CD-ROM disc included in this book contains many useful files and programs that can be used when working with JavaServer Pages. You will find a Web page providing one-click access to all the Internet links mentioned in this book, as well as several popular programs you can install and use on your computer. Before installing any of the programs on the disc, make sure a newer version of the program is not already installed on your computer. For information about installing different versions of the same program, contact the program's manufacturer.

SYSTEM REQUIREMENTS

While most programs on the CD-ROM disc have minimal system requirements, your computer should be equipped with the following hardware and software to use all the contents of the CD-ROM disc:

* A Pentium or faster processor.
* Microsoft Windows 95 or later.
* At least 32MB of RAM.
* At least 200MB of hard drive space.
* A double-speed (2x) or faster CD-ROM drive.
* A monitor capable of displaying at least 256 colors or grayscale.
* A modem with a speed of at least 14,400 bps.

AUTHOR'S SOURCE CODE

The CD provides files that contain all the sample code used throughout the book. You can browse the files directly from the CD-ROM disc or you can copy these files to your hard drive and use them as the basis for your own projects. You should open the files using a text editor such as WordPad.

WEB LINKS

This CD contains a Web page that provides one-click access to all the Web pages and Internet references in the book. To use these links, you must have an Internet connection and a Web browser, such as Internet Explorer, installed.

ACROBAT VERSION

The CD-ROM contains an e-version of this book that you can view and search using Adobe Acrobat Reader. You can also use the hyperlinks provided in the text to access all the Web pages and Internet references in the book. You cannot print the pages or copy text from the Acrobat files. An evaluation version of Adobe Acrobat is also included on the CD-ROM disc.

INSTALLING AND USING THE SOFTWARE

This CD-ROM disc contains several useful programs.

Before installing a program from this CD, you should exit all other programs. In order to use most of the programs, you must accept the license agreement provided with the program. Make sure you read any Readme files provided with each program.

Program Versions

Shareware programs are fully functional, free trial versions of copyrighted programs. If you like a particular program, you can register with its author for a nominal fee and receive licenses, enhanced versions and technical support.

Freeware programs are free, copyrighted games, applications and utilities. You can copy them to as many computers as you like, but they have no technical support.

GNU software is governed by its own license, which is included inside the folder of the GNU software. There are no restrictions on distribution of this software. See the GNU license for more details.

Trial, demo or evaluation versions are usually limited either by time or functionality. For example, you may not be able to save projects using these versions.

For your convenience, the software titles on the CD are listed in alphabetical order.

Acrobat Reader

For Microsoft Windows 95/98/NT/2000/Me. Evaluation version.

This disc contains an evaluation version of Acrobat Reader from Adobe. You will need this program to access the e-version of the book included on this disc. For more information about using Adobe Acrobat Reader, see page 270.

Apache

For Microsoft Windows 95/98/NT/2000. Freeware version.

Apache is a Web server from the Apache Software Foundation. It offers many new and improved features that make publishing Web pages faster and easier. The Apache Web server does not include support for Java components, however, these features are available as add-ons from the jakarta.apache.org Web site.

You can download the latest version of Apache as well as view information, such as troubleshooting tips and an FAQ, at the www.apache.org Web site.

Dreamweaver UltraDev

For Microsoft Windows 95/98/NT/2000/Me. Trial Version.

Dreamweaver UltraDev is a development tool that can be used to design and manage JSP applications. Dreamweaver UltraDev allows you to view and manage code while visually developing Web applications, as well as preview and edit live server data.

Dreamweaver UltraDev is available from Macromedia, Inc. and is fully functional for 30 days, after which time you must register it with the author. For more information, visit the www.macromedia.com Web site.

HomeSite

For Microsoft Windows 95/98/NT/2000/Me. Evaluation version.

HomeSite is a full featured HTML editor that is well-suited for use with other Web-related coding languages, such as JavaServer Pages. Homesite also includes powerful Web site management features.

HomeSite is an evaluation program from Allaire. It is fully functional for 30 days, after which time you are required to register it with the author. You can download the latest version of HomeSite as well as participate in message forums with other HomeSite users at www.allaire.com.

WHAT'S ON THE CD-ROM

JBuilder

For Windows 98/NT/2000. Demo version.

JBuilder is a set of development tools you can use to build and organize Java applications, components and JavaBeans.

JBuilder is a demo program from the Borland Software Corporation. It is fully functional for 60 days. To download JBuilder, visit the www.inprise.com Web site.

LiteWebServer

For Microsoft Windows and UNIX. Evaluation version.

LiteWebServer is a small, Java-based Web server that is ideal for personal or intranet use. LiteWebServer features support for Java components and JavaServer Pages.

LiteWebServer is offered by Gefion software. To download or purchase LiteWebServer, visit the www.gefionsoftware.com Web site.

Resin

For Microsoft Windows and UNIX. Evaluation version.

Resin is a Web server that allows you to quickly process and manage JSP files and Java components. It also includes XSL support, which helps you simplify and organize complex Web sites.

Resin is available from Caucho Technology. For more information about Resin, visit the www.caucho.com Web site.

ServletExec

For Microsoft Windows 98/NT/2000 and Linux. Evaluation version.

ServletExec is a Web server that uses JSP and component technology to build and power dynamic Web applications.

ServletExec is provided by the Unify Corporation. It is fully functional for 30 days, after which you are required to register it with the author. To ensure you have the latest version of ServletExec, visit the www.unifyewave.com Web site.

Tomcat

For Microsoft Windows, UNIX and Linux. Open Source.

Tomcat is a fully-functional Web server that you can install on your computer to create and deploy JSP pages. Tomcat is open source software, which means it is developed and maintained by volunteer programmers from around the world.

Tomcat is constantly being updated. This disc contains a recent release of the Tomcat Web server, but you should ensure you that you use the latest version of the server. The latest version of Tomcat is available at the jakarta.apache.org/tomcat Web site.

UltraEdit-32

For Microsoft Windows 95/98/NT/2000. Shareware version.

UltraEdit-32 is a text editor that can be used to write code in many languages, including HTML and Java. UltraEdit-32 has many features to make coding easier and more efficient, including syntax highlighting, multi-level undo and customizable templates.

UltraEdit-32 is a shareware program from IDM Computer Solutions, Inc. It is fully functional for 45 days, after which time you are required to register it with the author. Additional spelling, dictionaries, macros and support files for UltraEdit-32 are available at www.ultraedit.com.

WebSphere Application Server Advanced Edition

For Windows NT/2000. Evaluation version.

The WebSphere Application Server Advanced Edition by IBM is a high-performance server that supports multiple platforms and database programs. It includes powerful features that allow you to manage, store and deploy JavaBeans, Java components and JSP pages.

WebSphere Application Server Advanced Edition is fully functional for 60 days, after which you are required to register it with the author. Additional support files and resources are available at the www-4.ibm.com/software/webservers Web site.

TROUBLESHOOTING

We have tried our best to compile programs that work on most computers with the minimum system requirements. Your computer, however, may differ and some programs may not work properly for some reason.

The two most likely problems are that you do not have enough memory (RAM) for the programs you want to use or you have other programs running that are affecting the installation or running of a program. If you get error messages while trying to install or use the programs on the CD-ROM disc, try one or more of the following methods and then try installing or running the software again:

* Close all running programs.
* Restart your computer.
* Turn off any anti-virus software.
* Close the CD-ROM interface and run demos or installations directly from Windows Explorer.
* Add more RAM to your computer.

If you still have trouble installing the programs from the CD-ROM disc, please call the Hungry Minds Customer Care phone number: 800-762-2974.

USING THE E-VERSION OF THE BOOK

You can view *JavaServer Pages™: Your visual blueprint for designing dynamic content with JSP™* on your screen using the CD-ROM disc included at the back of this book. The CD-ROM disc allows you to search the contents of each chapter of the book for a specific word or phrase. The CD-ROM disc also provides a convenient way of keeping the book handy while traveling.

You must install Adobe Acrobat Reader on your computer before you can view the book on the CD-ROM disc. This program is provided on the disc. Acrobat Reader allows you to view Portable Document Format (PDF) files, which can display books and magazines on your screen exactly as they appear in printed form.

To view the contents of the book using Acrobat Reader, display the contents of the disc. Double-click the BookPDFs folder to display the contents of the folder. In the window that appears, double-click the icon for the chapter of the book you want to review.

USING THE E-VERSION OF THE BOOK

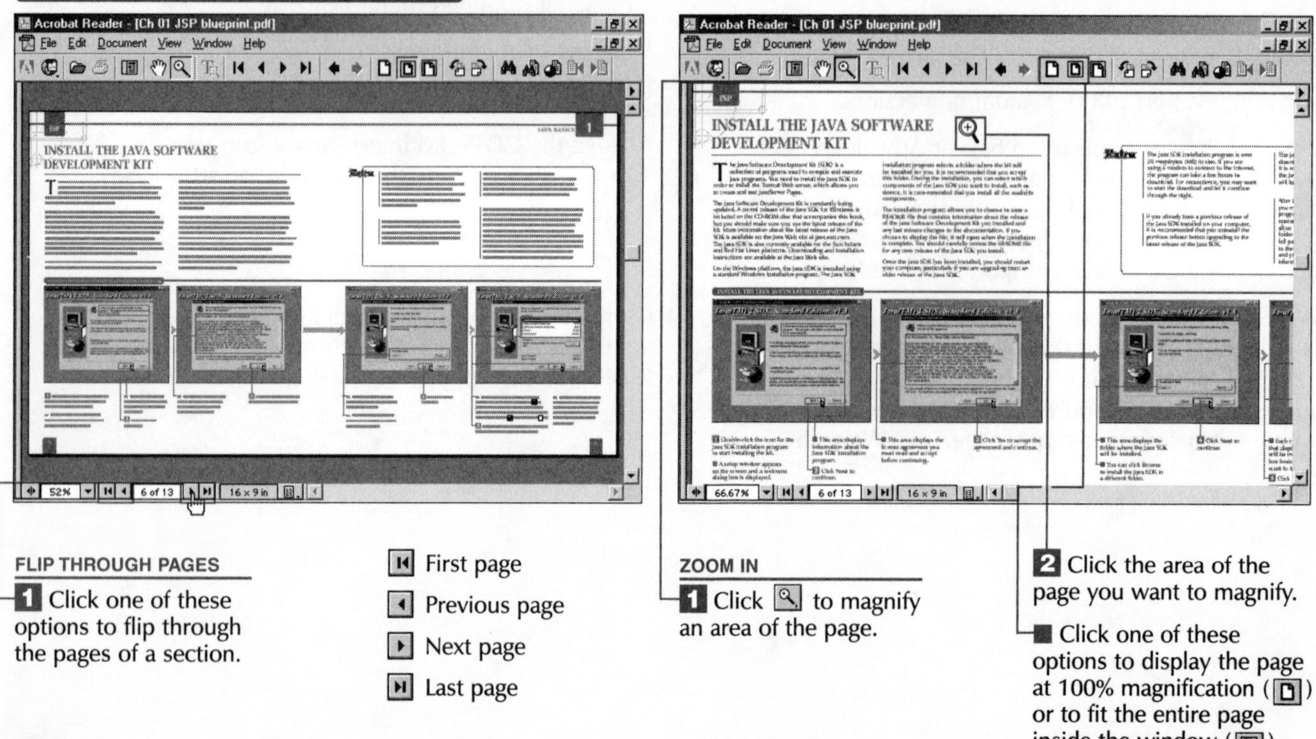

FLIP THROUGH PAGES

1 Click one of these options to flip through the pages of a section.

- First page
- Previous page
- Next page
- Last page

ZOOM IN

1 Click to magnify an area of the page.

2 Click the area of the page you want to magnify.

■ Click one of these options to display the page at 100% magnification ( ) or to fit the entire page inside the window ( ).

Extra

To install Acrobat Reader, insert the CD-ROM disc into a drive. In the screen that appears, click Software. Click Acrobat Reader and then click Install at the bottom of the screen. Then follow the instructions on your screen to install the program.

You can make searching the book more convenient by copying the .pdf files to your own computer. Display the contents of the CD-ROM disc and then copy the BookPDFs folder from the CD to your hard drive. This allows you to easily access the contents of the book at any time.

Acrobat Reader is a popular and useful program. There are many files available on the Web that are designed to be viewed using Acrobat Reader. Look for files with the .pdf extension. For more information about Acrobat Reader, visit the www.adobe.com/products/acrobat/readermain.html Web site.

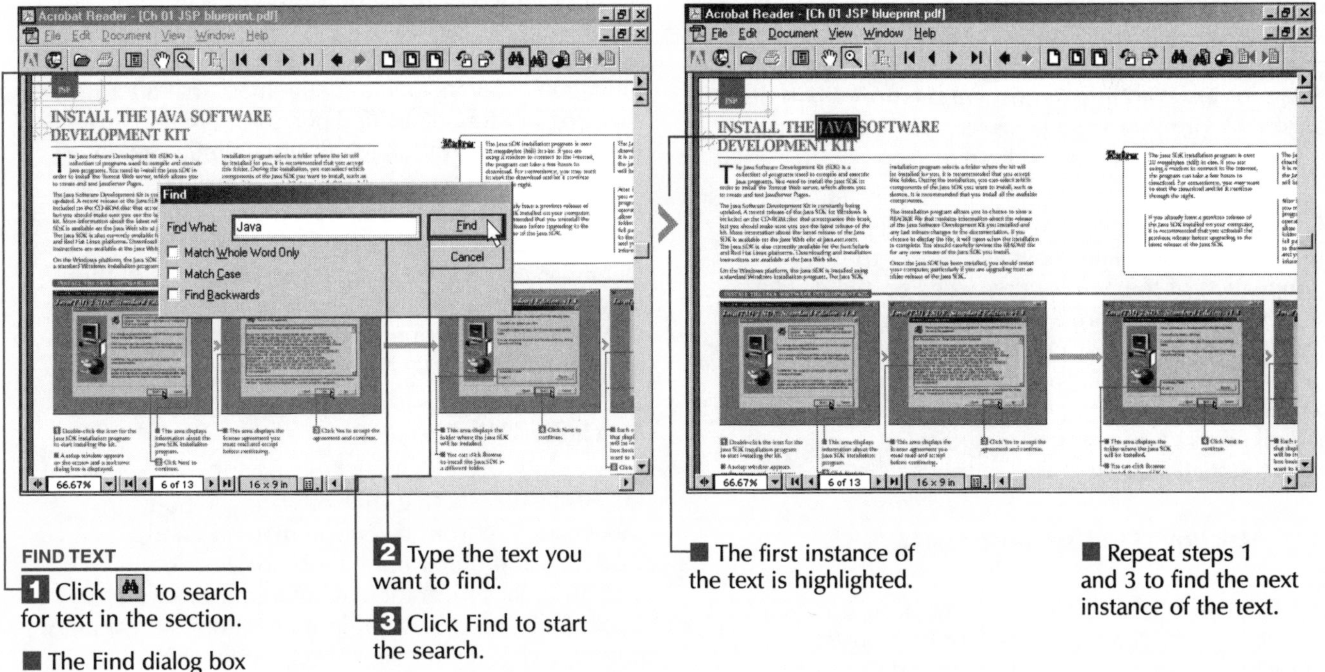

FIND TEXT

1 Click [binoculars icon] to search for text in the section.

■ The Find dialog box appears.

2 Type the text you want to find.

3 Click Find to start the search.

■ The first instance of the text is highlighted.

■ Repeat steps 1 and 3 to find the next instance of the text.

APPENDIX

HUNGRY MINDS, INC.
END-USER LICENSE AGREEMENT

READ THIS. You should carefully read these terms and conditions before opening the software packet(s) included with this book ("Book"). This is a license agreement ("Agreement") between you and Hungry Minds, Inc. ("HMI"). By opening the accompanying software packet(s), you acknowledge that you have read and accept the following terms and conditions. If you do not agree and do not want to be bound by such terms and conditions, promptly return the Book and the unopened software packet(s) to the place you obtained them for a full refund.

1. License Grant. HMI grants to you (either an individual or entity) a nonexclusive license to use one copy of the enclosed software program(s) (collectively, the "Software") solely for your own personal or business purposes on a single computer (whether a standard computer or a workstation component of a multi-user network). The Software is in use on a computer when it is loaded into temporary memory (RAM) or installed into permanent memory (hard disk, CD-ROM, or other storage device). HMI reserves all rights not expressly granted herein.

2. Ownership. HMI is the owner of all right, title, and interest, including copyright, in and to the compilation of the Software recorded on the disk(s) or CD-ROM ("Software Media"). Copyright to the individual programs recorded on the Software Media is owned by the author or other authorized copyright owner of each program. Ownership of the Software and all proprietary rights relating thereto remain with HMI and its licensers.

3. Restrictions On Use and Transfer.

(a) You may only (i) make one copy of the Software for backup or archival purposes, or (ii) transfer the Software to a single hard disk, provided that you keep the original for backup or archival purposes. You may not (i) rent or lease the Software, (ii) copy or reproduce the Software through a LAN or other network system or through any computer subscriber system or bulletin-board system, or (iii) modify, adapt, or create derivative works based on the Software.

(b) You may not reverse engineer, decompile, or disassemble the Software. You may transfer the Software and user documentation on a permanent basis, provided that the transferee agrees to accept the terms and conditions of this Agreement and you retain no copies. If the Software is an update or has been updated, any transfer must include the most recent update and all prior versions.

4. Restrictions on Use of Individual Programs. You must follow the individual requirements and restrictions detailed for each individual program in What's on the CD-ROM of this Book. These limitations are also contained in the individual license agreements recorded on the Software Media. These limitations may include a requirement that after using the program for a specified period of time, the user must pay a registration fee or discontinue use. By opening the Software packet(s), you will be agreeing to abide by the licenses and restrictions for these individual programs that are detailed in What's on the CD-ROM and on the Software Media. None of the material on this Software Media or listed in this Book may ever be redistributed, in original or modified form, for commercial purposes.

5. Limited Warranty.

(a) HMI warrants that the Software and Software Media are free from defects in materials and workmanship under normal use for a period of sixty (60) days from the date of purchase of this Book. If HMI receives notification within the warranty period of defects in materials or workmanship, HMI will replace the defective Software Media.

(b) HMI AND THE AUTHOR OF THE BOOK DISCLAIM ALL OTHER WARRANTIES, EXPRESS OR IMPLIED, INCLUDING WITHOUT LIMITATION IMPLIED WARRANTIES OF MERCHANTABILITY AND FITNESS FOR A PARTICULAR PURPOSE, WITH RESPECT TO THE SOFTWARE, THE PROGRAMS, THE SOURCE CODE CONTAINED THEREIN, AND/OR THE TECHNIQUES DESCRIBED IN THIS BOOK. HMI DOES NOT WARRANT THAT THE FUNCTIONS CONTAINED IN THE SOFTWARE WILL MEET YOUR REQUIREMENTS OR THAT THE OPERATION OF THE SOFTWARE WILL BE ERROR FREE.

(c) This limited warranty gives you specific legal rights, and you may have other rights that vary from jurisdiction to jurisdiction.

6. Remedies.

(a) HMI's entire liability and your exclusive remedy for defects in materials and workmanship shall be limited to replacement of the Software Media, which may be returned to HMI with a copy of your receipt at the following address: Software Media Fulfillment Department, Attn.: JavaServer Pages: Your visual blueprint for designing dynamic content with JSP, Hungry Minds, Inc., 10475 Crosspoint Blvd., Indianapolis, IN 46256, or call 1-800-762-2974. Please allow four to six weeks for delivery. This Limited Warranty is void if failure of the Software Media has resulted from accident, abuse, or misapplication. Any replacement Software Media will be warranted for the remainder of the original warranty period or thirty (30) days, whichever is longer.

(b) In no event shall HMI or the author be liable for any damages whatsoever (including without limitation damages for loss of business profits, business interruption, loss of business information, or any other pecuniary loss) arising from the use of or inability to use the Book or the Software, even if HMI has been advised of the possibility of such damages.

c) Because some jurisdictions do not allow the exclusion or limitation of liability for consequential or incidental damages, the above limitation or exclusion may not apply to you.

7. U.S. Government Restricted Rights. Use, duplication, or disclosure of the Software for or on behalf of the United States of America, its agencies and/or instrumentalities (the "U.S. Government") is subject to restrictions as stated in paragraph (c)(1)(ii) of the Rights in Technical Data and Computer Software clause of DFARS 252.227-7013, or subparagraphs (c) (1) and (2) of the Commercial Computer Software - Restricted Rights clause at FAR 52.227-19, and in similar clauses in the NASA FAR supplement, as applicable.

8. General. This Agreement constitutes the entire understanding of the parties and revokes and supersedes all prior agreements, oral or written, between them and may not be modified or amended except in a writing signed by both parties hereto that specifically refers to this Agreement. This Agreement shall take precedence over any other documents that may be in conflict herewith. If any one or more provisions contained in this Agreement are held by any court or tribunal to be invalid, illegal, or otherwise unenforceable, each and every other provision shall remain in full force and effect.

INDEX

Symbols and Numbers

A

B

C

D

INDEX

G

INDEX

H

I

J

K

M

N

O

Q

R

S

T

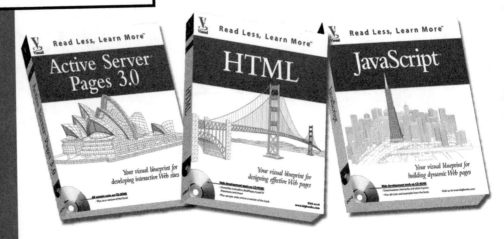

with these two-color Visual™ guides

The Complete Visual Reference

For visual learners who want an all-in-one reference/tutorial that delivers more in-depth information about a technology topic.

"Master It" tips provide additional topic coverage

Title	ISBN	Price
Master Active Directory™ VISUALLY™	0-7645-3425-4	$34.99
Master Microsoft® Access 2000 VISUALLY™	0-7645-6048-4	$39.99
Master Microsoft® Office 2000 VISUALLY™	0-7645-6050-6	$39.99
Master Microsoft® Word 2000 VISUALLY™	0-7645-6046-8	$39.99
Master Office 97 VISUALLY™	0-7645-6036-0	$39.99
Master Photoshop® 5.5 VISUALLY™	0-7645-6045-X	$39.99
Master Red Hat® Linux® VISUALLY™	0-7645-3436-X	$34.99
Master VISUALLY™ HTML 4 & XHTML™ 1	0-7645-3454-8	$34.99
Master VISUALLY™ Microsoft® Windows® Me Millennium Edition	0-7645-3496-3	$34.99
Master VISUALLY™ Windows® 2000 Server	0-7645-3426-2	$34.99
Master Windows® 95 VISUALLY™	0-7645-6024-7	$39.99
Master Windows® 98 VISUALLY™	0-7645-6034-4	$39.99
Master Windows® 2000 Professional VISUALLY™	0-7645-3421-1	$39.99

The *Visual*™ series is available wherever books are sold, or call 1-800-762-2974. Outside the US, call 317-572-3993

TRADE & INDIVIDUAL ORDERS

Phone: **(800) 762-2974**
or **(317) 572-3993**
(8 a.m.–6 p.m., CST, weekdays)
FAX : **(800) 550-2747**
or **(317) 572-4002**

EDUCATIONAL ORDERS & DISCOUNTS

Phone: **(800) 434-2086**
(8:30 a.m.–5:00 p.m., CST, weekdays)
FAX : **(317) 572-4005**

CORPORATE ORDERS FOR VISUAL™ SERIES

Phone: **(800) 469-6616**
(8 a.m.–5 p.m., EST, weekdays)
FAX : **(905) 890-9434**

Qty	ISBN	Title	Price	Total

Shipping & Handling Charges

	Description	First book	Each add'l. book	Total
Domestic	Normal	$4.50	$1.50	$
	Two Day Air	$8.50	$2.50	$
	Overnight	$18.00	$3.00	$
International	Surface	$8.00	$8.00	$
	Airmail	$16.00	$16.00	$
	DHL Air	$17.00	$17.00	$

Subtotal ______________

CA residents add applicable sales tax ______________

IN, MA and MD residents add 5% sales tax ______________

IL residents add 6.25% sales tax ______________

RI residents add 7% sales tax ______________

TX residents add 8.25% sales tax ______________

Shipping ______________

Total ______________

Ship to:

Name ______________________________

Address ______________________________

Company ______________________________

City/State/Zip ______________________________

Daytime Phone ______________________________

Payment: ☐ Check to Hungry Minds (US Funds Only)

☐ Visa ☐ Mastercard ☐ American Express

Card # ______________ Exp. ________ Signature ______________